The Essential Guide to Flash CS4 AIR Development

Marco Casario with Andrew Shorten,
Koen De Weggheleire, and Matteo Ronchi

friendsof

DESIGNER TO DESIGNER™

an Apress® company

The Essential Guide to Flash CS4 AIR Development

ISBN-13 (pbk): 978-1-4302-1588-2

ISBN-13 (electronic): 978-1-4302-1589-9

9 8 7 6 5 4 3 2 1

Distributed to the book trade worldwide by Springer-Verlag New York, Inc., 233 Spring Street, 6th Floor, New York, NY 10013. Phone 1-800-SPRINGER, fax 201-348-4505, e-mail orders-ny@springer-sbm.com, or visit www.springeronline.com.

For information on translations, please contact Apress directly at 2855 Telegraph Avenue, Suite 600, Berkeley, CA 94705. Phone 510-549-5930, fax 510-549-5939, e-mail info@apress.com, or visit www.apress.com.

Apress and friends of ED books may be purchased in bulk for academic, corporate, or promotional use. eBook versions and licenses are also available for most titles. For more information, reference our Special Bulk Sales–eBook Licensing web page at http://www.apress.com/info/bulksales.

The source code for this book is freely available to readers at www.friendsofed.com in the Downloads section.

Credits

Lead Editors
Clay Andres, Matthew Moodie

Associate Production Director
Kari Brooks-Copony

Technical Reviewer
Devon Wolfgang

Production Editor
Katie Stence

Editorial Board
Clay Andres, Steve Anglin,
Mark Beckner, Ewan Buckingham,
Tony Campbell, Gary Cornell,
Jonathan Gennick, Michelle Lowman,
Matthew Moodie, Jeffrey Pepper,
Frank Pohlmann, Ben Renow-Clarke,
Dominic Shakeshaft, Matt Wade, Tom Welsh

Compositor
Dina Quan

Proofreader
April Eddy

Indexer
Broccoli Information Management

Project Manager
Beth Christmas

Artist
April Milne

Copy Editor
Damon Larson

Interior and Cover Designer
Kurt Krames

Developmental Editor
Valerie Haynes Perry

Manufacturing Director
Tom Debolski

To the memory of my grandmother Maria.

CONTENTS AT A GLANCE

CONTENTS

vii

CONTENTS

FOREWORD

It's been over a decade since FutureSplash, the predecessor to Macromedia Flash, and then later Adobe Flash, was first released; who could have imagined back then that a simple vector-based animation tool would evolve to become a robust platform for delivering expressive content, rich Internet applications, and high-quality video across a multitude of browsers and operating systems.

Today, Flash encompasses more than just a browser plug-in and corresponding authoring tool; the Flash platform provides web, desktop, and mobile runtimes, together with frameworks, tools, servers, and services to enable designers and developers to create high-impact experiences.

Flash Player remains at the core of the platform, with each release offering new capabilities and further improving performance. Building upon the addition of a new high-performance virtual machine for executing ActionScript code in Flash Player 9, the release of Flash Player 10 adds support for 3D transformations, custom filters and effects, advanced audio processing, and GPU hardware acceleration, enabling an entirely new class of experiences not previously achievable on the Web.

As you look to deliver an engaging experience in a way that is convenient, relevant, and personal to the user, it is important to consider whether the browser is always the most appropriate access point. For example, applications deployed to the browser typically are not available when the user is offline, they are constrained within the browser chrome, they don't allow common application interactions such as drag-and-drop from the desktop, and they limit access to files and information on the user's local machine. For some applications, these limitations cause user frustration and a desire for a richer solution.

With the release of the Adobe AIR runtime, Flash designers and developers now have the opportunity to build Flash-based applications that run on the desktop, with new capabilities to extend application functionality and overcome some of the limitations experienced when running inside the web browser. Adobe AIR builds upon the features already found in Flash Player, offering, for example, unrestricted local file system access, as well as providing a version of WebKit for rendering HTML content and SQLite for the storage and retrieval of local data.

Expanding your knowledge of the Flash platform to understand the new capabilities provided by the AIR runtime is crucial if you want to deliver the most engaging experiences for your clients.

The Essential Guide to Flash CS4 AIR Development will help you get to grips with the AIR-specific features in Flash Professional CS4 and show how to leverage the new AIR APIs to create desktop applications that will work consistently on Mac, Windows, and Linux operating systems.

If you need inspiration for how you can leverage Adobe AIR, I recommend you visit the Adobe AIR Marketplace (www.adobe.com/go/marketplace/), where you will find AIR applications that you can download and try for yourself. Once you've built your own AIR applications, I encourage you to promote them on the AIR Marketplace so that others can discover and enjoy using them—we certainly look forward to seeing what you create!

Andrew Shorten
Platform Evangelist, Adobe

ABOUT THE AUTHORS

 **Marco Casario** is one of the most dynamic developers and consultants in the Adobe world.

He has been passionate about informatics since he was little more than a child and used to program games in Basic for Commodore 64 before dedicating himself, while still very young, to innovative projects for the Web using Flash and Director (as far back as versions 3 and 5).

In 2001, he began to collaborate with Macromedia Italy. Since that year, he has produced and headed a long series of presentations, conferences, and articles, which you can find listed in detail in his blog entitled "Hands on Adobe World" (http://casario.blogs.com/), which is currently receiving several thousands of visitors every day.

In 2005, Marco founded Comtaste (www.comtaste.com/en/), a company dedicated to exploring new frontiers in rich Internet applications and the convergence of the Web, the desktop, and the world of mobile devices. MobyMobile (www.mobymobile.com/) and YouThruBiz (www.youthrubiz.com/) are representative of Comtaste's recent work.

Marco is also the founder of the biggest worldwide Flash Lite user group (http://groups.yahoo.com/group/FlashLite/) and of AUGItaly (www.augitaly.com/), a reference point for the Italian community of Adobe users, in which he carries out the role of content manager for the section dedicated to Flex and AIR (www.augitaly.com/flexgala/).

He's a professional speaker who regularly speaks at international conferences like Adobe MAX, Flash on the Beach, Flex Camp, Multi-Mania, FITC, 360|Flex, AJAXWorld, O'Reilly Web 2.0 Summit, Adobe Live, and many other local events.

His company, Comtaste, is currently busy working on the development of some very ambitious projects concerning banks and financial agencies, and various Flex and Flash Media Server training activities for the creation of rich Internet applications on behalf of companies including Accenture, HP, Capgemini Engineering, and Adobe Systems Software Ireland.

Marco is also the author of the following books: *Adobe AIR Cookbook* (O'Reilly, 2008), *AdvancED AIR Applications* (friends of ED, 2009), and *Flex Solutions: Essential Techniques for Flex 2 and 3 Developers* (friends of ED, 2007).

Contributing Authors

Andrew Shorten is a platform evangelist for Adobe and is passionate about improving the quality, richness, and value of computer-based experiences. Andrew developed web, kiosk, and mobile user interfaces for government and enterprise customers while working at Fujitsu, and has since worked for Macromedia, Microsoft, and Adobe, where he has engaged with designers, developers, web agencies, and organizations to help them deliver rich, engaging, and successful web and desktop experiences.

Koen De Weggheleire is a faculty member of the Technical University of West Flanders (HOWEST) where he teaches Flash platform solutions (Flash, Flex, and AIR) with a smile.

As the Adobe user group manager for Belgium (www.adobeusergroup.be/) and an Adobe community expert for Flash, Koen is heavily addicted to the community and inspires it through his blog at www.newmovieclip.com/, and by speaking at various events including Adobe MAX, FITC, 360|Flex, Flashbelt, and Flash on the Beach.

He coordinates the yearly Belgian multimedia conference Multi-Mania (www.multi-mania.be/), where thousands of people come together to learn from industry experts and share knowledge.

Koen is a coauthor of *Foundation Flex for Developers: Data-Driven Applications with PHP, ASP. NET, ColdFusion, and LCSD* (friends of ED, 2007). He's currently working on *AdvancED AIR Applications* for friends of ED, and even more AIR books from Koen are on the way.

When there is still some time left, Koen can be found at his company Happy-Banana, together with Wouter Verweirder, doing Flash platform consultancy on advanced award-winning rich Internet applications.

When Koen is not talking ActionScript, you can find him producing music, collecting goodies, eating pizza, or renovating his 100-year-old house.

Matteo Ronchi is a Comtaste consultant. His main job is development in the multimedia and web technology fields. His professional path started in 2000 as a 3D graphics designer for product design and virtual environment visualization. Soon, following his passion for games and Internet technologies, he moved from 3D to web development, mainly using Flash and Director as core technologies. In the last two years, his work has mainly focused on ActionScript and Flex programming. In 2007, he began speaking at international conferences such as Adobe Live, From A to Web, and 360|Flex, mainly focusing on Adobe AIR development.

Fabio Bernardi has been a web developer since 2003. The passion for programming rich and friendly web applications brought him to investigate more on Flash, ActionScript, and Flex. In 2005 he joined Comtaste, where he's been involved in several international projects. He is channel manager of the Italian Flex user group FlexGala (www.augitaly.com/flexgala/), where he's an active contributor. He is an Adobe Certified Professional Flash developer and a consultant for Adobe Italy.

About the Technical Reviewer

 **Devon Wolfgang** is an avid Flash fan(atic) who's been fiddling and tinkering with ActionScript, Flash, Flex, and AIR since the dark web ages of 1999. He recently finished a six-year contract with the US Navy, and now resides in Ireland with his beautiful wife, Deirdre, where he holds the position of senior software developer with vStream Digital Media (www.vstream.ie/). When not wildly busy, you might just find him blogging about ActionScript or involved in one of his other preoccupations such as bad movies and bad music at http://blog.onebyonedesign.com/.

ACKNOWLEDGMENTS

Writing a book really is a huge undertaking. During the course of the journey, you often have the feeling that you will never reach the end. Not just because in the end you are reduced to working on it at night after a long day at work or during the weekends, but particularly because it is a task that absorbs all of your ideas and requires constant and assiduous concentration. This often brings you to the point of abstracting yourself from reality and putting personal and working relationships with the people around you to the test. It is for this reason that at the end of your work as an author, you realize how much patience your work colleagues, your clients, your partners, and most importantly, your family had to have to not turn their back on you.

I therefore want to acknowledge these people.

Thank you to my mother, who has always believed in me and has always pushed me to improve myself and to see beyond the surface of things. Thank you to my father who has finally come to understand that it is never too late to begin to hang out with his son. Thank you to my brother who for the period of the writing of the book respected all my insufferable requests.

Thank you to my beloved honey, Katia, whose patience was really put to the test. Being near me during the period in which I wrote this book was definitely more difficult than usual, but her unconditional love, support, and help was fundamental to encourage me to go on. Thanks for inspiring me to be my best. I love you, darling.

Thank you Andrew, Koen, Matteo, and Fabio for your help with this book. I am honored to work with you.

Thank you to my business partner Raffaele and my colleagues Emanuele, Constantine, Liviu, Kira, and Francesco, who were often abandoned by my presence but knew how to take care of their own (and often also my) work commitments. We will do great things together.

Thank you to my friends Fabrizio, Renato, Daniele, Juri, Marmotta, and Alessio, who even after all the refusals of their invitations because of this book, have not left my side. A special thanks to Clay Andres, who gave me the opportunity to write this book and whose ideas and corrections have rendered it better. Finally, an enormous thank you to the people who made this book possible and better, and without whose help and tips it could not have been a success—namely Beth Christmas, Damon Larson, Katie Stence, and the staff behind the scene at friends of ED. They are all passionate people whose primary job is to publish the very best content.

INTRODUCTION

If you want to learn more about AIR development using Flash CS4 and ActionScript 3, this is the book for you. You'll learn the AIR APIs for creating desktop applications with these technologies, and you'll learn to build them using object-oriented programming techniques. Whether you are a Windows, Mac, or Linux developer, this book will be useful for you, since Adobe AIR is a cross-platform desktop runtime, and the examples in this book are intended for all platforms. Throughout the chapters, you'll find detailed information that takes into account the differences between the different platforms.

The Essential Flash CS4 AIR Development site

I've created a companion site from which you can download all the code of the chapters and revised content: http://flashcs4air.comtaste.com/. The site will also be used for tracking the errata page for the book, so make sure to check back frequently for any updates.

What you need

In order to follow and create the examples shown in this book, you'll need the Flash CS4 authoring tool. You can download a 30-day trial here: www.adobe.com/products/flash/. You'll also need to install the AIR 1.5 runtime from wwww.adobe.com/go/air. Finally, all the examples used in this book are downloadable from http://flashcs4air.comtaste.com/.

AIR resources

Each topic in this book is presented in the context of an applied solution. Although a brief introduction exists for each solution, this book is not intended as a reference or documentation book.

The official Adobe AIR documentation is huge and very well written. It covers all the aspects of official Adobe AIR in a comprehensive way. You can download the complete official Adobe AIR documentation for free at http://www.adobe.com/support/documentation/en/air/.

Another important resource is the Adobe Flex Doc Team blog, where you'll find updates, new content, and other helpful information: http://blogs.adobe.com/flexdoc/.

Here is a list of useful resources dedicated to AIR:

- Adobe AIR Market place: http://www.adobe.com/go/marketplace
- http://feeds.adobe.com
- Adobe AIR Developer Center Feed: http://rss.adobe.com/developer_center_air_tutorials.rss?locale=en
- http://adobe.com/devnet/air/
- http://onair.adobe.com/blogs/videos/
- http://tech.groups.yahoo.com/group/flexcoders/
- http://InsideRIA.com
- http://casario.blogs.com
- http://flexsolutions.comtaste.com/

Questions and contacts

Please direct any technical questions or comments about the book to flexsolutions@comtaste.com. For more information about other Flex books, see the friends of ED website, at www.friendsofed.com/.

Layout conventions

To keep this book as clear and easy to follow as possible, the following text conventions are used throughout.

Important words or concepts are normally highlighted on the first appearance in **bold type**.

Code is presented in fixed-width font.

New or changed code is normally presented in **bold fixed-width font**.

Pseudocode and variable input are written in *italic fixed-width font*.

Menu commands are written in the form Menu ➤ Submenu ➤ Submenu.

Where I want to draw your attention to something, I've highlighted it like this:

> *Ahem, don't say I didn't warn you.*

Sometimes code won't fit on a single line in a book. Where this happens, I use an arrow like this: ➥.

```
This is a very, very long section of code that should be written all ➥
on the same line without a break.
```

CHAPTER 1
INTRODUCING ADOBE AIR

 Desktop Keeley
Desktop Keeley provides up
sport info, showbiz gossip a
direct to your desktop.

By ashorten 30-Jul-08 ⭐

 TweetDeck
TweetDeck evolves the exist
of Twitter by breaking it dow

By Iain Dodsworth 24-Jul-08
☆ ☆ ☆ ☆ ☆

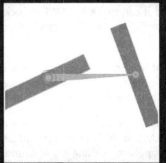

Share Your
Screen

Meet live over the web and
share your screen with up to
3 people

Collaborate with remote
participants using integrated
audio, chat, video and

In 2007, Adobe launched Apollo, the code name for a cross–operating system runtime that allows developers to leverage their existing web development skills to build and deploy rich Internet applications (RIAs) to the desktop.

With this runtime, web developers can leave the browser and its limitations, dictated by sandbox security, and add native functions of desktop applications that communicate and interact with Windows, Mac OS X, and Linux operating systems. The final version of Adobe's technology became AIR (Adobe Integrated Runtime).

Following are the ways in which AIR has added value over its natural competitor JRE (Java Runtime Environment):

- You can use it to create applications from scratch easily.
- You can port web applications to the desktop.
- You can deploy on different operating systems.

To create a desktop application with AIR, designers and developers don't need to learn a new language or development environment. They can create desktop applications using the same knowledge they use every day for web applications. Whether they use HTML, CSS, JavaScript, Ajax, ActionScript, or MXML, Adobe AIR can accommodate them and display the application on the desktop. And that's why learning another IDE (integrated development environment) isn't required. You can use Dreamweaver, Flash, Flex, Eclipse, Aptana, or any other environment that can use these languages. This also means that bringing a web application developed with Ajax or ActionScript (Flash or Flex) onto the desktop requires minimum effort apart from adding functions, which are provided by AIR SDKs (software development kits) to interact with the operating system.

Sun's "write once, run anywhere" motto has often shown its weakness in deploying desktop applications made with Java on different operating systems. Too many times, developers have had to rewrite entire pieces of code or find workarounds to make Java desktop applications work on Windows, Linux, or Mac OS X. With AIR, the time spent porting the application to different operating system will be null.

And if you don't believe what I'm telling you, you can trust Adobe's guarantee, which has already proved it can make any SWF (Shockwave Flash) application visible on Windows, Linux, Mac, and Sun Solaris. Check it out yourself at www.adobe.com/products/flashplayer/.

With the recent release of Flash CS4, Adobe provides an even more efficient tool to write ActionScript 3 code that can be exported natively not only as a web application in SWF format, but also as a desktop application in AIR format.

Congratulations on your choice to create a new generation of desktop applications with Flash CS4 and AIR. In this chapter, you'll learn the difference between developing a web and a desktop application using the AIR runtime.

Understanding the difference between browser and desktop applications

Browser or **web applications** are programs that work with an active Internet connection and that are loaded in a web browser. Facebook (www.facebook.com/) is an example of a well-known web application.

Desktop applications, on the other hand, are launched directly from a local computer, and don't necessarily require an Internet connection. OpenOffice Writer (www.openoffice.org/) is an example of a desktop application.

A few application features for the browser and the desktop are compared in Table 1-1.

Table 1-1. Comparison between a browser application's characteristics with those of a desktop application

Feature	Browser Apps	Desktop Apps
Internet	Required	Not necessary
Installation	None	Must be installed on the local system
Application management	Easy update	Update manager APIs
OS support	Multiple platforms	Multiple platforms
I/O support	None	File system access
Access to OS	Limited	Data stored locally via file access

As you can guess from this table, desktop applications can have more advanced functions that interact and integrate better with the local system than web applications.

Desktop and web applications are both widely used every day, so you can see how it would be advantageous to combine the features of the two. Doing so creates a single environment for developing hybrid applications. An early example of this was BuzzWord, a formerly web-only word-processing tool later released as an AIR desktop application (originally created by Virtual Ubiquity, BuzzWord was recently acquired by Adobe). The BuzzWord desktop application (shown in Figure 1-1) allows you to open and edit documents locally. Visit https://buzzword.acrobat.com/ to learn more about BuzzWord.

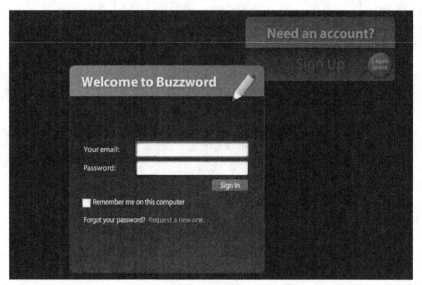

Figure 1-1. You can download BuzzWord from the Acrobat website.

With technologies like AIR, creating desktop applications that can interact with the operating system as well as easily access remote data is quite easy and fast. Maybe the era of "occasionally connected applications" has really arrived.

> *Occasionally Connected Computing (OCC) is a term coined by Macromedia and used to describe some aspects of a web application when not connected to the Internet. This is sometimes a feature of a rich Internet application. (Read more on Wikipedia at* http:// en.wikipedia.org/wiki/Occasionally_Connected_Computing*).*

In the next section of the chapter, you'll learn what's behind the AIR runtime and how to install the SDK to start developing applications.

Installing AIR and its SDKs

To be able to install and use AIR applications, you'll need the AIR runtime installed locally. The AIR runtime is free, and for Windows, you can download it from Adobe at http:// get.adobe.com/air/. For other systems, you can download the runtime from http:// get.adobe.com/air/otherversions/. Figure 1-2 shows this download page on the Adobe site.

Figure 1-2. Download and install the AIR runtime for your system.

Installing the runtime

Once you've downloaded the runtime, you can install it on your machine using the installation wizard. After you've done this, you'll be able to install and execute AIR applications.

Also on the Adobe website, you'll find the Adobe AIR Marketplace (shown in Figure 1-3) at the following address: http://www.adobe.com/cfusion/exchange/index.cfm?event=productHome&exc=24&loc=en_us. Here you'll find a list of applications you can download and install to help you understand what you can actually do (and what has already been done) with AIR technology.

Figure 1-3. You'll find many applications for inspiration in the Adobe AIR Marketplace.

Before you install AIR, I recommend that you can meet the following system requirements:

- For Windows systems
  - Intel Pentium 2GHz or faster processor
  - Windows Vista Home Premium, Business, Ultimate, or Enterprise; Windows XP with Service Pack 2 or Windows 2000 with Service Pack 4; 512MB of RAM; 32MB of VRAM
- For Mac OS X systems
  - PowerPC G4 1.8GHz or faster processor, or Intel Core Duo 1.33GHz or faster processor
  - Mac OS X v.10.4.9 or later, or 10.5.1 (Intel or PowerPC; Intel processor required for H.264 video)
  - 512MB of RAM; 32MB of VRAM

International language support

Installing an application can intimidate many users. Fortunately, AIR installation and other runtime dialog boxes have been translated into the following languages:

- Chinese traditional
- Chinese simplified
- English
- French
- German
- Italian
- Japanese
- Korean
- Portuguese
- Russian
- Swedish
- Dutch
- Czech
- Polish
- Turkish
- Spanish

The language used for the installation wizard will be taken from the language used by the local operating system. This means that if you have Windows installed in English, the AIR installation wizard will show English labels. Moreover, you can develop your AIR application to support the following:

- Building internationalized applications, including keyboard input for double-byte languages
- Localizing the name and description attributes in the application descriptor file
- Localizing error messages, such as SQLError.detailID and SQLError.detail➥ Arguments, in the SQLite database
- Obtaining an array of preferred user interface languages as set by the operating system using the Capabilities.languages property

The WebKit engine embedded in AIR

The AIR runtime allows you to load the three following types of formats and contents through its HTML engine:

- HTML
- JavaScript
- CSS

This is possible thanks to the WebKit engine, which is part of the WebKit Open Source Project (http://webkit.org/). This project is the same one used for the Apple WebKit Framework for Mac OS X and Google Chrome.

> AIR uses the code base directly from the WebKit project, not from Apple's WebKit Framework.

HTML and JavaScript within AIR are handled by the WebKit engine. The choice of this engine is very well explained in Adobe's FAQs (http://labs.adobe.com/wiki/index.php/ Apollo:developerfaq#Why_did_Adobe_choose_WebKit.3F):

> We [Adobe] spent a considerable amount of time researching a number of HTML rendering engines for use in AIR. We [Adobe] had four main criteria, all of which WebKit met:
>
> - Open project that we could contribute to
>
> - Proven technology, that web developers and end users are familiar with
>
> - Minimum effect on AIR runtime size
>
> - Proven ability to run on mobile devices
>
> While the final decision was difficult, we felt that WebKit is the best match for AIR at this time.

The SWF format is run because Flash Player is embedded in AIR. Finally, AIR can integrate with PDF documents, but only if Acrobat Reader is installed in the local computer.

Chapter 10 will discuss how to integrate HTML/JavaScript contents, while in Chapter 9, you'll learn how to open PDF content in your AIR applications.

Installing the AIR SDKs

Now that you've installed the runtime, you can install the AIR SDKs, which make up a library to develop and compile AIR applications. The AdobeAIRSDK file you'll download, once it's unzipped, will contain the following items:

- Schema and templates for the application.xml manifest file
- Default icons for the AIR application
- Framework for the AIR APIs
- Template for the AIR application install badge
- Command-line AIR Debug Launcher (ADL)
- Command-line AIR Developer Tool (ADT)

While you had to install the AIR extension with Flash CS3 to be able to add the AIR APIs to Flash's IDE, the SDKs have been natively included with the new version of Flash.

From Flash CS4, you can package and preview AIR application files without having to install AIR SDKs. However, even if it isn't necessary, I advise you to install the SDKs, which also provide interesting examples and the ADL and ADT command-line tools.

Using ADT and ADL

The AIR application compiler (a.k.a. AIR Developer Tool [ADT]) allows you to compile and package an AIR application to be distributed. With Flash CS4, there is a Preview mode that allows you to do this as well, but if you want to, you can also use a window terminal and the adt tool:

```
adt -package HelloWorld.air  HelloWorld-app.xml HelloWorld.swf
```

With this simple syntax, the file will be created and a HelloWorld.air preview will be launched.

ADL allows you to carry out debug sessions in AIR applications without having to create the package and install the application. Here's an example of its use:

```
adl HelloWorld-app.xml
```

The topics regarding packaging and debugging AIR applications will be discussed using Flash CS4 as a development environment. You can refer to Chapter 3 for more information.

In this book, you'll create AIR applications using Flash CS4. The programming language that will you use is ActionScript. In the next section, you'll learn more about the latest version of the ActionScript language.

The ActionScript 3 language

Before getting into detail about Flash CS4 and AIR APIs, I'd like to discuss the programming language that will be used throughout the book: ActionScript. ActionScript is executed by the Flash client runtime environment. More precisely, it's the ActionScript Virtual Machine (AVM) embedded in the Flash runtime that executes ActionScript programs.

> *A virtual machine is a module that takes the description of a computation as its input and performs that computation.*

ActionScript 3 marks an important evolution of the language compared to previous versions (you can find a lot of articles about this topic on the Adobe DevNet page (www.adobe.com/devnet/); see the "Consulting the Web: Resources" section near the end of the chapter). Finally, ActionScript is an object-oriented language with which you can create complex applications and maintain clean, robust, and reusable code. At this time, there are three Flash client runtime environments:

- **Flash Player**: This executes the applications in the web browser or in stand-alone mode directly on the desktop (without interacting with the operating system). The most recent version is Flash Player 10.

- **Flash Lite**: This is a light profile of Flash Player that runs on mobile devices. The latest version of Flash Lite is 3, which still doesn't execute ActionScript 3 code—only code that is written and compiled in ActionScript 2.

- **Adobe AIR**: This runtime runs applications directly on the desktop, accessing the operating system's features.

It's precisely the characteristic of being executed by the Flash runtime instead of the operating system that makes ActionScript a very portable and cross-platform system. Similarly to how your web application can be viewed on different browsers and operating systems, an application written with ActionScript and compiled for AIR will be compatible with Windows, Mac OS X, and Linux systems.

The latest version of the ActionScript language is 3; it was first introduced in Flash Player 9. ActionScript is based on the ECMAScript international standard (ECMA-262; see www.ecma-international.org/publications/standards/Ecma-262.htm for more information) in the ECMAScript fourth edition (www.ecmascript.org/es4/spec/overview.pdf). To execute code that is written in ActionScript 3, a new AVM is used in the Flash runtime: the ActionScript Virtual Machine 2 (AVM2). If you want to learn more about AVM2, you can read the official Adobe documentation on it at www.adobe.com/devnet/actionscript/articles/avm2overview.pdf.

In order to be executed by one of the Flash runtimes, an ActionScript application has to be converted into a binary format. This operation is called **compilation**. A binary format called ActionScript bytecode is used in the SWF file. This file contains all the assets (graphics, images, CSS files, SWF files, etc.) used in the projects, as well as the bytecode.

To compile an ActionScript program in a SWF file, you use a compiler. Flash CS4 has its own internal compiler, which allows it to compile ActionScript 3 code in bytecode and create the SWF wrapper (a container). In this book, we will simply use the internal compiler of the Flash CS4 environment.

Adobe's IDE isn't the only tool that allows you to compile SWF files. You can also find command-line compilers on the Web. One of the most famous ones is the haXe compiler, the successor of MTASC (Motion-Twin ActionScript 2 Compiler; see www.mtasc.org/).

haXe (see http://haxe.org/doc/intro) allows you to compile a haXe program to a SWF file. haXe can compile for Flash Player 6 through 9, with either a pre-Flash 8 API or the newer ActionScript 3/Flash 9 API. haXe offers very good performance and language features to develop Flash content.

According to Gary Grossman, the creator of ActionScript, ActionScript 3 has the four following goals:

- ■ *Safety*: *The language supports type safety so developers can write unambiguous, easily maintainable code.*

- ■ *Simplicity*: *The language is intuitive enough for developers to be able to read and write programs without constantly consulting a reference manual.*

- ■ *Performance*: *The language enables developers to write complex programs that perform efficiently and responsively.*

- ■ *Compatibility*: *The language provides a short backward and forward compatibility path and a significant overlap with industry standards. ActionScript 3 is a dialect of ECMAScript, which formalizes the features of ActionScript 2, adds the capabilities of ECMAScript for XML (E4X), and unifies the language into a coherent whole.*

You can read Gary's full article, "ActionScript 3.0 Overview," at www.adobe.com/devnet/actionscript/articles/actionscript3_overview.html.

ActionScript 3 consists of the core language, which includes statements, expressions, conditions, loops, and types, and the Flash Player APIs. The core language contains the basics of the ActionScript language, while the Flash Player APIs contain the classes that provide access to the Flash Player functionality.

There are many new features in ActionScript 3, and unfortunately it's beyond the scope of this book to talk about them all. However, on the Adobe site, in the ActionScript Technology Center (www.adobe.com/devnet/actionscript/), you'll find a lot more information. Also read the "Consulting the Web: Resources" section at the end of this chapter, where you can find a list of useful web resources.

In the next section, you'll get an overview of the AIR classes you'll use for developing desktop applications.

The AIR APIs

In programming, the term **API** stands for **application programming interface**. It usually refers to a set of functions, procedures, and classes that an operating system, runtime, library, or service provides to support requests made by computer programs.

AIR has its own APIs to program desktop applications and directly interact with the operating system. As well as AIR APIs, the developer can implement the standard ActionScript APIs used to program SWF files. A list of these APIs is provided by Adobe's online documentation for the ActionScript language, called LiveDocs. You'll find an overview of the ActionScript 3.0 Language and Components Reference at this address: http://livedocs.adobe.com/flash/9.0/ActionScriptLangRefV3/.

To this list, you can add all the new AIR runtime APIs (a complete list of AIR APIs can be found at http://livedocs.adobe.com/labs/air/1/aslr/index.html). Table 1-2 lists a few runtime classes (these are only a part of AIR's APIs). These classes aren't available to SWF content running in the Adobe Flash Player plug-in in the browser.

Table 1-2. The runtime classes tied to AIR

Class Name	Package
File	flash.filesystem
FileListEvent	flash.events
FileMode	flash.filesystem
FileStream	flash.filesystem
HTMLHistoryItem	flash.html
HTMLHost	flash.html
HTMLLoader	flash.html
HTMLPDFCapability	flash.html
NativeApplication	flash.desktop

For instance, developers can take advantage of AIR APIs to access the local file system by using the File class provided by the flash.filesystem package. In programming, a package is a container that includes a group of classes. Each package has its own set of names for types, which helps to prevent name conflicts, called a **package name**.

As a simple example, the class named HTMLLoader in flash.html is invoked as follows:

```
flash.html.HTMLLoader
```

> *Do not confuse packages with namespaces. Namespaces are used for controlling the visibility of declarations. Namespaces are custom access specifiers (public, private, protected) that can have names of your choosing.*

AIR also has APIs for the service monitoring framework. These classes are external to the Flash package. They are in the air.net package and include classes used for network detection. To be able to use these APIs, it's necessary to include the ServiceMonitor.swc file.

> *See Chapter 11 for a discussion of the ServiceMonitor.swc file.*

To be able to fully take advantage of AIR's potential, it's necessary to know all the APIs that the technology provides. As such, the next section includes a list of AIR's main features.

Getting under the hood of AIR 1.5

Regardless of the fact that AIR is quite young, there are already many desktop runtime features. To use a technology to program in the best possible way, you have to know what it provides and its limits. This section will provide an overview of AIR's potential, in terms of the APIs it provides to the developer, and a couple of its limitations.

To describe AIR's APIs, I'll follow the order of the table of contents of this book, so you can quickly refer to the chapter that discusses the feature you're interested in.

AIR native window APIs

This set of APIs allows you to create and edit cross-platform desktop windows. The class that creates a system window is NativeWindow, contained in the flash.display package. The native window APIs contain the following classes:

- NativeWindow
- NativeWindowInitOptions

They also contain these constants:

- NativeWindowDisplayState
- NativeWindowResize
- NativeWindowSystemChrome
- NativeWindowType

You can use the Flash stage and display a list to add a visual object to a NativeWindow as follows:

```
var winOptions:NativeWindowInitOptions = new NativeWindowInitOptions();
winOptions.systemChrome = NativeWindowSystemChrome.STANDARD;
winOptions.transparent = false;
var newWindow:NativeWindow = new NativeWindow(winOptions);
```

You can create these three types of windows:

- **Normal**: This is the classic window with the full-size chrome style. It appears on the taskbar or the OS X window menu.
- **Utility**: This is a tool palette window. It does not show on the taskbar or OS X window menu.
- **Lightweight**: This is a custom window with no chrome.

With the following properties, you can control the basic appearance and behavior of a window and create custom windows with custom shapes using alpha transparency:

- type
- systemChrome
- transparent

> *See Chapter 5 for a discussion of AIR's native window APIs.*

Menu classes

AIR implements two new classes in the flash.display package to create menus:

- NativeMenu
- NativeMenuItem

These classes allow you to create native system windows that can be used as the following:

- Application menus (on Mac OS X systems)
- Window menus (on Windows systems)
- Pop-up menus
- Context menus

The following native menu classes can be added onto the classes that are already available to create customized context menus:

- ContextMenu
- ContextMenuItem

The following types of menus can be created in AIR applications:

- **Application menus**: Global menus that apply to the entire application.
- **Window menus**: Menus that are associated with single windows and are displayed below the title bar. Window menus are supported on the Windows operating system, but not on Mac OS X.
- **Context menus**: Menus that you can open in response to a right-click or Cmd+click on an interactive object in SWF content or a document element in HTML content.
- **Dock and system tray icon menus**: Icon menus assigned to an application icon in the Mac OS X dock or Windows notification area.

- **Pop-up menus**: Menus that aren't necessarily associated with a particular application object or component.
- **Custom menus**: Menus that can be created using the AIR menu classes.

> *See Chapter 6 for a discussion of menus.*

File system integration

AIR provides complete access to the host file system, allowing your application to use all the files it needs to function correctly. You can move, create, copy, and remove files or entire folders. You can also access the system clipboard to create applications you can actually use and that are integrated with the host operating system. The `flash.filesystem` package provides the following classes to interact with the file system:

- `File`: The `File` class allows you to work with documents and folders that are on the local operating system by creating references to the files that you can interact with programmatically.
- `FileMode`: The `FileMode` class provides static constants that define the possible modes in which the `FileStream` class can access the binary content of any file (reading, writing, appending, etc.).
- `FileStream`: To access the content of a file, you have to use the `FileStream` class. The `FileStream` class can operate in synchronous and asynchronous mode. When you use the synchronous reading and writing mode, the class behaves very much like the `ByteArray` class.

> *See Chapter 7 for a discussion of file system integration.*

Interaction with the operating system

An AIR application is installed on the local computer and therefore allows it to react to startup or closure events. For example, it's possible to launch an application when the user logs onto the computer by using the following code property:

```
NativeApplication.nativeApplication.startAtLogin=true
```

It's also possible to carry out operations (such as saving data that the user has worked on) during the closure of the application itself using the exiting event dispatched by `NativeApplication`. You can also create event listeners for the `closing` and `close` events during the closing phase.

> *See Chapter 8 for a discussion of the operating system.*

Tracking user presence

Speaking of interaction with the operating system, another feature is being able to track user presence, meaning that you can be aware of when the user is actively using the computer. An AIR application can track user presence by using NativeApplication's idleThreshold property and the USER_IDLE and USER_PRESENT events.

> See Chapter 8 for a discussion of tracking user presence.

PDF support

The AIR runtime can render PDF contents using the HTMLLoader class and the Acrobat Reader browser plug-in. This means that it is possible to open PDF content directly from an AIR application if the Acrobat Reader plug-in is installed on the local computer. The HTMLLoader.pdfCapability property allows the application to detect if a user can render PDF content.

> See Chapter 9 for a discussion of PDF support.

Integrating HTML content

Through the WebKit engine, the AIR application can load HTML content such as an HTML page. It can load HTML, CSS, and JavaScript code with the HTMLLoader class, as shown here:

```
var spriteDiv:Sprite;
var html:HTMLLoader = new HTMLLoader;
html.width = 800;
html.height = 600;
var urlToLoad:URLRequest = new URLRequest("http://www.comtaste.com/");
html.load(urlToLoad);
spriteDiv.addChild(html);
```

> See Chapter 10 for a discussion of integrating HTML content.

Monitoring network connectivity

An Internet connection (or any other network connectivity) isn't necessary for some desktop applications. They can work without ever having to request remote information on the local client. Other desktop applications, on the other hand, could need to access remote information to load data from an external database or a network. This is why it's essential for an AIR application to monitor network connectivity. AIR allows you to check for changes in the network connectivity of the computer where the application is installed. You can monitor changes in a network connection (not only Internet connections, but also intranet, VPN, etc.) by using the Event.NETWORK_CHANGE event.

AIR also provides developers with a service monitor framework. With this framework, you can detect the HTTP connectivity and whether the application can make HTTPS requests. Here's an example of this:

```
var monitor:URLMonitor;
monitor = new URLMonitor(new URLRequest('http://www.comtaste.com'));
monitor.addEventListener(StatusEvent.STATUS, onStatusHandler);
monitor.start();
```

See Chapter 11 for a discussion of monitoring network connectivity.

SQLite support

AIR supports the creation of local databases with SQLite. SQLite offers databases contained in a single independent file without the necessity of server applications or configuration documents. The SQLite format is multiplatform. Therefore, you can import a database created with Windows onto an OS X system and vice versa, without any kind of conversion.

The AIR SQLite APIs are defined in the flash.data package, and they contain the following classes:

- SQLConnection, for connecting to local databases
- SQLStatement, for executing queries to relational databases
- SQLResult, for managing the data returned by database queries, and many other classes that support the aforementioned ones

See Chapter 12 for a discussion of SQLite.

Updating installed applications

Having an application that is **resident** on the desktop means that a new installation file has to be distributed to update the application, and the user has to launch it. AIR has a class that allows you to update the application easily and efficiently. The Updater class includes the update() method to update the currently running application with a different version. The version of the application is specified as the version parameter of the update() method. This string has to match the string in the attribute of the main element of the application descriptor file for the AIR file to be installed. It is therefore possible to provide the user of the application with a simple system to maintain the AIR application updated to the latest version.

> *See Chapter 13 to learn about updating installed applications.*

In this quick overview, I've provided only a few of the most relevant features of AIR 1.5. AIR APIs are huge, so it would be quite a long process to describe all of them. In the following list, you'll find other important AIR features that you'll be able to use for developing your applications:

- Drag and drop
- Clipboard
- Notifications
- Application/installer signing
- Application icons
- File type registrations
- Background applications
- XML-RPC/SOAP/REST-based web service support
- Binary and XML sockets
- Task managers or process lists
- Application shortcuts
- Localization (for the application descriptor, localized elements have been renamed to text and l:lang; moreover the application descriptor's lang attribute has been changed to xmchanges)
- Custom filters and effects using Adobe Pixel Bender
- High-speed JavaScript execution using SquirrelFish (WebKit)
- Enhanced 3D effects and visual performance improvements
- New text engine with advanced layout components and anti-aliasing
- Drawing API enhancements
- Color management

The next section will illustrate the current weaknesses of the AIR APIs.

AIR's limitations

Now that I've talked about the potential of the AIR APIs, it's only fair to talk about the limits of this new technology. You have to bear in mind that AIR is new and Adobe is already working on its future versions to implement new added features. These limitations concern the following items:

- Native libraries and executable files
- USB and serial port APIs
- Hardware acceleration processes
- Full support for accessibility

Starting with the features that a developer will surely miss, we have the problem of not being able to access native libraries or executable files. This means that it still isn't possible to launch an external program that is installed on the local system from AIR or use system libraries to enrich desktop applications. Therefore, even if it is possible to create a link between the AIR application and the operating system by dragging files back and forth or accessing the clipboard, you can't launch an executable program that is installed on the local system.

The two following third-party projects exist for allowing AIR applications to launch external executable programs:

- Merapi
- CommandProxy

Merapi (www.merapiproject.net/) is an open source project that functions as a framework for connecting AIR to Java on the desktop. CommandProxy, a proof-of-concept project created by Mike Chambers, shows how to integrate AIR applications with C#/.NET code on any operating system that AIR currently runs on (Mac and Windows). It provides a communication proxy between an AIR application and the underlying operating system, and could theoretically work with other web-based desktop runtimes (see www.mikechambers. com/blog/2008/01/17/commandproxy-net-air-integration-proof-of-concept/).

> Pay attention to potential concerns about security for these third-party libraries. For more on the subject, read "CommandProxy: It's cool, but is it a good idea?" by Mike Chambers, at www.mikechambers.com/blog/2008/01/22/commandproxy-its-cool-but-is-it-a-good-idea/.

Another limitation is the impossibility of supporting USB or serial port APIs. For desktop applications that need to interact with external devices that are connected to the computer via USB or serial ports, AIR 1.5 doesn't have any APIs. If you have to communicate with a printer or a barcode reader, you can't use AIR. All you can do is connect to webcams or microphones.

This weakness also translates into limited printing support. It's often necessary for a desktop application to be able to access a list of installed printers without having to resort to the classic Print dialog box. This isn't a supported option in the Adobe runtime, which manages the printing process like Flash Player does for web applications.

If you want to exploit the computer's hardware acceleration process to create 3D games or increase the performance of a video-compositing application, you'll have limited hardware acceleration. Hardware acceleration will only be used for full-screen videos (thanks to Flash Player).

Last but not least, there is limited support for accessibility. Evidently, the runtime still can't communicate well with the system libraries to make the content of the application accessible.

What's new in Flash with CS4

The new version of Flash, CS4, is full of new features that make a lot of wishes come true for the designers and developers who use this environment. First Macromedia and now Adobe have always given a lot of attention to the growing needs of the users of their IDE. This version of Flash solves a lot of the problems that the product had before, regarding the technical as well as the graphical aspects.

Flash CS4 tries to make everyone happy. Designers require a tool that keeps up with their ideas and allows them to create articulate animations. They also need a tool for creating 3D elements with complex and realistic movements, and that can combine video elements with sound and animation. Designers can now push their creativity to the limit with this IDE to produce innovative and surprising animations. All of this is included in a single environment with an intuitive interface. Developers need a tool that uses a powerful and object-oriented language that can increase their productivity in writing code, debugging an application, and collaborating. Developers can now write more robust and complex RIAs (rich Internet applications).

There are a lot of new features in Flash CS4. This section covers the most relevant ones, which are the following:

- AIR authoring support
- 3D graphics
- The Bone tool
- The Motion Editor panel
- Preconfigured motion tweens
- The Kuler panel
- Sound asset improvements
- The Project and Library panels
- Integration with Flex
- H.264 support for videos in high resolution
- ConnectNow integration
- Adobe Pixel Bender

AIR authoring support

While authoring your application, you can preview it without having to compile and install it on the computer. To launch the preview that has been loaded in the AIR runtime, choose the Control ➤ Test Movie menu option. This way, you can test the application before releasing it. Furthermore, a new dialog box to configure the application settings of the AIR application has been introduced: AIR – Application & Installer Settings. This panel allows you to specify the settings that will be written in the **application descriptor** file. The application descriptor file is an XML file that the AIR application uses for installation and startup.

With Flash CS4, publishing an AIR file is quite a simple operation. Follow these steps to compile a SWF file and an XML application descriptor file, and package them in an AIR installer file:

1. Click the Publish button in the Publish Settings dialog box.

2. Click Publish AIR File in the AIR – Application & Installer Settings panel.

3. Choose File ➤ Publish.

4. Choose File ➤ Publish Preview.

Figure 1-4 shows the dialog boxes you use to publish an AIR project.

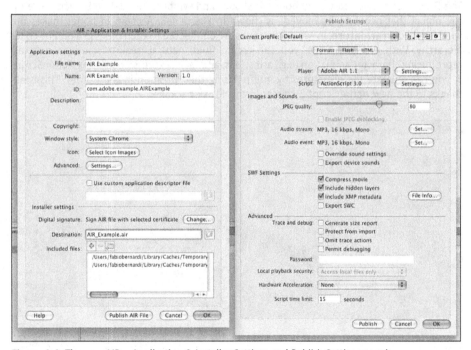

Figure 1-4. The new AIR – Application & Installer Settings and Publish Settings panels

3D graphics

This version of Flash finally has 3D effects that allow you to move and rotate movie clips in 3D space on the stage. Every movie clip now has a new property: the Z axis, which is similar to a 3D tool. Translation effects such as moving an object in 3D space on the stage and transformation (rotation of an object) are now possible. The following 3D tools, objects, and properties are available in Flash CS4:

- The Pointview and Camera objects
- The angle and vanishing point properties
- The 3D Translation tool
- The 3D Rotation tool
- The perspective angle property

The Bone tool

You can use the Bone tool to create animations using **inverse kinematics**. Wikipedia defines inverse kinematics as "the process of determining the parameters of a jointed flexible object (a kinematic chain) in order to achieve a desired pose" (see http://en.wikipedia.org/wiki/Inverse_kinematics). Inverse kinematics is relevant to 3D animation, which you'll see in this book.

The Bone tool allows you to add bones to shapes and symbols that define the structure of the object that needs to be moved, as shown in Figure 1-5. A chain of bones makes up what is called an **armature**, in which the bones are connected to each other in a parent-child hierarchy. With this technique, you can create fluid, natural, realistic motions such as reproducing character animation (e.g., arms, legs, and facial expressions). Using ActionScript 3, you can animate the armatures by interpolating their position in the frames. This is all thanks to the new ActionScript 3 classes in the fl.ik package.

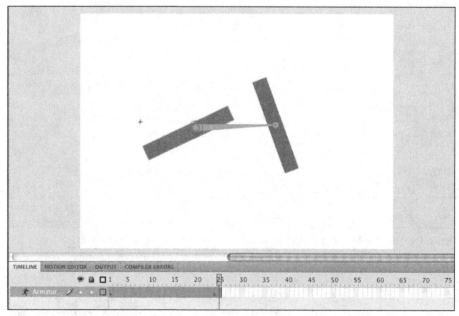

Figure 1-5. The Bone tool allows you to add bones, shapes, and symbols that define the structure of the object you want to move.

The Motion Editor panel

This new panel that has been added to Flash's IDE gives you absolute control over each keyframe parameter. It's a powerful tool for displaying, interacting with, and editing tween properties and their keyframes. This way, it's possible to have better control over tween animations and make them a bit more realistic. Here are some of the operations that you can carry out from the Motion Editor panel:

- Adding and removing filters
- Creating custom ease curves
- Creating complex curves for complex tweened effects
- Adding and removing keyframe properties
- Adding color effects
- Controlling the shape of tween curves

Figure 1-6 displays the Motion Editor panel.

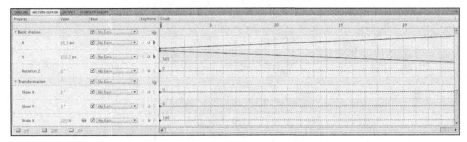

Figure 1-6. The Motion Editor panel

Using the preconfigured motion tweens

Often, the same animation will be used in a Flash project in different parts of the document. Flash CS4 allows you to save a lot of time by using motion presets. You can use the Motion Presets panel to do the following:

- Save a tween as a custom motion preset
- Apply a motion preset
- Preview a motion preset
- Import a motion preset
- Export a motion preset

Figure 1-7 displays the Motion Presets panel with the preconfigured motion tweens that can be applied to a graphic symbol.

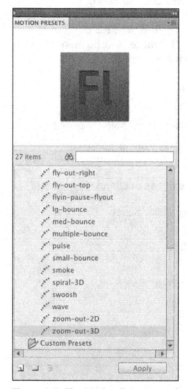

Figure 1-7. The Motion Presets panel

The Kuler panel

Kuler was one of the first AIR applications released by Adobe (see http://kuler.adobe.com/). The Kuler panel, which was already a panel in Illustrator CS3, allows you to generate color themes that can inspire any project. The Kuler panel is displayed in Figure 1-8.

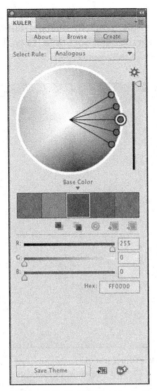

Figure 1-8. The Kuler panel allows you to generate color themes.

Improvements on sound assets

Flash CS4 is integrated with Adobe Soundbooth, which allows users to edit imported sounds directly from within Flash. Adobe has also created a new sound library with a series of sound effects that are ready to use.

> In Chapter 9, you'll learn how to work with sound assets in an AIR application.

The Project and Library panels

The new Project panel is displayed in Figure 1-9. Using this panel, you can manage multiple document files in a single project. This means you can optimize the management of complex projects, which include several files at the same time. In a Flash project, you can link any Flash file in FLA and SWF format, as well as another Flash project.

The new Library panel gives you more control over your project's assets than in previous versions of Flash. You can use this panel to manage different assets more easily than before. Now you can launch searches and sort data, as well as set properties on multiple library items at once.

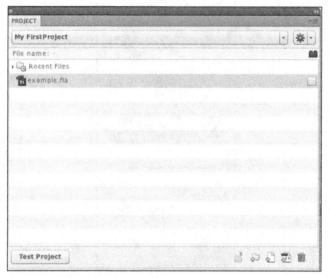

Figure 1-9. The new Project panel

Integration with Flex

The integration between Flash and Flex has been optimized with Flash CS4. You can save a Flash asset as a Flex component in SWC (compiled SWF file) format. This format can be imported into the Flex project as a library, and it can be used like any other component.

The components that will be created and exported by Flash CS4 are subclasses of the UIMovieClip class found in the mx.flash package. This class is, in turn, a subclass of the flash.display.MovieClip class, which implements the following interfaces: IDeferredInstantiationUIComponent, IToolTipManagerClient, IStateClient, IFocus➥ ManagerComponent, and IConstraintClient.

There are no particular constraints in the creation of Flash content that will be exported as a Flex component. Follow this advice to guarantee a successful export:

- You must export your content as a movie clip symbol.
- The registration point should be in the upper-left corner.
- The frame rate should be 24 to match Flex's default frame rate (this operation will be automatically performed when you execute the Make Flex Component command).
- The symbol name in the library should be a valid ActionScript class name.

The use of Flash to create components that will then be used in Flex is handy, especially when you want to use functions that only Flash has (e.g., using the timeline to create animations or using components of Flash to skin the Flex components).

H.264 support for video in high resolution

With Adobe Media Encoder integrated into Flash CS4, it's possible to encode the highest-quality video. This wasn't possible before in Flash—you had to use video products such as Adobe Premiere Pro and After Effects. Now, using Adobe Media Encoder, you can easily capture and broadcast Flash video in high resolution.

H.264 is a standard for video compression. It is also known as MPEG-4 Part 10 and MPEG-4 AVC (Advanced Video Coding). The goal of this format was to create a standard capable of providing good video quality at substantially lower bit rates than previous standards (e.g., half of the bit rate of MPEG-2, H.263, or MPEG-4 Part 2), without increasing the complexity of design so much that it would be impractical or excessively expensive to implement. Read more at http://en.wikipedia.org/wiki/H.264.

> In Chapter 9, you'll learn how to embed Flash video into an AIR desktop application.

Integration with ConnectNow

ConnectNow is a web application for organizing collaborative web conferences. With ConnectNow (www.adobe.com/acom/connectnow/), you can use screen sharing, chat, notes, audio, and video to conduct meetings online. These online interactions can be as productive as in-person meetings, and can accommodate up to three participants. You must create a web conference from Flash CS4 using Flash Player in order to use ConnectNow. ConnectNow is part of the Acrobat.com family of products. The interface for ConnectNow is displayed in Figure 1-10.

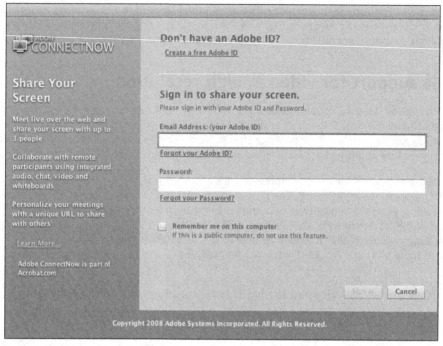

Figure 1-10. You can lauch a web conference directly from Flash CS4 with ConnectNow.

Adobe Pixel Bender

Adobe Pixel Bender is a new scripting language. You can use it to create custom filters, blends, and fills at runtime to add new and creative visual effects for the Flash runtime environment. To develop Pixel Bender custom filters, you need the Pixel Bender Toolkit.

Pixel Bender is used to implement image-processing algorithms in a hardware-independent manner with the following benefits:

- C-based language with a syntax based on GLSL (GLSL stands for GL Shading Language, often referred as glslang, and is defined by the Architectural Review Board of OpenGL)
- Allows the same filter to run efficiently on different GPU and CPU architectures
- Provides abstraction of the complexity of executing on heterogeneous hardware
- Supports third-party creation and sharing of filters and effects
- Delivers excellent image-processing performance in Adobe products

The final section of this chapter provides a list of web resources that you can use on a daily basis to stay updated on Flash CS4 and AIR.

Consulting the Web: Resources

Even if the AIR runtime is still a young piece of technology, there is already a lot of useful information for it on the Web for free. You should definitely start with the Adobe Developer Connection (ADC) site (www.adobe.com/devnet/), which provides articles and examples of code to learn from the experts. This site is organized as follows:

- **Adobe AIR Developer Center** (www.adobe.com/devnet/): The ADC site is divided into three sections according to the language you want to use:
  - **Develop with HTML/Ajax** (www.adobe.com/devnet/air/ajax/): This section is dedicated to Ajax AIR development.
  - **Adobe AIR Developer Center for Flash** (www.adobe.com/devnet/air/flash/): This section is dedicated to Flash AIR development.
  - **Adobe AIR Developer Center for Flex** (www.adobe.com/devnet/air/flex/): This section is dedicated to Flex AIR development.
- **Flash Developer Center** (www.adobe.com/devnet/flash/): This section is dedicated to Flash articles.
- **ActionScript Technology Center** (www.adobe.com/devnet/actionscript/): This section is dedicated to ActionScript 3 articles.

You can also access the following online documentation for free:

- Developing Adobe AIR 1.1 Applications with Adobe Flash CS4 Professional (http://help.adobe.com/en_US/AIR/1.1/devappsflash/)
- Programming ActionScript 3.0 (http://livedocs.adobe.com/flash/9.0/main)
- ActionScript 3.0 Language and Components Reference (includes AIR) (http://livedocs.adobe.com/flash/9.0/ActionScriptLangRefV3/)
- Quick Starts (for Flash CS3) (www.adobe.com/go/learn_air_flash_qs_en)
- Using Flash (http://livedocs.adobe.com/flash/9.0/UsingFlash)
- Using ActionScript 3.0 Components (http://livedocs.adobe.com/flash/9.0/main)

The blogs of the following AIR team members and Adobe evangelists are always useful sources of news, tips, and communication:

- Lee Brimelow (www.theflashblog.com/)
- Serge Jespers (www.webkitchen.be/)
- Ted Patrick (www.onflex.org/ted/)
- Andrew Shorten (http://ashorten.com/)
- James Ward (www.jamesward.org/wordpress/)
- Christian Cantrell (http://weblogs.macromedia.com/cantrell/)
- Mike Chambers (www.mikechambers.com/)
- Richard Galvan (http://blogs.adobe.com/rgalvan/)

- Christophe Coenraets (http://coenraets.org/)
- Mike Downey (http://madowney.com/blog/)
- Daniel Dura (www.danieldura.com/)
- Kevin Hoyt (http://blog.kevinhoyt.org/)
- Mike Potter (www.riapedia.com/)
- Ryan Stewart (http://blog.digitalbackcountry.com/)
- Ben Forta (www.forta.com/)
- Enrique Duvós (www.duvos.com/)

Finally, there is the following blogger ecosystem. It consists of communities and mailing lists you can refer to for day-to-day development problems with AIR technology:

- Marco Casario (http://casario.blogs.com/)
- David Tucker (www.davidtucker.net/)
- Peter Elst (www.peterelst.com/blog/)
- Rich Tretola (http://blog.everythingflex.com/)
- Renaun Erikson (http://renaun.com/blog/)
- Devon O. Wolfgang (http://blog.onebyonedesign.com/)
- Koen De Weggheleire (http://newmovieclip.wordpress.com/)

Summary

In this first chapter, you've learned the basics of the AIR APIs and some of the new features of Flash CS4. Basically, you aren't short on choices. Once you've read this book and learned how to use AIR APIs to develop desktop applications with Flash CS4, I hope you'll want to know how other developers create their applications.

You can only grow and improve through these kinds of dialogs.

Happy reading!

CHAPTER 2
INTRODUCING FLASH CS4

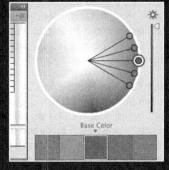 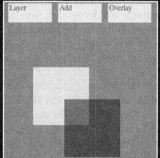 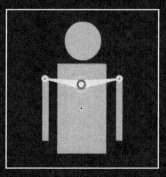

Adobe Flash has been one of the most important web development products for several years now. The fact that you can create animations, work with data from external sources, produce interactive games, and play high-resolution videos has made this software a stronghold for professional web developers and designers as well as amateurs.

The new version of Flash, CS4, part of the Adobe Creative Suite 4, allows you to create even more complex animations than the ones you could build in the previous versions, with the introduction of new features and tools. It's now possible to animate graphic assets with inverse kinematics, control objects during an animation, and create 3D animations using the new 3D Translation and 3D Rotation tools.

Given the enormous potential of Flash and Flash Player, today you can also create desktop applications in Flash through the Adobe AIR. This means you can port your web applications to the desktop and create all kinds of software without having to learn a new language or development technology.

ActionScript, now in its third version, is no longer Flash's faithful companion. ActionScript 3 has evolved into an object-oriented programming (OOP) language that can be used for developing complex and robust Rich Internet Applications (RIAs).

In this chapter, you will explore how the graphics programs of the Adobe family have been made to work together to be leaner and faster. You will also see how to create synergies among the development products: Flex and Flash. Additionally, you will experiment with the main new features of Flash CS4 and AIR. I'll tie together all of this information into a series of practical examples.

Let's start with the evolution of Flash—what it has become, what can you do with it, and what can you expect from Flash in the future.

The evolution of Flash CS

In 2005, Adobe acquired the Macromedia brand and products. Adobe assimilated these products well at the user interface level, but there was a need for them to be assimilated at both the graphical and integration levels as well. Most notably, users wanted to create graphical projects and import them directly into Flash without having to waste time with the various export and import procedures. With CS4, Adobe focused on these aspects to provide users better integration among its products.

As you will see in the following chapters, Illustrator CS4, like Photoshop CS4 and Fireworks CS4, allows you to convert graphical assets into symbols that Flash can use easily, cutting down on production and project development times. Flash CS4 can read Illustrator, Photoshop, and Fireworks CS4 project files. You can process each asset and import it into a Flash project as an editable layer (be it text, a vector shape, or a bitmap), and you can also convert layers into movie clips. This ability makes the initial graphics settings processes for your project a lot leaner.

Flash CS3 vs. Flash CS4

There are substantial differences between Flash CS4 and Flash CS3, both in the user interface and the new added features.

You can pretty safely say that Flash CS4 release tends to give more importance to the designer, the graphical aspects, and the animation development potential than its predecessor. Flash CS3 gave more importance to the potential that it could provide to developers. Flash CS3 did provide certain features for designers, though. For example, it allowed you to save, export, and import XML animations. These capabilities made it unnecessary to rebuild animations from scratch or import them into new projects. Flash CS4, on the other hand, actually targets designers.

The most attractive feature of Flash CS4 for designers and developers alike is the capability for creating animations of 2D objects in 3D environments. Also important are the new z and rotationZ properties of the DisplayObject class, which allow you to make objects move in space; and Pixel Bender, the new toolkit that allows you to manage custom filter effects.

Remember, however, that the objects you can manage are 2D (two-dimensional); you can't, for example, give a square or a circle a third dimension on its own. You can still create 3D animations, though, by using tweens set up on the timeline or in code. This chapter includes examples of how to create timeline-based animations that exploit the new features. You will also see how to repeat the same exercise using ActionScript 3 so that you'll be able to operate on 3D animations with code, not just with the Flash tools.

The user interface has also changed a lot between Flash CS3 and CS4. When you open the new version, you will probably feel disoriented at first. This is mainly due to the fact that there is a completely new approach to the use of the timeline, and therefore to creating even the simplest animations. However, anyone that has a little familiarity with programs like Adobe Premiere Pro CS4 or After Effects CS4 will be familiar with the tools you are about to analyze.

The upcoming sections will cover the following new features of Flash:

- Timeline frames
- Effects
- The Deco tool
- Audio
- The H.264 video compression standard
- XFL format
- Flash CS4 and Flex

Using the timeline

In Flash, the timeline has always been very important because it has typically contained most of the animation (obviously, except for cases in which the animation is exclusively controlled via code). Today things have changed, especially as far as the frames of the timeline are concerned.

The timeline frames aren't used like in the previous versions; only the ones that are actually inserted (keyframes) are processed and calculated, like in Premiere Pro CS4. And now you can actually control animations with **Bezier curves** (parametric curves used in computer graphics), simply by setting the length (number of frames) you want to use.

Each variation for any property (X, Y, alpha, etc.) will be displayed on the Flash timeline with a little diamond, as shown in frame 24 in Figure 2-1.

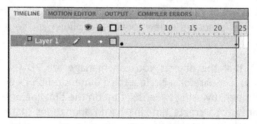

Figure 2-1. The new Flash CS4 timeline ready to work

> If you prefer to work in the traditional style, you can continue managing the animations like you're used to by using the Classic Tween option. This feature is described further in the "Using the main work panels to create animations" section.

Adding effects to improve presentations

To improve the presentation of your Flash projects, you can add effects to an object on the stage by following these steps:

1. Choose the Display option on the Properties panel.

2. Choose the type of blending (Normal, Layer, Darken, Multiply, Screen, etc.). The blending options are for fusing colors and symbols; you may be used to seeing these in graphic design programs like Photoshop.

3. Save the image in memory by selecting the Cache as bitmap option. This gives Flash the opportunity to cache the image so you don't have to render the clip all over again during the animation. This cuts down memory use and improves the performance of the application.

The Deco tool

Bearing in mind that the new version of Flash CS4 is aimed at designers, it would have been impossible for it to exclude the Deco tool. This new tool is quite interesting, even if not particularly advanced in terms of functions. This tool, which is quite easy to use, allows you to apply decorative patterns exclusively to vector shapes and traces. To use it, all you have to do is create a shape on the stage, select the Deco tool from the Tools panel, and select one of the items in the Properties panel, which displays all the Deco tool's options, as shown in Figure 2-2.

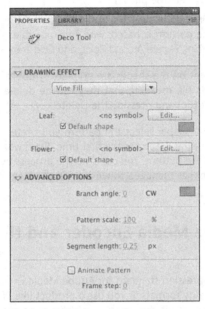

Figure 2-2. The Deco tool's options

The following list details the options of the Deco tool:

- Drawing Effect: In this section, you can choose from three types of predefined patterns: Vine Fill, Grid Fill, and Symmetry Brush.

  - Vine Fill: This creates a pattern that redesigns any element with a stylized leaf pattern. This, in turn, has two options: Leaf and Flower, which both allow you to set the color of the pattern to apply or change the pattern image with a movie clip from the library.

  - Grid Fill: This dotted-square pattern fills shapes with little squares in horizontal lines in the color you choose from the color picker under the Drawing Effect item. This effect also allows you to choose a movie clip from the library as a theme of the pattern.

  - Symmetry Brush: This dotted-square pattern is inserted symmetrically according to the position of the guide. You can place the position of the symmetrical point in the Advanced Options subpanel.

- Advanced Options: This section presents advanced options for each of the three drawing effects just mentioned:

  - For Vine Fill: You can set the angle of the pattern, the color, and the length of the segment that needs to be repeated (in pixels). The Animate Pattern option creates a brief animation on the timeline that lasts as long as the number of frames specified in the Frame step option, in which the pattern progressively covers the whole shape.

  - For Grid Fill: The advanced options are Horizontal Spacing (for the horizontal spacing of the dots), Vertical Spacing (for the vertical spacing of the dots), and Pattern Scale (to scale the pattern).

  - For Symmetry Brush: The available options regard setting the point on which the symmetry of the pattern is based, with four possible types: Reflect Across Line, Reflect Across Point, Rotate Around Point, and Grid Translation.

Remember that the patterns on the shapes are graphics symbols, and they don't interfere with the shape itself or its fill, meaning that they can be deleted at any time simply by selecting them with Select tool and pressing the Delete key.

To assign a decoration to a shape, select the pattern you prefer and click the shape you want to fill. When you click the shape for the first time, Flash will cover the shape by progressively covering it with the pattern. You can stop the process by clicking again, and only the part that the Deco tool has managed to work on in the meantime will stay covered by the pattern.

Support for Adobe Media Encoder and the new audio library

The new H.264 video compression standard for Adobe Media Encoder allows you to create or code videos in high-quality formats. If you use a product like Premiere Pro CS4 or After Effects CS4, you can export videos through this standard for Flash Player 10.

Also, Adobe couldn't exclude audio features from its new version of Flash. Flash CS4 presents a new sample library, which includes 186 small and brief audio samples.

The XFL format

The XFL (Extensible Flash) format is key in the integration of Flash with other Adobe CS products. XFL allows you to import open After Effects CS4 or InDesign CS4 files (in which you can read, edit, or delete assets). The XFL format is based on XML, which registers the same information that is saved in an FLA file, meaning that XFL files are actually lighter (in terms of KB) and more readable on various operating systems (because they're essentially compressed files) than FLA files. However, once you open an XFL file in Flash CS4, you have to save the project in FLA format. You can't actually save a file in XFL format in Flash CS4.

To see the content of an XFL file, all you have to do is open it as a common file (not through the Import option). All of the assets of the original file will appear in the timeline, and the original object will appear in the library.

Flash CS4/Flex integration

Finally, I'd like to mention the increasing integration of Flash CS4 and Flex. Today it is actually possible to import components built with ActionScript 3 code into your web or desktop Flex projects. Flex 3 allows you to develop RIAs from precreated and customizable components alike. Flash CS4 allows you to create components especially for Flex products. This integration is possible thanks to Flash's SWC (Shockwave Compiled) exportation format. This format allows you to generate components dynamically in Flash, insert ActionScript 3 code if necessary, and import the work into Flex. Everything you insert into an SWC file can be used perfectly in Flex.

Now that you've been introduced to the main new features of Flash CS4, it's time to get more specific, starting with the new IDE.

Learning the new Flash IDE

In this section, I'll discuss the following new features:

- The graphics panels (including the Tools panel and its settings, the stage's features, the Kuler panel, and the Swatches panel)
- The main work panels (including the Motion Presets panel, the timeline, and the animation tools)

> *The interfaces are quite similar among the CS4 versions of the Adobe products, as are the tasks of creating documents, managing work panels, and manipulating workspaces. These common approaches make going from one application to the other easy, without diminishing the particular characteristics of each one.*

Using the graphical panels

As mentioned, the new Flash IDE looks quite different from the previous version at first. However, if you look closely at the various panels, you'll see that the tools are the same: you still have the library and the Tools panel, which work in the same way. (The timeline is the only element that has varied significantly.) The Tools panel and library have acquired a few additions, though, which have improved the performance and management of the product. These are discussed next.

Enhancements to the Tools panel

The Tools panel, shown in Figure 2-3, has been improved thanks to the introduction of the 3D Rotation and 3D Translation tools, which, as mentioned previously, allow you to create and control 3D animation.

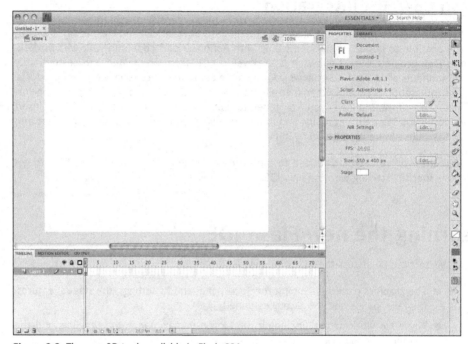

Figure 2-3. The new 3D tools available in Flash CS4

Enhancements to the library

The library has a new option that organizes elements into folders, which you can use when converting objects into button, movie clip, or graphic symbols. For example, if you try and convert a shape (Modify ➤ Convert to symbol) into a movie clip symbol, the Folder option on the Convert to Symbol panel will allow you to insert the new object into an existing folder or create a new one.

Changing panel settings

Just like any other Adobe CS4 product, Flash allows you to change the settings of the panels (position, visibility, etc.). You can modify and customize the defaults of the workspace on the Properties panel, as shown in Figure 2-4.

Figure 2-4. Using the Properties panel to customize the workspace

To set up the workspace so that it is more suitable for your needs, just follow these steps:

1. Click the Essentials item (in the upper-right corner of the screen).

2. Once you have moved, opened, or closed the panels as needed, select New Workspace from the drop-down menu.

3. The New Workspace panel will appear. On this panel, enter a name, and click the OK button. This will save the position of the panels of your work area so that you can reset them at any time. The new name you assign to the setting will appear in the list of workspaces, below the Essentials item.

The stage's improvements

The stage has also undergone a few interesting changes. The most important change to the stage concerns moving an object on the stage (e.g., a movie clip or shape). When you begin to move an object on the stage, Flash will leave a translucent copy of the object in the initial position, as shown in Figure 2-5. This feature makes it easier to manage objects on the stage.

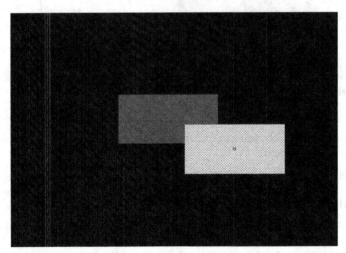

Figure 2-5. When you move an object, a copy of it stays in its initial position for reference.

Choosing the right color: the Adobe Kuler panel

Another important graphics tool introduced in CS4 is the Adobe Kuler panel. You can use this panel to create and save color themes, download them from the Web, and share your presets with the Kuler community. As you can see in Figure 2-6, the Kuler panel allows you to choose a set of five colors, either through hexadecimal code or RGB values.

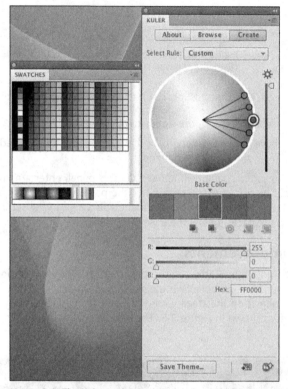

Figure 2-6. The Kuler and Swatches panels of Flash CS4

To use the Kuler panel, just click Window ➤ Other Panels ➤ Kuler. You will see the three following tabs:

- About: This tab gives a brief presentation of Adobe Kuler and its capabilities.
- Browse: On this tab, you can browse the various saved presets (or download new ones from the Web).
- Create: On this tab, you can create and save your own color presets.

Managing Kuler's colors: the Swatches

Each saved or newly created preset can be added to the Swatches panel and used at will. The Swatches panel allows you to manage the colors you want to use in your Flash projects. Each saved preset in the Kuler panel can be used in this panel, whether you created it or downloaded it from the Web.

Using the main work panels to create animations

Now that you have seen a few important new features in Flash CS4, you'll concentrate on the tools used to make animations:

- The Motion Presets panel
- The timeline

Working with animation presets: the Motion Presets panel

The Motion Presets panel, new in Flash CS4, is an amazing utility tool. Anyone telling the story of Flash always starts by saying that Flash was born as "the program that made the ball bounce" without using JavaScript, Java applets, or other powerful but more complex tools. This story entered the collective imagination of all Flash developers and designers, and they've now created a panel of preset animations: the Motion Presets panel. And the first preformatted animation was none other than the bouncing ball (the Bounce Smoosh effect). Let's take a look at this panel now.

To open the Motion Presets panel, go to Window ➤ Motion Presets. The panel shows a list of the 27 types of animations, as well as a brief preview of the selected animation. You can use this panel to create and save new presets, and alter existing presets.

Try and apply an animation to an object straight away. Bear in mind that you can only apply animations to movie clips, text fields, button symbols, and graphic symbols; you can't apply animations to shapes. If you forget to convert your shape into a movie clip or other type of symbol, Flash CS4 will do it automatically, after it has warned you about the conversion.

1. Create a new Flash CS4 document by clicking File ➤ New ➤ Flash File (Adobe AIR).
2. Draw a rectangle on the stage with the Rectangle tool.
3. Convert this new shape into a movie clip symbol by selecting it with the Selection tool and then choosing Modify ➤ Convert to symbol ➤ Type: Movie Clip.

The Convert to Symbol panel allows you to optimize the library of the object you use in a Flash project. In fact, if you don't keep the library under control, it can become a mess of elements that are impossible to organize. As you can see in Figure 2-7, the Convert to Symbol panel offers various options that allow you to optimize your library. The Folder option allows you to register or create a movie clip and save it in a preexisting or a newly created folder. Because you don't need to classify the folder, you can leave the Library root option selected so that the object will be saved in the main root directory.

Once the object has been converted, you can apply the desired effect to it.

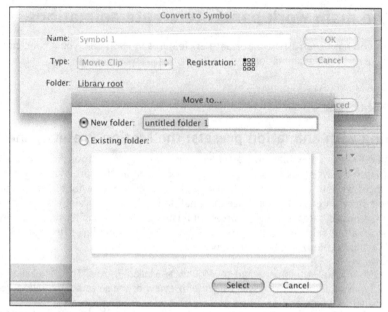

Figure 2-7. The Convert to Symbol panel with the options to optimize the organization of the material

To apply a motion preset animation, follow these steps:

1. Open the Motion Presets panel (Window ➤ Motion Presets).

2. Click the Default Presets folder.

3. Choose the item you prefer by clicking it.

4. If you like the preview, click Apply.

Now you've added the animation you chose to your element. You might notice a dotted line next to the movie clip on the stage. This line traces the movements of the animation, and is known as a **motion path**, which you may be familiar with from Adobe AfterEffects CS4. You can edit it by dragging the dots like a Bezier path, and if you open the timeline, you'll notice that it changes along with your edits.

Once you've applied a motion preset to an object on the stage, its layer in the timeline is converted into a motion tween layer. The animation will take up as many frames on the timeline as the selected motion preset needs.

Next, you'll look at one last aspect of the Motion Presets panel: importing and exporting your own animation. In the context menu activated by clicking the upper-right icon on the panel (shown in Figure 2-8), you can import and/or export a premade animation or create a new one. The context menu offers various options to manage the motion presets. The default animations, as well as the ones you can generate yourself, are saved in the XML file.

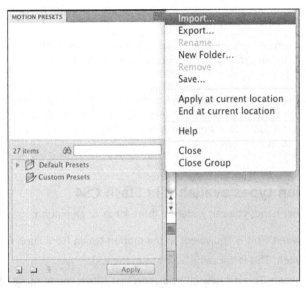

Figure 2-8. The options on the Motion Presets panel

To save an animation you have created, right-click the layer of the timeline that contains the animation. Then choose Save from the context menu. The animation must be a motion tween.

The next section explains how to create an animation using the timeline and the animation tools.

The timeline

You've probably noticed that the timeline in Flash CS4 has changed considerably since CS3. Animations today are more powerful than in the past, because the Motion Editor panel has been added to the timeline. The Motion Editor panel allows you to control the various parameters of your objects in 2D and 3D space during the animation. However, the types of frames of the timeline haven't changed much. They remain as follows:

- **Keyframe**: A frame containing various kinds of material (movie clips, buttons, etc.)
- **Blank keyframe**: An empty frame without any kind of element inside it
- **Frame**: A simple non-key frame

The animation types available in Flash CS3

Up to Flash CS3, it was possible to create two different kinds of animation on the timeline through interpolation:

- **Motion tween**: An interpolation that is generally used with movie clips, buttons, or graphics.
- **Shape tween**: An interpolation that can only be used with vector forms or elements of another type converted into vector forms.

> *Interpolation* is a method that uses numerical analysis of a finite amount of data. In Flash, this process translates into the creation of an animation between an initial condition (objects on a keyframe) and a final condition (objects on one of the following keyframes).

The animation types available in Flash CS4

Today, on the other hand, you can generate three kinds of animation:

- **Classic tween**: This is equivalent to the motion tween from Flash CS3.
- **Shape tween**: This is the same as it was in the CS3.
- **Motion tween**: This is a new interpolation that allows you to move objects in 3D as well as 2D environments, and to operate on the various parameters of the elements you want to animate through the Motion Editor panel.

Creating a 3D animation

Creating a simple 3D animation really isn't all that complicated. The important thing is that the object you are animating has to be a symbol (e.g., a movie clip). Try and test these 3D tools.

1. Open a new Flash document (choose File ➤ New ➤ Flash File (ActionScript 3.0)).

2. Draw a simple rectangle with the Rectangle tool.

3. Convert this shape into a movie clip symbol.

4. Select the shape, and go to Modify ➤ Convert to symbol ➤ Type: Movie Clip.

In the Properties panel, which is on the right-hand side of the screen by default, notice the items regarding 3D position and view settings of your movie clip object. To create your 3D animation, you have to set the number of frames you need to create the animation on the timeline, just like you're used to, and then perform the following steps:

5. Click any frame in the timeline to select it.

6. Go to Insert ➤ Timeline ➤ Frame (or press F5).

7. Right-click any frame between the first and the one you selected in step 5, and choose the first option from the context menu, Create Motion Tween.

To check that everything worked, see if the symbol on Layer 1 of the timeline has changed. The frames of the layer should be colored blue, as shown in Figure 2-9.

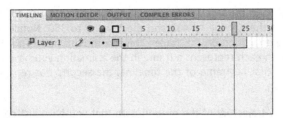

Figure 2-9. Here is your new layer, where you've applied the motion tween.

Now that you've applied a motion tween to the chosen layer, you are ready to apply 3D animation to your movie clip.

The Motion Editor panel

Take a look at the Motion Editor panel, next to the Timeline panel. This panel is populated with properties that allow you to manage objects in 3D environments. The main items on this panel are Basic Motion and Transformation. The other ones, Color Effect and Filters, pertain to the more graphical or aesthetic aspects of your object.

The Motion Editor panel is fundamentally divided into two separate parts: on the left are the various parameters with their relevant settings, and on the right is a timeline. The latter will allow you to edit the values of Basic motion (to place your objects on the X, Y, and Z axes), Transformation (to change the inclination or scaling of an object), and other parameters that allow you to insert, change, or delete keyframes.

To begin creating an animation using the Motion Editor panel, open the Motion Editor panel (Window ➤ Motion Editor) and place the head of the timeline on frame 1, as illustrated in Figure 2-10.

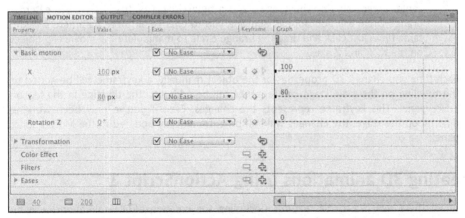

Figure 2-10. Using the the Motion Editor panel to create an animation

In the Basic motion section of the Motion Editor panel, you can change the X and Y parameters of an animation by double-clicking the value of this property and inserting a new value (or dragging the value). Try this by entering an X value of 100 and a Y value of 80.

Now, on the timeline in the Motion Editor panel, move to frame 10 and repeat the procedure. This time, set the X value to 400 and the Y value to 350. Notice that it traces the movements of the animation on the stage—this is a motion path. This motion path contains ten dots, which each represent a frame in the animation you have created. The first dot represents the first keyframe of the timeline, the second dot represents the second keyframe, and so on.

You can change the trajectory of the motion path that you have just created. To do this, select a dot on the motion path with the Selection tool and drag it with the mouse.

> When you want to change the trajectory, the motion path must be deselected.

Once you have carried out this change to the X and Y parameters, two curves will be drawn next to the X and Y parameters in the Basic motion section of the Motion Editor panel. These curves represent the movement you have just created, allowing you to see the position that the object assumes throughout the animation. If you go back to the timeline at this point, you'll see that a small diamond icon has been added at frame 10 of the layer containing the animation. The diamond icon indicates that the animation has been created.

You can easily turn this 2D animation into a 3D one, and there are two ways to do so:

- Right-click between the frames of the animation you created and choose the 3D Tween option from the context menu. Then go back to the Motion Editor panel and change the Z and Z Rotation options as you prefer.
- Select the 3D Rotation tool from the Tools panel, and then select the movie clip object. Three graphics will appear on the object, allowing you to change the parameters manually (by clicking and dragging): a vertical red bar (for the X axis), a horizontal green bar (for the Y axis), and a blue circle (for the Z axis). An external orange circle will also appear, allowing you to change all three parameters at the same time. Just click and drag the orange circle to manipulate the movie clip object on the X, Y, and Z axes.

Each time you change 3D properties of the object manually, a keyframe will be added to the timeline on the main stage, and another will be added to the timeline in the Motion Editor panel. This keyframe represents the changes. Even if you've only been working directly on the stage, the changes will still be automatically updated in the Motion Editor panel.

Creating 3D animations using ActionScript 3

All of these new Flash CS4 features (including the creation of 3D animations) can be accessed via the ActionScript 3 language. This means that the MovieClip class, for example, supports the properties z and rotationZ.

This next exercise will show you how to create a simple 3D animation using ActionScript, made up of a simple square containing a text field that will rotate on its Y axis:

1. Create a new Flash CS4 document (File ➤ New ➤ Flash File (ActionScript 3.0)).

2. Save your document in a directory of your choice (File ➤ Save).

3. Create a new ActionScript file (File ➤ New ➤ ActionScript File); this file will contain the code you need for your application.

4. In the directory you saved the Flash file in, create this folder path: com/comtaste/foed/essentialair/chapter02. In the chapter02 folder, save the ActionScript file as MyClip.as. In Chapter 4 (in the "Managing the Document Class" section), I'll explain the meaning of this path.

In the ActionScript file you have just opened, insert the following code:

```
package com.comtaste.foed.essentialair.chapter02
{
    import flash.display.Sprite;
    import flash.text.TextField;
    import flash.utils.setInterval;

    public class MyClip extends Sprite
    {
        private var mySquare:Sprite=new Sprite();
        private var myText:TextField=new TextField();
```

With this first piece of code, you've imported the classes you need and created two instances of the Sprite and TextField classes. The instance of the Sprite class will be your square, and the instance of the TextField class will be the text contained in the square.

Next, insert the following code:

```
public function MyClip():void
{
    designSquare();
    setInterval(rotateIt, 10);
}
```

In this portion of code, you have created the constructor of your class, which will call the designSquare() method and will continuously control the rotation of the square (setInterval(rotateIt, 10)).

The next piece of code will draw a square and rotate it on the Y axis:

```
private function rotateIt():void
{
    mySquare.rotationY+=2;
}

private function designSquare():void
{
    with(mySquare.graphics){
        beginFill(0xFF0000, 1);
```

```
        drawRect(0,0, 100,100);
        endFill();
    }
    mySquare.x=this.stage.stageWidth/2;
    mySquare.y=this.stage.stageHeight/2;
    myText.text="Hello World!";
    mySquare.addChild(myText);
    this.addChild(mySquare);
    }
}
}
```

With these last lines of code, you have drawn the square, inserted the text field into the movie clip, and finally set the movement of the square's rotation. Save this ActionScript file as `MyClip.as`.

Return to the initial FLA file (or reopen it if it's closed) and continue with these steps:

5. Insert the name of the ActionScript file (without the extension .as) with its path (com.comtaste.foed.essentialair.chapter02.MyClip) in the Class box of the Publish item in the Properties panel. This will link the two files.

6. Test your application to check what you have written so far (Control ➤ Test Movie). The final result should look like Figure 2-11.

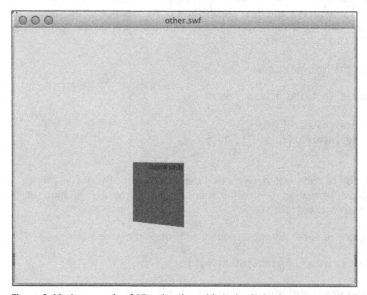

Figure 2-11. An example of 3D animation with ActionScript 3

Creating animations on the Z axis

In the 3D environments you can create in Flash, the Z property pertains to the axis perpendicular to the stage. As such, movement on this axis produces an animation that looks somewhat more like a zoom than an object moving in space.

To understand this better, consider the following example. Open a new Flash document, and display the Actions panel by clicking Window ➤ Actions (or pressing F9). Then enter the following code:

```
var square_mc:MovieClip=new MovieClip();
var typeZ_txt:TextField=new TextField();
var dir:Number=20;

addChild(square_mc);
addChild(typeZ_txt);

with(square_mc.graphics)
{
    beginFill(0xFF0000,1);
    drawRect(0,0,100,100);
    endFill();
}

function fwd():void
{
    square_mc.z-=dir;
    typeZ_txt.text=String("Z property: "+square_mc.z);
    if(square_mc.z==-500 || square_mc.z==1500)
    {
        dir*=-1;
    }
    square_mc.x=stage.stageWidth/2-square_mc.width/2;
    square_mc.y=stage.stageHeight/2-square_mc.height/2;
}
setInterval(fwd, 15);
```

If you test your application, you will see how an animation that works on the Z axis behaves.

> *The project you've just created will appear enlarged, as if you had created it using the scaleX and scaleY properties. However, don't confuse the two—the object is actually moving on the Z axis (perpendicular to the stage); it's not actually being made larger or smaller.*

The example in the following section incorporates the procedures covered in this section: we will analyze how an animated object behaves on each of the three axes, one at a time.

Creating a 3D inspector using ActionScript 3

This example will allow you to develop a simple 3D inspector, a small application that traces objects and shows how they behave in Flash when they are animated on the X, Y, and Z axes. This 3D inspector application will load an external image, so make sure you have an Internet connection to test this example.

Three different buttons of the application will allow you to move your image on the X, Y, and Z axes, respectively, as shown in Figure 2-12.

Figure 2-12. The 3D inspector, which allows you to analyze the image's movement on the X, Y, and Z axes

1. Create a new Flash file in ActionScript 3 (File ➤ New ➤ Flash File (ActionScript 3.0)).

2. In the Publish item on the Properties panel, enter your document class—com. comtaste.foed.essentialair.chapter02.Inspector—in the Class box.

3. Save this Flash file (File ➤ Save) in the directory you prefer, with the name 3DInspector.fla.

4. Create an ActionScript file (File ➤ New ➤ ActionScript File).

5. Save this document as Inspector.as in the following directory: com/comtaste/ foed/essentialair/chapter02. The 3DInspector.fla file and the com folder must be in the same directory.

With the ActionScript file opened, insert the following code:

```
package com.comtaste.foed.essentialair.chapter02
{
        import flash.display.MovieClip;
        import flash.display.Loader;
```

```
import flash.text.TextField;
import flash.utils.setInterval;
import flash.events.MouseEvent;
import flash.net.URLRequest;
```

As usual, start by inserting all the classes you need, and then proceed by instancing all the classes you need for the project:

```
public class Inspector extends MovieClip{

    public var rotateX_mc:MovieClip=new MovieClip();
    public var rotateY_mc:MovieClip=new MovieClip();
    public var rotateZ_mc:MovieClip=new MovieClip();
    public var resetAll_mc:MovieClip=new MovieClip();
    public var menu:Array=[[rotateX_mc,0xFFAACC, "X Rotation"],➡
    [rotateY_mc,0xAABBCC, "Y Rotation"],➡
    [rotateZ_mc,0xEEAA44, "Z Rotation"],➡
    [resetAll_mc,0xDD7766, "Reset All"]];

    public var rotationSquare:MovieClip=new MovieClip();
    public var speed:int=2;

    public var spacing:Number=60;
    public var squareWidth:Number=70;
    public var squareHeight:Number=30;

    public var rotateX:Boolean;
    public var rotateY:Boolean;
    public var rotateZ:Boolean;
```

With this portion of code, you've created the instances of your buttons. The menu property typed as Array contains the instance names and properties of the MovieClip objects.

Next, you'll set some useful variables for the various objects. These variables determine the space between buttons, the height and width of each of them, and the speed of object rotation.

```
public function Inspector():void{
    for(var i:Number=0; i<menu.length; i++){
        var rotationValue:TextField=new TextField();
        rotationValue.selectable=false;
        rotationValue.mouseEnabled=false;
        drawingSquare(menu[i][0], menu[i][1]);
        menu[i][0].x=(spacing+20)*i;
        rotationValue.text=menu[i][2];
        menu[i][0].addChild(rotationValue);
        menu[i][0].addEventListener(MouseEvent.CLICK, setRotation);
    }
drawingObject();
setInterval(rotateIt, 20);
}
```

With this portion of code, you've set up the buttons on the stage with a for loop, and you've generated a text field (rotationValue) to be inserted in each button. The drawing-Square() method will allow you to draw as many buttons as the loop requires.

The remaining code will place each button on the X axis at regular intervals, and will assign the setRotation() method to each of them for when the user interacts with a click:

```
private function drawingSquare(obj:MovieClip, color:uint):void{
    with(obj.graphics){
        beginFill(color, 1);
        moveTo(0,0);
        lineTo(squareWidth,0);
        lineTo(squareWidth,squareHeight);
        lineTo(0,squareHeight);
        endFill();
    }
    this.addChild(obj);
}
```

The drawingSquare() method will allow you to create a rectangular shape each time it's invoked.

```
private function drawingObject():void{
    var pathPhoto:URLRequest=new URLRequest ➡
    ("http://www.comtaste.com/img/logoComtaste.gif");
    var loader:Loader=new Loader();
    loader.load(pathPhoto);
    rotationSquare.addChild(loader);
    rotationSquare.x=stage.stageWidth/2;
    rotationSquare.y=stage.stageHeight/2;
    this.addChild(rotationSquare);
}
```

The drawingObject() method places the square on the stage, more or less at the center.

The following code will allow you to manage the animation using the setInterval() method:

```
private function rotateIt():void{
    if(rotateX){
    rotationSquare.rotationX+=speed;
    } if(rotateY){
        rotationSquare.rotationY+=speed;
    }if(rotateZ){
        rotationSquare.rotationZ+=speed;
    }
}
```

It's important to note how to change the rotationSquare instance in this script. To do so, simply work on the three new properties of the DisplayObject: rotationX, rotationY, rotationZ, as shown here:

```
private function setRotation(event:MouseEvent):void{
    switch(event.currentTarget){
        case rotateX_mc:
         rotateX=true;
         rotateY=false;
         rotateZ=false;
        break;
        case rotateY_mc:
         rotateX=false;
         rotateY=true;
         rotateZ=false;
        break;
        case rotateZ_mc:
         rotateX=false;
         rotateY=false;
         rotateZ=true;
        break;
        case resetAll_mc:
         rotateX=false;
         rotateY=false;
         rotateZ=false;
         rotationSquare.rotationX=0;
         rotationSquare.rotationY=0;

         rotationSquare.rotationZ=0;
        }
    }
  }
}
```

This last method monitors the status of the three Boolean variables rotateX, rotateY, and rotateZ.) According to each variable, the object will rotate on the X, Y, or Z axis. You can now save your documents and test the application (Control ➤ Test Movie).

The next example will create an ActionScript class that works with some of the classes contained in the flash.display package.

Creating a BlendType controller

ActionScript comes with some classes made for building graphical elements. In the next exercise, you'll use the BlendMode class to explore how objects interact graphically with visual effects.

1. Create a new Flash file in ActionScript 3 (File ➤ New ➤ Flash File (ActionScript 3.0)).

2. Enter the document class—com.comtaste.foed.essentialair.chapter02. GraphicBlend—in the Class box under the Publish item in the Properties panel.

3. Save this Flash file in the directory you prefer as GraphicBlend.fla.

4. Create the ActionScript file (File ➤ New ➤ ActionScript File).

5. Save this document as GraphicBlend.as in the directory com/comtaste/foed/
essentialair/chapter02/ (remember that the com folder and the GraphicBlend.
fla file must be in the same directory).

With the ActionScript file open, insert the following code:

```
package com.comtaste.foed.essentialair.chapter02{
    import flash.display.Sprite;
    import flash.display.MovieClip;
    import flash.events.MouseEvent;
    import flash.display.BlendMode;
    import flash.text.TextField;
    import flash.text.TextFieldAutoSize;
    import flash.geom.Matrix;
    import flash.display.GradientType;
    import flash.display.SpreadMethod;
```

Your code begins importing the classes you need. The following list explains some of the
less well-known classes:

- Matrix allows you to map points from one space (defined by coordinates) to
  another.

- SpreadMethod provides the beginGradientFill() method of the Graphics class
  with values.

- GradientType provides the type of gradient to the beginGradientFill() method
  of the Graphics class.

- BlendMode provides the visual effect of the fusion of two images.

These classes create the final result of the project, which is shown in Figure 2-13.

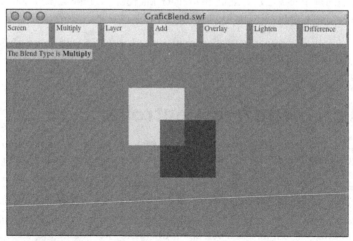

Figure 2-13. The BlendType controller shows the various methods of fusion
between two shapes.

Now proceed by adding the following code to your example:

```
public class GraphicBlend extends Sprite{
    public var square1_mc:Sprite=new Sprite();
    public var square2_mc:Sprite=new Sprite();
    public var squareWidth:Number=90;
    public var squareHeight:Number=90;
    public var labelButton:Array=["Screen", "Multiply", "Normal",➥
"Add", "Overlay", "Lighten", "Difference"];
    public var gradientMatrix:Matrix = new Matrix();
    public var textBlend:TextField=new TextField();
    public var gradientType:String = GradientType.LINEAR;
    public var gradientColor:Array = new Array;
    public var gradientAlphas:Array = [1, 1];
    public var gradientRatios:Array = [0x00, 0xFF];
    public var addRemoveGradient:Boolean;
```

The preceding code includes all the variables required for the GraphicBlend class. This example also contains three instances of the Array class to define the parameters for the beginGradientFill() method: gradientColor, gradientAlphas, and gradientRatios.

Next, continue with the class constructor, which will place all the objects you need on the stage:

```
public function GraphicBlend():void{
    drawingSquare(square1_mc, 0xAADDFF);
    drawingSquare(square2_mc, 0xCC22FF);
    square1_mc.x=200;
    square1_mc.y=100;
    square2_mc.x=250;
    square2_mc.y=150;
    square2_mc.addEventListener(MouseEvent.MOUSE_DOWN, takeIt);
    square2_mc.addEventListener(MouseEvent.MOUSE_UP, leaveIt);
    square1_mc.addEventListener(MouseEvent.CLICK, changeGradient);
    square2_mc.buttonMode=true;
    square1_mc.buttonMode=true;
```

Quite simply, this constructor code allows you to draw two squares, which, placed one on top of the other, will allow you to see how the various blend types interact.

> In digital image editing, blend modes are used to determine how two layers are blended into each other.

Next, you're varying the color of the first square from a flat color to a color with a gradient, with the changeGradient() method. The methods leaveIt() and takeIt() in square2_mc's handler allow you to drag and drop square2_mc on the stage.

```
function takeIt(event:MouseEvent):void
{
    square2_mc.startDrag(false);
}

function leaveIt(event:MouseEvent):void
{
    square2_mc.stopDrag();
}
```

Next, add the following for loop, which will make it easier to control the buttons:

```
for(var i:Number=0; i<labelButton.length; i++)
{
    var button:MovieClip=new MovieClip();
    var labelText:TextField=new TextField();
    labelText.selectable=false;
    labelText.mouseEnabled=false;
    labelText.autoSize=TextFieldAutoSize.LEFT;
    drawingSquareMenu(button, 0xAAFF88);
    button.addChild(labelText);
    button.x=(button.width+10)*i;
    labelText.text=labelButton[i];
    this.addChild(button);
    button.blendType=(labelButton[i]);
    button.buttonMode=true;
    button.addEventListener(MouseEvent.CLICK, changeBlend);
}
```

This code (like in the previous exercise) creates a button for each value in the labelButton array. Then it writes a label on the buttons and creates event listeners for each of them using the addEventListener() method.

The following instructions close the part of code regarding the constructor of your ActionScript file. This code block sets the various user interface buttons on your BlendType controller:

```
this.addChild(textBlend);
textBlend.y=button.height+10;
textBlend.autoSize=TextFieldAutoSize.LEFT;
textBlend.background=true;
textBlend.backgroundColor=0xFFAA00;
}
```

Now write the value of the type of blend you're adopting in the textBlend instance, as follows:

```
private function drawingSquare(obj:Sprite, color:uint):void{
    with(obj.graphics){
        beginFill(color, 1);
        moveTo(0,0);
```

```
            lineTo(squareWidth,0);
            lineTo(squareWidth,squareHeight);
            lineTo(0,squareHeight);
            endFill();
        }
        this.addChild(obj);
    }
    private function drawingSquareMenu(obj:Sprite, color:uint):void{
        with(obj.graphics){
            beginFill(color, 1);
            moveTo(0,0);
            lineTo(70,0);
            lineTo(70,30);
            lineTo(0,30);
            endFill();
        }
    this.addChild(obj);
    }
```

This code, like in the previous exercise, is exclusively for drawing the shapes that you will use in your application.

Next, add the following code, which uses the changeBlend() method to control the fusion between the two movie clips:

```
    private function changeBlend(event:MouseEvent):void{
        switch(event.currentTarget.blendType){
            case "Screen":
              square2_mc.blendMode=BlendMode.SCREEN;
            break;
            case "Multiply":
              square2_mc.blendMode=BlendMode.MULTIPLY;
            break;
            case "Layer":
              square2_mc.blendMode=BlendMode.NORMAL;
            break;
            case "Add":
             square2_mc.blendMode=BlendMode.ADD;
            break;
            case "Overlay":
            square2_mc.blendMode=BlendMode.OVERLAY;
            break;
            case "Lighten":
             square2_mc.blendMode=BlendMode.LIGHTEN;
            break;
            case "Difference":
             square2_mc.blendMode=BlendMode.DIFFERENCE;
            break;
        }
```

```
textBlend.htmlText="The Blend Type is <b>"+➡
event.currentTarget.blendType+"</b>";
}
```

With the switch command, you can manage the blendMode property of the square2_mc instance. The accepted values are the constants (SCREEN, MULTIPLY, LAYER, etc.) of the BlendMode class.

This example has been limited to the creation of seven types: Add, Overlay, Lighten, Difference, Normal, Multiply, and Screen. The BlendMode class actually has a lot more, though. For more information on the subject, consult the official Adobe documentation on ActionScript 3 at http://livedocs.adobe.com/flash/9.0/ActionScriptLangRefV3/.

```
private function changeGradient(event:MouseEvent):void
{
    addRemoveGradient=!addRemoveGradient;
    if(!addRemoveGradient){
        gradientColor=[0xAADDFF,0xAADDFF]

    }else{
        gradientColor=[0xAA33CC, 0x3399DD]
    }
    gradientMatrix.createGradientBox(event.currentTarget.width, ➡
    event.currentTarget.height,0, 0,0);
    gradientMatrix.createGradientBox(event.currentTarget.width, ➡
    event.currentTarget.height,0, 0,0);
    var colorDist:String = SpreadMethod.REFLECT;
    square1_mc.graphics.beginGradientFill(gradientType, ➡
    gradientColor, gradientAlphas, gradientRatios, gradientMatrix, ➡
    colorDist);
    square1_mc.graphics.drawRect(0, 0, square1_mc.width, ➡
    square1_mc.height);
    }
  }
}
```

In this last block of code, you've added the changeGradient() method. With the gradientMatrix object (an instance of the Matrix class), you can draw a rectangular shape (with the createGradientBox() method). You set the type of SpreadMethod, and then you draw your gradient thanks to the beginGradientFill() and drawRect() methods of the Graphics class.

Remember that this gradient, created with the createGradientBox() method of the Maxtrix class, will be applied on the square1_mc shape.

You have reached the end of this little exercise. Test the application (Control ➤ Test Movie), clicking the various buttons to see how the two rectangular shapes interact with BlendMode.

Next, I'll introduce the inverse kinematics feature.

Using inverse kinematics

Inverse kinematics (sometimes referred to as IK) is a tweening method. It allows you to create animations in which several interlinked objects move according to the position of the other objects they are linked to. For example, imagine that you have to animate an arm of the human body from the shoulder to the hand. The hand movement will depend on the forearm movement, which will in turn depend on the upper arm, which pivots on the shoulder of the body.

This kind of animation is simple today, thanks to the support of inverse kinematics in Flash CS4.

You can create movement with inverse kinematics in two different ways: you can use the timeline and animate the various interlinked objects, or you can use ActionScript 3 through the classes contained in the fl.ik package: IKArmature, IKBone, IKEvent, IKJoint, IKMover, and IKManager.

> Remember that when you use inverse kinematics for an animation, you can build it using only graphics, buttons, movie clip symbols, or simple shapes. However, if you're generating an inverse kinematic animation in ActionScript, you can only use movie clip symbols. Also, in ActionScript, you can only control elements that are linked to only one other element, not to several elements.

Follow these steps to create an animation with inverse kinematics. In this exercise, you'll create a little stylized man and move its arms using inverse kinematics:

1. Create a new Flash CS4 document (File ➤ New ➤ Flash File (ActionScript 3.0)).

2. Draw a sort of stylized human body using the following shapes:

   - A circle for the head, with these characteristics: width: 60, height: 60, X: 240, Y: 90

   - A rectangle for the body, with these characteristics: width: 80, height: 140, X: 230, Y: 160

   - A rectangle for the left arm, with these characteristics: width: 10, height: 100, X: 205, Y: 180

   - A rectangle for the right arm, with these characteristics: width: 10, height: 100, X: 325, Y: 180

3. Convert each element into a movie clip symbol.

4. Choose the Bone tool from the Tools panel. This tool will allow you to link the various symbols together to animate them with inverse kinematics.

5. Keeping the Bone tool selected, link the rectangle (body) of your stylized man with one arm and then the other by dragging and dropping, so that you obtain the result illustrated in Figure 2-14.

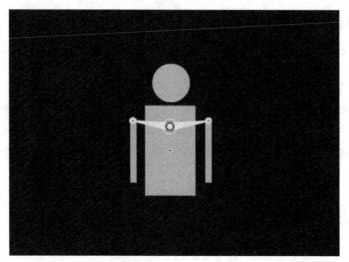

Figure 2-14. Your stylized man, ready to be animated with inverse kinematics

The first thing you should notice on the stage is the **bone**, which is the line that connects the body to the arms. Also notice the new layer, Armature, which has been created on the timeline. This layer incorporates all the objects that need to be animated by connecting them with the Bone tool.

Like in all the possible animations in Flash, you can click a frame and insert a keyframe by pressing F6 or choosing Insert ➤ Timeline ➤ Keyframe. You can also move the arms simply by using the Selection tool.

If you try and test this simple animation, you will notice that the objects have pivoted on the bone. The bone is the connection between the body clip and the arm clip.

However, it isn't simple to move these objects, seeing as each object depends on all the others. For example, if you only want to move the arm of your little man using the Bone tool, you have to keep the Shift key pressed during the movement. Try it.

You can change the bone in a variety of ways through the parameters available on the Properties panel, as shown in Figure 2-15.

To do this, click the bone, and then click the Properties panel.

The Constrain option allows you to set the maximum and minimum values of the rotation angles of the movie clip used with the Bone tool. If you select the Armature layer on the timeline, the Properties panel will be updated with the properties of the Armature layer.

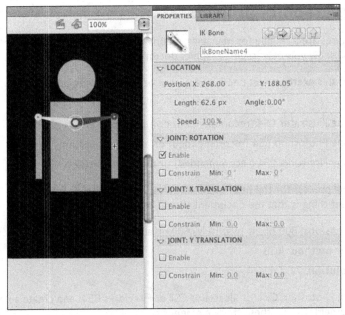

Figure 2-15. The parameters available for the Bone tool

In the Options item, you'll find the Type option, which offers two choices: Authortime and Runtime. These two options allow Flash to interpret the way to create inverse kinematic animations. When working with the timeline, you have to choose Authortime. If you want to work with ActionScript 3, you have to choose Runtime.

In the next section, I'll talk about another important aspect of Flash CS4: its integration with the other Adobe products.

Adobe product integration

When creating applications in Flash CS4 and Adobe AIR, not only do you have to write well-programmed code, but you need to provide your users with great-looking, easy-to-use user interfaces as well. While Flash gives you a lot of options in this regard, not being a graphic design product per se, it unfortunately has a few weaknesses. These, however, can be easily overcome thanks to Flash's integration with the editing and imaging products of the Adobe family: Photoshop CS4, Illustrator CS4, and Fireworks CS4, to name a few.

One thing that's made this integration possible is the new XFL format. XFL allows you to transfer files between Adobe video-editing programs (e.g., Premiere Pro CS4 and After-Effects CS4) or page layout programs (e.g., InDesign CS4). Chapter 3 deals with the various aspects of the integration among these products in more detail.

Importing graphics projects

Several features are available for managing graphical assets. This section presents an exercise that will show you how import graphics documents into Flash CS4.

To carry out this exercise, you need at least one of the following programs in addition to Flash CS4:

- Adobe Illustrator CS4 (recommended) or a previous version
- Adobe Photoshop CS4 (recommended) or a previous version
- Adobe Fireworks CS4 (recommended) or a previous version

Your working process for the next exercise will vary depending on the software you use—the important thing is that the document should use the following settings:

- **Dimensions**: 800 pixels (width) by 600 pixels (height)
- **Color method**: RGB
- **Resolution**: 72 dpi

1. Open Photoshop CS4 (or Illustrator CS4 or Fireworks CS4) and create a new graphic document. Design these three elements:
   - A text field with the text Hello World!.
   - A vector shape (any shape will do).
   - A bitmap image (any image, provided it isn't bigger than the document. If you work in Illustrator, however, you have to remember to deselect the Link option. This option will be fundamental when you want to convert this picture into a symbol, as you will see later in this section).
2. Place the objects in the order that you prefer, but make sure they are all visible in the document, as illustrated in Figure 2-16.
3. Save the document (e.g., with a name of importAI.ai, importPSD.psd, or importPNG.png).
4. Open Flash CS4 if you haven't already, and choose the Flash File (Adobe AIR) option from the welcome screen.
5. If the welcome screen doesn't open, you can choose the same option by clicking File ➤ New ➤ Flash File (Adobe AIR).
6. Now, with the File ➤ Import ➤ Import to Stage menu item, ask Flash CS4 to import your file directly onto the stage. This process will ensure that the document is inserted into the library as well as onto the stage.

Next, let's see what happens when you import an Illustrator project into a Flash project. Afterward, we'll look at importing Photoshop and Fireworks files as well.

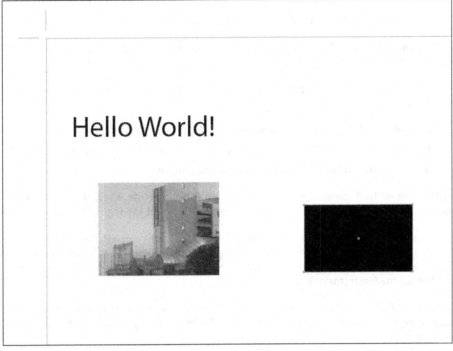

Figure 2-16. The example file you will import into Flash CS4 with three types of elements: a text field, a shape, and an image

Importing an Illustrator file

If the document you created previously was made with Adobe Illustrator, choose your importAI.ai file from the import panel in Flash. The panel that will open once you've started the import process (Import "importAi.ai" to Stage) will allow you to set various parameters. The left side, Check Illustrator layers to import, allows you to choose which layer you want to import, and the settings on the right side (Import options) will change according to the layer you choose. For example, if you choose the layer containing the bitmap image that you inserted into the Illustrator document, the import options that Flash will provide are the following:

- Flattened bitmap to maintain appearance: The image will be processed as a flattened image to maintain its original appearance.
- Create Movie Clip: This converts the photo into a movie clip, to which you can also add an instance name and choose a registration point.

If, on the other hand, you choose the vector form you drew in Illustrator, in the section on the right-hand side of the panel (Path import options for "Path"), you can choose to import it with the following options:

- Path editable: This will import your file as an editable vector path in Flash.
- Bitmap: This will import it as a noneditable image.

In both cases, you can choose if you want to convert it into a movie clip, give a name to the instance, and set the registration point.

The last option regards the importation of the text asset, which can be imported as one of the following:

- Editable text: This will import your text into Flash as static text.
- Vector outlines: This will import your text as a vector shape for each letter of text.
- Bitmap: This will import your text as a bitmap image.

Again, with each of these three options, you can further decide whether to convert the asset into a movie clip, assign a name to the instance, and set the registration point.

The Check Illustrator Layer to import section provides options to convert the asset into Flash layers, keyframes, or a single Flash layer. Since the best option for this exercise is Flash Layers, keep the Place object at original position option unchanged so as to keep the original position of the Illustrator drawing.

You can check the Set Stage to same size as Illustrator artboard option, which will automatically change the dimensions of the Flash stage according to the dimensions of the Illustrator document.

You can leave the last two options, Import unused symbols and Import as a single bitmap image, unselected.

Confirm your choices by clicking OK. The various layers of Illustrator will be imported onto the stage.

Adobe Illustrator still has a few important tricks. Both the CS4 and CS3 versions allow you to convert its objects natively into movie clips and/or buttons. This capability is very useful for exporting projects into Flash—once the document is imported, you can work with all the relevant settings already defined.

1. Go back to Illustrator and open the importAI.ai file you created for this exercise (if it isn't already open). Then click one of the three elements (image, shape, or text field).

2. Once you select an object on the stage, press F8 to open the Symbol Options panel, like you do in Flash, or open the Symbol Options panel (Window ➤ Symbol) and drag the element into it. This panel (shown in Figure 2-17) will offer you the following choices:

- Name: Name your future instance (e.g., mySquare).
- Type: Choose Movie Clip as the symbol type.
- Flash Registration: Choose the upper-left registration point.

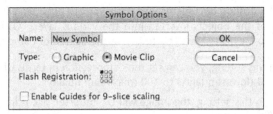

Figure 2-17. The Symbol Options panel to convert your shape, text, or images into a symbol

3. The new object will now appear in the Symbol dialog box. Save your Illustrator file again and restart the process of importing it into Flash. When the Import "importAI. ai" to Stage panel reopens, the layers that have been converted into symbols will already be movie clips.

With your file open in Illustrator, perform the following steps:

4. Copy one or more objects with Ctrl+C (Windows) or Cmd+C (Mac).

5. Go to Flash and press Ctrl+V (Windows) or Cmd+V (Mac) to paste the objects onto the stage. The Paste panel will open, offering you the choice of importing the selected objects as bitmaps (Paste as bitmap) or using Illustrator's importer (Paste using AI File Importer preferences).

6. Leave the Apply recommended import settings to resolve incompatibilities and maintain layers setting unchanged. Confirm by clicking OK, and your layers will be correctly imported.

Importing a Photoshop file

This exercise will show you how to import a Photoshop file, which is similar to importing an Illustrator file.

1. In Flash, choose File ➤ Import ➤ Import to Stage to begin the import process. This time, choose a file with a .psd extension.

2. The import panel will open. The left-hand section of this panel (Check Photoshop layers to import) will be populated by various layers that make up your PSD files. Start by selecting the layer containing the text.

The right-hand side of the import panel will offer you three options for importing the text layer:

- Editable text: This imports the text layer as static text.
- Vector outlines: This imports the text layer as a vector outline for each piece of text.
- Flattened bitmap image: This imports the text layer as a bitmap image.

When you import Photoshop documents into Flash, you are provided with options to manage some settings of the objects inserted into the various layers. Of importance is the Publish Settings option, which allows you to define the degree of compression, as follows:

- Lossy: With this setting, you can set the compression in terms of the quality of the image, from 0 (lowest quality) to 100 (maximum quality).

- Lossless: With this setting, the image will be imported according to the standards defined in Photoshop.

3. Next, choose an asset containing the imported image. There are two options:

  - Bitmap image with editable layer style: This imports the asset as a movie clip containing the image, so you assign a name to the instance and set the registration point.

  - Flattened bitmap image: This creates a noneditable flattened image; with this option, you can choose whether or not to convert it into a movie clip.

As with the text, you can choose between lossy and lossless compression with the Publish Settings option.

You'll be provided with two options for importing the vector shape:

- Editable path: This imports the asset as a vector shape. In this case, you can edit your shape immediately after importing it into Flash.

- Bitmap: This creates a noneditable flattened image. With this option, you can choose whether or not to convert it into a movie clip.

It's preferable to leave the Place layers at original position option under the list of Photoshop assets as it is, in order to maintain the original position of the various assets.

If you want to change the dimensions of the stage to those of the Photoshop document, you can select the Set Stage size to same size as Photoshop canvas option.

Importing a Fireworks file

If your project comes from Fireworks, you carry out the same procedure, with a few differences. Again, you follow the importation procedure (File ➤ Import ➤ Import to Stage), but this time choose importPNG.png.

Compared to Illustrator and Photoshop, Flash's import panel for Fireworks isn't very advanced, as shown in Figure 2-18.

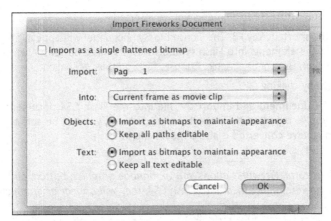

Figure 2-18. The Import Fireworks Document panel with its few options

The first option, Import as a single flattened bitmap, is for importing all the assets as a flat image. I suggest selecting this option, because it's the only way to manage your assets. This choice will make it possible to choose from the following items:

- Import: This option lets you choose the page number of the Fireworks layer you want to import.

- Into: This lets you choose whether to import the Fireworks layer as a new Flash layer or as a movie clip (if you use the latter option, you can't specify the name of the instance like you did in Illustrator).

- Objects: This option lets you choose between Import as a bitmaps to maintain appearance, which lets you import as a flattened image, and Keep all paths editable, which lets you import as editable layers (this is the recommended choice).

- Text: With this option, you can choose between Import as bitmaps to maintain appearance, which will import the asset as a flattened image, and Keep all text editable, which imports it as editable text.

Confirm your choices by clicking OK.

Once you've completed the importation, you can find the various assets that make up the Fireworks file in your project.

As with Illustrator, Fireworks also allows you to import the assets by the copying and pasting process explained previously.

1. Going back to the Fireworks file you created, copy the selected assets (Ctrl+C on Windows or Cmd+C on the Mac) and paste them onto the stage in Flash (Ctrl+V on Windows or Cmd+V on the Mac).

2. The Import Fireworks Document panel will reappear, allowing you to manage the import process with the specifications you indicated previously.

3. Return to the Fireworks document you created at the beginning of this section (importPNG.png).

4. Select one of the three elements you've inserted.

5. Press the shortcut key F8. The Convert to Symbol panel will appear, allowing you to convert the elements into Flash symbols with its three options: Animation (same as movie clip), Button, or Graphic. Choose, for example, Animation.

6. Confirm by clicking OK.

7. Save the document and import the file into the Flash CS4 document once again. Once you've repeated the importation procedure, you will be able to see that the symbol you've converted is also a movie clip in Flash.

> *Similar to Illustrator, Fireworks allows you to manage graphics, button, and movie clip symbols. When you import them into Flash CS4, they will appear as graphics, buttons, or movie clips.*

Next, check out what Flash CS4 has to offer regarding AIR development tools.

Creating and managing an AIR project

As you know, AIR gives you the ability to port web applications onto the desktop. As you will see in more detail in Chapter 3, Flash CS4 provides you with many tools to develop AIR applications.

Creating a document in Flash CS4 for Adobe AIR is very similar to creating a classic Flash document for the Web, but there is some additional information to consider. To create an AIR application in Flash, you can start from the welcome screen and choose File Flash (Adobe AIR) (or you can do it via the File ➤ New menu option). Be sure to use the latest version of ActionScript: ActionScript 3.0.

> *You can build AIR applications with Flash CS4 only with ActionScript 3.0.*

When you've finished creating an AIR project, you can test and debug your application using the same tools you use in Flash for web development projects. You can test the application using the Control ➤ Test Movie. There are two main debugging tools:

- The trace() method, which allows you to trace the values of variables and values returned by the methods on video.
- The debugger, which you can access from the Debug ➤ Debug Movie menu option. This tool, if used correctly, allows you to check the status of the various methods, properties, and variables that are instanced during the execution of your application.

A more detailed description of the debugging tools is provided in Chapter 3.

But before you can get started using Adobe AIR, you have to set it up properly. This is done using the AIR – Application & Installer Settings panel. This panel allows you to set up and edit, among other things, icons, external files to include, and some other features for packaging and deploying your AIR applications. You can open the panel via File ➤ AIR Settings. This panel will be covered in more detail in Chapter 3.

Packaging and deploying an AIR application

The workflow of a desktop AIR application goes through several different phases. But the last phase is always the package and deployment of the application, which creates the file that will be distributed to users.

Flash CS4 allows you to create the final installation file at the end of the process with an .air extension. Your application's users must have the AIR runtime installed to be able to run the program. The runtime is free and can be downloaded from the official website: http://get.adobe.com/air/?promoid=BUIGQ.

In order to create the final AIR installation file, all you have to do is reopen the AIR – Application & Installer Settings panel mentioned and click the Publish AIR File button. You can then distribute your application, which you can do by downloading or through the browser.

Flash provides a badge.fla file, which allows you to create an HTML page that includes a SWF file. With this SWF file, you can download the AIR runtime, if you don't already have it on your machine, or the whole AIR application you've created.

Creating and deploying a simple browser in AIR with Flash CS4

In this example, you will create a simple browser in AIR. The application will be then packaged into an AIR installation file.

Create a new Flash file in Adobe AIR (File ➤ New ➤ Flash File (Adobe AIR)). It's a good practice to set the width and height of the project in this phase so that they are big enough to contain an HTML page. For this example, set the Flash file to a width of 1000 pixels and a height of 700 pixels. To change these parameters, just click the Edit button in the Properties panel. In the next panel, you insert these values into the Width and Height boxes in the Dimensions option.

Now create a new ActionScript file (File ➤ New ➤ ActionScript File). Remember that you always have to save your files. Start by saving the Flash project file as MyBrowser.fla, and then save the ActionScript file as MyHTML.as, in the following directory: com/comtaste/ foed/essentialair/chapter02. Remember that the folder com and the Flash file (MyBrowser.fla) must be in the same directory.

With the Flash file open, start writing the code of your project, which, as usual, begins by importing the classes you need:

```
package com.comtaste.foed.essentialair.chapter02
{
    import flash.display.Sprite;
    import flash.html.HTMLLoader;
    import flash.net.URLRequest;
    import flash.events.Event;
    import flash.events.MouseEvent;
    import flash.events.KeyboardEvent;
    import flash.text.TextField;
    import flash.text.TextFieldAutoSize;
    import flash.text.TextFieldType;
```

Then proceed by inserting all the variables you need to develop your project:

```
public class MyHTML extends Sprite
{
    public var urlReq:URLRequest;
    public var myHtml:HTMLLoader = new HTMLLoader();
    public var address_txt:TextField=new TextField();
    public var address_btn:Sprite=new Sprite();
    public var addressLabel_txt:TextField=new TextField();
```

The urlReq variable will let you specify the address you want to insert. The HTMLLoader class will upload the HTML content of the page you've requested—but remember that this ActionScript 3 class only works in AIR projects, and cannot be reused for Flash web projects.

The remaining instances regard dynamic text and allow the user to insert the Internet address. The address_btn will work as a button that when clicked will load the URL into the AIR application.

You'll also give the user the option of clicking the button once the URL of the website has been inserted. Set up the constructor of your ActionScript file as follows:

```
public function MyHTML()
{
    myHtml.width = stage.stageWidth;
    myHtml.height = stage.stageHeight - address_txt.y - ➥
    address_txt.height;
    with(address_txt){
        border=true;
        type=TextFieldType.INPUT;
        x=18;
        y=20;
        width=360;
        height=22;
        background=true;
```

```
            backgroundColor=0xFFFFFF;
        }
```

In this portion of code, you have set some parameters (width and height) of the myHTML object. This object is an instance of the HTMLLoader class, which will allow you to view the requested web page.

You have set up all the parameters you need for the dynamic text field address_txt and included type to show that the dynamic text field is an input field, as well as background and backgroundColor for the color of the background.

In the next code block, you'll draw the address_btn button:

```
    with(address_btn){
        graphics.beginFill(0xFFCCAA, 1);
        graphics.drawRect(400, 20, 90, 20);
        graphics.endFill();
        buttonMode=true;
    }

    with(addressLabel_txt){
        x=420;
        y=20;
        text="Go!";
        autoSize=TextFieldAutoSize.LEFT;
        selectable=false;
        mouseEnabled=false;
    }
```

With these two with statements, you set the characteristics of the button (which you have designed using the Graphics class) and those of the text label to put on the button.

```
        addChild(myHtml);
        addChild(address_txt);
        addChild(address_btn);
        addChild(addressLabel_txt);
        myHtml.x=0;
        myHtml.y=this.address_txt.y+this.address_txt.height+10;
        address_btn.addEventListener(MouseEvent.CLICK, viewPageHandler);
        Stage .addEventListener(KeyboardEvent.KEY_DOWN, ➡
        viewPageHandlerByEnter);
    }
```

In the preceding code block, you've added the various elements to the stage, including the myHTML object. Then you've assigned an event to the stage that fires each time the user presses the Enter key on the keyboard. Another event listener is created to react to the click event of the address_btn button.

Both methods will allow the AIR application to load the web page from the address inserted into the address_txt dynamic text field.

Add the two event handlers viewPageHandler() and viewPageHandlerByEnter():

```
private function viewPageHandler(event:MouseEvent):void
{
    urlReq=new URLRequest(address_txt.text);
    myHtml.load(urlReq);
}

private function viewPageHandlerByEnter(event:KeyboardEvent):void
{
    if(event.keyCode==13){
        urlReq=new URLRequest(address_txt.text);
        myHtml.load(urlReq);
    }
  }
 }
}
```

The two event handlers are essentially identical—the only differences are in the event parameter automatically generated by the event itself. In the first case, the method is called by clicking the button, so event will be typed as a MouseEvent. In the second case, it will be typed as a KeyboardEvent, because it is an event that is generated from the keyboard.

Another difference is due to the fact that in the viewPageHandlerByEnter method, you need to check which keyCode corresponds to the keyboard event, and it is possible to guess how 13 corresponds to the Enter key.

You don't have to add anything else in your ActionScript file, so go back to your Flash project and insert the name of the ActionScript file you've created into the Class box in the Properties panel, including the full path: com.comtaste.foed.essentialair. chapter02.MyHTML.

Test the movie to check that everything is working properly (Control ➤ Test Movie). If everything is fine, you can create your AIR file to be distributed.

Begin by setting the parameters that AIR needs to save the file correctly. You manage these parameters through the AIR – Application & Installer Settings panel mentioned previously. This panel is also discussed in more detail in Chapter 3. For now, you'll only use it quickly for the sake of this example.

Open the AIR – Application & Installer Settings panel by choosing File ➤ AIR Settings, and then set the various items as follows:

- File Name: My Browser (displayed on/below the file icon)
- Name: Browser (displayed in the application window [if using system chrome] and in the Windows taskbar)
- Version: 1.0
- ID: com.comtaste.foed.essentialair.chapter02.MyBrowser

- Description: My first browser in Adobe AIR with Flash CS4
- Copyright: **Optional**
- Window Style: System Chrome
- Icon: **Keep the default settings—you'll use the default icons provided by Flash CS4.**
- Advanced: **Keep the default settings.**
- Digital Signature: **To create an AIR file, you have to create a digital signature, so click the** Change **button, and in the next panel, click the** Create **button. Considering the fact that many parameters are optional, populate the various fields in the** Create Self-Signed Digital Certificate **panel as follows:**

  - Publisher Name: Comtaste.com
  - Organization Unit: Comtaste
  - Organization Name: Comtaste Srl
  - Country: Italy
  - Password: mypass
  - Confirm Password: mypass
  - Type: 1024-RSA
  - Save As: **Save the file in the directory you prefer.**

Confirm everything by clicking OK. Back in the Digital Signature panel, insert your new password in the Password field and, if you want to, check the Remember password for this session check box. Then click OK to confirm. Leave the Timestamp option checked (this timestamp denotes the date when your digital signature is saved; Chapter 13 will go into more detail about digital signatures). For Destination, choose the folder where you want to save your file. You can skip the Include files option, because you don't need to add any more files.

Now all you have to do is actually publish your work. Click the Publish AIR File button. In a few seconds, Flash CS4 will warn you that the AIR file has been created with a pop-up message: AIR file has been created. Close the AIR – Application & Installer Settings panel by clicking OK.

Now you can browse for the folder where you saved your FLA file and see that the AIR file has been added to it.

Double-click the AIR file, and the Adobe AIR runtime will start the installation process, allowing you to choose which directory you want to install the file on, and whether or not to open the program at the end of the process.

Notice how, at the beginning of the installation process, AIR warns you of the risks related to installing an unknown product. This is due to the fact that your signature isn't officially registered. The author is and will remain unknown until you create a legally recognized digital signature. See Chapter 13 for more details on digital signatures.

Complete the installation process. If you keep the standard options that AIR provides unaltered, your file should open automatically. Notice that the default icon of your AIR project has been added to the stage, as usual when you install any program.

On Windows, your icon will appear under Start ➤ Programs ➤ MyBrowser. On the Mac, you can find it under User ➤ Application ➤ MyBrowser. In both cases, you can delete your product according to the normal procedures of your operating system:

- On Windows, choose Start ➤ Control Panel ➤ Add or Remove Programs. In the next panel, select your project (Browser) and delete it by clicking the Remove button.

- On Mac OS X, all you have to do is drag it from the Application folder to the Trash folder. In both cases, your project will be permanently deleted from your machine.

See Chapter 13 to learn more about installing and uninstalling AIR applications.

Summary

In the second chapter of this book, you have explored some of the new features of Adobe Flash CS4 and its new potential, especially in the field of graphic design.

As mentioned, Flash CS4 new features are aimed at graphic designers. The many innovations you have dealt with in this chapter regard managing 3D environments and the relevant animations, as well as managing the interface panels that are typical of CS4. You learned about inverse kinematics and how to create animations with several interlinked objects. You analyzed the Deco tool to design patterns, even animated ones, on your objects. Finally, you looked at how to create and distribute AIR products with Flash CS4.

Chapter 3 will cover the features of Flash CS4 in more detail to help you develop AIR applications. Finally, you will see how to set up an AIR project with Flash CS4.

CHAPTER 3

BUILDING YOUR FIRST AIR
APPLICATION

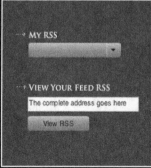

Creating an Adobe AIR application with Flash CS4 is similar to writing a Flash application for the Web. There are, however, important differences regarding the AIR publication settings and the version of ActionScript to use, as well as the AIR APIs. For example, in an AIR project developed with Flash CS4, you must use the latest version of ActionScript: ActionScript 3. Also, when you create AIR projects with Flash CS4, you are creating cross-platform projects—they should be able to run on Windows, Mac OS X, and Linux platforms. You don't need to study other languages; you don't have to learn other tools.

Furthermore, AIR projects don't have all the limitations that the browser normally has in Flash projects for the Web. For example, it's possible to work with the file system to save a local file, create local databases, manage system windows, and so on.

In AIR projects with Flash CS4, you can use the same methodologies you use when working with Flash projects. I am referring specifically to various drawing capabilities: creating and managing movie clips, buttons, and graphics, importing bitmaps, and generating animations over a timeline.

The use and management of the Flash timeline and its layers to create animations, however, are quite different in this new version. Flash CS4 provides three possibilities: Create Motion Tween, Create Shape Tween, and Create Classic Tween. These allow you to develop attractive and professional projects for your end users. You are able to offer users the same "flashy" experience that Flash provides for web applications with AIR.

At the code level, it is a good practice to apply the approach of **object-oriented programming** (**OOP**) and design patterns in your AIR projects. OOP is a widely used programming paradigm today, and the code in the examples in this book will follow it. If you're not familiar OOP, see the Wikipedia article on it, at http://en.wikipedia.org/wiki/Object_oriented.

A *design pattern* is a general reusable solution to a commonly occurring problem in software design. Object-oriented design patterns show relationships and interactions between classes or objects, without specifying the final application classes or objects that are involved. Using design patterns will improve your code considerably in terms of readability, performance, stability, and reusability. (See http://en.wikipedia.org/wiki/Design_pattern for more information on design patterns.)

OOP and design pattern practices come with many benefits. For example, OOP allows you to reuse the code in other applications and maintain it more easily. Also, with ActionScript, it is possible to use the same code libraries and objects you've developed across different projects.

Writing code on a frame of the timeline is not a good practice. It makes the code hard to maintain and sometimes difficult to modify.

In this chapter and through the entire book, you'll work with the OOP approach in mind, creating ActionScript classes to handle the logic of your AIR applications.

Creating an AIR project in Flash

As you're accustomed to with all versions of Flash, simply choose the type of document you want to create from the **welcome screen**. The welcome screen is the startup page that appears within the Flash IDE. It allows you to select the type of document you want to create. By default, this screen is displayed every time you open Flash CS4.

On the welcome screen, under the Create New column, is listed all the types of documents you can create in Flash, as shown in Figure 3-1.

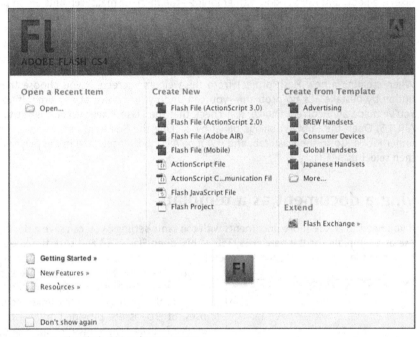

Figure 3-1. The Flash CS4 welcome screen

Creating an AIR project is the same as creating a Flash project. Open Flash CS4 and click the option Flash File (Adobe AIR). This will create an AIR project file in the Flash IDE.

The stage, the timeline, and all the rest of the Flash IDE panels appear as in previous versions of Flash. But creating an AIR file means that you intend to work using the AIR APIs to interact with the local operating system (to access the file system, to store data locally with SQLite support, etc.).

As in any Flash project, in AIR the width and height dimensions set for the stage are also those of the final project you will publish. You can easily change the settings regarding the dimensions of the stage of the AIR application. To do this, all you have to do is click the Edit button under the Size menu on the Properties panel.

The Document Properties panel will appear, allowing you to do the following:

- Change the dimensions of the document
- Change the background color
- Vary the frame rate of the document
- Change the ruler units

Changing the ruler units makes it possible to choose between pixels, inches, points, centi-meters, and millimeters. For obvious technical reasons, I suggest you choose pixels. The pixel is a good unit for working with graphics—the monitor measurements are in pixels, as are the measurements of the stage.

For the frame rate, leave the value at 24 fps. At 24 fps, animations look better. Flex, which doesn't use a timeline, also uses this frame rate for animations created with ActionScript.

When creating a new Flash project from the welcome screen, if you choose the wrong option by mistake, it's no problem—you can undo your choice at any time. If you think you've made an incorrect choice, just check that the Flash Player version is set to Adobe AIR 1.5. Open the Publish Settings panel by clicking the Edit item in the Properties panel under Profile. Go to the Flash tab, and if Adobe AIR 1.5 isn't selected in the player options, then select it.

Saving a document as a template

If you need to create more documents with the same settings, you can save a document to use as a template for the new ones. To do this, open Flash CS4 and click the Make Default button in the Document Properties panel. This opens the Adjust 3D perspective angle to pre-serve current stage projection option. Leave the box checked for this item. This will allow AIR to avoid problems of perspective linked to possible uses of 3D assets provided by Flash CS4. If you've followed these instructions, the data will be stored. You can also trust that when the new document is created, the settings you have cho-sen will be reused. You can close the Document Properties panel by clicking the OK button.

Figure 3-2. You can increase or decrease the frame rate of the timeline from the Properties panel.

Note that you can change the frame rate of the timeline by clicking the value of the frame rate next to the FPS option in the Properties panel, as shown in Figure 3-2. You can also change the frame rate by dragging the arrow to the right (to increase the frame rate) or the left (to decrease it).

The Properties panel will confirm the choices you have made so far, and the Edit button will be enabled.

Working with the Publish Settings panel

Before going any further, it is useful to discuss the Publish Settings panel, shown in Figure 3-3. From this panel, you can modify the settings related to the AIR document. To get into the Publish Settings panel, just click the Edit button for the Profile item on the Properties panel.

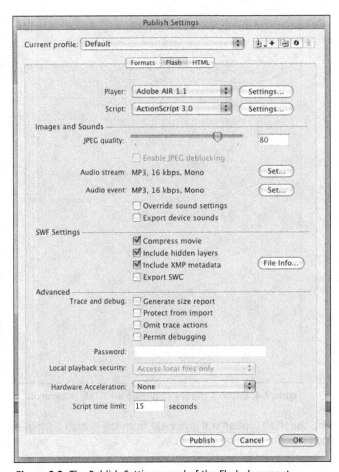

Figure 3-3. The Publish Settings panel of the Flash document

The Publish Settings panel lets you change the following items: formats, Flash, and HTML.

Confirm that all the parameters are set correctly by clicking the Flash item in the upper tab menu. Figure 3-3 shows settings for the player used (Adobe AIR) and script version (ActionScript 3.0) that you will use. You can create Flash projects that use Flash Player versions 1 through 10, as well as ActionScript versions 1.0, 2.0, and 3.0.

Unlike Flash files for web applications, in an AIR project, the application is compiled to an AIR package. This means that an HTML wrapper won't be created in the compiling phase.

To avoid this, open the Publish Settings panel and click the Formats item, and then uncheck the box next to the HTML item, as shown in Figure 3-4.

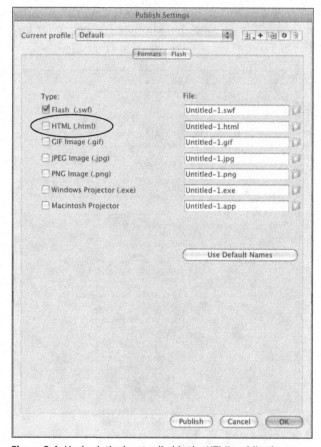

Figure 3-4. Uncheck the box to disable the HTML publication.

At this point, the HTML option will disappear from the Publish Settings panel. Confirm the settings and close the panel by clicking OK.

Saving the AIR project

You have set all the basic parameters to create an AIR project with Flash CS4. Now save your file, even though the project is effectively empty. To save the document, just go to File ➤ Save. The Save as window will appear and allow you to indicate the directory where you want to save your document.

> *It is a good practice to save your files after creating any project and setting the necessary parameters.*

Flash projects have the extension .fla. You can save FLA documents only for the CS4 or CS3 versions. However you can still work on Flash projects created with previous versions in Flash CS4 (such as Flash 8, Flash MX2004, etc.).

Now you are ready to set up the layout of your first AIR project.

Designing your application's layout

At this point, you should understand that there aren't many differences in Flash CS4 between creating an AIR desktop application layout and a web application layout. Designers can use the same tools they always have to design the look and feel of the project: Photoshop, Illustrator, and Fireworks. Now they are able to share their graphical assets with developers, who can integrate them into the code more easily.

In the following paragraphs, you'll learn how to make the work process among designers (who create graphical assets) and developers (who import and use them in the code) easier.

> *If you want to learn more about Flash and web application layout design, you can consult Adobe's Flash Design Center at www.adobe.com/cfusion/ designcenter/search.cfm?product=Flash&go=Go.*

Improvements in integration between Adobe products

Because of the recent developments in the family of Adobe products, Flash CS4 works well with Adobe's CS graphics software:

- Photoshop CS4 allows you to select a portion of a document and import it, with a simple cut-and-paste operation, into an HTML page in Dreamweaver. You can then save this slice and export it as a JPG file.

- Illustrator CS4 allows you to create movie clip symbols that are ready to be imported into Flash. The symbol's name, set in Illustrator, will be shown in Flash with the same instance name.

- Fireworks CS4 can export a complete HTML page of your graphical work, with CSS. You can also export CSS declarations for Flex components, as well as generate a complete MXML page (Macromedia Extensible Markup Language) that is ready to be opened in Flex.

The increased integration between these programs translates into a better collaboration between designers and developers. Today, designers who don't know much programming can work closely with developers by creating the graphical assets. This approach makes the work for the developer easier and cuts development time for the overall project.

Importing graphical assets

Flash can import Photoshop PSD files, Illustrator AI files, and Fireworks PNG files. You can import the various graphical assets that make up the projects into your AIR project in the Flash IDE and they will still be editable. This feature saves a lot of time, avoiding a whole series of exporting and importing operations each time there is a change. You can also convert assets into Flash movie clips, and for those you can set up a registration point or assign an instance name directly in Illustrator, Photoshop, or Fireworks.

In previous versions of Flash, importing graphical assets from Photoshop, Illustrator, or Fireworks was a more complicated process. You had to export the assets in several graphics files in a format that Flash would accept (e.g., JPG or PNG), place the elements on the stage of the Flash document in the exact position they needed to appear in, and convert the imported elements to movie clip symbols, if necessary.

Today these problems no longer exist. The following sections will show you just how simple it has become.

Importing Photoshop assets

Importing a Photoshop file in PSD format into Flash is pretty easy. Start by opening Flash and clicking File ➤ Import ➤ Import to Library. The Import to Library panel window will appear, as shown in Figure 3-5.

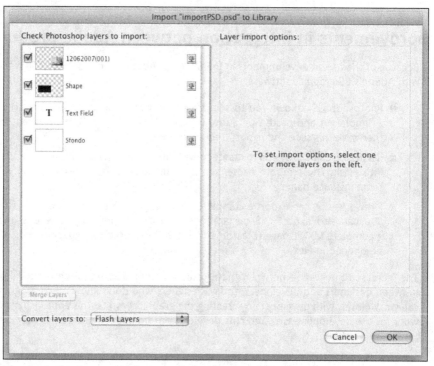

Figure 3-5. The Import to Library panel for a Photoshop file

You can choose which layers of the Photoshop document to import, and also whether to import it as a bitmap or a movie clip.

The Import to Library panel is divided into two main parts:

- Check Photoshop layers to import: This pane shows the list of available layers.
- Options for: This pane provides a list of importing options.

The Check Photoshop layers to import section displays each layer as a thumbnail, as shown in Figure 3-6. In this section, you can choose the layers you want to import into the Flash project by checking or unchecking the check boxes.

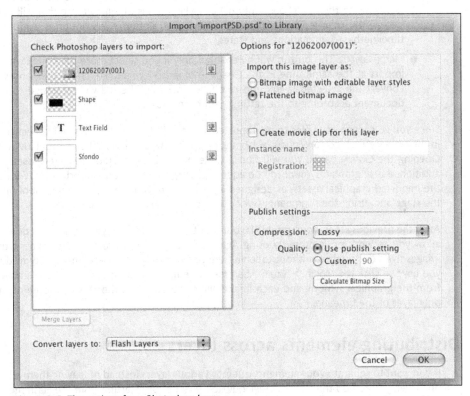

Figure 3-6. The options for a Photoshop layer

On the right-hand side of the Import to Library panel, the Options for settings allow you to manage the following characteristics of each layer:

- Import this image layer as: This allows you to indicate whether to import the layer as a bitmap (using the Flattened bitmap image option) or as a movie clip (using the Bitmap image with editable layer styles option).
- Create movie clip for this layer: You can select this option only if you're importing the layer as a flattened bitmap image. However, you can give the layer an instance name regardless of whether you're importing as a flattened image or an image with editable layer styles.

- Publish settings: This option allows you to further optimize the elements to import. The Compression option, which allows you to set the compression of the image, has two options: Lossless and Lossy. If you choose Lossless, you have no other parameters to set up. If you choose Lossy, you can choose the quality level of the image (from 0 to 100) with the Custom option of the Quality item, or keep the default publication setting (usually 80). The Calculate Bitmap Size button allows you to check the size of the layer (in kilobytes) you're importing according to the optimization setting you've chosen.

There are also some other important settings in this panel, including the following:

- Convert layers to: This option allows you to import the layers in two ways: as Flash layers (using the Flash layers options) or as keyframes of a movie clip that will contain all the required layers (using the Keyframes option). This option is useful for timeline-based animations and states.

- Merge Layers: This button will be enabled only if you select more than one layer to import at the same time in the Check Photoshop layers to import section, and will convert the selected layers into one layer in Flash. The file will be added to the document according to the settings you have chosen.

Since you've chosen your files to be imported into the library, your assets will be available in the Library panel (go to Window ➤ Library, or press Ctrl+L [Windows] or [Cmd+L (Mac)]). Opening the Library panel, you will find a folder with all the various imported assets. In addition, a new graphic symbol will be added, usually named as the imported file, with all the imported graphical assets, as designed in Photoshop. Drag this graphical symbol onto the stage and, using the Align panel (Window ➤ Align), place it at center stage.

After the previous steps, your graphic layout is put inside a graphic symbol, and this doesn't allow you to work on it properly using ActionScript code. You are forced to extract the images from this symbol, without touching the position of any of these images. To do this, you have to click the Modify ➤ Break Apart menu item. The graphic layout will be removed from the graphical symbol, and each image will stand alone on the only keyframe of the only layer of the timeline.

Distributing elements across layers

If you want to separate your elements out into various layers instead of leaving them all on one layer, you can do this with the Distribute to layers option. Starting from the Flash menu, click Modify ➤ Timeline ➤ Distribute to layers. Doing so will create one layer for each element and distribute each element to a separate layer of the timeline.

Importing Illustrator assets

In this section, you'll see how to import vector assets from Illustrator into Flash. The import process doesn't vary that much between Photoshop and Illustrator. Just open the Flash IDE, import an Illustrator file by clicking File ➤ Import ➤ Import to Library, and select an AI file from Illustrator. A dialog window will open (Import "file_name.ai" to Library), divided into two main parts: Check Illustrator layers to import and Layer import options for, as shown in Figure 3-7.

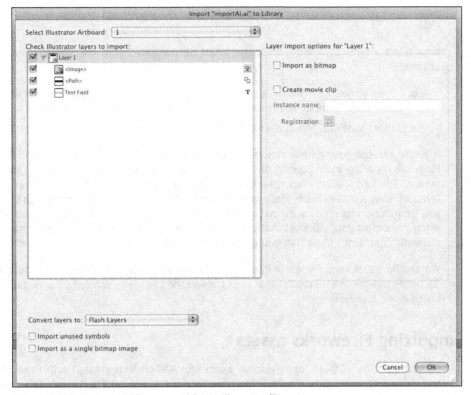

Figure 3-7. The Import to Library panel for an Illustrator file

In Check Illustrator layers to import, once again, you'll find the layers to be imported and their associated check boxes. Just check (or uncheck) the boxes to import (or not import) the Illustrator layers.

In contrast to Photoshop, the Illustrator importation phase allows you to import the layers with different properties. To explore this, with the Import to Library panel open, click a layer containing text. The Text Import Options items will offer you the three following options:

- Editable text: The element will remain a layer containing text.
- Vector outlines: The element will become vector outlines.
- Bitmap: The element will become a bitmap image.

With all three options, you can convert the text into a movie clip.

Now select a layer containing an outline. You'll be presented with the following import options:

- Editable path: This allows you to keep the outline as an editable vector shape.
- Bitmap: This converts the Illustrator outline into an image.

Again, both of these options allow you to convert the content of this layer into a movie clip.

Now select a layer containing an image. You'll be presented with the following import options:

- **Flatten bitmap to maintain appearance**: This optimizes the image to maintain its aspect ratio, without deformations, and includes all layers in one bitmap.
- **Create movie clip**: This converts the image into a movie clip.

If you've created your graphical asset in something other than RGB mode (e.g., CMYK), Flash will show the Incompatibility report button under the Check Illustrator layers to import section. The Incompatibility report button indicates a possible incompatibility between the layers of Illustrator and Flash. Flash will warn you about the discrepancy, but it won't stop you from importing if you want to proceed. However, the issue will become problematic when you export your work. At that point, you may notice that the colors of your graphic elements differ from those that you initially chose in Illustrator.

You should create vector assets in Illustrator that are already adapted to Flash AIR projects. It's better to work in RGB mode, or at least convert the assets you worked on previously in CMYK mode into RGB.

Importing Fireworks assets

You can use Flash CS4 to insert graphic assets into AIR projects created with Fireworks, too. Fireworks works with the PNG (Portable Network Graphics) file format. This poses some limitations compared to the formats that are available in Photoshop (PSD) and Illustrator (AI). However, that doesn't make it any less useful. Fireworks is a great tool for optimizing images for the Web, mixing vector and bitmap assets together, and exporting HTML, CSS, and MXML files.

In order to import a PNG Fireworks file into Flash, open Flash, choose File ➤ Import ➤ Import to Library, and then select the PNG file to import. The Import Fireworks Document panel will open, as shown in Figure 3-8. This window has fewer options compared to the equivalent Photoshop and Illustrator panels.

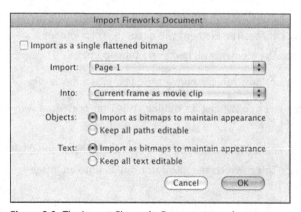

Figure 3-8. The Import Fireworks Document panel

The first option, Import as a single flattened bitmap, allows you to choose whether to import the file as a single image with flattened layers, as shown previously.

Below this is the Import option, where you specify the layer of the document to import, and the Into option, where you specify the import destination—either in the current keyframe of the timeline as a movie clip (Current frame as movie clip) or as a new layer of the timeline (New layer).

The next option regards the graphical assets that can be imported into the Flash file. You can choose whether to import the graphical objects or text fields, respectively, as editable shapes or text, or as bitmap images.

The file will be correctly imported into the library of the Flash file in the form of a graphic symbol. A folder will be created for the necessary files contained in the symbol itself. To use the elements imported from Fireworks onto the stage of the Flash document, you have only to drag the symbol from the library (by going to Window ➤ Library, or pressing Ctrl+L [Windows] or Cmd+L [Mac]) onto the stage.

Using CSS files in AIR applications

Cascading Style Sheets (CSS) is a style sheet language used to describe the presentation of a document written in markup languages (e.g., XHTML, SVG, or XUL). You can import CSS documents into Flash to change the look and feel of user interface elements in AIR applications.

Since ActionScript 2.0, it has been possible to use CSS to style Flash elements, but it was restricted to dynamic text fields. ActionScript 3.0 now supports many of the CSS1 properties declared by the W3C (you can read more about it at www.w3.org/TR/REC-CSS1).

In Flash, there are two ways to use CSS: by loading external style sheets or creating them via ActionScript.

The ActionScript StyleSheet class manages and controls the styles in a Flash application. This class allows you to create an object containing the formatting rules for the text contained in an instance of the TextField class.

> Remember that the text you modify via CSS can't be edited at runtime by users. If you want users to be able to modify the text, it's better to use the TextFormat class.

The content of dynamic text fields has to be assigned using the htmlText property. This is because the text field has to be able to read and interpret the text as HTML code.

Here is an example of an internal declaration of CSS using the ActionScript StyleSheet class:

```
var myStyle:StyleSheet=new StyleSheet();
var myStyleObj:Object=new Object();
myStyleObj.color="#AACC00";
```

91

```
myStyleObj.fontFamily="Verdana";
myStyleObj.fontSize=20;

myStyle.setStyle(".myColor", myStyleObj);

var textFieldCSS:TextField=new TextField();
textFieldCSS.styleSheet=myStyle;
textFieldCSS.htmlText="<span class='myColor'>Hello</span> world!";
addChild(textFieldCSS);
```

This code is quite simple. The dynamic text, named textFieldCSS, is associated with the instance of the CSS style sheet, which in turn loads the settings from the myStyleObj object.

The part that may look strange is the fontFamily property. In CSS declarations, you set the font-family property, whereas in ActionScript, the dash is eliminated and the following letter is uppercase: fontFamily.

Let's now examine the case of loading CSS as an external file. This option is very useful when you have a CSS file that styles a web application that you want to apply to format your AIR application.

Let's take the following CSS style, defined within a style.css file, as an initial example:

```
.myFormat {
    font-family: Verdana, Arial, Helvetica, sans-serif;
    font-size: 10px;
    font-youight: bold;
    color: #990000;
}
```

Next, insert the following ActionScript code to read and apply the style to a dynamic text field. Open the Flash IDE, create a Flash AIR project, and write this simple code on the first keyframe of the first layer of the timeline:

```
var textFieldCSS:TextField=new TextField();
var loaderCSS:URLLoader=new URLLoader();
var cssURLRequest:URLRequest=new URLRequest("style.css");
var myStyle:StyleSheet=new StyleSheet();

addChild(textFieldCSS);

with(textFieldCSS)
{
    width=300;
    height=80;
    x=30;
    y=30;
    autoSize=TextFieldAutoSize.LEFT;
    border=true;
}
```

```
loaderCSS.load(cssURLRequest);
loaderCSS.addEventListener(Event.COMPLETE, readCssHandler);

function readCssHandler(event:Event):void
{
    myStyle.parseCSS(loaderCSS.data);
    textFieldCSS.styleSheet=myStyle;
    textFieldCSS.htmlText="➥
    <span class='myFormat'>Hello World!</span>";
}
```

Let's analyze the code written in this brief example. An instance of the URLLoader class will load the CSS file. The instance of the StyleSheet class will code the style and interpret it correctly as a CSS style, and the dynamic text field, through the styleSheet properties, will apply the style to its content.

Now that you have learned how to import and use graphics assets from the most common Adobe products, you are able to set up an application layout.

Another important step in the workflow of an AIR application is the creation of the final file that you will distribute to clients. In the next section, you'll learn how to manage publishing settings and debug an AIR application.

Publishing an AIR application

Once you have finished your AIR application and everything is up and running, just package it in an AIR installation file to be distributed (the file extension will be .air).

Packaging an AIR application means generating a file with an AIR extension; this simply means that it is a compressed file (e.g., ZIP or RAR). It is a package containing the graphic elements, media assets, SWF files, and everything else your application requires to be installed and used.

To see the project, you need the AIR runtime, which you can download for free from the Adobe website (http://get.adobe.com/air/?promoid=BUIGQ).

The runtime (or runtime system) is a software package that allows a program to work correctly on a machine. The AIR 1.5 runtime is indispensable for the execution of various projects, including using Flash Player for the browser. Without it you couldn't do much! The AIR runtime therefore has to be installed on your machine, because it's responsible for installing (and uninstalling) your application, as well as making it executable so that the project can run. The AIR runtime installation is described in Chapter 1.

To create an AIR installation file, open the AIR – Application & Installer Settings panel of the Flash file, which you can do by clicking Properties ➤ AIR Settings ➤ Edit or File ➤ AIR Settings. This panel, shown in Figure 3-9, allows Flash CS4 to set up all the fundamental information for your application to work properly on the machines of your users. This information includes the icons to use and the transparency of the application window, among other things. As you will notice, the panel divides the information to be inserted into two categories: Application settings and Installer settings.

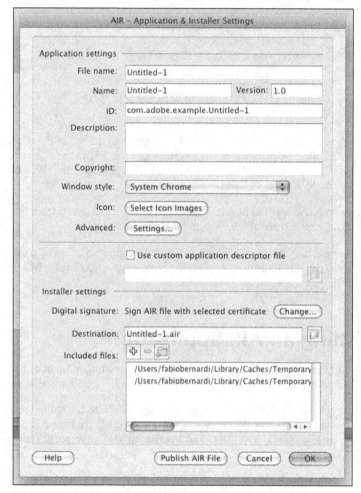

Figure 3-9. The AIR – Application & Installer Settings panel

Managing AIR with the Application & Installer Settings panel

You can use the AIR – Application & Installer Settings panel to set up all the options for packaging and distributing AIR applications. The Application settings section of this panel includes the following options:

The File name option is required and contains a string to use as the file name of the application when the application is installed.

The Name option—not mandatory but highly recommended—is displayed in the AIR application during installation and uninstallation.

Version is another important setting. This will allow you to let the user download updates for your application. In this example, however, you have to consider that the update isn't automatic, so it will have to be programmed via ActionScript. This will mainly consist of code that compares the local version number of the application to a remote version number. If there are discrepancies, the application can be programmed to update itself (this process is described in Chapter 13).

The ID setting is also important. The ID allows you to recognize every AIR project by a unique reference.

In Description, an optional field, you can include a brief description of your work.

In Copyright, you can insert rights information for your project.

In Window style, you can set the chrome quality of your window—meaning that you can make the application window more or less transparent. The first option, System Chrome, will allow the application to run inside a typical window in the operating system installed on the machine, as shown in Figure 3-10.

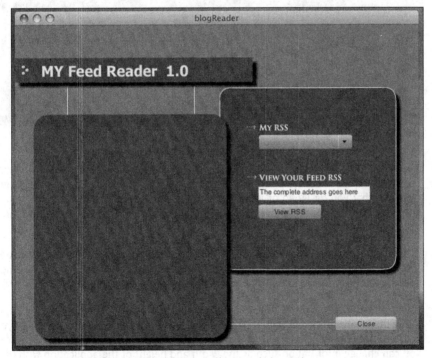

Figure 3-10. An application with the System Chrome window style

The second option available, Custom Chrome (opaque), will eliminate the borders of the window but leave the stage visible and use the color you selected in the Publish Settings panel (see Figure 3-11). With this option, you'll see only the stage and the graphic element you've used for your application. You can jump to Chapter 5 to learn more about AIR windows APIs.

Figure 3-11. An application with the Custom Chrome (opaque) window style

The third and last option, Custom Chrome (transparent), will eliminate all information regarding the transparency of the stage and the system window, and only show the graphic elements that you designed or imported into the document. With this option, you'll only see the graphic elements you've used in the application. The stage will be transparent, as shown in Figure 3-12.

In the Icon field, you can choose the icon images for your application. Once the application has been installed, the icons can be used as links on the desktop, in the menu of applications on the computer, in the taskbar as a system tray icon, or as a dock image.

If you click the Advanced ➤ Settings button, the Advanced Settings panel will open, allowing you to manage the settings of your application in more depth. In this panel, you can associate files necessary for your AIR application with the Associated file types option, and you can change information such as the width and height of the application with the Initial windows settings option.

Figure 3-12. An application with the Custom Chrome (transparent) window style

The settings you choose for Initial windows settings will overwrite the defaults in the Publish Settings panel. The Maximum height, Maximum width, Minimum width, and Minimum height options regard the minimum and maximum height and width of the application window when it is running on the user's machine. There are four more options regarding the possibility of restoring the window, making it maximizable or minimizable. The last option, Visible, allows you to decide whether the main window will be visible when your application starts up. These options are all selected by default, so leave them as they are unless you need them to be different.

With the last option, Other settings, you can insert the paths for the install folder and the program menu folder. These two items will tell the operating system where to create the installation folder and the program folder.

Managing digital signatures

The Installer settings section handles, most notably, the options relevant to the digital signature of an AIR file. The digital signature lets the users of your application know that it hasn't been altered by someone else (for malicious purposes).

A **digital signature** (or qualified electronic signature) is a document in electronic format based on cryptographic technology. The signature is used to authenticate digital documents and is equivalent to an autographic signature on paper documents. (Chapter 13 covers digital signatures and certificates in greater depth.)

Each AIR application must be signed using a digital signature. The signature is used to verify that the AIR application has not been altered since it was signed. In order to do this, it includes information about the signing certificate, which is used to verify the publisher identity.

The security assurances, limitations, and legal obligations involving the use of code-signing certificates are outlined in the certificate practice statements (CPSs) and subscriber agreements published by the issuing certificate authorities. Refer to the VeriSign CPS at www.verisign.com/repository/CPS/, the VeriSign Subscriber's Agreement at https://www.verisign.com/repository/subscriber/SUBAGR.html, the thawte CPS at www.thawte.com/cps/index.html, and the thawte Code Signing Certificate Agreement at www.thawte.com/ssl-digital-certificates/free-guides-whitepapers/pdf/develcertsign.pdf.

To sign AIR files, you can use an existing class 3 high-assurance code-signing certificate, or you can obtain a new one using one of the following:

- VeriSign:
  - Microsoft Authenticode Digital ID
  - Sun Java Signing Digital ID
- Thawte:
  - AIR Developer Certificate
  - Apple Developer Certificate
  - JavaSoft Developer Certificate
  - Microsoft Authenticode Certificate

In any case, an AIR product must have a signature, so you can create it in Flash CS4 or choose one. Click Digital signature ➤ Set to choose or create this file. The Digital signature panel contains two main options, as shown in Figure 3-13:

- Sign the AIR file with a digital certificate
- Prepare an AIR intermediate (AIRI) file that will be signed later

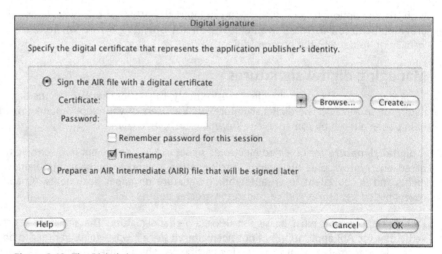

Figure 3-13. The Digital signature panel

Choose the first option because you are creating an AIR file to distribute this application. If you haven't already created the file (or if you don't have a digital signature), you have to click the Create button. The Create Self-Signed Digital Certificate panel will open, where you will be able to insert all the necessary information, as shown in Figure 3-14:

- Publisher name: The name of the person who will publish the project, normally the software house

- Organization unit: The unit of the publisher dedicated to the project

- Organization name: The name of the organization

- Country: The country of the organization

- Password/Confirm password: The control password to protect the digital signature

- Type: The type of digital signature

- Save as: The file name of the digital signature, which you can save in a directory of your choice

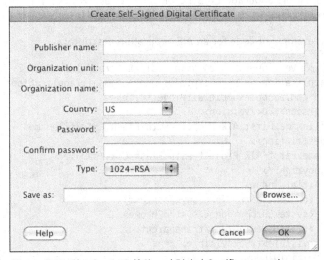

Figure 3-14. The Create Self-Signed Digital Certificate panel

This information is saved in a file with a .p12 or .pfx extension. This signature file can be reused every time you publish a new AIR, Flash, Flex, or Dreamweaver project. The signature is confirmed through the password that you assign when the document is created.

This P12 or PFX file is fictitious and has no legal value. Therefore, your AIR file will not indicate the name of the producer, nor any other information that you have inserted in the digital signature. The digital signature you have created is only useful to complete this phase of exporting the AIR file.

Once you save the digital signature, confirm by clicking OK. The path of the file will be inserted in the Certificate box. In the Password field below, insert the password that you declared in the digital signature. If you want, you can select the option Remember password for this session, so as to not have to insert the password each time you have to publish an AIR file. Close the Digital signature panel by clicking OK.

At this point, the Digital signature option on the AIR – Application & Installer Settings panel will show the message Sign AIR file with selected certificate.

The last two options on this panel, Destination and Included files, concern the path to the AIR file and the possible files to include in the project.

The application descriptor file

Each AIR application requires an **application descriptor** file, which is an XML file that describes the basic properties of the application. The application descriptor is usually named using the name of the project plus the -app suffix (e.g., projectName-app.xml). This XML-based file contains the information available in the AIR – Application & Installer Settings panel. The application descriptor file will be automatically generated every time you create a Flash file for AIR, and will be saved in the same folder as the FLA file. It contains the properties that affect the entire application.

You can open the application descriptor, since it's an XML file, with any text editor (e.g., Notebook on Windows or TextEdit on the Mac), or with Dreamweaver CS4.

Here is an example of code for an AIR application descriptor:

```
<?xml version="1.0" encoding="UTF-8" standalone="no" ?>
<application xmlns="http://ns.adobe.com/air/application/1.0">
<id>com.adobe.example.airProject</id>
<version>1.0</version>
<filename>First AIR Project with Flash CS4</filename>
<description/>
<name>First AIR Project with Flash CS4</name>
<copyright/>
<initialWindow>
    <content>airProject.swf</content>
    <systemChrome>none</systemChrome>
    <transparent>true</transparent>
    <visible>true</visible>
</initialWindow>
<icon>
    <image128x128>AppIconsForAIRPublish/AIRApp_128.png</image128x128>
    <image48x48>AppIconsForAIRPublish/AIRApp_48.png</image48x48>
    <image32x32>AppIconsForAIRPublish/AIRApp_32.png</image32x32>
    <image16x16>AppIconsForAIRPublish/AIRApp_16.png</image16x16>
</icon>
<customUpdateUI>false</customUpdateUI>
<allowBrowserInvocation>false</allowBrowserInvocation>
</application>
```

Notice how this code contains the same information that you have in the AIR – Application & Installer Settings panel.

Understanding what's in the application descriptor is useful, especially if you want to create AIR applications with Flex. You can edit all the information by hand. For example, to make the window of the system where the application will run transparent, as shown in Figure 3-12, you have to set the value of the systemChrome node to none and transparent to true. Things are slightly different in Flex Builder, where, in addition, it is necessary to set up a CSS style especially for the WindowedApplication tag with image and background shading set to 0.

Creating a transparent window

Following is an example of an application descriptor file that creates a transparent window for an AIR project:

```
<?xml version="1.0" encoding="UTF-8"?>
<application xmlns="http://ns.adobe.com/air/application/1.0">
<!-- The application identifier string, unique to this application.➨
        Required. -->
<id>AnalogicClock</id>
<!-- Used as the filename for the application. Required. -->
<filename>AnalogicClock</filename>
<!-- The name that is displayed in the AIR application installer. ➨
        Optional. -->
<name>AnalogicClock</name>
<!-- An application version designator➨
        (such as "v1", "2.5", or "Alpha 1"). ➨
        Required. -->
<version>v1</version>
<!-- Description, displayed in the AIR application installer. ➨
        Optional. -->
<!-- <description></description> -->
<!-- Copyright information. Optional -->
<!-- <copyright></copyright> -->
<!-- Settings for the application's initial window. Required. -->
<initialWindow>
    <!-- The main SWF or HTML file of the application. Required. -->
    <!-- Note: In Flex Builder, the SWF reference is set➨
            automatically. -->
    <content>[This value will be overwritten by Flex Builder➨
                    in the output app.xml]</content>
    <!-- The title of the main window. Optional. -->
    <!-- <title></title> -->
    <!-- The type of system chrome to use (either "standard" or ➨
            "none"). Optional. Default standard. -->
    <systemChrome>none</systemChrome>

    <!-- Whether the window is transparent. Only applicable when➨
            systemChrome is false. Optional. Default false. -->
    <transparent>true</transparent>
```

```
            <!-- Whether the window is initially visible. Optional.➡
                Default false. -->
            <!-- <visible></visible> -->
            <!-- Whether the user can minimize the window. Optional.➡
                Default true. -->
            <!-- <minimizable></minimizable> -->
            <!-- Whether the user can maximize the window. Optional.➡
                Default true. -->
            <!-- <maximizable></maximizable> -->
            <!-- Whether the user can resize the window. Optional.➡
                Default true. -->
            <!-- <resizable></resizable> -->
            <!-- The window's initial width. Optional. -->
            <!-- <width></width> -->
            <!-- The window's initial height. Optional. -->
            <!-- <height></height> -->
            <!-- The window's initial x position. Optional. -->
            <!-- <x></x> -->
            <!-- The window's initial y position. Optional. -->
            <!-- <y></y> -->
            <!-- The window's minimum size, specified ➡
                as a width/height pair, such as "400 200". ➡
                Optional. -->
            <!-- <minSize></minSize> -->
            <!-- The window's initial maximum size,specified ➡
                as a width/height pair, such as "1600 1200". ➡
                Optional. -->
            <!-- <maxSize></maxSize> -->
    </initialWindow>
    <!-- The subpath of the standard default installation.➡
            location to use. Optional. -->
    <!-- <installFolder></installFolder> -->
    <!-- The subpath of the Windows Start/Programs menu to use.Optional.-->
    <!-- <programMenuFolder></programMenuFolder> -->
    <!-- The icon the system uses for the application. For at least one➡
            resolution,specify the path to a PNG file included in the ➡
            AIR package. Optional. -->
    <!-- <icon>
        <image16x16></image16x16>
        <image32x32></image32x32>
        <image48x48></image48x48>
        <image128x128></image128x128>
    </icon> -->

    <!-- <customUpdateUI></customUpdateUI> -->
    <!-- Whether the application can be launched when the user clicks a➡
            link in a Web browser. Optional. Default false. -->
    <!-- <allowBrowserInvocation></allowBrowserInvocation> -->
    <!-- Listing of file types for which the application can register.➡
```

```
            Optional. -->
<!-- <fileTypes> -->
<!-- Defines one file type. Optional. -->
<!-- <fileType> -->
<!-- <name></name> -->
<!-- The extension to register. Required. -->
<!-- <extension></extension> -->
<!-- The description of the file type. Optional. -->
<!-- <description></description> -->
<!-- The MIME type. Optional. -->
<!-- <contentType></contentType> -->
<!-- The icon to display for the file type. Optional. -->
<!-- <icon>
     <image16x16></image16x16>
     <image32x32></image32x32>
     <image48x48></image48x48>
     <image128x128></image128x128>
</icon> -->
<!-- </fileType> -->
<!-- </fileTypes> -->
</application>.
```

This application descriptor file is automatically generated when you create an AIR project in Flex Builder.

> You can use an application descriptor file created by Flex Builder in your Flash project and vice versa.

Test the AIR applications to view all these settings. As for any project created in Flash, just click Control ➤ Test Movie (or press Ctrl+Enter [on Windows] or Cmd+Enter [on the Mac]) to get an idea of the window settings of your program.

If you have set up the window in Custom Chrome (transparent) mode, your window won't have maximize, minimize, or close buttons, so you'll have to create and code them manually. In Chapter 5, you'll learn more about creating transparent windows.

For now, close these projects by clicking Alt+F4 (on Windows) or Cmd+Q (on the Mac).

Installing AIR applications

Next, create an AIR file by clicking File ➤ Publish (or pressing Shift+F12), or clicking the Edit button of the Properties panel under the AIR settings item, and then clicking Publish AIR file. After a few seconds, a message will tell you that the publication file has been created correctly. You'll find the AIR file in the folder where you've saved the Flash file.

Installing and uninstalling an AIR application from the AIR file

Start the installation by double-clicking the file. At this point, the AIR runtime will start the installation, at the end of which your project will be available on the computer.

To uninstall an AIR application from Windows, just go to Start ➤ Control Panel ➤ Add or Remove Programs, select the AIR application from the list, and click Remove. On the Mac, just drag the application from the Application folder and drop it in the Trash folder, or run the AIR installer file again and choose the Uninstall option.

Distributing an AIR application with the badge installation

AIR's potential doesn't stop at enabling you to develop desktop applications with web tools. AIR also allows you to check if the AIR runtime is installed from the browser, and install an application from the browser.

Flash CS4 installs a file called badge.fla in the Adobe Flash CS4\AIK1.5\samples\ directory. Through this file, you can allow your users to download and install your AIR project, as well as the necessary AIR runtime, from an HTML page of your website.

Furthermore, it is possible to customize the installation interface that Flash CS4 provides for AIR applications. You can edit the files in the Adobe Flash CS4\AIK1.5\samples\badge folder to manage the AIR application from the browser. This folder contains

- The Flash project of the badge file, badge.fla
- The AIRBadge.as class
- The default_badge.html file

Open the default_page.html file with Dreamweaver CS4 or a text editor of your choice.

In this file, you can look for the JavaScript AC_FL_RunContent() function, and change the parameters of the FlashVars property according to the needs of your project.

> The FlashVars property provides a method of importing variables into the top layer of a movie when first instantiated. You can use FlashVars to pass values from ActionScript to JavaScript (and vice versa), as well as invoke functions.

You can edit the following parameters of FlashVars:

- appname: Identifies the name of the application (optional).
- appurl: Specifies the URL of the AIR file to download. It is a mandatory parameter, and the address has to be absolute (e.g., http://www.comtaste.com/air-app/myApp.air).

- airversion: Identifies the version of the AIR runtime (not your application). This is also a mandatory parameter.
- imageurl: Specifies the pathway of the image to show in the installation interface.
- buttoncolor: Indicates the color of the download button (in hexadecimal).
- messagecolor: Indicates the color of the text of the message to show under the download button if the runtime isn't installed.

Note that buttoncolor and messagecolor don't automatically appear in default_badge.html, but you can add them.

You can add the code contained in this page (default_badge.html) directly from the HTML document of the website from which the user downloads the AIR file. If you prefer, you can save it with another name in the folder of your project.

> *Do not move the default_badge.html file from its original folder, and do not save it with different settings from the default settings. This way, you'll always have a clean template file available.*

The badge.fla file contains a default (editable) image and a simple download button. You can open the badge.fla file and edit the settings regarding the dimensions, background color, and other elements. However, the JavaScript function you modified beforehand and the SWF file generated by this Flash document (badge.fla) have to coexist inside the HTML page.

In the workflow of an AIR application, the step preceding the publishing and distributing is the one that allows developers to make their applications bug-free: the debugging phase.

Flash CS4 has some new features to make the debugging phase easier. In the next section, you'll learn the basic techniques to debug an AIR application using the Flash IDE.

Debugging an AIR application in Flash CS4

In any kind of Flash project, from the simplest to the most complex, you need to check or test if your application works. That is, you need to debug it.

The term **debugging** originates from electronic calculators that crashed frequently because of insects that nested inside of them and got electrocuted. Fixing the calculators involved finding the short-circuited points and restarting the machine, and from then on it was known as debugging. Today, debugging an application means checking for, finding, and eliminating errors (at a code level) in your application.

A correct debugging procedure allows you to solve problems or malfunctions in your application, but it isn't as easy as it sounds. Making a good debugging system means not only finding and correcting errors, but also avoiding introducing new ones or otherwise generating abnormal activity in your application. Closing a fault in your code only to find out that you have created a new one somewhere else can happen frequently, with very frustrating consequences. But do not despair, because Flash CS4 provides you with some powerful debugging tools.

There are four main ways to debug a Flash or an AIR application:

- Using the trace() method
- Using the Debug tool
- Using remote debugging
- Using try...catch...finally ActionScript code.

We'll look at the differences between the four options next.

Using the trace method

The trace() method allows you to debug by tracing values through the Output panel. For example, you can monitor the content of the variables or values returned by a given method. However, you are the one who has to explicitly provide input by telling the trace() method which values you want it to return. You can use this method when you know exactly where to look, or exactly what you want to check.

Create a new Flash project for AIR by going to File ➤ New ➤ Flash File (Adobe AIR) or by clicking the Flash File (Adobe AIR) button from the initial welcome screen.

In Flash, you can insert ActionScript code through the Actions panel in the Window menu (or by pressing F9). Go ahead and open it. If you are used to previous versions of Flash, you will recognize this panel, which hasn't changed. According to many developers, the Actions panel isn't an optimal code-writing tool. The writing processes aren't very automatic, and therefore writing very large projects can be tiresome and difficult. But it is definitely good practice for beginners and those who want to perfect their programming skills.

Begin by writing the following code on the first frame of the timeline:

```
var myCompanyName:String=new String();
myCompanyName="Comtaste";
var completeString:String=new String();
completeString="My Company Name is: "+myCompanyName;
trace(completeString);
```

The previous example is extremely simple. The steps are as follows:

1. Create a variable.
2. Assign a value to the variable by inserting the name of the company.
3. Create another variable.
4. Assign a value to that as well.
5. Use the trace() method to trace a sentence in the Output panel (My Company Name is:), to which you connect the content of completeString.

Testing an application and using the trace() method is equivalent to publishing the SWF file. Let's see what happens. Click Control ➤ Test Movie (or Ctrl+Enter [on Windows] or Cmd+Enter [on the Mac]). The SWF document will be compiled, but at the same time the Output panel, available only during authoring time in Flash CS4, will open. Inside it is not only the sentence you have set (My Company Name is: Company Name), but also the following information:

```
[SWF] myApp.swf - 4777 bytes after decompression.
```

If you close the test file window you have created, another message will appear on the panel: Test Movie terminated.

Now, to understand the use of the trace() method better, try to generate a malfunction. To do so, disable a line of code that you have just written, like this:

```
var myCompanyName:String=new String();
myCompanyName="Comtaste";
var completeString:String=new String();
// completeString="My Company Name is: "+myCompanyName;
trace(completeString);
```

With this change, you don't generate an error, but you also don't get the required result, as the completeString variable hasn't been assigned any value.

Now, if you run another test with Control ➤ Test Movie, you'll see that no response is provided in the Output panel. The trace() method hasn't traced the content of the variable. This fact lets you know that the error regards the population (the assignment of a value) of the variable itself. Your bug is therefore not in the declaration of the variable, but in its population.

To understand the use of the trace() method for debugging a bit better, let's look at another example. Delete the previous code in the Flash timeline and insert the following:

```
var mySquare:MovieClip=new MovieClip();
var posX:Number=40;
var posY:Number=30;

addChild(mySquare);
with(mySquare.graphics)
{
    beginFill(0xFF0000, 1);
    drawRect(0,0,100,100);
    endFill();
}
mySquare.x=posX;
mySquare.y=posY;
```

This code is also simple enough: you have drawn a square (an instance of the MovieClip class) that is placed on the X and Y axes at 40 and 30 coordinates, respectively. When you test your work, once again everything should work properly. Now change the code to the following:

```
var mySquare:MovieClip=new MovieClip();
var posX:Number=40;
var posY:Number;

addChild(mySquare);
with(mySquare.graphics)
{
     beginFill(0xFF0000, 1);
     drawRect(0,0,100,100);
     endFill();
}
mySquare.x=posX;
mySquare.y=posY;
```

Test your application again. This time things won't work out! In this case, Flash doesn't warn you about any error. Everything seems to run smoothly, except you can't see your red square (the instance name of mySquare typed as MovieClip).

You can use the trace() method to debug the application. Try to make it return the coordinates of your square, just to see where it is. At the end of the lines of code you changed, add these two:

```
trace(mySquare.x);
trace(mySquare.y);
```

Then run your project again. You should now get 40 for the X axis and −107374182.4 for the Y axis. Here is the error: the square is there, but it is off the stage. This is because you have omitted the value of the posY variable. Flash, not being able to come to terms with the syntax error, inserted the maximum negative value for the Y axis.

Understanding compile-time errors

The examples provided so far have contained syntactically correct, working code, but haven't given the correct results. If, on the other hand, the code is syntactically incorrect, it will crash your application, rendering the trace() method useless. To deal with this, Flash provides the Compiler Errors panel.

To see how the Compiler Errors panel works, modify the previous code as follows:

```
var mySquare:MovieClip=new MovieClip();
var posX:Number=40;
var posY:Number=40z;

addChild(mySquare);
with(mySquare.graphics)
{
     beginFill(0xFF0000, 1);
     drawRect(0,0,100,100);
     endFill();
```

```
}
mySquare.x=posX;
mySquare.y=posY;

trace(mySquare.x);
trace(mySquare.y);
```

This time, you have indicated 40z as a value for the posY variable, which will cause an error because posY is a numerical variable, and it cannot accept textual values.

If you test the application with Control ➤ Test Movie, the Compiler Errors panel will open, displaying a list of all the possible errors in the code, as shown in Figure 3-15.

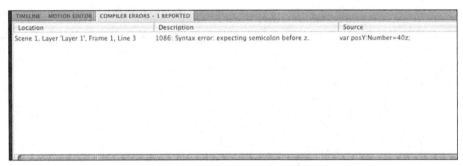

Figure 3-15. The Flash Compiler Errors panel with a short description of the error

The panel provides the following three pieces of information on the error:

- Location: The exact position of the error in terms of frame number, line, and layer of the timeline
- Description: The cause of the error
- Source: The exact line of the contested code

If you double-click the line of the error in the panel, the Go To Source button will be activated. If you click it, you'll be taken to the Actions panel, where the line of incorrect code will be highlighted.

Using the Debug tool

Now, you'll look at how to debug an application using the Debug tool. The Debug tool is a working area that contains the following windows:

- **The** Script **window**: This window contains your ActionScript code.
- **The** Variables **window**: This window is for monitoring the variables.
- **The** Debug **console**: This window is for checking the debugging process of the application.

The Debug tool is for checking the variables and methods you use in your code. It can be very useful for complex and detailed debug activities, and it can save you a lot of time.

In contrast to the trace() method, the Debug tool can block the execution of the ActionScript code at precise points in documents. These points are called **breakpoints**, and they need to be inserted before the debug operation is started.

Go back to the previous example, leaving the code unaltered so that you can detect the errors with the Debug tool. Open the Actions panel in Flash, and change the third line, var posY:Number=40z, to the following: var posY:Number=40. Then click the bar on the left side of the Actions panel, next to the line of suspect code you need to analyze, as shown in Figure 3-16 (the red dots indentify the breakpoints inserted).

Figure 3-16. Insert breakpoints in the Actions panel to find possible errors.

When you click the bar on the left side of the Actions panel, you're asking Flash's Debug tool to stop the execution of the application. That precise point of code will not be executed until you click the Continue button of the Debug console to restart the execution. Then, the debug operation will continue to read and execute the next line of code until the next breakpoint, if one exists. The execution will then continue until the end of the ActionScript code.

Now you can start the debug operation.

You can activate the Debug tool by clicking Debug ➤ Debug Movie or pressing Ctrl+Shift+Enter.

You can use the Debug *tool for applications where the code is inserted in the keyframes, as well as for applications with code in the AS file. However, it isn't possible to add breakpoints to ASC (ActionScript for Communication) or JSFL (JavaScript Flash) files.*

Once started, the Debug tool reads all the code until the first breakpoint, blocking the execution of the code at that point. The breakpoint is highlighted by a yellow arrow.

In this phase of debugging, the SWF file isn't visible, and will not actually be generated until after the complete execution of the application code. Now you can change the value of the properties and variables of your application via the Variables panel, as shown in Figure 3-17.

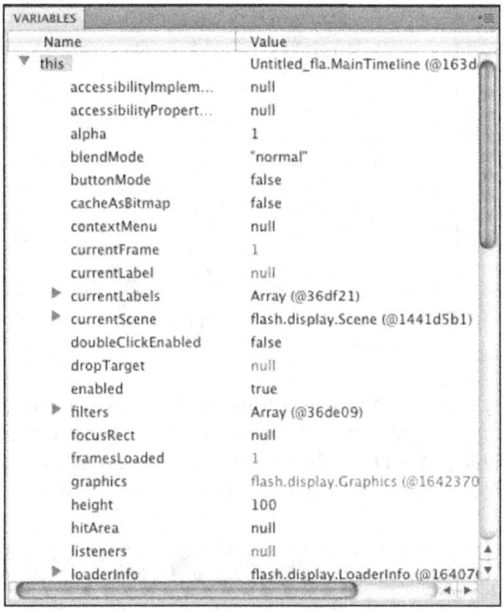

Figure 3-17. The Variables panel

Using the Variables panel

The Variables panel shows all the properties (with their related values) and objects that appear on the stage. To see the objects and properties, click the + sign in the Variables panel next to the this item, which identifies the stage of the application.

Going through this long list, you can find the mySquare object, the instance of the MovieClip class you drew previously using ActionScript code. mySquare, being an instance of the MovieClip class, inherits all the properties of this class.

If you click the + sign next to the name mySquare, you can see its properties, as shown in Figure 3-18. Notice the x and y properties at the end of the list for the mySquare object, which include the values that you set up in the code.

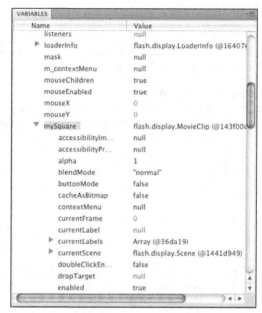

Figure 3-18. The mySquare properties shown in the Variables panel

All the properties and variables are editable in the Variables panel. So, change your error: double-click the numerical value of the y property of mySquare. Change the improbable value –107374182.4 to 10. Once the changes have been made, you can continue by clicking the Continue button (the green arrow) of the Debug console, as shown in Figure 3-19.

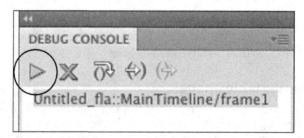

Figure 3-19. The Continue button

The debug operation will stop again at the following line because you have inserted a breakpoint there. Note that the Output panel shows the line number 40 to tell you that the previous line of code has been processed.

Now the code is complete, the SWF file is generated, and the properties aren't editable any more. This time, you can see the red square (the mySquare instance) on the stage, but don't let the result confuse you. The instance mySquare is visible because you have changed the y property with the Debug tool, but the code error is still there and needs to be eliminated.

To exit the Debug console, just close the SWF file or click the End Debug Session button on the Debug Console panel.

Remote debugging

The debugging possibilities in Flash don't stop with the trace() method and the Debug tool. Flash also allows you to debug a remote SWF file by using the stand-alone version of Flash Player, or a Flash Player debugger version (a.k.a. debug players or content debuggers) available in the C:\Program Files\Adobe\Adobe Flash CS3\Players\Debug directory. Remote debugging is only allowed for the files that are located in the same host of the application.

In order to debug a remote file, you must set certain options in its publication phase. These options are shown in Figure 3-20. Here's how to set them correctly:

1. Choose File ➤ Publish Settings.

2. On the Flash tab, check the Permit debugging option in the Advanced section.

> For security, you can enter a password that will be requested during debugging.

The procedure for remote debugging is the following:

1. Click Debug ➤ Begin Remote Debugging Session ➤ ActionScript 3.0. You'll have 2 minutes to open Flash Player and connect to the remote debugging session.

2. Open Flash Player for the debug: from the desktop, go to Programs ➤ Adobe ➤ Flash CS4 ➤ Players ➤ Debug.

3. Open a SWF file to carry out the debug directly from Flash Player.

Go back to Flash CS4 and note that the debug has been connected to your application, allowing you to carry out the debugging.

> Regarding remote files, you must remember not to connect to a SWF application on another computer (for example in an intranet). In this case, the debugger will not be able to read the data regarding the breakpoints in the Flash file.

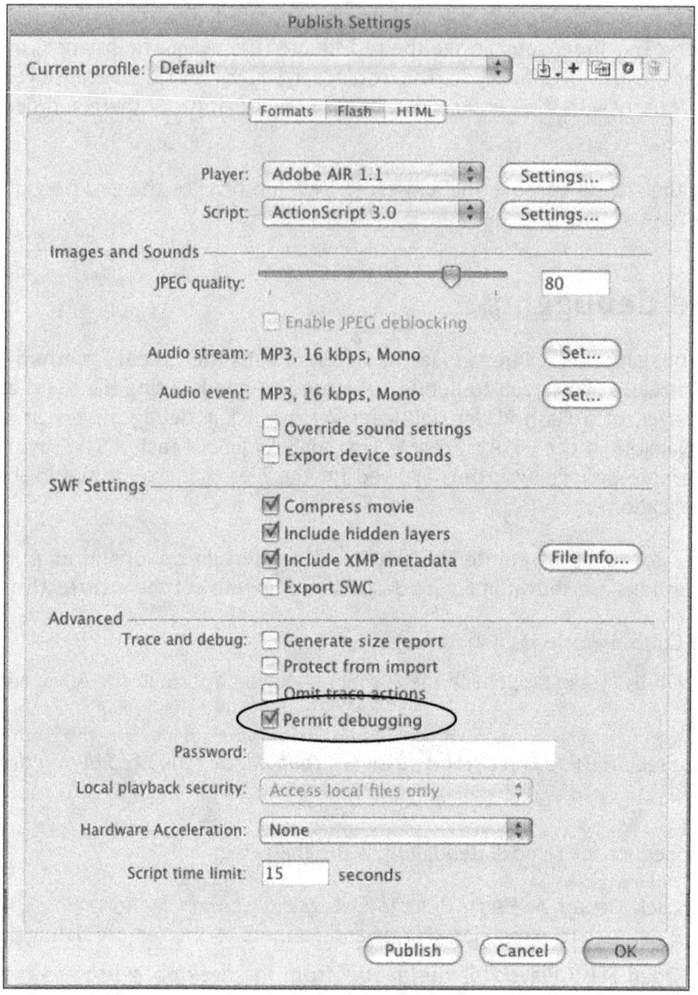

Figure 3-20. Check this option to permit remote debugging.

Debugging with the try...catch...finally statement

Another useful approach for debugging an application is to use the `try...catch...finally` statement in ActionScript 3. Here's an example:

```
try {
    // try block
} catch(error[:ErrorType1]) {
    // catch block
} catch(error[:ErrorTypeN]) {
    // catch block
```

```
} finally {
    // finally block
}
```

You can test the code (try), check the type of error (catch), and then go on to an instruction that will solve the error (finally). This kind of code is used especially when there is a runtime error. In the case of an error, Flash Player generates an exception, which in turn generates an Error object. If there is an error in the code, it gets passed on to the catch instruction. If the error in the try instruction isn't generated, the Flash compiler goes directly to the finally instruction. Here's an example that uses the try...catch... finally statement:

```
var mySprite:Sprite = new Sprite();
var error:Boolean=false;
try {
    mySprite["dynamicProperty"] = "foo";
}
catch (err:Error) {
    trace ("ERROR: "+err);
    error=true;
}
finally{
    if(error)
    {
        trace("An error occured");
    }else{
        trace("No error occured");
    }
}
```

If you run the example, the Output panel will open and show the following runtime error:

```
ReferenceError: Error #1056: Cannot create property ➥
dynamicProperty on. flash.display.Sprite.  ➥
An error occurred
```

Thanks to the try...catch...finally statement and the trace() method, you can easily intercept errors in your application.

Creating and deploying a simple feed reader in AIR

Now you can put everything you've read so far into practice with a real-world example. The example won't focus so much on the ActionScript code as on the setup, packaging, deploying, and distributing aspects of an AIR application using Flash CS4.

Open a new Flash file for AIR and save it in a folder on your computer with the name BlogReader.fla. You don't need many graphical elements for your application; it is enough for your file to have the following:

- A combo box with the instance name sites_cb
- An input field with the instance name yourFeed_txt
- A dynamic text area where you can view the various articles extracted from the RSS feed, with the instance name textArea_txt

First of all, with the opened FLA file, create a new ActionScript file (with an .as extension). Save it as BlogReader.as in the following directory: com/comtaste/foed/essentialair/ chapter03, remembering that the com folder and the file BlogReader.fla must be in the same directory. In Chapter 4 (in the "Managing the document classes" section), I'll explain the meaning of this path. This file is where you'll insert the necessary code. You can only insert actions into AS files. That is why the stage and other panels are not shown by Flash.

When you write code in an AS file, you should first insert everything between the braces after the package keyword, like this:

```
package {
// ActionScript 3.0 code
}
```

When you create an AS document, you need to import all the classes you'll be using. For example, if you want to insert a simple text field into your application, you have to import the TextField class. Here's the code that imports all the classes you need:

```
package com.comtaste.foed.essentialair.chapter03{
        import flash.display.MovieClip;
        import fl.controls.ComboBox;
        import flash.display.NativeWindow;
        import fl.transitions.Tween;
        import fl.transitions.easing.*;
        import fl.transitions.TweenEvent;
        import flash.text.TextField;
        import flash.events.MouseEvent;
        import flash.events.Event;
        import flash.events.KeyboardEvent;
        import flash.net.URLLoader;
        import flash.net.URLRequest;
```

The list is long but fundamental. Often, a good part of the initial code of the AS file for a project is a series of import statements.

Proceed by setting all the variables you will need for your BlogReader class:

```
public class BlogReader extends MovieClip
{

        private var blogXML:XML;
```

```
private var blogURLLoader:URLLoader=new URLLoader();
private var blogURLRequest:URLRequest;
private var blogArray:Array;
private var winControl:NativeWindow;
```

In the preceding code, the blogURLLoader property typed as URLLoader will load the RSS documents from a URL set in the blogURLRequest property. The blogXML property typed as XML will load the content of the parsed RSS document.

Proceed by setting the constructor of your AS file:

```
public function BlogReader():void
{
    winControl=Stage.nativeWindow;
    bar_mc.buttonMode=true;
    textArea_txt.multiline=true;
    textArea_txt.wordWrap=true;
    titleFeed_mc.x=titleFeed_mc.width;
    bar_mc.addEventListener(MouseEvent.MOUSE_DOWN, moveWin);
    sites_cb.addEventListener(Event.CHANGE, viewFeed);
    close_btn.addEventListener(MouseEvent.CLICK, closeWin);
    yourFeed_btn.addEventListener(MouseEvent.CLICK, yourFeed);
    yourFeed_txt.addEventListener(MouseEvent.CLICK, cleanIt);
    addEventListener(KeyboardEvent.KEY_DOWN, yourfeedClickHandler);
}
```

> The constructor is, in OOP, the backbone of a class. It is a special public method called when an object is created. The constructor can be omitted during the creation of a class, although one will be created automatically by the compiler.

Here you establish, if necessary, the initialization characteristics of a class (or simple AS file). In your case, you have established the events linked to the various buttons on the stage of the Flash file, and set certain properties of the text field that will contain the content of the RSS file.

Proceed with the following code:

```
public function viewFeed(event:Event):void
{
    blogURLRequest=new URLRequest(String(sites_cb.selectedItem.data));
    manageFeed();
}

public function yourFeed(event:MouseEvent):void
{
    blogURLRequest=new URLRequest(String(yourFeed_txt.text));
    manageFeed();
}
```

With these last two methods, you record the path of the RSS. There are two methods because you have two options in your application:

- Choosing an item from the combo box on the stage (viewFeed)
- Seeing the feed from the path introduced by the user in the text input field yourFeed_txt

The viewFeed() and yourFeed() methods, in turn, call another method (manageFeed()). This is to avoid rewriting the same code more than once. The yourFeed() and viewFeed() methods only differ as far as the path of the file to load is concerned.

Proceed by writing the manageFeed() method:

```
public function manageFeed():void
{
    textArea_txt.htmlText="";
    titleFeed_mc.feedTitle_txt.text="";
    blogURLLoader.load(blogURLRequest);
    blogURLLoader.addEventListener(Event.COMPLETE, showData);
}
```

The manageFeed() method empties the dynamic text fields regarding the name and content of the feeds. It loads the new indicated path and then, once the RSS file is finished loading, it starts the showData() method to effectively show the RSS news.

Proceed by writing the showData() method:

```
public function showData(event:Event):void
{
    blogXML=XML(blogURLLoader.data);
    blogArray=new Array();
    for each(var prop:XML in blogXML.channel.item){
        blogArray.push({urlPath:prop.title, urlLink:prop.link});
    }
    for(var i:Number=0; i<blogArray.length; i++){
        textArea_txt.htmlText+="<b><font color='#FFAA00'>"➥
                                            +(i+1)+") . </font></b><i>➥
        <a href='"+blogArray[i].urlLink+"'>".➥
        + blogArray[i].urlPath+"</a></i><br>";
    }
    titleFeed_mc.feedTitle_txt.text=blogXML.channel.title;
    var showFeedTitle:Tween=new Tween(titleFeed_mc, "x", ➥
    Regular.easeOut, titleFeed_mc.x, 0, 2, true);
}
```

This instruction is quite simple: the for loop populates the blogArray array of the content of the RSS file, and then the content itself is used to populate the dynamic text field textArea_txt to view the requested feeds, thanks to the second for...each loop.

The HTML tags for the htmlText property of the textArea_txt field are used to provide a minimum degree of formatting. The Tween class allows you to create a simple animation for the title box that will appear each time a new RSS feed is loaded.

Now you'll use some of the classes that are exclusive to the AIR ActionScript 3 APIs.

One of these is the NativeWindow. This class allows you to make the AIR applications interact with the file system. This subject will be explained in more depth in the Chapter 5.

Let's pick up the code where you left off:

```
public function moveWin(event:MouseEvent):void
{
    winControl.startMove();
}
```

This startMove() method of the NativeWindow class allows you to move the application on the screen of your user.

The following code closes your application:

```
public function closeWin(event:MouseEvent):void
{
    var pushOff:Tween=new Tween(this, "x", Regular.easeOut, ➥
        this.x, -700, 5, true);
    sites_cb.visible=false;
    textArea_txt.text="";
    event.currentTarget.label="";
    yourFeed_btn.label="";
    yourFeed_txt.visible=false;
    titleFeed_mc.visible=false;
    pushOff.addEventListener(TweenEvent.MOTION_FINISH, closeFinally);
}
private function closeFinally(event:TweenEvent):void
{
    winControl.close();
}
```

The closeFinally() method in the closeWin() method is synchronized with the closure of the animation that is generated by the instance of the Tween class: pushOff. At the end of this animation, the procedures in the function will be set off, and the function will close the window of your application. The closing action will then be managed once again by the NativeWindow class, thanks to the close() method.

The following code allows you to make your final project a little bit more captivating:

```
public function cleanIt(event:MouseEvent):void
{
    event.currentTarget.text="";
    textArea_txt.text="";
```

```
        var closeTitle:Tween=new Tween(titleFeed_mc, "x",  .➡
        Regular.easeOut, titleFeed_mc.x,   titleFeed_mc.width, 2, true);
}
```

This next instruction will be called when the user presses the Enter key:

```
public function yourfeedClickHandler (event:KeyboardEvent):void
{
    if(event.keyCode==13){
        blogURLRequest=new URLRequest(String(yourFeed_txt.text));
        manageFeed();
    }
  }
 }
}
```

When the user types the address into the input text field and then presses the Enter key, the manageFeed() method will start the data-loading procedure. In the yourfeedClickHandler() method, you ask ActionScript to check the keyCode. If it corresponds to the number 13 (which is the reference to the Enter key), then you can begin the process of loading the RSS data.

Your work is almost done. You have to finish the publication settings and associate this AS file (BlogReader.as) with your work; otherwise, it will be disconnected.

You also need to set the instance name and some other values of the ComboBox component. To do so, perform the following steps:

1. Open the BlogReader.fla file.

2. Select the combo box on the stage and set its instance name to sites_cb.

3. Open the Component Inspector (Window ➤ Component Inspector).

4. Click the magnifying glass icon on the DataProvider field to open the Values panel, as shown in Figure 3-21.

5. In the Values panel, you can enter the URLs of the RSS feeds you want to consume in your application. Fill it in with the following values:

- label: Adobe Labs; data: http://weblogs.macromedia.com/labs/index.xml
- label: Comtaste Blog; data: http://blog.comtaste.com/index.xml
- label: Marco Casario Blog; data: http://casario.blogs.com/mmworld/rss.xml

6. Click OK to confirm.

7. Close the Component Inspector panel.

Now you can test the application that you have created by clicking Control ➤ Test Movie, or pressing Ctrl+Enter (Windows) or Cmd+Enter (Mac).

If you want to make the window transparent, just change the Window style setting in the AIR – Application & Installer Settings panel from System Chrome to Custom Chrome (transparent).

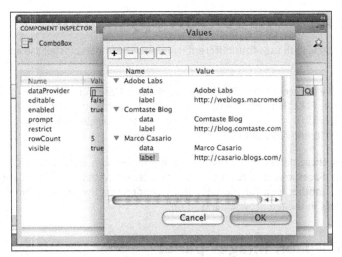

Figure 3-21. The DataProvider options

Returning to the BlogReader.fla file, open the publishing settings of AIR and indicate the following values as settings for the application descriptor:

- File name: Blog Reader
- Name: Blog Reader
- Version: 1.0
- ID: com.adobe.example.blogReader
- Description: My First Blog Reader in Adobe AIR with Flash CS4
- Copyright: Optional.
- Window style: Custom chrome (transparent)
- Icon: Keep the default settings.
- Advanced: Keep the default settings.
- Digital signature: Provide settings as explained in Chapter 2 and Chapter 13.
- Destination: Choose a directory to save the file in.
- Included files: None.

Now you can confirm by clicking OK, and then click Control ➤ Test Movie to test the application. If the project is working, you can click File ➤ Publish. A message will appear confirming the correct creation of an AIR file. You are now ready to publish the work for your potential clients. (Read Chapter 13 to learn the different options you have to distribute an AIR application.)

Creating icons for AIR applications

An AIR application uses four different icons shown after you install the application and run it in AIR.

These have to respect the dimensions required by Flash in the AIR – Icon Images panel and must be in PNG (Portable Network Graphics) format. You can create four different sizes for the icons: 16 × 16 pixels, 32 × 32 pixels, 64 × 64 pixels, and 128 × 128 pixels, to allow for the different views in which the icon appears.

You have these different icons with different dimensions because the icons can appear in different places: one icon for the Program folder on Windows or the Application folder on the Mac, another icon for the taskbar on Windows or the dock bar on the Mac, one for thumbnails in the file browser, and so on.

The AIR – Icon Images panel

The AIR – Icon Images panel, which allows you to manage the icons of your application, can be reached through the AIR – Application & Installer Settings panel. To open the AIR – Icon Images panel, do the following:

1. Click Properties ➤ Publish ➤ AIR Settings ➤ Edit.

2. In the AIR – Application & Installer Settings panel, click the Select Icon Images button.

The upper part of the panel (Preview) gives you a preview of each of the four icon images set up in the lower part (Icon file locations), as shown in Figure 3-22.

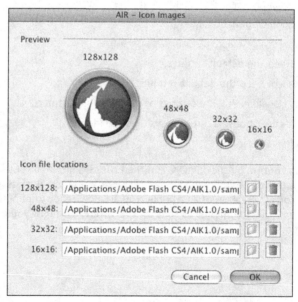

Figure 3-22. The AIR – Icon Images panel

You can click the folder button to choose or change the icon, and the trash button to delete it.

Managing icons in the application descriptor

The details regarding the icons are registered in the application descriptor file. Here is an example of an application descriptor, with the icon-related code shown in bold:

```
<application xmlns="http://ns.adobe.com/air/application/1.5">
<id>com.adobe.example.airProject</id>
<version>1.0</version>
<filename>First AIR Project with Flash CS4</filename>
<description/>
<name>First AIR Project with Flash CS4</name>
<copyright/>
<initialWindow>
     <content>airProject.swf</content>
     <systemChrome>none</systemChrome>
     <transparent>true</transparent>
     <visible>true</visible>
</initialWindow>
<icon>
     <image128x128>AppIconsForAIRPublish/AIRApp_128.png</image128x128>
     <image48x48>AppIconsForAIRPublish/AIRApp_48.png</image48x48>
     <image32x32>AppIconsForAIRPublish/AIRApp_32.png</image32x32>
     <image16x16>AppIconsForAIRPublish/AIRApp_16.png</image16x16>
</icon>
<customUpdateUI>false</customUpdateUI>
<allowBrowserInvocation>false</allowBrowserInvocation>
</application>
```

The various image nodes contained in the main icon node identify the various files to manage in your AIR application. Once you have created and managed your icons, the project is ready to be packaged in an AIR file and distributed to your clients. See Chapter 13 for a discussion of packaging AIR applications.

Summary

This chapter has covered the fundamental steps in creating an AIR application with Flash CS4. You've learned everything that makes up an AIR project in detail:

- What an AIR file is made up of
- How to manage each aspect of an AIR project
- The steps to follow when you want to create an AIR project

In the next chapter, you will learn more about building AIR applications and how to create an application descriptor file without using the Flash CS4 wizard through practical examples, including the creation of a media player and a weather widget.

CHAPTER 4
SETTING AIR APPLICATION
PROPERTIES

There are many important steps to consider when building an AIR project and distributing it to clients. Just to mention one of the main features you should consider, think about managing the system chrome of the windows in your project. For example, you have to think about whether to create transparent windows and how to handle fundamental functions such as minimizing, maximizing, and closing. (See Chapter 5 to learn more about native window classes.)

Among the other topics in this chapter, I'll talk about how to manage the icons that will be installed on your user's machine with your product, which kind of files you can use, and which characteristics they require. This chapter will also concentrate on the **application descriptor**, an XML file that defines the information in your AIR project.

So let's start by going through the typical steps when creating a Flash CS4 project.

Setting up an AIR project

As you saw in Chapter 3, there is a very important panel to manage the initial settings of Adobe AIR projects: AIR – Application & Installer Settings. This panel functions as a setup tool that allows you to manage the information necessary to generate the application descriptor. Because this file is a text document in XML format, you can manage it easily, or even create your own, like any other XML file.

One of the tasks you will face in this chapter is the generation of an AIR file without the help of Flash CS4 tools. Configuring an AIR program itself and creating the respective application descriptor isn't a particularly complex process. You just need to know the various nodes that make up the application descriptor and the appropriate values to insert.

You'll start by creating the AIR project that you will develop systematically throughout the chapter: a small multimedia player for audio MP3 files.

From the Flash CS4 welcome screen, choose Flash File (Adobe AIR). (If the welcome screen doesn't open, just click File ➤ New, and then select Flash File (Adobe AIR).) With your Flash CS4 document for AIR open, immediately save the document in the directory you prefer, with the name audioPlayer.fla.

> As good general practice, save the file immediately, even if it's empty.

Managing the document classes

The next step is the creation of an ActionScript file where you will insert all the code you need. Except for cases that explicitly require the use of different working methods during other exercises, from now on you will only enter your code in ActionScript files that are external to the Flash files. These ActionScript files that you will create are also called **document classes**. The Class item in the Properties panel allows the Flash (FLA) file to process the code contained in the ActionScript (AS) file.

Basically, writing code in a document class is a bit like moving the code that you would normally write in a timeline frame into an ActionScript file. Working with document classes allows you to improve the use of the code. In this way, the ActionScript code will only be in one file, not distributed over the various timelines of the Flash project.

Furthermore, because ActionScript files are text files, you can edit them with text-editing programs such as Notepad or TextEdit, as well as with Adobe products that can open text files, such as Dreamweaver CS4, for example.

Having said this, you can return to your audioPlayer.fla project and type com.comtaste. foed.essentialair.chapter04.AudioPlayer in the Class box.

Why com.comtaste.foed.essentialair.chapter04.AudioPlayer? It's purely a question of the organization of the classes that can make up an application. In OOP logic, it's essential to divide the classes (ActionScript files) according to the purpose they're created for. For example, you might create a folder called data for all the classes that manage external information (XML, RSS, etc.), and a folder called media to create multimedia elements, and a folder called utility to manage utility functions in the application.

Another reason for this type of file naming has to do with the **reverse domain name system** (**reverse DNS**), a standard adopted from Java. As the name suggests, this system is based on the inversion of the domain name (e.g., www.comtaste.com becomes com. comtaste, and the www is omitted), so you can organize all its content into folders according to their use (e.g., com.comtaste.utility).

In an ActionScript file, every part of the reverse DNS corresponds to a same-named folder. This means that your ActionScript file will have to be saved in the following directory, starting from the com folder of the directory that contains the audioPlayer.fla file: com/ comtaste/foed/essentialair/chapter04.

Next, you will create an ActionScript file that contains the code for your application, which you will name AudioPlayer.as. Unlike the name of the FLA file you've created (audioPlayer.fla), the ActionScript class must begin with a capital letter.

To create the AudioPlayer.as file, from the File ➤ New menu, choose ActionScript File, and save your ActionScript file in the following directory: com/comtaste/foed/essentialair/ chapter04.

Now you'll see the link between the audioPlayer.fla and AudioPlayer.as files in the Class box in the Properties panel, as well as in the Target box, as shown in Figure 4-1.

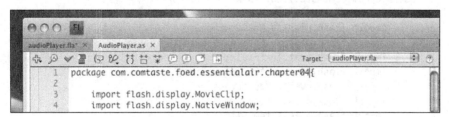

Figure 4-1. The Target box, showing the link between the ActionScript and Flash files

Creating a media player in AIR

If it's not open already, open the Flash document you created (audioPlayer.fla). In this section, you'll be programming the various graphical elements you will use in this project; however, you first need to insert at least one component in the project's library. To do so, open the Components panel (Window ➤ Components) and choose the DataGrid component from the User Interface section. Once you've inserted the component on the stage, you can delete the instance itself, because you are only actually interested in the object in the library.

> You can also insert an instance of the DataGrid component by dragging the component straight into the library instead of dragging it to the stage and deleting it.

Call your component using ActionScript to create an instance of the DataGrid class (var dataList:DataGrid=new DataGrid()); Flash will call the object in the library.

If you observe the DataGrid object in the library carefully, you'll notice the following item in the Linkage column: Export: fl.controls.DataGrid, as shown in Figure 4-2.

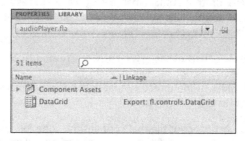

Figure 4-2. The Library panel with the DataGrid component linked with its own class

The presence of Export: fl.controls.DataGird means that the DataGrid in the library is connected to the relevant DataGrid ActionScript class.

At the beginning of this chapter, you created the ActionScript file, AudioPlayer.as, which you will use to insert the application code. Open it and enter the following code:

```
package com.comtaste.foed.essentialair.chapter04{
    import flash.display.MovieClip;
    import flash.display.NativeWindow;
    import flash.display.NativeWindowInitOptions;
    import flash.text.TextField;
    import flash.text.TextFieldAutoSize;
    import flash.events.MouseEvent;
    import flash.events.Event;
    import flash.filesystem.File;
    import flash.media.Sound;
    import flash.media.SoundMixer;
```

```
import flash.media.SoundChannel;
import flash.net.URLRequest;
import fl.controls.DataGrid;
import fl.data.DataProvider;
```

Creating and importing classes

As mentioned in Chapter 3, at the beginning of the creation of a class, the code has to start with the keyword package. This will contain all the code you will write in the file, and all the classes you need to import.

Among the classes you're importing for your project are File and NativeWindow. These classes will be explained in greater detail in Chapter 5. For now, you just need to know that they're there to create your media player correctly.

There is no hierarchy among the classes, so you can import them in any order that you wish.

Generating variables

Now, proceed by generating all the variables that you will use. (Note that these variables will become properties in ActionScript files.) After the code you just entered, enter the following:

```
public class AudioPlayer extends MovieClip
{
    private var open_btn:MovieClip=new MovieClip();
    private var play_btn:MovieClip=new MovieClip();
    private var stop_btn:MovieClip=new MovieClip();
    private var pause_btn:MovieClip=new MovieClip();
    private var prev_btn:MovieClip=new MovieClip();
    private var next_btn:MovieClip=new MovieClip();
    private var background_mc:MovieClip=new MovieClip();
    private var info_txt:TextField=new TextField();
    private var dataList:DataGrid=new DataGrid();
    private var dataSource:DataProvider=new DataProvider();
    private var dataListArray:Array=new Array();
    private var thisStage:NativeWindow;
    private var song:Sound;
    private var mySoundChannel:SoundChannel;
    private var pathSong:URLRequest;
    private var fileSong:File;
```

All the objects you will use are in the list of properties provided in the preceding code. Notably, you have a DataGrid to manage in your interface, which you will use as a playlist. You also need a DataProvider, which is the data source of the DataGrid, and an Array, which you will use to store the data and call it back later on. The thisStage instance of the NativeWindow class is used to control the system window where your application will run, and the fileSong instance of the File class is used to control file selection.

The class constructor

Next, enter the code for the class constructor, as follows:

```
public function AudioPlayer():void
{
        var menu:Array=new Array();
        drawBackground(background_mc);
        menu=[
                {button:open_btn, labelText:"Browse.."},
                {button:play_btn, labelText:"Play"},
                {button:stop_btn, labelText:"Stop"},
        ];
```

In the constructor, you generated an instance of the Array class (menu) to control the menu, as the name suggests. Next, you called the drawBackground() method, which allows you to draw the background of the stage. Then you populated the menu variable as an associative array so as to insert a dynamic text field (labelText) for each button.

Setting up and placing buttons

Now you have to set up and place your buttons. Here's the code to do so:

```
for(var i:Number=0; i<menu.length; i++)
{
    menu[i].button.itsLabel=menu[i].labelText;
    drawButton(menu[i].button);
    menu[i].button.x=5+(menu[i].button.width+10)*i;
    menu[i].button.y=5;
    menu[i].button.addEventListener(MouseEvent.CLICK, manageAudio);
}
```

With the for loop, you can control the various items in the menu of the application. You placed the various buttons on the X and Y axes, and then you called the drawButton() method (which, as you will see, is very similar to the drawBackground() method), which will allow you to actually draw the buttons on the stage by exploiting ActionScript's drawing APIs.

Finally, you have made it so all the buttons, once the user clicks any of them, call the manageAudio() method to control the flow of audio from your media player.

Building and managing the application interface

Proceed with building the application interface:

```
thisStage=stage.nativeWindow;
addChild(info_txt);
addChild(dataList);
```

In the preceding code, you set up the stage of the main window. Then you added the objects on the stage to the display list (the instance of the TextField class, info_txt) to display the song's information during its execution, as well as to the DataGrid (dataList) to display the songs that are opened each time.

```
with(info_txt){
     x=5;
     y=30;
    width=320;
    autoSize=TextFieldAutoSize.LEFT ;
    multiline=true;
    wordWrap=true;
    selectable=false;
    border=true;
    background=true;
    backgroundColor=0xAACC99;
}

with(dataList){
     x=0;
    y=info_txt.y+50;
    dataProvider=dataSource;
    width=stage.stageWidth;
    height=stage.stageHeight-info_txt.y-50;
    columns=["SONGS"];
    addEventListener(MouseEvent.CLICK, datagridSongHandler);
}
}
```

In the preceding code block, you set the X and Y positions on the stage of both elements (info_txt and dataList), and then you set some useful properties for each instance. For info_txt, you set a background color, and you set the multiline property so that the text will wrap. For dataList, you set the width and height, and then, with the columns property, you set the grid to only show the data from the SONGS column.

Listening to a song

Finally, if the user starts to listen to a song (so that the dataSource array is populated), they can replay previously chosen songs by clicking the DataGrid.

```
private function drawBackground(obj:MovieClip):void
{
    with(obj.graphics)
    {
        beginFill(0x883311, 0.7);
        drawRect(0,0,stage.stageWidth, stage.stageHeight);
        endFill();
    }
    addChild(obj);
}
```

In the preceding code, you used the drawBackground() method to draw the background of the stage of your application. This background, an instance of the MovieClip class, will have the width and height of the stage.

The following code handles the drawing of the buttons of the application (play_btn, open_btn, and stop_btn):

```
private function drawButton(obj:MovieClip):void
{
    with(obj.graphics)
    {
        beginFill(0xFFAACC, 1);
        drawRect(0,0,100,20);
        endFill();
    }
    addChild(obj);
    var textLabel:TextField=new TextField();
    textLabel.selectable=false;
    textLabel.text=obj.itsLabel;
    textLabel.autoSize=TextFieldAutoSize.LEFT;
    obj.addChild(textLabel);
    obj.buttonMode=true;
}
```

In this code, you used the drawButton() method to draw the buttons using the graphics property of the MovieClip class. Then you inserted a dynamic text field that will contain the value set up in the menu array.

Managing audio files

At this point, you can proceed with the manageAudio() method:

```
private function manageAudio(event:MouseEvent):void
{
    switch(event.currentTarget)
    {
        case open_btn:
        fileSong=new File();
        fileSong.browse();
        fileSong.addEventListener(Event.SELECT, chooseSong);
        break;
        case stop_btn:
        SoundMixer.stopAll();
        info_txt.text="";
        break;
        case play_btn:
        if(pathSong!=null){
            SoundMixer.stopAll();
            playSong(pathSong);
```

```
            }
            break;
        }
    }

    private function chooseSong(event:Event):void
    {
        SoundMixer.stopAll();
        dataList.addItem({SONGS:fileSong.name, PATH:fileSong.url});
        dataListArray.push({path:fileSong.url});
        pathSong=new URLRequest(String(fileSong.url));
        playSong(pathSong);
    }
```

A control on one of the buttons of the menu array allows you to control the various situations. If the user clicks the stop_btn button, the audio will stop; if the user clicks the play_btn button, the audio will start. If the user clicks the open_btn button, the File class makes it possible to view the file selection screen through the fileSong instance and its browse() method, and choose among all the files in the computer at that time.

Once the song has been selected (fileSong.addEventListener(Event.SELECT, chooseSong)), the loading process begins, so the array as well as the DataProvider for your DataGrid is populated.

Playing the song

The playSong() method, which follows, is responsible for actually playing the song:

```
    private function playSong(url:URLRequest):void
    {
        song=new Sound();
        song.load(url);
        mySoundChannel=song.play();
        song.addEventListener(Event.COMPLETE, showInfo);
    }

        private function showInfo(event:Event):void
        {
            if(song.id3.songName!=null || song.id3.artist!=null){
                info_txt.htmlText="<b>Song name:</b>: <i>"+(song.id3.
songNa➡
me)+"</i> ["+song.id3.year+"]        <br><b>Artist</b>: "+➡
song.id3.artist+"<br><b>Album</b>: "+song.id3.album;
            }else{
                info_txt.text="Undefined song";
            }
        }
```

In addition to starting the audio of the song, the playSong() method also calls the MP3 files' metatags.

As you may know, MP3 files contain **metatags**, which contain information regarding the music's author, title, year, genre, and so on. This information can be collected by ActionScript and displayed on the monitor thanks to the id3 property of the Sound class. After the song has been loaded by the song.addEventListener(Event.COMPLETE, showInfo) method, this information will become available and, if it has been duly compiled, will appear in the info_txt text field.

Setting the id3 tags

To let the user of your media player know which song is being executed, you must set the id3 tags correctly. To set the id3 tags of an MP3 file on a Windows machine, follow these steps:

1. Right-click the audio file.
2. Click Summary, and then Advanced.
3. Set the values for Author, Year, and Genre for the song you have chosen.

Playing the song selected by the DataGrid component

Next, enter the following code:

```
private function datagridSongHandler(event:MouseEvent):void
{
   //in case user clicks on header
    if(event.currentTarget.selectedIndex>-1)
    {
        SoundMixer.stopAll();
        pathSong=new URLRequest(dataListArray[dataList.
selectedIndex].path);
        playSong(pathSong);
      }
    }
  }
}
```

This last method, datagridSongHandler(), allows the user to restart the selected song from the DataGrid on the stage.

Now you can save your ActionScript file and return to the Flash file (audioPlayer.fla). To test your application so far, press Ctrl+Enter (on Windows) or Cmd+Enter (on the Mac), or click Control ➤ Test Movie. Your application should look like Figure 4-3.

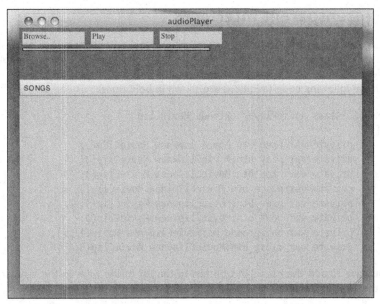

Figure 4-3. Your first AIR media player

When you test the application, you should be able to load an MP3 file by browsing through the various folders on your computer (by clicking the Browse button).

Next, you'll work with the system chrome of the application window.

AIR application system chrome

If you try working with your application as it is, you can control the window with the default buttons provided by the operating system. However, you can do without the system windows and make your own buttons. In this section, you'll see how to make the main window background transparent and insert a button to close the window.

Go back to your Flash document (audioPlayer.fla) and open the AIR – Application & Installer Settings panel by clicking File ➤ AIR Settings, or AIR Settings from the Properties panel. In the Window style option, choose the Custom Chrome (transparent) option, and confirm by clicking OK.

If you try to restart the application, you will run into two problems: you won't be able to move the window on the desktop (it's impossible to do so at this time), and you won't be able to close the window either.

This means that when you create transparent interfaces for your project, you have to solve these graphical problems yourself, and make some changes in your application.

Creating transparent interfaces

Return to your ActionScript document (AudioPlayer.as) and change your code, starting with the creation of another instance of the MovieClip class, this time for a new button to close the application. To do this, just insert another instance of the MovieClip class, as shown in the following code (additions are shown in bold print):

```
public class AudioPlayer extends MovieClip
{
      private var open_btn:MovieClip=new MovieClip();
      private var play_btn:MovieClip=new MovieClip();
      private var stop_btn:MovieClip=new MovieClip();
      private var pause_btn:MovieClip=new MovieClip();
      private var prev_btn:MovieClip=new MovieClip();
      private var next_btn:MovieClip=new MovieClip();
      private var background_mc:MovieClip=new MovieClip();
      private var close_btn:MovieClip=new MovieClip();
```

Now you have to add the close_btn button to the list of the ones in the menu array, so change the array as follows:

```
menu=[
{button:open_btn, labelText:"Browse.."},
{button:play_btn, labelText:"Play"},
{button:stop_btn, labelText:"Stop"},
{button:close_btn, labelText:"Close"}
];
```

Now you have to insert the options to assign to this button if the user interacts with it. Quite simply, you have to tell ActionScript that the AIR document has to be closed. To do so, you will have to use a class you've only explored briefly until now: the File class. The switch you've used will have to be changed as follows:

```
switch(event.currentTarget)
{
      case open_btn:
      fileSong=new File();
      fileSong.browse();
      fileSong.addEventListener(Event.SELECT, chooseSong);
      break;
      case stop_btn:
      SoundMixer.stopAll();
      info_txt.text="";
      break;
      case play_btn:
      if(pathSong!=null){
            SoundMixer.stopAll();
            playSong(pathSong);
      }
      break;
```

```
            case close_btn:
            thisStage.close();
             break;
        }
```

If you test your application again, you'll see the new button on the stage, and if you click it, the program will close. This way, you've solved one problem, but you still have to solve another: moving the window on the desktop.

Moving the window on the desktop

Once again, the File class comes to the rescue with its startMove() method, which makes it possible to drag your application on the user's desktop.

To drag the application on the desktop, you have to modify the constructor of the class. After the for loop and before the with(info_txt) loop, change the code as follows:

```
        thisStage=stage.nativeWindow;
        background_mc.addEventListener(MouseEvent.MOUSE_DOWN, ➡
                                                        startMoveHandler);

        addChild(info_txt);
        addChild(dataList);
```

Now the background_mc movie clip will allow you to actually move your application on the stage.

Before testing the application, you have to insert the startMove() method that you have assigned to the background_mc movie clip on MOUSE_DOWN. Insert the method after the with(dataList) code block, as shown here:

```
        private function startMoveHandler(event:MouseEvent):void
        {
                thisStage.startMove();
        }
```

At this point, you can test your application. If you keep the mouse button pressed (MOUSE_DOWN) on the background (background_mc), you will be able to move the application window.

Everything seems to be working well . . . but your application may need one extra adjustment. If you try loading non-audio files, the application won't be able to load the data. To remedy this, you have to filter the choices in the selection box so that only audio files are available.

Filtering audio files

The browse() method of the File class gives you the option of inserting an array of values for the file extensions to filter. This array can in turn be inserted as an instance of the FileFilter class.

4

To begin, you need to add the following to the class importation section:

```
import flash.net.FileFilter;
```

Now, at the section concerning the creation of the various variables, add this at the end:

```
private var audioFilter:FileFilter = new FileFilter("Audio Files➥
  [*.mp3; *.wav] ", "*.mp3;*.wav;");
```

This instance of the FileFilter class imports a reference text value and the various extensions associated with it.

Change the browse() method as follows:

```
private function manageAudio(event:MouseEvent):void
{
    switch(event.currentTarget)
    {
        case open_btn:
        fileSong=new File();
        fileSong.browse([audioFilter]);
```

Now, the text Audio Files [*.mp3, *.wav] will be the text that will appear in the system panel when browsing for files.

Save your ActionScript file and test your application. This time, notice how the AIR application doesn't show all the files on your computer—only the ones that have .mp3 or .wav extensions, as required by the audioFilter variable (see Figure 4-4).

Figure 4-4. When the audio player browses your machine, it will show only MP3 and WAV files.

Working with advanced properties

In the Advanced Settings panel, it is possible to adjust some important parameters such as the initial size of the window and its position on the stage. You can also specify whether your system window is maximizable, minimizable, and so on.

Adjusting the initial size and position of windows

Returning to your Flash document (audioPlayer.fla), open the Advanced Settings panel by clicking File ➤ AIR Settings ➤ Advanced Settings. Deselect the Maximizable, Minimizable, and Resizable options, and make sure the values of the X and Y parameters are set to 0. Then close the panel by clicking OK.

Before testing the project, change the Window style option from Custom Chrome (transparent) to System Chrome. Confirm by clicking OK.

Now test your application. As shown in Figure 4-5, the only button on your interface is the X to close the window, and the window of your program is at the top-left corner of the screen, since you set the X and Y coordinates to 0.

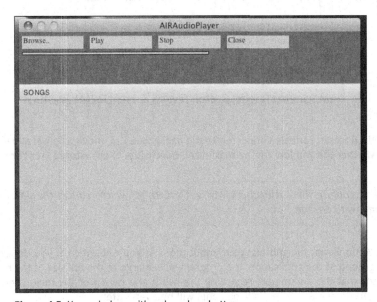

Figure 4-5. Your window, with only a close button

In the next section, you'll see how to allow the application to be maximized to full-screen size.

Modifying the application's window

Now return to the ActionScript file (AudioPlayer.as) to make further changes to the project. Through the following code, you will be able to maximize your application to full-screen size. However, please note that it won't be completely full screen. The application will fill the screen except for the Windows taskbar and the Mac dock bar. Add the following bold code between the for and with(info_txt) loops:

```
thisStage=stage.nativeWindow;
background_mc.doubleClickEnabled=true;
background_mc.addEventListener(MouseEvent.DOUBLE_CLICK, maximizeWin);
background_mc.addEventListener(MouseEvent.MOUSE_DOWN, startMove);
```

In this block of code, you enabled the background to support double-clicking (doubleClickEnabled), and then assigned the maximizeWin() method to the double-click function.

Now you can move to the startMoveHandler() method in your ActionScript file and write the following code underneath it:

```
private function maximizeWin(event:MouseEvent):void
{
    if(!event.currentTarget.maxWin){
        thisStage.maximize();
    }else{
        thisStage.restore();
    }
    event.currentTarget.maxWin=!event.currentTarget.maxWin;
}
```

The maxWin Boolean variable connected to the background_mc movie clip will allow you to control whether the window can be maximized (maximize()) or restored (restore()).

> Don't confuse these with the minimize() method, which reduces the system window to an icon.

Save the ActionScript file and test your application. As you will notice, if you double-click the background of the application, the program will enlarge to the full size of the monitor. This means that the parameters regarding the width and height of the main windows in the AIR – Application & Installer Settings panel will be overwritten.

If you try to move the window to 200 on the X axis, it won't consider this request because the settings in the ActionScript code are subordinate to the settings specified in the application descriptor. If you put this request (thisStage.x=200) into the maximizeWin() method as follows, the window, when it is resized, will move on the X axis to 200:

```
function maximizeWin(event:MouseEvent):void
{
    if(!event.currentTarget.maxWin){
        thisStage.maximize();
    }else{
        thisStage.restore();
        thisStage.x=200;
    }
    event.currentTarget.maxWin=!event.currentTarget.maxWin;
}
```

> Recall that the application descriptor is an XML file that Flash generates automatically.
> I'll discuss it further shortly.

4

Specifying the installation and program menu folders

Finally, you can specify the installation folder and the one containing the menu of your program through the AIR – Application & Installer Settings panel:

1. Return to the audioPlayer.fla Flash file and click File ➤ AIR Settings.

2. Click the Settings button of the Advanced option.

3. In the Advanced Settings panel, type AIR Audio Player in the Install Folder and Program menu folder fields.

4. Close the Advanced Settings panel by clicking OK.

5. Restore the Window style parameter to Custom Chrome (transparent), and confirm by clicking OK.

6. Save the Flash project and check your application one last time, before publication to ensure that everything runs according to plan.

Distributing the application

In this section, you'll get your project ready for distribution. With the Flash file (audioPlayer.fla) open, display the AIR – Application & Installer Settings panel (File ➤ AIR Settings). Now click the Publish AIR File button to actually create your installation file, which will be saved in the same directory as the Flash project file.

A message like AIR file has been created will tell you that the operation has completed successfully. Now you can install or distribute your product. In the folder containing your exercise, you can find your final file.

> *As mentioned, in order for you to use this product, you must have the AIR runtime on your machine. You can download it for free from the official Adobe website:* www.adobe.com/. *Once you've installed the runtime, you can install your product and use it according to the specifications you've given it.*

Move to the folder where you have saved the Flash file, where the AIRAudioPlayer.air installation file should be, and then double-click the AIR file to open it and start the installation process. If you leave the options unaltered during the process, your program will start as soon as the installation process is over. To make sure that everything works properly, do the following:

1. Load a file.
2. Listen to it.
3. Stop the audio.
4. Close the program.

> *AIR products are regular programs, just as any other program you install on your computer normally. This means that your file is available in the* All Programs *list on Windows or the* Application *folder on the Mac.*

Let's browse on your computer toward the folders that usually contain the applications that are stored on your computer.

- **On Windows**: Go to Start ➤ All Programs, and you will notice that the program has been installed in the folder you specified in the installation panel when you were working on the project.
- **On the Mac**: The program is in a folder (AIR audio player) contained in the Application folder.

Opening the AIR file

The installation file (AIRAudioPlayer.air) is actually a ZIP file. Rename it with a .zip or .rar extension, so that it's called AIRAudioPlayer.zip or AIRAudioPlayer.rar. Then open the file.

Inside the compressed file, you will find all the files and folders for your application, as shown in Figure 4-6.

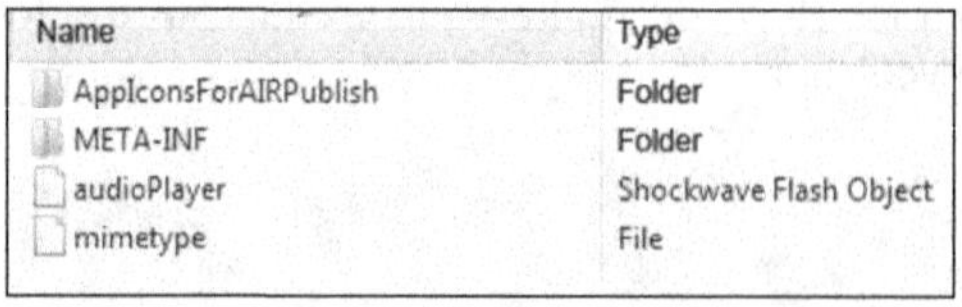

Name	Type
AppIconsForAIRPublish	Folder
META-INF	Folder
audioPlayer	Shockwave Flash Object
mimetype	File

Figure 4-6. The ZIP folder of your AIR application

These files are as follows:

- The SWF file
- The folder with the icons
- The `mimetype` file, which contains information about the AIR package
- A `META-INF` folder to manage the product information

Now that you've seen how an AIR file is made, change the compressed file's extension from `.zip` or `.rar` back to `.air`.

On Windows, if you go to the folder in which the AIR file is installed on the machine (e.g., `C:\Programs\AIR Audio Player\AIR Audio Player`), you will find the same files that you found just a moment ago. You will also find the application descriptor—the XML file that controls the main information of the application.

You've now seen the whole process of creating an AIR application, so let's look at a more advanced topic: the application descriptor file.

The application descriptor

Now go to the folder containing the FLA file of your project, where the XML file, `audioPlayer-app.xml`, should be. The application descriptor file is a text file, so you can open it with Dreamweaver CS4 (recommended), or with Windows Notepad or Mac TextEdit.

If you have any familiarity with XML or HTML, you won't have any difficulty understanding this file, which should be similar to the one that follows:

```
<?xml version="1.0" encoding="UTF-8" standalone="no" ?><application ➥
xmlns="http://ns.adobe.com/air/application/1.5">
<id>com.comtaste.foed.essentialair.chapter04.audioPlayer</id>
<version>1.0</version>
<filename>AIR Audio Player</filename>
<description>My First Audio Player in Adobe AIR 1.5</description>
<name>AIR Audio Player</name>
<copyright/>
<initialWindow>
    <content>audioPlayer.swf</content>
    <systemChrome>none</systemChrome>
    <transparent>true</transparent>
    <visible>true</visible>
    <maximizable>false</maximizable>
    <minimizable>true</minimizable>
    <resizable>true</resizable>
</initialWindow>
<customUpdateUI>false</customUpdateUI>
<allowBrowserInvocation>false</allowBrowserInvocation>
```

```
<icon>
    <image128x128>AppIconsForAIRPublish/AIRApp_128.png</image128x128>
    <image48x48>AppIconsForAIRPublish/AIRApp_48.png</image48x48>
    <image32x32>AppIconsForAIRPublish/AIRApp_32.png</image32x32>
    <image16x16>AppIconsForAIRPublish/AIRApp_16.png</image16x16>
</icon>
<installFolder>AIR Audio Player</installFolder>
<programMenuFolder>AIR Audio Player</programMenuFolder>
</application>
```

Your file is divided into two separate sections. All the nodes (id, version, filename, description, etc.) up to the resizable node regard the initial information you entered in the AIR – Application & Installer Settings panel. The other nodes of the application descriptor file (customUpdateUI, allowBrowserInvocation, icon, installFolder, and programMenuFolder) have to do with the settings of the Advanced Settings panel. The paths for the icon node are the same as the paths of the icon images on the local computer.

This application descriptor will be used by the AIR application each time you open the application.

Removing transparency

Next, you'll make a simple change to the application descriptor to stop your application window from being transparent. In the initialWindow node, change the nodes regarding the transparency of the window as follows:

```
<initialWindow>
<content>audioPlayer.swf</content>
<systemChrome>standard</systemChrome>
<transparent>false</transparent>
<visible>true</visible>
<maximizable>false</maximizable>
<minimizable>true</minimizable>
<resizable>true</resizable>
</initialWindow>
```

According to the changes you have made, the window shouldn't be transparent any more. Save the application descriptor file and return to Flash.

Now test your application. Notice that the window isn't transparent any more, and the system buttons to control the window itself have become visible again, as shown in Figure 4-7.

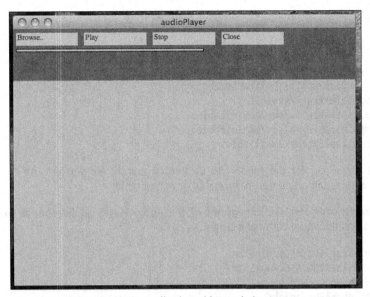

Figure 4-7. The Audio Player application without window transparency

As you can see, changes to transparency can be made manually without having to use the Flash CS4 wizard. In fact, you can create an application descriptor file manually. The next section shows you how to do this.

Creating an XML application descriptor without using a wizard

To add the code, open Dreamweaver CS4 or a text editor of your choice. (You can also use FlashDevelop [www.flashdevelop.org/], a good alternative for code editing.) Start writing the code, beginning with the initial settings:

```
<?xml version="1.0" encoding="UTF-8" standalone="no" ?>
<application xmlns="http://ns.adobe.com/air/application/1.0">
<id>com.mycompany.example.AIRAudioPlayer</id>
```

Proceed with the general settings of the AIR product:

```
<version>1.0</version>
<filename>AIR Audio Player</filename>
<description>My First Audio Player in Adobe AIR</description>
<name>AIR Audio Player</name>
<copyright>companyCopyright</copyright>
```

Similarly to how you set the values in the Flash project panel, in this case you've inserted the various parameters between the filename, description, name, and copyright nodes.

Next, enter the various items regarding the main window:

```
<initialWindow>
<content>audioPlayer.swf</content>
<systemChrome>standard</systemChrome>
<transparent>false</transparent>
<visible>true</visible>
<maximizable>false</maximizable>
<minimizable>false</minimizable>
<resizable>true</resizable>
```

With this code, you set the window to be nontransparent (so you will use the system chrome) and resizable, but not maximizable or minimizable.

The following code sets the dimensions of the Audio Player application, as well as its maximum and minimum width and height.

```
<minSize>600 450</minSize>
<maxSize>700 550</maxSize>
<width>600</width>
<height>450</height>
</initialWindow>
```

With this code, you set the minSize and maxSize properties, which assign the maximum and minimum sizes that your application will have (in your case, respectively, 700 × 500 pixels and 600 × 450 pixels). With the width and height parameters, you set the window size to 600 × 450 pixels.

The last part of your application descriptor will almost exclusively regard the path of the installation file and the control of the program's icons. It will specify which file to use for the various dimensions of the icons, as well as the installation folder that will be created on the user's machine.

```
<customUpdateUI>false</customUpdateUI>
<allowBrowserInvocation>false</allowBrowserInvocation>
<icon>
    <image128x128>AppIconsForAIRPublish/AIRApp_128.png</image128x128>
    <image48x48>AppIconsForAIRPublish/AIRApp_48.png</image48x48>
    <image32x32>AppIconsForAIRPublish/AIRApp_32.png</image32x32>
    <image16x16>AppIconsForAIRPublish/AIRApp_16.png</image16x16>
</icon>

<installFolder>AIR Audio Player</installFolder>
<programMenuFolder>AIR Audio Player</programMenuFolder>
</application>
```

Now save the file as audioPlayer-app.xml (make sure that you use the -app suffix).

> *The –app suffix in the name of the file is very important because it is interpreted as a key for AIR to actually recognize the name of the file.*

Once you've saved the file, perform the following steps:

1. Return to Flash CS4.
2. Open the AIR – Application & Installer Settings panel.
3. Select the Use custom application descriptor file option.
4. Choose the file that you have just created in Dreamweaver CS4 (by clicking the folder button).
5. Confirm by closing the AIR – Application & Installer Settings panel.

Test the preview of your project, and if all has gone well, your file should work properly.

Creating an AIR application with Flex 3

Flash CS4 isn't the only software that allows you to create AIR products; it's also possible with Flex 3, which shares Flash's ActionScript 3 programming language. When you create an AIR file for distribution, Flex also produces an XML file for the application descriptor.

The following code is an example of a project built with Flex:

```
<?xml version="1.0" encoding="UTF-8"?>
<application xmlns="http://ns.adobe.com/air/application/1.5">
<id>MyBrowser</id>
<filename>MyBrowser</filename>
<name>MyBrowser</name>
<version>v1</version>
<description></description/>
<copyright></copyright>
<initialWindow>
    <content>[This value will be overwritten by Flex Builder in the ➥
output app.xml]</content>
    <title></title>
    <systemChrome>standard</systemChrome>
    <transparent>none</transparent>
    <visible>true</visibile>
    <!-- <minimizable></minimizable> -->
    <!-- <maximizable></maximizable> -->
    <!-- <resizable></resizable> -->
    <!-- <width></width> -->
    <!-- <height></height> -->
    <!-- <x></x> -->
    <!-- <y></y> -->
    <!-- <minSize></minSize> -->
    <!-- <maxSize></maxSize> -->
```

4

```
        </initialWindow>
        <!-- <installFolder></installFolder> -->
        <!-- <programMenuFolder></programMenuFolder> -->
        <icon>
                <image16x16></image16x16>
                <image32x32></image32x32>
                <image48x48></image48x48>
                <image128x128></image128x128>
        </icon>

        <!-- <customUpdateUI></customUpdateUI> -->
        <!-- <allowBrowserInvocation></allowBrowserInvocation> -->
        <!-- <fileTypes> -->
        <!-- <fileType> -->
        <!-- <name></name> -->
        <!-- <extension></extension> -->
        <!-- <description></description> -->
        <!-- <contentType></contentType> -->
        <!-- <icon>
        <image16x16></image16x16>
        <image32x32></image32x32>
        <image48x48></image48x48>
        <image128x128></image128x128>
        </icon> -->
        <!-- </fileType> -->
        <!-- </fileTypes> -->
        </application>
```

From a quick overview of Flex's application descriptor, you will notice many similarities. (One difference is that Flex disables empty items instead of omitting them.) You can create your application descriptor file with or without Flash CS4, and associate it with the AIR products created with Flex.

Let's close this chapter with one last example to summarize the concepts you have learned. In this example, you'll generate the application descriptor file yourself.

Creating a weather widget in AIR

In this last section, you will create a weather widget in AIR. First, create a new Flash CS4 document for AIR. Once you've created the document, save it as Weather.fla. In your application, you will need two components: a Button to close the application and a ComboBox to select the city whose weather you are interested in.

For this exercise, you will use the free information distributed by Yahoo Weather. This information is released in RSS format (i.e., XML format). You'll only use a few cities as examples (Rome, Berlin, Paris, New York, Moscow, and Tokyo). If you want to increase the choices, you can take the references from the Yahoo Weather website at the following address: http://weather.yahoo.com/.

Open the Components panel (Window ➤ Components) and drag an instance of a ComboBox and a Button onto the stage.

As mentioned previously, dragging these instances onto the stage will also add the objects to the library. You can eliminate the instances on the stage because the code you will insert will call these components directly from the library itself. It is also possible to insert the component by dragging it straight into the library.

At this point, create a new ActionScript file (File ➤ New) and save it as Weather.as in the following directory: com/comtaste/foed/essentialair/chapter04.

> Remember, the com folder must be in the same directory as the Weather.fla Flash file.

Start writing your code:

```
package com.comtaste.foed.essentialair.chapter04{

    import flash.display.MovieClip;
    import flash.display.NativeWindow;
    import flash.events.Event;
    import flash.events.MouseEvent;
    import flash.text.TextField;
    import flash.text.TextFormat;
    import flash.net.URLRequest;
    import flash.net.URLLoader;
    import fl.controls.ComboBox;
    import fl.controls.Button;
    import fl.data.DataProvider;
```

This code, as you should already understand from the previous example, includes all the classes you need in your application.

Now insert the instances of the classes that you will use in the application:

```
public class Weather extends MovieClip
{
    private var background_mc:MovieClip=new MovieClip();
    private var info_txt:TextField=new TextField();
    private var myFormat:TextFormat=new TextFormat();
    private var xmlData:XML;
    private var xmlPath:URLRequest=new URLRequest();
    private var xmlUrlLoad:URLLoader=new URLLoader();
    private var infoArray:Array;
    private var urlDataProvider:DataProvider=new DataProvider();
    private var comboCity:ComboBox=new ComboBox();
    private var close_btn:Button=new Button();
    private var thisWin:NativeWindow;
    private var now:Date=new Date();
```

Proceed writing with the class constructor:

```
public function Weather():void
{
        drawBackground(background_mc);
        addChild(info_txt);
        addChild(comboCity);
        addChild(close_btn);

        insertCity();
        init();


}
```

This time, your constructor is very simple: you've added the three following main elements to your application:

- info_txt, for displaying the information from the Yahoo Weather service
- comboCity, for controlling the list of available cities
- close_btn, for closing the application

Proceed by populating the ComboBox to select the city.

Populating the ComboBox

Let's continue with the insertCity() method to populate the DataProvider of the ComboBox:

```
private function insertCity():void
{
    urlDataProvider.addItem({label:"Berlin",  ➥
data:"http://xml.weather.yahoo.com/forecastrss? ➥
        p=GMXX0007&u=c"});
    urlDataProvider.addItem({label:"Rome",  ➥
data:"http://xml.weather.yahoo.com/forecastrss?p=➥
        ITXX0067&u=c"});
    urlDataProvider.addItem({label:"New York",  ➥
data:"http://xml.weather.yahoo.com/forecastrss?p=➥
        USNY0996&u=c"});
    urlDataProvider.addItem({label:"Moscow",  ➥
data:"http://xml.weather.yahoo.com/forecastrss?p=➥
        RSXX0063&u=c"});
    urlDataProvider.addItem({label:"Tokyo",  ➥
data:"http://xml.weather.yahoo.com/forecastrss?p=➥
        JAXX0085&u=c"});
    urlDataProvider.addItem({label:"Paris",  ➥
```

```
data:"http://xml.weather.yahoo.com/forecastrss?p=➡
        FRXX0076&u=c"});
    urlDataProvider.sortOn("label");
comboCity.dataProvider=urlDataProvider;
}
```

With the insertCity() method, you populated the DataProvider (urlDataProvider) to control the ComboBox information regarding the name of the city (label) and the path of the RSS file for the information you want to recover (data). Then you used the sortOn() method of the DataProvider class to order the various items alphabetically.

Next, enter the second method called in the constructor, init():

```
private function init():void
{
    thisWin=stage.nativeWindow;
    info_txt.htmlText="<b>Choose Your City</b>";
    myFormat.font="Verdana";
```

In the first part of the previous code, you set the instance of the NativeWindow class (thisWin). Then you wrote a generic text in the dynamic text field info_txt. Finally, you set the font property of the myFormat instance.

Setting up and managing the interface

The following code will set up the various objects your application needs:

```
with(comboCity)
{
    x=0;
    y=0;
    addEventListener(Event.CHANGE, showIt);
}
with(info_txt)
{
    x=comboCity.x+comboCity.width+10;
    y=comboCity.y;
    width=stage.stageWidth-(comboCity.x)-comboCity.width-15;
    height=stage.stageHeight-1;
    border=true;
    background=true;
    selectable=false;
    addEventListener(MouseEvent.MOUSE_DOWN, moveIt);
}

with(close_btn)
{
    x=comboCity.x;
```

4

```
            y=stage.stageHeight-close_btn.height;
            label="Close";
            addEventListener(MouseEvent.CLICK, closeWin);
        }
    }
```

With these three with cycles, you set the three main elements of your interface and assigned events to each of them:

- The closeWin() method will be called by the close_btn button to close the application window.
- The moveIt() method will move the window.
- The showIt() method will be called by the comboCity button when the user changes a city in the list.

With the next block of code, you will manage the information extracted from the Yahoo service (with the showit() method), the closure of the application (with the closeWin() method), and the possibility of moving the application itself around the stage (with the moveIt() method).

```
        private function showIt(event:Event):void
        {
            parseCityInfo();
        }

        private function closeWin(event:MouseEvent):void
        {
            thisWin.close();
        }

        private function moveIt(event:MouseEvent):void
        {
            thisWin.startMove();
        }
```

Let's look the last three methods:

- showIt() calls the parseCityInfo() method, which will parse the XML file containing the information and display it on video.
- closeWin() closes the application window.
- moveIt() allows the user to move the window.

The parseCityInfo() method regards the effective parsing of the data extracted from the Yahoo XML file:

```
        private function parseCityInfo():void
        {
            xmlPath.url=String(comboCity.selectedItem.data);
            xmlUrlLoad.load(xmlPath);
```

```
        xmlUrlLoad.addEventListener(Event.COMPLETE, showAllInfo);
    }
```

The parseCityInfo() method will call the XML file path through the load() method.

Then, at the end of the loading process, the information will be displayed with the showAllInfo() method:

```
    private function showAllInfo(e:Event)
    {
        infoArray=new Array();
        xmlData=XML(xmlUrlLoad.data);
        for each(var prop:XML in xmlData.channel.item)
        {
            info_txt.htmlText="<b><font size='16'>"+(prop.title).➥
    toUpperCase()+"</font></b><br>"+prop.description;
        }
            if(now.getHours()>7 && now.getHours()<15)
            {
                info_txt.backgroundColor=0x0066FF;
                 myFormat.color=0xFFAAAA;
            }else if(now.getHours()>15 && now.getHours() <19){
                info_txt.backgroundColor=0xFFCB65;
                myFormat.color=0xFFFFAA;
            }else{
                info_txt.backgroundColor=0x003366;
                myFormat.color=0xFFFFFF;
            }
            info_txt.autoSize="left";
            info_txt.setTextFormat(myFormat);
    }

    private function drawBackground(obj:MovieClip):void
    {
        with(obj.graphics)
        {
            beginFill(0xFFAACC, 0.3);
            drawRect(0,0, stage.stageWidth, stage.stageHeight);
            endFill();
        }
         addChild(obj);
      }
     }
    }
```

In the preceding code, you populated the xmlData variable with the content of the XML file from the Web. Then, with a for loop, you retrieved the data and entered the information that you need in the dynamic text field (info_txt).

The parameters of interest from the XML file (or the RSS file, in this case) are contained in the title node (for the title) and the description node (for the general information), which in turn are contained in the item node of the channel node.

Then, with an if condition, you checked the time, and according to the time of day (morning, afternoon, or night), you set the background color of the dynamic text field to change.

Finally, you used the drawBackground() method to draw the background of your application.

Now that you've finished writing your code, save the file and return to the Flash document (Weather.fla). From the Properties panel, enter com.comtaste.foed.essentialair.chapter04. Weather in the Class box, and by doing so connect the class you created a few lines ago to your Flash project.

Now the Flash project is ready. Test the project to check everything is correct, and the final result should look like Figure 4-8.

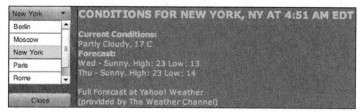

Figure 4-8. Here is your application.

Setting up the application descriptor

As with any good widget, you should give your application a transparent background, and you have to set the installation file, the title of the application, and so on. Basically, you have to set up your application descriptor. In this exercise, you'll be creating the file yourself so that your application will have the following characteristics:

- File name: Weather Gadget
- Name: Weather Gadget
- Version: 1.0
- ID: com.company.example.Weather
- Description: Weather Gadget in AIR
- Copyright: Leave this field blank.
- Window style: Custom Chrome (transparent)
- Icon: Use the default parameters.
- Advanced: Deselect the Maximizable, Minimizable, and Resizable options.
  - Install folder: Weather Gadget
  - Program menu folder: Weather Gadget

- Digital signature: Choose your own digital signature file or create it now. (For more information about digital signatures, refer to Chapter 3.)
- Destination: Weather.air

You can populate the AIR – Application & Installer Settings panel with this information, or you can create the XML file yourself. To do so, open Dreamweaver CS4 or the text editor you prefer, and save the application descriptor as Weather-app.xml in the same directory as the application. Then enter the following in the file:

```xml
<?xml version="1.0" encoding="UTF-8" standalone="no" ?>
<application xmlns="http://ns.adobe.com/air/application/1.5">

<id>com.company.example.Weather</id>

<version>1.0</version>

<filename>Weather Gadget</filename>

<description>Weather Gadget in Adobe AIR</description>


<name>Weather Gadget</name>

<copyright/>

<initialWindow>
  <content>Weather.swf</content>
  <systemChrome>none</systemChrome>
  <transparent>true</transparent>
  <visible>true</visible>
  <maximizable>false</maximizable>
  <minimizable>false</minimizable>
  <resizable>false</resizable>
</initialWindow>

<icon/>

<customUpdateUI>false</customUpdateUI>

<allowBrowserInvocation>false</allowBrowserInvocation>

<installFolder>Weather Gadget</installFolder>

<programMenuFolder>Weather Gadget</programMenuFolder>

</application>
```

4

If you write your application descriptor yourself, you have to open the AIR – Application & Installer Settings panel and select the Use custom application descriptor file option to disable the options and enable the ones in the file you've created. Click the folder button to choose the file and select the Weather-app.xml file.

Now you can publish your AIR file for distribution.

Summary

In this chapter, you have learned how to do the following:

- Build an AIR product
- Set the correct installation and publication parameters of an AIR product
- Create and manage a digital certificate
- Use and create an application descriptor without using the Flash AIR – Application & Installer Settings panel

In the next chapter, you will see how to manage the system windows to control your project.

CHAPTER 5

WORKING WITH THE WINDOW APIS AND THE SCREEN CLASS

One of the main features that a desktop runtime should provide is a window API system to create native windows. AIR offers you a totally customizable way of generating native windows, giving total control over their look and feel. Developing with Adobe AIR, you can create the following different window types:

- Windows that match the classic Apple style when run on the Mac, or the classic Microsoft style when run on Windows
- The skinnable chrome provided by the Flex SDK, which allows you to create custom window styles independent from the operating system where your application is run
- Custom windows with vector and bitmap assets with full support for transparency and alpha blending

The window APIs allow you to manage, create, edit, and/or delete system windows for an AIR project built with Flash CS4.

Working with system windows is a bit like working with browser pop-up windows. You may need to open, in your AIR application, an additional window to display content or provide information to your users.

In Chapter 3, you learned how to create transparent windows for your application. In this chapter, you'll learn how to minimize, maximize, and restore windows, as well as the following window classes provided by AIR:

- NativeWindow: This class is for creating and managing system windows.
- NativeWindowInitOptions: This class is for managing the properties of system windows (making it possible to restore or maximize them).
- NativeWindowSystemChrome: This class is for managing the system chrome of the window (to make it more or less transparent).

When working with windows another important class is the Screen class that allows you to control secondary monitors linked to user's machine. A paragraph is oriented to this class. Later in the chapter, you'll also see how to manage your application's icons for the Mac dock bar. Creating windows in AIR is a pretty simple operation with Flash. You can animate system windows like Flash movie clips. For example, you can adjust their depth (i.e., place one window on top of another), change their size and position, and edit their look and feel.

The NativeWindow class allows to you create and modify native operating system windows. The options vary according to whether the application is being run on Windows, Mac OS X, or Linux.

In AIR projects (including those involving Flex and Dreamweaver), there are three APIs for working with windows:

- **ActionScript window**: This API is for managing windows built via ActionScript 3. To add content to a window created with code, just assign the content to the display list of the window's stage.

- **Flex window**: This API is for windows that have been created in the Flex frame-work. These components (e.g., WindowedApplication) can only be used in Flex projects.

- **HTML window**: This API is for windows that have been created in Dreamweaver CS4 with HTML and JavaScript, such as in classical web projects where it is possible to inherit JavaScript methods and properties.

Native windows dispatch events when a change is about to happen. You can handle these events, for example, to maximize a window when the user clicks a button or change the position of user interface elements when a resize event is dispatched.

Understanding native window classes

AIR automatically creates a default window for an application using the content specified in the XML application descriptor file. It's up to you to create any additional windows you need.

The application descriptor file also allows you to manage things like the dimensions of the file, the transparency of the system chrome, and the window title. You can set the same information for windows created with the NativeWindow class using the NativeWindowInitOptions, NativeWindowType, and NativeWindowSystemChrome classes, setting the following properties:

- Type: This property allows you to set three types of windows:

  - **Normal**: A typical window of your operating system.

  - **Utility**: A tool palette system window. This type of window is usually narrower than normal windows, and it doesn't appear in the Windows taskbar or the Mac dock bar.

  - **Lightweight**: A system window without chrome settings—typical for tooltips and warning windows.

- SystemChrome: This property manages the transparency of the windows, and has two settings:

  - Standard: This property provides the standard window controls (minimize, close, and maximize).

  - None: This provides invisible standard control properties for windows.

- Transparent: This Boolean (true/false) property is directly linked to the SystemChrome property. It allows you to set the transparency of the window if it's set to true. In this case, the SystemChrome has to be set to None; otherwise, you wouldn't achieve the desired transparent effect.

Here are a few methods of the main NativeWindow class to manage the windows:

- startMove(): Allows you to move the window on the screen (e.g., for windows with a transparent SystemChrome)

- startResize(): Allows you to change the dimensions of the window (resize it)

- close(): Closes the open system window
- minimize(): Reduces the window to an icon
- maximize(): Makes the window as wide as the monitor
- restore(): Restores the window to its initial size after it has been minimized or maximized

Creating your first native window

In this next section, you will learn how to create system windows with ActionScript and resize the windows. Building on this, later in the chapter you will create a simple text editor application to apply the concepts you've learned so far.

Begin the process of creating a native window by following these steps:

1. Open Flash and create a new AIR document.
2. Save your Flash file as FirstNativeWindow.fla in the directory you prefer.
3. Create a new ActionScript file.
4. Save this file in the following directory: com.comtaste.foed.essentialair. chapter05, and call it FirstNativeWin.as. Remember that the com folder and the Flash file must be in the same directory. For more details about this path, you can read the "Managing the document classes" section in Chapter 4.

Enter the following code in the ActionScript file. This initial code allows you to correctly set the class for this example.

```
package com.comtaste.foed.essentialair.chapter05{
    import flash.display.MovieClip;
    import flash.display.NativeWindow;
    import flash.display.NativeWindowSystemChrome;
    import flash.display.NativeWindowInitOptions;
    import flash.events.MouseEvent;

public class FirstNativeWin extends MovieClip
{
    public var initOptionNewWin:NativeWindowInitOptions=➡
    new NativeWindowInitOptions();
    public var newWin:NativeWindow;
    public var myButton:MovieClip=new MovieClip();
```

You've imported all the classes you need in an ActionScript file. You've also imported the three classes mentioned at the beginning of this chapter:

- NativeWindow
- NativeWindowInitOptions
- NativeWindowSystemChrome

Now set up your class constructor:

```
public function FirstNativeWin():void
{
    initOptionNewWin.systemChrome=NativeWindowSystemChrome.STANDARD;
    initOptionNewWin.resizable=false;
    initOptionNewWin.maximizable=false;
    drawButton(myButton);
    myButton.addEventListener(MouseEvent.CLICK, openWindow);
}
```

This code sets the following characteristics of your new window:

- The window will have a standard system chrome, resembling those of the windows in the operating system the program is running on.
- The window can't be resized (resize property).
- The window can't be maximized (maximize property).

5

The method drawButton(myButton) refers to the instance of the button of your application.

Proceed with the following code:

```
private function drawButton(obj:MovieClip):void
{
    with(obj.graphics)
    {
        beginFill(0xAAEECC, 1);
        drawRect(10, 10, 100, 20);
        endFill();
    }
    addChild(obj);
    obj.buttonMode=true;
}

private function openWindow(event:MouseEvent):void
{
    newWin=new NativeWindow(initOptionNewWin);
    newWin.title="My First New Win";
    newWin.activate();
    newWin.width=200;
    newWin.height=200;
}
}
}
```

This last portion of code uses the drawButton() method to the draw button and the openWindow() method to create the new window. Look at the openWindow() method closely. You'll notice the constructor of the NativeWindow class requires the settings of the initOptionNewWin instance, whereas the title, width, and height properties allow you to set the relevant parameters. The `activate()` method initializes your window by making it visible on video, without which you wouldn't have been able to finish the project.

Assigning the document class to the project

Now you can save your file and go back to the Flash document you created at the beginning of this exercise.

In the Properties panel of Flash, enter the path and the name of the ActionScript file (com.comtaste.foed.essentialair.chapter05.FirstNativeWindow) you created in the Class box. Now you can test your application.

The result, as shown in Figure 5-1, shows how the new window you've created is set up like in any Windows system window. This new window is nonscalable and nonresizable.

Figure 5-1. Your first window in AIR

You can animate the windows just like you can create Flash projects with movie clips. Furthermore, like browser windows or movie clips in Flash, system windows can have a depth order (e.g., you can bring a window to the foreground or the background).

Continuing with the previous example, let's set the dimension of the main window to 200 pixels. Perform the following steps:

1. Open the `FirstNativeWindow.fla` file.
2. Open the Properties panel and click the Edit button on the Properties item.

3. The Document Properties panel will open. Set the Width and Height parameters both to 200 pixels.

4. Close the panel by clicking OK.

5. Open the FirstNativeWin.as ActionScript class.

Continue with the example by entering the following new code, displayed in bold:

```
package com.comtaste.foed.essentialair.chapter05{
    import flash.display.MovieClip;
    import flash.display.NativeWindow;
    import flash.display.NativeWindowSystemChrome;
    import flash.display.NativeWindowInitOptions;
    import flash.events.MouseEvent;
    import flash.events.Event;

    public class FirstNativeWin extends MovieClip
    {
        public var initOptionNewWin:NativeWindowInitOptions=➥
        new NativeWindowInitOptions();
        public var newWin:NativeWindow;
        public var mainWin:NativeWindow;
        public var windowCreated:Boolean=new Boolean();
        public var myButton:MovieClip=new MovieClip();
        public var dir:Number=10;
        public function FirstNativeWin():void
        {
            initOptionNewWin.systemChrome=➥
            NativeWindowSystemChrome.STANDARD;
            initOptionNewWin.resizable=false;
            initOptionNewWin.maximizable=false;
            mainWin=this.stage.nativeWindow;
            drawButton(myButton);
            myButton.addEventListener(MouseEvent.CLICK, openWindow);
        }

        private function drawButton(obj:MovieClip):void
        {
            with(obj.graphics)
            {
                beginFill(0xAAEECC, 1);
                drawRect(10, 10, 100, 20);
                endFill();
            }
            addChild(obj);
            obj.buttonMode=true;
            obj.stat=false;
        }
```

```
private function openWindow(event:MouseEvent):void
{
    windowCreated=!windowCreated;
    if(windowCreated){
        newWin=new NativeWindow(initOptionNewWin);
        newWin.title="My First New Win";
        newWin.activate();
        newWin.width=200;
        newWin.height=200;
        addEventListener(Event.ENTER_FRAME, moveWin);
    }else{
        newWin.close();
        mainWin.close();
    }
}

private function moveWin(event:Event):void
{
    if (!mainWin.closed && !newWin.closed) {
        newWin.y += dir;
        if(newWin.y<(mainWin.y-newWin.height) || newWin.y>➡
(mainWin.y+mainWin.height)){
            dir*=-1;
            if(dir<0){
                newWin.orderToBack();
            }else{
                newWin.orderToFront();
            }
        }
    }
}
}
```

The result is shown in Figure 5-2.

What has actually happened? First of all, you imported the Event class to manage the animation. Then you added code for moving the new window forward or back in the window order. You also initialized the main window as NativeWindow. Now you can control the main window position in relation to the new window you will create once you click the button.

In the openWindow() function, you created a Boolean variable, which is instanced in the button when it is created. If the variable is set to true, a new window will be created and animated; otherwise, all the windows (the main one and the new one) will be closed.

With the moveWin() method, you animate your window.

Figure 5-2. Your new window in AIR—this time it's animated.

The `dir` numerical property sets the speed of movement, and the `orderToBack()` and `orderToFront()` methods set the position of the new window in relation to the previous and any other open windows.

Now you can go back to Flash and test your application. If you click once on `myButton`, the new window will be created, and if you click it twice, both windows will be closed.

Animating a new window

The next example will show you how to animate a new window.

As always, create a new Flash file for AIR, and save it as `TestAnimationNW.fla` in a directory of your choice. Then create a new ActionScript file named `AnimationWindow.as` and save it in the following directory: com/comtaste/foed/essentialair/chapter05 (remember that the com folder and the Flash file must be in the same directory).

Write the following code in the new document:

```
package com.comtaste.foed.essentialair.chapter05{

    import flash.display.MovieClip;
    import flash.display.NativeWindow;
    import flash.display.NativeWindowType;
    import flash.display.NativeWindowInitOptions;
    import flash.display.NativeWindowSystemChrome;
    import flash.display.StageDisplayState;
    import flash.display.StageAlign;
    import flash.display.StageScaleMode;
    import flash.text.TextField;
    import flash.events.MouseEvent;
    import flash.system.Capabilities;
    import fl.transitions.Tween;
    import fl.transitions.easing.Bounce;
    import fl.transitions.TweenEvent;
```

As usual, you've imported all the classes you need, including two useful ones: Tween and TweenEvent. These two classes allow you to manage the animation you want to apply to the new window.

Next, insert the code to initialize your ActionScript file:

```
public class AnimationWindow extends MovieClip{
    public var mainWindow:NativeWindow;
    public var newWinInit:NativeWindowInitOptions=new Native➡
WindowInitOptions();
    public var newWin:NativeWindow;
    public var labelText:TextField=new TextField();
    public var createIt:MovieClip=new MovieClip();
    public var moveWin:MovieClip=new MovieClip();
    public var thisTime:Date=new Date();
```

Again, you've declared all the properties you are going to need, and you've also included the Date class, which tells your application to return the date to insert as content in your new window.

Now set the constructor of your ActionScript class:

```
public function AnimationWindow():void
{
    mainWindow = stage.nativeWindow;
    stage.scaleMode=StageScaleMode.NO_SCALE;
    stage.align=StageAlign.TOP_LEFT;

    labelText.htmlText=String("Today is <b>"+thisTime.getDate()+"/"+➡
(thisTime.getMonth()+1)+"/"+thisTime.getFullYear()+"</b>");
```

```
        addChild(createIt);
        addChild(moveWin);
        designButton(createIt, 100, 30, 0, 0);
        designButton(moveWin, 100, 30, 0, 100);
        createIt.addEventListener(MouseEvent.CLICK, createWindow);
        moveWin.addEventListener(MouseEvent.CLICK, moveWindow);
}
```

At this point, you must remember that the new window you will create has to keep the content unaltered. To do this, you have assigned the StageScaleMode.NO_SCALE value to the scaleMode property and the StageAlign.TOP_LEFT value to the align properties. If you hadn't done this, the content would be bigger than the real measure. Then you assigned functions to the two buttons: one to create a new window and another to move it on the user's desktop.

Next are the methods that create the new window:

```
        private function createWindow(event:MouseEvent):void
        {
                newWinInit.systemChrome=NativeWindowSystemChrome.STANDARD;
                newWinInit.type=NativeWindowType.UTILITY ;
                newWin=new NativeWindow(newWinInit);
                newWin.activate();
                newWin.stage.addChild(labelText);
                newWin.title="Calendar - WINDOW";
                newWin.x=0;
                newWin.width=300;
                newWin.height=100;
                newWin.stage.addEventListener(MouseEvent.CLICK, closeMe);
        }
```

Again, as you did for the previous exercise, you set the systemChrome, and you set the type property of the newWinInit instance to utility. By doing so, you create a utility window.

With the following code, you'll close the window:

```
        function closeMe(event:MouseEvent):void
        {
                newWin.close();
                mainWindow.close();
        }
```

The closeMe() method allows you to close both of the windows once the user clicks the utility window. The next method, moveWindow(), allows you to move the window on the user's desktop.

```
        private function moveWindow(event:MouseEvent)
        {
                var moveIt:Tween=new Tween(newWin, "x", Bounce.easeOut, ➥
                newWin.x, ((Capabilities.screenResolutionX)-newWin.width), ➥
                5, true);
```

```
            moveIt.addEventListener(TweenEvent.MOTION_FINISH, backIt);
            function backIt(event:TweenEvent)
            {
                  moveIt.yoyo();
            }
      }

      private function designButton(obj:MovieClip, objWidth:Number, ➥
      objHeight:Number, objX:Number, objY:Number)
      {
            with(obj.graphics)
            {
                  beginFill(0xAACCDD, 1);
                  drawRect(objX,objY,objWidth,objHeight);
                  endFill();
            }
            obj.buttonMode=true;
      }
   }
}
```

These last two methods move the window once the moveWin() function is recalled. Also, to move the window, you used the Tween class.

The constructor of the Tween class is made up of some parameters, which are all the class needs to animate the new window. The parameters are as follows:

- The object (newWin)
- The property on which you will create the animation (in this case, on the X axis)
- The animation (Bounce, to make the animation bouncy, with an ease-out property to slow down the animation at the end)
- The initial position of the animation (the starting point on the X axis)
- The final position of the animation (the endpoint on the X axis)
- The number of seconds or frames (five—this option depends on the next parameter)
- The unit of measure (seconds or frames) (if set to true, seconds are used; otherwise, frames are used)

Now save the file. Go back to the Flash file and, in the Properties panel, enter the name and the path of the ActionScript file you created—com.comtaste.foed.essentialair. chapter05.AnimationWindow—in the Class box. Then test your application.

To close all the windows, click the newWin window (the new one). (Don't close it using the standard window close button—it will crash the application.)

In this example, you have seen how to create a new window in AIR, and how to manage the basic animation of the window. Over the next sections, you will analyze the properties and functions of each native window class in more detail.

Managing windows

In the following exercises, you'll see how to manage the windows without the system default controls (minimize, close, maximize/reduce). You'll start by adding content to a new system window.

Adding content to a new window

As you have seen, it isn't difficult to create a new window. However, you have to populate it and add some content as well.

> *In this example, you will see how to load a simple picture into a window. The method that allows you to add content to a window is addChild(). If you are familiar with ActionScript 3, you know that this method is used to add objects to the DisplayObject list and display them on the stage of your AIR project.*

As always, create a new Flash file for AIR, and save it as AddContent.fla in a directory of your choice. Then create a new ActionScript file named AddContent.as and save it in the com/comtaste/foed/essentialair/chapter05 directory.

Write the following code in the new ActionScript class (AddContent.as):

```
package com.comtaste.foed.essentialair.chapter05{

    import flash.display.MovieClip;
    import flash.display.NativeWindow;
    import flash.display.NativeWindowInitOptions;
    import flash.display.NativeWindowSystemChrome;
    import flash.display.Loader;
    import flash.display.StageScaleMode;
    import flash.display.StageAlign;
    import flash.net.URLRequest;
    import flash.events.MouseEvent;
    import flash.events.Event;
```

Now proceed with the rest of your code:

```
    public class AddContent extends MovieClip
    {
        public var loader:Loader=new Loader();
        public var urlLoader:URLRequest=new URLRequest➥
        ("http://www.comtaste.com/img/logoComtaste.gif");
        public var newWin:NativeWindow;

    public function AddContent():void
    {
        createNewWin();
```

```
        newWin.stage.addEventListener(MouseEvent.CLICK, closeMe);
        loader.load(urlLoader);
        loader.contentLoaderInfo.addEventListener(Event.COMPLETE, showIt);
    }
```

The AddContent() class allows you to insert external content (downloaded from the Web). As with any other Flash project for the Web, the Loader class will allow you to load the picture into your project. The URLRequest class will tell the Loader the path of the JPG file you want to load.

Proceed with the following code:

```
    private function createNewWin():void
    {
        var initOptions:NativeWindowInitOptions=new➡
        NativeWindowInitOptions();
        initOptions.transparent=true;
        initOptions.systemChrome=NativeWindowSystemChrome.NONE;
        newWin=new NativeWindow(initOptions);
        newWin.alwaysInFront=true;
        newWin.stage.align=StageAlign.TOP_LEFT;
        newWin.stage.scaleMode=StageScaleMode.NO_SCALE;
        newWin.activate();
    }

    private function showIt(event:Event):void
    {
        newWin.stage.addChild(event.target.content);
        newWin.stage.stageWidth=event.target.content.width;
        newWin.stage.stageHeight=event.target.content.height;
    }
    private function closeMe(event:MouseEvent):void
    {
        newWin.close();
    }
    }
    }
```

The two methods createNewWin() and showIt() allow you to create a new window, which will have no content at first. The showIt() function will add the content loaded from the instance of the Loader class (with the addChild() method).

Now you can tell the window to resize itself according to the size of the loaded image, which you can add in later. The closeMe() method will close the newWin window.

Now you can return to your Flash file and associate the document class of the project with the ActionScript class you've just created. Enter the name of the ActionScript file you've just created (com.comtaste.foed.essentialair.chapter05.AddContent) in the Class box in Flash's Properties panel, and then test your application.

As you can see from Figure 5-3, the new window has been created, and is only populated with the image you have requested.

Figure 5-3. The picture loaded in the new window

> To close the main window, click the close button. To close the new window, click the image.

Creating a photo gallery with native window classes

The next example will show you how to manage the dimensions of a new system window. This time, you will load some images into the main window. Then, when you click each of them, a new window will open with the same picture, with the same dimensions as the image.

As always, create a new Flash file for AIR, and save it as PhotoGallery.fla in a directory of your choice. Then create a new ActionScript file named PhotoGallery.as and save it in the following directory: com/comtaste/foed/essentialair/chapter05.

> To complete this exercise, you need an internet connection.

Type the following code in the ActionScript file:

```
package com.comtaste.foed.essentialair.chapter05{

    import flash.display.MovieClip;
    import flash.display.Loader;
    import flash.display.NativeWindow;
    import flash.display.NativeWindowInitOptions;
    import flash.display.NativeWindowSystemChrome;
    import flash.display.StageAlign;
    import flash.display.StageScaleMode;
    import flash.net.URLRequest;
    import flash.text.TextField;
    import flash.events.MouseEvent;
    import flash.events.Event;
```

Continue with the following code:

```
public class PhotoGallery extends MovieClip
{
    public var loader:Loader;
    public var menu:Array=new Array();
    public var dist:int=90;
    public var newWin:NativeWindow;
    public var initOption:NativeWindowInitOptions=new ➥
    NativeWindowInitOptions();

    // Class constructor
    public function PhotoGallery():void
    {
        menu=[{photoURL:"http://www.comtaste.com/img/contacts.jpg",➥
    titlePhoto:"Photo Number 1"}, {photoURL:"http://www.comtaste.com/img/➥
    how.jpg", titlePhoto:"Photo Number 2"},{photoURL:"http://www.comtaste➥
    .com/img/our_creatures.jpg", titlePhoto:"Photo Number 3"}, ➥
    {photoURL:"http://www.comtaste.com/img/support.jpg", ➥
    titlePhoto:"Photo Number 4"}, {photoURL:"http://www.comtaste.com/img/➥
    working.jpg", titlePhoto:"Photo Number 5"},➥
    {photoURL:"http://www.comtaste.com/img/caseStudiesList.gif",➥
    titlePhoto:"Photo Number 6"}];
        for(var i:Number=0; i<menu.length; i++)
        {
            var myPhoto:MovieClip=new MovieClip();
            var photoURL:URLRequest=new ➥
    URLRequest(menu[i].photoURL);
            addChild(myPhoto);
            loader=new Loader();
            loader.load(photoURL);
            myPhoto.titlePhoto=menu[i].titlePhoto;
            myPhoto.photoURL=menu[i].photoURL;
            myPhoto.scaleX=.3;
```

```
            myPhoto.scaleY=.3;
            myPhoto.x=dist*i;
            myPhoto.addChild(loader);
            myPhoto.addEventListener(MouseEvent.CLICK, showIt);
            myPhoto.buttonMode=true;
        }
    }
```

In this block of code, you've populated the array that includes the pictures you want to display. Progressively, you've added your photos to the stage with a for loop. The photos are loaded by the instance of the Loader class at first (loader), and then by the instance of the MovieClip class (myPhoto).

Managing windows with added content

Next, you'll position the six photos on the stage in the main window. To do this, you have to set two properties for the myPhoto instance (photoURL and titlePhoto) in order to pass the parameters regarding the image to the new window you will open.

Now let's examine the next method of your ActionScript file, showIt(), to create the window that will display the photos:

```
    private function showIt(event:MouseEvent):void
    {
        createWin(event.currentTarget.photoURL, ➡
        event.currentTarget.titlePhoto);
    }

    private function createWin(url:String, itsText:String):void
    {
        initOption.systemChrome=NativeWindowSystemChrome.STANDARD;
        newWin=new NativeWindow(initOption);
        newWin.stage.align=StageAlign.TOP_LEFT;
        newWin.stage.scaleMode=StageScaleMode.NO_SCALE;
        var loader:Loader=new Loader();
        var path:URLRequest=new URLRequest(url);
        loader.load(path);
        loader.contentLoaderInfo.addEventListener(Event.COMPLETE, ➡
        showPhoto);
        function showPhoto(event:Event):void
        {
            newWin.stage.addChild(loader);
            newWin.stage.stageWidth =event.target.content.width;
            newWin.stage.stageHeight =event.target.content.height;
            newWin.title=itsText;
            newWin.activate();
        }
    }
}
}
```

The showIt() method passes the parameters that the window needs to the createWin() method: the absolute path of the photo you want to load and the caption of the image. This method includes, in turn, the event handler (showPhoto()), which is registered to the COMPLETE event and invoked when the photo has been loaded. At the time the photo is loaded and the exact dimensions of the image are available, the images can be mirrored in the dimensions of the window.

Return to your Flash file, PhotoGallery.fla, and associate the document class of the project with the ActionScript class you've just created by inserting the name and the path of the ActionScript file (com.comtaste.foed.essentialair.chapter05.PhotoGallery) in the Class box in Flash's Properties panel. Then test your application.

The result, which should resemble Figure 5-4, shows the images you have loaded in the main window. By clicking each of them, a new window should open, containing the same image (at its original size).

Figure 5-4. The photo gallery you've created

When the user clicks a photo, the close() method is invoked and the native window is closed.

Next, create the event handler for the CLICK event on the window by adding the following code to the ActionScript class (the new code is displayed in bold):

```
private var newWin:NativeWindow;
private var loader:Loader=new Loader();

private function createWin(url:String, itsText:String):void
{
    initOption.systemChrome=NativeWindowSystemChrome.STANDARD;
    newWin=new NativeWindow(initOption);
    newWin.stage.align=StageAlign.TOP_LEFT;
    newWin.stage.scaleMode=StageScaleMode.NO_SCALE;
    newWin.stage.addEventListener(MouseEvent.CLICK, destroyIt);
    var path:URLRequest=new URLRequest(url);
    loader.load(path);
    loader.contentLoaderInfo.addEventListener(Event.COMPLETE,

showPhoto);
}

function showPhoto(event:Event):void
{
    newWin.stage.addChild(loader);
    newWin.width=event.target.content.width;
    newWin.height=event.target.content.height;
    newWin.title=itsText;
    newWin.activate();
}
function destroyIt(event:MouseEvent):void
{
    newWin.close();
}
```

Now return to the `PhotoGallery.fla` file and run it again. This time, when you click the image, the new window should close.

Next, let's examine how to manage a window with a transparent system chrome. In the next example, you'll create an application using your own buttons to close, minimize, and restore the window.

Creating a transparent window with custom chrome

Windows with transparent backgrounds are very attractive from the user's point of view. In this section, you'll create a window with the system chrome set to transparent.

As always, create a new Flash file for AIR, and save it as `OpenCloseWindow.fla` in a directory of your choice. Then create a new ActionScript file named `OpenCloseWindow.as`, and save it in the following directory: com/comtaste/foed/essentialair/chapter05.

Enter this code within the ActionScript file:

```
package com.comtaste.foed.essentialair.chapter05{
    import flash.display.MovieClip;
    import flash.display.NativeWindow;
    import flash.events.MouseEvent;
    import flash.text.TextField;

public class OpenCloseWindow extends MovieClip
{
    public var closeWinButton:MovieClip=new MovieClip();
    public var minimizeWinButton:MovieClip=new MovieClip();
    public var maximizeWinButton:MovieClip=new MovieClip();
    public var restoreWinButton:MovieClip=new MovieClip();
    public var mainWindow:NativeWindow;
    public var menu:Array=new Array();
    public var widthButton:Number=100;
    public var heightButton:Number=30;
```

Up to here, there isn't anything new—you're just importing the classes your application needs and creating the relevant properties.

Let's proceed with the class constructor:

```
public function OpenCloseWindow():void
{
    menu=[[closeWinButton, "Close"], [minimizeWinButton, "Minimize"],
        [maximizeWinButton, "Maximize"],
        [restoreWinButton, "Restore"]];
    mainWindow= stage.nativeWindow;
    mainWindow.title="Main Window";
    for(var i:Number=0; i<menu.length; i++)
    {
        drawButton(menu[i][0]);
        var labelText:TextField=new TextField();
        labelText.selectable=false;
        labelText.autoSize="left";
        labelText.text=String(menu[i][1]);
        menu[i][0].x=(widthButton+10)*i;
        menu[i][0].addChild(labelText);
        menu[i][0].addEventListener(MouseEvent.CLICK, controlWin);
        menu[i][0].addEventListener(MouseEvent.MOUSE_OVER, ➡
        rollOverMe);
        menu[i][0].addEventListener(MouseEvent.MOUSE_OUT, rollOutMe);
        menu[i][0].addEventListener(MouseEvent.MOUSE_DOWN, dragMe);
    }
}
```

In this code block, you created an array for the various items on the menu, and you drew four buttons with a for() loop. Within the for() loop, you added a text label to every

button and created the event listeners for the following events: CLICK, MOUSE_OVER, MOUSE_
OUT, and MOUSE_DOWN.

Each button has four event handlers: controlWin(), rollOverMe(), rollOutMe(), and
dragMe() (with this last method, you'll also see how to move your application on the
desktop).

Add the code within these event handlers:

```
private function drawButton(obj:MovieClip):void
{
    with(obj.graphics)
    {
        beginFill(0xAAEECC, 1);
        drawRect(0, 0, widthButton, heightButton);
        endFill();
    }
    this.addChild(obj);
    obj.buttonMode=true;
}

private function rollOverMe(event:MouseEvent):void
{
     event.currentTarget.y+=3;
}

private function rollOutMe(event:MouseEvent):void
{
    event.currentTarget.y-=3;
}
```

The drawButton() method will draw the various buttons on the stage. The other two event
handlers (rollOverMe() and rollOutMe()) will set a light rollover and rollout effect on the
buttons, respectively. This effect is a simple movement along the Y axis.

To move the application on the user's desktop, just invoke the startMove() method of the
NativeWindow class. You have to associate the stage with an instance of the NativeWindow
class to make movement happen:

```
private function dragMe(event:MouseEvent):void
{
    mainWindow.startMove();
}
```

The last part of your script includes the main methods of the NativeWindow class:

```
private function controlWin(event:MouseEvent):void
{
     switch(event.currentTarget)
    {
       case closeWinButton:
```

```
                mainWindow.close();
                break;
                case minimizeWinButton:
                mainWindow.minimize();
                break;
                case maximizeWinButton:
                mainWindow.maximize();
                break;
                case restoreWinButton:
                mainWindow.restore();
              break;
          }
        }
      }
    }
```

The four methods used in this portion of code are as follows:

- close(): This is for closing a system window.
- minimize(): This is for reducing a window to an icon (in the taskbar on Windows or the dock bar on the Mac).
- maximize(): This is for enlarging the application to full screen.
- restore(): This is for restoring the window to its initial size.

Now you can associate your ActionScript file (OpenCloseWindow.as) with your Flash file (OpenCloseWindow.fla). In the Properties panel of Flash, enter the name and the path of the ActionScript file you created in the Class box: com.comtaste.foed.essentialair. chapter05.OpenCloseWindow.

At this point, only one thing is missing: you have to make the main window of your application transparent. Open the Flash file OpenCloseWindow.fla. Click the Edit button in the AIR Settings section of the Properties panel. The AIR – Application & Installer Settings panel will appear. On this panel, choose the Custom Chrome (transparent) option from the Window Style item, and confirm the choice by clicking OK.

> *See Chapter 4 for more information on correctly setting the window publication options.*

Now you can test your application. The result, as you can see in Figure 5-5, shows your application with four buttons. If you click each of them, you can test the various methods of the NativeWindow class.

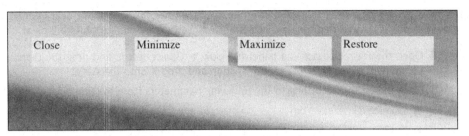

Figure 5-5. The window with the system chrome set to transparent

You can drag the window on the stage if you keep a button pressed down.

Creating a simple text editor using native window classes

5

Now that you understand native window classes in more depth, you can put your work into practice and apply what you've learned so far. In this section, you'll create a simple text editor, in which some windows will be controlled by native window classes.

As always, create a new Flash file for AIR, and save it as TextEdit.fla in a directory of your choice.

Adding components in an AIR project

This time, before creating the ActionScript file, you need to insert some useful user interface elements as well as a few components that Flash CS4 provides in the Components panel, as shown in Figure 5-6.

1. Set up the project: leave the dimensions of the stage at the default size: 550 pixels wide and 400 pixels high. As a background color, you can choose pure black (#000000). To change the background color of the application, just click the Background color button and select black from the color picker.

2. Click the first keyframe of the first layer of the timeline.

3. Create a text input field with the following characteristics:

   - X: 21
   - Y: 64
   - Instance name: text_txt
   - Width: 495
   - Height: 320

Figure 5-6.
The Components panel

181

As far as the font and the color are concerned, pick the ones you prefer, but bear in mind that your project is a text editor, so try to choose those that are comfortable to look at.

4. Open the Flash Components panel (Window ➤ Components), and drag the Button component from the User Interface section and drop it onto the stage.

5. Place the button according to the following parameters from the Properties panel:

- Instance name: save_btn
- X: 437
- Y: 30

6. Set some parameters for the button in the Component Inspector, which you can reach from Window ➤ Component Inspector.

7. Select the Label item and enter the following text in the Value field: Save file.

8. Next, from the Components panel, in the User Interface section, drag the UIScrollBar component onto the stage.

When dragging the UIScrollBar component onto the stage, you have to be careful to place it exactly on the right-hand side of the input text field, inside the text field, as shown in Figure 5-7.

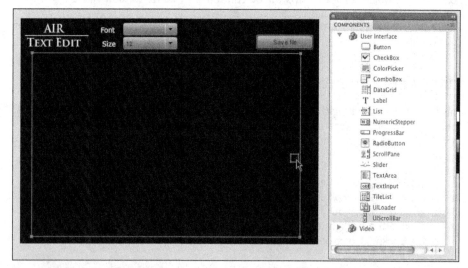

Figure 5-7. Place the UIScrollBar component inside the input field on the right-hand side.

The UIScrollBar component doesn't need anything else. It controls the text-scrolling functionality by default.

Managing the ComboBox component

Next, you'll insert two ComboBox components to control the text (in this example, to change the font face and the dimensions). Select the ComboBox from the Components panel, and set it up on the stage according to the following parameters from the Properties panel:

- X: 190
- Y: 8
- Instance Name: font_cb

Now insert a new ComboBox to control the dimensions of the font. Drag a new ComboBox onto the stage and set up the following parameters for this instance as well:

- X: 190
- Y: 32
- Instance Name: size_cb

As you will see when you insert the code, the ComboBox allows you to set up the DataProvider with ActionScript as well as with the Component Inspector:

1. Select the size_cb component.

2. Open the Component Inspector (if it isn't already open).

3. Select the dataProvider item.

4. Select the Value item, and click the magnifying glass button in the upper-right corner, as shown in Figure 5-8.

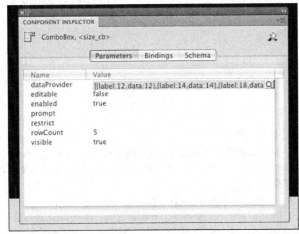

Figure 5-8. Insert the data in the ComboBox by clicking the dataProvider item

5. Click the + symbol on the Values panel to set the dataProvider.

6. In the two fields (label and data), enter the value 12.

7. Repeat the last two steps, this time using 14 and 18 as values.

Creating the Save Document panel

Before finishing the user interface elements, you have to create the panel that will be used as the Save As dialog. It will resemble the one shown in Figure 5-9.

Figure 5-9.
The Save As dialog that you'll create in this section.

1. Insert a new symbol (Insert ➤ New Symbol).

2. Drag a movie clip from the panel and name it panelSaving.

3. Click the Advanced button. The Create New Symbol panel will now provide you with more options.

4. In the Linkage section, select the Export to ActionScript option.

5. In the Class box, which will become active, type PanelSaving, and confirm by clicking OK.

6. Inside this new movie clip, panelSaving, draw a black rectangular shape 240 pixels wide and 170 pixels high.

7. Insert three static text fields with the following labels for your user interface: Save file as..., File Name, and File Type, as shown previously in Figure 5-9.

8. Next, add an input text field (placed under the File Name heading) with the following parameters:

   - X: 8
   - Y: 59
   - Width: 215
   - Height: 19
   - Instance Name: title_txt

9. Click the Show border around text button in the Character section of the Properties panel. By doing so, you'll be able to see a text field with a visible black border and a white background.

10. Drag a Button component from the Components panel (Window ➤ Components) and put it inside the panelSaving movie clip. Drag the ComboBox from the Components panel and put it inside the panelSaving movie clip.

11. Enter the following parameters for the button on the Properties panel:

    - Instance name: file_btn
    - X: 145
    - Y: 110

12. From the Component Inspector, choose Label: Save.

13. Enter the following parameters for the ComboBox:

    - Instance name: fileType_cb
    - X: 8
    - Y: 110

14. From the Component Inspector, click the dataProvider field and set the following values:

- label: Simple Text File
- data: txt
- label: HTML Format
- data: html

15. Confirm by clicking OK, and close the Component Inspector if it's still open.

You finish the work on the user interface assets of your panel with one last button: close_btn. In the panelSaving movie clip, write close with the text tool, select this text and convert it to a button symbol, and name the instance close_btn.

Now you've finished the graphical part, and you can write the code for your application.

Writing the text editor ActionScript code

To complete your project, you need some ActionScript code. In this section, you'll learn how to code with the NativeWindow class.

First, open Flash. In the Properties panel, enter the name of the ActionScript file, com.comtate.foed.essentialair.chapter05.TextEdit, in the Class box. Select ActionScript File from the File ➤ New menu in the next panel. Save this file in the com/comtaste/foed/essentialair/chapter05 directory as TextEdit.as.

Start by adding the code to import all the classes you need:

```
package com.comtaste.foed.essentialair.chapter05{
    import flash.display.MovieClip;
    import flash.display.NativeWindow;
    import flash.display.NativeWindowType;
    import flash.display.NativeWindowInitOptions;
    import flash.display.NativeWindowSystemChrome;
    import flash.text.TextField;
    import flash.filesystem.*;
    import flash.events.Event;
    import flash.events.MouseEvent;
    import flash.text.TextFormat;
    import flash.text.Font;
    import flash.display.StageAlign;
    import flash.display.StageScaleMode;
```

Notice that you're importing the filesystem package along with all the other classes. The filesystem package includes some of the classes that you use to work with local files and folders. These classes (File, FileStream, and FileMode) are introduced in this example, and will be discussed further in Chapter 7.

Next, prepare the TextEdit class:

```
public class TextEdit extends MovieClip
{
    public var myFormat:TextFormat=new TextFormat();
    public var panel_mc:PanelSaving=new PanelSaving();
    public var newWin:NativeWindow;
    public var openWin:NativeWindow;
    public var initWin:NativeWindowInitOptions=new➠
    NativeWindowInitOptions();
```

As usual, in this portion of code, you've inserted all the variables you need, including the panel_mc instance of the PanelSaving class you created before.

> Remember, panelSaving *is the movie clip shown in Figure 5-9.*

Now set up the class constructor:

```
public function TextEdit():void
{
    stage.focus=text_txt;
    createSaveWin();
    save_btn.addEventListener(MouseEvent.CLICK, savePanel);
    panel_mc.file_btn.addEventListener(MouseEvent.CLICK, finalReg);
    panel_mc.close_btn.addEventListener(MouseEvent.CLICK, savePanel);
    init();
}
```

With the line stage.focus=text_txt, you set the focus on the input text field so that the cursor will already be inside the text field. Then you set up the various events for the buttons that save the file.

The class constructor also calls two methods: createSaveWin() and init(). Have a look at them:

```
public function createSaveWin():void
{
    initWin.systemChrome = NativeWindowSystemChrome.STANDARD;
    initWin.type = NativeWindowType.UTILITY;
    newWin = new NativeWindow(initWin);
    openWin = this.stage.nativeWindow;
    newWin.stage.stageWidth=panel_mc.width;
    newWin.stage.stageHeight=panel_mc.height;
    newWin.stage.align=StageAlign.TOP_LEFT;
    newWin.stage.scaleMode=StageScaleMode.NO_SCALE;
    newWin.stage.addChild(panel_mc);
    newWin.title = "Save Document";
    newWin.x += openWin.x+openWin.width/2-newWin.width/2;
```

```
        newWin.y += openWin.y+openWin.height/2-newWin.height/2;
    }
```

The createSaveWin() method accomplishes the following tasks:

- Setting up the system chrome of the new window that will open
- Setting the system chrome type to UTILITY
- Creating an instance of NativeWindow named openWin, which will contain the main stage

Instancing the second NativeWindow variable, newWin, allows you to identify the main window of this application. You can place the new window at the center of the main one.

Finally, you set up the scaleMode and stageAlign properties of the new window to NO_SCALE and TOP_LEFT to maintain the aspect ratio of the window's content.

Initializing the TextEdit application

The following code initializes the component that you've inserted on the stage:

```
public function init():void
{
    with(font_cb){
        x=190;
        y=8;
        width=160;
        rowCount=10;
        labelField="fontName";
        dropdown.iconField = null;
        dataProvider = new DataProvider(Font.enumerateFonts(true) ➡
        .sortOn("fontName"));
        addEventListener(Event.CHANGE, changeFont);
    }

    with(size_cb){
        rowCount=5;
        addEventListener(Event.CHANGE, changeFont);
    }
}
private function changeFont(event:Event):void
{
    myFormat.font=font_cb.selectedItem.fontName;
    myFormat.size=size_cb.selectedItem.data;
    text_txt.setTextFormat(myFormat);
}
```

The init() method controls a whole series of initial application settings. You start with the font_cb ComboBox, for which you define the width and the number of rows. Using the Font class, you set the various fonts installed on the operating system. The enumerateFont() method allows you to read all the characters installed on the computer the AIR application is running on, on video (in alphabetical order by font name). Any change to the font_cb ComboBox (e.g., a simple selection of a font in the list) will invoke the changeFont() event handler. For the size_cb ComboBox, you're just setting a few simple parameters in the changeFont() function, which is assigned to the onChange event of the Event class.

The last part of the previous code is the changeFont() method. Thanks to the instance of the TextFormat class myFormat, you have set the font and size properties, which you will assign to the text_txt instance. These changes will then be applied to the text field.

Here's the last part of your code:

```
private function savePanel(event:MouseEvent):void
{
    createSaveWin();
    newWin.activate();
}


private function finalReg(event:MouseEvent){
    var file:File = File.desktopDirectory;
    var fileName:String = unescape(escape(panel_mc.title_txt.text ➡
    + "." + ➡
    panel_mc.fileType_cb.selectedItem.data).split("%0D").join(""));
    file = file.resolvePath(fileName);
    var writeIt:FileStream = new FileStream();
    writeIt.open(file, FileMode.WRITE);
    writeIt.writeUTFBytes(text_txt.text);
    writeIt.close();
    newWin.close();
    }
  }
}
```

The savePanel() method activates the new window, calling the createWin() method, which will allow you to carry out the saving process. The finalReg() method uses the File class to register your actual file with its content.

> In Chapter 7, you'll see how to read and write from text files.

Now I'll give a quick overview of the methods of the File and FileStream classes that control the process of saving data:

- resolvePath(): This indicates the path to the file (in your case, the desktop directory of your operating system) and its content.
- write(): This is for actually writing the file to the system.
- close(): This closes the file registration process.

Now save your file, return to the Flash project file of your AIR application (TextEdit.fla), and test your work. The result should be similar to the one in Figure 5-10.

Figure 5-10. Your text editor in AIR

Creating full-screen windows

AIR allows you to create full-screen applications. Some well-known web applications give users the ability to maximize video content to full screen (e.g., YouTube). AIR applications make it is possible to use all the available space in the interface, too.

> *The FLVPlayback component in Flash allows you to see videos in AIR and web projects. It covers the whole space available on the stage when you enlarge the application to full screen. This means that the user will only be able to see the video—the other elements won't be visible. The user can press the Esc button to exit the application, as usual for full-screen modes.*

The StageDisplayState class allows you to control the full-screen mode through the FULL_SCREEN, FULL_SCREEN_INTERACTIVE, and NORMAL constants. Remember that when you widen an interface to full screen, you have to make sure that the various elements in your user interface aren't distorted by the enlargement. To avoid this, you must set the scaling of the stage so that you don't deform the elements it contains.

The classes delegated for alignment and scaling are StageAlign, StageScaleMode, and StageDisplayState.

The following example will show you how to maximize your application.

Create your Flash file in AIR and save it as FullScreenWin.fla. Create a new ActionScript file and save it as FullScreen.as in the following directory: com.comtaste.foed. essentialair.chapter05.

Begin writing your code within the FullScreen.as class:

```
package com.comtaste.foed.essentialair.chapter05{
    import flash.display.MovieClip;
    import flash.display.StageAlign;
    import flash.display.StageScaleMode;
    import flash.display.StageDisplayState;
    import flash.events.MouseEvent;
    import flash.text.TextField;
    import flash.events.Event;
```

In this part, as usual, import the classes you need:

```
public class FullScreen extends MovieClip{

    public var fullScreen_mc:MovieClip=new MovieClip();
    public var stopFullScreen_mc:MovieClip=new MovieClip();
    public var textLabel:TextField=new TextField();
    public var toolTip:TextField=new TextField();
```

The properties typed as MovieClip objects (fullScreen_mc and stopFullScreen_mc) will control the two buttons to activate and deactivate full-screen mode.

The textLabel TextField property gives the application focus and makes it active. The toolTip property, as its name suggests, will act as a tooltip when the user moves the mouse over the buttons.

Now proceed with the class constructor:

```
public function FullScreen():void{
    stage.align=StageAlign.TOP_LEFT;
    stage.scaleMode=StageScaleMode.NO_SCALE;
    stage.addEventListener(Event.ENTER_FRAME, checkStatus);
    drawButton(fullScreen_mc);
    drawButton(stopFullScreen_mc);
    writeText(textLabel);
    writeText(toolTip);
    toolTip.visible=false;
    fullScreen_mc.x=0;
    stopFullScreen_mc.x=fullScreen_mc.width+10;
    textLabel.y=0;

    with(fullScreen_mc){
        addEventListener(MouseEvent.CLICK, putFullScreen);
        addEventListener(MouseEvent.ROLL_OVER, rollOverMe);
        addEventListener(MouseEvent.ROLL_OUT, rollOutMe);
    }
```

```
        with(stopFullScreen_mc){
            addEventListener(MouseEvent.CLICK, stopFullScreen);
            addEventListener(MouseEvent.ROLL_OVER, rollOverMe);
            addEventListener(MouseEvent.ROLL_OUT, rollOutMe);
        }
    }
```

Until here there is nothing new, except for the ENTER_FRAME event, which allows you to check the StageDisplayState as soon as you see it. The drawButton() and writeText() methods deal with the look and feel of the buttons and text fields (textLabel and toolTip), in which you will write the instructions about the status of the window.

The textLabel and toolTip properties will handle with the rollover and rollout effects of the buttons themselves:

```
public function rollOverMe(event:MouseEvent):void
{
    toolTip.visible=true;
    switch(event.currentTarget){
        case stopFullScreen_mc:
        toolTip.htmlText="<b>End Full Screen Mode</b>";
        break;
        case fullScreen_mc:
        toolTip.htmlText="<b> Full Screen Mode</b>";
        break;
    }
}

public function rollOutMe(event:MouseEvent):void
{
    toolTip.text="";
    toolTip.visible=false;
}

public function drawButton(obj:MovieClip):void
{
    with(obj.graphics){
        beginFill(0xFF0000, 1);
        drawRect(0, 50, 120, 30);
        endFill();
    }
    addChild(obj);
    obj.buttonMode=true;
}

public function writeText(obj:TextField):void
{
    obj.autoSize="left";
    obj.border=true;
    obj.background=true;
```

5

```
            obj.backgroundColor=0xCCFF99;
            addChild(obj);
        }
```

The previous code is exclusively dedicated to the creation of the user interface elements of the AIR application.

Now move on to the most interesting part—how to control the window in its two modes:

```
        public function putFullScreen(event:MouseEvent):void
        {
            stage.displayState=StageDisplayState.FULL_SCREEN;
            textLabel.htmlText="The AIR application is in <b> ➥
            Full Screen Mode </b>. ➥
            Press the other button or press ➥
            <b>ESC </b>button to escape";
        }
        public function stopFullScreen(event:MouseEvent):void
        {
            stage.displayState=StageDisplayState.NORMAL;
            textLabel.text="";
        }
```

The StageDisplayState class, through its two constants, FULL_SCREEN and NORMAL, allows users to control the two view states of the application. These instructions are set up in the displayState property.

Now finish the class by adding the following code:

```
        public function checkStatus(event:Event):void
        {
            if(stage.displayState==StageDisplayState.NORMAL){
            textLabel.htmlText="The AIR application is in <b>Normal➥
        Screen Mode</b>. Press the first button for Full Screen Mode";
            }
          toolTip.x=mouseX+20;
          toolTip.y=mouseY+20;
          }
        }
    }
```

Through the Event class, you can constantly monitor the StageDisplayState and place the mouse next to your dynamic toolTip text field.

Save your file and come back to the Flash document, FullScreenWin.fla. Now, in the Properties panel, enter the name and the path of the ActionScript file you've created—com.comtaste.foed.essentialair.chapter05.FullScreen—in the Class box. Save your Flash file and test your video. Click the first button to activate full-screen mode. The result should be similar to that illustrated in Figure 5-11.

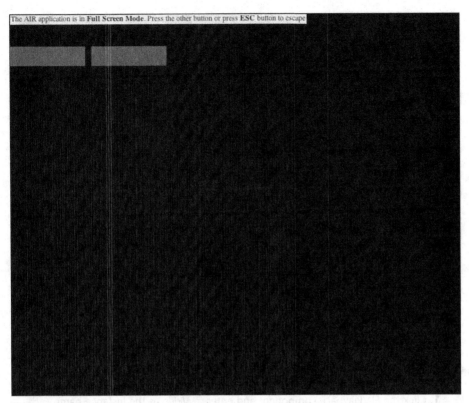

The AIR application is in **Full Screen Mode**. Press the other button or press **ESC** button to escape

Figure 5-11. The window in full-screen mode

Remember, things change if you use the FLVPlayback video component in an AIR application. First of all, you have to obtain a Flash video file in FLV format.

Open FullScreenWin.fla in Flash CS4 and follow these steps:

1. Open the Components panel.

2. Insert an instance of the FLVPlayback component and name it myVideo.

3. Open the Component Inspector (Window ➤ Component Inspector).

4. Insert the path of the relevant FLV file in the source field.

5. Save your Flash file again and retest your application.

As soon as you click the fullScreen_mc button, you will notice how the video component covers the entire screen. All you have to do to exit full-screen mode is press Esc. The final result should look like Figure 5-12.

Figure 5-12. The window in full-screen mode, with a FLVPlayBack video component

In the case you prefer that the FLVPlayback component doesn't cover the entire area, you can set its scaleMode property. To do so, open the FullScreen.fla Flash document and follow these steps:

1. Click the FLVPlayback component and enter myVideo as the instance name.

2. Return to the ActionScript file FullScreen.as.

3. Change the putFullScreen() method to the following:

```
public function putFullScreen(event:MouseEvent):void
{
    stage.displayState=StageDisplayState.FULL_SCREEN;
    myVideo.scaleMode= VideoScaleMode.NO_SCALE;
    textLabel.htmlText="The AIR application is in <b>➥
    Full Screen Mode </b>. Press the other button or ➥
     press <b>ESC </b>button to escape";
}
```

Now the video won't cover the entire area of the stage, leaving the width and height of the FLVPlayback component unchanged.

In the next sections, you will see the last two important aspects of managing windows: working with multiple screens and managing taskbar icons.

Working with multiple screens

When designing AIR projects, you should keep in mind that some users use several monitors on the same computer. You can set up and control this in ActionScript 3 and AIR using the Screen class. You can use this class to check how many monitors the user is using, and which one you want to use for displaying your application in.

Screens, in ActionScript 3, are considered rectangles on a virtual desktop. Each monitor that is connected to a computer is actually a rectangular area on the virtual desktop itself.

> You will need to test the examples in this section on a computer that is using more than one monitor.

The following example shows you how to make an application return the coordinates of your monitor in a dynamic text field on the stage of your AIR application.

Begin your new example by creating a new Flash file, and save it as MyScreen.fla. Create a new ActionScript file called MyScreen.as and save it in the following directory: com/comtaste/foed/essentialair/chapter05.

As usual, begin the code of the MyScreen.as class by importing the ActionScript classes you need:

```
package com.comtaste.foed.essentialair.chapter05{

    import flash.display.Screen;
    import flash.display.StageAlign;
    import flash.display.StageScaleMode;
    import flash.display.MovieClip;
    import flash.display.NativeWindow;
    import flash.text.TextField;
    import flash.text.TextFieldAutoSize;
    import flash.events.Event;
```

Proceed with the code for the class constructor:

```
public class MyScreen extends MovieClip{

    public var labelText:TextField= new TextField();

    public function MyScreen():void
    {
        addChild(labelText);
        stage.align = StageAlign.TOP_LEFT;
        stage.scaleMode = StageScaleMode.NO_SCALE;
        stage.addEventListener(Event.ENTER_FRAME, showMeasure);
        labelText.autoSize=TextFieldAutoSize.LEFT;
        labelText.background=true;
```

5

```
labelText.border=true;
labelText.backgroundColor=0xFFAACC;

function showMeasure(event:Event):void
{
    var screens:Array = Screen.getScreensForRectangle➡
    (stage.nativeWindow.bounds);
    labelText.text=String(screens[0].bounds);
}
            }
        }
    }
```

You have inserted a TextField object (labelText) where the application will write the various measurements of the monitor contained in the screen's Array property, and the coordinates of the monitor. These measurements are registered in the getScreensForRectangle() method. This method identifies the boundaries (coordinates, width, and height) of the primary monitor. By inserting these values in the showMeasure() function, you can make the application return the actual measurements of your monitor in real time, as well as the x and y position of the monitor itself.

> The coordinates of any additional monitors are also given in x and y coordinates in relation to the main monitor.

In the preceding code, you've also avoided the deformation of the objects on the stage by setting the scaleMode property to StageScaleMode.NO_SCALE.

The monitor coordinates are provided by the getScreensForRectangle() method in the showMeasure() method.

Save the ActionScript file, and go back to the MyScreen.fla Flash file. In the Properties panel, enter the name and the path of the ActionScript file—com.comtaste.foed. essentialair.chapter05.MyScreen—in the Class box.

Save your Flash file and test your movie. During the execution of your project, move the window of your AIR application in the second monitor. The result is shown in Figure 5-13.

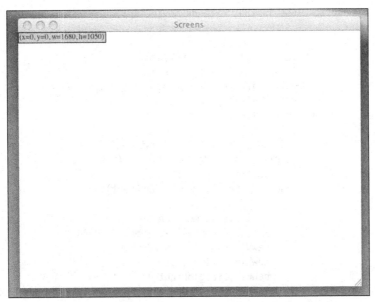

Figure 5-13. The window displays the values of the monitor on which you are viewing your application.

Managing taskbar icons

In your AIR project, you can control the icons of your application using ActionScript. In the following example, you'll learn how to work with the Windows taskbar using status notifications (highlighting), which is a typical way that an application sends a notification to the user.

Begin your new example by creating a Flash file in AIR, and save it as TaskBar.fla. Create a new ActionScript file, and save it as TaskBar.as in the following directory: com/comtaste/foed/essentialair/chapter05.

Insert the following code in the ActionScript file:

```
package com.comtaste.foed.essentialair.chapter05{

    import flash.display.MovieClip;
    import flash.desktop.NotificationType;
    import flash.display.NativeWindow;
    import flash.display.NativeWindowInitOptions;
    import flash.display.NativeWindowSystemChrome;
    import flash.events.MouseEvent;
```

```
public class TaskBar extends MovieClip
{

    public var mainWin:NativeWindow;
    public var newWin:NativeWindow;
    public var initOp:NativeWindowInitOptions=new➡
    NativeWindowInitOptions();
    public function TaskBar():void
    {
        mainWin=this.stage.nativeWindow;
        mainWin.stage.addEventListener(MouseEvent.CLICK, showIt);
        mainWin.title="MY TASKBAR";
        function showIt(event:MouseEvent):void
        {
            initOp.systemChrome =➡
            NativeWindowSystemChrome.STANDARD;
            newWin=new NativeWindow(initOp);
            newWin.activate();
            newWin.orderToFront();
            mainWin.notifyUser(NotificationType.INFORMATIONAL);
        }
    }
}
```

The most interesting part of the previous code concerns the notifyUser() method. This method allow you to send the notification to the system taskbar through the INFORMATIONAL constant of the NotificationType class.

Save the ActionScript file and go back to the Flash file (TaskBar.fla). In the Properties panel, enter the name of the ActionScript file—com.comtaste.foed.essentialair. chapter05.TaskBar—in the Class box. Save your Flash file and test your video. As you will notice, as soon as you click the main window, a new system window will open in the foreground (thanks to the orderToFront() method). Then the icon of the main window (MY TASKBAR) will turn orange (only for Windows users).

Managing windows without taskbar icons

Working with native windows and screens, it is also possible to create windows that aren't displayed on the Windows taskbar or on the Mac dock bar. The LIGHTWEIGHT constant of the NativeWindowType class, which you've already seen in the previous text editor example, allows you to do just that. Creating a window that doesn't appear on the taskbar can be useful, for example, if you want the window to appear only for alert messages. The following example will show you how to do this.

Begin your new example by creating a Flash file in AIR, and save it as Lightweight.fla. Create a new ActionScript file, and save it as Lightweight.as in the following directory: com/comtaste/foed/essentialair/chapter05.

Write the following code in the ActionScript file:

```
package com.comtaste.foed.essentialair.chapter05{

    import flash.display.MovieClip;
    import flash.events.MouseEvent;
    import flash.display.NativeWindow;
    import flash.display.NativeWindowInitOptions;
    import flash.display.NativeWindowType;
    import flash.display.NativeWindowSystemChrome;

    public class Lightweight extends MovieClip{

        public var openButton:MovieClip=new MovieClip();
        public var newWin:NativeWindow;
        public function Lightweight():void{

            drawButton(openButton);
            openButton.addEventListener(MouseEvent.CLICK, createWin);
        }

        private function drawButton(obj:MovieClip):void
        {
            with(obj.graphics){
                beginFill(0xFFEE11, 1);
                drawRect(0,0,100,30);
                endFill();
            }
            this.addChild(obj);
        }

        private function createWin(event:MouseEvent):void
        {
            if(!newWin){
                var initOptions:NativeWindowInitOptions=new➡
                NativeWindowInitOptions();
                initOptions.transparent=false;
                initOptions.systemChrome=NativeWindowSystemChrome.NONE;
                initOptions.type=NativeWindowType.LIGHTWEIGHT;
                newWin=new NativeWindow(initOptions);
                newWin.activate();
                newWin.alwaysInFront=true;
                newWin.width=300;
                newWin.height=100;
                newWin.x=200;
                newWin.y=100;
                newWin.stage.addEventListener(MouseEvent.CLICK, ➡
                closeWin);
            }
        }
```

5

```
            private function closeWin(event:MouseEvent):void
            {
                  newWin.close();
            }
      }
}
```

The most interesting part of this code is the use of the type property of the NativeWindowInitOptions. If it is set to LIGHTWEIGHT or UTILITY, like in this case, it will create a system window that isn't displayed in the taskbar.

The LIGHTWEIGHT value is a particular system window that doesn't include the system chrome, like all the other application windows. It only includes one window background (white by default).

Now save the Lightweight.as file. Return to your Flash file (Lightweight.fla) and enter the name and path of the ActionScript file—com.comtaste.foed.essentialair. chapter05.Lightweight—in the Class box in the Properties panel. Then save the Flash file and test your application.

As you will notice, as soon as you click the yellow square on the stage, the new window will appear on the screen, but not in the taskbar. To close the lightweight window, just click it.

Figure 5-14 shows the taskbar before you click, and Figure 5-15 shows it after you click.

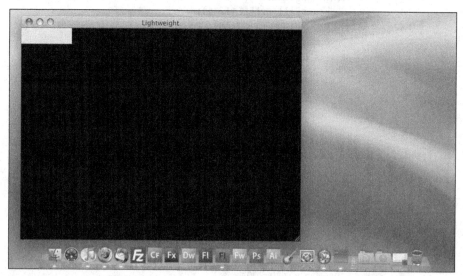

Figure 5-14. The new window before you click the button

Figure 5-15. The new window doesn't appear in the system taskbar after you click the button.

Summary

In this chapter, you have learned how to handle the main features of windows in AIR applications using the classes of the windows APIs contained in the flash.display package.

Through the exercises shown in this chapter, you've seen how to manage the native window classes. In particular, you've learned how to do the following:

- Generate and manage the system chrome with ActionScript
- Create animations with the system windows
- Insert content in the new system windows
- Manage native window classes in AIR applications
- Use the Screen class for multiple screens
- Create normal, utility, and lightweight windows

CHAPTER 6

CREATING MENUS FOR FLASH APPLICATIONS

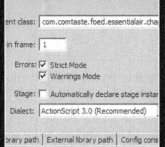

Menus are an integral part of your life as a software user. You find them on the Web, in desktop applications, on your own operating system, and even on mobile devices like cell phones and personal digital assistants (PDAs). You often don't realize how important menus are when you use them. It's so obvious to have them that you only realize how important they are when they aren't available.

On the Web, you normally have menus regarding the browser, which allow you to access the content of the site you are using. You rarely have menus that give you access to the specific commands and functions of the website. However, things are changing slowly with the advent of Web 2.0 applications, and menus—not only browsing menus but those specifically related to the web application—are becoming more and more frequent.

As Flash web developers, you have the following options to create menus for your applications:

- Adding items to the context menu provided by Flash Player
- Creating your own menus

Both options work very well, but the option of using Flash Player's context menu doesn't give you much flexibility. The other option requires a substantial amount of time and effort to obtain valid results if you create the menus for your web application from scratch.

When you develop Adobe AIR applications with Flash CS4, you don't need to worry about how to offer advanced functions with a menu. The framework itself provides various solutions to choose from according to your needs. AIR implements two new classes that aren't available for Flash Player in a web environment in the flash.display package:

- NativeMenu
- NativeMenuItem

These classes allow you to create native system menus to use as application menus (on Mac OS X systems), window menus (on Windows systems), pop-up menus, and context menus. The native menu classes are an addition to the following classes that are already available to create personalized context menus:

- ContextMenu
- ContextMenuItem

The native menu classes provide more flexibility than the traditional classes for context menus. This chapter will provide information on the options you have to create menus for your applications.

We'll begin with a tour of the various types of menus that you can use for your AIR applications.

Introducing the menu types

This section provides an overview of the following types of menus:

- Window menus (Microsoft Windows systems)
- Application menus (Mac OS X systems)
- System tray and dock icon menus
- Context menus
- Pop-up menus

Window menus

Window menus are associated with a specific window of the application and are placed just under the title bar. As mentioned, this type of menu is only available on Microsoft Windows systems. Window menus can only be displayed if the window they are associated with implements standard system chrome; they can't be displayed on windows with custom chrome.

You can assign a different menu to each window of your application. You can add a menu to a window by assigning an instance of the NativeMenu class to the menu property. This property is displayed by the NativeWindow class, from which AIR application windows derive. To check if the operating system where your application is running supports window menus, you have to check the static supportsMenu property of the NativeWindow class.

> Window menus can't contain commands as top-level items; only submenus.

Application menus

Application menus are associated with the entire AIR application. They aren't displayed in a single window, but are placed at the top of the desktop. This type of menu is only available for Mac OS X systems. While window menus don't exist for a given window until you create them, application menus, on the other hand, are always created by AIR's runtime for the executing application.

The automatically created menu contains the standard commands such as open, close, copy, and paste, and you can add or remove commands and items from the default menu as you prefer, or overwrite it completely. If you decide to maintain the default menu, you can register event listener functions on the items that are already there, so you'll have full control over the operations that are associated with each command on the menu.

> Application menus, like window menus, can't contain actions as top-level items; only submenus.

System tray and dock icon menus

These menus are associated with the icons in the system tray or the dock bar, depending on the operating system. They are displayed when the user right-clicks the icon. Microsoft Windows systems don't have any default menus associated with the icons in the system tray. Mac OS X systems implement a default menu, which, contrary to the application menu, can't be edited or removed. The menu you create for the dock icon is placed above the default menu. It isn't even possible to register event listener functions for the default items in a dock icon menu.

Context menus

A **context menu** is a menu that appears when you right-click on Microsoft Windows systems, and when you Ctrl-click on Mac OS X. A context menu can be associated with any instance of an object that derives from the InteractiveObject class, so you can have as many context menus as you need for your application.

In a traditional Flash application for the Web, Flash Player automatically generates a context menu containing items that you can't remove. In an AIR application, there isn't any default menu, but you can create one if necessary.

You can create context menus by using either the NativeMenu class provided by AIR or the ContextMenu provided by Flash Player.

Pop-up menus

These menus share the same functions as context menus, but they aren't associated with right-clicks or Ctrl-clicks on a specific object. These menus, once they've been created, can be displayed anywhere on the stage of your application. They can appear both as a response to an event generated by the user or from the execution of ActionScript code.

Obviously, these are types of menus that are available if you are using AIR's built-in APIs. No one stops you from creating menus that are graphically or functionally different to satisfy the aesthetic or functional needs of your application. If you create your own menus, you simply choose not to use the built-in menus provided by AIR.

> It's important to remember that the built-in menus provided by AIR with the NativeMenu and ContextMenu classes are rendered outside of your application. Any custom menus you create are rendered inside the running application.

The next section will discuss the internal structure of native menu objects in more depth.

Examining the structure and elements of a native menu

Menus are hierarchical structures: they have a root, and in the case of native menus, they are represented by an instance of the NativeMenu class. A menu is a series of nodes that can be commands or, in turn, menus themselves. Any node is represented by instances of the NativeMenuItem class. When a command is selected, it generates an event, which conveys the information regarding the element of the relevant menu. This event is conveyed as an instance of the flash.events.Event class.

Recall that application and window menus can't contain commands as top-level elements. Therefore all the instances of the NativeMenuItem class that are top-level nodes contain instances of the NativeMenu class to define the submenus.

It's possible to associate the following types of information to each instance of the NativeMenuItem class:

- **The** name **property**: A single and unique identification that won't be displayed
- **The** label **property**: A text label that will be displayed in the menu
- **The** data **property**: An object of any kind, containing information regarding the selected item on the menu

In addition to the selection event, the elements of the menu also generate a display event. The display event is generated a moment before a drop-down menu is rendered by Flash Player. This event allows you to update the content of the menu before it is displayed. You can register the display event both on the instance of the NativeMenu class that contains the menu and one of its items.

A good example of how to use the display event is in a menu that lists the recent web pages that the user has visited. Each time the user accesses the list, the application regenerates the list by checking which pages have been visited lately. It is also possible to use the display event to disable or hide the items on the menu when necessary. You might want to do this if the user doesn't have the necessary privileges to access some of the functions of your application.

Creating a native menu

When you work on native menus in AIR, you always deal with instances of the NativeMenu class.

To create a native menu, start up Flash CS4 and open the AIR ch06p01.fla project. The project has been set up so that it doesn't automatically declare the variables of the elements on the screen. This option is defined by the Automatically declare stage instances check box in the Advanced ActionScript 3.0 Settings panel, which can be reached through the Publish Settings panel (see Figure 6-1).

6

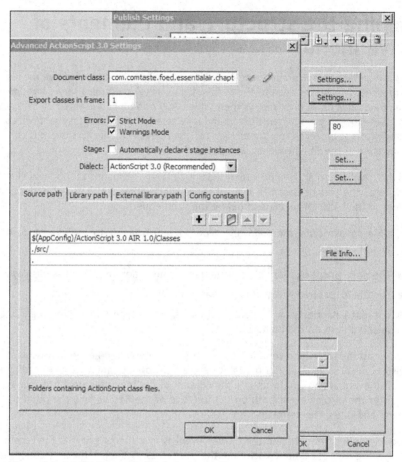

Figure 6-1. Set the Automatically declare stage instances property in the Advanced ActionScript 3.0 Settings panel.

Two objects have been set up on the stage of the project, as you can see in Figure 6-2:

- The custom menu button, which has the instance name button, provided by the Button component

- A TextArea with the instance name output, provided by the TextArea component

The menu created as a native context menu will be associated with the button, whereas the TextArea will act as an output console for the application.

The project document class is the com.comtaste.foed.essentialair.chapter6.Ch06p01 class. Click the Edit class definition icon (which looks like a pencil) in the Publish section of the Document Properties panel to open it.

If you don't want to use the class from the Chapter06 folder, you can create a new ActionScript class and save it as Ch06p01.as.

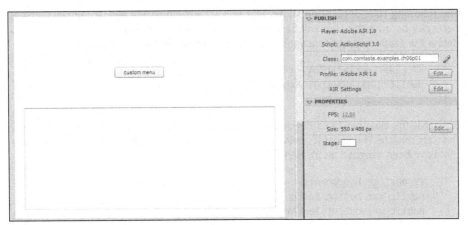

Figure 6-2. The stage of the ch06p01.fla project

The class creates a native menu and associates it with the custom menu button with the instance name button as a context menu on the stage. To create a menu object, you have to create an instance of the NativeMenu class, like this:

```
var menu:NativeMenu = new NativeMenu();
```

To populate the native menu with some elements, you can use the following addItem() and addSubMenu() functions, which respectively allow you to add commands and sub-menus to the native menu:

```
// add a NativeMenuItem to native menu
menu.addItem( new NativeMenuItem( "menu element" ) );

// add a submenu to native menu
menu.addSubMenu( new NativeMenu(), "submenu element" );
```

Following is the code of the Ch06p01.as class. Notice the details: as you may already know, the class defines the package it belongs to. Then it declares all the classes it has to import to make the ActionScript code work properly:

```
package com.comtaste.foed.essentialair.chapter6
{
import fl.controls.Button;
import fl.controls.TextArea;

import flash.display.MovieClip;
import flash.display.NativeMenu;
import flash.display.NativeMenuItem;
import flash.events.Event;
import flash.filesystem.File;
```

Among others, the NativeMenu and NativeMenuItem classes are imported, from the flash. display package, making it possible to create and use the native menus.

6

The following class declaration shows that you are extending the MovieClip class. This is necessary because the class will be associated with the Flash project and therefore has to define the properties and functions it needs to be rendered by Flash Player.

```
// class declaration
public class Ch06p01 extends MovieClip
{
```

Now that the class has been defined, you can declare the variables that the elements of the class can use. The variables have to include all the instances of the objects on the stage that have been assigned an ID. Here's the code:

```
// onstage components
public var button:Button;
public var output:TextArea;

// class properties
private var menuRoot:NativeMenu;
```

The menuRoot variable will contain the native menu that will be associated with the button button. The menu will be created and associated with the button in the constructor method of the class.

The **constructor method** of a class is a method with the same name as the class. Flash Player executes this method automatically each time an instance of the class is created. That's why it's called a constructor method. Its purpose is to allow the initialization of the elements and the functions the class needs to make the class work. This method doesn't have a return type, as it can't be used arbitrarily. It can only be launched when the class is instantiated. Also note that the constructor method must be public in ActionScript 3.

Here's an example of how to use the menuRoot variable:

```
// class constructor
public function Ch06p01()
{
    // call super class constructor
    super();
        // generate native menu to use
    createNativeMenu();
        // assign menu to right-click on button
    button.contextMenu = menuRoot;
}
```

Next, launch the createNativeMenu() method in the class constructor. This method is in charge of instantiating and populating the native menu. Then you assign the menuRoot variable, which contains your native menu, to the contextMenu property of the component of the Button class. Assign an instance of a native menu to this property. Doing so tells Flash Player that the relevant menu should be displayed on the button when the user right-clicks (on Windows) or Ctrl-clicks (on the Mac).

To create the native menu, the createNativeMenu() method executes the following instructions:

```
// create a complete native menu
private function createNativeMenu():void
{
```

An instance of the NativeMenu class is assigned to the menuRoot variable as follows:

```
// instantiate main menu object
menuRoot = new NativeMenu();
```

Then two submenus are added to the native menu you've just created. The two following functions have been prepared to generate the submenus:

```
createFirstSubMenu()
createSecondSubMenu()
```

These functions are in charge of creating the submenus and returning the instances. Here's the code:

```
// append subMenus to menu root
menuRoot.addItem( createFirstSubMenu() );
menuRoot.addItem( createSecondSubMenu() );
}
```

The context menu that you want to create will have the structure shown in Figure 6-3.

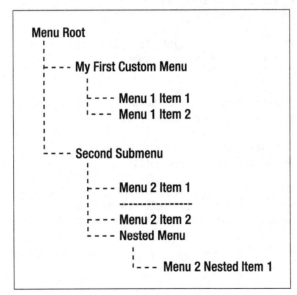

Figure 6-3. Graphical representation of the menu's structure

This is the complete ActionScript class that you have created:

```
package com.comtaste.foed.essentialair.chapter6
{
import fl.controls.Button;
import fl.controls.TextArea;

import flash.display.MovieClip;
import flash.display.NativeMenu;
import flash.display.NativeMenuItem;
import flash.events.Event;
import flash.filesystem.File;

public class Ch06p01 extends MovieClip
{
    // onstage components
    public var button:Button;
    public var output:TextArea;

    // class properties
    private var menuRoot:NativeMenu;

    public function Ch06p01()
    {
        super();

        // generate native menu to use
        createNativeMenu();

        // assign menu to right-click on button
        button.contextMenu = menuRoot;
    }

    // create a complete native menu
    private function createNativeMenu():void
    {
        // instantiate main menu object
        menuRoot = new NativeMenu();

        // append subMenus to menu root
        menuRoot.addItem( createFirstSubMenu() );
        menuRoot.addItem( createSecondSubMenu() );
    }
}
}
```

Creating submenus for a native menu

To create a submenu item, you use the NativeMenuItem class. Begin by opening the Ch06p01.as class and add the createFirstSubMenu() method, which creates an item of the NativeMenuItem class and adds two elements. This item will be used as a first submenu of the native menu you're creating. Here's the code:

```
private function createFirstSubMenu():NativeMenuItem
{
```

Next, create an instance of the NativeMenuItem class by showing the label that it needs to be associated with. Assign an instance of the NativeMenu class to the submenu property of the element you've just created. The native menu object associated with the submenu property will contain the subitems you'll create for this element of the menu.

```
// create first submenu
var subMenu:NativeMenuItem =
 new NativeMenuItem( "My first custom submenu" );
    // initialize child container
subMenu.submenu = new NativeMenu();
```

Follow these steps to define the elements that will be displayed as children of the element of the menu you've just created:

1. Instantiate an object of the NativeMenuItem class by giving the constructor a label for the element.

2. Register an event listener method for the SELECT event (Event.SELECT). Each time the user selects this element from the menu, the menuItemSelected() method will be executed.

3. Finally, add the element of the menu you've created to the submenu property of the submenu you're creating with the addItem() method of the NativeMenuItem class. Here's the code:

```
// create first submenu child
var subMenuItem1:NativeMenuItem =
new NativeMenuItem( "menu 1 item 1" );
// register event listener for menu item
subMenuItem1.addEventListener( Event.SELECT, menuItemSelected );
// add item to submenu
subMenu.submenu.addItem( subMenuItem1 );
```

Create a second object of the NativeMenuItem class. Then register the selection event of the element to the menuItemSelected() method. Finally, add the element to the submenu you're creating. Here's the code:

```
// create a second child, register event listener for
// selection event and assign to submenu
var subMenuItem2:NativeMenuItem =
new NativeMenuItem( "menu 1 item 2" );
subMenuItem2.addEventListener( Event.SELECT, menuItemSelected );
subMenu.submenu.addItem( subMenuItem2 );
```

6

Next, return the menu you've created so that it can be added as a child of the main context menu.

```
        return subMenu;
    }
```

The first submenu has been created and is ready to use. Before testing your application, you have to define the createSecondSubMenu() method, which will deal with initializing the second submenu of the context menu you're creating. The following sequence of operations to execute is very similar to the procedure to create the first submenu:

1. Create an object of the NativeMenuItem class.

2. Assign an instance of the NativeMenu class to its submenu property.

3. Populate the submenu object with the elements you like.

This menu will also have a submenu and will contain an element separator. For each item on the menu, you will have to register a selection event on the menuItemSelected() event listener method. Here's the code:

```
    private function createSecondSubMenu():NativeMenuItem
    {
        // create first submenu
        var subMenu:NativeMenuItem =
        new NativeMenuItem( "Second submenu" );
        // initialize child container
        subMenu.submenu = new NativeMenu();
        // create first submenu child
        var subMenuItem1:NativeMenuItem =
         new NativeMenuItem( "menu 2 item 1" );
        // register event listener for menu item
        subMenuItem1.addEventListener( Event.SELECT, menuItemSelected );
        // add item to submenu
        subMenu.submenu.addItem( subMenuItem1 );
```

Creating element separators

The element separators in a native menu are in turn instances of the NativeMenuItem class. The separators display a horizontal line instead of a text label. The line shows the border between different groups of elements. To create an element separator, you instantiate an object of the NativeMenuItem class, providing it with a Boolean value (true) as a second argument. This second argument is false by default, and tells the object that it has to ignore the text label property and show a separator line.

Now create an element separator and add it to the menu, under the first element you created previously:

```
        // add a separator item
        // label will be ignored for separator items
        var subMenuSeparator:NativeMenuItem =
         new NativeMenuItem( "", true );
```

```
// add separator to menu
subMenu.submenu.addItem( subMenuSeparator );
```

Adding items to the submenu

After the element separator, you create and add a new item to the submenu. Then you create and add an element that will contain another submenu. To populate the internal submenu, populate the submenu property of a native element of the menu with the necessary items. Here's the code:

```
// create a second child, register event listener for
// selection event and assign to submenu
var subMenuItem2:NativeMenuItem =
        new NativeMenuItem( "menu 2 item 2" );
subMenuItem2.addEventListener( Event.SELECT, menuItemSelected );
subMenu.submenu.addItem( subMenuItem2 );
// create a new item as an internal submenu
// using addSubmenu command
var childSubMenu:NativeMenuItem =
    subMenu.submenu.addSubmenu( new NativeMenu(), "Nested menu" );
// initialize child container
childSubMenu.submenu = new NativeMenu();
// create a child, register event listener for
// selection event and assign to internal submenu
var subMenuItem3:NativeMenuItem =
        new NativeMenuItem( "menu 2 nested item 1" );
subMenuItem3.addEventListener( Event.SELECT, menuItemSelected );
childSubMenu.submenu.addItem( subMenuItem3 );
        return subMenu;
}
```

Using the menuItemSelected() method

Next, you'll employ the menuItemSelected() method, which will be launched each time the user selects one of the items on the context menu. When a selection event is generated, the event listener method receives an instance of the flash.events.Event class as an argument. The selection events are transmitted by the selected element on the menu, through the hierarchical structure of the menu, to the root element.

The object received as an argument has the two following properties:

- target
- currentTarget

If the event has been registered directly on the elements of the menu (like in this case), the two properties will have the same value. In this case, both properties refer to the instance of the selected NativeMenuItem class. However, if the event is registered on the root menu or on one of the roots of the submenus, the target property of the received event object will always refer to the selected element. The currentTarget property will always refer to the object the event is registered on.

When an item is selected, the `menuItemSelected()` method writes the label of the selected element in the `TextArea`, which acts as a text output console. Here's the code:

```
// called on click on menu items
private function menuItemSelected( evt : Event ):void
{
    // access NativeMenuItem instance selected
    var item:NativeMenuItem = evt.target as NativeMenuItem;
    // write in the textarea selected item's label
    output.appendText( "CLICKED ON: " + item.label + File.lineEnding );
}
```

Displaying the code for the native submenus

This is the complete Ch06p01.as class that you have created:

```
package com.comtaste.foed.essentialair.chapter6
{
import fl.controls.Button;
import fl.controls.TextArea;

import flash.display.MovieClip;
import flash.display.NativeMenu;
import flash.display.NativeMenuItem;
import flash.events.Event;
import flash.filesystem.File;

public class Ch06p01 extends MovieClip
{
    // onstage components
    public var button:Button;
    public var output:TextArea;

    // class properties
    private var menuRoot:NativeMenu;

    public function Ch06p01()
    {
        super();

        // generate native menu to use
        createNativeMenu();

        // assign menu to right-click on button
        button.contextMenu = menuRoot;
    }

    // create a complete native menu
    private function createNativeMenu():void
    {
```

```
        // instantiate main menu object
        menuRoot = new NativeMenu();

        // append subMenus to menu root
        menuRoot.addItem( createFirstSubMenu() );
        menuRoot.addItem( createSecondSubMenu() );
    }

    private function createFirstSubMenu():NativeMenuItem
    {
        // create first submenu
        var subMenu:NativeMenuItem =
        new NativeMenuItem( "My first custom submenu" );

        // initialize child container
        subMenu.submenu = new NativeMenu();

        // create first submenu child
        var subMenuItem1:NativeMenuItem =
        new NativeMenuItem( "menu 1 item 1" );

        // register event listener for menu item
        subMenuItem1.addEventListener( Event.SELECT,

menuItemSelected );

        // add item to submenu
        subMenu.submenu.addItem( subMenuItem1 );

        // create a second child, register event listener for
        // selection event and assign to submenu
        var subMenuItem2:NativeMenuItem =
                    new NativeMenuItem( "menu 1 item 2" );
        subMenuItem2.addEventListener( Event.SELECT,

menuItemSelected );
        subMenu.submenu.addItem( subMenuItem2 );

        return subMenu;
    }

    private function createSecondSubMenu():NativeMenuItem
    {
        // create first submenu
        var subMenu:NativeMenuItem =
            new NativeMenuItem( "Second submenu" );

        // initialize child container
        subMenu.submenu = new NativeMenu();
```

```
                    // create first submenu child
                    var subMenuItem1:NativeMenuItem =
                        new NativeMenuItem( "menu 2 item 1" );

                    // register event listener for menu item
                    subMenuItem1.addEventListener( Event.SELECT,

menuItemSelected );

                    // add item to submenu
                    subMenu.submenu.addItem( subMenuItem1 );

                    // add a separator item
                    // label will be ignored for separator items
                    var subMenuSeparator:NativeMenuItem =
                        new NativeMenuItem( "", true );

                    // add separator to menu
                    subMenu.submenu.addItem( subMenuSeparator );

                    // create a second child, register event listener for
                    // selection event and assign to submenu
                    var subMenuItem2:NativeMenuItem =
                        new NativeMenuItem( "menu 2 item 2" );
                    subMenuItem2.addEventListener( Event.SELECT,

menuItemSelected );
                    subMenu.submenu.addItem( subMenuItem2 );

                    // create a new item as an internal submenu
                    // using addSubmenu command
                    var childSubMenu:NativeMenuItem =
                        subMenu.submenu.addSubmenu( new NativeMenu(),

"Nested menu" );

                    // initialize child container
                    childSubMenu.submenu = new NativeMenu();

                    // create a child, register event listener for
                    // selection event and assign to internal submenu
                    var subMenuItem3:NativeMenuItem =
                        new NativeMenuItem( "menu 2 nested item 1" );
                    subMenuItem3.addEventListener( Event.SELECT,
                                                    menuItemSelected );
                    childSubMenu.submenu.addItem( subMenuItem3 );
```

```
            return subMenu;
        }



        // called on click
        private function menuItemSelected( evt : Event ):void
        {
            var item:NativeMenuItem = evt.target as NativeMenuItem;
            output.appendText( "CLICKED ON: "
                + item.label + File.lineEnding );
        }
    } // close class
} // close package
```

Testing the native menus

Now the application is ready to be tested. To test it, go back to the Flash ch06p01.fla. project. Then run the application by selecting the Test Movie command from the Flash CS4 Controls menu. Once it has been compiled and executed, right-click (or on Mac OS X systems, Ctrl-click) the button at the center of the stage. The native menu you've prepared will appear. You can see the application in Figure 6-4.

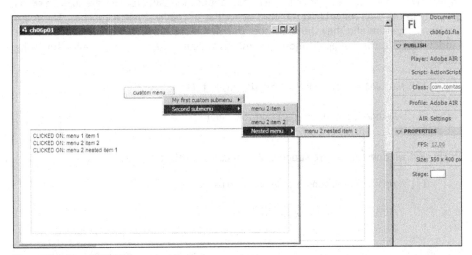

Figure 6-4. The ch06p01.fla project in Flash

Each time you select an item from the context menu, the label of the selected element will be displayed in the TextArea. In the next section, you'll learn how to use window- and application-level menus in real-world applications.

Working with application and window menus

When you interact with a desktop application, you're used to using general menus that guide you and introduce you to the functions you can choose from. For example, if you're using a word-processing program and you want to know which formats you can save the document in, you will almost definitely look for the Save as command from the File menu, without even thinking about it. Likewise, if you need to copy the selected text, you'll look for the Copy command from the Edit menu. These operations are strongly embedded in every user that has experience with modern computers. Regardless of any previous knowledge about the program you're working on, the menu bar will always be a safe haven where you can look for the commands and functions you need.

Some modern software applications have interfaces that mimic the standards of many web applications. These applications don't have traditional menus—they only provide icons in the application, and these are sometimes difficult to interpret. When users access one of these programs for the first time, they may feel disoriented, and may not even understand how to start using the application.

AIR puts users at ease by supporting a traditional menu bar that guides them through the features of your application. As mentioned at the beginning of the chapter, there are two types of menus for AIR applications: application menus (on Mac OS X systems) and window menus (on Microsoft Windows systems).

To know which type of menu you can use in your application, AIR provides the supportsMenu property in the NativeApplication class as well as in the NativeWindow class. These are Boolean properties and they show whether the menus are supported at the application or window level. To check if application-level menus are supported, you can use the following code:

```
If( NativeApplication.supportsMenu == true )
{
    // code to manage application menu
}
```

To check if window menus are supported, you can use the following:

```
If( NativeWindow.supportsMenu == true )
{
    // code to manage windows menu
}
```

The procedure to create application menus is identical to the procedure for window menus. The only thing that changes is the object you need to assign the menus to and how the end user will use them.

Creating a menu for multiple operating systems

This exercise is intended to show you how to create an application that provides its own menu bar. It's also intended to show you how to make the menu behave properly on operating systems that require application menus as well as on systems that require window menus.

Start by opening the Flash CS4 ch06p02.fla project. As you can see in Figure 6-5, the stage of your project only contains a TextArea component. Like in the previous exercise, you'll use it as a console for your messages. These messages keep track of the operations that occur during the execution of your application. The real important part of your application is the menu bar you'll create with ActionScript code.

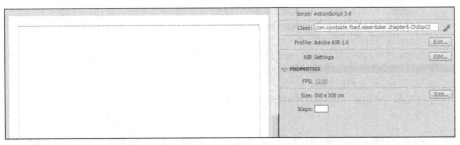

Figure 6-5. The ch06p02.fla project layout

Next, access the Ch06p02.as class, which is the document class of the project. Click the Edit class definition icon on the Document Properties panel, as shown in Figure 6-6.

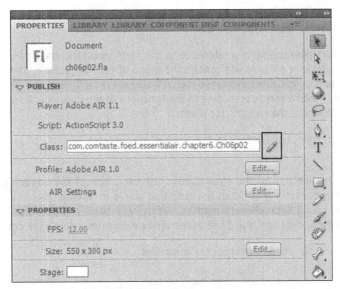

Figure 6-6. The Edit class definition icon

As usual, the class begins by defining its namespace and importing the external classes it depends on:

```
package com.comtaste.foed.essentialair.chapter6
{
// Flash CS4 specific components classes
import fl.controls.TextArea;

// Adobe AIR and ActionScript classes
import flash.desktop.NativeApplication;
import flash.display.MovieClip;
import flash.display.NativeMenu;
import flash.display.NativeMenuItem;
import flash.display.NativeWindow;
import flash.events.Event;
import flash.filesystem.File;

// class definition
public class Ch06p02 extends MovieClip
{
```

After the opening declarations of the classes, you set the variables that the whole class can use:

```
// onstage components
public var output:TextArea;

// class properties
private var menuRoot:NativeMenu;
```

The output variable represents a reference to the TextArea on the stage of the Flash CS4 project. The menuRoot variable will contain the menu of your application. The constructor method of the class initializes the native menu. It also checks if it has to be assigned to the application or window menu, according to the functions of the local operating system. The following code opens the constructor method:

```
public function Ch06p02()
{
```

The constructor method of the class invokes the execution of the **super constructor**, meaning the constructor method of the class that you're extending. Then it calls the execution of the createNativeMenu() method, which instantiates and prepares the instance of the NativeMenu class that you'll use as the application menu. Here's the code:

```
// call super constructor function
super();
    // generate native menu to use
createNativeMenu();
```

Once you've created the menu, you have to assign it to the application. First, you have to establish whether to associate it with the main window or the application.

Using application menus

To check if you can assign the menu to the application, you have to check the value of the supportsMenu variable of the NativeApplication class. If it's true, it means that you can use the application-level menus. Then you assign the menuRoot object, which is an instance of the NativeMenu class, to the menu property of the nativeApplication object of the NativeApplication class. Now the application-level menus are only available on Mac OS X operating systems. Here's the code to accomplish these tasks:

```
// assign to application menu if we are on Mac OS X
if ( NativeApplication.supportsMenu )
{
    NativeApplication.nativeApplication.menu = menuRoot;
}
```

Using window menus

To check if you can use window menus, you have to test if the value of the supportsMenu property of the NativeWindow class is true. To assign a menu object to a native window, you have to use the menu property of the nativeWindow object of the reference to the stage object owned by the window. The code is as follows:

```
// assign to window menu if we are on Microsoft Windows
if ( NativeWindow.supportsMenu )
{
    stage.nativeWindow.menu = menuRoot;          }

}
```

The constructor method invokes the createNativeMenu() method to instantiate and populate the native menu you are going to work with. This method instantiates an object of the NativeMenu class and assigns it to the menuRoot class variable, which you created previously. To populate the menu, the value returned by the createFirstSubMenu() method—which populates the native menu—is given to the addItem() method of the NativeMenu class as an argument.

```
// create a complete native menu
private function createNativeMenu():void
{
    // instantiate main menu object
    menuRoot = new NativeMenu();
        // append subMenus to menu root
    menuRoot.addItem( createFirstSubMenu() );
}
```

This is the complete Ch06p02.as class that you have created:

```
package com.comtaste.foed.essentialair.chapter6
{
import fl.controls.TextArea;
```

```
import flash.desktop.NativeApplication;
import flash.display.MovieClip;
import flash.display.NativeMenu;
import flash.display.NativeMenuItem;
import flash.display.NativeWindow;
import flash.events.Event;
import flash.filesystem.File;

public class Ch06p02 extends MovieClip
{
    // onstage components
    public var output:TextArea;

    // class properties
    private var menuRoot:NativeMenu;

    public function Ch06p02()
    {
        super();

        // generate native menu to use
        createNativeMenu();

        // assign to application menu if we are on Mac OS X
        if ( NativeApplication.supportsMenu )
        {
            NativeApplication.nativeApplication.menu = menuRoot;
        }

        // assign to window menu if we are on Microsoft Windows
        if ( NativeWindow.supportsMenu )
        {
            stage.nativeWindow.menu = menuRoot;
        }

    }

    // create a complete native menu
    private function createNativeMenu():void
    {
        // instantiate main menu object
        menuRoot = new NativeMenu();

        // append subMenus to menu root
        menuRoot.addItem( createFirstSubMenu() );
    }
}
}
```

Defining the menu and its functions

Now, let's assign the application menu to the main window or the whole application. It will only contain one item: 'App settings' to which you will associate three elements with as many commands. These three elements will be constructed in the createFirstSubMenu() method. The following ActionScript code defines the createFirstSubMenu():

```
private function createFirstSubMenu():NativeMenuItem
{
```

Start by creating a local variable, subMenu, an instance of the NativeMenuItem class, which will be the return value of the method createFirstSubMenu(). When you create the NativeMenuItem object, you tell AIR which text label it will have (App settings in the following code). This NativeMenuItem child of the application menu will be a drop-down menu that contains some commands. To add these child elements to the following instance of the NativeMenuItem class, you have to instantiate an object of the NativeMenu class. This object will then be assigned to its subMenu property. The following code accomplishes these tasks:

```
// create submenu
var subMenu:NativeMenuItem = new NativeMenuItem( "App settings" );
    // initialize child container
subMenu.submenu = new NativeMenu();
```

Next, populate the submenu you've just created with three instances of the NativeMenuItem class. Then register a different event listener method on each of them for the selection event. Remember, to create an element of the menu, you generate an instance of the NativeMenuItem class. Then you tell the constructor method which label has to be associated with the object. At that point, register an event listener method for the Event.SELECT event. Finally, add the element you've created to the submenu. Do this through the addItem() method of the instance of the NativeMenu class, which is assigned to the subMenu property of the object of the NativeMenuItem class.

```
// create first child, register event listener for
// selection event and assign to submenu
var aboutCommand:NativeMenuItem = new NativeMenuItem( "About.." );
aboutCommand.addEventListener( Event.SELECT, getInformation );
subMenu.submenu.addItem( aboutCommand );
// create second child, register event listener for
// selection event and assign to submenu
var minimizeCommand:NativeMenuItem =
    new NativeMenuItem( "Minimize" );
minimizeCommand.addEventListener( Event.SELECT,
                                    minimizeApplication );
subMenu.submenu.addItem( minimizeCommand );
// create third child, register event listener for
// selection event and assign to submenu
var closeCommand:NativeMenuItem = new NativeMenuItem( "Close" );
closeCommand.addEventListener( Event.SELECT, closeApplication );
```

6

```
            subMenu.submenu.addItem( closeCommand );
                return subMenu;
    }
```

All you have to do now is define the event listener functions you need for the selection events. Your menu will allow you to do the following:

1. Minimize the application

2. Close the application

3. Access the saved description in the XML configuration file of the AIR project

The closeApplication() method will call the immediate closure of the application and, consequently, all its open windows. To close the application, you use the exit() method of the static nativeApplication property of the NativeApplication class. The code follows:

```
// close application
private function closeApplication( e : Event ):void
{
    NativeApplication.nativeApplication.exit();
}
```

To minimize the active window of the application, you launch the minimizeApplication() method, which uses the minimize() method of the instance of the NativeWindow class. Here's the code:

```
// minimize application
private function minimizeApplication( e : Event ):void
{
    stage.nativeWindow.minimize();
}
```

This is the complete ActionScript class that you've just created:

```
package com.comtaste.foed.essentialair.chapter6
{
import fl.controls.TextArea;

import flash.desktop.NativeApplication;
import flash.display.MovieClip;
import flash.display.NativeMenu;
import flash.display.NativeMenuItem;
import flash.display.NativeWindow;
import flash.events.Event;
import flash.filesystem.File;

public class Ch06p02 extends MovieClip
{
    // onstage components
    public var output:TextArea;
```

```
// class properties
private var menuRoot:NativeMenu;

public function Ch06p02()
{
    super();

    // generate native menu to use
    createNativeMenu();

    // assign to application menu if we are on Mac OS X
    if ( NativeApplication.supportsMenu )
    {
        NativeApplication.nativeApplication.menu = menuRoot;
    }

    // assign to window menu if we are on Microsoft Windows
    if ( NativeWindow.supportsMenu )
    {
        stage.nativeWindow.menu = menuRoot;
    }

}

// create a complete native menu
private function createNativeMenu():void
{
    // instantiate main menu object
    menuRoot = new NativeMenu();

    // append subMenus to menu root
    menuRoot.addItem( createFirstSubMenu() );
}

private function createFirstSubMenu():NativeMenuItem
{
    // create submenu
    var subMenu:NativeMenuItem =
        new NativeMenuItem( "App settings" );

    // initialize child container
    subMenu.submenu = new NativeMenu();

    // create first child, register event listener for
    // selection event and assign to submenu
    var aboutCommand:NativeMenuItem =
        new NativeMenuItem( "About.." );
    aboutCommand.addEventListener( Event.SELECT, getInformation );
    subMenu.submenu.addItem( aboutCommand );
```

```
        // create second child, register event listener for
        // selection event and assign to submenu
        var minimizeCommand:NativeMenuItem =
                new NativeMenuItem( "Minimize" );
        minimizeCommand.addEventListener( Event.SELECT,
                                                minimizeApplication );
        subMenu.submenu.addItem( minimizeCommand );

        // create third child, register event listener for
        // selection event and assign to submenu
        var closeCommand:NativeMenuItem =
                new NativeMenuItem( "Close" );
        closeCommand.addEventListener( Event.SELECT,
                                                closeApplication );
        subMenu.submenu.addItem( closeCommand );

        return subMenu;
    }

    // close application
    private function closeApplication( e : Event ):void
    {
        NativeApplication.nativeApplication.exit();
    }

    // minimize application
    private function minimizeApplication( e : Event ):void
    {
        stage.nativeWindow.minimize();
    }
} // close class
} // close package
```

Accessing the XML file descriptor

Through ActionScript 3, you can access the XML document used by AIR's runtime to execute your application correctly. Flash CS4 generates the XML document in the authoring phase. In this document, you can see a lot of information regarding the application in execution. The document also includes the description of the application, if provided by the developer.

Flash CS4 provides a specific menu that allows you to create the XML configuration file of the application. You can access this menu through the Edit AIR Settings button on the Document Properties panel in the Flash project. You can see the menu in Figure 6-7. Among the various fields, there is a Description field where you can provide a description of the application that will be presented to the user when the application is being installed.

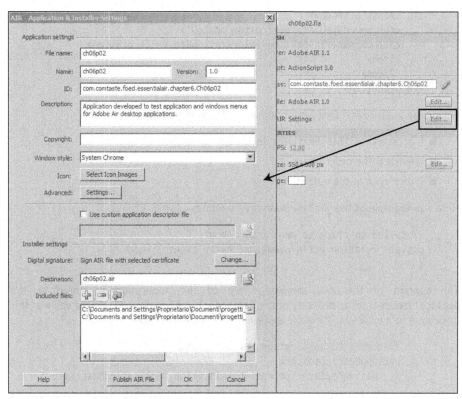

Figure 6-7. The Edit AIR Settings button

The XML document that is automatically generated by Flash CS4's menus for the ch06p02.
fla project is the following:

```
<?xml version ="1.0" encoding="utf-8" ?>
<application xmlns="http://ns.adobe.com/air/application/1.0">
    <id>com.adobe.example.ch06p02</id>
    <version>1.0</version>
    <filename>ch06p02</filename>
    <description>
        Application developed to test application
        and windows menus for Adobe Air desktop
        applications.
    </description>
    <name>ch06p02</name>
    <copyright></copyright>
    <initialWindow>
        <content>ch06p02.swf</content>
        <systemChrome>standard</systemChrome>
        <transparent>false</transparent>
        <visible>true</visible>
```

```
        </initialWindow>
        <customUpdateUI>false</customUpdateUI>
        <allowBrowserInvocation>false</allowBrowserInvocation>
        <icon>
        </icon>
    </application>
```

Calling the getInformation() method has the following effects:

- It accesses the XML descriptor document.
- It extracts the description.
- It displays it in the output TextArea.

Here's an example of the getInformation() method:

```
// called on click on menu item "About.."
private function getInformation( evt : Event ):void
{
```

The content of the XML descriptor file of the application is stored in the applicationDescriptor property of the NativeApplication class. Assign the value of this document to a local XML variable, appDescriptor, as shown here:

```
// access to application XML descriptor
var appDescriptor:XML =
    NativeApplication.nativeApplication.applicationDescriptor;
```

To be able to access the nodes of the XML document, first you have to know which XML namespace they've been defined in. You can access this information through the namespace() method of the XML class, as shown here:

```
// retrieve XML descriptor namespace
var nsDeclaration:Namespace = appDescriptor.namespace();
```

Now you have the content of the XML descriptor file of the application. You've also defined the XML namespace to access. Next, you can use the E4X syntax to extract the information you're interested in.

> E4X is a programming language extension that adds native XML support to ECMAScript (which ActionScript is based on). E4X provides a simpler syntax for accessing XML documents and treats XML as a primitive data type.

The form you use for the XML query is the following:

```
//<XML instance>.<namespace>::<node name>
    // read description node from XML
    var informationText:String =
        String( appDescriptor.nsDeclaration::description[ 0 ] );
```

Finally, write the definition extracted from the XML descriptor file of the application in the output TextArea.

To wrap the text in the TextArea, use the AIR lineEnding variable of the File class instead of the ActionScript Unicode \n sequence. This variable correctly reports the native line ending for the local operating system. This will be useful if the text gets copied and pasted into an external text document. Here's the code:

```
        // write into textare 'output' description contents
        output.appendText( "Adobe Air, test application for " +
                        "menus functionalities." + File.lineEnding );
        output.appendText( informationText + File.lineEnding );
    }
```

This is the complete ActionScript class that you've just created:

```
    package com.comtaste.foed.essentialair.chapter6
    {
    import fl.controls.TextArea;

    import flash.desktop.NativeApplication;
    import flash.display.MovieClip;
    import flash.display.NativeMenu;
    import flash.display.NativeMenuItem;
    import flash.display.NativeWindow;
    import flash.events.Event;
    import flash.filesystem.File;

    public class Ch06p02 extends MovieClip
    {
        // onstage components
        public var output:TextArea;

        // class properties
        private var menuRoot:NativeMenu;

        public function Ch06p02()
        {
            super();

            // generate native menu to use
            createNativeMenu();

            // assign to application menu if we are on Mac OS X
            if ( NativeApplication.supportsMenu )
            {
                NativeApplication.nativeApplication.menu = menuRoot;
            }
```

```
            // assign to window menu if we are on Microsoft Windows
            if ( NativeWindow.supportsMenu )
            {
                stage.nativeWindow.menu = menuRoot;
            }

    }

    // create a complete native menu
    private function createNativeMenu():void
    {
        // instantiate main menu object
        menuRoot = new NativeMenu();

        // append subMenus to menu root
        menuRoot.addItem( createFirstSubMenu() );
    }

    private function createFirstSubMenu():NativeMenuItem
    {
        // create submenu
        var subMenu:NativeMenuItem =
            new NativeMenuItem( "App settings" );

        // initialize child container
        subMenu.submenu = new NativeMenu();

        // create first child, register event listener for
        // selection event and assign to submenu
        var aboutCommand:NativeMenuItem =
            new NativeMenuItem( "About.." );
        aboutCommand.addEventListener( Event.SELECT, getInformation );
        subMenu.submenu.addItem( aboutCommand );

        // create second child, register event listener for
        // selection event and assign to submenu
        var minimizeCommand:NativeMenuItem =
            new NativeMenuItem( "Minimize" );
        minimizeCommand.addEventListener( Event.SELECT,
                                minimizeApplication );
        subMenu.submenu.addItem( minimizeCommand );

        // create third child, register event listener for
        // selection event and assign to submenu
        var closeCommand:NativeMenuItem =
            new NativeMenuItem( "Close" );
```

```
                closeCommand.addEventListener( Event.SELECT,
                                        closeApplication );
            subMenu.submenu.addItem( closeCommand );

            return subMenu;
        }


        // called on click
        private function getInformation( evt : Event ):void
        {
            var appDescriptor:XML =
                NativeApplication.nativeApplication.applicationDescriptor;
            var nsDeclaration:Namespace = appDescriptor.namespace();
            var informationText:String =
                String( appDescriptor.nsDeclaration::description[ 0 ] );
            output.appendText( "Adobe Air, test application for " +
                    + "menus functionalities." + File.lineEnding );
            output.appendText( informationText + File.lineEnding );
        }

        // close application
        private function closeApplication( e : Event ):void
        {
            NativeApplication.nativeApplication.exit();
        }

        // minimize application
        private function minimizeApplication( e : Event ):void
        {
            stage.nativeWindow.minimize();
        }
    } // close class
} // close package
```

Your application is finished and is ready to use. To do so, go back to Flash, and run the application by selecting the Test Movie command from the Control menu. If you're working in a Microsoft Windows environment, your application will use a window menu and will look like Figure 6-8. If, on the other hand, you're working in a Mac OS X environment, it will use an application menu, like all native Mac OS X applications.

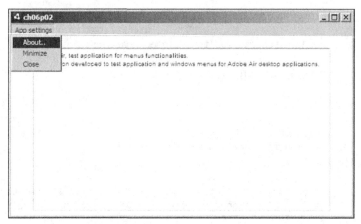

Figure 6-8. The ch06p02.fla project in execution

The next section will show you how to work with context menus in AIR applications.

Working with context menus

As mentioned at the beginning of this chapter, context menus appear at the cursor when the user right-clicks (on Windows) or Ctrl-clicks (on the Mac). Contrary to Flash applications for the Web, AIR applications don't offer any default context menus, so it's up to the developer to create and populate context menus for the application if necessary.

Context menus can be created with two different ActionScript classes:

- The NativeMenu class
- The ContextMenu class

You can only use the NativeMenu class for AIR applications, whereas you can use the ContextMenu class for both AIR applications and those that have been created to be executed in a web environment with Flash Player. The ContextMenu class is less flexible and offers fewer possibilities to developers, regardless of the fact that it extends the NativeMenu class.

> The ContextMenu *class extends the* NativeMenu *class in AIR applications as well as in traditional Flash applications. The* NativeMenu *class can be used only for AIR applications.*

Now you can create an AIR application that uses both types of context menus.

Creating context menus

In this section, you will create native and nonnative context menus. Start by opening the ch06p03.fla project in Flash CS4. You'll notice that the stage of the project contains the following two buttons, in addition to the output TextArea:

- nativeBtn
- contextBtn

Next, you'll associate a different context menu with each button and use the TextArea as a console for the application. Open the document class that is associated with the Flash project by clicking the Edit class definition icon in the Document Properties panel. Figure 6-9 displays the stage of the application.

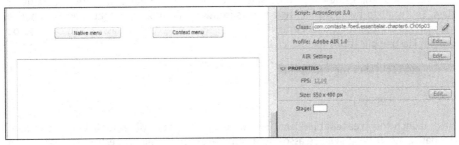

Figure 6-9. The stage and Document Properties panel of the ch06p03.fla project

The Ch6p03.as class starts by declaring its namespace and the external classes it needs to import for the correct execution of the application. Here's the code:

```
package com.comtaste.foed.essentialair.chapter6
{
import fl.controls.Button;
import fl.controls.TextArea;

import flash.display.MovieClip;
import flash.display.NativeMenu;
import flash.display.NativeMenuItem;
import flash.events.ContextMenuEvent;
import flash.events.Event;
import flash.filesystem.File;
import flash.ui.ContextMenu;
import flash.ui.ContextMenuItem;

public class Ch06p03 extends MovieClip
{
```

After declaring the external classes, you have to list the necessary class variables. These variables include the components on the stage of the Flash project. Finally, you need to show the instances of the two menus that you will build and populate. The code is as follows:

```
// onstage components
public var nativeBtn:Button;
public var contextBtn:Button;
public var output:TextArea;

// class properties
private var nativeMenuRoot:NativeMenu;
private var contextMenuRoot:ContextMenu;
```

Continue by defining the class constructor method and executing the super constructor class. You want to build two context menus in this application: one that uses AIR's native menus, and another that uses context menus of the ContextMenu class, which can also be used in Flash applications for the Web.

```
public function ch06p03()
{
    super();
```

Next, launch the createNativeMenu() method. This method will instantiate and populate the native menu, which will be associated with the contextMenu property of the nativeBtn button on the stage.

```
// generate native menu to use
createNativeMenu();
 // assign native menu to right-click on button
nativeBtn.contextMenu = nativeMenuRoot;
```

Next, you execute the createContextMenu() method to instantiate and populate a context menu of the ContextMenu class. This menu will be stored in the contextMenuRoot class variable and also assigned to the contextMenu property of the contextBtn button. Here's the code:

```
// generate context menu to use
createContextMenu();
 // assign context menu to right-click on button
contextBtn.contextMenu = contextMenuRoot;
}
```

Once you've completed the execution of the constructor method, your application will be ready. Each of the two buttons on the stage of the Flash project will have its own context menu. The nativeBtn button will use a context menu based on the instance of the NativeMenu class. The contextBtn button will use an instance of the ContextMenu class for its context menu.

This is the complete ActionScript class:

```
package com.comtaste.foed.essentialair.chapter6
{
import fl.controls.Button;
import fl.controls.TextArea;

import flash.display.MovieClip;
import flash.display.NativeMenu;
import flash.display.NativeMenuItem;
import flash.events.ContextMenuEvent;
import flash.events.Event;
import flash.filesystem.File;
import flash.ui.ContextMenu;
import flash.ui.ContextMenuItem;

public class Ch06p03 extends MovieClip
{
    // onstage components
    public var nativeBtn:Button;
    public var contextBtn:Button;
    public var output:TextArea;

    // class properties
    private var nativeMenuRoot:NativeMenu;
    private var contextMenuRoot:ContextMenu;

    public function Ch06p03()
    {
        super();

        // generate native menu to use
        createNativeMenu();

        // assign native menu to right-click on button
        nativeBtn.contextMenu = nativeMenuRoot;

        // generate context menu to use
        createContextMenu();

        // assign context menu to right-click on button
        contextBtn.contextMenu = contextMenuRoot;
    }
}
}
```

Native context menus

To create a native context menu, you populate the nativeMenuRoot context menu. This menu belongs to the NativeMenu class, in the body of the createNativeMenu() method in the Ch06p03.as class. Here's the code:

```
// create a complete native menu
private function createNativeMenu():void
{
```

Next, assign an instance of the NativeMenu class to the nativeMenuRoot class property. You add two submenus as the first elements of the menu, which are respectively generated by the createFirstSubMenu() and createSecondSubMenu() methods. To add elements to the menu, you use the addItem() method of the NativeMenu class.

```
// instantiate main menu object
nativeMenuRoot = new NativeMenu();
    // append subMenus to menu root
nativeMenuRoot.addItem( createFirstSubMenu() );
nativeMenuRoot.addItem( createSecondSubMenu() );
```

After the two submenus, you add a separator element to the menu. Remember, you have to create an instance of the NativeMenuItem class to add an item separator, and then you assign the true Boolean value as a second argument to the constructor of the class, as shown here:

```
// append item separator to root of menu
var itemSeparator:NativeMenuItem = new NativeMenuItem( "", true );
nativeMenuRoot.addItem( itemSeparator );
```

Finally, you add two more elements after the separator. These elements aren't submenus, but selectable items, so you register an event listener method for the selection event on each of them. The items are instances of the NativeMenuItem class.

```
// append command directly to root of menu
var subCommand1:NativeMenuItem =
        new NativeMenuItem( "subCommand 1" );
subCommand1.addEventListener( Event.SELECT, menuItemSelected );
nativeMenuRoot.addItem( subCommand1 );

// append another command directly to root of menu
var subCommand2:NativeMenuItem =
        new NativeMenuItem( "subCommand 2" );
subCommand2.addEventListener( Event.SELECT, menuItemSelected );
nativeMenuRoot.addItem( subCommand2 );
}
```

The createNativeMenu() method uses the createFirstSubMenu() and create➡ SecondSubMenu() methods to define its first two elements. These methods are similar to the ones you used in the ch06p01.fla project to instantiate and populate the items of a native menu. The code looks like this:

```
private function createFirstSubMenu():NativeMenuItem
{
    // create first submenu
    var subMenu:NativeMenuItem =
                new NativeMenuItem( "My first custom submenu" );
        // initialize child container
    subMenu.submenu = new NativeMenu();
        // create first submenu child
    var subMenuItem1:NativeMenuItem =
        new NativeMenuItem( "menu 1 item 1" );
        // register event listener for menu item
    subMenuItem1.addEventListener( Event.SELECT, menuItemSelected );
        // add item to submenu
    subMenu.submenu.addItem( subMenuItem1 );
        // create a second child, register event listener for
    // selection event and assign to submenu
    var subMenuItem2:NativeMenuItem =
        new NativeMenuItem( "menu 1 item 2" );
    subMenuItem2.addEventListener( Event.SELECT, menuItemSelected );
    subMenu.submenu.addItem( subMenuItem2 );
        return subMenu;
}

private function createSecondSubMenu():NativeMenuItem
{
    // create first submenu
    var subMenu:NativeMenuItem =
        new NativeMenuItem( "Second submenu" );
        // initialize child container
    subMenu.submenu = new NativeMenu();
        // create first submenu child
    var subMenuItem1:NativeMenuItem =
        new NativeMenuItem( "menu 2 item 1" );
        // register event listener for menu item
    subMenuItem1.addEventListener( Event.SELECT, menuItemSelected );
        // add item to submenu
    subMenu.submenu.addItem( subMenuItem1 );
        // add a separator item
    // label will be ignored for separator items
    var subMenuSeparator:NativeMenuItem =
        new NativeMenuItem( "", true );
        // add separator to menu
    subMenu.submenu.addItem( subMenuSeparator );
        // create a second child, register event listener for
    // selection event and assign to submenu
    var subMenuItem2:NativeMenuItem =
        new NativeMenuItem( "menu 2 item 2" );
    subMenuItem2.addEventListener( Event.SELECT, menuItemSelected );
    subMenu.submenu.addItem( subMenuItem2 );
```

6

```
// create a new item as an internal submenu
// using addSubmenu command
var childSubMenu:NativeMenuItem =
    subMenu.submenu.addSubmenu( new NativeMenu(), "Nested menu" );
// initialize child container
childSubMenu.submenu = new NativeMenu();
// create a child, register event listener for
// selection event and assign to internal submenu
var subMenuItem3:NativeMenuItem =
        new NativeMenuItem( "menu 2 nested item 1" );
subMenuItem3.addEventListener( Event.SELECT, menuItemSelected );
childSubMenu.submenu.addItem( subMenuItem3 );
    return subMenu;
}
```

The two methods create two submenus. For each of the selectable items on the context menu, you register the menuItemSelected() method as an event listener for the SELECT event of the Event class. The event listener method accesses the instance of the NativeMenuItem class. The latter generates the selection event through the target variable of the instance of the Event class it receives as an argument of the method. Through the reference to the instance of the NativeMenuItem class, you access the text label of the element—the label property of the NativeMenuItem class. You write the text label in the body of the output TextArea on the stage of the Flash project. The following code accomplishes these tasks:

```
// called on click on native menu items
private function menuItemSelected( evt : Event ):void
{
    var item:NativeMenuItem = evt.target as NativeMenuItem;

    output.appendText( "NATIVE MENU CLICKED ON: "
                        + item.label + File.lineEnding );
}
```

The menuItemSelected() method completes the steps that are required to create, populate, and make the native context menu assigned to the nativeBtn button work.

Nonnative context menus

The constructor method of the Ch06p03.as class contains the createContextMenu() method. You must execute this method in order to instantiate and populate the context menu that uses the ContextMenu class. Menus that are based on instances of the ContextMenu class have fewer functions than native menus that are based on the NativeMenu class.

The instances of the ContextMenu class can't contain submenus, only top-level elements. Furthermore, the selection events aren't retransmitted to the root of the menu from the selected elements through the hierarchical structure, so you have to register the event listener functions straight on the single items. Because there can't be any submenus, no display event is generated for the items that instantiate the ContextMenu class. The following code opens the createContextMenu() method:

```
// create a complete native menu
private function createContextMenu():void
{
```

Next, assign an instance of the ContextMenu class to the contextMenuRoot variable to initialize the context menu that the contextBtn button will use:

```
// initialize context menu
contextMenuRoot = new ContextMenu();
```

Create an instance of the ContextMenuItem class. This will be the first element on the context menu you're creating. You assign a text label to the object when you instantiate the ContextMenuItem class.

```
// create first item
var item1:ContextMenuItem = new ContextMenuItem( "First Item" );
```

Register an event listener method for the new item on the menu. When the user selects the item, it will execute the contextMenuItemSelected() method. The instances of the ContextMenuItem class don't generate an Event.SELECT event when they're selected, but a ContextMenuEvent.MENU_ITEM_SELECT event.

```
// register event listener for menu item
item1.addEventListener(
        ContextMenuEvent.MENU_ITEM_SELECT,
        contextMenuItemSelected );
```

Remember that the ContextMenu class extends the NativeMenu class. But it would be wrong to use the inherited methods to add child items to the menu. If you use native methods like addItem(), for example, the menu could be rendered wrong or not work properly.

The ContextMenu class requires its items to be added or removed via the customItems property. This property is an instance of the Array class that lists the instances of the ContextMenuItem class that will be displayed on the menu. Here's an example of the customItems property:

```
// add item to context menu
contextMenuRoot.customItems.push( item1 );
```

In native menus, you've seen how to create elements that act as separators between various groups of items. Menus based on the ContextMenu class can also contain item separators. Unlike the NativeMenuItem class, the ContextMenuItem class allows you to define both the separator and the following item in the same instance.

As with the NativeMenuItem class, to create an item separator, follow these steps:

1. Assign the true Boolean value to the constructor method as a second argument.

2. Create a new item for the context menu.

3. Specify that an item separator will have to come before the item itself.

4. Register the selection event for this item on the contextMenuItemSelected() event listener method, like you did for the first item on the context menu.

5. Add the item under the customItems array of the instance of the ContextMenu class you're working on.

The following code accomplishes these tasks:

```
// create a separator
var itemSeparator:ContextMenuItem =
new ContextMenuItem( "second Item with separator before", true );

// register event listener for menu item
itemSeparator.addEventListener( ContextMenuEvent.MENU_ITEM_SELECT,
                    contextMenuItemSelected )

// add item to context menu
contextMenuRoot.customItems.push( itemSeparator );
}
```

To complete the class, and therefore the application, you have to define the contextMenuItemSelected() event listener method. The method acts like the menuItemSelected() method—the only difference is that the event object it receives is an instance of the ContextMenuEvent class. Furthermore, its target property is a reference to an instance of the ContextMenuItem class instead of an object of the NativeMenuItem class.

Each time an element of the context menu based on the ContextMenu class is selected, its label will be written in the body of the output TextArea.

The following code completes the class:

```
// called on click on context menu items
private function contextMenuItemSelected( evt : ContextMenuEvent ):void
{
    var item:ContextMenuItem = evt.target as ContextMenuItem;

    output.appendText( "CONTEXT MENU CLICKED ON: "
                        + item.label + File.lineEnding );
}
```

Testing the context menus

This is the complete ActionScript class that you just created:

```
package com.comtaste.foed.essentialair.chapter6
{
import fl.controls.Button;
import fl.controls.TextArea;
```

```
import flash.display.MovieClip;
import flash.display.NativeMenu;
import flash.display.NativeMenuItem;
import flash.events.ContextMenuEvent;
import flash.events.Event;
import flash.filesystem.File;
import flash.ui.ContextMenu;
import flash.ui.ContextMenuItem;

public class Ch06p03 extends MovieClip
{
    // onstage components
    public var nativeBtn:Button;
    public var contextBtn:Button;
    public var output:TextArea;

    // class properties
    private var nativeMenuRoot:NativeMenu;
    private var contextMenuRoot:ContextMenu;

    public function Ch06p03()
    {
        super();

        // generate native menu to use
        createNativeMenu();

        // assign native menu to right-click on button
        nativeBtn.contextMenu = nativeMenuRoot;

        // generate context menu to use
        createContextMenu();

        // assign context menu to right-click on button
        contextBtn.contextMenu = contextMenuRoot;
    }

    // create a complete native menu
    private function createNativeMenu():void
    {
        // instantiate main menu object
        nativeMenuRoot = new NativeMenu();

        // append subMenus to menu root
        nativeMenuRoot.addItem( createFirstSubMenu() );
        nativeMenuRoot.addItem( createSecondSubMenu() );
```

```
        // append item separator to root of menu
        var itemSeparator:NativeMenuItem =
            new NativeMenuItem( "", true );
        nativeMenuRoot.addItem( itemSeparator );

        // append command directly to root of menu
        var subCommand1:NativeMenuItem =
            new NativeMenuItem( "subCommand 1" );
        subCommand1.addEventListener( Event.SELECT, menuItemSelected );
        nativeMenuRoot.addItem( subCommand1 );

        // append another command directly to root of menu
        var subCommand2:NativeMenuItem =
            new NativeMenuItem( "subCommand 2" );
        subCommand2.addEventListener( Event.SELECT, menuItemSelected );
        nativeMenuRoot.addItem( subCommand2 );
    }

    private function createFirstSubMenu():NativeMenuItem
    {
        // create first submenu
        var subMenu:NativeMenuItem =
            new NativeMenuItem( "My first custom submenu" );

        // initialize child container
        subMenu.submenu = new NativeMenu();

        // create first submenu child
        var subMenuItem1:NativeMenuItem =
            new NativeMenuItem( "menu 1 item 1" );

        // register event listener for menu item
        subMenuItem1.addEventListener( Event.SELECT,
                menuItemSelected );

        // add item to submenu
        subMenu.submenu.addItem( subMenuItem1 );

        // create a second child, register event listener for
        // selection event and assign to submenu
        var subMenuItem2:NativeMenuItem =
            new NativeMenuItem( "menu 1 item 2" );
        subMenuItem2.addEventListener( Event.SELECT,
                menuItemSelected );
        subMenu.submenu.addItem( subMenuItem2 );

        return subMenu;
    }
```

```
private function createSecondSubMenu():NativeMenuItem
{
    // create first submenu
    var subMenu:NativeMenuItem =
            new NativeMenuItem( "Second submenu" );

    // initialize child container
    subMenu.submenu = new NativeMenu();

    // create first submenu child
    var subMenuItem1:NativeMenuItem =
            new NativeMenuItem( "menu 2 item 1" );

    // register event listener for menu item
    subMenuItem1.addEventListener( Event.SELECT,
                menuItemSelected );

    // add item to submenu
    subMenu.submenu.addItem( subMenuItem1 );

    // add a separator item
    // label will be ignored for separator items
    var subMenuSeparator:NativeMenuItem =
            new NativeMenuItem( "", true );

    // add separator to menu
    subMenu.submenu.addItem( subMenuSeparator );

    // create a second child, register event listener for
    // selection event and assign to submenu
    var subMenuItem2:NativeMenuItem =
            new NativeMenuItem( "menu 2 item 2" );
    subMenuItem2.addEventListener( Event.SELECT,
                menuItemSelected );
    subMenu.submenu.addItem( subMenuItem2 );

    // create a new item as an internal submenu
    // using addSubmenu command
    var childSubMenu:NativeMenuItem =
            subMenu.submenu.addSubmenu( new NativeMenu(),
                                "Nested menu" );

    // initialize child container
    childSubMenu.submenu = new NativeMenu();

    // create a child, register event listener for
    // selection event and assign to internal submenu
    var subMenuItem3:NativeMenuItem =
```

```
                      new NativeMenuItem( "menu 2 nested item 1" );
            subMenuItem3.addEventListener( Event.SELECT,
                    menuItemSelected );
            childSubMenu.submenu.addItem( subMenuItem3 );

            return subMenu;
    }

    // called on click on native menu items
    private function menuItemSelected( evt : Event ):void
    {
        var item:NativeMenuItem = evt.target as NativeMenuItem;
        output.appendText( "NATIVE MENU CLICKED ON: " +
                    item.label + File.lineEnding );
    }


    // create a complete native menu
    private function createContextMenu():void
    {
        // initialize context menu
        contextMenuRoot = new ContextMenu();

        // create first item
        var item1:ContextMenuItem =
                    new ContextMenuItem( "First Item" );
        item1.addEventListener( ContextMenuEvent.MENU_ITEM_SELECT,
                    contextMenuItemSelected )
        contextMenuRoot.customItems.push( item1 );

        // create a separator
        var itemSeparator:ContextMenuItem =
    new ContextMenuItem( "second Item w/ separator before", true );

        itemSeparator.addEventListener( ContextMenuEvent.MENU_ITEM_➥
    SELECT,
                    contextMenuItemSelected )
        contextMenuRoot.customItems.push( itemSeparator );


    }

    // called on click on context menu items
    private function contextMenuItemSelected(
                                        evt : ContextMenuEvent ):void
    {
```

```
                var item:ContextMenuItem = evt.target as ContextMenuItem;
                output.appendText( "CONTEXT MENU CLICKED ON: " +
                        item.label + File.lineEnding );
        }

    } // close class
    } // close package
```

Now you're ready to compile and test your application. To do so, go back to the ch06p03.fla project and start the compilation by selecting the Test Movie item from the Control menu, as shown in Figure 6-10.

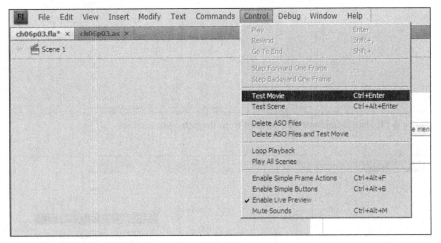

Figure 6-10. The command to compile and test the movie

Now try interacting with the application by right-clicking (on Windows) or Ctrl-clicking (on the Mac) on the two buttons. When you click, the context menus should appear at the cursor.

Finally, try selecting different items to display the selection messages in the TextArea. You can see what the two context menus look like on Microsoft Windows XP in Figures 6-11 and 6-12.

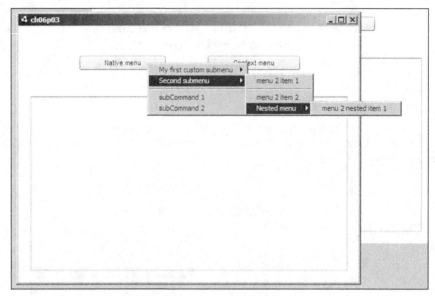

Figure 6-11. NativeMenu instance opened from the nativeBtn instance

Figure 6-12. ContextMenu instance opened from the contextBtn instance

In the next section, you'll learn how to create custom menus for dock icons and system tray icons.

Managing dock and system tray icon menus

Many applications offer context menus associated with the application's icon. On Windows systems, these menus are located in the system tray. If you're working on a Mac OS X system, you'll find these menus in the dock bar. Generally, these menus have shortcuts for the most common functions of the application you're using. These menus might also contain commands that must be accessible even when the application is minimized or hidden by the desktop.

The AIR runtime allows you to manage and interact with the system tray and dock bar icons of your application. You can define context menus for them. On Microsoft Windows systems, the icons in the system tray don't have any default context menus, so unless you have a specially prepared menu to display, it won't provide a context menu.

Mac OS X systems, on the other hand, have a default menu for dock bar icons. The menus you create will be added to the default menu provided by the operating system. You can't modify or remove the default menus provided by the system for dock bar icons.

The application you will create in the next section will run on both Windows and Mac OS X.

6

Assigning a menu to an application icon

Start by opening the ch06p04.fla file in Flash CS4. The project, like the previous ones, only has an output TextArea. This TextArea will display the messages regarding the status of your application.

The project, as shown in Figure 6-13, displays an icon in the system tray or dock bar of the local system, which is why a symbol has been prepared in the library. The symbol is a movie clip: Application Icon, which represents the way you want to show the application icon. In the Symbol Properties panel, shown in Figure 6-14, the class name of the symbol has been specified: ApplicationIcon. This class name allows you to instantiate the symbol in the library via ActionScript.

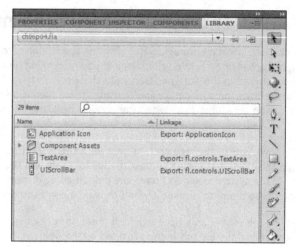

Figure 6-13. The stage and Library panel of the ch06p04.fla project

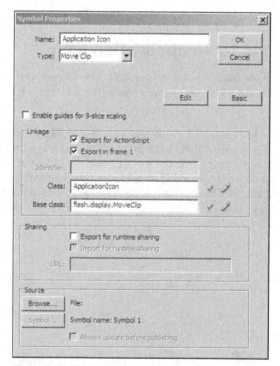

Figure 6-14. The Symbol Properties panel

You access the document class of the Flash project by clicking the Edit class definition icon on the Document Properties panel. Like for the other projects in this chapter, the Flash project has been set up to not declare the variables automatically for the elements on the stage. You'll have to specify them yourself in the class associated with the project.

The class starts by declaring the namespace and the dependence on external classes, as shown here:

```
package com.comtaste.foed.essentialair.chapter6
{
import fl.controls.TextArea;

import flash.desktop.DockIcon;
import flash.desktop.NativeApplication;
import flash.desktop.SystemTrayIcon;
import flash.display.BitmapData;
import flash.display.MovieClip;
import flash.display.NativeMenu;
import flash.display.NativeMenuItem;
import flash.display.NativeWindow;
import flash.events.Event;
import flash.filesystem.File;

public class Ch06p04 extends MovieClip
{
```

Then you declare two class properties: one that refers to the component of the TextArea class on the stage of the project, and one to contain the native menu that the application will use:

```
// onstage components
public var output:TextArea;

// class properties
private var menuRoot:NativeMenu;
```

Next, the constructor method of the class will call the initialization of the native menu. It will check which options are supported by the local operating system. This method will also assign the menu to the menu bar of the application or window. Finally, it will assign the menu to the icon in the system tray or to the icon in the dock bar, depending on which one is available.

```
public function Ch06p04()
{
    super();
```

You call the createNativeMenu() function to instantiate and populate the menu that will be used for the application as well as the application's icon. Here's the code:

```
// generate native menu to use
createNativeMenu();
```

6

Next, you check if the operating system supports application-level or window-level menus. After that, you assign the menu to the correct property on the basis of the functions of the operating system. This code accomplishes these tasks:

```
// assign to application menu if we are on Mac OS X
if ( NativeApplication.supportsMenu )
{
    NativeApplication.nativeApplication.menu = menuRoot;
}
    // assign to window menu if we are on Microsoft Windows
if ( NativeWindow.supportsMenu )
{
    stage.nativeWindow.menu = menuRoot;          }
```

Finally, you call the initIcon() method, which instantiates the ApplicationIcon symbol and uses its graphical representation as the application icon:

```
    initIcon();
}
```

To instantiate and populate the native menu, you use the createNativeMenu() method, which assigns an instance of the NativeMenu class to the menuRoot class property. Then you add a submenu to the menu using the addItem() function of the NativeMenu class:

```
// create a complete native menu
private function createNativeMenu():void
{
    // instantiate main menu object
    menuRoot = new NativeMenu();
        // append subMenus to menu root
    menuRoot.addItem( createFirstSubMenu() );
}
```

The submenu is created and returned by the createFirstSubMenu() function, as shown here:

```
private function createFirstSubMenu():NativeMenuItem
{
```

Next, you create an instance of the NativeMenuItem class with a label of App settings. This object will be the element of the menu returned by the function. Then you assign an instance of the NativeMenu class to the submenu property of the element, so as to populate its list of items.

```
// create submenu
var subMenu:NativeMenuItem = new NativeMenuItem( "App settings" );
    // initialize child container
subMenu.submenu = new NativeMenu();
```

You'll add three methods to the menu, which will allow you to do the following:

- Access the description of the application
- Minimize the active window
- Close the application

Each menu item is registered to an event listener method for the selection event, as shown here:

```
// create first child, register event listener for
// selection event and assign to submenu
var aboutCommand:NativeMenuItem = new NativeMenuItem( "About.." );
aboutCommand.addEventListener( Event.SELECT, getInformation );
subMenu.submenu.addItem( aboutCommand );
// create second child, register event listener for
// selection event and assign to submenu
var minimizeCommand:NativeMenuItem =
                new NativeMenuItem( "Minimize" );
minimizeCommand.addEventListener( Event.SELECT,
                minimizeApplication );
subMenu.submenu.addItem( minimizeCommand );
// create third child, register event listener for
// selection event and assign to submenu
var closeCommand:NativeMenuItem = new NativeMenuItem( "Close" );
closeCommand.addEventListener( Event.SELECT, closeApplication );
subMenu.submenu.addItem( closeCommand );
    return subMenu;
}
```

The event listener functions for the three items on the native menu are the following, and have already been explained in detail in the previous exercise regarding application menus:

```
// get application description
private function getInformation( evt : Event ):void
{
    // access to application XML descriptor
    var appDescriptor:XML =
        NativeApplication.nativeApplication.applicationDescriptor;

    // retrieve XML descriptor namespace
    var nsDeclaration:Namespace = appDescriptor.namespace();

    // read description node from XML
    var informationText:String =
        String( appDescriptor.nsDeclaration::description[ 0 ] );
```

6

```
            // write into textarea 'output' description contents
            output.appendText( "Adobe Air, test application for "
                + "menus functionalities." + File.lineEnding );
            output.appendText( informationText + File.lineEnding );
        }

        // close application
        private function closeApplication( e : Event ):void
        {
            NativeApplication.nativeApplication.exit();
        }

        // minimize application
        private function minimizeApplication( e : Event ):void
        {
            stage.nativeWindow.minimize();
        }
```

Preparing the application icon

Now all you have to do is correctly prepare the application icon. This is the task of the following initIcon() method, which is called at the end of the class constructor method:

```
        // set up application icons
        private function initIcon():void
        {
```

First, you have to obtain an object of the BitmapData class to use as a graphical representation of the application icon. To do so, you have to instantiate the ApplicationIcon symbol in the ch06p04.fla project library.

Then create a local icon property, to which you assign an instance of the ApplicationIcon symbol. The local icon property is declared as a MovieClip, not an ApplicationIcon. This is possible because the ApplicationIcon symbol extends the MovieClip class, so it's correct to say it's a MovieClip. **Inheritance** is a fundamental concept for object-oriented programming languages like ActionScript 3.

```
            // instanstiate icon symbol available in proj library
            var icon:MovieClip = new ApplicationIcon();
```

Creating an object for raster representation

Now that you've instantiated the ApplicationIcon symbol, you have to create an object to be its raster representation. Begin by creating a BitmapData object. You specify the dimensions of its canvas as the dimensions of the icon instance you've just created. Then you draw the instance of the icon in the raster object using the draw() function of the BitmapData class. The draw() function allows you to draw any object that implements the IbitmapDrawable interface on the canvas of a BitmapData object. You can use this function to draw any object that implements the interface on the canvas of an object. In

ActionScript, this interface is implemented by the DisplayObject class and the Bitmap class. The following code accomplishes these tasks:

```
// access and save bitmapdata of icon
var iconImg:BitmapData = new BitmapData( icon.width, icon.height );
iconImg.draw( icon );
```

Next, you assign the raster representation of the icon for the application to the bitmaps property of the icon object of your AIR application. The bitmaps property is an array of raster representations of icons provided by an AIR application.

The runtime will use a representation with dimensions as similar as possible to the ones you've chosen (but exactly how similar depends on the local operating system and its graphical settings). The definition of the list of available icons for the application doesn't depend on the local system, and you always proceed as follows:

```
// define application icon
NativeApplication.nativeApplication.icon.bitmaps = [ iconImg ];
```

Using the correct class type for an application icon

6

According to the local operating system, the icon property of the nativeApplication object of the NativeApplication class can refer to instances of various classes. On Microsoft Windows systems, the icon represents an instance of the SystemTrayIcon class. On Mac OS X systems, the icon represents an instance of the DockIcon class. You can check which type of icon is supported by checking the Boolean supportsDockIcon and supportsSystemTrayIcon properties of the NativeApplication class, which let's you know if the system supports dock icons or system tray icons, respectively.

Here's an example of the NativeApplication class:

```
if ( NativeApplication.supportsDockIcon )
{
```

If the system supports DockIcon icons, you simply assign the native menu to the menu property of the icon object. The menu will be added on the one that is natively provided by the operating system. Here's an example of the DockIcon icons:

```
// assign dock icon custom menu
DockIcon( NativeApplication.nativeApplication.icon ).menu
                = menuRoot;
}else if ( NativeApplication.supportsSystemTrayIcon )
{
```

If, on the other hand, the system supports SystemTrayIcon icons, you also define a string of text to be used as the icon's tooltip. SystemTrayIcon icons don't have a menu from the operating system—just the one you provided them. DockIcon icons don't support tooltips. Here's an example of a SystemTrayIcon icon:

```
        // assign system tray icon custom menu
    SystemTrayIcon( NativeApplication.nativeApplication.icon ).menu
                        = menuRoot;
        // tooltip for tray icon, available only on Windows
    SystemTrayIcon( NativeApplication.nativeApplication.icon ).tooltip
                        = "Application settings";
        }
    }
```

Executing the application

Go back to the Flash ch06p04.fla project to execute the application and see the results of your work (Control ➤ Test Movie). You can see the application icon with its activated context menu in Figures 6-15 and 6-16. The application will work both on operating systems that support SystemTrayIcon icons (Microsoft Windows) and systems that support DockIcon icons (Mac OS X).

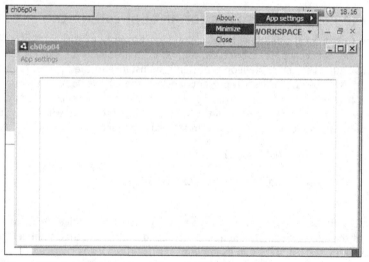

Figure 6-15. Application icon on Microsoft Windows systems

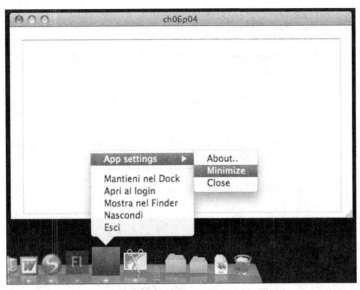

Figure 6-16. Application icon on Mac OS X systems

This is the complete ActionScript class that you have just created:

```
package com.comtaste.examples
{
import fl.controls.TextArea;

import flash.desktop.DockIcon;
import flash.desktop.NativeApplication;
import flash.desktop.SystemTrayIcon;
import flash.display.BitmapData;
import flash.display.MovieClip;
import flash.display.NativeMenu;
import flash.display.NativeMenuItem;
import flash.display.NativeWindow;
import flash.events.Event;
import flash.filesystem.File;

public class Ch06p04 extends MovieClip
{
    // onstage components
    public var output:TextArea;

    // class properties
    private var menuRoot:NativeMenu;

    public function Ch06p04()
    {
        super();
```

```
        // generate native menu to use
        createNativeMenu();

        // assign to application menu if we are on Mac OS X
        if ( NativeApplication.supportsMenu )
        {
            NativeApplication.nativeApplication.menu = menuRoot;
        }

        // assign to window menu if we are on Microsoft Windows
        if ( NativeWindow.supportsMenu )
        {
            stage.nativeWindow.menu = menuRoot;
        }

        initIcon();
    }

    // create a complete native menu
    private function createNativeMenu():void
    {
        // instantiate main menu object
        menuRoot = new NativeMenu();

        // append subMenus to menu root
        menuRoot.addItem( createFirstSubMenu() );
    }

    private function createFirstSubMenu():NativeMenuItem
    {
        // create submenu
        var subMenu:NativeMenuItem =
                new NativeMenuItem( "App settings" );

        // initialize child container
        subMenu.submenu = new NativeMenu();

        // create first child, register event listener for
        // selection event and assign to submenu
        var aboutCommand:NativeMenuItem =
                new NativeMenuItem( "About.." );
        aboutCommand.addEventListener( Event.SELECT, getInformation );
        subMenu.submenu.addItem( aboutCommand );

        // create second child, register event listener for
        // selection event and assign to submenu
        var minimizeCommand:NativeMenuItem =
                new NativeMenuItem( "Minimize" );
        minimizeCommand.addEventListener( Event.SELECT,
```

```
                minimizeApplication );
        subMenu.submenu.addItem( minimizeCommand );

        // create third child, register event listener for
        // selection event and assign to submenu
        var closeCommand:NativeMenuItem =
                new NativeMenuItem( "Close" );
        closeCommand.addEventListener( Event.SELECT,
                closeApplication );
        subMenu.submenu.addItem( closeCommand );

        return subMenu;
    }

// set up application icons
private function initIcon():void
{
        // instanstiate icon symbol available in proj library
        var icon:MovieClip = new ApplicationIcon();

        // access and save bitmapdata of icon
        var iconImg:BitmapData =
                new BitmapData( icon.width, icon.height );
        iconImg.draw( icon );

        // define application icon
        NativeApplication.nativeApplication.icon.bitmaps = [iconImg];

        if ( NativeApplication.supportsDockIcon )
        {
            // assign dock icon custom menu
            DockIcon( NativeApplication.nativeApplication.icon ).menu
                = menuRoot;

        }else if ( NativeApplication.supportsSystemTrayIcon )
        {
            // assign system tray icon custom menu
     SystemTrayIcon( NativeApplication.nativeApplication.icon ).menu
                = menuRoot;

            // tooltip for tray icon, available only on Windows
     SystemTrayIcon( NativeApplication.nativeApplication.icon ).tooltip
                = "Application settings";
        }
    }

// called on click
private function getInformation( evt : Event ):void
{
```

```
            var appDescriptor:XML =
            NativeApplication.nativeApplication.applicationDescriptor;
            var nsDeclaration:Namespace = appDescriptor.namespace();
            var informationText:String =
            String( appDescriptor.nsDeclaration::description[ 0 ] );
            output.appendText( "Adobe Air, test application for "
            + "menus functionalities." + File.lineEnding );
            output.appendText( informationText + File.lineEnding );
        }

        // close application
        private function closeApplication( e : Event ):void
        {
            NativeApplication.nativeApplication.exit();
        }

        // minimize application
        private function minimizeApplication( e : Event ):void
        {
            stage.nativeWindow.minimize();
        }
    } // close class
} // close package
```

The next section will show how to build and launch pop-up menus in AIR applications.

Creating and accessing pop-up menus

So far, you've worked with menus that are associated with tangible elements of your applications, such as the following:

- Context menus that are activated on objects on the stage
- Context menus associated with icons in the system tray or dock bar
- Menus associated with windows and menus of the application itself

AIR applications also allow you to create **pop-up menus**. These are native menus like all the other ones you've seen so far—the only difference is that pop-up menus aren't natively associated with any element on the interface of the application. It's up to the developer to define and implement the logic and the way in which a pop-up menu can be activated. An AIR application can have any number of pop-up menus.

You can show a pop-up menu anywhere on the stage. It can be activated in the following ways: if the user clicks a button, if the mouse rolls over any object, if the user presses a combination of keys, and on any other condition you want for your application.

Activating pop-up menus

The NativeMenu class has the display() method to activate a pop-up menu. Every time this method is called, the pop-up menu appears at the specified coordinates. The display() method requires the three following arguments:

- **Destination stage**: Specifies which stage has to display the pop-up menu. If the AIR application is on only one NativeWindow-type window, the destination stage is automatically the window that displays the application. If you're making a multi-window application, you will have to specify the stage of the window you want to display the pop-up menu on.
- **Coordinate (X axis)**: Specifies the position on the X axis of the pop-up menu. This coordinate specifies the position from the top left corner of the menu. The coordinate will apply to the stage you've specified as a first argument of the function.
- **Coordinate (Y axis)**: Specifies the position on the Y axis where you want to display the pop-up menu. This coordinate specifies the position from the top left corner of the menu. The coordinate will apply to the stage you've specified as a first argument of the function.

Creating pop-up menus

Open the ch06p05.fla project, which will allow you to create a pop-up menu. You can see the stage of the application and the elements it contains in Figure 6-17. The point is to obtain a native pop-up menu that will be displayed at specific coordinates in response to a click of the button with an instance name of button. The menu will be also displayed in response to the press of the M key on the keyboard.

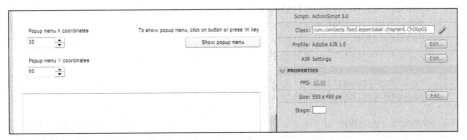

Figure 6-17. Stage of the ch06p05.fla project

To offer more flexibility to the user, two components of the NumericStepper class have been provided, with a posX and posY ID. These components allow you to dynamically change the coordinates where you want the pop-up menu to appear. Finally, there is a TextArea with an output ID. From the beginning of this chapter, you've seen this component being used as the destination of the messages that are generated during the execution of the application.

Access the document class of the project by clicking the Edit class definition icon on the Document Properties panel in Flash CS4. The class begins by defining its namespace and specifying the following external classes it depends on:

```
package com.comtaste.foed.essentialair.chapter6
{
import fl.controls.Button;
import fl.controls.NumericStepper;
import fl.controls.TextArea;

import flash.desktop.NativeApplication;
import flash.display.MovieClip;
import flash.display.NativeMenu;
import flash.display.NativeMenuItem;
import flash.events.Event;
import flash.events.KeyboardEvent;
import flash.events.MouseEvent;
import flash.filesystem.File;

public class Ch06p05 extends MovieClip
{
```

Before creating the constructor method, you define the class properties the application needs. Among the properties, you'll find a reference to every element on the stage of the Flash project. You'll also find the menuRoot property, which contains the instance of the NativeMenu class you'll use as a pop-up menu. The following code accomplishes these tasks:

```
// onstage components
public var posX:NumericStepper;
public var posY:NumericStepper;
public var button:Button;
public var output:TextArea;

// class properties
private var menuRoot:NativeMenu;
```

The constructor method of the class instantiates and populates the native menu. Then it registers the event listener functions that will activate the pop-up menu, as shown here:

```
public function Ch06p05()
{
    super();
```

After calling the super constructor of the class, you call the createNativeMenu() method, which populates the pop-up menu. You also register the event listener function that will be called when the user selects one of the items on the menu. Here's the code:

```
// generate native menu to use
createNativeMenu();
```

Next, you'll register two event listener functions. One will be used when the user presses the keys on the keyboard, and the other is for the click event on the button on the stage. Here's the code for these event listener functions:

```
// assign event listener to key press
NativeApplication.nativeApplication.addEventListener(
                KeyboardEvent.KEY_UP,
                showPopupMenuFromKeyboard );

// assign event listener to click on button
this.addEventListener( MouseEvent.CLICK, showPopupMenu );
}
```

The createNativeMenu() method instantiates and populates the pop-up menu in the application. To populate the pop-up menu you use the same procedure as all the previous examples. You assign an instance of the NativeMenu class to the menuRoot class property. Then you create and add three objects of the NativeMenuItem class to the native menu. Each element of the menu is registered on the menuItemSelected() method for when the user selects it on the menu. The following code accomplishes these tasks:

```
// create a complete native menu
private function createNativeMenu():void
{
    // instantiate main menu object
    menuRoot = new NativeMenu();
        // append items to menu root

    var item1:NativeMenuItem = new NativeMenuItem( "Item 1" );
    item1.addEventListener( Event.SELECT, menuItemSelected );
    menuRoot.addItem( item1 );

    var item2:NativeMenuItem = new NativeMenuItem( "Item 2" );
    item2.addEventListener( Event.SELECT, menuItemSelected );
    menuRoot.addItem( item2 );

    var item3:NativeMenuItem = new NativeMenuItem( "Item 3" );
    item3.addEventListener( Event.SELECT, menuItemSelected );
    menuRoot.addItem( item3 );
}
```

Each time the user selects an element from the pop-up menu, the menuItemSelected() method is launched. This accesses the text label of the object of the selected NativeMenuItem class. The name of the selected element on the menu will appear in the TextArea on the stage. Here's the code:

```
// called on click on menu item selection
private function menuItemSelected( evt : Event ):void
{
    var item:NativeMenuItem = evt.target as NativeMenuItem;
```

```
output.appendText( "CLICKED ON: " + item.label + File.lineEnding );
}
```

In the constructor method of the class, the showPopupMenuFromKeyboard() method is linked to pressing the keys on the keyboard. This method will be launched each time the application is active and the user presses any key. Here's the code:

```
// called when user presses a key on his keyboard
private function showPopupMenuFromKeyboard( evt : KeyboardEvent ):void
{
```

Next, you assign the key the user presses to a local variable. To obtain the pressed key, you use the static fromCharCode() method of the String class. You pass the value of the charCode property, which is transported by the object of the KeyboardEvent class received as an argument of the function to the method:

```
// access pressed key
var keyString:String =
    String.fromCharCode( evt.charCode ).toLowerCase();
```

You check if the value associated with the key on the keyboard is the letter M. If it is, you show the pop-up menu in the window of the application using the values of NumericStepper components on the stage, with posX and posY as coordinates. Here's the code:

```
// if key pressed is valid show pop-up menu
if( keyString == "m"  )
{
    menuRoot.display( this.Stage, posX.value, posY.value );
}
}
```

Finally, the showPopupMenu() method is registered on the click event of the button with the instance name button in the class constructor method. When the user clicks the button, it shows the pop-up menu at the coordinates that have been specified by the two NumericStepper components on the stage of the application.

```
// called when button is clicked
private function showPopupMenu( evt : MouseEvent ):void
{
    // show pop-up menu
    menuRoot.display( this.Stage, posX.value, posY.value );
}
```

Now, go back to the Flash ch06p05.fla project to see the results of your work. Select the Test Movie item from the Control menu to execute the application. Try clicking the button or pressing the m key on your keyboard. You can see an example of the activated pop-up menu in Figure 6-18.

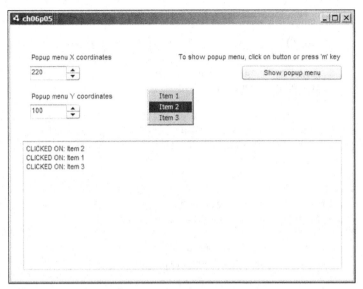

Figure 6-18. The ch06p05.fla project on execution

This is the complete ActionScript class that you just created:

```
package com.comtaste.foed.essentialair.chapter6
{
import fl.controls.Button;
import fl.controls.NumericStepper;
import fl.controls.TextArea;

import flash.desktop.NativeApplication;
import flash.display.MovieClip;
import flash.display.NativeMenu;
import flash.display.NativeMenuItem;
import flash.events.Event;
import flash.events.KeyboardEvent;
import flash.events.MouseEvent;
import flash.filesystem.File;

public class Ch06p05 extends MovieClip
{
    // onstage components
    public var posX:NumericStepper;
    public var posY:NumericStepper;
    public var button:Button;
    public var output:TextArea;

    // class properties
    private var menuRoot:NativeMenu;
```

```
public function Ch06p05()
{
    super();

    // generate native menu to use
    createNativeMenu();

    // assign menu to click on button
    NativeApplication.nativeApplication.addEventListener(
        KeyboardEvent.KEY_UP, showPopupMenuFromKeyboard );
    this.addEventListener( MouseEvent.CLICK, showPopupMenu );
}

// create a complete native menu
private function createNativeMenu():void
{
    // instantiate main menu object
    menuRoot = new NativeMenu();

    // append items to menu root
    var item1:NativeMenuItem = new NativeMenuItem( "Item 1" );
    item1.addEventListener( Event.SELECT, menuItemSelected );
    menuRoot.addItem( item1 );
    var item2:NativeMenuItem = new NativeMenuItem( "Item 2" );
    item2.addEventListener( Event.SELECT, menuItemSelected );
    menuRoot.addItem( item2 );
    var item3:NativeMenuItem = new NativeMenuItem( "Item 3" );
    item3.addEventListener( Event.SELECT, menuItemSelected );
    menuRoot.addItem( item3 );

}

// called when user presses a key on his keyboard
private function showPopupMenuFromKeyboard(
                                    evt : KeyboardEvent ):void
{
    var keyString:String =
        String.fromCharCode( evt.charCode ).toLowerCase();
    if( keyString == "m"  )
    {
        menuRoot.display( this.stage, posX.value, posY.value );
    }
}

// called when button is clicked
private function showPopupMenu( evt : MouseEvent ):void
{
    menuRoot.display( this.stage, posX.value, posY.value );
}
```

```
        // called on click on menu item selection
        private function menuItemSelected( evt : Event ):void
        {
            var item:NativeMenuItem = evt.target as NativeMenuItem;
            output.appendText( "CLICKED ON: " +
                        item.label + File.lineEnding );
        }
    } // close class
    } // close package
```

The display() method of the NativeMenu class only works properly on Microsoft Windows systems. Flash Player doesn't work properly on Mac OS X systems, and displays the pop-up menu on the cursor of the mouse instead of at the specified coordinates. This occurs if the call to the display() function happens as a consequence of an event of the MouseEvent class. If the call happens in response to other events, the application doesn't display the pop-up menu at all. In the next section, you'll see how to create flexible native menus defined via external configuration documents.

Creating native menus dynamically

The menus you've created in the examples so far have all been generated through pre-defined ActionScript code. If you wanted to change the label of an item on the menu, change the order of the items, or remove or add elements, you would have to recompile the Flash project. You would also have to generate a new installation file for the application, or provide an update, if the application supports updates.

> See Chapter 8 for a discussion of how to manage updates in an AIR application.

When you're developing real applications, it's advisable to create applications that don't need to be recompiled every time you make minor changes. If your user had to update the whole application (not just a few configuration files) every week or every month, you'd probably lose your audience quite quickly.

To avoid or at least limit these situations, you can extend the NativeMenu class. You can create a class that allows the menu items to be generated dynamically from an XML structure. Because native menus are hierarchal, it's relatively easy to represent a native menu skeleton to an XML structure. Another advantage is the possibility of changing the localization of the menu of the application by loading different XML documents.

First, you have to define the structure of the XML document so that each item on the menu is represented by a MenuItem node. The attributes of each node will define the properties to be assigned to the corresponding instance of the NativeMenuItem class that will be created. You can also embed MenuItem nodes in other MenuItem nodes to generate submenus.

A MenuItem node will have the following skeleton:

```
<MenuItem label="" isSeparator="" mnemonicIndex=""
          keyEquivalent="" name="" select="" />
```

The attributes provided allow you to define the structure and behavior of the corresponding menu items. Here is an analysis of the attributes:

- label: This is the text label that will be assigned to the element, be it a command or a submenu.

- isSeparator: This is a Boolean value that specifies if the element will be a separator or not. If the value is true, the element will be a separator, so all other attributes will be ignored.

- mnemonixIndex: This specifies the index that corresponds to the letter of the text label that is recognized as a shortcut key. You can use this shortcut when you are exploring the items on the menu with the keyboard arrows. This parameter can only be applied in AIR projects with window and application menus.

- keyEquivalent: This specifies the letter that will select an item on the menu when it's pressed in conjunction with the Ctrl key on Windows or the Cmd key on Mac OS X. In order for this shortcut to work, the application has to be active and in the foreground. This parameter can only be applied to window and application menus.

- name: This is a unique ID that doesn't depend on the localization of the element.

- select: This is the name of the method that has to be called upon a selection event. This attribute allows you to easily activate, deactivate, or change the functions that are associated with an element on the menu.

Extending the NativeMenu class

Now you can create the class that will dynamically generate native menus for your application. The class is called XMLMenu. You can find it in the com.comtaste.foed.essentialair. chapter6 namespace in the src folder of the ch06p06.fla project. The class begins by declaring its namespace and the classes to import in the compilation phase of the application:

```
package com.comtaste.foed.essentialair.chapter6
{
import flash.display.NativeMenu;
import flash.display.NativeMenuItem;
import flash.events.Event;
```

The following class declaration tells Flash that you're extending the NativeMenu class:

```
public class XMLMenu extends NativeMenu
{
```

Then you define the necessary class properties. A property will keep track of the context in which the methods of the select attributes in the `MenuItem` nodes will be executed. A property will store a copy of the original source XML of the menu.

```
// execution scope for mapped functions
private var _scope:Object;

// stored xml source
private var _source:XML;
```

The constructor method of the class requires the two following arguments. The first is the XML that defines the structure of the menu, and the second is the scope in which the functions that are associated with the selection events in the XML are executed.

```
public function XMLMenu( XMLSource:XML, scope:Object )
{
    // call super constructor
    super();
```

Then you assign the received XML instance to the class variables, as well as the object that will be the execution scope for the functions you need to map:

```
// store mapped function scope
_scope = scope;
    // store xml source
_source = XMLSource;
```

Next, you extract an instance of the XMLList class that contains all the top-level MenuItem nodes of the received XML document by using E4X syntax:

```
// generate xmlList of all top-level <menuItem> xml nodes
var menuItems:XMLList = XMLSource.MenuItem;
```

Now that everything has been prepared correctly, you call the `createItemFromXML()` method. You provide the list of elements to create as an argument. You also specify that they need to be added as children of the class itself, as shown here:

```
// generate menu items from xml
createItemFromXML( this, menuItems );
}
```

The recursive createItemFromXML() method starts from a list of XML nodes, like the ones that you've defined as MenuItem. You generate a native menu in which each element corresponds to an XML node. The first argument of the method requires an instance of the NativeMenu class. Finally, you add the elements you've created to this instance from the nodes you've provided as a second argument of the function. Here's the code:

```
// initialize xml-defined menu items
private function createItemFromXML( menu:NativeMenu,
                                    source:XMLList ):NativeMenu
{
```

Then you define the following instance of the NativeMenuItem class, which you'll use to generate the items of the native menu in a for...each loop:

```
// menu item that will be created
var item:NativeMenuItem;
```

For each XML node, you access its attributes and use them to populate the properties of the NativeMenuItem object you're creating. Here's the code:

```
// iterate on any top-level node
// and create a submenu for each element
var xmlItem:XML;
for each( xmlItem in source )
{
    // access menu item details
```

To access the attributes of the node, you used the E4X syntax. The syntax requires the attributes to be accessed by specifying xmlItem.@attributeName. For each MenuItem node, you access all the properties provided by the XML object. Each attribute has to be saved in the right kind of local variable for the received data. These operations are shown in the following code:

```
// label for item
 var itemLabel:String = String( xmlItem.@label );
// item's ID, not displayed
var itemName:String = String( xmlItem.@name );
// mnemonic index key
var itemMnemonicIndex:int = int( xmlItem.@mnemonicIndex );
// key equivalent associated with item,
// need COMMAND key on Mac and Control key on Windows
var itemKeyEquivalent:String = String(xmlItem.@keyEquivalent);
// indicates if item is a separator
 var itemIsSeparator:Boolean = false;
 if( String( xmlItem.@isSeparator ) == 'true' )
 {
     itemIsSeparator = true;
 }
// callback function name to recall when item is selected
var itemSelectLabel:String = String( xmlItem.@select );
```

The last attribute to check, select, allows you to register an event listener function dynamically for the selection event of a given node. The XML node, via this attribute, specifies the name of the required event listener method, but doesn't specify where the method actually is. The execution environment of the method is provided to the constructor of the class and stored in the _scope variable. Finally, the getFunction() method checks for the presence of the function in the given execution environment and returns a reference to the event listener function or the null value:

```
// try to retrieve requested callback on defined scope
var itemSelect:Function = getFunction( itemSelectLabel );
```

After having extracted and validated the values assigned to all the attributes of the node in question, you can assign the reference to a new instance of the NativeMenuItem class to the local item variable. This variable is declared outside of the iterative loop. The label defined by the XML node is provided to the constructor method. You also specify whether the instance you're creating is an item separator in the method. You assign the value of the corresponding attribute to the name property of the NativeMenuItem class. The property won't be displayed in the menu but will be the unique ID for the element. Here's the code:

```
// instantiate menu item
item = new NativeMenuItem( itemLabel, itemIsSeparator );
// assign values to correct properties
item.name = itemName;
```

All the other properties provided by the XML node are only necessary if the item isn't an item separator, so next, you check the value of the Boolean itemIsSeparator variable before assigning the rest of the information:

```
// all other properties are needed
// only if menu item is not a separator
if( !itemIsSeparator )
{
    // assign given mnemonic index
    item.mnemonicIndex = itemMnemonicIndex;

    // assign given key equivalent shortcut
    item.keyEquivalent = itemKeyEquivalent;
```

If the itemSelect variable isn't null, it means that a correspondence has been found in the relevant execution environment (_scope) for the required event listener method (attribute select). Here's an example:

```
// if available, map callback to select event
if( itemSelect != null )
{
    item.addEventListener( Event.SELECT, itemSelect );
}
}
```

Once you've completed the object of the NativeMenuItem class, you can add it to the menu as an item. Do so by calling the addItem() function of the NativeMenu class, as shown here:

```
// add menu item created to parent
menu.addItem( item );
```

Before creating another menu item, you check if the XML node contains child MenuItem nodes. If so, it means that the element you've created will become a submenu of the menu.

Next, you create an XMLList object containing the subnodes. Then you assign an instance of the NativeMenu class to the submenu property of the NativeMenuItem item you're creating. Finally, you call the createItemFromXML() method, specifying that the list of XML nodes will have to populate the initialized submenu property.

```
// if menu item is itself a menu
// populate it
var subMenuItems:XMLList = xmlItem.MenuItem;
if( subMenuItems.length() > 0 )
{
    // instantiate submenu object
    item.submenu = new NativeMenu();
            // populate submenu
    createItemFromXML( item.submenu, subMenuItems );
}
}
```

At the end of the for...each loop, you return the populated menu to the calling method, like this:

```
// return menu
return menu;
}
```

The createItemFromXML() method uses the following getFunction() function to check if the event listener method is valid. The value becomes the attribute of the XML node.

```
private function getFunction( name:String ):Function
{
```

The method receives a string, which corresponds to the name of the function, as an argument. You create a local variable of the Function class, specifying that its initial value is null. Before proceeding, you check that the function name received as an argument for the function isn't null or an empty text string. If it isn't valid, you interrupt the execution of the function and return the null value to the calling method. Here's the code:

```
var f:Function = null;
// if name is not valid do not proceed
if( name == null || name == "" )
    return null;
```

Open a try...catch construct. In the construct, you assign the reference to the required method from the local variable you've set up for this purpose. Then you obtain a reference to the required method through the literal access to the relevant execution environment.

If the relevant execution method is a dynamic object and the required method doesn't exist, the variable will keep its null value. If the execution environment is an instance of a class, the attempt to access a nonexistent property will cause an exception in Flash Player. The exception will be intercepted by the try...catch construct, avoiding unwanted error messages during the execution of the application. The following example accomplishes these tasks:

```
// use try...catch to avoid unwanted runtime exceptions
try
{
    // try access callback function in defined scope
    f = _scope[ name ];
        } catch ( e:TypeError )
{
    // The callback specified in source file
    // is something other than a method
    trace('The callback "' + name +
            '" is invalid for object type XMLMenu' );

} catch ( e:ReferenceError )
{
    // The callback does not exist
    trace( 'The callback "' + name +
            '" does not exist for object type XMLMenu');
}

// return retrieved function's pointer
return f;
}
```

The XMLMenu class is now ready to be used when you need to generate native menus dynamically in your applications. In the next section, you'll create an AIR application that will use this class.

Using the XMLMenu class to create dynamic menus

The purpose of this exercise is to improve the previous example of the ch06p02.fla project, making the creation of the application menu dynamic. Begin by opening the ch06p06.fla project in Flash CS4. The project is the same as the ch06p02.fla project at first, as you can see in Figure 6-19.

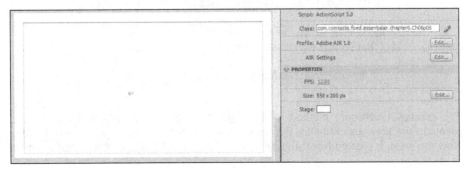

Figure 6-19. The stage of the ch06p06.fla project

Access the document class for this project by clicking the Edit class definition icon on the Document Properties panel of the Flash project. This will open the class associated with the project. The class starts by declaring its namespace, followed by the classes it needs to import during compilation to make the application work properly. Then come the class properties, which are the same ones as the ch06p02.fla project. The code is as follows:

```
package com.comtaste.foed.essentialair.chapter6
{
    import fl.controls.TextArea;
    import flash.desktop.NativeApplication;
    import flash.display.MovieClip;
    import flash.display.NativeMenu;
    import flash.display.NativeMenuItem;
    import flash.display.NativeWindow;
    import flash.events.Event;
    import flash.filesystem.File;
    import flash.filesystem.FileMode;
    import flash.filesystem.FileStream;

    public class ch06p06 extends MovieClip
    {
    // onstage components
    public var output:TextArea;
    // class properties
    private var menuRoot:NativeMenu;
```

Next, the constructor method of the class creates and populates the native menu. The menu object is then assigned to the application or window menu, depending on the functions of the local operating system:

```
public function ch06p06()
{
    super();
    // generate native menu to use
    createNativeMenu();
    // assign to application menu if we are on Mac OS X
    if ( NativeApplication.supportsMenu )
    {
        NativeApplication.nativeApplication.menu = menuRoot;
    }
    // assign to window menu if we are on Microsoft Windows
    if ( NativeWindow.supportsMenu )
    {
        stage.nativeWindow.menu = menuRoot;        }
}
```

The createNativeMenu() method is in charge of initializing and populating the native menu. In the previous examples, the menus were created directly via ActionScript code. Now the menu is created from an external XML structure. The external XML document is read and its content is assigned to an instance of the class you've created, XMLMenu. The class will populate the menu using the XML document.

```
// create a complete native menu
private function createNativeMenu():void
{
```

In this example, the source XML document is in the xml folder in the installation folder of the AIR application, so you create the following instance of the File class that determines the path of the XML file:

```
// specify path for xml menu source
var xmlSourceFile:File =
File.applicationDirectory.resolvePath( "xml/menuSource.xml" );
```

Next, create an object of the FileStream class and use it to access the XML document in read-only mode. The XML document contains the structure of the native menu that you want to create. You will access the file in synchronous mode.

```
// create a FileStream object
var fileStream:FileStream = new FileStream();
    // open stream for reading xml menu source
fileStream.open( xmlSourceFile, FileMode.READ );
```

You save the content of the opened file in an XML variable. Then you close the stream to the external XML document, as shown here:

```
// load XML source content
var xmlSource:XML =
    XML( fileStream.readUTFBytes( fileStream.bytesAvailable ) );
    // close fileStream connection to xml file
fileStream.close();
```

Now you can assign the instance of the XMLMenu class to the menuRoot property. This instance is created from the loaded XML structure. You specify that the execution environment of possible event listener functions will be the active instance of the application, in the constructor of the XMLMenu class. This information is provided as a second argument, as shown here:

```
// instantiate main menu object
menuRoot = new XMLMenu( xmlSource, this );
```

Finally, you register an event listener event for the selection event of the whole native menu. Each time the user selects an item on the menu, an event listener event that is associated with the item will be invoked. Then the genericMenuSelection() method will be launched, which will write the label of the selected item on the TextArea on the stage.

```
// register event listener at menu root level
menuRoot.addEventListener( Event.SELECT, genericMenuSelection );
}
```

6

The createNativeMenu() method accesses an external XML document to define the structure of the native menu that you want to use.

During the creation of the native menu, an event listener method has been created for the selection event of the whole menu. This method is genericMenuSelection(). It accesses the instance of the selected item via the target property of the event object that the function receives, and extracts its text label and writes it in the output TextArea. Here's an example of the genericMenuSelection() method:

```
// minimize application
public function genericMenuSelection( e : Event ):void
{
    // get reference to menu item selected via target property of event
    var target:NativeMenuItem = e.target as NativeMenuItem;
        // write into output textarea
    output.appendText( "Selected item with name: '" +
                target.name + "'" + File.lineEnding );
}
```

The XML document that defines the structure specifies the following event listener methods for some items. These methods are the same as the ones in the ch06p02.fla project:

```
// get application description
public function getInformation( evt : Event ):void
{
    // access to application XML descriptor
    var appDescriptor:XML =
        NativeApplication.nativeApplication.applicationDescriptor;

    // retrieve XML descriptor namespace
    var nsDeclaration:Namespace = appDescriptor.namespace();

    // read description node from XML
    var informationText:String =
        String( appDescriptor.nsDeclaration::description[ 0 ] );

    // write into textarea 'output' description contents
    output.appendText( "Adobe Air, test application for "
        + "menus functionalities." + File.lineEnding );
    output.appendText( informationText + File.lineEnding );
}

// close application
public function closeApplication( e : Event ):void
{
    NativeApplication.nativeApplication.exit();
}
```

```
    // minimize application
    public function minimizeApplication( e : Event ):void
    {
        stage.nativeWindow.minimize();
    }
```

Now the application is complete. Go back to the Flash project and execute it by selecting Control ➤ Test Movie. You can see the application in execution in Figure 6-20. Try interacting with the menu by selecting different items. Close the application, change the external XML document, and execute it again. As you can see, updating and editing the application menu is now a very simple operation.

The XML document for your example is the following:

```xml
<?xml version ="1.0" encoding="utf-8" ?>
<menu>
    <MenuItem label="File" isSeparator="false"
        mnemonicIndex="0" keyEquivalent=""
        name="fileMenu" select="">
        <MenuItem label="New File" isSeparator="false"
            mnemonicIndex="0" keyEquivalent="n"
            name="newFileCommand" select=""/>
        <MenuItem label="Open File" isSeparator="false"
            mnemonicIndex="0" keyEquivalent="o"
            name="openFileCommand" select=""/>
        <MenuItem label="" isSeparator="true"
            mnemonicIndex="" keyEquivalent=""
            name="fileMenuSeparator1" select=""/>
        <MenuItem label="Minimize" isSeparator="false"
            mnemonicIndex="0" keyEquivalent="i"
            name="minimizeCommand" select="minimizeApplication"/>
        <MenuItem label="Close File" isSeparator="false"
            mnemonicIndex="0" keyEquivalent="l"
            name="closeFileCommand" select="closeApplication"/>
        <MenuItem label="" isSeparator="true"
            mnemonicIndex="" keyEquivalent=""
            name="fileMenuSeparator2" select=""/>
        <MenuItem label="About..." isSeparator="false"
            mnemonicIndex="0" keyEquivalent="a"
            name="minimizeCommand" select="getInformation"/>
    </MenuItem>
    <MenuItem label="Edit" isSeparator="false"
        mnemonicIndex="0" keyEquivalent=""
        name="editMenu" select="">
        <MenuItem label="Copy" isSeparator="false"
            mnemonicIndex="0" keyEquivalent="c"
            name="copyCommand" select=""/>
        <MenuItem label="Cut" isSeparator="false"
            mnemonicIndex="1" keyEquivalent="x"
            name="cutCommand" select=""/>
```

6

277

```
        <MenuItem label="Paste" isSeparator="false"
            mnemonicIndex="0" keyEquivalent="v"
            name="pasteCommand" select=""/>
    </MenuItem>
    <MenuItem label="Custom" isSeparator="false"
        mnemonicIndex="0" keyEquivalent=""
        name="customMenu" select="">
        <MenuItem label="Generic 1" isSeparator="false"
            mnemonicIndex="0" keyEquivalent=""
            name="genericCommand1" select=""/>
        <MenuItem label="Generic 2" isSeparator="false"
            mnemonicIndex="0" keyEquivalent=""
            name="genericCommand2" select=""/>
    </MenuItem>
</menu>
```

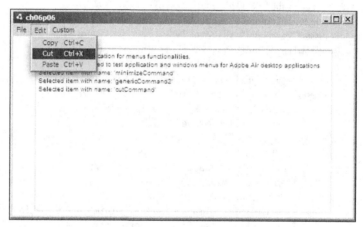

Figure 6-20. The ch06p06.fla project on execution

This is the complete ActionScript class that you just created:

```
package com.comtaste.foed.essentialair.chapter6
{
import fl.controls.TextArea;

import flash.desktop.NativeApplication;
import flash.display.MovieClip;
import flash.display.NativeMenu;
import flash.display.NativeMenuItem;
import flash.display.NativeWindow;
import flash.events.Event;
import flash.filesystem.File;
import flash.filesystem.FileMode;
import flash.filesystem.FileStream;
```

```
public class Ch06p06 extends MovieClip
{
    // onstage components
    public var output:TextArea;

    // class properties
    private var menuRoot:NativeMenu;

    public function Ch06p06()
    {
        super();

        // generate native menu to use
        createNativeMenu();

        // assign to application menu if we are on Mac OS X
        if ( NativeApplication.supportsMenu )
        {
            NativeApplication.nativeApplication.menu = menuRoot;
        }

        // assign to window menu if we are on Microsoft Windows
        if ( NativeWindow.supportsMenu )
        {
            stage.nativeWindow.menu = menuRoot;
        }

    }

    // create a complete native menu
    private function createNativeMenu():void
    {
        // specify path for xml menu source
        var xmlSourceFile:File =
        File.applicationDirectory.resolvePath( "xml/menuSource.xml" );

        // create a FileStream object
        var fileStream:FileStream = new FileStream();

        // open stream for reading xml menu source
        fileStream.open( xmlSourceFile, FileMode.READ );

        // load XML source content
        var xmlSource:XML =
            XML(fileStream.readUTFBytes(fileStream.bytesAvailable));

        // close fileStream connection to xml file
        fileStream.close();
```

```
            // instantiate main menu object
            menuRoot = new XMLMenu( xmlSource, this );

            // register event listener at menu root level
            menuRoot.addEventListener( Event.SELECT,
                genericMenuSelection );
        }

        // called on click
        public function getInformation( evt : Event ):void
        {
            var appDescriptor:XML =
            NativeApplication.nativeApplication.applicationDescriptor;
                var nsDeclaration:Namespace = appDescriptor.namespace();
            var informationText:String =
                String( appDescriptor.nsDeclaration::description[ 0 ] );
            output.appendText( "Adobe Air, test application for "
                + "menus functionalities." + File.lineEnding );
            output.appendText( informationText + File.lineEnding );
        }

        // close application
        public function closeApplication( e : Event ):void
        {
            NativeApplication.nativeApplication.exit();
        }

        // minimize application
        public function minimizeApplication( e : Event ):void
        {
            stage.nativeWindow.minimize();
        }

        // minimize application
        public function genericMenuSelection( e : Event ):void
        {
            // get reference to menu item selected
            // via target property of event
            var target:NativeMenuItem = e.target as NativeMenuItem;

            // write into output textarea
            output.appendText( "Selected item with name: '" +
                        target.name + "'" + File.lineEnding );
        }
    } // close class
} // close package
```

Summary

This chapter presented the differences in how Windows and Mac OS X operating systems display native menus. You learned how to create flexible multiplatform menu that are easy to maintain. In the final part of this chapter, you created a customized class to generate native menus from XML documents. The XMLMenu class was integrated in a functioning AIR application as an example. The class you created only shows a part of its potential functionality.

Now it's up to you to improve and extend this class by adding functions to make it more flexible and useful for your specific needs.

6

CHAPTER 7
ACCESSING THE FILE SYSTEM

Developing websites or web applications with Adobe Flash can be fun and creative. It's possible to obtain spectacular graphical effects for your portals and create easy-to-use browsing systems. However, it can be a little more frustrating to work with ActionScript if you need to interact with data to access local files and their content or write data to the user's computer.

All of Flash Player's limitations for accessing remote content on the Web have solid reasons that are based on user safety. However, when it comes to desktop applications and AIR, things change completely.

AIR provides complete access to the host file system, allowing your applications to use all the file system resources it needs to function correctly. You can move, create, copy, and remove files or entire folders. You can also access the system clipboard, and drag and drop files and items from the operating system or other desktop applications into your applications. It allows you to create applications that are fully integrated with the host operating system.

The FileReference and FileStream classes are available to work with the file system. The File class extends the FileReference class, and the FileStream class allows you to access documents on the host machine in **synchronous** or **asynchronous** modes. When you access the file system in synchronous mode, all the other operations in your application are put on standby until the running synchronous process has been completed. These operations include rendering objects or interactions with the user. Until the process has finished, the user won't be able to interact with the application.

When you access the file system in asynchronous mode, on the other hand, your application continues to function normally while it's reading or writing to disk, leaving the user oblivious to the fact that the application is processing information. Asynchronous access to the file system requires event listener functions for each operation to confirm the success or failure of the operation. Further on in this chapter, you'll see how to make both ways of accessing the file system work.

The next section will introduce the ActionScript classes in the flash.filesystem package.

The flash.filesystem package classes

The flash.filesystem package, which has been added to the AIR APIs, provides the following classes:

- File
- FileMode
- FileStream

The File class

Each instance of the File class is a reference to a specific file or folder on the host operating system. You can use this class to identify the complete path of a file or folder, access detailed information regarding the file or folder, or manipulate its content.

The File class also allows you to work with documents and folders that are on the local operating system by creating references to the files that you can interact with programmatically. The methods to access the files or folders are almost identical to one another.

To make multiplatform application development easier, AIR includes properties to point to standard folders as static constants of the File class. These standard folders allow you to point a File object to a folder on the local system on Windows, Mac OS X, and Linux. These standard folders will be covered shortly. The following code shows how to point to the readme.txt file on the user's desktop using the File class:

```
var fileObj:File = File.desktopDirectory.resolvePath("readme.txt");
```

The FileMode class

This class provides various static constants that define the possible modes in which the FileStream class can access the binary content of any file. AIR allows you to open a file in the following modes:

- **Read**: The FileStream object can read data from the file.
- **Write**: The FileStream object can write data to the file.
- **Create**: The FileStream object creates a file upon opening.
- **Truncate upon opening**: Data in the file is deleted upon opening (before any data is written).
- **Append written data**: Data is always written to the end of the file (when any write method is called).

The FileStream class

The FileStream class is responsible for accessing the content of a document and provides various methods to write to and read from the file. You have to provide an instance of the File class to the FileStream class to tell it which document you are interested in. The following code opens the readme.txt file on the user's desktop in read-only mode:

```
var fileObj:File = File.desktopDirectory.resolvePath("readme.txt");
var streamObj:FileStream = new FileStream();
streamObj.open( fileObj, FileMode.READ );
```

Now let's take a look at folders.

AIR folder shortcuts

AIR provides you a set of shortcuts to access the more common folders on the user's local system. The following sections discuss these.

The user folder

This folder corresponds to the user's home folder on Windows (C:\Documents and settings*userName*\) as well as on Mac OS X (/User/*userName*/). The user folder generally contains all the user's files and data. It occasionally contains subfolders for configuration documents or data associated with the application.

You can create a reference to a file or folder in the main user folder by using the userDirectory constant, as shown here:

```
var fileObject:File = File.userDirectory.resolvePath( "readme.txt" );
```

This is an example of creating a reference to a text document in the root of the relevant folder.

The user documents folder

This folder is normally in the main user folder and is meant to contain the user's personal data and documents. You can use this folder to let the user save documents that can be used even outside the application, such as generated reports or exported images. You can access the files and the folder by using the documentsDirectory constant, like this:

```
var fileObject:File = File.documentsDirectory.resolvePath(
                          "readme.txt" );
```

The application folder

This folder contains the installed application and the files that are distributed along with the program. From here, you can also access the application descriptor XML file and the icons associated with it.

When you define a file or folder path using a URL (as opposed to the native system path), you can refer to this folder as app:/. You can access the files and folders contained in it by using the applicationDirectory constant, as shown here:

```
var file:File = File.applicationDirectory.resolvePath("readme.txt");
```

The application storage folder

For each AIR application you install, a separate folder is created for files containing the user's preferences or any partially saved documents.

This storage folder is different for every user of the local operating system and uses the combination of the application ID and the publisher ID of the application to generate a unique name for itself.

On Mac OS X systems, the path to access this folder follows this pattern: /User/ UserName/Library/Preference/applicationID.publisherID/Local Store/.

On Microsoft Windows, the path is as follows: C:\Document and Settings\UserName\ Application data\applicationID.publisherID\Local Store\.

When you define a file or folder path using a URL, you can refer to this folder as app-storage:/. You can access the files and folders contained in it by using the applicationStorageDirectory constant, like this:

```
var fileObject:File =
    File.applicationStorageDirectory.resolvePath( "readme.txt" );
```

The desktop folder

The desktop folder is a shortcut to access the active user's desktop. You can access the files and the folders it contains like this:

```
var fileObject:File =
    File.desktopDirectory.resolvePath( "readme.txt" );
```

The file system root

On Mac OS X systems, when you want to access the root of the operating system, it always returns the reference to the only root file that's available: /. On Microsoft Windows systems, the system returns a list of all the installed disks that are associated with a drive letter (e.g., C:, D:, etc.). To access the root folders, you use the static getRootDirectories() function of the File class, as shown here:

```
File.getRootDirectories();
```

The getRootDirectories() method returns an array of File objects. Any returned File object is a root folder of the local operating system.

Accessing files and folders

AIR provides standard ways to access the most commonly used folders during the execution of a desktop application. These folders allow the developer to point to the files more quickly and easily. However, these shortcuts may not give you quite the freedom you would like. To reach any file in the computer, the File class gives you a few options:

- The use of relative paths
- The use of native paths
- The use of URLs
- The ability to browse and select files

The next few sections will illustrate each of these approaches.

Using relative paths

The File class, as already mentioned, allows you to access the files or folders from a known path of another file. Using this technique, you can start from one of the standard folders provided by AIR and then choose the path of your explicit destination. To determine the path of a file using this approach, you use the resolvePath() method of the File class.

The following line of code returns an instance of the File class that refers to the readme. txt file in the installation folder of the application:

```
var file:File = File.applicationDirectory.resolvePath("readme.txt");
```

Using this technique, you can access all the files and folders you are interested in just by starting from a known folder.

You can also calculate the relative path between two different files by using the getRelativePath() function. This function returns a string of text with the relative path between the two files you choose. To obtain the relative path between two files, you have to have two File objects that represent the relevant documents:

```
// Point two file objects to two different files
var file1:File = File.desktopDirectory.resolvePath(
                          "my works/test/august/report.txt" );
var file2:File = File.desktopDirectory.resolvePath( "my works" );

// calculate relative path
var relativePath:String = file2.getRelativePath( file1 );
```

The response path will be test/august/report.txt.

Using native paths

Instead of using relative paths, you can use the native path of a file or folder. The native path corresponds to the absolute path of the file, as defined by the local operating system. For Windows systems, native paths use either the backslash (\) or the forward slash (/) as a separator. Mac OS X systems only use the forward slash.

> The File class provides developers with the static separator variable to facilitate run-time construction of native paths. This variable recognizes the path-building pattern for the host operating system and returns the correct separator.

If you want to create a File object on Windows systems using the native path, you use the nativePath property, with which you associate the following path:

```
var fileObj:File = new File();
fileObj.nativePath = "C:/Test Folder/readme.txt";
```

You can specify the same file on a Mac OS X system as follows:

```
var fileObj:File = new File();
fileObj.nativePath = "/Users/Matteo/Test Folder/readme.txt";
```

You can also obtain the native paths straight from the constructor of the File class like this:

```
var fileObj:File = new File("C:/Test Folder/readme.txt" );
trace(fileObj.nativePath);
```

The global trace() method returns the URI-encoded version of the URL: c:/Test%20Folder/readme.txt.

Using system URLs

Another alternative to native paths are file or folder URLs. You can specify the path of a given document by using its URL instead of its native path. The URLs that AIR accepts for the file system are defined by three possible roots:

- file:///, for a random path on the hosting system
- app:/, for a relative path to the application installation folder
- app-storage:/, for a relative path to the application data folder

You can create a File object by using the url property, as follows:

```
var fileObj:File = new File();
fileObj.url = "file:///c:/Test Folder/readme.txt";
```

You can also write the following code to obtain the URL straight from the constructor of the File class, like you would for native paths:

```
fileObj:File = new File("file:///c:/Test Folder/readme.txt" );
```

When you assign the URL of a File object, it gets converted into its URI-encoded version, where all spaces are replaced by %20. So, when you access the url property of the preceding fileObj variable in reading mode, this will be the result:

```
file:///c:/Test%20Folder/readme.txt
```

Browsing and selecting a file

The last option to define a File object is to let the user choose through a dialog box. The File class provides four different browsing system dialog boxes and the same number of methods:

- browseForOpen() shows a system dialog box that allows the user to select a single file on his computer. It is possible to choose some filters to limit the selection to a certain number of files.
- browseForSave() shows a system dialog box that allows the user to select a single file on his computer. You can't choose any filters—only a string to display in the title bar of the box.

7

- browseForOpenMultiple() shows a system dialog box that allows the user to select an indefinite number of files on his computer. You can choose filters to limit the selection to a certain type of files.

- browseForDirectory() shows a system dialog box that allows the user to select a single folder on his computer. You can choose a string to be displayed in the title bar of the box.

The browseForOpen(), browseForSave(), and browseForDirectory() methods dispatch the select event of the Event class when the user selects a file or a folder. The target property of the auto-generated event object contains a reference to the file object you are interested in.

The browseForOpenMultiple() method, on the other hand, dispatches the selectMultiple event of the FileListEvent class. The generated event object provides the files property, which represents a list of file objects regarding the selection that the user makes in the dialog box.

Follow these steps to use a dialog box to select a folder on a local system:

1. Open Flash CS4 and open the ch07p01.fla project, or create a new Flash file. This project will allow the user to select any folder from the local operating system. To access the Browse for Folder dialog box, click the button with the instance name choose and the label Select a Folder on the application stage. Every time the user selects a file, the path will be entered in a TextArea with an instance name of output, visible on the stage.

2. Now you associate an ActionScript class with the Flash document you've just created. You can create this class from scratch as a new ActionScript class (saved it in the following folders structure: com/comtaste/foed/essentialair/chapter7), or use the Ch07p01.as class, which you can download from the downloads section at www.friendsofed.com/.

3. Now click the Edit class definition icon from the Document Properties panel of the Flash project (shown in Figure 7-1) to access the document class containing the ActionScript code.

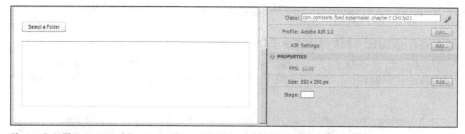

Figure 7-1. The stage and Document Properties panel for the ch07p01.fla project

Now enter the code for the Ch07p01.as class, which starts by specifying the namespace of the package it is contained in and indicates the external classes it depends on to execute correctly, as shown here:

```
package com.comtaste.foed.essentialair.chapter7
{
import fl.controls.Button;
import fl.controls.TextArea;
import flash.display.MovieClip;
import flash.events.Event;
import flash.events.MouseEvent;
import flash.filesystem.File;
```

Next, you'll declare the class and extend the MovieClip class. You have to extend from the MovieClip or the Sprite class so that the Flash CS4 compiler can associate the document class with the stage of the ch07p01.fla project. Here's how to accomplish this task:

```
public class Ch07p01 extends MovieClip
{
```

The properties that have to be available to all the functions implemented by the class itself are defined in the body of the class. These properties contain references to the instances of objects on the stage of the Flash project. Also, a property of the File class will contain the reference to the folder the user will select from time to time.

You have to declare the variables that refer to the objects on the stage. This is because the project has been designed so that it doesn't generate the declaration of variables for the graphical elements automatically. This choice is specified on the Advanced ActionScript 3.0 Settings panel of the project, which you can access through the Publish Settings panel (see Figure 7-2).

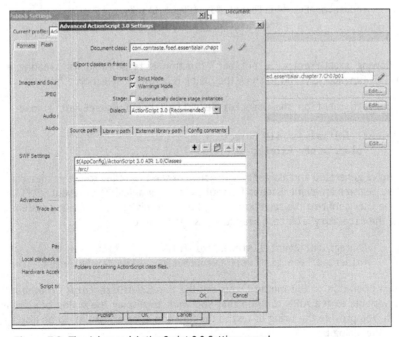

Figure 7-2. The Advanced ActionScript 3.0 Settings panel

Here is the ActionScript that opens the body of the Ch07p01.as class:

```
public class Ch07p01 extends MovieClip
{
// on stage components
public var choose:Button;
public var output:TextArea;

// class properties
private var folder:File;
```

Now you can prepare the constructor of the class correctly, where you can register an event listener for the click event on the choose button. When the user clicks the button, it will execute the showDirectorySelection() function.

> See Chapter 6 to learn more about creating constructor classes.

After the declaration of the properties, enter the following code:

```
// class properties
private var folder:File;

public function Ch07p01()
{
    // register event listener for button
    choose.addEventListener( MouseEvent.CLICK,
                showDirectorySelection );
}
```

The following showDirectorySelection() function is responsible for creating a File object. This function asks AIR to show the dialog box for the selection a folder:

```
private function showDirectorySelection( event:MouseEvent ):void
{
    // initialize file object
    folder = new File();
```

Once you've generated and assigned an instance of the File class to the folder class variable, you register an event listener function to the variable for the Event.SELECT event. When the user confirms the selection of the folder on his or her operating system, it will execute the directorySelected() function, as shown here:

```
// register event listener for folder selection
folder.addEventListener( Event.SELECT, directorySelected );
```

As a final operation of the method, you call the browseForDirectory() method of the folder variable to tell AIR's runtime that you want to display the dialog box for folder selection. You provide the string of text to the function as an argument, to be displayed as a title of the dialog box, like this:

```
        // show system dialog
        folder.browseForDirectory( "Choose a folder on your system" );
    }
```

When the user clicks the choose button, a Browse for Folder dialog box will appear. If the user clicks the Cancel button in the dialog box, nothing will happen, but if a folder is selected, it will call the directorySelected() function. Figure 7-3 shows the open dialog box.

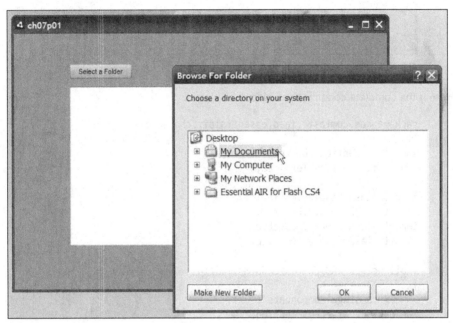

Figure 7-3. The Browse for Folder dialog box opened from your AIR application

The directorySelected() method accesses the native path of the selected folder and writes it in the output TextArea on the application stage, as shown here:

```
    private function directorySelected( event:Event ):void
    {
        // write out selected folder's path
        output.appendText( "Selected folder: " + folder.nativePath +"\n" );
    }
    }
    }
```

Now go back to the ch07p01.fla project, and execute it by selecting the Test Movie command from the Flash CS4 Control menu. In Figure 7-4, you can see the application in execution after a few folders have been selected. Open the Browse for Folder dialog box by clicking the choose button. Each time you confirm the selection of a folder, it's native path will appear in the output TextArea.

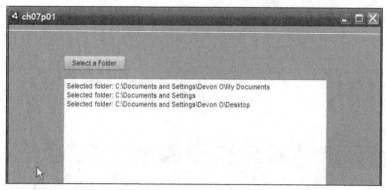

Figure 7-4. The ch07p01.fla project during execution

Here is the complete code for the Ch07p01.as class:

```
package com.comtaste.foed.essentialair.chapter7
{
import fl.controls.Button;
import fl.controls.TextArea;

import flash.display.MovieClip;
import flash.events.Event;
import flash.events.MouseEvent;
import flash.filesystem.File;

public class Ch07p01 extends MovieClip
{
    // on stage components
    public var choose:Button;
    public var output:TextArea;

    // class properties
    private var folder:File;

    public function Ch07p01()
    {
        super();

        // register event listener for button
        choose.addEventListener( MouseEvent.CLICK,
                    showDirectorySelection );
    }


    private function showDirectorySelection( event:MouseEvent ):void
    {
        // initialize file object
        folder = new File();
```

```
                // register event listener for folder selection
                folder.addEventListener( Event.SELECT, directorySelected );

              // show system dialog
              folder.browseForDirectory("Choose a directory on your system");
            }

            private function directorySelected( event:Event ):void
            {
                // write out selected folder's path
                output.appendText("Selected folder: "+folder.nativePath+"\n");
            }
        } // class end
        } // package end
```

The next section will show how to list a folder's contents.

Accessing the contents of a folder

AIR allows you to obtain a list of files and folders in a particular folder. This can be very useful if, for example, you want to create an application to load and display all images in a given folder. For each file and folder, you can also access detailed information such as the size, the extension (if it's a file), the remaining disk room, the creation date, and so on. To access the list of files and documents in a folder, you have to use the getDirectoryListing() function provided by the File class. This method returns a list of File objects contained in the relevant folder.

In this section, you will see how to use the getDirectoryListing() method.

Listing the contents of a folder

The example AIR application ch07p02.fla will allow you to select a folder and display a list of files and folders in a DataGrid control.

It will trace the following information for each object in the folder:

- Name
- Size
- Extension (for files only)
- Creation date

Open the ch07p02.fla project in Flash CS4 or create a new one. Access its document class as you have already done in the previous exercise—by clicking the Edit class definition icon on the Document Properties panel (see Figure 7-5).

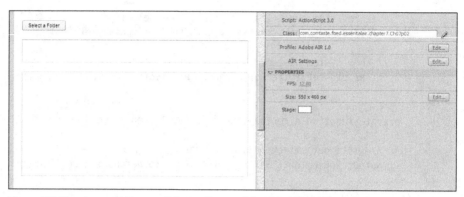

Figure 7-5. The stage and Document Properties panel for the ch07p02.fla project

You start the class as follows, by declaring its namespace and the external classes it needs to import during compilation. Create a new ActionScript class and save it with the name Ch07p02.as. Insert the following code:

```
package com.comtaste.foed.essentialair.chapter7
{
import fl.controls.Button;
import fl.controls.DataGrid;
import fl.controls.TextArea;
import fl.controls.dataGridClasses.DataGridColumn;
import fl.data.DataProvider;

import flash.display.MovieClip;
import flash.events.Event;
import flash.events.MouseEvent;
import flash.filesystem.File;

public class Ch07p02 extends MovieClip
{
```

Next, you declare the class properties, as shown here:

```
public class Ch07p02 extends MovieClip
{

// onstage components
public var choose:Button;
public var output:TextArea;
public var directoryList:DataGrid;

// class properties
private var folder:File;
```

Like in the previous exercise, you have the choose button to open the dialog box. The folder property contains a reference to the folder the user selects and the output TextArea. The DataGrid component is there to display the details of the files in the relevant folder.

The constructor prepares the elements of the class: it registers the necessary event listeners and sets the required columns in the DataGrid component.

The following code invokes the super constructor function and registers an event listener function for the click event of the choose button. When the user clicks the button, the application will call the showDirectorySelected() function and show the Browse for Folder dialog box.

```
public function Ch07p02()
{    super();
    // register event listener for button
    choose.addEventListener( MouseEvent.CLICK,
                  showDirectorySelection );
    // set up DataGrid
```

Now you need to specify the columns for the DataGrid component. Each column is represented by an instance of the DataGridColumn class. For each DataGridColumn object, you specify a header by assigning it to the headerText property, as shown here:

```
    // register event listener for button
    choose.addEventListener( MouseEvent.CLICK,
                  showDirectorySelection );
    // set up DataGrid
    // instantiate new DataGrid column
    var col1:DataGridColumn = new DataGridColumn();

    // set column header
    col1.headerText = "File name";
```

Then it is necessary to define a value for the dataField property, which indicates the name of the property to display. The dataField property of a DataGridColumn object takes on the value in the DataProvider of the DataGrid. The following code accomplishes these tasks:

```
    // set column datafield to use from dataprovider
    col1.dataField = "name";
```

Now that the column has been initialized correctly, you can add it to the DataGrid by calling the addColumn() method of the DataGrid class, like this:

```
    // append the column to our DataGrid
    directoryList.addColumn( col1 );
```

Next, instantiate and add the other columns you need to the DataGrid as well:

```
    // generate other needed columns

    var col2:DataGridColumn = new DataGridColumn();
    col2.headerText = "File size";
    col2.dataField = "size";
    directoryList.addColumn( col2 );
```

7

```
        var col3:DataGridColumn = new DataGridColumn();
        col3.headerText = "File extension";
        col3.dataField = "extension";
        directoryList.addColumn( col3 );
        var col4:DataGridColumn = new DataGridColumn();
        col4.headerText = "Creation date";
        col4.dataField = "creationDate";
        directoryList.addColumn( col4 );
    }
```

The showDirectorySelection() function does the following:

1. Regenerates the instance of the File class that is assigned to the folder variable

2. Registers an event listener function for when the user selects a folder

3. Displays the dialog box to select a folder

That code is shown here:

```
    private function showDirectorySelection( event:MouseEvent ):void
    {
        // initialize file object
        folder = new File();
        // register event listener for folder selection
        folder.addEventListener( Event.SELECT, directorySelected );
        // show system dialog
        folder.browseForDirectory( "Choose a folder on your system" );
    }
```

The event listener function that is associated with the selection of a folder is directorySelected(). It obtains the list of objects in the selected folder and displays them in the DataGrid, as shown here:

```
    private function directorySelected( event:Event ):void
    {
```

Next, you write the complete native path of the selected folder in the output TextArea, as follows:

```
        // write out selected folder's path
        output.appendText( "Selected folder: " + folder.nativePath +"\n" );
```

Next, you extract the list of objects contained in the selected folder in the local directoryContents variable. To access the list, you use the getDirectoryListing() function of the folder variable. The getDirectoryListing() method is a synchronous method, so the application will wait for it to finish during its execution. This could mean that the application will freeze for a few seconds if the selected folder has a large number of files and folders. Further on in this chapter, you'll see how to change this exercise to avoid the problem by using the asynchronous getDirectoryListingAsync() method. Here's the code:

```
// get selected folder contents
var directoryContents:Array = folder.getDirectoryListing();
```

Now that you've obtained the list of objects in the selected folder, you create the following instance of the DataProvider class, which will be your data source to populate the DataGrid:

```
// DataGrid dataprovider
var dp:DataProvider = new DataProvider();
```

You want the DataGrid to list all the available folders first, and then all the files, like it would normally do in Windows. To obtain this result, create the following folderNum variable as a counter for the folders on the system:

```
// folder counter
var folderNum:int = -1;
```

Next, you populate your DataProvider object with the list of objects returned by the getDirectoryListing() function by using a for each loop. You know for sure that each object in the directoryContents array is an instance of the File class.

```
// populate dataprovider
var item:File;
for each( item in directoryContents )
{
```

In any for each loop, you check if the object represented by the item variable, an instance of the File class, is a folder by checking its isDirectory property.

If the item is a folder, you increase the folder counter to 1 and add the folder to the DataProvider dp in the position given by the folderNum variable. This way, all the folders will be listed before the files.

To add an element in an explicit position, use the addItemAt() method of the DataProvider class, as shown here:

```
// if item is a folder, show it before files
if( item.isDirectory )
{
    // increments folder count
    folderNum++;

    // put folder after last folder
    // present in dataprovider
    dp.addItemAt( item, folderNum );
}
else
{
```

7

If the object represented by the item variable isn't a folder, you add it below the dp using the addItem() function of the DataProvider class, like this:

```
// add files after folders
dp.addItem( item );
}
}
```

You've created and populated the dp DataProvider object with the instances of the File class returned by the getDirectoryListing() method. Next, you assign the dp variable to the dataProvider property of the directoryList DataGrid to display the extracted information:

```
// assign dataprovider to DataGrid
directoryList.dataProvider = dp;
}
```

Here is the complete code for the Ch07p02.as class:

```
package com.comtaste.foed.essentialair.chapter7
{
import fl.controls.Button;
import fl.controls.DataGrid;
import fl.controls.TextArea;
import fl.controls.dataGridClasses.DataGridColumn;
import fl.data.DataProvider;

import flash.display.MovieClip;
import flash.events.Event;
import flash.events.MouseEvent;
import flash.filesystem.File;

public class Ch07p02 extends MovieClip
{
    // on stage components
    public var choose:Button;
    public var output:TextArea;
    public var directoryList:DataGrid;

    // class properties
    private var folder:File;

    public function Ch07p02()
    {
        super();

        // register event listener for button
        choose.addEventListener( MouseEvent.CLICK,
                showDirectorySelection );
```

```
    // set up DataGrid
    var col1:DataGridColumn = new DataGridColumn();
    col1.headerText = "File name";
    col1.dataField = "name";
    directoryList.addColumn( col1 );

    var col2:DataGridColumn = new DataGridColumn();
    col2.headerText = "File size";
    col2.dataField = "size";
    directoryList.addColumn( col2 );

    var col3:DataGridColumn = new DataGridColumn();
    col3.headerText = "File extension";
    col3.dataField = "extension";
    directoryList.addColumn( col3 );

    var col4:DataGridColumn = new DataGridColumn();
    col4.headerText = "Creation date";
    col4.dataField = "creationDate";
    directoryList.addColumn( col4 );
}


private function showDirectorySelection( event:MouseEvent ):void
{
    // initialize file object
    folder = new File();

    // register event listener for folder selection
    folder.addEventListener( Event.SELECT, directorySelected );

    // show system dialog
    folder.browseForDirectory("Choose a directory on your system");
}

private function directorySelected( event:Event ):void
{
    // write out selected folder's path
    output.appendText("Selected folder: "+folder.nativePath+"\n");

    // get selected directory contents
    var directoryContents:Array = folder.getDirectoryListing();

    // DataGrid dataprovider
    var dp:DataProvider = new DataProvider();

    // folder counter
    var folderNum:int = -1;
    // populate dataprovider
```

7

```
            var item:File;
            for each( item in directoryContents )
            {
                if( item.isDirectory )
                {
                    folderNum++;
                    dp.addItemAt( item, folderNum );
                }
                else
                {
                    dp.addItem( item );
                }
            }

            // assign dataprovider to DataGrid
            directoryList.dataProvider = dp;
        }
    } // class end
} // package end
```

When you create the columns for the DataGrid in the constructor function, you specify a value for each of them in the dataField property. The value you assign corresponds to the property of the File class to be displayed.

Now the application is complete. Go back to the ch07p02.fla project, and compile and execute the AIR application (Test Movie ➤ Control). A preview is shown in Figure 7-6.

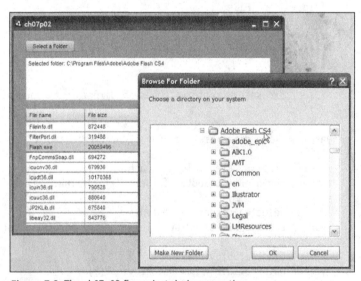

Figure 7-6. The ch07p02.fla project during execution

In the following section, you'll see how to use asynchronous methods to carry out file and folder listing operations in a given folder.

Listing the contents of a folder with asynchronous functions

The Flash CS4 project in the preceding section uses a synchronous approach to obtain the list of objects contained in a folder. As you already know, synchronous functions can cause the application to freeze temporarily when it is carrying out fairly complex operations. Users may not understand that the application has frozen because it is handling a large quantity of data, not because of an error. As such, users might shut the application down and lose part of their work unnecessarily.

To avoid these kinds of situations, you can use asynchronous methods instead of synchronous ones. When you use asynchronous methods, the application doesn't wait for a given operation to finish, but it continues to work correctly. When the asynchronous operation has completed, it generates an event to tell you and let you prepare event listener functions.

For this example, create a new Flash file and save it as ch07p03.fla.

The ch07p03.fla project is almost the same as the ch07p02.fla project as far as the user interface elements on the stage are concerned. The only differences regard the operation of requesting the contents of a given folder, which is asynchronous in this new example. Even the code of the ActionScript class doesn't change that much.

Take the Ch07p02.as class and save it as Ch07p03.as. Then associate it with the ch07p03.fla project as a document class.

Open the Ch07p03.as class and go to the directorySelected() method, where you'll make the following small changes to make the operations asynchronous:

```
private function directorySelected( event:Event ):void
{
```

Like in the previous version, access the native path of the selected folder. Next, write it in the output TextArea, which you'll use as a console for the messages to be generated during the execution of the application. Here's the code:

```
// write out selected folder's path
output.appendText( "Selected folder: " + folder.nativePath +"\n" );
```

Then, instead of calling the synchronous getDirectoryListing() method and processing the returned data, you register an event listener to the instance of the File class, which represents the folder selected by the user. You register the showDirectoryContents() event handler on the DIRECTORY_LISTING event of the FileEvent class. Finally, you launch the asynchronous getDirectoryListing() method to start extracting the contents of the relevant folder. That code is shown here:

```
// register event listener for folder listing
folder.addEventListener( FileListEvent.DIRECTORY_LISTING,
                         showDirectoryContents );
```

7

303

```
        // request folder contents
    folder.getDirectoryListingAsync();
}
```

When the asynchronous function has finished, it generates the FileListEvent.DIRECTORY_
LISTING event and executes the showDirectoryContents() event handler. When you use
the getDirectoryListingAsync() method, remember to import the flash.events.
FileListEvent class. The function accesses the generated list, which contains the objects
in the folder selected by the user, and uses it to populate the dataProvider of the
DataGrid.

Write the following showDirectoryContents() event handler in the Ch07p03.as class after
the closure of the directorySelected() method:

```
    private function showDirectoryContents( event:FileListEvent ):void
    {
```

You can access the list of elements in the folder through the files property of the event
object of the FileListEvent class, received as an argument of the method.

You set this list to the directoryContents variable, which is typed as Array. Then populate
the DataGrid, as has already been described in detail for the ch07p02.fla project:

```
        // get selected folder contents
        var directoryContents:Array = event.files;
        // DataGrid dataprovider
        var dp:DataProvider = new DataProvider();
        // folder counter
        var folderNum:int = -1;

        // populate dataprovider
        var item:File;
        for each( item in directoryContents )
        {
            if( item.isDirectory )
            {
                folderNum++;
                dp.addItemAt( item, folderNum );
            }
            else
            {
                dp.addItem( item );
            }
        }

        // assign dataprovider to DataGrid
        directoryList.dataProvider = dp;
        // clear event listener for folder listing
        folder.removeEventListener( FileListEvent.DIRECTORY_LISTING,
                                    showDirectoryContents );
    }
```

With these changes, the ActionScript code will only execute asynchronous operations. There is no more risk of the application freezing or making the user wait a long time during execution.

Go back to the Flash ch07p03.fla project and execute it to check if the changes have worked.

In this first part of the chapter, you've been introduced to the preliminary concepts regarding AIR's I/O (input/output) operations. In the second part, you'll see how to copy, move, and delete files and folders on the local system.

Performing operations on files and folders

Until now, you've seen how to access a given file or folder and how you can obtain more detailed information on them. You've also seen how to access the objects contained in a given folder. The File class allows you to perform many operations on files and folders, and you can carry out each operation in either synchronous or asynchronous mode.

An AIR application can execute the following operations on files or folders:

- Copying
- Moving
- Moving to the system Recycle Bin (on Windows) or Trash (on the Mac)
- Deletion

It's also possible to create new files and folders. In the following sections, you'll analyze these operations.

Copying files and folders

The File class provides methods that allow you copy files or folders. When you copy a file, you can also choose to overwrite it if it already exists on that destination path.

The method provided by the AIR's file APIs to execute a synchronous copy is copyTo(). The following code is an example of how to use the method:

```
// original file on user desktop
var source:File = File.desktopDirectory.resolvePath( "test.txt" );

// destination file on user documents folder, may exist or not
var destination:File =
            File.documentsDirectory.resolvePath( "test.txt" );

// copy source file to destination file
// the second parameter set true overwriting if necessary
source.copyTo( destination, true );
```

7

To execute the same copy operation in asynchronous mode, you use the copyToAsync() method.

When working with asynchronous methods, you have to create event listeners for the events that are generated during the life cycle of the operation. The following code shows an example of how to use the copyToAsync() method:

```
// original file on user desktop
var source:File = File.desktopDirectory.resolvePath( "test.txt" );

// destination file on user documents folder, may exist or not
var destination:File =
            File.documentsDirectory.resolvePath( "test.txt" );

// register event listener functions to source file object
source.addEventListener( Event.COMPLETE, copyCompleted );
source.addEventListener( IOErrorEvent.IO_ERROR, copyFailed );

// copy source file to destination file using async method
// the second parameter set true overwriting if necessary
source.copyToAsync( destination, true );

// event listener functions
function copyCompleted( event:Event ):void
{
    // copy completed! put your code here
}

function copyFailed ( event: IOErrorEvent):void
{
    // copy failed! put your code here
}
```

Moving files and folders

It's possible to move files or folders to locations other than their original one. As with the copy operation, you can choose whether to use synchronous or asynchronous mode to move them. To execute a synchronous move, you have to use the moveTo() method of the File class, as shown here:

```
// original file on user desktop
var source:File = File.desktopDirectory.resolvePath( "test.txt" );

// destination path on user documents folder, may exist or not
var destination:File =
            File.documentsDirectory.resolvePath( "test.txt" );
```

```
// move source file to destination path
// the second parameter set true overwriting if necessary
source.moveTo( destination, true );
```

You can execute the same method in asynchronous mode by launching the moveToAsync() method. The following code shows how to move a file asynchronously:

```
// original file on user desktop
var source:File = File.desktopDirectory.resolvePath( "test.txt" );

// destination path on user documents folder, may exist or not
var destination:File =
            File.documentsDirectory.resolvePath( "test.txt" );

// register event listener functions to source file object
source.addEventListener( Event.COMPLETE, fileMoved );
source.addEventListener( IOErrorEvent.IO_ERROR, moveFailed );

// move source file to destination path using async method
// the second parameter set true overwriting if necessary
source.moveToAsync( destination, true );

// event listener functions
function fileMoved ( event:Event ):void
{
    // file moved correctly!, put your code here
}

function moveFailed ( event: IOErrorEvent):void
{
    // failed to move requested file!, put your code here
}
```

As with copying, moving a file in asynchronous mode requires you to register event listeners to manage the events that are dispatched from the moveToAsync() method.

The File class also provides the movetoTrash() and moveToTrashAsync() methods, which behave the same way as the moving operation. The only difference is that the destination is the operating system's trash.

Deleting files and folders

You can also permanently remove files and folders from the user's operating system.

In the following example, ch07p04.fla, you'll see how to create a simple AIR application that allows the user to select a file and decide whether to move it to the trash or delete it permanently. It also allows you to choose whether you want to use synchronous or asynchronous mode. Figure 7-7 shows the stage of the ch07p04.fla project and the Document Properties panel where the com.comtaste.foed.essentialair.chapter7.Ch07p04 document class is defined.

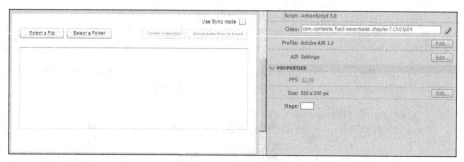

Figure 7-7. The stage and Document Properties panel for the ch07p04.fla project

Follow these steps to create the Flash project:

1. Create a new Flash file and save it as ch07p04.fla.

2. Insert a Button control on the stage and name it chooseFile. When this button is clicked, it opens a dialog box allowing the user to select a file from the local system.

3. Insert another two Button controls called deleteFile and trashFile, which will be disabled when the application starts up. These buttons will make it possible for the user to choose whether to delete the file or move it to the trash. They will only be activated when the user actually selects a file.

4. Now drag a CheckBox control to the stage and name it syncMode. This will allow you to choose whether the operations should be synchronous or asynchronous.

5. Finally, insert a TextArea and call it output, to display the messages that are generated during the execution of the application.

> *If you like, you can open the completed* ch07p04.fla *file, which has all these elements already added. You can retrieve it from the* /chapter07 *folder in the book's source code files (available from the* downloads *section at* www.friendsofed.com/).

In the next section, you'll learn how to create the ActionScript class that is associated with the ch07p04.fla file as a document class, which will carry out the operations of file selection, moving files to the trash, and deleting them.

Controlling deletion methods

Create a new ActionScript class and save it as Ch07p04.as, and then associate it with the ch07p04.fla file as a document class.

Next, open the document class you've just created by selecting the Edit class definition icon on the Document Properties panel in Flash CS4. The class begins by defining its namespace and importing the external classes it will need in the code, as shown here:

```
package com.comtaste.foed.essentialair.chapter7
{
import fl.controls.Button;
import fl.controls.CheckBox;
import fl.controls.TextArea;

import flash.display.MovieClip;
import flash.errors.IOError;
import flash.events.Event;
import flash.events.IOErrorEvent;
import flash.events.MouseEvent;
import flash.filesystem.File;
```

The properties containing references to the elements on the stage of the Flash project are declared in the body of the class.

Next, create the fileObject variable, which will contain a reference to the file the user selects through the dialog box:

```
public class Ch07p04 extends MovieClip
{
// on stage components
public var chooseFile:Button;
public var chooseFolder:Button;
public var deleteFile:Button;
public var trashFile:Button;
public var output:TextArea;
public var syncMode:CheckBox;

// class properties
private var fileObject:File;
```

The class constructor registers the event listeners for the MouseEvent.CLICK for the four buttons in the application. The event handlers will display the dialog box to allow the user to select the file or folder, delete the file, or move it to the trash. That code is shown here:

```
public function Ch07p04()
{
    super();

    // register event listener for buttons
    chooseFile.addEventListener( MouseEvent.CLICK, showFileSelection );
    chooseFolder.addEventListener( MouseEvent.CLICK,
                    showFolderSelection );
    deleteFile.addEventListener( MouseEvent.CLICK,
                    deleteSelectedFile );
    trashFile.addEventListener( MouseEvent.CLICK, trashSelectedFile );
}
```

7

The first two event listeners are called showFileSelection() and showFolderSelection(). They allow the user to select the file or folder he or she wants to delete. To allow the user to select a file or a folder, a new instance of the File class is assigned to the fileObject variable. Then the fileObjSelected() function is registered on the event of selection, which displays the correct version of the dialog box for the chosen selection. Here's the code to accomplish these tasks:

```
private function showFileSelection ( event:MouseEvent ):void
{
    // initialize file object
    fileObject = new File();
    // register event listener for folder selection
    fileObject.addEventListener( Event.SELECT, fileObjSelected );
    // show system dialog
    fileObject.browseForOpen( "Choose a file to delete" );
}

private function showFolderSelection( event:MouseEvent ):void
{
    // initialize file object
    fileObject = new File();
    // register event listener for folder selection
    fileObject.addEventListener( Event.SELECT, fileObjSelected );
    // show system dialog
    fileObject.browseForDirectory( "Choose a folder to delete" );
}
```

When a file or folder is selected, the fileObjSelected() function will write the native path of the relevant object in the output TextArea, and then it will enable the buttons to delete or move the file to the trash, as shown here:

```
private function fileObjSelected( event:Event ):void
{
    // write out selected folder's path
    output.appendText( "Selected file: "
                + fileObject.nativePath + File.lineEnding );
    // enable deletion buttons
    deleteFile.enabled = true;
    trashFile.enabled = true;
}
```

Once a file or folder has been selected, the user can choose whether to remove it completely or move it to the trash. If the user chooses the former, the application launches the deleteSelectedFile() function. The function will then proceed deleting the file using the synchronous or asynchronous method, depending on the syncMode CheckBox. Add the deleteSelectedFile() event handler as follows:

```
private function deleteSelectedFile( event:MouseEvent ):void
{
```

First, the buttons that allow the user to select a file or folder are temporarily disabled, so as to prevent the user from selecting another file while a file is being deleted. To enable or disable a button, you use the enabled property, as shown here:

```
// disable selection button
chooseFile.enabled = false;
chooseFolder.enabled = false;
```

Then you check the value of the selected property of the syncMode CheckBox. If it's true, then it's selected, and it will delete the file using the synchronous methods provided by the File class, as shown here:

```
// act based on user preferences
if( syncMode.selected )
{
```

Next, execute the operation in a try...catch construct to manage possible errors in the synchronous deletion process:

```
try
{
```

If the selected object is a folder, you use the deleteDirectory() method; otherwise, you use the deleteFile() method to remove the selected file. The deleteDirectory() method accepts an argument that shows whether the folder should be removed in any case (true) or only if it's empty (false); the default value is false. This code is as follows:

```
if( fileObject.isDirectory )
{
    // if it's a folder, remove it with all its contents
    fileObject.deleteDirectory( true );
} else
{
    // delete file
    fileObject.deleteFile();
}
                output.appendText( "Selection's deleted [SYNC]"
                    + File.lineEnding );
} catch( e:IOError )
{
```

If the deletion process isn't successful, you write the notification in the output TextArea, as shown here:

```
output.appendText( "Selection's NOT deleted [SYNC]"
                    + File.lineEnding );
}
```

When the synchronous operation is complete, regardless of the obtained result, you reactivate the buttons that select a new file or folder, and you disable the removal buttons. Here's the code:

```
        // enable selection button
        chooseFile.enabled = true;
        chooseFolder.enabled = true;
            // disable deletion buttons
        deleteFile.enabled = false;
        trashFile.enabled = false;
    } else
    {
```

Next, if the asynchronous option is selected, you register the event listener functions to the File object for the events that are triggered by a successful or failed deletion.

```
        // register event listener
        fileObject.addEventListener( Event.COMPLETE, fileObjDeleted );
        fileObject.addEventListener( IOErrorEvent.IO_ERROR,
                            fileObjDeletionError );
```

If the selected object is a folder, you use the deleteDirectoryAsync() function, specifying that the folder should be deleted even if it isn't empty. If the selected object is a file, you delete it with the deleteFileAsync() function.

Both functions will generate an event when the operation completes successfully or fails. Here are examples of these functions:

```
        if( fileObject.isDirectory )
        {
            // if it's a folder, remove it with all its contents
            fileObject.deleteDirectoryAsync( true );
        } else
        {
            // delete file
            fileObject.deleteFileAsync();
        }
    }
}
```

If the user decides to delete the file asynchronously, the method fileObjDeleted() will be called when the operation is completed. Here's an example of this method:

```
    private function fileObjDeleted( event:Event ):void
    {
```

Next, write a message in the TextArea to indicate the correct execution of the requested asynchronous operation, and reactivate the buttons to select a new file or folder and disable the removal buttons:

```
        // file removed correctly
        output.appendText( "Selection's deleted [ASYNC]"
                + File.lineEnding );
        // enable selection button
        chooseFile.enabled = true;
        chooseFolder.enabled = true;
        // disable deletion buttons
        deleteFile.enabled = false;
        trashFile.enabled = false;
```

Finally, remove the event listener functions that are registered on the fileObject class variable:

```
        // remove event listener
        fileObject.removeEventListener( Event.COMPLETE, fileObjDeleted );
        fileObject.removeEventListener( IOErrorEvent.IO_ERROR,
                fileObjDeletionError );
    }
```

If the deletion fails for some reason, an IOErrorEvent.IO.Error event is generated and the fileObjDeletionError() method is generated. The function executes the same operations as the fileObjDeleted() function, except if the message in the TextArea shows that the file hasn't been deleted. Here's the code:

```
    private function fileObjDeletionError( event:IOErrorEvent ):void
    {
        // file NOT removed
        output.appendText( "Selection's NOT deleted [ASYNC]"
                + File.lineEnding );
        // enable selection button
        chooseFile.enabled = true;
        chooseFolder.enabled = true;
        // disable deletion buttons
        deleteFile.enabled = false;
        trashFile.enabled = false;
        // remove event listener
        fileObject.removeEventListener( Event.COMPLETE, fileObjDeleted );
        fileObject.removeEventListener( IOErrorEvent.IO_ERROR,
                fileObjDeletionError );
    }
```

The user might want to move the file or folder he has selected to the system trash, instead of removing it permanently from the system. In this case, the trashSelectedFile() function is executed, as shown here:

```
    private function trashSelectedFile( event:MouseEvent ):void
    {
```

7

Next, temporarily disable the buttons that allow the user to select a file or folder to pre-vent the user from choosing another file while the removal operation is still running:

```
// disable selection button
chooseFile.enabled = false;
chooseFolder.enabled = false;
```

Based on the value of the selected property of the syncMode CheckBox, move the selected file or folder to the trash by using the synchronous function if the property is set to true, and the asynchronous function if it's set to false. Here's the code:

```
// act based on user preferences
if( syncMode.selected )
{
```

Now execute the synchronous move to the trash in a try...catch construct. Doing so allows you to intercept and manage possible failures in the operation.

```
// move to trash
try
{
```

Here, you use the synchronous moveToTrash() function of the File class to move the file or folder to the trash:

```
fileObject.moveToTrash();
output.appendText( "Selection's deleted [SYNC]"
        + File.lineEnding );
} catch( e:IOError )
{
    output.appendText( "Selection's NOT deleted [SYNC]"
        + File.lineEnding );
}
```

Once the operation is finished, you reactivate the buttons to select a new file or folder and disable the buttons to remove the selected item. That code is shown here:

```
// enable selection button
chooseFile.enabled = true;
chooseFolder.enabled = true;
        // disable deletion buttons
deleteFile.enabled = false;
trashFile.enabled = false;
} else
{
```

If the selected property of the syncMode CheckBox is set to false, you register two event listener functions on the fileObject class variable. These functions manage the success or failure of the moving operation. Then you execute the moveToTrashAsync() method. The following event listener functions are the same ones you used for the asynchronous per-manent removal of the selected item.

```
        // register event listener
        fileObject.addEventListener( Event.COMPLETE, fileObjDeleted );
        fileObject.addEventListener( IOErrorEvent.IO_ERROR,
                                            fileObjDeletionError );

        // move to trash
        fileObject.moveToTrashAsync();
    }
}
```

Reviewing the code and executing the file

Here is the complete code for the Ch07p04.as class:

```
package com.comtaste.foed.essentialair.chapter7
{
import fl.controls.Button;
import fl.controls.CheckBox;
import fl.controls.TextArea;

import flash.display.MovieClip;
import flash.errors.IOError;
import flash.events.Event;
import flash.events.IOErrorEvent;
import flash.events.MouseEvent;
import flash.filesystem.File;

public class Ch07p04 extends MovieClip
{
    // on stage components
    public var chooseFile:Button;
    public var chooseFolder:Button;
    public var deleteFile:Button;
    public var trashFile:Button;
    public var output:TextArea;
    public var syncMode:CheckBox;

    // class properties
    private var fileObject:File;

    public function Ch07p04()
    {
        super();

        // register event listener for buttons
        chooseFile.addEventListener( MouseEvent.CLICK,
                showFileSelection );
        chooseFolder.addEventListener( MouseEvent.CLICK,
                showFolderSelection );
        deleteFile.addEventListener( MouseEvent.CLICK,
```

```actionscript
            deleteSelectedFile );
        trashFile.addEventListener( MouseEvent.CLICK,
            trashSelectedFile );
}

private function showFileSelection( event:MouseEvent ):void
{
    // initialize file object
    fileObject = new File();

    // register event listener for folder selection
    fileObject.addEventListener( Event.SELECT, fileObjSelected );

    // show system dialog
    fileObject.browseForOpen( "Choose a file to delete" );
}

private function showFolderSelection( event:MouseEvent ):void
{
    // initialize file object
    fileObject = new File();

    // register event listener for folder selection
    fileObject.addEventListener( Event.SELECT, fileObjSelected );

    // show system dialog
    fileObject.browseForDirectory( "Choose a folder to delete" );
}

private function fileObjSelected( event:Event ):void
{
    // write out selected folder's path
    output.appendText( "Selected folder: "
            + fileObject.nativePath + File.lineEnding );

    // enable deletion buttons
    deleteFile.enabled = true;
    trashFile.enabled = true;
}

private function deleteSelectedFile( event:MouseEvent ):void
{
    // disable selection button
    chooseFile.enabled = false;
    chooseFolder.enabled = false;

    // act based on user preferences
    if( syncMode.selected )
    {
```

```
        try
        {
            if( fileObject.isDirectory )
            {
                // if is a directory,
                // remove it with all it's contents
                fileObject.deleteDirectory( true );
            } else
            {
                // delete file
                fileObject.deleteFile();
            }

            output.appendText( "Selection's deleted [SYNC]"
                    + File.lineEnding );

        } catch( e:IOError )
        {
            output.appendText( "Selection's NOT deleted [SYNC]"
                    + File.lineEnding );
        }

        // enable selection button
        chooseFile.enabled = true;
        chooseFolder.enabled = true;

        // disable deletion buttons
        deleteFile.enabled = false;
        trashFile.enabled = false;

    } else
    {
        // register event listener
        fileObject.addEventListener( Event.COMPLETE,
                fileObjDeleted );
        fileObject.addEventListener( IOErrorEvent.IO_ERROR,
                fileObjDeletionError );

        if( fileObject.isDirectory )
        {
            // if is a directory, remove it with all it's contents
            fileObject.deleteDirectoryAsync( true );
        } else
        {
            // delete file
            fileObject.deleteFileAsync();
        }
    }
}
```

7

```
private function trashSelectedFile( event:MouseEvent ):void
{
    // disable selection button
    chooseFile.enabled = false;
    chooseFolder.enabled = false;

    // act based on user preferences
    if( syncMode.selected )
    {
        // move to trash
        try
        {
            fileObject.moveToTrash();
            output.appendText( "Selection's deleted [SYNC]"
                    + File.lineEnding );

        } catch( e:IOError )
        {
            output.appendText( "Selection's NOT deleted [SYNC]"
                    + File.lineEnding );
        }

        // enable selection button
        chooseFile.enabled = true;
        chooseFolder.enabled = true;

        // disable deletion buttons
        deleteFile.enabled = false;
        trashFile.enabled = false;

    } else
    {
        // register event listener
        fileObject.addEventListener( Event.COMPLETE,
                fileObjDeleted );
        fileObject.addEventListener( IOErrorEvent.IO_ERROR,
                fileObjDeletionError );

        // move to trash
        fileObject.moveToTrashAsync();
    }
}

private function fileObjDeleted( event:Event ):void
{
    // file removed correctly
    output.appendText( "Selection's deleted [ASYNC]"
                    + File.lineEnding );
```

```
                    // enable selection button
                    chooseFile.enabled = true;
                    chooseFolder.enabled = true;

                    // disable deletion buttons
                    deleteFile.enabled = false;
                    trashFile.enabled = false;

                    // remove event listener
                    fileObject.removeEventListener( Event.COMPLETE,
                                    fileObjDeleted );
                    fileObject.removeEventListener( IOErrorEvent.IO_ERROR,
                                    fileObjDeletionError );
            }

            private function fileObjDeletionError( event:IOErrorEvent ):void
            {
                    // file NOT removed
                    output.appendText( "Selection's NOT deleted [ASYNC]"
                                    + File.lineEnding );

                    // enable selection button
                    chooseFile.enabled = true;
                    chooseFolder.enabled = true;

                    // disable deletion buttons
                    deleteFile.enabled = false;
                    trashFile.enabled = false;

                    // remove event listener
                    fileObject.removeEventListener( Event.COMPLETE,
                                    fileObjDeleted );
                    fileObject.removeEventListener( IOErrorEvent.IO_ERROR,
                                    fileObjDeletionError );
            }
    } // class end
    } // package end
```

Now that the application is completed, open the ch07p04.fla project and execute the file (Test Movie ➤ Control). Once the AIR application is running, create a few copies of the files on your computer and try selecting them and removing them using the application. Figure 7-8 shows the application being executed.

Pay attention to the files and folders you delete permanently, because they can't be restored. On the other hand, if you move files and folders to the trash, you'll be able to restore them. For this example, delete only the ch07p04.fla file and the folders you created.

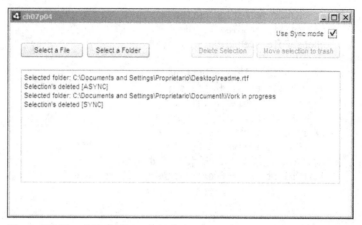

Figure 7-8. The ch07p04.fla project during execution

The next section will show how to read the content of files.

Accessing a file's content

So far, you've mainly learned about the management and maintenance of files and folders. AIR provides even more control, and also allows you to access the content of these files in reading and writing mode. To access the content of a file, you have to use the FileStream class.

Using the FileStream class

The FileStream class can operate in synchronous and asynchronous mode. When you use the synchronous reading and writing modes, the class behaves very much like the ByteArray class.

The ByteArray class allows developers to access data at the byte level and provides methods and properties to optimize reading, writing, and working with binary data.

When you use asynchronous functions, the FileStream class behaves like the URLStream class, which receives the data contained in the file in a continuous stream instead of all at once.

The URLStream class provides low-level access to the download operation. The data is provided to the application code immediately as it's downloaded (it doesn't wait until the entire file is complete, as is the case with the URLLoader class). Additionally, the URLStream class lets you close a stream before the downloading has completed. The downloaded file content is provided as raw binary data (see the Livedocs ActionScript documentation at http://livedocs.adobe.com/flash/9.0/ActionScriptLangRefV3/flash/net/ URLStream.html for more information).

You can operate in reading and writing modes on individual bytes of the file, or on whole serialized objects by using FileStream class objects. There are many functions for working with the native data types provided by ActionScript 3 (e.g., decimal numbers, integers, and text strings).

The process of accessing file content with the FileStream class could be summed up as follows:

1. Creating a FileStream object

2. Opening the connection to the file

3. Reading/writing data from/to the file

4. Closing the open connection to the file

Once an instance of the FileStream class has been created, you can open the connection to a file as shown here:

```
var stream:FileStream = new FileStream();
```

The connection can be synchronous, using the open() function, as in this example:

```
var fileObj:File = File.desktopDirectory.resolvePath( "Readme.txt" );
stream.open(fileObj, FileMode.READ );
```

Or it can be asynchronous, using the openAsync() function, as follows:

```
stream.openAsync(fileObj, FileMode.READ );
```

An asynchronous connection requires the use of event listener functions to manage the success or failure of the operation. Both functions require two arguments: the files to access and the access mode; the access modes are defined as constants of the FileMode class, and are as follows:

- FileMode.READ: Allows access to the file in read-only mode. When you use this connection mode, it isn't possible to write to the file. If the file doesn't exist, it won't be created automatically when the connection is opened.

- FileMode.WRITE: Allows access to the file in write-only mode. When you use this method, it isn't possible to read the content of the document. If the file doesn't exist, it will be created automatically when the connection is opened. This mode deletes the previous content of the document when the connection is opened and completely overwrites it.

- FileMode.APPEND: Allows access to the file in reading-and-writing mode. When you use this method, all content inserted through writing functions are added on at the end of the existing content, and it doesn't overwrite preexisting data. If the file doesn't exist, it will be created automatically when the connection is opened.

- FileMode.UPDATE: Allows access to the file in reading-and-writing mode. When you use this connection method, you provide full writing, overwriting, and reading rights on the content of the file. If the file doesn't exist, it is created automatically when the connection is opened.

Once the connection to the file has been opened, you are free to manipulate the data in it as required. Finally, the close() function is called to interrupt the opened connection:

```
stream.close();
```

In the next section, you will put the theory of accessing file content into practice.

Reading and writing to a text file

In this section, you will create an AIR application that can read from and write to document files with a .txt extension. Open the ch07p05.fla project in Flash CS4 or create a new Flash file. The application allows you to select a text file from the local computer, display it, and even edit it. The text is shown in an editable TextArea. The user can edit the text and save the changes to the original file.

Figure 7-9 shows the elements on the ch07p05.fla stage. There are two buttons, which have been associated with two instance names: choose and save, which will be used to open the dialog box for selecting a text file and saving the changes. Then there are two TextArea components: one with the instance name output, which will act as a console for the messages generated by the application, and one with the instance name text, which will display the content of the document chosen by the user.

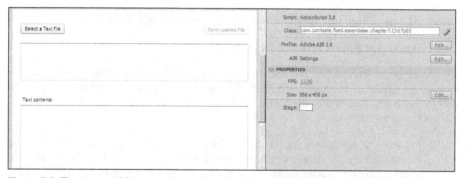

Figure 7-9. The stage and Document Properties panel for the ch07p05.fla project

Once you've created a new ActionScript class and saved it as Ch07p05.as, associate it as a document class with the ch07p05.fla file.

Then click the Edit class definition icon from the Document Properties panel to open the document class associated with the project. The Ch07p05.as class, like the other ones you have seen so far, is in the com.comtaste.foed.essentialair.chapter7 package. After declaring the external classes it depends on, the class lists the variables that refer to the components on the Flash project stage. The Ch07p05.as class is shown here:

```
package com.comtaste.foed.essentialair.chapter7
{
import fl.controls.Button;
import fl.controls.TextArea;
```

```
import flash.display.MovieClip;
import flash.events.Event;
import flash.events.MouseEvent;
import flash.filesystem.File;
import flash.filesystem.FileMode;
import flash.filesystem.FileStream;
import flash.net.FileFilter;

public class Ch07p05 extends MovieClip
{
// onstage components
public var choose:Button;
public var save:Button;
public var output:TextArea;
public var text:TextArea;
```

Then the class defines the fileObject properties, typed as File, and the stream properties, typed as FileStream, which will define a reference to the text file selected by the user and provide access to its content.

The stream property of the FileStream class is instanced immediately during its declaration, so that it is immediately available for all the elements of the class. Here's the code:

```
// class properties
private var fileObject:File;
private var stream:FileStream = new FileStream();
```

Next, the class constructor registers two event listener functions—for the click events on the choose and save buttons. Then an event listener function is registered on the stream object for the complete event. This event is generated when the object opens an asynchronous connection and the content of the relevant file is ready to be used:

```
public function Ch07p05()
{
    super();
    // register event listeners
    choose.addEventListener( MouseEvent.CLICK, showSelection );
    save.addEventListener( MouseEvent.CLICK, saveFile );
    stream.addEventListener( Event.COMPLETE, fileStreamOpened );
}
```

When the user clicks the choose button to select a text file, the application executes the showSelection() function. This function regenerates the fileObject variable, assigning it to a new instance of the File class. Then it registers an event listener function on the fileObject object. That listener will be executed when the user confirms the selection of a file from the dialog box provided by AIR. Finally, the opening of the dialog window is requested to select a single file, as you have already seen in the previous exercises, with the browseForOpen() method:

```
private function showSelection( event:MouseEvent ):void
{
    // initialize file object
    fileObject = new File();
    // register event listener for folder selection
    fileObject.addEventListener( Event.SELECT, textFileSelected );
```

The first element that is assigned to the browseForOpen() function is the title to display in the dialog box. The title is followed by an array containing the list of valid file formats for the selected item. The array is created using the array notation, meaning by directly writing a sequence of objects, separated by commas, between square brackets.

The application only manages text files, so you will assign only one valid format to the list. Each valid format has to be provided as an instance of the FileFilter class, which requires two arguments. The first one specifies the textual definition to be provided to the user for the defined file format, and the second provides the valid extensions for the format. Both arguments are assigned as text strings. Here's the code:

```
    // show system dialog
    fileObject.browseForOpen( "Choose a txt file...",
                [ new FileFilter( "Plain text files", "*.txt" ) ]);
}
```

The user will select a file from the dialog box opened by AIR as a response to the execution of the browseForOpen() method of the File class. When a file is selected, the relevant event listener, textFileSelected(), is executed, as shown here:

```
    private function textFileSelected( event:Event ):void
    {
```

Once the file has been selected in the dialog box, you write the complete native path of the selected file in the output TextArea, like this:

```
    // write out selected folder's path
    output.appendText( "Selected file: "
                    + fileObject.nativePath + File.lineEnding );
```

Then you tell the stream object to open the file asynchronously. To open an asynchronous connection to the file, you use the openAsync() method, specifying that the access to the content is in read-only mode.

```
    // read file
    stream.openAsync( fileObject, FileMode.READ );
}
```

Once the connection to the content of the selected file has been established by the user, the fileStreamOpened() method is executed, as you've established in the constructor function of the class. Here's the code:

```
    private function fileStreamOpened( event:Event ):void
    {
```

Next, write a message in the output TextArea to show that the connection to the file has been opened correctly, and activate the save button by setting the enabled property to true.

```
output.appendText( "file stream opened" + File.lineEnding );
// enable save button when file stream is opened
save.enabled = true;
```

Now that the connection to the file is open, you can access its content without editing it, because the connection has been opened in read-only mode. To obtain the textual representation as a text string of the file's content, you have to use the readUTFBytes() method of the FileStream class.

This method requires the quantity of bytes to be read and returned as a text string as an argument. The bytesAvailable property of the stream object provides the current number of bytes that are available for the open document:

```
// put file contents on textarea 'text'
text.text = stream.readUTFBytes( stream.bytesAvailable );
```

After extracting the textual content of the document, you interrupt the open connection using the close() method of the FileStream class, as shown here:

```
// close file stream
stream.close();
}
```

> Other applications can't edit the file until the connection to it has been closed; it's good to be aware of this.

If the user wants to save his work after editing the open text document, the user will click the save button and trigger the execution of the saveFile() function that is registered on it for the click event:

```
private function saveFile( event:Event ):void
{
```

When you execute the connection and writing operations of the updated content of the document in synchronous mode, you write the instructions in a try...catch construct. Doing so allows you to intercept possible exceptions that could be generated in case of error during the connection or writing operations.

Next, you ask for the opening of a single connection to the relevant file by using the open() method of the FileStream class. You also specify that the connection will be carried out in overwriting mode of the current document. Therefore, the previous content of the text document will be completely replaced by the content of the text TextArea when the operation is finished.

7

```
    try
    {
    // open sync stream to write on file
    stream.open( fileObject, FileMode.WRITE );
```

Next, you assign the new content of the text document by using the writeUTFBytes() function of the FileStream class. This function accepts a string as an argument, and writes it in the open document in binary format. Then you close the open connection to the text file.

```
        // overwrites file contents
        stream.writeUTFBytes( text.text );
        // close file stream
        stream.close();
    }
    catch( e:Error )    {
```

If errors occur during the attempts at writing to the file, you intercept the exception and warn the user by writing a failure message in the output TextArea, as shown here:

```
        output.appendText( "Error occourred trying to save file!"
                + File.lineEnding );
    }
}
```

Here is the complete code for the Ch07p05.as class:

```
package com.comtaste.foed.essentialair.chapter7
{
import fl.controls.Button;
import fl.controls.TextArea;

import flash.display.MovieClip;
import flash.errors.IOError;
import flash.events.Event;
import flash.events.MouseEvent;
import flash.filesystem.File;
import flash.filesystem.FileMode;
import flash.filesystem.FileStream;
import flash.net.FileFilter;

public class Ch07p05 extends MovieClip
{
    // on stage components
    public var choose:Button;
    public var save:Button;
    public var output:TextArea;
    public var text:TextArea;
```

```
// class properties
private var fileObject:File;
private var stream:FileStream = new FileStream();

public function Ch07p05()
{
    super();

    // register event listeners
    choose.addEventListener( MouseEvent.CLICK, showSelection );
    save.addEventListener( MouseEvent.CLICK, saveFile );
    stream.addEventListener( Event.COMPLETE, fileStreamOpened );
}

private function showSelection( event:MouseEvent ):void
{
    // initialize file object
    fileObject = new File();

    // register event listener for folder selection
    fileObject.addEventListener( Event.SELECT, textFileSelected );

    // show system dialog
    fileObject.browseForOpen( "Choose a txt file...",
    [new FileFilter( "Plain text files", "*.txt" );]);
}

private function textFileSelected( event:Event ):void
{
    // write out selected folder's path
    output.appendText( "Selected file: "
            + fileObject.nativePath + File.lineEnding );

    // read file
    stream.openAsync( fileObject, FileMode.READ );
}

private function fileStreamOpened( event:Event ):void
{
    output.appendText( "file stream opened" + File.lineEnding );

    // enable save button when file stream is opened
    save.enabled = true;

    // put file contents on textarea 'text'
    text.text = stream.readUTFBytes( stream.bytesAvailable );
```

```
                    // close file stream
                    stream.close();
                }

                private function saveFile( event:Event ):void
                {
                    try
                    {
                        // open sync stream to write on file
                        stream.open( fileObject, FileMode.WRITE );

                        // overwrites file contents
                        stream.writeUTFBytes( text.text );

                        // close file stream
                        stream.close();
                    }
                    catch( e:IOError )
                    {
                        output.appendText( "Error occourred trying to save file!"
                            + File.lineEnding );
                    }
                }

            } // class end
            } // package end
```

Return to the ch07p05.fla project and execute the AIR application (Test Movie ➤ Control). Select a text file, edit its content, and save it. The result should be similar to Figure 7-10.

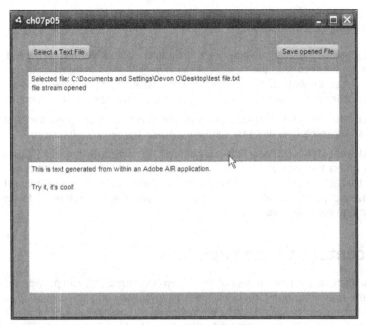

Figure 7-10. The ch07p05.fla project during execution

The next section will introduce how to interact with the local system clipboard.

Using the clipboard

AIR provides the possibility of accessing the system clipboard in **reading-and-writing mode**. This feature allows you to use the copied content of the clipboard from other applications and to make the copied content from your applications available to the operating system. It's possible to copy and paste the following kinds of content:

- Text strings
- Raster images
- Formatted HTML content
- Correctly formatted web addresses
- Serialized instances of ActionScript objects
- References to files and folders

A representation of the current content of the system can be accessed in AIR applications through the static generalClipboard property of the Clipboard class, as shown here:

```
var systemClipboard:Clipboard = Clipboard.generalClipboard;
```

AIR provides the following classes in the flash.desktop package to access and interact with the hosting system clipboard:

- Clipboard: This class provides the functions that access the system clipboard. There are methods to read the content of the clipboard and to add new data to it. When you read or write data in standard formats, AIR automatically converts it from ActionScript format to the operating system's native format at runtime.

- ClipBoardFormats: This class provides the constants that define the data formats that AIR recognizes and that can be used with the system clipboard.

- ClipboardTransferMode: This class defines the constants that specify the methods to access the data obtained from the clipboard of the system. When you use the getData() function of the Clipboard class, you can tell AIR whether you want to have a copy of the data on the clipboard, if possible, or a reference to the original data on the clipboard.

Adding content to the clipboard

When you want to add new content to the system clipboard, you can provide various formats for the relevant content. If, for example, you want to add a screenshot of your application to the system clipboard, you can provide the BitmapData object to represent an image, the serialized Bitmap object, and an instance of a File object containing the generated image. When another application accesses the content of the system clipboard, it can choose the most practical format from the three available formats. A web address, for example, can be provided as a hypertext link as well as a text string, so a browser can use the link, whereas a text editor will probably use the text string.

Say the content you want to add is a series of objects that require a certain amount of work from the computer. This content might be large images or long text documents. In this case, you could tell AIR to call a function only when the content is required by another application. In this way, you avoid transporting large quantities of data if it isn't necessary.

To add content to the clipboard, you use the setData() method of the Clipboard class, as follows:

```
// content to be added to clipboard
var webAddress:String = "http://www.adobe.com";

// add plain text format
Clipboard.generalClipboard.setData( ClipboardFormats.TEXT_FORMAT,
                    webAddress );

// add url formatted format
Clipboard.generalClipboard.setData( ClipboardFormats.URL_FORMAT,
                    webAddress );
```

If, on the other hand, you want to add content that will be generated only when required by another application, you have to use the setDataHandler() method of the Clipboard class. Here's the code:

```
// content to be added to clipboard
var webAddress:String = "http://www.adobe.com";

// add plain text format
Clipboard.generalClipboard.setDataHandler (
          ClipboardFormats.TEXT_FORMAT, getTexWebAddress );

// add url formatted format
Clipboard.generalClipboard.setDataHandler (
          ClipboardFormats.URL_FORMAT, getTexWebAddress );

public function getTexWebAddress():String
{
    return webAddress;
}
```

There is no guarantee that the content of the system clipboard from your application will remain available for other applications after the application itself has been closed, especially if you use the setDataHandler() function.

Accessing the content of the system clipboard

When you want to access the content of the system clipboard, you have to use the getData() function of the Clipboard class and specify the format you are interested in. Here's an example of this function:

```
var textClipboardData:String = Clipboard.generalClipboard.getData(
               ClipboardFormats.TEXT_FORMAT );
```

It's good practice to check if the system clipboard already contains data in the format required by your application before accessing the content in a given format. You can carry out this check by using the hasFormat() method of the Clipboard class, as shown here:

```
if( Clipboard.generalClipboard.hasFormat(
                 ClipboardFormats.TEXT_FORMAT ) )
{
  var textClipboardData:String =
  Clipboard.generalClipboard.getData( ClipboardFormats.TEXT_FORMAT );
}
```

Now you'll see how to create an AIR application that accesses and displays the content of the system clipboard. The project allows the user to access the content of the system clipboard and do the following:

- Display text content
- Display raster images
- Display hypertext links and load them in a new window of your application
- Display information that is associated with the copied files

Begin by opening the ch07p06.fla project in Flash CS4 (Figure 7-11). Then access its document class by clicking the Edit class definition icon on the Document Properties panel.

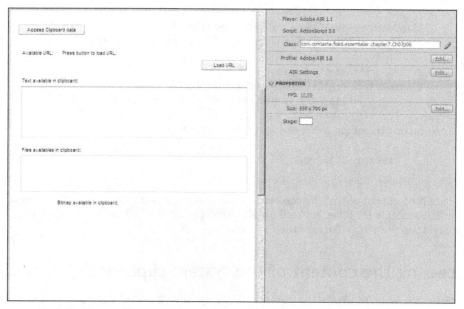

Figure 7-11. The stage and Document Properties panel for the ch07p06.fla project

You start the document class as usual, by declaring its package and the external classes it needs to import during compilation:

```
package com.comtaste.foed.essentialair.chapter7
{
import fl.controls.Button;
import fl.controls.DataGrid;
import fl.controls.Label;
import fl.controls.TextArea;
import fl.controls.dataGridClasses.DataGridColumn;
import fl.data.DataProvider;

import flash.desktop.Clipboard;
import flash.desktop.ClipboardFormats;
import flash.display.Bitmap;
import flash.display.BitmapData;
import flash.display.MovieClip;
import flash.display.NativeWindowInitOptions;
import flash.events.MouseEvent;
import flash.filesystem.File;
import flash.geom.Rectangle;
import flash.html.HTMLLoader;
import flash.net.URLRequest;
```

```
public class Ch07p06 extends MovieClip
{
```

First, you declare the variables that refer to the elements on the stage of the Flash project. The application has the two following buttons:

- loadData, to ask for the content of the system clipboard and display it
- loadHTML, to open a new native window in the application containing an HTMLLoader object that is opened on the hyperlink on the clipboard

Declare the variables as follows:

```
// onstage components
public var loadData:Button;
public var loadHTML:Button;
```

The application also has the following DataGrid to display the details of the files in the system clipboard:

```
public var filesInClipboard:DataGrid;
```

Additionally, the application includes the following TextArea, clipboardText. This TextArea will load textual content and a text label that will display the hyperlink, if a hyperlink will be available from the system clipboard.

```
public var clipboardText:TextArea;
public var availableURL:Label;
```

Then you define some other class variables that are necessary for the application to function correctly. You will instance the following URLRequest object when a hyperlink is available.

```
// class properties
private var webUrl:URLRequest;
```

Use the following Bitmap object to draw a BitmapData representation of the raster images on the clipboard:

```
private var image:Bitmap;
```

In the constructor function of the class, the columns in the DataGrid are defined, and then the event listener functions are registered for the two buttons on the stage, followed by the request to load the data on the clipboard when the application opens. Here's that code:

```
public function ch07p06()
{
```

Next, assign three columns to the DataGrid that will display the details of the files on the system clipboard. The DataGridColumn class instances will display the name, size, and extension of the files, as shown here:

```
// set up DataGrid
var col1:DataGridColumn = new DataGridColumn();
col1.headerText = "File name";
col1.dataField = "name";
filesInClipboard.addColumn( col1 );

var col2:DataGridColumn = new DataGridColumn();
col2.headerText = "File size";
col2.dataField = "size";
filesInClipboard.addColumn( col2 );

var col3:DataGridColumn = new DataGridColumn();
col3.headerText = "File extension";
col3.dataField = "extension";
filesInClipboard.addColumn( col3 );
```

Register the following event listener functions on the loadData and loadHTML buttons:

```
// register event listeners
loadData.addEventListener( MouseEvent.CLICK, readSystemClipboard );
loadHTML.addEventListener( MouseEvent.CLICK, loadHTMLcontents );
```

Next, load the data that is on the clipboard when the application is opened. To do this, force the generation of a click event on the loadData button to execute the readSystemClipboard() event listener function:

```
// access system clipboard contents
loadData.dispatchEvent( new MouseEvent( MouseEvent.CLICK ) );
}
```

When the application is opened, and each time the user clicks the loadData button, the readSystemClipboard() function is executed. This function accomplishes the following actions:

1. It removes any previous data loaded from the system clipboard.

2. It accesses the current content of the clipboard.

3. It displays it in the components on the stage of the application.

Here's the code for the readSystemClipboard() function:

```
private function readSystemClipboard( event:MouseEvent ):void
{
```

Now assign the representation of the system clipboard to the local clipboard variable by accessing the static generalClipboard property of the Clipboard class:

```
// access to system clipboard
var clipboard:Clipboard = Clipboard.generalClipboard;
```

Before processing the data currently on the clipboard, you have to remove the data that was loaded from the clipboard before and reset the components to display them. The following code accomplishes this task:

```
// clear previous clipboard-loaded contents
webUrl = null;
availableURL.text = "";
loadHTML.enabled = false;
clipboardText.text = "";
if( image != null )
{
    if( this.contains( image ) )
    {
        this.removeChild( image );
    }
}
filesInClipboard.dataProvider = new DataProvider();
```

Once the interface of the application has been cleared, you can proceed by checking the data on the clipboard and loading the data you want to display. Use the following hasformat() function to check the formats:

```
// access new available textual contents
if( clipboard.hasFormat( ClipboardFormats.TEXT_FORMAT ) )
```

Displaying text images

If the clipboard contains data in text format, you extract it by telling the getData() function to return the content associated with the TEXT_FORMAT constant of the ClipboardFormats class, and assign it to the clipboardText TextArea. Here's the code:

```
    // get plain-text contents
    var text:String = String( clipboard.getData(
            ClipboardFormats.TEXT_FORMAT ) );
    // show text
    clipboardText.text = text;
}
    // access new available bitmap contents
if( clipboard.hasFormat( ClipboardFormats.BITMAP_FORMAT ) )
```

Displaying raster content

If the clipboard contains data in raster format, you extract it by telling the getData() function to return the content associated with the BITMAP_FORMAT constant of the ClipboardFormats class. Then you assign that content to a BitmapData object, as shown here:

```
    // get bitmap contents
    var bmp:BitmapData = clipboard.getData(
            ClipboardFormats.BITMAP_FORMAT ) as BitmapData;
```

Then you assign a new instance of the Bitmap class, where you draw the BitmapData object obtained from the clipboard to the image class variable:

```
// create image object
image = new Bitmap( bmp, "auto", true );
```

Next, you assign the display coordinates to the Bitmap object on the stage of the application and scale it proportionally by setting its width to 250 pixels:

```
// set image position
image.x = 271;
image.y = 417;
        // scale image proportionally
var maxImageWidth:Number = 250;
image.scaleX = maxImageWidth / image.width;
image.scaleY = image.scaleX;
```

Then add the Bitmap object to the display list of the application to render the image and make it visible, as shown here:

```
// show image on stage
this.addChild( image );
}
    // access new available URL-formatted contents
if( clipboard.hasFormat( ClipboardFormats.URL_FORMAT ) )
```

Displaying and loading hypertext links

If the clipboard contains a hyperlink, you extract it by telling the getData() function to return the content associated with the URL_FORMAT constant of the ClipboardFormats class. You assign the URL_FORMAT data to the url property of the webUrl object. Before assigning the hyperlink to the property, you assign a new instance of the URLRequest class to the webUrl variable. The following code accomplishes these tasks:

```
// get copied URL
webUrl = new URLRequest();
webUrl.url = String( clipboard.getData(
            ClipboardFormats.URL_FORMAT ) );
```

Next, you enable the loadHTML button to allow the user to open the hyperlink in a new window. You also show the textual representation of the hyperlink in the availableURL component:

```
loadHTML.enabled = true;
availableURL.text = webUrl.url;
}
    // access new available files
if( clipboard.hasFormat( ClipboardFormats.FILE_LIST_FORMAT ) )
{
```

If the clipboard contains files, you extract them by telling the getData() function to return the content that is associated with the FILE_LIST_FORMAT constant of the ClipboardFormats class. You assign the FILE_LIST_FORMAT data to the local files variable:

```
// get file references on clipboard
var files:Array = clipboard.getData(
                    ClipboardFormats.FILE_LIST_FORMAT ) as Array;
```

Once you've obtained the list of files on the clipboard, you populate a DataProvider object with the instances of the available File objects. Then you assign the dataProvider as a source of data for the filesInClipboard DataGrid. The DataGrid's columns have been set in the constructor function of the class to access the property of the File class objects you've used to represent the content of each row. The code looks like this:

```
// DataGrid dataprovider
var dp:DataProvider = new DataProvider();
        // populate dataprovider
var item:File;
for each( item in files )
{
    dp.addItem( item );
}
// assign dataprovider to DataGrid
filesInClipboard.dataProvider = dp;
        }
    }
```

The readSystemClipboard() function has read the content of the host system clipboard and displayed it if it contained data. If the data extracted from the clipboard contains hyperlinks, the loadHTML button is enabled to allow the user to open it in a new window in the application. When the user clicks the loadHTML button, the loadHTMLcontents() method is executed. The loadHTMLcontents() method is registered as an event listener function for the click event on the button. Here's the code:

```
private function loadHTMLcontents( event:MouseEvent ):void
{
```

When a request is made to open a hyperlink obtained from the clipboard, you check that the webUrl object of the URLLoader class isn't equal to null. If it is for some reason, you interrupt the execution of the function. Here's how to check the webUrl object:

```
// load HTML contents from Web
if( webUrl == null )
{
    return;
}
```

7

Before opening the link, you instance a NativeWindowInitOptions object to provide the right initialization information to the window you'll create. You also prepare an object of the Rectangle class, which will define the position and the initial dimensions of the window. Here's the code:

```
// prepare HTML container to be shown in a new native window
var initOptions:NativeWindowInitOptions =
                    new NativeWindowInitOptions();
var bounds:Rectangle = new Rectangle(50, 30, 500, 400);
```

Next, you use the static createRootWindow() function of the HTMLLoader class to instance a new native window containing an object of the HTMLLoader class. You give the function the initialization options and the dimensions you created previously. You call the activate() function of the new native window to tell AIR to bring it to the foreground on the desktop.

```
// init visible, windows options, show scrollbars, bounding box
var html:HTMLLoader = HTMLLoader.createRootWindow(
                    false, initOptions, true, bounds );
html.stage.nativeWindow.activate();
```

Finally, you use the load() function of the instanced HTMLLoader object to load the hyperlink defined by the webUrl variable, as shown here:

```
// init HTML loading
html.load( webUrl );
}
```

Executing the application

Go back to the ch07p06.fla project and execute the application (Test Movie ➤ Control). Try it out by performing the following actions:

- Copy an image from your browser or from a graphical editing program.
- Copy a hyperlink from your browser.
- Copy some text from a word-processing program or copy some files from your file system.

After each of these operations, click the loadData button in the AIR application and you'll see the content appear in the relevant display components. You can see a few previews of the results you should obtain in Figures 7-12, 7-13, and 7-14.

Figure 7-12. The ch07p06 project during execution, with an image loaded from the clipboard

7

Figure 7-13. The ch07p06.fla project during execution, with a hyperlink loaded and opened from the clipboard

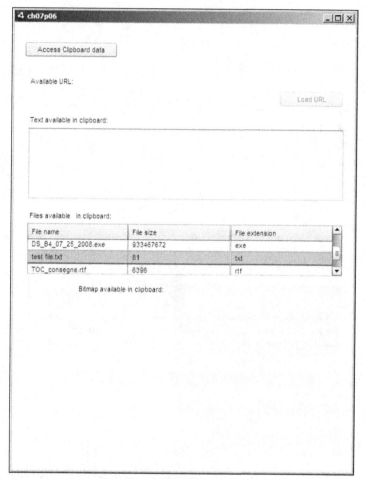

Figure 7-14. The ch07p06.fla project during execution, with files loaded from the clipboard

The next section will introduce you to AIR's drag-and-drop capabilities. You will see how to drag items from the local system desktop to an AIR application and vice versa.

Performing drag-and-drop actions

So far, you've seen how to create applications that interact with the host system clipboard to exchange data with other applications. With AIR, you can also exchange data between other applications and the file system with drag-and-drop actions.

AIR applications allow both drag-in and drag-out operations. You can move the same data formats in both directions, so you can use them in reading and writing operations to the system clipboard.

AIR provides the following classes from the flash.desktop package to manage drag-and-drop operations:

- NativeDragManager: This class coordinates and manages the dragging process from and to AIR applications. It also manages dragging operations between different components of the same application. When you start a dragging operation, a Clipboard class object is created, which contains saved data from the dragged elements. This object will be made available through the clipboard property of the NativeDragEvent class, which will be provided to the receiver of the dragging operation.

- NativeDragActions: This class defines the constants that set the possible dragging methods of available objects. The dragging options are copy, move, and reference.

- NativeDragOptions: This class allows you to specify which actions, defined by the NativeDragActions class, are valid for a given dragging action. The object that receives the dragging action will have to check if the receiving action (copy, move, or reference) is allowed with the object the user is dragging before accepting the operation.

The phases of a dragging operation

A dragging operation is made up of the following three separate phases:

- Start
- Drag
- Release

Read the following sections to find out more about these phases.

Starting a dragging operation

A dragging operation starts when the user clicks an element (but before releasing the mouse button). At that moment, a Clipboard class object has to be built in an event listener function associated with the mouse-down event. The Clipboard class object will transport the information associated with the dragging action and provided to the doDrag() function of the NativeDragManager class as an argument. The call to the doDrag() function actually starts the operation and generates a nativeDragStart event.

Dragging objects

This phase lasts until the user releases the mouse. During the movement, each time the dragged object reaches a possible valid destination for the dragging operation, a nativeDragEnter event is generated by the possible destination. If the destination can receive the object, it has to call the acceptDragDrop() method of the NativeDragManager class in the event listener function. That function must be associated with the nativeDragEnter event to confirm that the event will receive the object. When the object hovers over the possible destination, it will continue to generate a nativeDragOver event, and when it leaves the possible destination, it will generate a nativeDragExit event.

Releasing the mouse

When the user releases the mouse, a nativeDragDrop event is generated. The event is generated if the object is over a valid destination that has accepted the release by calling the acceptDragDrop() function of the NativeDragManager class. The event listener function for this event will receive the Clipboard object that was generated at the beginning of the action, and can manage it any way it likes. The object that has started the dragging operation will generate a nativeDragComplete event to mark the end of the dragging action. This is the case whether or not the dragging operation has been completed on a valid destination.

Dragging text documents to the TextArea

The best way to understand a new concept is to put in into practice, so now you'll learn how to create a program that extends the application presented in the ch07p05.fla exercise. This new application will allow the user to drag text documents into the TextArea to load and edit them.

Start by opening the ch07p07.fla project in Flash CS4. The stage of the application contains the same objects as the stage of the ch07p05.fla project, as you can see in Figure 7-15. Even the associated document class has the same functions, with a few additional ones to support dragging operations of files to the TextArea.

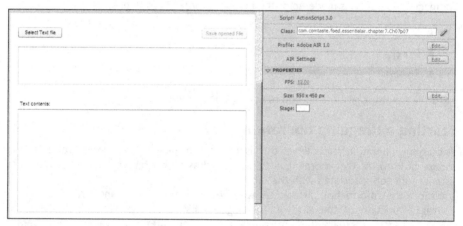

Figure 7-15. The stage and Document Properties panel for the ch07p07.fla project

Opening dragged files in the application

Access the document class of the project by clicking the Edit class definition icon on the Document Properties panel. As you can see in the following code sample, the class has a few extra external classes than the ch07p05.fla project. The class variables, though, are the same.

```
package com.comtaste.foed.essentialair.chapter7
{
import fl.controls.Button;
import fl.controls.TextArea;
```

```
import flash.desktop.Clipboard;
import flash.desktop.ClipboardFormats;
import flash.desktop.NativeDragActions;
import flash.desktop.NativeDragManager;
import flash.display.MovieClip;
import flash.events.Event;
import flash.events.MouseEvent;
import flash.events.NativeDragEvent;
import flash.filesystem.File;
import flash.filesystem.FileMode;
import flash.filesystem.FileStream;
import flash.net.FileFilter;

public class ch07p07 extends MovieClip
{
// on stage components
public var choose:Button;
public var save:Button;
public var output:TextArea;
public var text:TextArea;

// class properties
private var fileObject:File;
private var stream:FileStream = new FileStream();
```

In the constructor method, three event listeners have been registered to the TextArea (with the instance name text) to allow you to manage drag-and-drop actions to it, in addition to the event listener functions related to the buttons to open the connection of the stream object.

```
public function ch07p07()
{
    super();
    // register event listeners
    choose.addEventListener( MouseEvent.CLICK, showSelection );
    save.addEventListener( MouseEvent.CLICK, saveFile );
    stream.addEventListener( Event.COMPLETE, fileStreamOpened );

    // register native drag events on textarea component
    text.addEventListener(
            NativeDragEvent.NATIVE_DRAG_ENTER, enterDrag );
    text.addEventListener(
            NativeDragEvent.NATIVE_DRAG_DROP, confirmDrag );
    text.addEventListener(
            NativeDragEvent.NATIVE_DRAG_EXIT, exitDrag );
}
```

The showSelection(), saveFile(), and fileStreamOpened() event listener functions are the same ones as in the ch07p05.fla project. Also note that some functions have been added to manage the drag-and-drop operations. When a dragging action involves the TextArea, an enterDrag() function is executed, which will verify whether the object can be imported into the application or not. Here's the code:

```
public function enterDrag( event : NativeDragEvent ):void
{
```

Now write the following message to mark the beginning of the dragging operation in the output TextArea:

```
output.appendText( "DRAG STARTED" + File.lineEnding );
```

Next, access the Clipboard object that transports the information on the dragged elements through the clipboard property of the event object of the NativeDragEvent class. That class is received as an argument of the enterDrag() method:

```
// access dragged file list
var clipBoard:Clipboard = event.clipboard;
```

As shown in the preceding clipboard exercise, you check if the received Clipboard object contains data in the format you've specified. To do so, you use the hasFormat() function of the Clipboard class, like this:

```
// proceed only if there are files dragged
if( clipBoard.hasFormat( ClipboardFormats.FILE_LIST_FORMAT ) )
{
```

If the transported data contains references to files, you confirm whether the dragging action will be received. Do so by calling the acceptDragDrop() function of the NativeDragManager class, specifying that the potential object is the text TextArea:

```
        // validate dragging action
        NativeDragManager.acceptDragDrop( text );
    }
}
```

When the user releases the mouse over the TextArea and confirms the dragging operation, the confirmDrag() function is executed. That action is in response to the nativeDragDrop event of the NativeDragEvent class. This is the case if the enterDrag() function has accepted the action by calling the acceptDragDrop() method. Here's the code:

```
public function confirmDrag( event : NativeDragEvent ):void
{
```

Next, access the Clipboard object associated with the action to obtain the elements that are transported by the dragging actions. Do this through the clipboard property of the event object of the NativeDragEvent class. This event object is propagated as an argument of the even handler.

```
// access clipboard
var clipBoard:Clipboard = event.clipboard;
```

Then check that the received data is in a format that the application can recognize by using the hasFormat() function of the Clipboard class. The type of data that your application recognizes is defined by the FILE_LIST_FORMAT constant of the ClipboardFormats class.

```
// ensure that valid files are still available
if( clipBoard.hasFormat( ClipboardFormats.FILE_LIST_FORMAT ) )
{
```

When the validity of the received data has been verified, extract the array containing the dragged files. Do this by using the getData() function of the Clipboard class, as shown here:

```
// extract dragged file list
    var fileList:Array = clipBoard.getData(
        ClipboardFormats.FILE_LIST_FORMAT ) as Array;
```

If more than one file is being dragged, you can't proceed, as your application can only receive one text file at a time. This code is as follows:

```
// proceed only if one file has been dragged
if( fileList.length == 1 )
{
    // access file instance
    var file:File = fileList[ 0 ] as File;
```

Next, make sure that the object being dragged is a text file. Do so by checking the extension of the File object that the listener function receives. If the extension property of the File object, which represents the extension of the document, is txt, you can open the file.

```
// test file extension
if( file.extension == "txt" )
{
```

Once you've received confirmation that the object is a valid text file, you store its reference in the variable of the fileObject class. Then you ask the stream object to open an asynchronous connection with that fileObject in read-only mode. To open the connection to the file, you use the openAsync() asynchronous method of the FileStream class. The completion of the connection to the file generates a completion event that will execute the fileStreamOpened() function. Here's the code:

```
// store dragged file
fileObject = file;
                    // open async stream to file contents
    stream.openAsync( file, FileMode.READ );
} else
{
```

If the received object isn't a text file, you warn the user about the error. Do so by writing a message in the output TextArea, like this:

```
            output.appendText( "You must drag a valid TXT file"
                    + File.lineEnding );
    }
} else
{
```

If more than one file is being dragged at the same time, again you warn the user about the error. Do so by writing the following message in the output TextArea:

```
        output.appendText( "You must drag a single TXT file"
                + File.lineEnding );
    }
}else
{
```

Once again, if the received object isn't a file, you warn the user about the error. Do so by writing the following message in the output TextArea:

```
        output.appendText( "Attention, draged objects are not valid!"
                + File.lineEnding );
    }
}
```

If the operation is successful, the text in the file will be loaded in the text TextArea; otherwise, an error message will appear in the output TextArea. When the user continues to move by exiting the rollover action instead of releasing the mouse over the text TextArea, a nativeDragExit event is generated. This event will start the execution of the exitDrag() function. This function simply writes a message in the output TextArea to notify the user of the event, as shown here:

```
    public function exitDrag( e : NativeDragEvent ):void
    {
        output.appendText( "DRAG ENDED" + File.lineEnding );
    }
```

Go back to the Flash project and execute it (Test Movie ➤ Control). You can see the application running during a drag-in action in Figure 7-16.

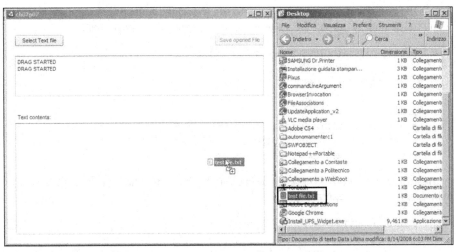

Figure 7-16. The ch07p07.fla project during a drag-in

Dragging files onto the desktop

To complete the ch07p07.fla project, you still have to add the possibility of dragging a copy of the opened text file to any location on the file system or directly into a word-processing program. The application with the new added functions is defined in the ch07p08.fla project. On the stage of this project, a new button has been added on textDragOut, which you can use to carry out drag-out operations (see Figure 7-17).

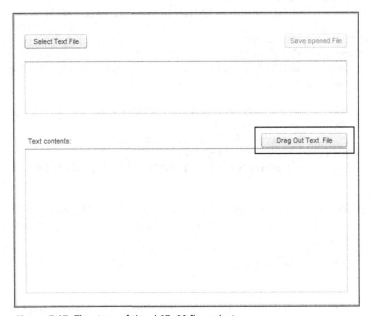

Figure 7-17. The stage of the ch07p08.fla project

Access the document class of the project to see the added functions. A class variable that refers to the new button on the stage has also been added, as shown here:

```
public class ch07p08 extends MovieClip
{
// onstage components
public var choose:Button;
public var save:Button;
public var textDragOut:Button;
public var output:TextArea;
public var text:TextArea;
```

In the constructor function, the following event listener functions have been added to manage the drag-out operations:

```
public function ch07p08()
{
    // register event listeners
    choose.addEventListener( MouseEvent.CLICK, showSelection );
    save.addEventListener( MouseEvent.CLICK, saveFile );
    stream.addEventListener( Event.COMPLETE, fileStreamOpened );
    // register native drag events on textarea component
    text.addEventListener(
            NativeDragEvent.NATIVE_DRAG_ENTER, enterDrag );
    text.addEventListener(
            NativeDragEvent.NATIVE_DRAG_DROP, confirmDrag );
    text.addEventListener(
            NativeDragEvent.NATIVE_DRAG_EXIT, exitDrag );
```

Next, register two event listener functions on the textDragOut button regarding the mouseDown and nativeDragComplete events. The function associated with the mouseDown event will start the drag-out action of the text file, whereas the function for the nativeDragComplete event will close the drag-out action.

```
    // register native drag events on textDragOut button
    textDragOut.addEventListener(
            MouseEvent.MOUSE_DOWN, initDragOut );
    textDragOut.addEventListener(
            NativeDragEvent.NATIVE_DRAG_COMPLETE, completeDragOut );
}
```

When the user clicks the textDragOut button, the following initDragOut() function will be executed. This function prepares the data that is going to be dragged and starts the drag-out action.

```
private function initDragOut( event : MouseEvent ):void
{
```

Next, if the text TextArea doesn't contain any text strings, you interrupt the execution of the function. You do this because there is no content associated with the drag-out operation.

```
        // get text from textarea
        var txt:String = text.text;
        if( txt.length == 0 )
        {
            // do nothing
            return;
        }
```

Create a text file in the applicationStorageDirectory folder of the AIR application and populate it with the textual content of the text TextArea. To write to the file, you use the synchronous functions of the FileStream class, as shown here:

```
        // creates new file containing textarea text
        tempFile = File.applicationStorageDirectory.resolvePath(
                "Adobe AIR generated txt files.txt" );
        // open stream to file
        stream.open( tempFile, FileMode.WRITE );
        // write in file
        stream.writeUTFBytes( txt );
        // close stream
        stream.close();
```

Once you've created a new text file containing the text to be exported, you're ready to create the Clipboard object that will be associated with the dragging action. You create an instance of the Clipboard class and add the text file to it. You specify that the file has to be saved in the format defined in the FILE_LIST_FORMAT constant of the ClipboardFormats class. You also add the textual representation of the document by saving it in the format of the data defined by the TEXT_FORMAT constant. By doing so, if the object is being dragged onto the desktop of the operating system, it will use the File format, whereas if it is being dragged into a word-processing program, it will use the plain-text format. The following code accomplishes these tasks:

```
        // create clipboard object instance
        var clipBoard:Clipboard = new Clipboard();
        // append file reference to clipboard object
        clipBoard.setData( ClipboardFormats.FILE_LIST_FORMAT,
                [ tempFile ], false );
        // append textual representation to clipboard object
        clipBoard.setData( ClipboardFormats.TEXT_FORMAT, txt, false );
```

During dragging actions, the operating system automatically creates a graphical preview of the dragged object. AIR allows you to define a customized graphical representation for your dragging actions. As such, you now create a raster object that represents the preview of the TextArea as it is displayed:

```
        // create textArea bitmapdata
        var bmp:BitmapData = new BitmapData( text.width, text.height );
        bmp.draw( text );
```

You don't want the dragging operation to create a duplicate of the text file you've created, but to move the existing instance. To do so, you create a NativeDragOptions object that

7

specifies that the only way to access the data is to move it. This object will be provided to the call to the doDrag() function. This function starts the dragging action as an argument, like this:

```
// set drag-out option to move file created to desired position
var opt:NativeDragOptions = new NativeDragOptions();
opt.allowCopy = false;
opt.allowLink = false;
opt.allowMove = true;
```

Next, make sure that the application moves the text file without copying it. Do so by telling the NativeDragManager class that the default option for dragging actions is the movement of data, as shown here:

```
// force default drag action
NativeDragManager.dropAction = NativeDragActions.MOVE;
```

Finally, you call the doDrag() function and provide the necessary arguments. You do this so that the image you have generated is used as a preview, and the dragging action generates the movement of the data and doesn't copy it. Here's the code:

```
// validate drag-out action
NativeDragManager.doDrag( textDragOut, clipBoard, bmp, null, opt );
```

Next, warn the user that the dragging operation has been started properly with a message in the output TextArea:

```
    output.appendText( "Start to drag-out" + File.lineEnding );
}
```

When the user releases the mouse and completes the drag-out operation, regardless of the result, a nativeDragComplete event is generated. That event starts the execution of the completeDragOut() function. This function writes the following message in the output TextArea to tell the user that the drag-out operation has completed:

```
private function completeDragOut( event : NativeDragEvent ):void
{
    output.appendText( "Completed drag-out of type: "
            + event.dropAction + File.lineEnding );
}
```

Compiling and executing the application

Now go back to the ch07p08.fla project, and compile and execute the AIR application (Test Movie ➤ Control). Write some text in the text TextArea and try dragging the textDragOut button to the desktop or into a word-processing program to use the functions you've just added. You can see the application in action in Figure 7-18.

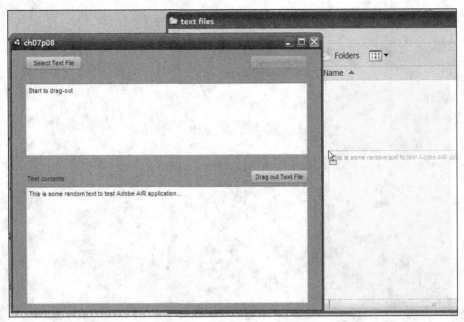

Figure 7-18. The ch07p08 project during a drag-out

7

Summary

This chapter has provided you with the basic knowledge to create applications that access features provided by operating systems, such as file systems, dialog boxes, clipboards, and drag-and-drop actions. All these topics require a certain amount of background knowledge, and covering all the possible functions in detail would require a lot more than a chapter. Nevertheless, this chapter has introduced a good share of the main parts of the most difficult points for each of the features.

With these tools and this basic knowledge, you should be able to start experimenting and create more advanced AIR applications.

CHAPTER 8

WORKING WITH THE OPERATING SYSTEM

In this chapter, some of the coolest advanced features provided by Adobe AIR will be shown. These features allow the applications you create to be completely integrated with the operating system. You'll learn how to do the following:

- Pass command-line arguments from the operating system shell to an AIR application
- Start an installed AIR application from a web page (installation is covered in more detail in Chapter 13)
- Create applications that start up with the operating system
- Associate file types with an AIR application
- Call the user's attention through operating system notifications

The next section will introduce you to the options that AIR applications can use upon startup.

Invoking an application

You can start an AIR application in various ways, but the following are the most common:

- By requesting the execution through command-line shells, such as a DOS prompt (on Windows) and the console (on Mac OS X)
- By starting the application from a link or an operating system menu
- By clicking an icon in the dock bar (only for Mac OS X systems)
- By requesting the opening of a type of file that is associated with the AIR application
- By accessing a web page that recognizes the application's ID and launches the application. This is only possible if the allowBrowserInvocation option has been enabled. This concept will be discussed further in the sections regarding application startup from web pages.

Each time an application is launched, the AIR runtime generates an InvokeEvent event. This event is conveyed through a singleton instance of the application (NativeApplication. nativeApplication). An application that wants to receive this event has to register itself for the InvokeEvent.INVOKE event, as shown here:

```
NativeApplication.nativeApplication.addEventListener(
                        InvokeEvent.INVOKE, functionName );
```

The registration of the event should occur during the initialization of the class, normally in the constructor method. The InvokeEvent.INVOKE event is usually used to initialize the application, using optional parameters. The InvokeEvent.INVOKE event is generated as soon as the application is launched, meaning before the application can register on it. To avoid this situation, AIR saves all the InvokeEvent.INVOKE events in a list. As soon as the application registers the event, it begins to receive all the InvokeEvent.INVOKE events that have occurred, one at a time. Events are passed one at a time, in brief intervals. Any time the local system or other application invokes the AIR application, a new InvokeEvent. INVOKE event is generated.

An InvokeEvent.INVOKE event is generated the first time the application is launched. Once the application is in execution, each subsequent user action to open the AIR application generates a new InvokeEvent.INVOKE event. You have to remember that if an InvokeEvent. INVOKE event is registered during the execution of the application, the associated function will receive all the events that have occurred previously. It's up to the developer to prepare different behaviors for the InvokeEvent.INVOKE events that are generated when the application is launched and during its execution.

The following code shows how to register an event listener function for the InvokeEvent. INVOKE event and access the information contained in the event object:

```
NativeApplication.nativeApplication.addEventListener(
                        InvokeEvent.INVOKE, onInvoke );
function onInvoke( evt : InvokeEvent ):void
{
    // folder where invocation started
    var invocationDirectory:File = evt.currentDirectory;

    // arguments passed
    var argumentsPassed:Array = evt.arguments;
}
```

An InvokeEvent object contains all the possible arguments that are passed to the application during its invocation. If the application is started by a command-line shell or a web page, the received arguments will all be explicitly defined by the caller. If a request is made to open a type of file that is associated with the application, the complete native path of the file itself will be passed on as an argument. The arguments are transported by the arguments property of the InvokeEvent object. This property is an Array object. The InvokeEvent object also has a currentDir property, which is a File object that specifies the path from which the application is invoked.

In the next section, you'll see how to interact with the arguments passed on via command lines.

Accessing command-line arguments

The command-line arguments are provided to the application as a space-separated text string. The list of arguments that are provided are converted into an Array object. If an argument is made up of values that contain spaces (e.g., a file path), you have to enclose it in quotation marks.

On Windows, you can pass arguments to an application by using the DOS prompt or **batch** files. Batch files are text files, with .bat extensions, that allow you to define a group of operations to be executed. To pass the name and password of a user through command-line arguments, you have to create a myFile.bat file and write the following code in it, in a single line:

8

```
"C:\Program File\Air Applications\myApplication.exe"
                         "Matteo Ronchi" secretPassword
```

On Mac OS X operating systems you can use the bash console or executing a script file. Script file are text files with a .scpt extension that allow you to define a group of operations to be executed. To pass the name and password of a user through command-line arguments, you have to create a myFile.scpt file and write the following code in it:

```
do shell script "/Application/myApplication.app/Contents/MacOS/
                 myApplication 'Matteo Ronchi' secretPassword;exit;"
```

Each time the batch file is executed, the myapplication application will receive an Array object containing two items: Matteo Ronchi and secretPassword. The following table shows various cases of conversion from command-line arguments to arrays.

Command-line arguments passed	Array received by AIR application
Matteo Ronchi SecretPassword	[Matteo, Ronchi, SecretPassword]
"Matteo Ronchi" SecretPassword	[Matteo Ronchi, SecretPassword]
"Matteo Ronchi" "SecretPassword"	[Matteo Ronchi, SecretPassword]

If the application is started because it's associated with a type of file the user wants to open, it will receive the path to the relevant file as an argument. The onInvoke() function shows how you can access the file that requires the AIR application to be launched:

```
function onInvoke( evt : InvokeEvent ):void
{
    // folder where invocation started
    var invocationDirectory:File = evt.currentDirectory;

    // arguments passed
    var argumentsPassed:Array = evt.arguments;

    // access file
    if( argumentsPassed.length > 0 )
    {
        // path of file opened
        var filePath:String = String( argumentsPassed[ 0 ] );

        // pointer to file to open
        var requestedFile:File = new File( filePath );

        // test if file exists
        var fileExists:Boolean = requestedFile.exists;
    }
}
```

The preceding code accesses the first argument passed by the InvokeEvent object in order to know which file requires the application to be opened. A File object will be created with this file path. Then, to be on the safe side, the code verifies the existence of the file through the fileInstance.exists property. This check is necessary because the application doesn't know which of the user's actions requested it to be launched.

When you request the launch of several files associated with an AIR application, there are differences between Windows systems and Mac OS X systems. On Mac OS X, only one InvokeEvent event is generated, which contains all the files requested by the user. Windows systems generate as many InvokeEvent events as the requested files.

In the next section, you'll create an application that demonstrates the use of command-line arguments.

Reading command-line arguments

The application you want to create will register with the InvokeEvent.INVOKE event. The application will write the arguments it receives and the path it has been opened from in a TextArea. Follow these steps to create the Flash CS4 project:

1. Create a new Flash file (Adobe AIR) and name it commandLineArguments.fla.
2. Create a TextArea component on the stage and assign it output as instance name. This component will display all the information received by the InvokeEvent object. If you prefer, you can open the file, which already has all the elements, from the Chapter08 folder in the source code files for the book (available from the downloads section at www.friendsofed.com/).
3. Open the Publish Settings panel (File ➤ Publish Settings).
4. Click the Settings button next to the Script: ActionScript 3 item, and the Advanced ActionScript 3.0 Settings panel will open, as shown in Figure 8-1.
5. Deselect the Automatically declare stage instances option. The properties that are associated with the components on the stage will be declared in the class you'll create soon.
6. Add the ./src/ item to the Source path tab. This operation tells Flash that it will have to look for ActionScript classes inside the path relating to the commandLine➥Arguments.fla project.
7. Click OK on the opened panels to close them.
8. Create a new src folder in the folder that contains the commandLineArguments.fla project. In this folder, you'll create the classes used in the application. The ActionScript code of the commandLineArguments.fla project is created in the CommandLineArguments.as class, in the com.comtaste.foed.essentialair.chapter8 package.

8

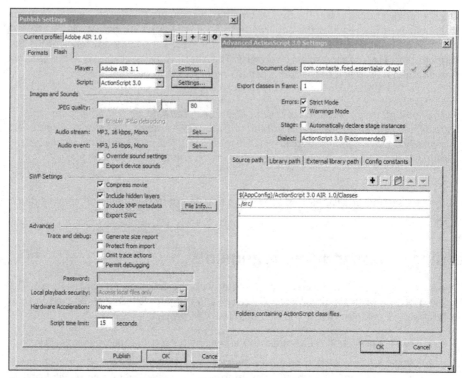

Figure 8-1. Setting the ActionScript properties for the commandLineArguments.fla project

The package of an ActionScript class corresponds to the path where Flash can find it. A package is defined by a group of dot-separated names (this syntax is called dot syntax). Each element of the package corresponds to a folder of the file system. The structure of folders to create for the com.comtaste.foed.essentialair.chapter8 package is the following: com/comtaste/foed/essentialair/chapter8.

9. Create the folders you need for the com.comtaste.foed.essentialair.chapter8 package, and create a new ActionScript file in the chapter8 folder. The file should be called CommandLineArguments.as. If you like, you can find the complete CommandLineArguments.as file in the source code of the project.

10. Go back to the Flash commandLineArguments.fla project and write the complete name of the com.comtaste.foed.essentialair.chapter8.CommandLineArguments class in the Class field of the Document Properties panel, as shown in Figure 8-2. The complete name of the class has to be written without the .as extension.

11. As mentioned in previous chapters, a class associated with a Flash project is called a document class. To access this class, click the Edit class definition icon (which looks like a pencil) next to the Class field. The CommandLineArguments.as class, which is now an empty document, will open in Flash CS4.

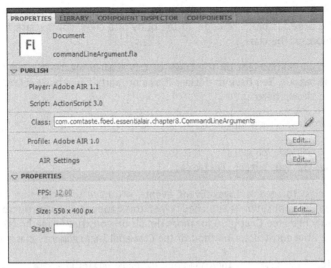

Figure 8-2. Defining the document class of the commandLineArguments.fla project

The ActionScript class has to begin with the declaration of its package, so enter the following code:

```
package com.comtaste.foed.essentialair.chapter8
{
```

This code shows the declaration of the external classes that you need to import:

```
package com.comtaste.foed.essentialair.chapter8
{
// Flash-specific classes
import fl.controls.TextArea;

// Adobe AIR-specific classes
import flash.desktop.NativeApplication;
import flash.display.MovieClip;
import flash.events.InvokeEvent;
import flash.filesystem.File;
```

Once you've declared the package and external dependencies of the class, declare the body of the class, as shown here:

```
public class CommandLineArguments extends MovieClip
{

}// close class
}// close package
```

As a refresher, the body of a class is delimited by curly braces ({}) that are indented with respect to the previous block of code. In the body of a class, you declare the properties and the methods of the class.

There is only one component on the stage of this Flash project—the TextArea with the instance name output. You have to declare it as a property typed as TextArea in the body of the class, as shown here:

```
public class CommandLineArguments extends MovieClip
{
    // onstage objects
    public var output:TextArea;
```

To allow the class to receive InvokeEvent events, you have to register an event listener function when the application is launched. When this happens, the constructor method of the class is launched (see Chapter 6 for more details on constructor methods). The following code shows the constructor method of the CommandLineArguments class:

```
public class CommandLineArguments extends MovieClip
{
    // onstage objects
    public var output:TextArea;

    // class constructor
    public function CommandLineArguments()
    {
        // register event listener function for INVOKE event
        NativeApplication.nativeApplication.addEventListener(
                    InvokeEvent.INVOKE, applicationInvoked );
    }
```

In the preceding code, the applicationInvoked() method is registered on the InvokeEvent.INVOKE event. Each time the application is launched, AIR will generate an InvokeEvent object that will be passed to the applicationInvoked() method of the class. The applicationInvoked() method, shown next, accesses the folder where the request for the application-launching process is made, and writes the native path of this folder in the TextArea:

```
// event listener method for application INVOKE event
private function applicationInvoked( evt : InvokeEvent ):void
{
    var currentDir:File = evt.currentDirectory;
    output.appendText( "Application invoked from position: "
                    + currentDir.nativePath + File.lineEnding );
```

Then the method accesses the array that contains the arguments passed to the application. This array is contained in the arguments property of the InvokeEvent object. The following code shows how the value of each of the arguments the application receives for the event is written in the TextArea. You use a for loop to cycle through the arguments:

```
        var arguments:Array = evt.arguments;
        for( var i:int = 0; i < arguments.length; i++ )
        {
            output.appendText( "Argument[" + i + "]: "
                            + arguments[ i ] + File.lineEnding );
        }
    }
```

Now the application is complete and ready to be tested. The complete code for the ActionScript CommandLineArguments.as class is shown here:

```
package com.comtaste.foed.essentialair.chapter8
{
// Flash-specific classes
import fl.controls.TextArea;

// Adobe AIR-specific classes
import flash.desktop.NativeApplication;
import flash.display.MovieClip;
import flash.events.InvokeEvent;
import flash.filesystem.File;

public class CommandLineArguments extends MovieClip
{
    // onstage objects
    public var output:TextArea;

    // class constructor
    public function CommandLineArguments()
    {
        // register event listener function for INVOKE event
        NativeApplication.nativeApplication.addEventListener(
                    InvokeEvent.INVOKE, applicationInvoked );
    }

    // event listener method for application INVOKE event
    private function applicationInvoked( evt : InvokeEvent ):void
    {
        var currentDir:File = evt.currentDirectory;
        output.appendText( "Application invoked from position: "
                    + currentDir.nativePath + File.lineEnding );

        var arguments:Array = evt.arguments;
        for( var i:int = 0; i < arguments.length; i++ )
        {
            output.appendText( "Argument[" + i + "]: "
                        + arguments[ i ] + File.lineEnding );
        }
    }
```

8

```
}// close class
}// close package
```

Go back to the Flash project and execute it by selecting the Test Movie command from the Control menu in Flash CS4. The application should look something like Figure 8-3. The TextArea only displays the launching folder; it doesn't display any arguments. This is because you can't pass arguments to an AIR application during the debugging phase.

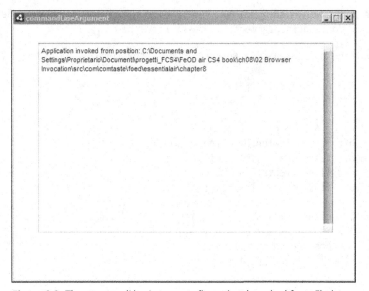

Figure 8-3. The commandLineArguments.fla project launched from Flash

Compiling and testing the commandLineArguments.fla project

In this section, I'll show you how to create the installation file of the application generated by the `commandLineArguments.fla` project. I'll also provide an example of how to pass command-line arguments through a batch file.

1. To create an installation file, click the Edit button next to the AIR Settings item in the Publish Settings panel. The AIR – Application & Installer Settings panel will open, allowing you to define various application options. In this chapter, you will see a few of these options in detail (see Chapter 4 for more information).

2. In the AIR – Application & Installer Settings panel, it's necessary to import the certificate to be associated with the application. To specify the certificate to be used, click the Set button next to the Digital Signature item, which will open the Digital Signature panel (see Figure 8-4).

3. Click the Create button to generate a certificate of your own. If you prefer, you can use the test certificate, testCertificate.p12, from the source code of the book in the Chapter08 folder. The password for the testCertificate.p12 certificate is test.

4. Once you've specified the certificate you want to use, click OK, and then click the Publish AIR File button to create the installation file.

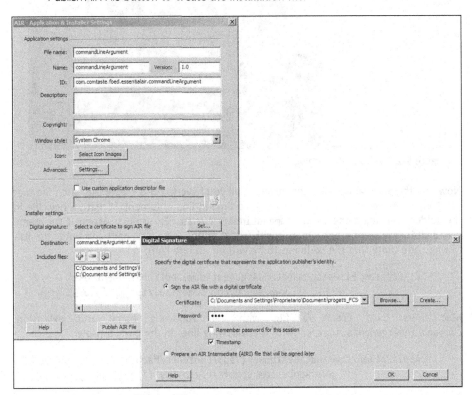

Figure 8-4. Specifying the digital certificate

5. In the folder that contains your commandLineArguments.fla project, the command➥ LineArgument.air file has been created. Start the installation of the commandLine➥ Argument.air application. Figure 8-5 shows the default settings provided during the installation.

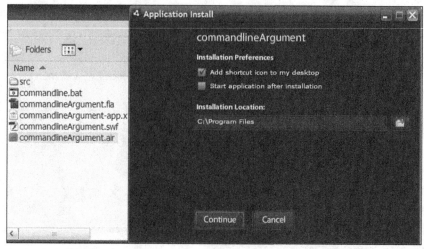

Figure 8-5. The installation dialog

Now that the application has been installed, all you have to do is create the batch file that will launch its execution by passing some command-line arguments. Create a new file in the folder containing the Flash commandLineArguments.fla project. Assign it the name commandLineArguments.bat. Open it with a text editor (e.g., Notepad) and enter the following code (note that the code has to be written on one line):

```
"C:\Program Files\commandLineArgument\commandLineArgument.exe"
                        www.adobe.com somefile.zip 'my file 33.jpg'
```

Mac users must create a file with the following name and extension: commandLineArguments.scpt, or write the following lines in the bash console:

```
/Application/commandLineArgument.app/Contents/MacOS/commandLineArgument
              www.adobe.com somefile.zip 'my file 33.jpg'; exit;
```

If your installation path is different from the one shown here, correct it as necessary. Save and close the document, and then launch the commandLineArguments.bat file. The application will start up, and you will see a list of command-line arguments. The launched application is shown in Figure 8-6.

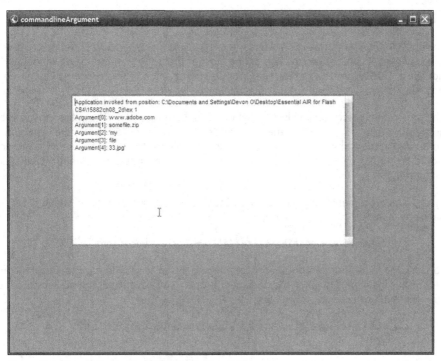

Figure 8-6. The application launched from a batch file

In the next section, you'll see how to launch an AIR application from a web page.

Using the browser to invoke the AIR application

AIR allows you to launch an application from a web page. For this to be possible, you have to make sure a few specific conditions are satisfied:

- The AIR application invoked from the web page has to have the allowBrowserInvocation option set to true.
- The web page has to recognize the application ID and publisher ID of the AIR application.

If a web page invokes an AIR application that is already in execution, it will be activated and brought to the foreground of the screen.

Setting the allowBrowserInvocation option

As shown in Chapter 4, Flash CS4 offers the AIR Settings dialog window to define the properties of an AIR application. You can define most of the options in this dialog window, but not the allowBrowserInvocation property. To set the value of this property, you have to edit the XML application descriptor file manually.

The application descriptor file is automatically generated by Flash CS4 in the same folder as the AIR project. The name of the file is made up of the AIR project plus the -app suffix. For example, the name of the application descriptor file for the myAIRproject.fla project would be myAIRproject-air.xml. (Application descriptors are discussed in more detail in Chapter 4.)

In this XML document, you can see the allowBrowserInvocation node, which is set to false by default:

```
<allowBrowserInvocation>false</allowBrowserInvocation>
```

To allow the invocation of an AIR application from a web page, you have to edit the content of this file manually. Once the document is open, you have to set the value associated with this node to true, as shown here:

```
<allowBrowserInvocation>true</allowBrowserInvocation>
```

Accessing the application ID and publisher ID of an AIR application

The web page that invokes the application has to recognize the application ID and publisher ID. The **application ID** is the unique ID of an AIR application. You can also access the application ID during the execution of the application through the property of the NativeApplication.nativeApplication object. The following code shows how you can access the value of the application ID:

```
var applicationID:String =
        NativeApplication.nativeApplication.applicationID;
```

Unlike the application ID, the **publisher ID** can't be freely defined. Flash CS4 generates the publisher ID during the compilation of the application. Each publisher ID is unique because it's made up of the information in the certificate you use to create the AIR file. If several applications are created using the same certificate, they'll have the same publisher ID. You can access the publisher ID during the execution of the AIR application, through the publisherID property of the NativeApplication.nativeApplication object, as shown here:

```
var publisherID:String =
        NativeApplication.nativeApplication.publisherID;
```

You can also access the publisher ID in the META-INF/AIR/publisherid file, which you can find in the folder where you've installed the AIR application. The web page will have to use both properties to invoke the required AIR application.

The BrowserInvokeEvent object

When an AIR application is invoked from a web page, the NativeApplication.native➡
Application object generates a BrowseInvokeEvent event. This event, like the InvokeEvent
events, is generated before the initialization code of the application has been executed. To
allow the application to receive all the events at the same time, the events are saved in
a list.

When an event listener function is registered for the BrowserInvokeEvent event, it will
receive all the listed events. The events will be passed on one at a time, separated by brief
intervals. You must remember that if a function is registered on the BrowserInvokeEvent
event after the application has been initialized, it will receive all the events that have
occurred previously.

The following code shows how to register an event listener function for a
BrowserInvokeEvent:

```
NativeApplication.nativeApplication.addEventListener(
                BrowserInvokeEvent.BROWSER_INVOKE, onInvoke );
```

The BrowserInvokeEvent object conveys various information to the AIR application. This
information allows the web page to provide specific data to the AIR application. The information is also necessary to validate the received data before it's used. Here are the properties provided by a BrowserInvokeEvent object:

- arguments: This is an Array object containing the information provided by the web
  page to the AIR application. All the elements of the Array object are typed as
  String.
- isHTTPS: This is a Boolean object that specifies whether the web page that has
  invoked the application uses an HTTP URL scheme (true) or not (false).
- isUserEvent: This is a Boolean object that specifies whether the invocation has
  been generated by a user's action, such as a mouse click. Since the 1.5 version of
  AIR doesn't allow the invocation of an application without the direct action of
  a user, at this time, this property is always set to true.
- sandboxType: This specifies the sandbox for the content of the web page. The values accepted are those that can be assigned to the Security.sandboxType property. Possible values are the following:
  - Security.APPLICATION: The web content shares the same security sandbox of
    the AIR application.
  - Security.LOCAL_TRUSTED: The web content is in the local-with–file system secu-
    rity sandbox.
  - Security.LOCAL_WITH_FILE: The web content is in the local-with–file system
    security sandbox.
  - Security.LOCAL_WITH_NETWORK: The web content is in the local-with-networking
    security sandbox.
  - Security.REMOTE: The web content is in a remote domain.

8

- securityDomain: This is the security domain for content from a remote domain. It represents the domain name (e.g., www.mySite.com). This property is only defined for content that is from a remote domain. Its value is null for the other possible security sandboxes.

The arguments property allows you to pass information to the invoked AIR application. It's important to avoid passing confidential data and execution instructions through events received from web pages. This precaution is necessary to reduce the possibilities of a third-party website manipulating an AIR application created by someone else. To guarantee better security, you can verify the isHTTPS and securityDomain properties before using the information that is passed on by the arguments property.

In the next section, you'll see how to create an AIR application and invoke it from a web page.

Creating an AIR application that allows browser invocation

In this section, you'll create an AIR application distributed from a web page. The end user will be able to launch and install the application by clicking it. Follow these steps to create the project:

1. Create a new Flash file (Adobe AIR) and name it browserInvocation.fla.

2. Create a TextArea component on the stage with an instance name of output. This component will display the information received by the BrowserInvokeEvent object. If you prefer, you can open the browserInvocation.fla file, which contains all the elements, from the Chapter08 folder.

3. Prepare the browserInvocation.fla project as shown in the commandLine➡ Argument.fla project at the beginning of the chapter.

4. Create a new ActionScript file that you will define as the document class of the project, and name it BrowserInvocation.as. The BrowserInvocation class has to be created in the package com.comtaste.foed.essentialair.chapter8. If you prefer, you can find the complete BrowserInvocation.as file in the source code of the browserInvocation.fla project.

Creating the document class for browserInvocation.fla

Go back to the Flash browserInvocation.fla project. Write the complete name of the com.comtaste.foed.essentialair.chapter8.BrowserInvocation class in the Class field of the Document Properties panel. Now that the document class has been defined, click the Edit class definition icon next to the Class field. The BrowserInvocation.as file will open in Flash CS4. Declare the package it belongs to at the beginning of the document:

```
package com.comtaste.foed.essentialair.chapter8
{
```

After the declaration of the package comes the list of the external classes you need. As you can see in the following code, you have to import a few specific classes from Flash CS4's framework and a few specific classes from the AIR framework:

```
// flash CS4 imports
import fl.controls.TextArea;

// Adobe AIR imports
import flash.desktop.NativeApplication;
import flash.display.MovieClip;
import flash.events.BrowserInvokeEvent;
import flash.filesystem.File;
```

The application you are building has the purpose of receiving BrowserInvokeEvent events and writing the information it receives from the browser in the output TextArea. The class is associated with a Flash project and therefore extends the MovieClip class. After the class declaration, you declare the output property, typed as TextArea, as shown here:

```
public class BrowserInvocation extends MovieClip
{
    // onstage objects
    public var output:TextArea;
```

In order to receive BrowserInvokeEvent events, you have to register an event listener function to the BrowserInvokeEvent.BROWSER_INVOKE event. In the constructor method of the class, you register the BROWSER_INVOKE event on the applicationInvoked() class method, which you will define shortly. In the constructor method, you also access the applicationID and publisherID properties of the AIR application.

> *Remember that the publisher ID of an AIR application is only accessible if the application has been installed correctly on the local system. If you launch the application from Flash CS4, the publisher ID won't be available. The publisher ID won't be available because it is generated from the certificate that is provided to complete the AIR application.*

The previously mentioned operations are shown in the following code:

```
// class constructor
public function BrowserInvocation()
{
    // write publisherID and applicationID
    output.appendText( "publisher ID: " +
        NativeApplication.nativeApplication.publisherID
        + File.lineEnding );
    output.appendText( "application ID: " +
        NativeApplication.nativeApplication.applicationID
        + File.lineEnding );

    // register event listener function for INVOKE event
    NativeApplication.nativeApplication.addEventListener(
      BrowserInvokeEvent.BROWSER_INVOKE, applicationInvoked );
}
```

8

It's important to access the publisher ID and application ID of the application. This information will be used further on to create a web page that can invoke the BrowserInvocation. air application. In the constructor method, you've specified that the application➥ Invoked() method has to be called when the application receives a BrowserInvokeEvent event. This method accesses the properties provided in the BrowserInvokeEvent object and displays its value in the TextArea on the stage of the browserInvocation.fla project. The properties of the event object provide information regarding the web page that invokes the AIR application. The arguments property transports information that can be used by the invoked AIR application. The applicationInvoked() function is in the following code:

```
// event listener method for application INVOKE event
private function applicationInvoked(evt:BrowserInvokeEvent):void
{
    // write BrowserInvokeEvent details
    output.appendText( "Application invoked from Web: "
                    + File.lineEnding );
    output.appendText( "Invoked from HTTP protocol: "
                    + evt.isHTTPS + File.lineEnding );
    output.appendText( "SAND BOX TYPE: "
                    + evt.sandboxType + File.lineEnding );
    output.appendText( "Security domain value: "
                    + evt.securityDomain + File.lineEnding );

    // write BrowserInvokeEvent received arguments, if any
    var arguments:Array = evt.arguments;
    for( var i:int = 0; i < arguments.length; i++ )
    {
        output.appendText( "Browser argument[" + i + "]: "
                        + arguments[ i ] + File.lineEnding );
    }
}

}// close class
}// close package
```

Here is the complete code for the BrowserInvocation.as class:

```
package com.comtaste.foed.essentialair.chapter8
{
// flash CS4 imports
import fl.controls.TextArea;

// Adobe AIR imports
import flash.desktop.NativeApplication;
import flash.display.MovieClip;
import flash.events.BrowserInvokeEvent;
import flash.filesystem.File;
```

```
public class BrowserInvocation extends MovieClip
{
    // onstage objects
    public var output:TextArea;

    // class constructor
    public function BrowserInvocation()
    {
        // write publisherID and applicationID
        output.appendText( "publisher ID: "
                + NativeApplication.nativeApplication.publisherID
                + File.lineEnding );
        output.appendText( "application ID: "
                + NativeApplication.nativeApplication.applicationID
                + File.lineEnding );

        // register event listener function for INVOKE event
        NativeApplication.nativeApplication.addEventListener(
          BrowserInvokeEvent.BROWSER_INVOKE, applicationInvoked );
    }

    // event listener method for application INVOKE event
    private function applicationInvoked(evt:BrowserInvokeEvent):void
    {
        output.appendText( "Application invoked from Web: "
                    + File.lineEnding );
        output.appendText( "Invoked from HTTP protocol: "
                    + evt.isHTTPS + File.lineEnding );
        output.appendText( "SAND BOX TYPE: "
                    + evt.sandboxType + File.lineEnding );
        output.appendText( "Security domain value: "
                    + evt.securityDomain + File.lineEnding );

        var arguments:Array = evt.arguments;
        for( var i:int = 0; i < arguments.length; i++ )
        {
            output.appendText( "Browser argument[" + i + "]: "
                    + arguments[ i ] + File.lineEnding );
        }
    }

}// close class
}// close package
```

8

Setting the allowBrowserInvocation option

As mentioned previously in the chapter, you need to set the allowBrowserInvocation option to true for an AIR application to be invoked by a web page. This option can't be defined in the AIR – Application & Installer Settings panel. You have to change the application descriptor file manually.

The file has been created by Flash CS4 in the same folder that contains the browser➡Invocation.fla project. Open the file, called browserInvocation-app.xml, in Flash CS4. The content of the XML document is the following:

```xml
<?xml version="1.0" encoding="UTF-8" standalone="no" ?>
<application xmlns="http://ns.adobe.com/air/application/1.5">

  <id>com.comtaste.foed.essentialair.chapter8.BrowserInvocation</id>
  <version>1.0</version>
  <filename>BrowserInvocation</filename>
  <description/>
  <name>BrowserInvocation</name>
  <copyright/>

  <initialWindow>
    <content>BrowserInvocation.swf</content>
    <systemChrome>standard</systemChrome>
    <transparent>false</transparent>
    <visible>true</visible>
    <maximizable>true</maximizable>
    <minimizable>true</minimizable>
    <resizable>true</resizable>
  </initialWindow>

  <icon/>
  <customUpdateUI>false</customUpdateUI>
  <allowBrowserInvocation>false</allowBrowserInvocation>
</application>
```

The XML node that refers to the allowBrowserInvocation option is highlighted in bold. This option is set to false by default. To allow the invocation from the Web, you have to set it to true, as shown here:

```xml
<allowBrowserInvocation>true</allowBrowserInvocation>
```

Testing and packaging the browserInvocation.air application

The browserInvocation.fla project is now ready to be tested and packaged. The final AIR application will be installed on the local system.

1. Go back to the Flash browserInvocation.fla project and execute it (Control ➤ Test Movie). The AIR application, launched by Flash CS4, will look like Figure 8-7.

   You can only see the application ID in the TextArea. In fact, neither the publisher ID nor the information regarding BrowserInvokeEvent events are available in an AIR application launched in Flash CS4. To create the installer for the browser➥ Invocation.air application, you have to proceed as explained in detail in the "Compiling and testing the CommandLineArguments.fla project" section.

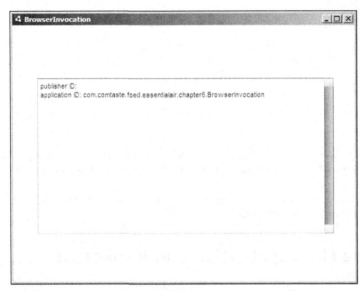

Figure 8-7. The browserInvocation.fla project launched from Flash

2. Open the AIR – Application & Installer Settings panel, and click the Set button next to the Digital Signature item.

3. Create a new certificate or use the testCertificate.p12 test certificate from the book's source code in the Chapter08 folder. The password for the test➥ Certificate.p12 certificate is test.

4. Click the Publish AIR File button. The browserInvocation.air file will be created in the folder that contains the browserInvocation.fla project.

5. Start the installation of the browserInvocation.air application. Leave the default settings provided by the installation procedure. At the end of the operation, the application will be launched, as shown in Figure 8-8. The publisher ID and application ID are displayed in the TextArea. Write them down, as you will need them to invoke the browserInvocation.air application from a web page.

8

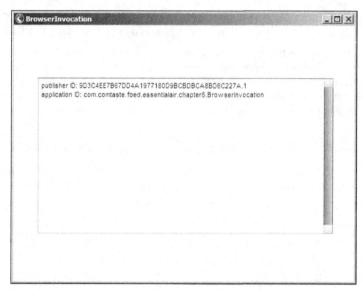

Figure 8-8. The browserInvocation.air application launched after installation

You'll see how to create a Flash application that invokes the browserInvocation.air application from a web page in the next section.

Creating a Flash application that invokes AIR applications

As mentioned previously, you can invoke an AIR application from a web page. A web page that invokes an AIR application has to contain a traditional Flash application. This Flash application will be in charge of launching the AIR application. Adobe provides ActionScript developers with the air.swf file, which offers the functions you need to carry out operations like the following:

- Checking if the AIR runtime is installed
- Checking if an AIR application is installed
- Installing an AIR application
- Invoking an AIR application

In the application you will create, you'll use a few of these functions. The air.swf file is hosted at http://airdownload.adobe.com/air/browserapi/air.swf. To use this file, a Flash application has to load it from the URL specified in its application domain. Once it's been loaded, you can use its functions.

Let's create the application:

1. Open a new Flash file (ActionScript 3) and name it browserLauncher.fla.

2. Create a TextArea component on the stage with an instance name of output.

3. Create a Button with an instance name of launchBtn, and set its enabled property to false from the Component Inspector panel.

4. Assign the label Launch AIR Application to the Button. If you prefer, you can open the complete browserLauncher.fla file from the source code of the book in the Chapter08 folder. You can see what the stage of the browserLauncher.fla project should look like in Figure 8-9.

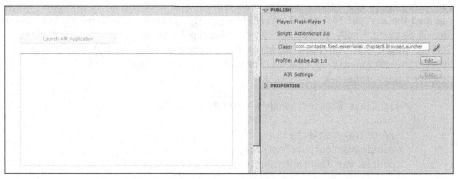

Figure 8-9. The stage and Document Properties panel of the browserLauncher.fla project

5. Prepare the project as already shown for the previous projects in this chapter.

6. Create a new ActionScript file called BrowserLauncher.as, which will be defined as the document class of the project. The BrowserLauncher class has to be created in the package com.comtaste.foed.essentialair.chapter8. If you prefer, you can find the complete BrowserLauncher.as file in the source code of the browser➡ Launcher.fla project.

Creating the document class for the browserLauncher.fla project

Next, you'll create the document class for your application. Go back to the browser➡ Launcher.fla project. Write the complete name of the com.comtaste.foed.➡ essentialair.chapter8.BrowserLauncher class in the Class field in the Document Properties panel. Click the Edit class definition icon next to the Class field. The BrowserLauncher.as file will open in Flash CS4. The following code shows the declaration of the package and the classes to import:

```
package com.comtaste.foed.essentialair.chapter8
{
import fl.controls.Button;
import fl.controls.TextArea;

import flash.display.*;
import flash.events.*;
import flash.net.URLRequest;
import flash.system.*;
```

A few import declarations use the * wildcard instead of a specific class name. The * wildcard allows you to tell the Flash CS4 compiler that you want to use several classes in a package. Instead of importing one for one of the classes you need, the * wildcard asks for all the classes in a package to be imported.

You start the body of the class by declaring the properties associated with the components on the stage of the browserLauncher.fla project: output, typed as TextArea; and launchBtn, typed as Button. Then you declare the loader property, typed as Loader, which will load the air.swf file; and the airFile property, typed as Object, where the loaded file will be saved. Finally, you declare the appID and publisherID properties, both typed as String, where you will have to insert the application ID and publisher ID of the browserInvocation.air application. The following code regards the declaration of the described class properties:

```
public class BrowserLauncher extends MovieClip
{
    // onstage objects
    public var output:TextArea;
    public var launchBtn:Button;

    // class properties
    private var loader:Loader;
    private var airFile:Object;

    // ID of application to launch
    private var appID:String = "PUT HERE THE ADOBE AIR APPLICATION ID";

    // publisher ID of application
    private var publisherID:String =
            "PUT HERE THE ADOBE AIR APPLICATION PUBLISHER ID";
```

The constructor method of the BrowserLauncher class starts by registering an event listener function for the MouseEvent.CLICK event, as shown here:

```
public function BrowserLauncher()
{
    // register event listener for button launchBtn
    launchBtn.addEventListener( MouseEvent.CLICK,
            launchApplication );
```

Each time the user clicks the launchBtn button, the launchApplication() method will be invoked. To load the air.swf file, you prepare the loader class property. The loader is assigned an instance of the Loader class. Then an object is created and instanced: loaderContext, typed as LoaderContext. The value of loaderContext will tell the loader object that the air.swf file has to be loaded in the application domain of the browserLauncher.fla project. An event listener function is registered on the loader object for the successful load of the air.swf file.

> *Please note the use of the INIT event instead of the COMPLETE event. This is necessary when you load SWF files. The COMPLETE event happens when the file has been loaded but the scripts in the file haven't been initialized yet. The INIT event occurs when all the scripts in the air.swf file are ready to use.*

When the air.swf file is loaded, the onRemoteFileLoaded() method will check if AIR is installed on the local system and if the browserInvocation.air application is installed. The following block of code shows how to create and initialize the loader object, as mentioned previously:

```
// create loader object
loader = new Loader();

// define application domain for loaded swf
var loaderContext:LoaderContext = new LoaderContext();
loaderContext.applicationDomain =
        ApplicationDomain.currentDomain;

// register event listener for loaded swf
loader.contentLoaderInfo.addEventListener( Event.INIT,
        onRemoteFileLoaded );
```

The load() method for the loader object is executed in a try...catch block. If the operation starts without any problems, the constructor method has completed its task. If there are errors, they will be intercepted and reported in the output TextArea, as shown here:

```
// try to load swf file
try
{
    loader.load( new URLRequest(
    "http://airdownload.adobe.com/air/browserapi/air.swf" ),
      loaderContext );
} catch (error : Error)
{
    // error loading file
    output.appendText( "Error accessing air.swf file: "
    + error.message + "\n" );
}
}
```

When the onRemoteFileLoaded() method is invoked, the air.swf file has been loaded and is ready to use. The air.swf file is assigned to the airFile class property. Then, as shown in the code of the onRemoteFileLoaded() method, the getStatus() method in the air.swf file is called. The getStatus() method determines whether the AIR runtime is there or not. A string is returned, with the following possible values:

8

- installed: AIR is correctly installed on the local system.
- available: AIR isn't installed on the local system, but it's possible to download it if necessary.
- unavailable: AIR cannot be installed on the current local system.

If AIR is installed, the application continues to execute. If AIR isn't installed or isn't available, you won't be able to interact with local AIR applications. The online application will simply display the status in the output TextArea. The following code provides the definition of the onRemoteFileLoaded() function:

```
private function onRemoteFileLoaded(e:Event):void
{
    // access and store loaded swf file
    airFile = e.target.content;

    // test Adobe AIR runtime status on user system
    switch ( airFile.getStatus() )
    {
        case "installed" :
```

If AIR is installed, you have to check if the browserInvocation.air application is installed on the local system. The air.swf file provides the getApplicationVersion() method to check if an AIR application is installed or not. If the application is installed, it returns the available version. The method requires three arguments:

- The application ID of the application to search for
- The publisher ID of the application to search for
- A function to invoke once the search is over

The following code shows the invocation of the getApplicationVersion() method:

```
            // OK, you can launch your application
            // now verify if requested AIR app
            // is installed on local system
            airFile.getApplicationVersion( appID,
                        publisherID, applicationSearchResult );
            break;

        case "available" :
            // Adobe AIR needs to be installed
            output.appendText( "Adobe AIR is not " +
                        "installed on user system" + "\n" );
            break;

        case "unavailable" :
            // Adobe AIR not available for your operating system
            output.appendText( "Adobe AIR is not " +
            "available for user system" + "\n" );
```

```
                break;
        }
    }
```

Once the search is over, the getApplicationVersion() method will invoke the applicationSearchResult() method. The method will receive a string as an argument, which contains the version of the requested application. If the returned version is null, the requested application isn't installed on the local system. As shown in the following code, if the browserInvocation.air application is installed, you set the enabled property of launchBtn to true. Otherwise, the output will display that the application is not installed on the local system.

```
        // callback defined for getApplicationVersion() method
        public function applicationSearchResult( version:String ):void
{
        if ( version == null )
        {
            // app is not available
            output.appendText( "Application requested is not " +
                "installed on local system.\n" );
        }
        else
        {
            // app is available
            // so enable application launch button
            launchBtn.enabled = true;
        }
    }
```

If the application is installed, the launchBtn button will be enabled. When the user clicks this button, the launchApplication() method will be invoked. This method creates an array that contains the information that needs to be passed to the AIR browserInvocation.air application. The method then invokes the launchApplication() method, provided by the air.swf file. The launchApplication() method requires the two following arguments, plus a third optional one:

- applicationID **(required)**: The application ID of the AIR application to invoke
- publisherID **(required)**: The publisher ID of the AIR application to invoke
- arguments **(optional)**: An array containing the information to pass to the AIR application. You can only pass text strings as additional information.

Here is the launchApplication() method:

```
        // event handler for launchBtn button
        private function launchApplication( evt : MouseEvent ):void
        {
            // custom arguments to pass to application
            var args:Array = [ "launchedFromBrowser", "Custom Data" ];
```

8

```
            // launch application
            airFile.launchApplication( appID, publisherID, args );
        }
```

Now the application is ready to be used. Here is the complete code of the BrowserLauncher. as class:

```
package com.comtaste.foed.essentialair.chapter8
{
import fl.controls.Button;
import fl.controls.TextArea;

import flash.display.*;
import flash.events.*;
import flash.net.URLRequest;
import flash.system.*;

public class BrowserLauncher extends MovieClip
{
    // onstage objects
    public var output:TextArea;
    public var launchBtn:Button;

    // class properties
    private var loader:Loader;
    private var airFile:Object;
    // ID of application to launch
    private var appID:String =
            " PUT HERE THE AIR APPLICATION ID ";

    // publisher ID of application
    private var publisherID:String =
            "PUT HERE THE AIR APPLICATION PUBLISHER ID";

    // class constructor
    public function BrowserLauncher()
    {
        // register event listener for button launchBtn
        launchBtn.addEventListener( MouseEvent.CLICK,
            launchApplication );

        // create loader object
        loader = new Loader();

        // define application domain for loaded swf
        var loaderContext:LoaderContext = new LoaderContext();
        loaderContext.applicationDomain =
            ApplicationDomain.currentDomain;
```

```
    // register event listener for loaded swf
    loader.contentLoaderInfo.addEventListener( Event.INIT,
        onRemoteFileLoaded );

    // try to load swf file
    try
    {
        loader.load( new URLRequest(
         "http://airdownload.adobe.com/air/browserapi/air.swf" ),
        loaderContext );
    } catch (error : Error)
    {
        // error loading file
        output.appendText( "Error accessing air.swf file: "
        + error.message + "\n" );
    }
}

private function onRemoteFileLoaded(e:Event):void
{
    // access and store loaded swf file
    airFile = e.target.content;

    // test Adobe AIR runtime status on user system
    switch ( airFile.getStatus() )
    {
        case "installed" :
            // ok, you can launch your application
            // now verify if requested AIR app
            // is installed on local system
            airFile.getApplicationVersion( appID,
                    publisherID, applicationSearchResult );
            break;
        case "available" :
            // Adobe AIR needs to be installed
            output.appendText( "Adobe AIR is not " +
                    "installed on user system" + "\n" );
            break;
        case "unavailable" :
            // Adobe AIR not available for your operating system
            output.appendText( "Adobe AIR is not " +
                    "available for user system" + "\n" );
            break;
    }
}

// callback defined for getApplicationVersion() method
public function applicationSearchResult( version:String ):void
{
```

8

```
                        if ( version == null )
                        {
                            // app is not available
                            output.appendText( "Application requested is not " +
                                        "installed on local system.\n" );
                        }
                        else
                        {
                            // app is available
                            // so enable application launch button
                            launchBtn.enabled = true;
                        }
                    }

                    // event handler for launchBtn button
                    private function launchApplication( evt : MouseEvent ):void
                    {
                        // custom arguments to pass to application
                        var args:Array = [ "launchedFromBrowser", "Custom Data" ];

                        // launch application
                        airFile.launchApplication( appID, publisherID, args );
                    }
            }// close class
            }// close package
```

Compiling and testing the browserLauncher.fla project

Follow these steps to launch and test the browserInvocation.air application from the browserLauncher.fla web application:

1. Go back to the browserLauncher.fla project.

2. Select the Publish command from the File menu to compile the application and create the HTML file you need to display it.

3. Open the folder containing the browserLauncher.fla project and launch the browserLauncher.html file. Your default browser will open the HTML page and look for the browserInvocation.air application. If the AIR application is installed on the local system, the launchBtn button will be activated. When the user clicks the button, the browserInvocation.air application will be invoked and its TextArea will display the information it receives from the web page. Figure 8-10 shows the browserInvocation.air application invoked by the browserLauncher.html web page.

The browserLauncher.fla *application needs the* air.swf *file. You can download it from the Adobe website. If the web page is run locally, an error will be thrown by Flash Player. When the error message appears, you'll be able to click the* Settings *button to open the Flash Player* Settings Manager. *The* Settings Manager *lets you manage global privacy settings, storage settings, security settings, and automatic notification settings. From this panel, you can turn on the ability to run web content from local folders.*

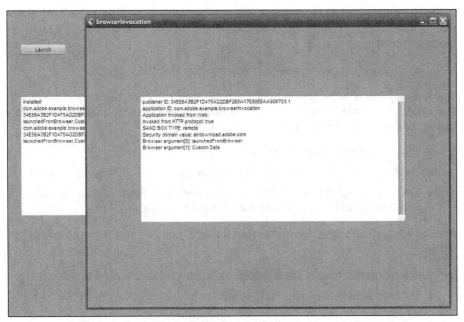

Figure 8-10. browserInvocation.air invoked from the browserLauncher.html web page

In the next section, you'll see how to work with the local operating system.

8

Local operating system integration

AIR provides good integration between its own applications and supported local operating systems, allowing AIR applications to improve the user's experience. Here are a few of the possibilities:

- Launching an AIR application when the user logs in.
- Associating certain types of files with an AIR application.
- Warning the user via system notification.

In the following sections, you'll learn how to use these functions, starting with how to launch an AIR application when a user logs in.

Start on login

Sometimes it's necessary for an application to be launched when the user accesses the local system. This way, the user can receive notices and communications from the application without having to worry about starting it manually. The AIR application won't be launched when the operating system starts up, but when the user logs in. This will make it possible for the AIR application to adopt different behaviors for different users of the same operating system. The **start on login** option is specific to the user who requests it.

In order to set the start on login option, you have to set the startAtLogin property of the running NativeApplication instance to true. The following code shows you how to set this option to true:

```
NativeApplication.nativeApplication.startAtLogin = true;
```

This property can only be set up after an application has been correctly installed and started up. So, to make an application launch automatically when the user logs in, the following conditions have to be met:

- The AIR runtime has to be installed.
- The AIR application to be launched has to be installed.
- The application to be launched when the user logs in has to have its NativeApplication startAtLogin property set to true.

After an AIR application has been set to start on login, there are three ways to modify this option:

- The application has the NativeApplication startAtLogin property set to false.
- The user changes the startup setting with the commands provided by the operating system.
- The user uninstalls the application.

If you try to set the value of the startAtLogin property during the execution of the AIR application launched by Flash, an exception will be generated by the AIR runtime. The startAtLogin property reflects the settings of the operating system. If the user disables the launch at login, the startAtLogin property will automatically be set to false by the AIR runtime.

Creating an AIR application with the start on login option

This section will show how to create an AIR application that starts on user login. You can set the startAtLogin property using a CheckBox on the application stage. Follow these steps to create the project:

1. Create a new Flash file (Adobe AIR) and name it startOnLogin.fla.
2. Create a TextArea component on the stage with an instance name of output. This component will be used as a console for the messages that are generated by the application.
3. Create a CheckBox with autoStart as its instance name.
4. Assign the following text string to the label property of the CheckBox: Start application on user login. If you prefer, you can open the complete startOnLogin.fla file from the Chapter08 folder.
5. Prepare the project as shown in the previous projects in this chapter.

6. Create a new ActionScript file and name it StartOnLogin.as; it will be defined as the document class of the project. The StartOnLogin document class has to be created in the package com.comtaste.foed.essentialair.chapter8. If you prefer, you can find the complete StartOnLogin.as file in the source code of the startOnLogin.fla project.

Creating the document class for startOnLogin.fla

Enter the complete name of the com.comtaste.foed.essentialair.chapter8. StartOnLogin class in the startOnLogin.fla project in the Class field of the Document Properties panel. Once you've defined the document class, click the Edit class definition icon next to the Class field, and the StartOnLogin.as file will open in Flash CS4.

The StartOnLogin.as class begins with the package declaration, like the classes illustrated previously in this chapter. In the body of the package, the external dependencies of the class are declared before the class declaration. In the following code, you can see the imported classes and the declaration of the StartOnLogin.as class's package:

```
package com.comtaste.foed.essentialair.chapter8
{
// Flash CS4-specific imports
import fl.controls.CheckBox;
import fl.controls.TextArea;

// Adobe AIR-specific imports
import flash.desktop.NativeApplication;
import flash.display.MovieClip;
import flash.events.Event;
import flash.filesystem.File;
```

The properties of the class are declared in the class body. The output property is declared, typed as TextArea, as well as the autoStart property, typed as CheckBox. These two properties represent the two components on the stage of the startOnLogin.fla project. The two properties are declared as follows:

```
public class StartOnLogin extends MovieClip
{
// onstage objects
public var output:TextArea;
public var autoStart:CheckBox;
```

The CheckBox on the stage allows the user to choose whether the application should be launched automatically at login to the operating system. To know what choice the user makes, an event listener is registered on the CHANGE event of the CheckBox. Each time the CheckBox changes its status, the setAutoStartOption() method will update the preferences of the AIR application.

When the constructor method of the StartOnLogin.as class is invoked, you access the actual value of the startAtLogin property. If the value of the startAtLogin property is available, it's associated with the selected property of the autoStart CheckBox. This operation, as shown in the code, is executed in a try...catch block. This is a necessary

8

step because the startAtLogin property is only accessible from a correctly installed AIR application. Trying to access startAtLogin from an application launched by Flash generates an exception in the AIR runtime. If an exception is generated, the try...catch block writes a message in the output TextArea, as shown here:

```
// class constructor
public function StartOnLogin()
{
    super();

    // try...catch block to manage unwanted exceptions
    try
    {
        // set actual initial value for CheckBox
        autoStart.selected =
            NativeApplication.nativeApplication.startAtLogin;

    } catch( error:Error )
    {
        output.appendText( "Impossible read autoStart value. "
                + "You cannot access this value from Flash IDE."
                + File.lineEnding );
    }
```

The following code shows how to register the setAutoStartOption() method to the Event.CHANGE event of the autoStart CheckBox:

```
    // register event listener for CheckBox
    autoStart.addEventListener( Event.CHANGE, setAutoStartOption );
}
```

Each time the user changes the status of the CheckBox, the setAutoStartOption() method is invoked. The method reads the value of the selected property of the CheckBox and assigns it to the startAtLogin property. Once you've updated the property, the choice is displayed in the output TextArea. Like in the constructor method, the operations on the startAtLogin property are carried out in a try...catch block. If the application isn't installed on the system, but has been launched by the Flash IDE, an exception will be generated. The exception is intercepted by the try...catch block and the detail of the error is displayed in the output TextArea. The code for the setAutoStartOption() function is the following:

```
// event listener for CheckBox
private function setAutoStartOption( evt : Event ):void
{
    // try...catch block to manage unwanted exceptions
    try
    {
        // set up autostart property based on CheckBox value
        NativeApplication.nativeApplication.startAtLogin =
                autoStart.selected;
```

```
        output.appendText( "AutoStart enabled: "
                + NativeApplication.nativeApplication.startAtLogin
                + File.lineEnding );

    } catch( error:Error )
    {
        output.appendText( "Impossible set autoStart. "
                + "You cannot set this value from Flash IDE."
                + File.lineEnding );
    }
}
```

Testing the startOnLogin.fla project

The StartOnLogin.as document class is now complete. In this section, you will see how to test and package the startOnLogin.fla project. Follow these steps to test the project:

1. Go back to the Flash startOnLogin.fla project and launch the application (Control ➤ Test Movie).

2. When the application has been launched, try interacting with the CheckBox on the stage. The error messages will be displayed in the output component because you're trying to access the startAtLogin property from a noninstalled AIR application. You can see the project launched by Flash in Figure 8-11.

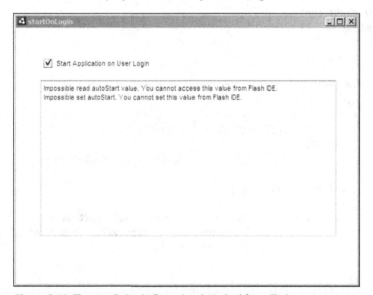

Figure 8-11. The startOnLogin.fla project launched from Flash

3. Publish the project in an AIR file as described in the "Testing and packaging the browserInvocation.air application" section.

4. Install the application and set it to be launched when the user logs in.

5. Restart the user's session, and you'll see that the application will be automatically invoked by the operating system.

Here is the complete code of the StartOnLogin.as class:

```
package com.comtaste.foed.essentialair.chapter8
{
// Flash CS4-specific imports
import fl.controls.CheckBox;
import fl.controls.TextArea;
// Adobe AIR-specific imports
import flash.desktop.NativeApplication;
import flash.display.MovieClip;
import flash.events.Event;
import flash.filesystem.File;

public class StartOnLogin extends MovieClip
{
// onstage objects
public var output:TextArea;
public var autoStart:CheckBox;

// class constructor
public function StartOnLogin()
{
    super();

    // try...catch block to manage unwanted exceptions
    try
    {
        // set actual initial value for CheckBox
        autoStart.selected =
            NativeApplication.nativeApplication.startAtLogin;

    } catch( error:Error )
    {
        output.appendText( "Impossible read autoStart value. "
                    + "You cannot access this value from Flash IDE."
                    + File.lineEnding );
    }

    // register event listener for CheckBox
    autoStart.addEventListener( Event.CHANGE, setAutoStartOption );
}

// event listener for CheckBox
private function setAutoStartOption( evt : Event ):void
{
```

```
            // try...catch block to manage unwanted exceptions
            try
            {
                // set up startAtLogin property based on CheckBox value
                NativeApplication.nativeApplication.startAtLogin =
                        autoStart.selected;
                output.appendText( "AutoStart enabled: "
                        + NativeApplication.nativeApplication.startAtLogin
                        + File.lineEnding );

            } catch( error:Error )
            {
                output.appendText( "Impossible set autoStart. "
                        + "You cannot set this value from Flash IDE."
                        + File.lineEnding );
            }
        }

    } // close class
}// close package
```

In the next section, you'll see how to associate an AIR application to a given file type.

File associations

Normally, you double-click a document when you want to open it. Otherwise, you select the document and press the Enter key on the keyboard (only on Windows systems). The operating system opens the document in the default application for the type of file you've selected. If a given file type hasn't been associated with a default editor, a dialog box is displayed, providing a list of possible programs to open the file with.

The AIR runtime allows the developer to associate one or more file types to an AIR application. You can do this during the installation procedure as well as during the execution of the application. During execution, you can only associate the file types that have been declared by the developer in the authoring phase of the application. You can also remove the association between a file type and an AIR application.

The file types that have been registered in the installation phase of an AIR application don't overwrite the associations that may already exist on the local system. For example, if an application is registered for the FLA file type during installation, the installation won't replace the default editor, since the FLA file type is already associated with Flash. In this case, it's preferable for the AIR application to ask whether it should become the default editor for the FLA file type when it starts up. During the execution of an AIR application, you can overwrite the default editor that is associated with certain file types.

The file types to associate with an AIR application have to be declared during its creation. The Flash CS4 IDE allows you to specify the file types to be associated with an AIR application through the AIR – Application & Installer Setting panel. An explanation of the procedure will be provided shortly. When you associate a file type with an AIR application, you have to provide certain information to the AIR runtime. The following section discusses infor-mation that you can specify.

File type settings

For each file type associated with an AIR application, you can specify the following infor-mation in the File Type Settings panel (see Figure 8-12):

- **Name (required)**: The name to associate with the file type.
- **Extension (required)**: The extension of the documents of the relevant file type. In the Extension field, the extension has to be provided without a dot (e.g., jpg, not .jpg).
- **Description (optional)**: The description to associate with the relevant file type.
- **Content type (optional)**: The MIME type of the file content.
- **Icons (optional)**: The icons to associate with the relevant file type. You can pro-vide four different formats for the icons: 128 × 128 pixels, 48 × 48 pixels, 32 × 32 pixels, and 16 × 16 pixels.

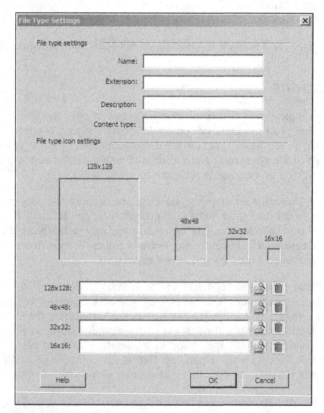

Figure 8-12. The File Type Settings panel

In the next section, you'll create an AIR application and set it as the default editor for certain file types.

Associating an AIR application with given file types

In this section, you'll create an application associated with two file types: JPG and CUST. The JPG file type is one of the most popular formats to save images. The JPG format has the benefit of balancing between quality and file size. The CUST file type will be created especially for the application. The application will register itself as a default editor for both file types. Controls will be provided to check which application is associated with these two file types. It will also be possible to change these associations. Follow these steps to create the project:

1. Create a new Flash file (Adobe AIR) and name it `fileAssociations.fla`.

2. Create a TextArea component on the stage and assign it the instance name `output`.

3. Create a CheckBox with `isDefaultForCustomCheck` as its instance name, and Set as default Editor for extension: .cust as its label.

4. Under the CheckBox, create a label with an instance name of `customTypeDefault➡ Editor`.

5. Create a second CheckBox with an instance name of `isDefaultForJpgCheck` and the following label: Set as default Editor for extension: .jpg.

6. Under the second CheckBox, create a new label with `jpgTypeDefaultEditor` as its instance name.

7. Finally, insert a Button on the stage with `readFileAssociationBtn` as its instance name.

If you prefer, you can open the complete `fileAssociations.fla` file from the `Chapter08` folder. Figure 8-13 shows the stage of the `fileAssociations.fla` project.

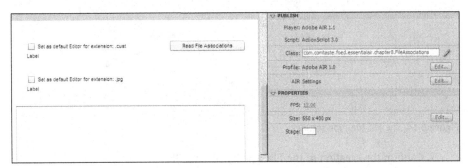

Figure 8-13. The stage and Document Properties panel of the fileAssociations.fla project

Prepare the `fileAssociations.fla` project as shown in the previous projects in this chapter.

Registering file type associations. Before creating the document class of the `fileAssociations.fla` project, you have to register the necessary file types. Follow these steps to do so:

1. Open the AIR – Application & Installer Settings panel and click the Advanced ➤ Settings button to access the advanced options.

2. In the Associated file types section, click the button to add a new file type. The File Type Settings panel will open, allowing you to insert the information regarding the new file type (see Figure 8-14).

3. You want to register the JPG file type. In the fields provided, enter the following values:

   - Name: Images
   - Extension: jpg
   - Description: Raster images
   - Content type: image/jpeg

4. In the lower part of the panel, there are four editable fields with controls to select the icons to be associated with the file type. In the fileIcons/jpg/ folder of the fileAssociations.fla project, there are four icons you can use. You can assign the icons you see in this folder, or create your own if you'd like. Figure 8-14 shows the File Type Settings panel with the aforementioned settings.

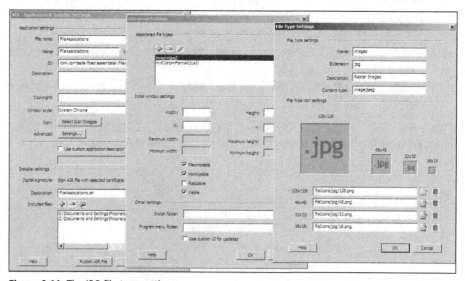

Figure 8-14. The JPG file type settings

5. Confirm the creation of the file type by clicking OK.

6. Repeat the previous steps to create another file type. The information to insert for this new file type is the following:

   - Name: myCustomFormat
   - Extension: cust
   - Description: My Custom Format
   - Content type: Leave empty

You can find some icons you can use for this file type in the fileIcons/myCustomIcon/ folder in the root folder of the fileAssociations.fla project. Figure 8-15 shows the File Type Settings panel with the settings for file types with a .cust extension.

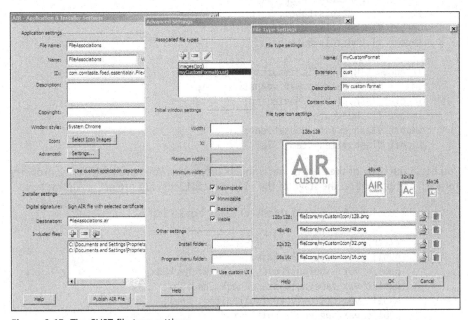

Figure 8-15. The CUST file type settings

7. Confirm the creation of this second file type and close the open dialog windows. The icons associated with the file types are automatically added to the fileAssociations.fla project. When you create the fileAssociations.air file, they will be automatically embedded.

Creating the document class. Next, you'll create the document class. To do so, create a new ActionScript file and name it FileAssociations.as; it will be defined as the project's document class. The FileAssociations class has to be created in the package com. comtaste.foed.essentialair.chapter8. If you prefer, you can find the complete FileAssociations.as file in the source code for the fileAssociations.fla project.

Write the complete name of the com.comtaste.foed.essentialair.chapter8. FileAssociations class in the Flash fileAssociations.fla project, in the Class field of the Document Properties panel. Once you've defined the document class, click the Edit class definition icon next to the Class field. The FileAssociations.as file will open in Flash CS4.

The FileAssociations.as class starts by declaring its package. In the body of the package, before declaring the class, the external dependencies are declared. The following code shows the imported classes and the declaration of the package of the FileAssociations.as class:

```
package com.comtaste.foed.essentialair.chapter8
{
// Flash-specific imports
import fl.controls.CheckBox;
import fl.controls.Label;
import fl.controls.TextArea;
import fl.controls.Button;

// Adobe AIR-specific imports
import flash.desktop.NativeApplication;
import flash.display.MovieClip;
import flash.events.Event;
import flash.events.MouseEvent;
import flash.filesystem.File;
```

You begin the body of the class by declaring its properties. You have to declare a property for each component on the stage of the fileAssociations.fla project, as shown here:

```
public class FileAssociations extends MovieClip
{
    // onstage objects
    public var output:TextArea;
    public var isDefaultForCustomCheck:CheckBox;
    public var isDefaultForJpgCheck:CheckBox;
    public var customTypeDefaultEditor:Label;
    public var jpgTypeDefaultEditor:Label;
    public var readFileAssociationBtn:Button;
```

The constructor method of the FileAssociations.as class registers the event listener methods for the controls on the stage and initializes the status of the application. The following code registers the readFileAssociation() method on the MouseEvent.CLICK events that are generated by the readFileAssociationBtn button:

```
    // class constructor
    public function FileAssociations()
    {
        // register event listener method
        //for button readFileAssociationBtn
        readFileAssociationBtn.addEventListener(
                MouseEvent.CLICK, readFileAssociation );
```

Then you have to register two event listener methods for the Event.CHANGE events of the two CheckBox components on the stage, as shown here:

```
        // register event listener methods for CheckBox components
        isDefaultForCustomCheck.addEventListener( Event.CHANGE,
                updateCustomTypeAssociation );
        isDefaultForJpgCheck.addEventListener( Event.CHANGE,
                updateJpgTypeAssociation );
```

Once you've registered the event listener methods, you have to initialize the status of the application controls. To do so, you simulate the mouse click on the readFileAssociationBtn button. By doing so, you generate a MouseEvent.CLICK event on the component.

The invoked event listener method, readFileAssociation(), checks which applications the file types with .jpg and .cust extensions are associated with. The application controls are updated according to the obtained information. The following code simulates the mouse click on the readFileAssociationBtn button:

```
            // read current file associations
            readFileAssociationBtn.dispatchEvent(
                    new MouseEvent( MouseEvent.CLICK ) );

    }
```

Each time you ask for the displayed data to be updated by clicking the readFile➡ AssociationBtn button, the readFileAssociation() method is invoked. This method checks if the AIR application in execution is set as the default editor for both the JPG and CUST file types. The method asks the AIR runtime for the complete path of the editor that is associated with each of the file types. The obtained information is used to update the components on the stage.

The NativeApplication class provides some methods to access information regarding the file types associated with an AIR application. You use the isSetAsDefaultApplication() method to check if the AIR application is set as the default editor for a given file type. The file type is passed to the isSetAsDefaultApplication() method as an argument.

The operations regarding the file types are executed in a try...catch block to intercept exceptions generated by the runtime. If exceptions are generated, a message containing information on the error is written in the output TextArea. The following code checks if the AIR application is set as the default editor for files with a .cust extension:

```
        private function readFileAssociation( evt  : MouseEvent ):void
        {
            try
            {
                // test if application is default editor for type: .cust
                var isDefaultForCustomType:Boolean =
        NativeApplication.nativeApplication.isSetAsDefaultApplication(
                        "cust" );
```

The isDefaultForCustomCheck CheckBox is selected if the AIR application is set as the default editor for files with a .cust extension. If the application isn't the default editor, the CheckBox will be deselected. The following code sets the status of the isDefaultFor➡ CustomCheck CheckBox:

```
            // set value for related CheckBox
            isDefaultForCustomCheck.selected = isDefaultForCustomType;
```

Then the getEditorPath() method, which you will create shortly, is invoked to obtain the path of the default editor for the CUST file type. The following code assigns the path of the default editor to the customTypeDefaultEditor label:

```
// show default editor path
customTypeDefaultEditor.text = getEditorPath( "cust" );
```

If an exception is generated during the execution of the preceding operations, the following code is executed. The information on the error is reported in the output TextArea:

```
} catch( error : Error )
{
    output.appendText( "[type .cust] Error: "
        + error.message + File.lineEnding );
}
```

The preceding operations for the CUST file type have to be repeated for the JPG file type, as shown here:

```
try
{
    // test if application is default editor for type: .jpg
    var isDefaultForJpegType:Boolean =
NativeApplication.nativeApplication.isSetAsDefaultApplication(
        "jpg" );

    // set value for related CheckBox
    isDefaultForJpgCheck.selected = isDefaultForJpegType;

    // show default editor path
    jpgTypeDefaultEditor.textField.text =
        getEditorPath( "jpg" );

} catch( error : Error )
{
    output.appendText( "[type .jpg] Error: "
        + error.message + File.lineEnding );
}
}
```

The readFileAssociation() method uses the getEditorPath() method to obtain the path of the default editor of a given file type. The getEditorPath() method requires as an argument the extension of the file type you want to identify as the default editor. You use the getDefaultApplication() method of the NativeApplication class to ask the AIR runtime for the path of the default editor of a given file type.

You have to pass the extension of the relevant file type as an argument to the getDefault➥ Application() method. The following code shows the invocation of the get➥ DefaultApplication() method, passing the extension received as an argument of the getEditorPath() method to the function:

```
private function getEditorPath( extension:String ):String
{
    // get default editor reference for given extension
```

```
        var defaultEditorPath:String =
NativeApplication.nativeApplication.getDefaultApplication( extension );
```

If the relevant file type doesn't have any default editor associated with it, the value returned by the getDefaultApplication() method is null. The path returned by getDefaultApplication() is memorized in the local defaultEditorPath variable. The following code assigns the string Default Editor Not Defined to defaultEditorPath if the file type doesn't have a default editor, and then returns the value of defaultEditorPath:

```
        // return default editor path
        if( defaultEditorPath == null )
        {
            return "Default Editor Not Defined";
        } else
        {
            return defaultEditorPath;
        }
    }
```

When the user changes the value of the isDefaultForCustomCheck CheckBox, the update➡ CustomTypeAssociation() method is invoked. This method checks the status of the CheckBox and acts accordingly. If the CheckBox is selected, the fileAssociations.air application will be set as the default editor for the CUST file type. To register the application in execution as the default editor for the CUST file type, the setAsDefaultApplication() method of the NativeApplication class is invoked. The setAsDefaultApplication() method requires the extension of the file type to be registered as an argument.

If the isDefaultForCustomCheck CheckBox isn't selected, the AIR application will no longer be the default editor for the CUST file type. To remove the association with the file type, you use the removeAsDefaultApplication() method of the NativeApplication class. This method requires as an argument the file extension to unregister from the association with the AIR application. Both operations are executed in a try...catch block to intercept errors generated by the runtime. If the operations fail, the information regarding the problems will be reported in the output TextArea.

Finally, the path of the default editor displayed by the customTypeDefaultEditor label is updated. The string of text returned by the getEditorPath() method is assigned to the customTypeDefaultEditor text property. The following code shows the complete implementation of the updateCustomTypeAssociation() method:

```
        //  manage file association for custom type .cust
        private function updateCustomTypeAssociation( evt : Event ):void
        {
            try{

                if( isDefaultForCustomCheck.selected == true )
                {
                    // register file format to this application
    NativeApplication.nativeApplication.setAsDefaultApplication( "cust" );
                } else
```

8

```
            {
                // remove file format association
NativeApplication.nativeApplication.removeAsDefaultApplication("cust");
            }

                // show default editor path
                customTypeDefaultEditor.text = getEditorPath( "cust" );

        } catch( error : Error )
        {
            output.appendText( "[type .cust] Error: "
                + error.message + File.lineEnding );
        }
    }
```

When the user changes the value of the isDefaultForJpgCheck CheckBox, the update➥ JpgTypeAssociation() method is invoked. The updateJpgTypeAssociation() method executes the same operations just mentioned for the updateCustomTypeAssociation() method. But in this case, the association for the JPG file type is updated instead of the CUST file type.

The following code shows the implementation of the updateJpgTypeAssociation() method:

```
        //  manage file association for image type .jpg
        private function updateJpgTypeAssociation( evt : Event ):void
        {
            try{

                if( isDefaultForJpgCheck.selected == true )
                {
                    // register file format to this application
NativeApplication.nativeApplication.setAsDefaultApplication( "jpg" );
                } else
                {
                    // remove file format association
NativeApplication.nativeApplication.removeAsDefaultApplication➥
( "jpg" );
                }

                // show default editor path
                jpgTypeDefaultEditor.text = getEditorPath( "jpg" );

        } catch( error : Error )
        {
            output.appendText( "[type .jpg] Error: "
                + error.message + File.lineEnding );
        }
    }
```

Testing the fileAssociations.fla project. Now that the document class for the fileAssociations.fla project is complete, it's time to test the project as follows:

1. Go back to the fileAssociations.fla project.

2. Launch the application from Flash (Control ➤ Test Movie).

3. Once the application has been launched, try interacting with the components on the stage.

Keep in mind that an AIR application launched in Flash CS4 can't require the association with a file type. The file type won't be registered in the application because the operating system doesn't have an installed application to refer to. Therefore, the operation will only remove the default editor that is actually registered for the relevant file type. If the fileAssociations.air application is compiled and installed, the association will turn out correctly.

You can see the fileAssociations.fla project launched from Flash in Figure 8-16.

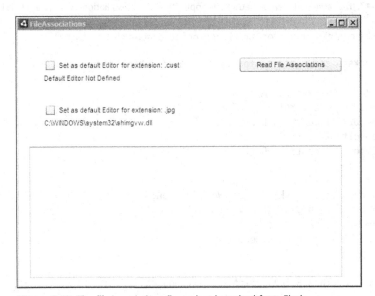

Figure 8-16. The fileAssociations.fla project launched from Flash

Figure 8-17 shows the fileAssociations.air application in execution after installation, and a document with a .cust extension next to it. The document uses the icon provided by the fileAssociations.air application.

399

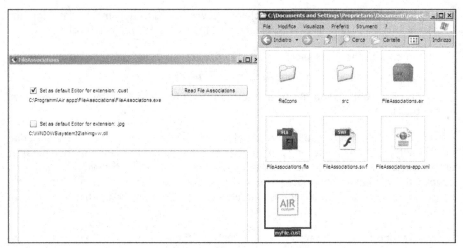

Figure 8-17. The launched fileAssociations.air application after installation (left), and a CUST file

Here is the complete code for the FileAssociations.as class:

```
package com.comtaste.foed.essentialair.chapter8
{
// Flash-specific imports
import fl.controls.CheckBox;
import fl.controls.Label;
import fl.controls.TextArea;
import fl.controls.Button;

// Adobe AIR-specific imports
import flash.desktop.NativeApplication;
import flash.display.MovieClip;
import flash.events.Event;
import flash.events.MouseEvent;
import flash.filesystem.File;

public class FileAssociations extends MovieClip
{
    // onstage objects
    public var output:TextArea;
    public var isDefaultForCustomCheck:CheckBox;
    public var isDefaultForJpgCheck:CheckBox;
    public var customTypeDefaultEditor:Label;
    public var jpgTypeDefaultEditor:Label;
    public var readFileAssociationBtn:Button;

    // class constructor
    public function FileAssociations()
    {
        // register event listener method
```

```
                // for button readFileAssociationBtn
                readFileAssociationBtn.addEventListener( MouseEvent.CLICK,
                        readFileAssociation );

                // register event listener methods for CheckBox components
                isDefaultForCustomCheck.addEventListener( Event.CHANGE,
                        updateCustomTypeAssociation );
                isDefaultForJpgCheck.addEventListener( Event.CHANGE,
                        updateJpgTypeAssociation );

                // read current file associations
                readFileAssociationBtn.dispatchEvent(
                        new MouseEvent( MouseEvent.CLICK ) );
        }

        private function getEditorPath( extension:String ):String
        {
                // get default editor reference for given extension
                var defaultEditorPath:String =
                  NativeApplication.nativeApplication.getDefaultApplication(
                        extension );

                // return default editor path
                if( defaultEditorPath == null )
                {
                    return "Default Editor Not Defined";
                } else
                {
                    return defaultEditorPath;
                }
        }

        //  manage file association for custom type .cust
        private function updateCustomTypeAssociation( evt : Event ):void
        {
                try{

                    if( isDefaultForCustomCheck.selected == true )
                    {
                        // register file format to this application
NativeApplication.nativeApplication.setAsDefaultApplication( "cust" );
                    } else
                    {
                        // remove file format association
NativeApplication.nativeApplication.removeAsDefaultApplication➡
( "cust" );
                    }
```

```
                // show default editor path
                customTypeDefaultEditor.text = getEditorPath( "cust" );

        } catch( error : Error )
        {
            output.appendText( "[type .cust] Error: "
                    + error.message + File.lineEnding );
        }
    }

    //  manage file association for image type .jpg
    private function updateJpgTypeAssociation( evt : Event ):void
    {
        try{

            if( isDefaultForJpgCheck.selected == true )
            {
                // register file format to this application
NativeApplication.nativeApplication.setAsDefaultApplication( "jpg" );
            } else
            {
                // remove file format association
NativeApplication.nativeApplication.removeAsDefaultApplication➡
( "jpg" );
            }

            // show default editor path
            jpgTypeDefaultEditor.text = getEditorPath( "jpg" );

        } catch( error : Error )
        {
            output.appendText( "[type .jpg] Error: "
                    + error.message + File.lineEnding );
        }
    }

    // read actual file associations and update application controls
    private function readFileAssociation( evt  : MouseEvent ):void
    {
        try
        {
            // test if application is default editor for type: .cust
            var isDefaultForCustomType:Boolean =
NativeApplication.nativeApplication.isSetAsDefaultApplication("cust");

            // set value for related CheckBox
            isDefaultForCustomCheck.selected = isDefaultForCustomType;
```

```
                    // show default editor path
                    customTypeDefaultEditor.text = getEditorPath( "cust" );

            } catch( error : Error )
            {
                    output.appendText( "[type .cust] Error: " +
                            error.message + File.lineEnding );
            }

            try
            {
                    // test if application is default editor for type: .jpg
                    var isDefaultForJpegType:Boolean =
        NativeApplication.nativeApplication.isSetAsDefaultApplication("jpg");

                    // set value for related CheckBox
                    isDefaultForJpgCheck.selected = isDefaultForJpegType;

                    // show default editor path
                    jpgTypeDefaultEditor.textField.text =
                            getEditorPath( "jpg" );

            } catch( error : Error )
            {
                    output.appendText( "[type .jpg] Error: " +
                            error.message + File.lineEnding );
            }
        }

    }// close class
    }// close package
```

You will see how to get the user's attention when an AIR application doesn't have the system's focus in the next section.

System notifications

Sometimes it's necessary for an application to get the user's attention. This necessity can depend on the completion of a requested operation or the reception of remote information to communicate. In any case, when the AIR application is in the foreground, it's pretty easy to find ways to attract the user's attention. If the application has been minimized or hidden by windows of other applications, however, it can be a little more difficult.

To help developers, AIR allows you to use system notifications to attract the user's attention. On Windows systems, system notifications allow you to make the window icon in the taskbar flash. On Mac OS X systems, you can bounce the dock icon of the application.

System notifications offer two levels of urgency. The values associated with these two levels are defined as constants in the NotificationType class. The possible values are the following:

- NotificationType.INFORMATIONAL: This kind of notification notifies the user discreetly. On Windows, the icon of the window in the taskbar flashes once, and then remains highlighted. On Mac OS X, the dock icon bounces only once.

- NotificationType.CRITICAL: This kind of notification notifies the user insistently. On Windows, the icon of the window in the taskbar flashes until the user returns to the AIR application. On Mac OS X, the dock icon bounces continuously until the user returns to the application.

In the following sections, you will see how to use system notifications in AIR applications.

Creating an AIR application that sends system notifications

You'll create an AIR application that generates system notifications after the application has lost system focus for 3 seconds. The user can choose if the system notification is INFORMATIONAL or CRITICAL through a CheckBox. Follow these steps to create this application:

1. Create a new Flash file (Adobe AIR) and name it systemNotification.fla.

2. Create a TextArea component on the stage with the instance name output.

3. Create a CheckBox with an instance name isNotificationCritical.

4. Assign the following text string as a label to the CheckBox: Select to send critical notification. If you prefer, you can open the complete systemNotification.fla file from Chapter08 folder of the book's source code.

5. Prepare the project as shown for the previous projects in this chapter. Create a new ActionScript file and name it SystemNotification.as; it will be used as the project's document class. The SystemNotification class has to be created in the package com.comtaste.foed.essentialair.chapter8. If you prefer, you can find the complete file in the source code of the systemNotification.fla project.

Creating the document class for systemNotification.fla

In the systemNotification.fla project, write the complete name of the com.comtaste. foed.essentialair.chapter8.SystemNotification class in the Class field in the Document Properties panel. Then click the Edit class definition icon next to the Class field. The SystemNotification.as file will open in Flash. The SystemNotification.as class begins with the package declaration.

In the body of the package, before declaring the class, the external dependencies are declared, as shown here:

```
package com.comtaste.foed.essentialair.chapter8
{
// Flash-specific imports
import fl.controls.CheckBox;
import fl.controls.TextArea;
```

```
// Adobe AIR-specific imports
import flash.desktop.DockIcon;
import flash.desktop.NativeApplication;
import flash.desktop.NotificationType;
import flash.display.MovieClip;
import flash.display.NativeWindow;
import flash.events.Event;
import flash.events.TimerEvent;
import flash.utils.Timer;
```

The project has two components on the stage: a TextArea and a CheckBox. You have to create two class properties for these two components. You create the output property, typed as TextArea, and the isNotificationCritical property, typed as CheckBox, as shown here:

```
public class SystemNotifications extends MovieClip
{
    // onstage objects
    public var output:TextArea;
    public var isNotificationCritical:CheckBox;
```

The class will need a timer to check when it's necessary to trigger system notifications. The following code declares the alarm property, typed as Timer:

```
// class properties
private var alarm:Timer;
```

You want the application to generate a system notification a few seconds after it has lost focus. In the constructor method, you register the onWindowsDeactivate() method on the Event.DEACTIVATE event generated by the application.

The event has to be registered on the NativeApplication.nativeApplication property. Each time the application loses focus, the onWindowsDeactivate() method will be invoked. The following code registers the event listener function for the Event.DEACTIVATE event:

```
// class constructor
public function SystemNotifications()
{
    // register event listener function to idle event
    NativeApplication.nativeApplication.addEventListener(
            Event.DEACTIVATE, onWindowsDeactivate );
```

When the onWindowsDeactivate() method is invoked, it starts the alarm timer. The following code initializes the alarm property, specifying that the timer will last 3000 milliseconds (3 seconds):

```
// set up timer object
alarm = new Timer( 3000, 1 );
```

When the timer object completes the countdown, it generates a TimerEvent.TIMER_ COMPLETE event. The following code registers the sendNotificationToUser() method on the completion event of the timer object:

```
alarm.addEventListener( TimerEvent.TIMER_COMPLETE,
        sendNotificationToUser );
}
```

Each time the user minimizes the systemNotification.air application or starts working on another program, the onWindowsDeactivate() method is invoked. This method resets the alarm timer object and restarts it, as shown here:

```
// event listener method for Event.DEACTIVATE
private function onWindowsDeactivate( evt : Event ):void
{
    // reset timer
    alarm.reset();

    // start timer
    alarm.start();
}
```

When the alarm timer object reaches the time limit, the sendNotificationToUser() method is launched. The sendNotificationToUser() method checks the status of the isNotificationCritical CheckBox. If the CheckBox is selected, the sendCritical➥ Notification() method is invoked, which sends a CRITICAL system notification. If the CheckBox isn't selected, the sendStandardNotification() method is invoked, which sends an INFORMATIONAL system notification. This code is the sendNotificationToUser() method:

```
// event listener method for timer completion
private function sendNotificationToUser( evt : TimerEvent ):void
{
    if( isNotificationCritical.selected == true )
    {
        sendCriticalNotification();

    } else
    {
        sendStandardNotification();
    }
}
```

The sendCriticalNotification() method is invoked to send CRITICAL system notifications. The method first checks if the notifications are supported for the application windows. This type of notification is supported when the NativeWindow.supportsNotification property is set to true. If window notifications are supported, the notifyUser() method of the NativeWindow class is invoked.

The notifyUser() method requires an optional argument to define the type of notification to generate. The possible valid values for the notifyUser() method are defined as constants in the NotificationType class. The default value is NotificationType. INFORMATIONAL. These operations are shown in the following code:

```
private function sendCriticalNotification():void
{
    // used on Windows
    if( NativeWindow.supportsNotification )
    {
        this.stage.nativeWindow.notifyUser(
                NotificationType.CRITICAL );
    }
```

Then you check if dock icons are supported. The dock icons are supported when the NativeApplication.supportsDockIcon property is set to true. If the dock icon of the application is available, it is used to display the system notification. As shown in the following code, you invoke the bounce() method of the DockIcon class to send the system notification:

```
    // used on Mac OS X
    if( NativeApplication.supportsDockIcon )
    {
     DockIcon( NativeApplication.nativeApplication.icon ).bounce(
            NotificationType.CRITICAL );
    }
}
```

The bounce() method, like the notifyUser() method, requires an optional argument to define the type of notification to generate. The possible valid values for the bounce() method are defined as constants in the NotificationType class. The default value is NotificationType.INFORMATIONAL.

The sendStandardNotification() method is invoked to send INFORMATIONAL system notifications. This method behaves exactly like the aforementioned sendCritical➡ Notification() method, except for the type of system notification it requires. When an INFORMATIONAL notification is requested, the NotificationType.INFORMATIONAL value is passed to the notifyUser() and bounce() methods as an argument. Here is the body of the sendStandardNotification()method:

```
private function sendStandardNotification():void
{
    // used on Windows
    if( NativeWindow.supportsNotification )
    {
        this.stage.nativeWindow.notifyUser(
            NotificationType.INFORMATIONAL );
    }
```

```
                    // used on Mac OS X
                    if( NativeApplication.supportsDockIcon )
                    {
                    DockIcon( NativeApplication.nativeApplication.icon ).bounce(
                            NotificationType.INFORMATIONAL );
                    }
        }
```

The document class of the project is complete. Here is the complete code of the ActionScript SystemNotification.as class:

```actionscript
package com.comtaste.foed.essentialair.chapter8
{
// Flash-specific imports
import fl.controls.CheckBox;
import fl.controls.TextArea;

// Adobe AIR-specific imports
import flash.desktop.DockIcon;
import flash.desktop.NativeApplication;
import flash.desktop.NotificationType;
import flash.display.MovieClip;
import flash.display.NativeWindow;
import flash.events.Event;
import flash.events.TimerEvent;
import flash.utils.Timer;

public class SystemNotifications extends MovieClip
{
    // onstage objects
    public var output:TextArea;
    public var isNotificationCritical:CheckBox;

    // class properties
    private var alarm:Timer;

    // class constructor
    public function SystemNotifications()
    {
        // register event listener function to idle event
        NativeApplication.nativeApplication.addEventListener(
                Event.DEACTIVATE, onWindowsDeactivate );

        // set up timer object
        alarm = new Timer( 3000, 1 );
        alarm.addEventListener( TimerEvent.TIMER_COMPLETE,
                sendNotificationToUser );
    }
```

```
// event listener method for timer completion
private function sendNotificationToUser( evt : TimerEvent ):void
{
    if( isNotificationCritical.selected == true )
    {
        sendCriticalNotification();

    } else
    {
        sendStandardNotification();
    }
}

// event listener method for Event.DEACTIVATE
private function onWindowsDeactivate( evt : Event ):void
{
    // reset timer
    alarm.reset();

    // start timer
    alarm.start();
}

private function sendCriticalNotification():void
{
    // used on Windows
    if( NativeWindow.supportsNotification )
    {
        this.stage.nativeWindow.notifyUser(
                NotificationType.CRITICAL );
    }

    // used on Mac OS X
    if( NativeApplication.supportsDockIcon )
    {
    DockIcon( NativeApplication.nativeApplication.icon ).bounce(
                NotificationType.CRITICAL );
    }
}

private function sendStandardNotification():void
{
    // used on Windows
    if( NativeWindow.supportsNotification )
    {
        this.stage.nativeWindow.notifyUser(
                NotificationType.INFORMATIONAL );
    }
```

```
                                // used on Mac OS X
                                if( NativeApplication.supportsDockIcon )
                                {
                                DockIcon( NativeApplication.nativeApplication.icon ).bounce(
                                        NotificationType.INFORMATIONAL );
                                }
                        }

                }// close class
                }// close package
```

Testing the systemNotification.fla project

Follow these steps to compile and test the project:

1. Go back to the systemNotification.fla Flash project.
2. Launch the application from Flash CS4 (Control ➤ Test Movie).
3. Once the application has been launched, minimize it or place it in the background behind another application.

Three seconds after you've minimized the application, it will send a system notification. If you are a Windows user, the notification will be shown by an application icon in the taskbar. If you are a Mac OS X user, the notification will be displayed in the dock icon of the application.

You'll see how to manage updates in an AIR application in Chapter 13.

Summary

This chapter has presented many features provided by AIR to Flash developers to allow a high level of integration with the local operating system. The purpose of these functions is to improve the AIR experience for end users and provide freedom to developers.

You've learned how to

- Pass command-line arguments from the operating system shell to an AIR application
- Start an installed AIR application from a web page (installation is covered in more detail in Chapter 13)
- Create applications that start up with the operating system
- Associate file types with an AIR application
- Call the user's attention through operating system notifications

In the next chapter, you will see how AIR allows you to interact with multimedia content such as PDF, video, and audio files.

CHAPTER 9

ADDING RICH MEDIA: PDF, VIDEO, AND AUDIO FILES

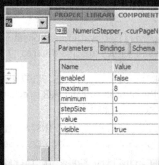

The use of rich media is a fundamental to creating attractive applications. Adobe AIR applications can import and display PDF (Portable Document Format) files, and play local and remote video and audio files. In the past few years, Flash Player's capabilities for playing audio and video files has grown considerably. Today, Flash Player (and consequently AIR applications) can play videos in high definition (HD), using the H.264 video format. This option offers many possibilities to AIR application developers. Support for MP3 audio has grown tremendously as well, allowing for the creation of new and interesting audio effects in AIR applications. The video format supported by Flash Player (FLV) has become a standard for video distribution on the Web. With AIR applications, it's also possible to bring this video format onto the desktop.

The AIR runtime uses the WebKit engine and the Adobe Reader browser plug-in to render PDF content. The WebKit engine is embedded in the AIR runtime, so you can use it in any AIR application you create. In addition, the WebKit engine is used to render both local and remote HTML content.

The Adobe Reader plug-in isn't distributed with the AIR runtime, so you have to install it on the local system. The AIR runtime requires version 8.1 or higher to be installed. If the local system has an earlier version than 8.1, you won't be able to render PDF files in your AIR applications. You can download the Adobe Reader plug-in for free from Adobe's homepage (www.adobe.com/).

In this chapter, you'll learn how to access and use PDF documents, video, and audio in your AIR applications. First, we'll take a look at using PDFs, the first step of which is detecting PDF capability.

Detecting PDF capability

In order for an AIR application to render PDF files, the application must first check if the local system can do it. The HTMLLoader class has the pdfCapability property to check if AIR can render PDF files correctly. The pdfCapability property returns a numerical code that shows whether AIR can render PDF files or not. If AIR can't use PDF files, an error code is generated.

The HTMLPDFCapability class defines constants for the possible values of the pdfCapability property. The valid values are listed here:

- HTMLPDFCapability.STATUS_OK: The Adobe Reader plug-in is installed and the version of the plug-in satisfies AIR's requirements. This constant shows that HTMLLoader objects can load PDF files.

- HTMLPDFCapability.ERROR_INSTALLED_READER_NOT_FOUND: The Adobe Reader plug-in isn't installed. It won't be possible to load PDF files in AIR applications.

- HTMLPDFCapability.ERROR_INSTALLED_READER_TOO_OLD: The version of Adobe Reader that is installed on the computer is earlier than 8.1, so it won't be possible to load PDF files in AIR applications.

- HTMLPDFCapability.ERROR_PREFERRED_READER_TOO_OLD: There are several versions of the Adobe Reader plug-in on the computer. The version set as the default editor for PDF files is an earlier version than 8.1, so the AIR application can't load PDF files.

> *On Windows systems, if a 7.x version of Adobe Reader is running, AIR will use it even if a later version is installed but not running. If these conditions persist and an AIR application tries to display a PDF file, an error window will be displayed by Adobe Reader. If this happens in your AIR application, you should provide users with instructions on how to avoid the problem.*

In this section, you'll see how to do the following:

- Detect PDF capability in AIR applications
- Create a document class for detecting PDF capability
- Test out your project to ensure that it works

Creating the DetectPDF.fla project

AIR provides the HTMLLoader.pdfCapability property for detecting whether it's possible to display PDF files. In the following exercise, you'll create an AIR application that notifies the user whether it's possible to load and display PDF files. The application will behave like a traffic light, showing a green light if it's possible to access PDF files and a red light if it isn't. If the version of the installed Adobe Reader plug-in is too old, the application will show a yellow light. A text message will always be displayed as well to notify the user about the situation.

Follow these steps to detect PDF capability:

1. Create a new Flash file (Adobe AIR) called DetectPDF.fla. If you prefer, you can open the complete file from the chapter09 folder of the book's source code (available from the downloads section of the friends of ED website, at www.friendsofed.com/).
2. Create a Label component on the stage and assign it the instance name PDFstatus. This component will tell if it's possible to display PDF files in AIR applications.
3. Create a shape with the Oval tool, and convert it into a movie clip, as shown in Figure 9-1. Right-click the shape you've just created to access the Convert to symbol command.
4. Assign the symbol name TrafficLight to the movie clip.
5. Select the Export for ActionScript check box and assign it the class name TrafficLight in the Class field.
6. Confirm the creation of the movie clip by clicking OK.
7. Assign the instance name trafficLightItem to the symbol.

9

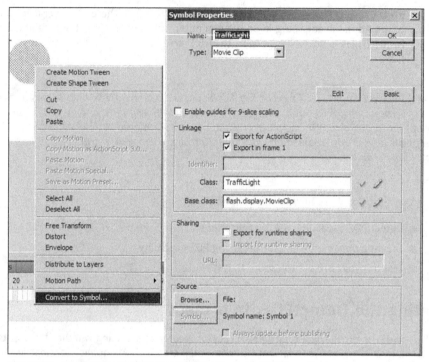

Figure 9-1. Creating the TrafficLight symbol in the DetectPDF.fla project

8. Open the Publish Settings panel of the project by selecting the Publish Settings command from the File menu in Flash CS4.

9. In the Publish Settings panel, click the Settings button next to the Script: ActionScript 3 item. The Advanced ActionScript 3.0 Settings panel will open, as shown in Figure 9-2.

10. Deselect the Automatically declare stage instances option. The properties associated with the components on the stage will be declared in the class you'll create shortly.

11. Add the ./src/ item on the Source path tab. This operation will tell Flash CS4 that it has to look for the ActionScript classes in this relative path to the DetectPDF.fla project.

12. Confirm the setup operations to close the open dialog windows.

13. Create a new src folder in the folder that contains the DetectPDF.fla project. In this folder, you'll create the classes the application will use. The ActionScript code of the DetectPDF.fla project will be written in the DetectPDF.as class in the com.comtaste.foed.essentialair.chapter9 package.

The structure of the folder you need to create for the com.comtaste.foed.essentialair.chapter9 package is com/comtaste/foed/essentialair/chapter9.

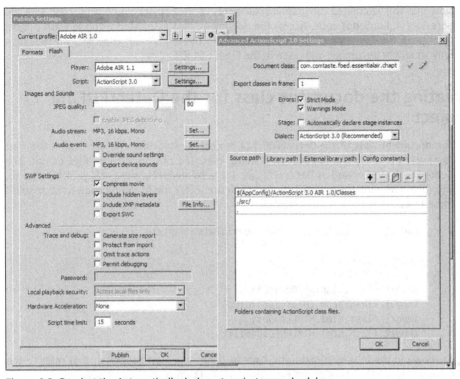

Figure 9-2. Deselect the Automatically declare stage instances check box.

14. Create the folders you need for the com.comtaste.foed.essentialair.chapter9 package and create a new ActionScript file in the chapter9 folder. If you prefer, you can find the complete DetectPDF.as file in the source code of the project.

15. Go back to the Flash DetectPDF.fla project and enter the complete name of the com.comtaste.foed.essentialair.chapter9.DetectPDF class in the Class field of the Document Properties panel, as shown in Figure 9-3. The complete name of the class has to be entered without the .as extension.

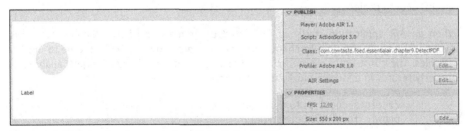

Figure 9-3. Defining the document class of the DetectPDF.fla project

Now that you've created the graphical elements of the project, you can proceed with the necessary ActionScript code. Access the document class associated with the Flash project by clicking the Edit class definition button next to the Class field. The class, which is now only an empty document, will open in the Flash CS4 IDE.

Creating the document class for the DetectPDF.fla project

The document class of the DetectPDF.fla project is responsible for checking if the host computer on which the application is being executed can display PDF files or not. The ActionScript class, saved as DetectPDF.as, starts by declaring the package it belongs to, and then it imports the external classes it will use. Enter the following code to accomplish these tasks:

```
package com.comtaste.foed.essentialair.chapter9
{
import fl.controls.Label;

import flash.display.MovieClip;
import flash.geom.ColorTransform;
import flash.html.HTMLLoader;
import flash.html.HTMLPDFCapability;
```

As shown in the following code, you have to define the class properties that refer to the components on the stage of the Flash DetectPDF.fla project:

```
public class DetectPDF extends MovieClip
{
    // onstage objects
    public var PDFstatus:Label;
    public var trafficLightItem:TrafficLight;
```

There are two objects on the stage, so the document class defines two class properties: PDFstatus, typed as Label, and trafficLightItem, typed as TrafficLight. (TrafficLight is the class name assigned to the symbol you created previously in the library of the DetectPDF.fla project.)

When an AIR application starts up, the constructor method of the document class is invoked. The application has to check if the local system allows the AIR runtime to display PDF files. The constructor method checks the value that the HTMLLoader.pdfCapability property returns in a switch block, as shown here:

```
// class constructor
public function DetectPDF()
{
    // test system pdf capability
    switch( HTMLLoader.pdfCapability )
    {
```

If AIR can load and display PDF files properly, the pdfCapability property returns the HTMLPDFCapability.STATUS_OK value. The text of the PDFstatus component is updated and the setGreenLight() method is called to color the TrafficLight instance green. The following code defines the preceding operations:

```
case HTMLPDFCapability.STATUS_OK:
    PDFstatus.text = "Your system is ready to open "
                            + "PDF documents in Adobe AIR";
    setGreenLight();
    break;
```

If the AIR runtime can't access any version of the Adobe Reader plug-in (HTMLPDFCapability. ERROR_CANNOT_LOAD_READER or HTMLPDFCapability.ERROR_INSTALLED_READER_NOT_FOUND), or if the installed version is too old (HTMLPDFCapability.ERROR_INSTALLED_READER_TOO_OLD), the traffic light turns red. To color the TrafficLight instance red, the setRedLight() method is invoked. The following code shows how you can notify the user that it isn't possible to display PDF files:

```
case HTMLPDFCapability.ERROR_CANNOT_LOAD_READER:
    PDFstatus.text = "Adobe AIR is not able to access "
    + "Acrobat Reader installation";
    setRedLight();
    break;

case HTMLPDFCapability.ERROR_INSTALLED_READER_NOT_FOUND:
    PDFstatus.text = "Acrobat Reader is not installed!";
    setRedLight();
    break;

case HTMLPDFCapability.ERROR_INSTALLED_READER_TOO_OLD:
    PDFstatus.text = "Acrobat Reader installed is a "
    + "version too old! Minimun version is
        Acrobat reader 8.1";
    setRedLight();
    break;
```

If AIR can display PDF documents, but only if the user changes the local system settings, the traffic light turns yellow. In this case, the user has to set the most recent version of Adobe Reader as the default player. To make the TrafficLight instance turn yellow, when HTMLLoader.pdfCapability has a value of HTMLPDFCapability.ERROR_PREFERRED_READER_TOO_OLD, you invoke the setYellowLight() method. As mentioned, this can happen if there are different versions of the Adobe Reader plug-in on the system, and an older version than 8.1 has been set as the preferred version. In this case, the application will tell the user to change the settings of the local system, as shown here:

```
case HTMLPDFCapability.ERROR_PREFERRED_READER_TOO_OLD:
    PDFstatus.text = "Multiple version of Acrobat Reader "
    + "are installed. The preferred is a too old version! "
    + "change your system settings.";
    setYellowLight();
```

```
            break;
        }
    }
```

This constructor method checks if AIR can display PDF files and notifies the user about the situation.

Now you have to create the methods that change the color of the trafficLightItem. The setGreenLight(), setRedLight(), and setYellowLight() methods use the transform. colorTransform property of the trafficLightItem to change its color.

The ColorTransform class allows you to change the color of a MovieClip instance in various ways. The class acts on the single color channels (red, green, blue, and alpha), allowing you to change its value. The following code shows the three methods you can use to change the color of the trafficLightItem:

```
        private function setGreenLight():void
        {
            trafficLightItem.transform.colorTransform =
                new ColorTransform( 0, 0, 0, 1, 0, 255, 0, 0 );
        }

        private function setRedLight():void
        {
            trafficLightItem.transform.colorTransform =
                new ColorTransform( 0, 0, 0, 1, 255, 0, 0, 0 );
        }

        private function setYellowLight():void
        {
            trafficLightItem.transform.colorTransform =
                new ColorTransform( 0, 0, 0, 1, 255, 255, 0, 0 );
        }
```

This is the complete code of the DetectPDF.as class:

```
        package com.comtaste.foed.essentialair.chapter9
        {
        import fl.controls.Label;

        import flash.display.MovieClip;
        import flash.geom.ColorTransform;
        import flash.html.HTMLLoader;
        import flash.html.HTMLPDFCapability;

        public class DetectPDF extends MovieClip
        {
            // onstage objects
            public var PDFstatus:Label;
            public var trafficLightItem:TrafficLight;
```

```
// class constructor
public function DetectPDF()
{
    // test system pdf capability
    switch( HTMLLoader.pdfCapability )
    {
        case HTMLPDFCapability.STATUS_OK:
            PDFstatus.text = "Your system is ready to open "
            + "PDF documents in Adobe AIR";
            setGreenLight();
            break;

        case HTMLPDFCapability.ERROR_CANNOT_LOAD_READER:
            PDFstatus.text = "Adobe AIR is not able to access "
            + "Acrobat Reader installation";
            setRedLight();
            break;

        case HTMLPDFCapability.ERROR_INSTALLED_READER_NOT_FOUND:
            PDFstatus.text = "Acrobat Reader is not installed!";
            setRedLight();
            break;

        case HTMLPDFCapability.ERROR_INSTALLED_READER_TOO_OLD:
            PDFstatus.text = "Acrobat Reader installed is a "
            + "version too old! Min version is Acrobat reader 8.1";
            setRedLight();
            break;

        case HTMLPDFCapability.ERROR_PREFERRED_READER_TOO_OLD:
            PDFstatus.text = "Multiple version of Acrobat Reader "
    + "are installed. The preferred is a too old version! "
    + "change your system settings.";
            setYellowLight();
            break;
    }
}

private function setGreenLight():void
{
    trafficLightItem.transform.colorTransform =
        new ColorTransform( 0, 0, 0, 1, 0, 255, 0, 0 );
}

private function setRedLight():void
{
    trafficLightItem.transform.colorTransform =
        new ColorTransform( 0, 0, 0, 1, 255, 0, 0, 0 );
}
```

9

```
        private function setYellowLight():void
        {
            trafficLightItem.transform.colorTransform =
                new ColorTransform( 0, 0, 0, 1, 255, 255, 0, 0 );
        }

    }// close class
    }// close package
```

Now that the DetectPDF.as class is complete, you can test the project.

Testing the DetectPDF.fla project

Go back to the Flash CS4 IDE and the DetectPDF.fla project. Select the Test Movie command from the Control menu to compile and start up the AIR application, as shown in Figure 9-4. You can also use Ctrl+Enter on Windows, or Cmd+Enter on Mac OS X. The AIR application will start up and display the status of your system. If AIR can display PDF documents in AIR applications, the traffic light will be green. You can see the application launched on a local system that displays PDF files in AIR in Figure 9-5.

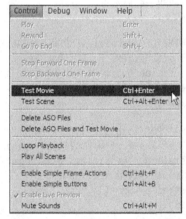

Figure 9-4. Launching the DetectPDF.fla project for testing

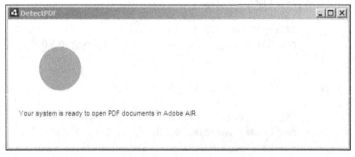

Figure 9-5. The DetectPDF.fla file launched from Flash. You've got the green light.

You'll see how to load and display a PDF document in an AIR application in the next section.

Loading and displaying PDF files in AIR

In the previous section, you saw how to check whether AIR can display PDF documents. In this section, your attention will move on to loading PDF documents in an AIR application. You want to create an application that allows the user to load PDF files on the local system. The operation will only be successful if AIR can display PDF documents. Each open document will be displayed in a different native window. The following steps will allow you to create the project:

1. Create a new Flash file (Adobe AIR) called LoadingPDF.fla. If you prefer, you can open the complete LoadingPDF.fla file from the chapter09 folder of the book's source code.

2. Create a Label component on the stage and don't assign it an instance name.

3. Assign the string "Click button to browse and open PDF files; if button is disabled, Acrobat Reader is not installed!" to the text property of the Label component from the Component Inspector, as shown in Figure 9-6.

4. Create a Button component with an openPDFBtn instance name and a "Browse PDF files" label. The Button will be used to request the opening of the dialog window for the selection of the PDF files to open.

5. Open the Publish Settings panel of the project by selecting the Publish Settings command from the File menu in Flash CS4. Carry out the configuration operations described in the previous Flash project in this chapter.

6. Create a new ActionScript file and call it LoadingPDF.as. If you prefer, you can find the complete LoadingPDF.as file in the source code of the project.

7. Go back to the Flash LoadingPDF.fla project and enter the complete name of the com.comtaste.foed.essentialair.chapter9.LoadingPDF class in the Class field in the Document Properties panel, as shown in Figure 9-7 (remember to exclude the .as extension).

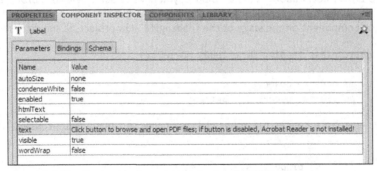

Figure 9-6. The Component Inspector for the LoadingPDF.fla project

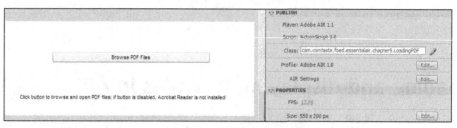

Figure 9-7. Defining the document class of the LoadingPDF.fla project

To access the document class associated with the LoadingPDF.fla project, click the Edit class definition icon next to the field, and the LoadingPDF.as class will open in Flash.

Creating the document class for the LoadingPDF.fla project

Enter the following code in the LoadingPDF.as document. It will open the package of the LoadingPDF class and declare which external classes Flash will have to import during the compilation phase of the LoadingPDF.fla project.

```
package com.comtaste.foed.essentialair.chapter9
{
import fl.controls.Button;
import flash.display.MovieClip;
import flash.display.NativeWindowInitOptions;
import flash.events.Event;
import flash.events.MouseEvent;
import flash.filesystem.File;
import flash.geom.Rectangle;
import flash.html.HTMLLoader;
import flash.html.HTMLPDFCapability;
import flash.net.FileFilter;
import flash.net.URLRequest;
```

After the import declarations in the class body, you have to define the class properties you need. First, declare the openPDFBtn property, typed as Button. This property represents the Button component on the stage of the LoadingPDF.fla project, as shown here:

```
public class LoadingPDF extends MovieClip
{
    // onstage objects
    public var openPDFBtn:Button;
```

The following code creates the other class property you need: fileBrowser, typed as File:

```
    // class properties
    private var fileBrowser:File;
```

The File fileBrowser object will allow the user to select the PDF documents to load. The HTMLLoader object will be used to display the requested PDF files in different NativeWindow instances. The constructor method initializes the status of the application. First, it checks if AIR can display PDF documents, as shown here:

```
// class constructor
public function LoadingPDF()
{
    // test system pdf capability
    if( HTMLLoader.pdfCapability == HTMLPDFCapability.STATUS_OK )
    {
```

If PDF documents can be displayed in AIR, the enabled property of openPDFBtn is set to true. You also register an event listener method for the click event on the button. When the button is clicked, the browsePDF() method is invoked. The following code carries out these operations:

```
// enable openPDFBtn button
openPDFBtn.enabled = true;

// register event listener for click event
openPDFBtn.addEventListener( MouseEvent.CLICK, browsePDF );
}
else
{
```

If AIR can't display PDF documents, the openPDFBtn button is disabled, as shown here:

```
// disable openPDFBtn button
openPDFBtn.enabled = false;
}
```

The File object is initialized and an event listener method is registered for the Event. SELECT event. This event is generated when the user selects a file from the selection window opened from the fileBrowser object. The dialog window to select the file you want to display will be opened in the installation of the folder of the application. The following code shows the initialization of the fileBrowser property:

```
// instantiate file instance
fileBrowser = File.applicationDirectory;

// register event listener for file browser object
fileBrowser.addEventListener( Event.SELECT, openPDF );
}
```

Now you have to write the ActionScript code you need to select a PDF document and display it in AIR. This is the ActionScript class just created:

```
package com.comtaste.foed.essentialair.chapter9
{
import fl.controls.Button;
```

```
import flash.display.MovieClip;
import flash.display.NativeWindowInitOptions;
import flash.events.Event;
import flash.events.MouseEvent;
import flash.filesystem.File;
import flash.geom.Rectangle;
import flash.html.HTMLLoader;
import flash.html.HTMLPDFCapability;
import flash.net.FileFilter;
import flash.net.URLRequest;

public class LoadingPDF extends MovieClip
{
    // onstage objects
    public var openPDFBtn:Button;

    // class properties
    private var fileBrowser:File;

    // class constructor
    public function LoadingPDF()
    {
        // test system pdf capability
        if( HTMLLoader.pdfCapability == HTMLPDFCapability.STATUS_OK )
        {
            // enable openPDFBtn button
            openPDFBtn.enabled = true;

            // register event listener for click event
            openPDFBtn.addEventListener( MouseEvent.CLICK, browsePDF );
        }
        else
        {
            // disable openPDFBtn button
            openPDFBtn.enabled = false;
        }

        // initiate file instance
        fileBrowser = File.applicationDirectory;

        // register event listener for file browser object
        fileBrowser.addEventListener( Event.SELECT, openPDF );

    }

}// close class
}// close package
```

Each time the user clicks the openPDFBtn button, it invokes the browsePDF() method. This method tells the fileBrowser to open a dialog window where the user can select the PDF document to display. (The fileBrowser is an instance of File.) The dialog window is opened by invoking the browseForOpen() method, which will be assigned an array containing the file types you can choose from. PDF documents are the only types of files you can open. This is the code for the browseForOpen() method:

```
// open browse dialog to choose PDF to open
private function browsePDF( event:MouseEvent ):void
{
    var filter:Array = new Array()
    filter.push( new FileFilter( "PDF documents", "*.pdf" ) );
    fileBrowser.browseForOpen( "Choose PDF to open..", filter );
}
```

When you select a PDF document to display, you invoke the openPDF() method. PDF documents are displayed using the WebKit engine and the Adobe Reader plug-in, so the HTMLLoader object will load the PDF document the user selects. Each PDF document will be opened in a new NativeWindow instance. The following code defines the dimensions and positions of the windows you want to create:

```
// open PDF in a new window
private function openPDF( event:Event ):void
{
    // prepare HTML container to be shown in a new native window
    var initOptions:NativeWindowInitOptions =
                    new NativeWindowInitOptions();
    var bounds:Rectangle = new Rectangle( 50, 350, 600, 400 );
```

To create a NativeWindow that contains an HTMLLoader object, you invoke the createRootWindow() method of the HTMLLoader class, which will be assigned four arguments:

- visible: This shows whether the window will be visible or not.
- options: This asks for a NativeWindowInitOption instance, and allows you to assign additional information to the window.
- scrollbars: This shows if the scrollbars will always have to be visible.
- bounds: This provides the dimensions and position of the window you're creating.

The following code invokes the createRootWindow() method and assigns the instance returned to a local variable:

```
// create new HTMLLoader instance
// passed arguments visible,
// windows options, show scrollbars, bounding box
var htmlViewPort:HTMLLoader = HTMLLoader.createRootWindow(
                    true, initOptions, true, bounds);
```

9

The URL of the PDF document to open is assigned to the load() method of the HTMLLoader object. The URL is assigned as an instance of the URLRequest class, as shown here:

```
        // creates remote request instance
        var urlReq:URLRequest = new URLRequest( fileBrowser.url );
        htmlViewPort.load( urlReq );
    }
```

This is the complete ActionScript class you created:

```
package com.comtaste.foed.essentialair.chapter9
{
import fl.controls.Button;

import flash.display.MovieClip;
import flash.display.NativeWindowInitOptions;
import flash.events.Event;
import flash.events.MouseEvent;
import flash.filesystem.File;
import flash.geom.Rectangle;
import flash.html.HTMLLoader;
import flash.html.HTMLPDFCapability;
import flash.net.FileFilter;
import flash.net.URLRequest;

public class LoadingPDF extends MovieClip
{
    // onstage objects
    public var openPDFBtn:Button;

    // class properties
    private var fileBrowser:File;

    // class constructor
    public function LoadingPDF()
    {
        // test system pdf capability
        if( HTMLLoader.pdfCapability == HTMLPDFCapability.STATUS_OK )
        {
            // enable openPDFBtn button
            openPDFBtn.enabled = true;

            // register event listener for click event
            openPDFBtn.addEventListener( MouseEvent.CLICK, browsePDF );
        }
        else
        {
            // disable openPDFBtn button
            openPDFBtn.enabled = false;
        }
```

```
            // initiate file instance
            fileBrowser = File.applicationDirectory;

            // register event listener for file browser object
            fileBrowser.addEventListener( Event.SELECT, openPDF );
        }

        // open browse dialog to choose PDF to open
        private function browsePDF( event:MouseEvent ):void
        {
            var filter:Array = new Array()
            filter.push( new FileFilter( "PDF documents", "*.pdf" ) );
            fileBrowser.browseForOpen( "Choose PDF to open..", filter );
        }

        // open browse dialog to choose PDF to open
        private function openPDF( event:Event ):void
        {
            // prepare HTML container to be shown in a new native window
            var initOptions:NativeWindowInitOptions =
                    new NativeWindowInitOptions();
            var bounds:Rectangle = new Rectangle( 50, 350, 600, 400 );

            // create new HTMLLoader instance
            // passed arguments visible, windows options,
            // show scrollbars, bounding box
            var htmlViewPort:HTMLLoader = HTMLLoader.createRootWindow(
                    true, initOptions, true, bounds);

            // creates remote request instance
            var urlReq:URLRequest = new URLRequest( fileBrowser.url );
            htmlViewPort.load( urlReq );
        }

    }// close class
}// close package
```

Now the document class for project LoadingPDF.fla is complete.

Testing the LoadingPDF.fla project

Follow these steps to test the LoadingPDF.fla project:

1. Go back to the Flash CS4 IDE and the LoadingPDF.fla project.

2. Select the Test Movie command from the Control menu to compile and start up the AIR application. The AIR application will start up, and if AIR can display PDF documents on your local system, the button on the stage will be enabled.

3. Click the button to open the dialog window and select a PDF document.

You can see the application during the PDF document selection process in Figure 9-8. You can find a PDF file in the folder that contains the source code of the chapter, if you don't already have a PDF on your local system.

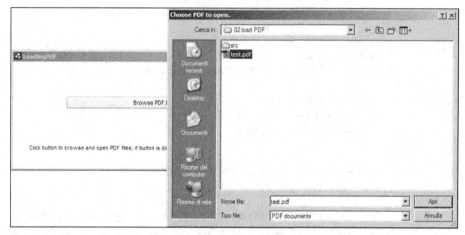

Figure 9-8. The LoadingPDF.fla project during PDF file selection

You can see the LoadingPDF.air application with a PDF document already open in Figure 9-9. The next section will show you how to directly control a few functions of a PDF document directly from AIR.

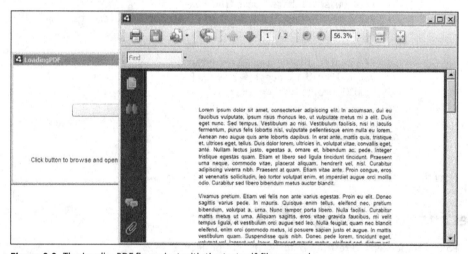

Figure 9-9. The LoadingPDF.fla project with the test.pdf file opened

Scripting PDFs

AIR allows you to communicate with PDF documents like a web page can through JavaScript code. The Adobe Reader plug-in allows the JavaScript code in a web page or the ActionScript code in an AIR application to control its behavior. The plug-in allows you to perform the following actions:

- Navigate through the pages
- Magnify the pages
- Interact with PDF forms
- Manage the events generated by the multimedia content embedded in the PDF document

> You can find more information on how to use JavaScript code in PDF documents on the Adobe website, at www.adobe.com/devnet/acrobat/javascript.html.

A PDF document can incorporate JavaScript code to allow the user to execute advanced operations—for example, the possibility of changing the displayed page or adjusting the zoom level of the PDF document. The JavaScript code can be inserted into the whole document or a single page. To insert the JavaScript code into a PDF document, you have to use Adobe Acrobat Professional.

A web page can invoke JavaScript code in a PDF document through the HTML DOM. Once you've obtained a reference to the element of the DOM that contains a PDF document, you can call the postMessage() method. This method, provided by the HTML DOM, allows you to pass information or requests to JavaScript code in the PDF document.

A PDF document can register an event listener method using JavaScript to call when the DOM of the HTML page invokes the postMessage() method. To register the event listener method, you have to assign the reference to the method you want to invoke to the messageHandler property. This property is exposed by the hostContainer object provided by the PDF document to the incorporated JavaScript.

The following code shows a PDF document incorporated in a web page:

```
<html>
    <head>
    </head>
    <body>
        <object id="pdfDoc"
            data="myDocument.pdf"
            type="application/pdf"
            width="100%" height="100%"/>
    </body>
</html>
```

9

To pass the information from the web page to the PDF document, you can write the following code in the head node:

```
<head>
    <script>
        function sendMessageToPDF()
        {
            pdfNode = document.getElementById( "pdfDoc" );
            try
            {
                pdfNode.postMessage( [ "Message 1",
                                "Message 2", "Message 3" ] );
            } catch (error)
            {
                alert( "Error trying to send message to PDF element" );
            }
        }
    </script>
</head>
```

Add the onload attribute to the body node to tell the HTML page to invoke the sendMessageToPDF() function when the loading process has completed, as shown here:

```
<body onload="sendMessageToPDF()">
```

Each time the web page is loaded, the JavaScript code passes three strings of text—Message 1, Message 2, and Message 3—to the PDF documents. If the operation fails, the application will display an alert window. The PDF myDocument.pdf document will contain JavaScript code that can manage the messages it receives from the HTML DOM.

Controlling PDF navigation from AIR

AIR can't communicate directly with the JavaScript code in a PDF document. This communication is possible thanks to the WebKit engine. So, to communicate with a PDF document, you have to go through an HTMLLoader object.

Let's create an application to understand how AIR can interact with JavaScript code in PDF documents. This application will allow the user to navigate between the pages of the document using the AIR interface. The user will also be able to change the zoom level of the PDF document by using the interface offered by the AIR application.

Follow these steps to create the ScriptingPDF.fla project:

1. Create a new Flash file (Adobe AIR) and name it ScriptingPDF.fla. If you prefer, you can open the complete ScriptingPDF.fla file from the chapter09 folder of the book's source code. Figure 9-10 shows what the stage of the ScriptingPDF.fla project should look like.

2. Create two Button components on the stage and give them the instance names zoomInBtn and zoomOutBtn. These will increase and decrease the zoom level of the PDF document, respectively.

3. Create a NumericStepper component with instance name curPageNs.

4. In the Component Inspector, set the maximum property to 8 and the minimum property to 0, as shown in Figure 9-11. The three components you've created have to have the enabled property set to false.

5. Finally, create a TextArea and assign it the instance name output.

Figure 9-10. The stage of the ScriptingPDF.fla project

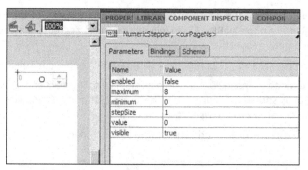

Figure 9-11. The Component Inspector for the NumericStepper object

Creating the document class for the ScriptingPDF.fla project

Follow these steps to create the document class of the ScriptingPDF.fla project:

1. Open the Publish Settings panel of the project by selecting the Publish Settings command from the File menu of Flash CS4.

2. Carry out the configuration operations described in the first project in this chapter.

3. Create a new ActionScript file and name it ScriptingPDF.as. If you prefer, you can find the complete ScriptingPDF.as file in the source code of the project.

4. Go back to the ScriptingPDF.fla project and write the complete name of the com.comtaste.foed.essentialair.chapter9.ScriptingPDF class in the Class field in the Document Properties panel, as shown in Figure 9-12 (remember to exclude the .as file extension).

5. To access the document class that is associated with the ScriptingPDF.fla project, click the Edit class definition icon next to the field, and the ScriptingPDF.as class will open in Flash.

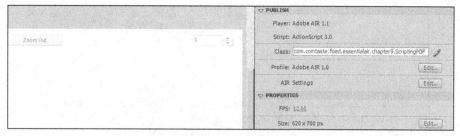

Figure 9-12. Defining the document class of the ScriptingPDF.fla project

Start the ScriptingPDF.as class by inserting the package of the class and the declaration of the necessary classes to import, as shown here:

```
package com.comtaste.foed.essentialair.chapter9
{
import fl.controls.Button;
import fl.controls.NumericStepper;
import fl.controls.TextArea;

import flash.display.MovieClip;
import flash.events.Event;
import flash.events.MouseEvent;
import flash.filesystem.File;
import flash.html.HTMLLoader;
import flash.html.HTMLPDFCapability;
import flash.net.URLRequest;
```

Then declare the class properties. There are four components on the stage of the ScriptingPDF.fla project. The following code declares the properties that correspond to the four components on the stage:

```
public class ScriptingPDF extends MovieClip
{
    // onstage objects
    public var output:TextArea;
    public var zoomInBtn:Button;
    public var zoomOutBtn:Button;
    public var curPageNs:NumericStepper;
```

Then you have to create two properties—file, typed as File, and htmlViewPort, typed as HTMLLoader—as shown here:

```
    // class properties
    private var file:File;
    private var htmlViewPort:HTMLLoader;
```

These two properties will load and display the PDF document the application will interact with. The following code defines the constructor method of the ScriptingPDF.as class:

```
    // class constructor
    public function ScriptingPDF()
    {
```

The constructor method starts by checking if AIR can display PDF documents, as shown here:

```
        // test system pdf capability
        if( HTMLLoader.pdfCapability == HTMLPDFCapability.STATUS_OK )
        {
```

If AIR can display PDF documents, the application is initialized. An event listener method is registered for the two buttons and for the NumericStepper component, as shown here:

```
// register event listener for components
zoomInBtn.addEventListener( MouseEvent.CLICK, zoomIn );
zoomOutBtn.addEventListener( MouseEvent.CLICK, zoomOut );
curPageNs.addEventListener(Event.CHANGE, gotoPage );
```

In order to interact with the PDF document, AIR has to load and display the HTML document that imports it. Next, you'll create the HTML document: testPDFScripting.html. The following code creates a File object for the HTML document you want to display:

```
// initiate File instance
file = File.applicationDirectory.resolvePath(
                "testPDFScripting.html" );
```

The HTML document is loaded and displayed by an HTMLLoader object. The following code creates an HTMLLoader object and defines its dimensions and position:

```
// create and position HTMLLoader instance
htmlViewPort = new HTMLLoader();
htmlViewPort.width = 600;
htmlViewPort.height = 400;
htmlViewPort.x = 10;
htmlViewPort.y = 60;
```

Now you have to register an event listener method for the HTML_DOM_INITIALIZE event, which is generated by the HTMLLoader object. This event is generated when the loaded HTML document has completed the initialization of its DOM. Register the event as shown here:

```
// register event listener for html DOM loader
htmlViewPort.addEventListener( Event.HTML_DOM_INITIALIZE,
                htmlLoaded );
```

The following code adds the HTMLLoader object to the stage:

```
// put html viewport on stage
addChild( htmlViewPort );
```

Finally, you have to start loading the HTML document. To do so, you invoke the load() method of the HTMLLoader class. The load() method requires an instance of the URLRequest class. Create a URLRequest object and assign it to the load() method, as shown here:

```
// creates remote request instance
var urlReq:URLRequest = new URLRequest( file.url );
htmlViewPort.load( urlReq );
    }
    else
    {
```

If the AIR runtime can't display PDF documents because Reader isn't installed or because the installed version is too old, write a message in the output TextArea, as shown here:

```
        output.appendText( "Impossible Load PDF. PDFCapability " +
                "value:    " + HTMLLoader.pdfCapability +
                File.lineEnding );
        }
    }
```

The constructor method initializes the application and starts the loading process of the
testPDFScripting.html file. When the loading process has been completed and the HTML
DOM has been initialized properly, the htmlLoaded() method is invoked. This method has
the task of enabling the two Button components and the NumericStepper component on
the stage of the project. This is the code for the htmlLoaded() method:

```
    private function htmlLoaded( event:Event ):void
    {
        // enable components
        zoomInBtn.enabled = true;
        zoomOutBtn.enabled = true;
        curPageNs.enabled = true;
    }
```

This is the complete ActionScript class you created:

```
    package com.comtaste.foed.essentialair.chapter9
    {
    import fl.controls.Button;
    import fl.controls.NumericStepper;
    import fl.controls.TextArea;

    import flash.display.MovieClip;
    import flash.events.Event;
    import flash.events.MouseEvent;
    import flash.filesystem.File;
    import flash.html.HTMLLoader;
    import flash.html.HTMLPDFCapability;
    import flash.net.URLRequest;

    public class ScriptingPDF extends MovieClip
    {
        // onstage objects
        public var output:TextArea;
        public var zoomInBtn:Button;
        public var zoomOutBtn:Button;
        public var curPageNs:NumericStepper;

        // class properties
        private var file:File;
        private var htmlViewPort:HTMLLoader;
```

9

```
                    // class constructor
                    public function ScriptingPDF()
                    {
                        // test system pdf capability
                        if( HTMLLoader.pdfCapability == HTMLPDFCapability.STATUS_OK )
                        {
                            // register event listener for components
                            zoomInBtn.addEventListener( MouseEvent.CLICK, zoomIn );
                            zoomOutBtn.addEventListener( MouseEvent.CLICK, zoomOut );
                            curPageNs.addEventListener(Event.CHANGE, gotoPage );

                            // initiate File instance
                            file = File.applicationDirectory.resolvePath(
                                    "testPDFScripting.html" );

                            // create and position HTMLLoader instance
                            htmlViewPort = new HTMLLoader();
                            htmlViewPort.width = 600;
                            htmlViewPort.height = 400;
                            htmlViewPort.x = 10;
                            htmlViewPort.y = 60;

                            // register event listener for html DOM loader
                            htmlViewPort.addEventListener( Event.HTML_DOM_INITIALIZE,
                                    htmlLoaded );

                            // put html vieport on stage
                            addChild( htmlViewPort );

                            // creates remote request instance
                            var urlReq:URLRequest = new URLRequest( file.url );
                            htmlViewPort.load( urlReq );
                        }
                        else
                        {
                            output.appendText( "Impossible Load PDF.PDFCapability " +
                                    "value:  " + HTMLLoader.pdfCapability +
                                    File.lineEnding );
                        }
                    }

                    private function htmlLoaded( event:Event ):void
                    {
                        // enable components
                        zoomInBtn.enabled = true;
                        zoomOutBtn.enabled = true;
                        curPageNs.enabled = true;
                    }
                }// close class
            }// close package
```

To complete the class, you still have to define the methods that communicate with the JavaScript code in the PDF document. When the user clicks the zoomInBtn button to increase the zoom of the PDF document, the zoomIn() method is invoked. This method accesses the PDF document through the HTML DOM and invokes the postMessage() method provided by the DOM. The following code accesses the element of the DOM that contains the PDF document:

```
private function zoomIn( event:MouseEvent ):void
{
    try
    {
        var pdfObj:Object =
        htmlViewPort.window.document.getElementById("PDFObj");
```

The invocation of the postMessage() method is launched in a try...catch block to intercept possible errors generated by the PDF document or by AIR. An array containing the ZoomIn string is passed to the postMessage() method as an argument. The JavaScript in the PDF receives the string and increases the zoom of the document. The following code makes the ZoomIn action request to the loaded PDF:

```
        pdfObj.postMessage([ "ZoomIn" ]);
    }
    catch (error:Error)
    {
```

If the postMessage() method fails, an error is generated. This error is intercepted by the try...catch block. If an error is generated, the following code writes a message in the output TextArea regarding what is going on:

```
        output.appendText( "ZoomIn error: " + error.name +
                File.lineEnding + "Error message: "
                + error.message + File.lineEnding );
    }
}
```

The zoomOut() and gotoPage() methods are implemented like the zoomIn() method. The difference is in the arguments passed to the method of the DOM, postMessage(). The zoomOut() method passes the ZoomOut string to postMessage(). The gotoPage() method passes the GotoPage string and the page number of the PDF document to postMessage().

This is the complete ScriptingPDF.as class you created:

```
package com.comtaste.foed.essentialair.chapter9
{
import fl.controls.Button;
import fl.controls.NumericStepper;
import fl.controls.TextArea;

import flash.display.MovieClip;
import flash.events.Event;
import flash.events.MouseEvent;
```

```
import flash.filesystem.File;
import flash.html.HTMLLoader;
import flash.html.HTMLPDFCapability;
import flash.net.URLRequest;

public class ScriptingPDF extends MovieClip
{
    // onstage objects
    public var output:TextArea;
    public var zoomInBtn:Button;
    public var zoomOutBtn:Button;
    public var curPageNs:NumericStepper;

    // class properties
    private var file:File;
    private var htmlViewPort:HTMLLoader;

    // class constructor
    public function ScriptingPDF()
    {
        // test system pdf capability
        if( HTMLLoader.pdfCapability == HTMLPDFCapability.STATUS_OK )
        {
            // register event listener for components
            zoomInBtn.addEventListener( MouseEvent.CLICK, zoomIn );
            zoomOutBtn.addEventListener( MouseEvent.CLICK, zoomOut );
            curPageNs.addEventListener(Event.CHANGE, gotoPage );

            // initiate File instance
            file = File.applicationDirectory.resolvePath(
                    "testPDFScripting.html" );

            // create and position HTMLLoader instance
            htmlViewPort = new HTMLLoader();
            htmlViewPort.width = 600;
            htmlViewPort.height = 400;
            htmlViewPort.x = 10;
            htmlViewPort.y = 60;

            // register event listener for html DOM loader
            htmlViewPort.addEventListener( Event.HTML_DOM_INITIALIZE,
                    htmlLoaded );

            // put html vieport on stage
            addChild( htmlViewPort );

            // creates remote request instance
            var urlReq:URLRequest = new URLRequest( file.url );
            htmlViewPort.load( urlReq );
```

```
        }
        else
        {
            output.appendText( "Impossible Load PDF.PDFCapability " +
                    "value:   " + HTMLLoader.pdfCapability +
                    File.lineEnding );
        }
    }

    private function htmlLoaded( event:Event ):void
    {
        // enable components
        zoomInBtn.enabled = true;
        zoomOutBtn.enabled = true;
        curPageNs.enabled = true;
    }

    private function zoomIn( event:MouseEvent ):void
    {
        try
        {
            var pdfObj:Object =
            htmlViewPort.window.document.getElementById("PDFObj");
            pdfObj.postMessage([ "ZoomIn" ]);
        }
        catch (error:Error)
        {
            output.appendText( "ZoomIn error: " + error.name +
                    File.lineEnding + "Error message: "
                    + error.message + File.lineEnding );
        }
    }

    private function zoomOut( event:MouseEvent ):void
    {
        try
        {
            var pdfObj:Object =
            htmlViewPort.window.document.getElementById("PDFObj");
            pdfObj.postMessage([ "ZoomOut" ]);
        }
        catch (error:Error)
        {
            output.appendText( "ZoomOut error: " + error.name +
                    File.lineEnding + "Error message: "
                    + error.message + File.lineEnding );
        }
    }
```

9

```
        private function gotoPage( event:Event ):void
        {
            try
            {
                var pdfObj:Object =
                htmlViewPort.window.document.getElementById("PDFObj");
                pdfObj.postMessage(
                  [ "GotoPage", curPageNs.value.toString() ]);
            }
            catch (error:Error)
            {
                output.appendText( "GotoPage error: " + error.name +
                        File.lineEnding + "Error message: " +
                        error.message + File.lineEnding );
            }
        }
    }// close class
}// close package
```

The document class of the ScriptingPDF.fla project is complete. Now you have to add the JavaScript code that the PDF file needs and create the HTML testPDFScripting.html document. Let's start by creating the PDF file.

Adding JavaScript code to PDF files

In order to add JavaScript code to a PDF document, you'll have to use Adobe Acrobat Professional. If you don't have this software, you can use the testPDFScripting.pdf file from the folder that contains the source code of the ScriptingPDF.fla project.

Open a PDF document with Acrobat Professional or create a new one. If you create a new one, populate at least nine pages of the document. Select the Advanced ➤ Document Processing ➤ Document JavaScripts menu command, as shown in Figure 9-13. This will open the JavaScript Functions dialog box, where you write myOnMessage in the Script Name field and click the Add button. Then the JavaScript Editor will open, as shown in Figure 9-14.

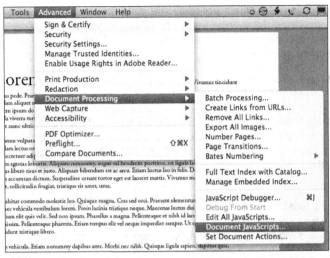

Figure 9-13. Opening the JavaScript Functions dialog in Acrobat Professional

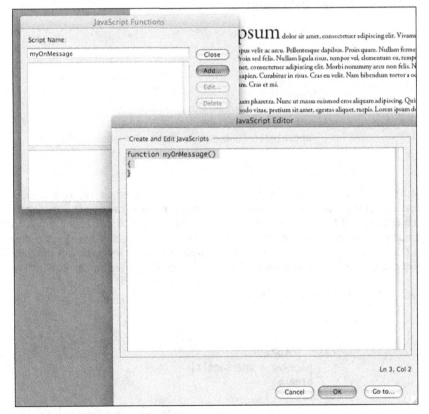

Figure 9-14. The JavaScript Editor

The JavaScript Editor will contain the JavaScript code for the ScriptingPDF.air applica-tion. Start by declaring the myOnMessage() function you will use as an event listener for the messages that come from the postMessage() DOM method. The function receives only one argument, as shown here:

```
function myOnMessage( aMessage )
{
```

In the ActionScript code you created previously, the argument passed to the postMessage() method is an Array object. You check if the received Array object has one or more elements. If it has one element, the method receives a ZoomIn or ZoomOut request. The string the method receives as a first element of the Array object is controlled in a switch construct.

If the string is a ZoomIn or ZoomOut, the zoom applied to the PDF document is doubled or halved. If the string contains a value that the method doesn't recognize, it will generate an error message in a window. The following JavaScript code carries out these operations:

```
if (aMessage.length==1)
{
    switch( aMessage[0] )
    {
        case "ZoomIn":
            zoom *= 2;
            break;
        case "ZoomOut":
            zoom /= 2;
            break;
        default:
            app.alert( "Unknown message: " + aMessage[0] );
    }
}
```

If the Array object contains two elements, it means the method receives a GotoPage request. The string that is received as a first element of the Array object is managed in a switch construct. If the value of the string is GotoPage, the PDF document moves to the page number provided as a second element of the Array object. If the string contains a value that the method doesn't recognize, it generates an error message in a window. The following JavaScript code shows how to change the page displayed by the PDF document:

```
else if ( aMessage.length==2 )
{
    switch( aMessage[0] )
    {
        case "GotoPage":
            pageNum = aMessage[1];
            break;
        default:
            app.alert( "Unknown message: " + aMessage[0] +
```

```
                                    " - " + aMessage[1] );
        }
    }
```

If the Array object is empty, an error message is displayed, as shown here:

```
        else
        {
            app.alert( "Message from hostContainer: \n" + aMessage );
        }
    }
```

To complete the code, you need to create two more functions: myOnDisclose(), which is called when the PDF document receives an onDisclose event, and myOnError(), which returns a true value, as shown here:

```
    function myOnDisclose(cURL,cDocumentURL)
    {
        return true;
    }
```

The myOnError() function is the event listener called when the communication between the HTML environment containing the PDF document and the document itself generates an error. The myOnError() event listener function shows an error message to tell the user that something hasn't worked properly. This is the code for the myOnError() function:

```
    function myOnError(error, aMessage)
    {
        app.alert(error);
    }
```

Now that the necessary event listener functions have been created, you need to make them the property of an object. This object will be associated with the messageHandler property of the hostContainer object exposed by the PDF document. After the declaration of the functions, create an Object instance and assign the event listener functions to it, as shown here:

```
    var msgHandlerObject = new Object();
    msgHandlerObject.onMessage = myOnMessage;
    msgHandlerObject.onError = myOnError;
    msgHandlerObject.onDisclose = myOnDisclose;
```

Finally, assign the object msgHandlerObject to the messageHandler property, as shown here:

```
    this.hostContainer.messageHandler = msgHandlerObject;
```

The JavaScript code is now complete. Confirm the insertion of the JavaScript code by clicking OK on the open window. Save the changes to the PDF document and close Acrobat Professional.

This is the complete JavaScript code:

```javascript
function myOnMessage(aMessage)
{
    if (aMessage.length==1) {
        switch(aMessage[0])
        {
            case "ZoomIn":
                zoom *= 2;
                break;
            case "ZoomOut":
                zoom /= 2;
                break;
            default:
                app.alert("Unknown message: " + aMessage[0]);
        }
    }
    else if (aMessage.length==2) {
        switch(aMessage[0])
        {
            case "GotoPage":
                pageNum = aMessage[1];
                break;
            default:
                app.alert("Unknown message: " + aMessage[0] +
                                " - " + aMessage[1]);
        }
    }
    else
    {
        app.alert("Message from hostContainer: \n" + aMessage);
    }
}

function myOnDisclose(cURL,cDocumentURL)
{
    return true;
}

function myOnError(error, aMessage)
{
    app.alert(error);
}

var msgHandlerObject = new Object();
msgHandlerObject.onMessage = myOnMessage;
msgHandlerObject.onError = myOnError;
msgHandlerObject.onDisclose = myOnDisclose;

this.hostContainer.messageHandler = msgHandlerObject;
```

Now you have to create the HTML document that will import the PDF file you've just created.

Creating an HTML page to show a PDF file

The AIR application that is generated by the ScriptingPDF.fla project loads an HTML file containing a PDF document. You've just learned how to create the PDF document you need, and now you need to create an HTML file that will display the PDF document.

Create a new HTML file and name it testPDFScripting.html. You can create the file with any kind of text editor (e.g., Notepad or WordPad), or with any HTML editor (e.g., Dreamweaver). If you prefer, you can find the complete file in the folder that contains the source code of this chapter.

Now you need to import the testPDFScripting.pdf document in the HTML document. To do so, create an object node to load the PDF file, as shown here:

```html
<html>
    <body>
        <object id="PDFObj"
            data="testPDFScripting.pdf"
            type="application/pdf"
            width="100%" height="100%"/>
    </body>
</html>
```

In the node, you specify that the PDF document's width and height will be set to 100% to make the PDF document occupy the whole space that is available on the HTML page. You can see the open HTML document in a web browser in Figure 9-15.

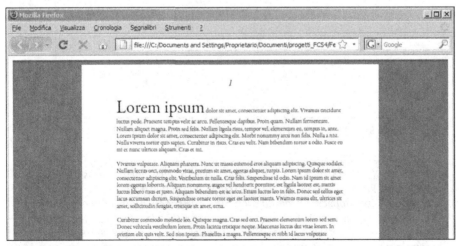

Figure 9-15. The testPDFScripting.html file opened in a web browser

Now you have all the elements you need to make the ScriptingPDF.fla project work.

Testing the ScriptingPDF.fla project

Go back to the Flash CS4 IDE and the project. Select the Test Movie command from the Control menu to compile and start up the AIR application. The AIR application will start up, and if AIR can display PDF documents on your local system, it will load the testPDFScripting. html file. The HTML document will display the testPDFScripting.pdf file. Try interacting with the PDF document by using the controls on the stage of the ScriptingPDF.fla proj- ect. You can see the compiled and started-up ScriptingPDF.fla project in Figure 9-16.

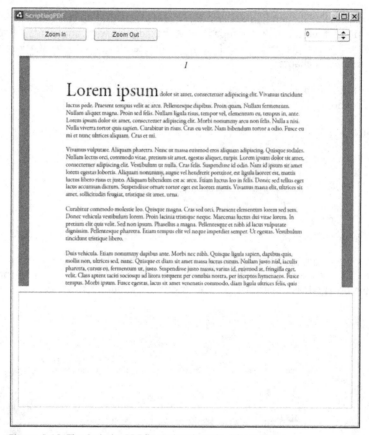

Figure 9-16. The ScriptingPDF.fla project launched from Flash

On Mac OS X systems, generally the default viewer for PDF documents is the Preview application. When you try to access JavaScript code in a PDF document from an AIR application, this application displays an error message. The requested operations will be executed anyway, but only after you confirm the alert. To avoid the problem, you need to set the Adobe Reader viewer as the default viewer for PDF files. If this is a potential situation, you should warn the users of your application about how to pro- ceed to solve the problem.

In the next section, you will see how to load and play video and audio files.

Working with video

An AIR application can import and display as many videos as possible. The limit to the number of videos that can be played is given by the amount of memory available on the operating system. AIR allows you to reproduce video files in these three formats:

- FLV (Flash video format)
- MOV (QuickTime file format)
- MP4 (MPEG-4 video format)

> *The MOV and MP4 formats can only be reproduced if the video track uses the H.264 codec. The FLV format allows you to obtain lightweight files with reasonably good reproduction quality. MOV and MP4 formats using the H.264 codec video provide high-quality videos with an acceptable file weight.*

Loading and playing video files

Follow these steps to load and play a video in an AIR application:

1. Create a new Flash file (Adobe AIR) and name it LoadingVideo.fla.

2. Create a TextArea on the stage and give it the instance name output. If you prefer, you can open the complete LoadingVideo.fla file from the chapter09 folder of the book's source code.

3. Open the Publish Settings panel of the project by selecting the Publish Settings command from the File menu in Flash.

4. Carry out the configuration operations described in the first project in this chapter.

5. Create a new ActionScript file and name it LoadingVideo.as. If you prefer, you can find the complete LoadingVideo.as file in the source code of the project.

6. Go back to the LoadingVideo.fla project and write the complete name of the com.comtaste.foed.essentialair.chapter9.LoadingVideo class in the Class field in the Document Properties panel, as shown in Figure 9-17 (remember to exclude the .as extension).

7. To access the document class associated with the Flash project, click the Edit class definition button next to the Class field. This will open the LoadingVideo.as class in Flash.

9

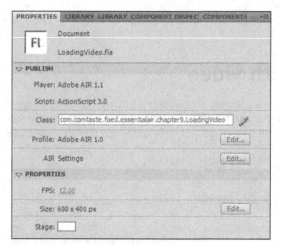

Figure 9-17. Defining the document class of the LoadingVideo.fla project

Creating the document class for the LoadingVideo.fla project

Create a new ActionScript class with Flash CS4. Save it with the name LoadingVideo.as. Write the package declaration of the class and the external classes it depends on in the LoadingVideo.as document, as shown here:

```
package com.comtaste.foed.essentialair.chapter9
{
import fl.controls.Button;
import fl.controls.TextArea;

import flash.display.MovieClip;
import flash.events.Event;
import flash.events.MouseEvent;
import flash.events.NetStatusEvent;
import flash.filesystem.File;
import flash.net.NetConnection;
import flash.net.NetStream;
import flash.media.Video;
```

The following code, which must be entered just after the import declarations, opens the class body. This code also defines the output class property, typed as TextArea, which refers to the TextArea on the stage of the LoadingVideo.fla project:

```
public class LoadingVideo extends MovieClip
{
    // onstage objects
    public var output:TextArea;
```

To access a video stream, you need three objects, for which you need to create three properties: video, typed as Video; netConn, typed as NetConnection; and stream, typed as NetStream—as shown here:

```
// class properties
private var video:Video;
private var netConn:NetConnection;
private var netStream:NetStream;
```

These three objects will allow the application to access video files and play them. They will be initialized in the constructor method of the class. First, you have to initialize the NetConnection object. The following code shows how to instantiate and start up a NetConnection object:

```
// class constructor
public function LoadingVideo()
{
    // init netconnection object
    netConn = new NetConnection();

    // open connection
    netConn.connect(null);
```

Now that you have a NetConnection object, you have to assign it to a NetStream instance. The NetStream class requires that a NetConnection object be passed to the constructor method during the creation of a new instance, as shown here:

```
// init stream object and attach it to netconnection object
netStream = new NetStream( netConn );
```

In ActionScript 3, when you want to manage events generated by a certain object, you register an event listener method for each event you are interested in. This is also valid for the NetStream class. This class, however, will generate some events that can't be registered with the addEventListener() method.

These particular events look for specific methods within the object assigned to the client property of the NetStream instance. Each time one of these events is invoked, it looks for the corresponding callback method in the client object. Assign the reference to the LoadingVideo.as class using the this object to the client property of the NetStream object, as shown here:

```
// set this class as client listener for stream events
netStream.client = this;
```

The following code registers an event listener method for each NET_STATUS event of the NetStream object:

```
// register event listener for NetStatus events
netStream.addEventListener( NetStatusEvent.NET_STATUS,
            netStatusHandler );
```

9

Now you need to create the Video object. The following code creates a new Video instance, places it on the stage, and defines a temporary dimension to use until the video stream is received:

```
// init video object
video = new Video();

// position video object
video.x = 5;
video.y = 140;

// initial fake size
video.width = 400;
video.height = 300;

// put video on stage
addChild(video);
```

The Video object created shows the video stream received by the NetStream object. To allow the reception of the video stream, you have to invoke the attachNetStream() method of the Video object. This method associates the video object with the NetStream instance it has to use, as shown here:

```
// attach video to NetStream object
video.attachNetStream( netStream );
```

The following code starts up the reproduction of the test-video.mp4 file by invoking the play() method of the NetStream object:

```
// launch video reproduction
netStream.play("test-video.mp4");
}
```

In this and the following Flash projects regarding the use of video content, you will always use the test-video.mp4 file. This file is a high-resolution (HD) video encoded in MP4 format; you can find it in the folder that contains the LoadingVideo.fla project in the source code of the book. If you prefer, you can use any video you like, provided that Flash Player and AIR support the format.

> *Flash Player, beginning with the 9.0.115 version, allows you to reproduce compressed videos in formats that derive from the standard MP4. Among these formats are the following: F4V, MP4, M4A, MOV, MP4V, 3GP, and 3G2.*
>
> *Videos in these formats have to contain compressed video using the H.264 video codec and/or compressed audio using the HE-AAC v2 audio codec. These audio and video formats allow you to distribute content in high resolution while keeping the size of the file relatively small.*

This is the complete ActionScript class you created:

```
package com.comtaste.foed.essentialair.chapter9
{
import fl.controls.Button;
import fl.controls.TextArea;

import flash.display.MovieClip;
import flash.events.Event;
import flash.events.MouseEvent;
import flash.events.NetStatusEvent;
import flash.filesystem.File;
import flash.net.NetConnection;
import flash.net.NetStream;
import flash.media.Video;

public class LoadingVideo extends MovieClip
{
    // onstage objects
    public var output:TextArea;

    // class properties
    private var video:Video;
    private var netConn:NetConnection;
    private var netStream:NetStream;

    // class constructor
    public function LoadingVideo()
    {
        // init netconnection object
        netConn = new NetConnection();

        // open connection
        netConn.connect(null);

        // init stream object and attach it to netconnection object
        netStream = new NetStream( netConn );

        // set this class as client listener for stream events
        netStream.client = this;

        // register event listener for NetStatus events
        netStream.addEventListener( NetStatusEvent.NET_STATUS,
                    netStatusHandler );

        // init video object
        video = new Video();

        // position video object
        video.x = 5;
        video.y = 140;
```

```
            // initial fake size
            video.width = 400;
            video.height = 300;

            // put video on stage
            addChild(video);

            // attach video to NetStream object
            video.attachNetStream( netStream );

            // launch video reproduction
            netStream.play("test-video.mp4");
        }
    }// close class
}// close package
```

The NET_STATUS event has been registered on the netStatusHandler() method in the constructor method of the class. This method will be invoked for each NET_STATUS event generated by the NetStream object. The netStatusHandler() method checks if it's an error event and, if it is, it writes the error in the output TextArea. The type of NET_STATUS event is defined by the info.code property of the Event object. The following code corresponds to the whole netStatusHandler() method:

```
        // called for any net status event
        private function netStatusHandler( event:NetStatusEvent ):void
        {
            if( event.info.code == "NetStream.FileStructureInvalid" )
            {
                // if video file is not valid, show message in output
                output.appendText("The video file structure is invalid.");
            }
            else if( event.info.code == "NetStream.NoSupportedTrackFound" )
            {
                // if video file doesn't contain valid video track,
                // show message in output
                output.appendText("The video doesn't contain any " +
                            "supported tracks");
            }
        }
```

Once you've declared the document class (the this object) as the client of the NetStream object, you have to create the onMetaData() method in the class. This method is invoked when Flash Player receives the metadata associated with the video that is being played.

> **Metadata** is the additional information that is associated with a video object. Video metadata provides information such as the size and length of the video.

The methods that can be invoked on the client object of a NetStream instance are the following:

- onMetaData()
- onCuePoint()
- onImageData()
- onPlayStatus()
- onTextData()

These methods are especially used when you reproduce videos that are on streaming servers, such as Flash Media Server and RED5. The onMetaData() method writes a message in the output TextArea to show that the metadata has been received, as shown here:

```
// called when metadata, if available, is received from stream
public function onMetaData( info:Object ):void
{
    output.appendText( "Video Metadata received");
}
```

Now the application is complete and ready to be tested. This is the complete ActionScript class you created:

```
package com.comtaste.foed.essentialair.chapter9
{
import fl.controls.Button;
import fl.controls.TextArea;

import flash.display.MovieClip;
import flash.events.Event;
import flash.events.MouseEvent;
import flash.events.NetStatusEvent;
import flash.filesystem.File;
import flash.net.NetConnection;
import flash.net.NetStream;
import flash.media.Video;

public class LoadingVideo extends MovieClip
{
    // onstage objects
    public var output:TextArea;

    // class properties
    private var video:Video;
    private var netConn:NetConnection;
    private var netStream:NetStream;
```

9

```
// class constructor
public function LoadingVideo()
{
    // init netconnection object
    netConn = new NetConnection();

    // open connection
    netConn.connect(null);

    // init stream object and attach it to netconnection object
    netStream = new NetStream( netConn );

    // set this class as client listener for stream events
    netStream.client = this;

    // register event listener for NetStatus events
    netStream.addEventListener( NetStatusEvent.NET_STATUS,
            netStatusHandler );

    // init video object
    video = new Video();

    // position video object
    video.x = 5;
    video.y = 140;

    // initial fake size
    video.width = 400;
    video.height = 300;

    // put video on stage
    addChild(video);

    // attach video to NetStream object
    video.attachNetStream( netStream );

    // launch video reproduction
    netStream.play("test-video.mp4");
}

// called for any net status event
private function netStatusHandler( event:NetStatusEvent ):void
{
    if( event.info.code == "NetStream.FileStructureInvalid" )
    {
        // if video file is not valid, show message in output
        output.appendText("The MP4's file structure is invalid.");
    }
    else if( event.info.code == "NetStream.NoSupportedTrackFound" )
```

```
        {
            // if video file doesn't contain valid video track,
            // show message in output
            output.appendText("The MP4 doesn't contain " +
                "any supported tracks");
        }
    }

    // called when metadata, if available, is received from stream
    public function onMetaData( info:Object ):void
    {
        output.appendText( "Video Metadata received");
    }

}// close class
}// close package
```

Now that you've completed the document class for the LoadingVideo.fla project, it's time to test it.

Testing the LoadingVideo.fla project

Go back to the LoadingVideo.fla project in Flash. Select the Test Movie command from the Control menu to start up the AIR application. Once it has started, AIR will load the video files you've specified on the stage and start playing the video, as you can see in Figure 9-18.

Figure 9-18. The LoadingVideo.fla project launched from Flash

As you have just seen, it's extremely easy to load and display video content in an AIR application. In the following sections, you'll access video streams using the functions provided by ActionScript 3 and AIR. Flash also offers the FLVPlayback component, which implements some of the techniques discussed in this chapter.

In the next section, you'll extend this application by using the metadata you receive with the video and regulating the volume of the video.

Working with video sound and metadata

From the Flash File menu, select the Save as command to save the LoadingVideo.fla project with a different name. Save the copy with the name LoadingVideoAdvanced.fla. If you prefer, you can open the file from the source code in the chapter09 folder. Figure 9-19 shows what the stage of the LoadingVideoAdvanced.fla project should look like.

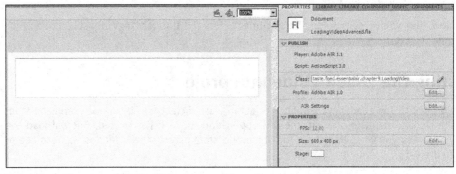

Figure 9-19. The stage of LoadingVideoAdvanced.fla project

It isn't necessary to add new elements on the stage of the project. Click the Edit class definition icon on the Document Properties panel to access the LoadingVideo.as class you created earlier in this chapter. You want to add access to the volume of the video to the application. To do so, you have to import a few new external classes to access the audio functions provided by AIR. Add the import statements as shown here:

```
package com.comtaste.foed.essentialair.chapter9
{
import fl.controls.Button;
import fl.controls.TextArea;

import flash.display.MovieClip;
import flash.display.Stage;
import flash.display.StageDisplayState;
import flash.display.StageAlign;
import flash.display.StageScaleMode;
import flash.events.Event;
import flash.events.MouseEvent;
import flash.events.NetStatusEvent;
import flash.filesystem.File;
```

```
import flash.geom.Rectangle;
import flash.net.URLRequest;
import flash.net.NetConnection;
import flash.net.NetStream;
import flash.media.Video;
import flash.media.SoundTransform;

public class LoadingVideo extends MovieClip
{
```

Setting the video volume

To access the audio track of the video in order to adjust the volume, you have to associate it with a SoundTransform object. The following code shows the addition of the declaration of the audioTrack class property, typed as SoundTransform:

```
public class LoadingVideo extends MovieClip
{
    // onstage objects
    public var output:TextArea;

    // class properties
    private var video:Video;
    private var netConn:NetConnection;
    private var netStream:NetStream;
    private var audioTrack:SoundTransform;
```

In the constructor method, you invoke the play() method of the NetStream object to start the test-video.mp4 video. After the video has been started, you can access the soundTransform property of the NetStream object. The soundTransform property is the SoundTransform object of the audio track of the video you are playing. The SoundTransform object controls the volume of the Sound object. The soundTransform property also controls the output on the right and left speakers for stereo sounds. The volume of an audio track accepts values from 0 to 1, where 0 indicates the absence of volume and 1 is the maximum volume. The following code, inserted at the end of the constructor method, adjusts the volume of the audio track of the video:

```
// attach video to NetStream object
video.attachNetStream( netStream );

// launch video reproduction
netStream.play("test-video.mp4");

// get access to video sound track
audioTrack = netStream.soundTransform;

// set initial audio value for video
audioTrack.volume = .5;

// update audio on video file
netStream.soundTransform = audioTrack;
```

9

The LoadingVideo.fla project loads the video at a fixed size defined in the class. In the LoadingVideoAdvanced.fla project, the video will be displayed at its real size. The real dimensions of the video can be accessed in the metadata of the video.

Accessing video metadata

In the LoadingVideo.fla project, you already learned how it's possible to set a method to be invoked when the metadata of a video in execution is available for the AIR application. This method receives a dynamic object as an argument. The argument contains the metadata information for the video in reproduction. The metadata of a video can contain various kinds of information, including the following:

- Video width and height
- Video an audio codecs
- A cue points list
- Video duration, expressed in seconds

The following code accesses all the information in the metadata in a for...in loop. Every piece of available information is displayed in the output TextArea, as shown here:

```
public function onMetaData( info:Object ):void
{
    // cycle on metadata properties
    for( var propName:String in info )
    {
        output.appendText( propName + " = "
                        + info[propName] + File.lineEnding );
    }
```

Next, assign the original dimensions of the video to the Video object on the stage, as shown here:

```
    // set video to real size
    video.width = info.width;
    video.height = info.height;
}
```

The code added to the onMetaData() method allows the application to display the video at its original dimensions.

This is the complete ActionScript class you created:

```
package com.comtaste.foed.essentialair.chapter9
{
import fl.controls.Button;
import fl.controls.TextArea;

import flash.display.MovieClip;
import flash.display.Stage;
import flash.display.StageDisplayState;
```

```actionscript
import flash.display.StageAlign;
import flash.display.StageScaleMode;
import flash.events.Event;
import flash.events.MouseEvent;
import flash.events.NetStatusEvent;
import flash.filesystem.File;
import flash.geom.Rectangle;
import flash.net.URLRequest;
import flash.net.NetConnection;
import flash.net.NetStream;
import flash.media.Video;
import flash.media.SoundTransform;

public class LoadingVideo extends MovieClip
{
    // onstage objects
    public var output:TextArea;

    // class properties
    private var video:Video;
    private var netConn:NetConnection;
    private var netStream:NetStream;
    private var audioTrack:SoundTransform;

    // class constructor
    public function LoadingVideo()
    {
        // set up scaling rules
        stage.scaleMode = StageScaleMode.NO_SCALE;
        stage.align = StageAlign.TOP_LEFT;

        // init netconnection object
        netConn = new NetConnection();

        // open connection
        netConn.connect(null);

        // init stream object and attach it to netconnection object
        netStream = new NetStream( netConn );

        // set this class as client listener for stream events
        netStream.client = this;

        // register event listener for NetStatus events
        netStream.addEventListener( NetStatusEvent.NET_STATUS,
                    netStatusHandler );

        // init video object
        video = new Video();
```

9

```
        // position video object
        video.x = 20;
        video.y = 140;

        // initial fake size
        video.width = 400;
        video.height = 300;

        // put video on stage
        addChild(video);

        // attach video to NetStream object
        video.attachNetStream( netStream );

        // launch video reproduction
        netStream.play("test-video.mp4");

        // get access to video sound track
        audioTrack = netStream.soundTransform;

        // set initial audio value for video
        audioTrack.volume = .5;

        // update audio on video file
        netStream.soundTransform = audioTrack;
    }

    // called for any net status event
    private function netStatusHandler( event:NetStatusEvent ):void
    {
        if( event.info.code == "NetStream.FileStructureInvalid" )
        {
            // if video file is not valid,show message in output
            output.appendText("The MP4's file structure is invalid.");
        }
        else if( event.info.code == "NetStream.NoSupportedTrackFound" )
        {
            // if video file doesn't contain valid video track,
            // show message in output
            output.appendText("The MP4 doesn't contain " +
                    "any supported tracks");
        }
    }

    // called when metadata, if available, is received from stream
    public function onMetaData( info:Object ):void
    {
        // cycle on metadata properties
        for( var propName:String in info )
```

```
        {
            output.appendText( propName + " = " + info[propName]
                    + File.lineEnding );
        }

        // set video to real size
        video.width = info.width;
        video.height = info.height;
    }

}// close class
}// close package
```

Testing the LoadingVideoAdvanced.fla project

Go back to the LoadingVideoAdvanced.fla project in Flash. Select the Test Movie command from the Control menu to start up the AIR application. Once you've started up the AIR application, it loads the video you've specified on the stage and displays it in its original dimensions. The original dimensions and the other metadata are shown in the output TextArea.

The video in its original size is a lot bigger than the stage of the AIR application and can only be displayed in part. Even if you maximize the window, as shown in Figure 9-20, you can't see the whole video. In the next section, you'll extend the LoadingVideoAdvanced.fla project to show the video in full-screen format.

Figure 9-20. The LoadingVideoAdvanced.fla project launched from Flash, with a maximized window

Showing full-screen videos

Select the Save as command from the Flash File menu to save the LoadingVideoAdvanced. fla project with the name LoadingVideoFullscreen.fla. If you prefer, you can open the complete LoadingVideoFullscreen.fla file from the chapter09 folder of the book's source code.

You want to add a button to allow the user to activate full-screen mode for the video. Place a Button component on the stage and assign it the instance name fullscreenBtn. In Figure 9-21, you can see what the stage of the LoadingVideoFullscreen.fla project should look like.

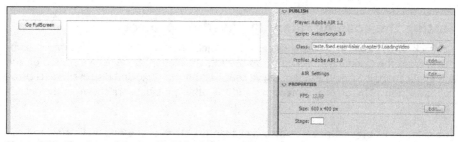

Figure 9-21. The stage of the LoadingVideoFullscreen.fla. project

Click the Edit class definition icon on the Document Properties panel to access the LoadingVideo.as class. Add a new class property, fullscreenBtn, typed as Button, as shown here:

```
// onstage objects
public var output:TextArea;
public var fullscreenBtn:Button;

// class properties
private var video:Video;
private var netConn:NetConnection;
private var netStream:NetStream;
private var audioTrack:SoundTransform;
```

In the constructor method, you need to register an event listener method for the CLICK event of the fullscreenBtn button. The following code registers the CLICK event of the button on the goFullScreenMode() method:

```
// launch video reproduction
netStream.play("test-video.mp4");

// get access to video sound track
audioTrack = netStream.soundTransform;

// set initial audio value for video
audioTrack.volume = .5;
```

```
// update audio on video file
netStream.soundTransform = audioTrack;

// register event listeners for click event
fullscreenBtn.addEventListener( MouseEvent.CLICK,
                goFullScreenMode );
```

The goFullScreenMode() method has the task of displaying the full-screen format of the video. You don't want the whole stage of the application shown in full-screen—only the video. To only show the video, you have to tell AIR which part of the stage you want to show. To do so, create a Rectangle object that displays the coordinates of the video on the stage, as shown here:

```
// invoked when user clicks fullscreenBtn
private function goFullScreenMode( event:MouseEvent ):void
{
    // define video rect on stage
    var scalingRect:Rectangle = new Rectangle(
                video.x, video.y, video.width, video.height );
```

The Rectangle object has to be assigned to the fullScreenRectSource property of the stage to tell AIR which area has to be displayed in full-screen mode, as shown here:

```
// force fullscreen only to video rect
stage.fullScreenSourceRect = scalingRect;
```

Now it's possible to activate full-screen mode for the application. To request full-screen mode, you have to assign the StageDisplayState.FULL_SCREEN value to the displayState property of the stage. This is the code to activate full-screen mode:

```
// toggle fullscreen
stage.displayState = StageDisplayState.FULL_SCREEN;
}
```

This is the complete ActionScript class you created:

```
package com.comtaste.foed.essentialair.chapter9
{
import fl.controls.Button;
import fl.controls.TextArea;

import flash.display.MovieClip;
import flash.display.Stage;
import flash.display.StageDisplayState;
import flash.display.StageAlign;
import flash.display.StageScaleMode;
import flash.events.Event;
import flash.events.MouseEvent;
import flash.events.NetStatusEvent;
import flash.filesystem.File;
import flash.geom.Rectangle;
```

9

465

```
import flash.net.URLRequest;
import flash.net.NetConnection;
import flash.net.NetStream;
import flash.media.Video;
import flash.media.SoundTransform;

public class LoadingVideo extends MovieClip
{
    // onstage objects
    public var output:TextArea;
    public var fullscreenBtn:Button;

    // class properties
    private var video:Video;
    private var netConn:NetConnection;
    private var netStream:NetStream;
    private var audioTrack:SoundTransform;

    // class constructor
    public function LoadingVideo()
    {
        // set up scaling rules
        stage.scaleMode = StageScaleMode.NO_SCALE;
        stage.align = StageAlign.TOP_LEFT;

        // init netconnection object
        netConn = new NetConnection();

        // open connection
        netConn.connect(null);

        // init stream object and attach it to netconnection object
        netStream = new NetStream( netConn );

        // set this class as client listener for stream events
        netStream.client = this;

        // register event listener for NetStatus events
        netStream.addEventListener( NetStatusEvent.NET_STATUS,
                    netStatusHandler );

        // init video object
        video = new Video();

        // position video object
        video.x = 5;
        video.y = 140;
```

```actionscript
        // initial fake size
        video.width = 400;
        video.height = 300;

        // put video on stage
        addChild(video);

        // attach video to NetStream object
        video.attachNetStream( netStream );

        // launch video reproduction
        netStream.play("test-video.mp4");

        // get access to video sound track
        audioTrack = netStream.soundTransform;

        // set initial audio value for video
        audioTrack.volume = .5;

        // update audio on video file
        netStream.soundTransform = audioTrack;

        // register event listeners for click event
        fullscreenBtn.addEventListener( MouseEvent.CLICK,
                        goFullScreenMode );
    }

// called for any net status event
private function netStatusHandler( event:NetStatusEvent ):void
{
    if( event.info.code == "NetStream.FileStructureInvalid" )
    {
        // if video file is not valid, show message in output
        output.appendText("The MP4's file structure is invalid.");
    }
    else if( event.info.code == "NetStream.NoSupportedTrackFound" )
    {
        // if video file doesn't contain valid video track,
        // show message in output
        output.appendText("The MP4 doesn't contain " +
                    "any supported tracks");
    }
}

// called when metadata, if available, is received from stream
public function onMetaData( info:Object ):void
{
    // cycle on metadata properties
    for( var propName:String in info )
```

9

```
                    {
                        output.appendText( propName + " = " + info[propName] +
                                File.lineEnding );
                    }

                    // set video to real size
                    video.width = info.width;
                    video.height = info.height;
                }

                // invoked when user clicks fullscreenBtn
                private function goFullScreenMode( event:MouseEvent ):void
                {
                    // define video rect on stage
                    var scalingRect:Rectangle = new Rectangle(
                                video.x, video.y, video.width, video.height );

                    // force fullscreen only to video rect
                    stage.fullScreenSourceRect = scalingRect;

                    // toggle fullscreen
                    stage.displayState = StageDisplayState.FULL_SCREEN;
                }

        }// close class
        }// close package
```

Now the application is ready to be used in full-screen mode.

Testing the LoadingVideoFullscreen.fla project

Go back to the LoadingVideoFullscreen.fla project in Flash. Select the Test Movie command from the Control menu to start the AIR application. Once you've started the AIR application, load the video file on the stage and display it in its original format. Click the button to show it in full-screen mode. Figure 9-22 shows the LoadingVideoFullscreen. fla project in execution.

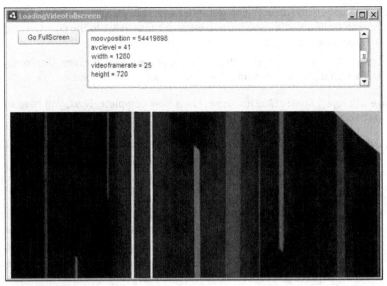

Figure 9-22. The LoadingVideoFullscreen.fla project launched from Flash

Now you know how to display video content in AIR applications. Next, you'll see how to reproduce an MP3 file.

Working with sound

AIR allows you to play back local as well as remote audio files. The only audio format available is the MP3 format. It isn't possible to access other audio formats such as AIFF, WAV, or Ogg Vorbis directly. Using audio files in AIR applications isn't very different from importing and displaying images, videos, and PDFs. In the next section, you'll see how to import and play back an audio file in an AIR application.

Loading and playing audio files

In this section, you'll see how to create an AIR application that can play an audio file and allows you to adjust the volume. Follow these steps to create the project:

1. Create a new Flash file (Adobe AIR) and name it ControlAudioVolume.fla. If you prefer, you can open the complete ControlAudioVolume.fla file from the chapter09 folder of the book's source code. In Figure 9-23, you can see the complete stage for the ControlAudioVolume.fla project.

2. Create a TextArea on the stage and assign it the instance name output.

3. Create two Button objects with instance names playBtn and stopBtn. Both of them have to be disabled, so you have to assign a false value to the enabled property in the Component Inspector.

4. Lastly, create a Slider object with an instance name sliderVolume. Disable the Slider, and assign it 0 as a minimum value and 1 as a maximum value.

The stage of project ControlAudioVolume.fla is now complete. Next, you have to define the project's document class, as shown here:

1. Open the Publish Settings panel of the project by selecting the Publish Settings command from the Flash File menu.

2. Carry out the configuration operations described in the first project in this chapter.

3. Create a new ActionScript file and name it ControlAudioVolume.as. If you prefer, you can find the complete ControlAudioVolume.as file in the source code of the project.

4. Go back to the ControlAudioVolume.fla project and write the complete name of the com.comtaste.foed.essentialair.chapter9.ControlAudioVolume class in the Class field in the Document Properties panel, as shown in Figure 9-23.

5. To access the document class that is associated with the ControlAudioVolume.fla project, click the Edit class definition icon next to the Class field on the Document Properties panel. This will open the ControlAudioVolume.as class in Flash.

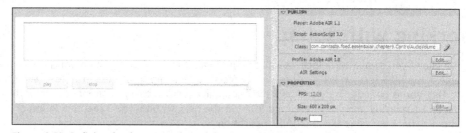

Figure 9-23. Defining the document class of the ControlAudioVolume.fla project

Creating the document class for the ControlAudioVolume.fla project

In the ControlAudioVolume.as file, enter the package declaration of the class and the external classes to import, as shown here:

```
package com.comtaste.foed.essentialair.chapter9
{
import fl.controls.Button;
import fl.controls.TextArea;
import fl.controls.Slider;
```

```
import flash.display.MovieClip;
import flash.events.Event;
import flash.events.IOErrorEvent;
import flash.events.MouseEvent;
import flash.net.URLRequest;
import flash.media.SoundTransform;
import flash.media.Sound;
import flash.media.SoundChannel;
import flash.media.ID3Info;
```

On the stage of the ControlAudioVolume.fla project, there are four components. Create the class properties associated with them: playBtn and stopBtn, typed as Button; output, typed as TextArea; and sliderVolume, typed as Slider.

The following code declares these properties:

```
public class ControlAudioVolume extends MovieClip
{
    // onstage objects
    public var output:TextArea;
    public var stopBtn:Button;
    public var playBtn:Button;
    public var sliderVolume:Slider;
```

AIR uses different channels to play multiple audio files. Each channel is identified with a SoundChannel object. An AIR application can use up to 20 channels at the same time. The imported audio file will be assigned to the class audioFile property, typed as Sound. The SoundChannel object you use to reproduce the file will be associated with the audio property, typed as SoundChannel. The following code declares the two properties used to reproduce audio files:

```
    // class properties
    private var audioFile:Sound;
    private var audio:SoundChannel;
```

The constructor method of the ControlAudioVolume.as class initializes the application and requests the reproduction of an audio file. First, three event listener methods are registered for the three controls on the stage, as shown here:

```
    // class constructor
    public function ControlAudioVolume()
    {
        playBtn.addEventListener( MouseEvent.CLICK, startPlay );
        stopBtn.addEventListener( MouseEvent.CLICK, stopPlay );
        sliderVolume.addEventListener( Event.CHANGE, updateVolume );
```

Then a Sound object is instantiated, and event listener methods are registered to the Sound object for the Event.COMPLETE, Event.ID3, and IOErrorEvent.IO_ERROR events. The following code instantiates the Sound object and registers the necessary event listener methods:

```
audioFile = new Sound();
audioFile.addEventListener( Event.COMPLETE, audioReady );
audioFile.addEventListener( Event.ID3, ID3Received );
audioFile.addEventListener( IOErrorEvent.IO_ERROR,
        audioIOError );
```

Once you've initialized the Sound object, you create a URLRequest object for the audio file to load. The URLRequest object is passed to the load() method of the Sound class, as shown here:

```
var audioURL:URLRequest =
        new URLRequest( "Mozart - Fantasy No. 2.mp3" );
audioFile.load( audioURL );
}
```

You can find the audio file Mozart - Fantasy No. 2.mp3 in the folder containing the ControlAudioVolume.fla project in the source code of the book. If you prefer, you can use another MP3 file. When the requested audio file has been loaded in the application, the audioReady() method is invoked. This method enables the two Button objects and the Slider object on the stage so the user can interact with the application.

This is the code for the audioReady() method:

```
private function audioReady( event:Event ):void
{
    stopBtn.enabled = true;
    playBtn.enabled = true;
    sliderVolume.enabled = true;
}
```

If errors occur during the loading process of the audio file, the audioIOError() method is invoked. The method displays an error message in the output TextArea, as shown here:

```
private function audioIOError( event:Event ):void
{
    output.appendText( "Error accessing Audio file!" );
}
```

In the previous sections, you've seen how a video file can have metadata associated with it, which transports additional information regarding the video. MP3 files can also have metadata, which are known as **ID3 tags**. When the AIR application receives the metadata of the audio file, the ID3Received() method is invoked. This method accesses the ID3Info object in the Event object received as an argument. The ID3Received() method displays the value of some of the metadata from the ID3Info object in the output TextArea, as shown here:

```
private function ID3Received( event:Event ):void
{
    var id3Data:ID3Info = audioFile.id3;
```

```
output.appendText( "ID3 tag received \n" );
output.appendText( "ARTIST: " + id3Data.artist + "\n" );
output.appendText( "SONG NAME: " + id3Data.songName + "\n" );
output.appendText( "ALBUM: " + id3Data.album+ "\n" );
}
```

When the user clicks the playBtn button, the startPlay() method is invoked. The invoked method starts the playback of the audio file and assigns the playback channel to the SoundChannel audio object. This is the code for the startPlay() method:

```
private function startPlay( event:MouseEvent ):void
{
    audio = audioFile.play();
}
```

To interrupt the reproduction of the file, the user clicks the stopBtn button, which invokes the stopPlay() method. The stopPlay() method invokes the stop() method of the SoundChannel class to interrupt the playback, as shown here:

```
private function stopPlay( event:MouseEvent ):void
{
    audio.stop();
}
```

Finally, you define the updateVolume() method, which is invoked every time the user changes the value of the sliderVolume slider on the stage. To change the volume of an audio file, you have to change the value of the volume property of the SoundTransform object. The following code assigns the current value of sliderVolume to the SoundTransform object:

```
function updateVolume( event:Event ):void
{
    var audioVol:SoundTransform = new SoundTransform();
    audioVol.volume = sliderVolume.value;
    audio.soundTransform = audioVol;
}
```

This is the complete ActionScript class you created:

```
package com.comtaste.foed.essentialair.chapter9
{
import fl.controls.Button;
import fl.controls.TextArea;
import fl.controls.Slider;

import flash.display.MovieClip;
import flash.events.Event;
import flash.events.IOErrorEvent;
import flash.events.MouseEvent;
import flash.net.URLRequest;
import flash.media.SoundTransform;
```

```
import flash.media.Sound;
import flash.media.SoundChannel;
import flash.media.ID3Info;

public class ControlAudioVolume extends MovieClip
{
    // onstage objects
    public var output:TextArea;
    public var stopBtn:Button;
    public var playBtn:Button;
    public var sliderVolume:Slider;

    // class properties
    private var audioFile:Sound;
    private var audio:SoundChannel;

    // class constructor
    public function ControlAudioVolume()
    {
        playBtn.addEventListener( MouseEvent.CLICK, startPlay );
        stopBtn.addEventListener( MouseEvent.CLICK, stopPlay );

        sliderVolume.addEventListener( Event.CHANGE, updateVolume );

        audioFile = new Sound();
        audioFile.addEventListener( Event.COMPLETE, audioReady );
        audioFile.addEventListener( Event.ID3, ID3Received );
        audioFile.addEventListener( IOErrorEvent.IO_ERROR,
                audioIOError );

        var audioURL:URLRequest =
                new URLRequest( "Mozart - Fantasy No. 2.mp3" );
        audioFile.load( audioURL );
    }

    private function audioReady( event:Event ):void
    {
        stopBtn.enabled = true;
        playBtn.enabled = true;
        sliderVolume.enabled = true;
    }

    private function ID3Received( event:Event ):void
    {
        var id3Data:ID3Info = audioFile.id3;
        var songName:String = id3Data.songName;
        var artist:String = id3Data.artist;
```

```
        output.appendText( "ID3 tag received \n" );
        output.appendText( "ARTIST: " + id3Data.artist + "\n" );
        output.appendText( "SONG NAME: " + id3Data.songName + "\n" );
        output.appendText( "ALBUM: " + id3Data.album+ "\n" );
    }

    private function audioIOError( event:Event ):void
    {
        output.appendText( "Error accessing Audio file!" );
    }

    private function startPlay( event:MouseEvent ):void
    {
        audio = audioFile.play();
    }

    private function stopPlay( event:MouseEvent ):void
    {
        audio.stop();
    }

    function updateVolume( event:Event ):void
    {
        var audioVol:SoundTransform = new SoundTransform();
        audioVol.volume = sliderVolume.value;
        audio.soundTransform = audioVol;
    }

}// close class
}// close package
```

Now the document class of the `ControlAudioVolume.fla` project is complete.

Testing the ControlAudioVolume.fla project

Go back to the project in Flash. Select the Test Movie command from the Control menu to start the AIR application. If the audio file is loaded correctly, the components on the stage will be enabled. You can see the ControlAudioVolume.fla project in execution in Figure 9-24.

9

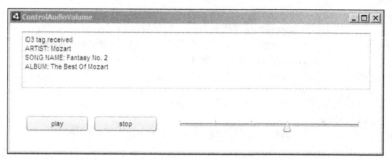

Figure 9-24. The ControlAudioVolume.fla project launched from Flash

Click the play button to start playing the file. Once the file is playing, try using the slider to change the volume of the file. Be careful not to use it before the file starts playing; otherwise, AIR will generate an error.

Summary

This chapter introduced AIR's capabilities for handling PDF documents, importing and displaying video files, and importing and playing back audio files.

These capabilities allow you to obtain a high level of integration between the application interface and displayed documents. The purpose of these features is to improve the user experience, making AIR applications more attractive and innovative.

CHAPTER 10

WORKING WITH HTML CONTENT

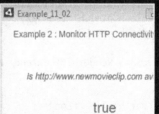

At this point in the book, you've already explored many of the features of Adobe AIR. And those of you who are Flash developers that create web applications have already begun to appreciate the APIs that allow you to interact with the host system. As if this wasn't enough, Adobe has embedded a proper HTML engine in AIR to load HTML content into desktop applications.

AIR includes the WebKit engine (www.webkit.org/), the same engine used for the Safari browser; Google Chrome; and the Nokia browser on mobile devices, S60 (www.s60.com/). Having an HTML engine means you can parse, lay out, and render HTML as well as JavaScript content in your AIR applications. But that's not all; AIR treats HTML content like a display object and, like all display objects in ActionScript 3, it can be manipulated via code by applying effects such as blurring, masking, and so on.

AIR represents HTML content in the HTMLLoader class in the flash.html package. This object is contained in turn in a NativeWindow object.

This chapter will illustrate the AIR functions that use the HTML engine to load, display, and interact with HTML content. We'll begin with an example that uses the HTMLLoader object.

Using the HTMLLoader object

The HTMLLoader class manages the content you need to load and display web pages, which can be directly loaded by a URL, or assigned to the object as a string. In fact, there are two different methods the HTMLLoader object can use: load() and loadString(). The first method, load(), is assigned to a URLRequest object, which contains the URL resource to render. The second method, loadString(), accepts HTML content typed as String.

Here is an example that loads a web page using the HTMLLoader object:

```
package com.comtaste.foed.essentialair.chapter10
{
import flash.display.MovieClip;
import flash.html.HTMLLoader;
import flash.net.URLRequest;

public class RenderHTML extends MovieClip
{

public var html:HTMLLoader;

public function RenderHTML()
{
    html = new HTMLLoader()
    html.width = 800;
    html.height = 600;
    var urlReq:URLRequest = new URLRequest➥
("http://www.comtaste.com/en" );
```

```
    html.load( urlReq );
    addChild(html);
}
}
}
```

The RenderHTML class creates all the code you need to obtain the final result in the constructor to render the HTML page from the URL http://www.comtaste.com.

The public html property creates an instance of the HTMLLoader class and uses the load() method to load the content. The parameter that is assigned to the load() method is the urlReq local variable, typed as URLRequest.

The HTMLLoader object is a Display object that exposes the width and height properties, which have to be set in order to make it visible. In fact, the default dimensions of an HTMLLoader are 0 X 0 pixels.

In the following example, you'll see how to load HTML content with the loadString() method, which is programmatically assigned to the HTML code that has to be rendered. This is the loadString() method syntax:

```
loadString(htmlContent:String):void
```

The only difference compared to the load() method is in the parameter that the method accepts: a string. Here is an ActionScript class that loads HTML content with an HTML string:

```
package com.comtaste.foed.essentialair.chapter10
{
import flash.display.MovieClip;
import flash.html.HTMLLoader;
import flash.net.URLRequest;

public class RenderHTML extends MovieClip
{

public var html:HTMLLoader;

public function RenderHTML()
{
    html = new HTMLLoader()
    html.width = 800;
    html.height = 600;
    var htmlContent:String = "<html>
        <body><p>Hello World!</p>
        </body></html>";
    html.loadString ( htmlContent );
    addChild(html);
}
}
}
```

10

481

The HTMLLoader object renders the string Hello World! with the loadString() method, as shown here:

```
var htmlContent:String = "<html>
    <body><p>Hello World!</p>
    </body></html>";
html.loadString ( htmlContent );
```

The HTMLLoader object inherits many methods that can be used to create transitions or particular effects on the HTML content. For example, it is possible to change the alpha property to operate on the transparency of HTMLLoader's content, or to apply graphic filters on the HTML display (such as a blur effect). These operations require particular care, as they may make the text content illegible.

Once you understand how to use the methods of the HTMLLoader object to load HTML content, you can create the first Flash project that displays the content in an AIR application.

Unlike the ActionScript classes you've created so far, this new class uses the addChild() method to display the HTML content loaded by the HTMLLoader object in the application.

Open Flash CS4 and create a new ActionScript class, and save it as RenderComplexHTML.as. The class is created in the following folder structure: com/comtaste/foed/essentialair/ chapter10. You have to create the com/ folder from the root of the project, where you have saved the Flash file.

Enter the following ActionScript code:

```
package com.comtaste.foed.essentialair.chapter10
{
import flash.display.MovieClip;
import flash.display.NativeWindowInitOptions;
import flash.display.SimpleButton;
import flash.display.Sprite;
import flash.display.StageAlign;
import flash.display.StageScaleMode;
import flash.events.MouseEvent;
import flash.geom.Rectangle;
import flash.html.HTMLLoader;
import flash.net.URLRequest;
import fl.controls.TextArea;

public class RenderComplexHTML extends MovieClip
{
public function RenderComplexHTML ()
{
this.stage.scaleMode = StageScaleMode.NO_SCALE;
this.stage.align = StageAlign.TOP_LEFT;

initLayout();
}
```

```
public var html:HTMLLoader;
public var textInput:TextArea;
public var loadURL:SimpleButton;

protected function initLayout():void
{
// draw HTML container
html = new HTMLLoader();
html.width = 400;
html.height = 300;
html.x = 50;
html.y = 30;
this.addChild( html );

loadURL.addEventListener(MouseEvent.CLICK, loadHTMLcontents);

textInput.text =
"<html>"+"\n"
+"<head>"+"\n"
+"<style>"+"\n"
+"table.myTable{"+"\n"
+ "border-collapse:collapse;"+"\n"
+ "font-size:10pt;"+"\n"
+ "background-color:#808080;"+"\n"
+ "width:350px;"+"\n"
+ "border-style:solid;"+"\n"
+ "border-color:black;"+"\n"
+ "border-width:2px;"+"\n"
  +"}"+"\n"

+"th.myTable{"+"\n"
 +"font-size:10pt;"+"\n"
 +"color:white;"+"\n"
 + "}"+"\n"

+"td.myTable{"+"\n"
+ "font-size:10pt;"+"\n"
+ "background-color:#409040;"+"\n"
+ "color:white;"+"\n"
+ "border-style:solid;"+"\n"
+ "border-width:1px;"+"\n"
+ "text-align:center;"+"\n"
  + "}"+"\n"
+"</style>"+"\n"
+"</head>"+"\n"
+"<body>"+"\n"
+"<h1>HTML header</h1><table class='myTable'>"+"\n"
+"<tr>"+"\n"
+"<th class='myTable'>Column 1</th>"+"\n"
+"<th class='myTable'>Column 2</th>"+"\n"
```

10

```
+"</tr>"+"\n"
+"<tr>"+"\n"
+"<td class='myTable'>row 1</td>"+"\n"
+"<td class='myTable'>row 1</td>"+"\n"
+"</tr>"+"\n"
+"<tr>"+"\n"
+"<td class='myTable'>row 2</td>"+"\n"
+"<td class='myTable'>row 2</td>"+"\n"
+"</tr>"+"\n"
+"<tr>"+"\n"
+"<td class='myTable'>row 3</td>"+"\n"
+"<td class='myTable'>row 3</td>"+"\n"
+"</tr>"+"\n"
+"</table>"+"\n"
+"</body>"+"\n"
+"</html>";


}


protected function loadHTMLcontents( event:MouseEvent ):void
{
// load HTML contents from textAreaContent
if( textInput.text == "" )
return;

html.loadString( textInput.text );
}


}
}
```

The RenderComplexHTML class uses the loadString() method of the object to load the HTML content, which is a table. The rows and columns of the table are formatted with CSS code in the style tag. The whole HTML code is displayed in a TextArea component, textInput. This way, the HTML code can be changed in real time.

The HTML code isn't loaded in the HTMLLoader object until you click the loadURL button. In the initLayout() method, you create the following event listener associated with the loadHTMLcontents method:

```
loadURL.addEventListener(MouseEvent.CLICK, loadHTMLcontents);
```

The loadString() method will be invoked and the HTML content will be loaded in the loadHTMLcontents() event handler, as you can see here:

```
protected function loadHTMLcontents( event:MouseEvent ):void
{
// load HTML contents from textAreaContent
if( textInput.text == "" )
return;
```

```
html.loadString( textInput.text );
}
```

Note that the HTMLLoader class will be instantiated in the initLayout() method, launched by the constructor of the class. The instance of the object also includes specifications on the width, height, and X,Y position. Finally, the instance has to be added to the display object to be displayed. This is why you use this method.

In the following code, a new instance of the HTMLLoader class is created:

```
html = new HTMLLoader();
html.width = 400;
html.height = 300;
html.x = 50;
html.y = 30;
this.addChild( html );
```

This ActionScript class can now be associated with a Flash document as a document class, as follows:

1. Create a Flash AIR project and save it.

2. Open the document class you've just created and associated with the Flash project by selecting the Edit class definition icon in the Document Properties panel.

3. Create the following elements on the stage by dragging the components from the Components panel:

   ■ A TextArea component

   ■ A Button component

4. Assign the following instance names to the components added to the stage:

   ■ textInput for the TextArea component

   ■ loadURL for the Button component

5. Test the AIR application by compiling the file.

The SimpleButton ActionScript class allows you to control all instances of button symbols in a SWF file. After you create an instance of a button within the Flash IDE, you can use the methods and properties of the SimpleButton class to manipulate buttons with ActionScript. Read more information from the official documentation, at http://livedocs.adobe.com/flash/9.0/ActionScriptLangRefV3/flash/display/SimpleButton.html.

Caching content

When HTML content is loaded in the HTMLLoader object, AIR caches content locally. This means that the first time HTML content is loaded, its content (images, CSS, JavaScript, etc.) is saved locally, and every time it is requested again, it is loaded from the cache (unless it's out of date).

10

This shouldn't surprise you that much because it's exactly the same thing that applies to web browsers when you're on the Web. This approach allows you to optimize HTTP calls and enhance the user experience by cutting down on waiting time.

In AIR, you can choose whether to use cached content or request the web page all over again. The HTMLLoader class exposes the two following properties, which allow you to control how AIR loads the HTML content:

- useCache: This Boolean property specifies whether the local cache should be consulted before HTTP requests issued by this object fetch data. The default value is initialized from URLRequestDefaults.useCache.

- cacheResponse: This Boolean property specifies whether successful response data should be cached for HTTP requests issued by this object. When set to true, the HTMLLoader object uses the operating system's HTTP cache. The default value is initialized from URLRequestDefaults.cacheResponse.

To force AIR not to cache the HTML content, the cacheResponse property has to be set to false before invoking the load() method, like in the following example:

```
package com.comtaste.foed.essentialair.chapter10
{
import flash.display.MovieClip;
import flash.html.HTMLLoader;
import flash.net.URLRequest;

public class RenderHTML extends MovieClip
{

public var html:HTMLLoader;

public function RenderHTML()
{
   html = new HTMLLoader()
   html.width = 800;
   html.height = 600;
   var urlReq:URLRequest = new URLRequest➥
("http://www.comtaste.com/en" );

   html.cacheResponse = false;

   html.load( urlReq );

}
}
}
```

To force AIR not to use the content that has previously been saved locally in the cache, you have to set the useCache property to false, like in the following example:

```
package com.comtaste.foed.essentialair.chapter10
{
import flash.display.MovieClip;
import flash.html.HTMLLoader;
import flash.net.URLRequest;

public class RenderHTML extends MovieClip
{

public var html:HTMLLoader;

public function RenderHTML()
{
   html = new HTMLLoader()
   html.width = 800;
   html.height = 600;
   var urlReq:URLRequest = new URLRequest➡
("http://www.comtaste.com/en" );

   html.useCache = false;

   html.load( urlReq );

}
}
}
```

The default value of both properties (useCache and cacheResponse) is true.

Autoscrolling HTML content

When HTML content is loaded, it is often necessary to give the user the option to scroll the content. In fact, when an HTMLLoader object is created and a web page is loaded with the load() method, the content is loaded in the object. But if its dimensions aren't the same width and height of its content, the user won't have a scrollbar.

Most of the time, it's impossible for the developer to be aware of the exact dimensions of the page he wants to load. With ActionScript 3, you can programmatically scroll the content of an HTMLLoader using the scrollH and scrollV properties of the ScrollBar class.

Horizontal and vertical scrolling with scrollH and scrollV

The following example creates an ActionScript class that loads an HTML web page with the HTMLLoader objects and has horizontal and vertical scrollbars:

```
package com.comtaste.foed.essentialair.chapter10
{
import flash.display.MovieClip;
import flash.html.HTMLLoader;
```

```
import flash.net.URLRequest;
import fl.controls.ScrollBar;
import flash.events.Event;

public class ScrollHTML extends MovieClip
{

private var html:HTMLLoader;
private var scrollBarHor:ScrollBar;
private var scrollBarVer:ScrollBar;

public function ScrollHTML()
{

scrollBarHor = new ScrollBar();
scrollBarHor.direction = "horizontal";
scrollBarHor.width = stage.stageWidth - 50;
scrollBarHor.x = 0;
scrollBarHor.y = stage.stageHeight - 50;
scrollBarHor.addEventListener (Event.SCROLL, scrollHorHandler);

addChild(scrollBarHor)

scrollBarVer  = new ScrollBar();
scrollBarVer.direction = "vertical";
scrollBarVer.height = stage.stageHeight - 50;
scrollBarVer.x = stage.stageWidth - 50;
scrollBarVer.y = 0;
scrollBarVer.addEventListener (Event.SCROLL, scrollVerHandler);

addChild(scrollBarVer);


html = new HTMLLoader();
html.width = stage.stageWidth - 50;
html.height = stage.stageHeight - 50;

html.addEventListener(Event.COMPLETE, completeHandler);

html.addEventListener(Event.SCROLL, scrollHandler);

var urlReq:URLRequest = new URLRequest("http://www.comtaste.com/en" );
html.load( urlReq );

addChild(html);

}
```

```
    private function completeHandler(event:Event):void
    {
        html.scrollH = 0;
        html.scrollV = 0;
        // Set scrollbar properties
        scrollBarHor.setScrollProperties(
                            html.width,
                            0,
                html.contentWidth - html.width);

     scrollBarVer.setScrollProperties(html.height,
                                    0,
         html.contentHeight - html.height);


    }

    private function scrollVerHandler(event:Event):void
    {
        html.scrollV = scrollBarVer.scrollPosition;
    }

    private function scrollHorHandler(event:Event):void
    {
        html.scrollH = scrollBarHor.scrollPosition;
    }

    private function scrollHandler(event:Event):void
    {
    // Update scrollbars
    scrollBarVer.scrollPosition =    html.scrollV;

    scrollBarHor.scrollPosition =    html.scrollH;

    }

    }
    }
```

You create the instances of the ScrollBar class to manage the horizontal and vertical scrollbars in the class constructor:

```
    scrollBarHor = new ScrollBar();
    scrollBarHor.direction = "horizontal";
    scrollBarHor.width = stage.stageWidth - 50;
    scrollBarHor.x = 0;
    scrollBarHor.y = stage.stageHeight - 50;
    scrollBarHor.addEventListener(Event.SCROLL, scrollHorHandler);

    addChild(scrollBarHor)
```

10

```
scrollBarVer  = new ScrollBar();
scrollBarVer.direction = "vertical";
scrollBarVer.height = stage.stageHeight - 50;
scrollBarVer.x = stage.stageWidth - 50;
scrollBarVer.y = 0;
scrollBarVer.addEventListener (Event.SCROLL, scrollVerHandler);

addChild(scrollBarVer);
```

> A ScrollBar *must be added to the library of the Flash file.*

Then you create an event handler for the horizontal scrollbar and another for the vertical scrollbar, which are triggered every time the Event.SCROLL event is raised. The scrolling of the HTML content is carried out in these two event handlers:

```
private function scrollVerHandler(event:Event):void
{
    html.scrollV = scrollBarVer.scrollPosition;
}

private function scrollHorHandler(event:Event):void
{
    html.scrollH = scrollBarHor.scrollPosition;
}
```

Managing the scrollbars with createRootWindow

The HTMLLoader object has a method that manages the horizontal and vertical scrollbars automatically: createRootWindow().

This static method creates a new NativeWindow object that contains an HTMLLoader object. You use the HTMLLoader object that is returned by this method to load HTML content. Finally, the method returns a new HTMLLoader object that is on the stage of the new NativeWindow object.

> See Chapters 1 and 5 for discussions of the NativeWindow *class.*

The createRootWindow() method accepts the following optional parameters that you can use to change the properties of the new window:

- visible: Boolean (defaults to true); specifies whether the window is visible.

- windowInitOptions: NativeWindowInitOptions (defaults to null); specifies window initialization options; if null, uses default NativeWindowInitOptions values.

- scrollBarsVisible: Boolean (defaults to true); specifies whether the window provides scrollbars.

- bounds: Rectangle (defaults to null); if not null, specifies the window boundaries. If any of x, y, width, or height is NaN (not a number), the corresponding dimensions of the window are left at their default values.

The following example uses the createRootWindow() method to load HTML content:

```
package com.comtaste.foed.essentialair.chapter10
{
import flash.display.MovieClip;
import flash.display.NativeWindowInitOptions;
import flash.display.SimpleButton;
import flash.display.Sprite;
import flash.display.StageAlign;
import flash.display.StageScaleMode;
import flash.events.MouseEvent;
import flash.geom.Rectangle;
import flash.html.HTMLLoader;
import flash.net.URLRequest;
import flash.text.TextField;
import flash.text.TextFieldAutoSize;
import flash.text.TextFieldType;
import flash.text.TextFormat;
import flash.text.TextFormatAlign;

public class AutoScrollHTML extends MovieClip
{

public var html:HTMLLoader;
public var textInput:TextField;
public var loadURL:SimpleButton;

public function AutoScrollHTML()
{
this.stage.scaleMode = StageScaleMode.NO_SCALE;
this.stage.align = StageAlign.TOP_LEFT;

initLayout();
}


protected function initLayout():void
{
loadURL.addEventListener(MouseEvent.CLICK, loadHTMLcontents);
}

protected function loadHTMLcontents( event:MouseEvent ):void
{
var urlReq:URLRequest;
```

10

```
                // load HTML contents from Web
                if( textInput.text == "" )
                {
                urlReq = new URLRequest( "http://www.comtaste.com/en");

                } else {

                urlReq = new URLRequest( textInput.text );

                }

                // prepare HTML container to be shown in a new native window
                var initOptions:NativeWindowInitOptions =
                        new NativeWindowInitOptions();
                var bounds:Rectangle = new Rectangle(50, 30, 500, 400);

                // init visible, windows options, show scrollbars, bounding box
                html = HTMLLoader.createRootWindow(false, initOptions, true, bounds);
                html.stage.nativeWindow.activate();

                var urlReq:URLRequest = new URLRequest( textInput.text );
                html.load( urlReq );
                }
                }
                }
```

In the event handler loadHTMLcontents(), which is called when the user clicks the button with the instance name loadURL, the createRootWindow() method is invoked. The following parameters are assigned to the method with these values:

```
                html = HTMLLoader.createRootWindow(false,
                initOptions,
                true,
                bounds);
```

Here are some brief comments on the values assigned to the parameters:

- visible = false: This sets the window to be invisible.
- windowInitOptions = initOptions: This value is typed as NativeWindowInitOptions, and allows you to initialize the window options.
- scrollBarsVisible = true: This provides the scrollbars for the window.
- bounds = bounds: This value is typed as Rectangle, and represents the area and the position where the window will be created.

The NativeWindowInitOptions and Rectangle values are created in the same event handler, loadHTMLcontents, which is highlighted in bold in the following code:

```
protected function loadHTMLcontents( event:MouseEvent ):void
{
// load HTML contents from Web
if( textInput.text == "" )
var urlReq:URLRequest = new URLRequest( "http://www.comtaste.com/en");

// prepare HTML container to be shown in a new native window
var initOptions:NativeWindowInitOptions =
new NativeWindowInitOptions();
var bounds:Rectangle = new Rectangle(50, 30, 500, 400);

// init visible, windows options, show scrollbars, bounding box
html = HTMLLoader.createRootWindow(false, initOptions, true, bounds);
html.stage.nativeWindow.activate();

var urlReq:URLRequest = new URLRequest( textInput.text );
html.load( urlReq );
}
```

This ActionScript class uses the createRootWindow() method, which automatically creates the scrolling function of the HTML content.

The next section illustrates a technique for making ActionScript objects available to JavaScript and vice versa.

Accessing ActionScript from JavaScript

The HTMLLoader doesn't render HTML and JavaScript content as static content. AIR allows for communication between JavaScript and ActionScript by invoking functions from the AIR application (ActionScript) to JavaScript functions that are loaded in the HTMLLoader object. Conversely, ActionScript can access functions and variables from JavaScript.

For example, save the following HTML page as testJS.htm. You can use any text editor to create it. This example uses Dreamweaver CS4 to make the code easier to write.

The HTML page will then be loaded in an AIR application using the HTMLLoader object.

Here is the HTML code for the testJS.htm page:

```
<!DOCTYPE html PUBLIC "-//W3C//DTD
HTML 4.01//EN"
"http://www.w3.org/TR/html4/strict.dtd">
<html>
<script>
var messageFromAir = "Not Defined";
function showMessageFromAir()
{
    alert( messageFromAir );
```

```
    }
    </script>
    <body>
    <h2>Show an alert message displaying
    an Actionscript generated strings</h2>
    <button onClick="showMessageFromAir()">
    Which message comes from Adobe AIR ?
    </button>

    <h2>Send a trace action into Adobe AIR
    output console from Javascript</h2>
    <p><button onClick="linkedToAIR(
    'This is a javascript generated string.')">
    Call Adobe Air function.
    </button></p>
    </body>
    </html>
```

This is a pretty simple HTML page, made up of two headers and two buttons. The first button, on the onClick event, invokes a JavaScript function, which is declared in the page within the script tag, as shown here:

```
    <script>
    var messageFromAir = "Not Defined";
    function showMessageFromAir()
    {
        alert( messageFromAir );
    }
    </script>

    <button onClick="showMessageFromAir()">
    Which message comes from Adobe AIR ?
    </button>
```

The showMessageFromAir() function simply executes an alert to which it assigns the messageFromAir variable. This variable is initially set to the value Not Defined. This variable will use a value that is passed by the ActionScript code.

The second button invokes an ActionScript function on the onClick event, like this:

```
    <h2>Send a trace action into Adobe AIR
     output console from Javascript</h2>
    <p><button onClick="linkedToAIR(
    'This is a javascript generated string.')">
    Call Adobe Air function.
    </button></p>
```

The linkedToAIR() function isn't declared in JavaScript in the HTML page, but will be an ActionScript method in the class you will create later in this chapter.

Now open Flash and create a new ActionScript class. Save it as CrossScripting.as, with the same path as the other classes you've saved in this book (com.comtaste.foed. essentialair.chapter10).

Insert the following ActionScript code in the class:

```
package com.comtaste.foed.essentialair.chapter10
{
import flash.display.MovieClip;
import flash.display.NativeWindowInitOptions;

import flash.display.Sprite;
import flash.display.StageAlign;
import flash.display.StageScaleMode;
import flash.events.Event;
import flash.events.MouseEvent;
import flash.geom.Rectangle;
import flash.html.HTMLLoader;
import flash.net.URLRequest;


public class CrossScripting extends MovieClip
{
public var html:HTMLLoader;


public function CrossScripting()
{
this.stage.scaleMode = StageScaleMode.NO_SCALE;
this.stage.align = StageAlign.TOP_LEFT;

initLayout();

var urlReq:URLRequest = new URLRequest( "testJS.htm" );
html.load( urlReq );
}


protected function initLayout():void
{
// draw HTML container
html = new HTMLLoader();
html.width = 400;
html.height = 350;
html.x = 50;
html.y = 10;
html.addEventListener(Event.COMPLETE, htmlLoaded);
this.addChild( html );
}
```

10

```
    private function htmlLoaded(e:Event):void
    {
        html.window.messageFromAir =
        "Attention, this is an Actionscript
         generated Alert String!!";
        html.window.linkedToAIR = linkedToJS;
    }

    private function linkedToJS( messageFromJS:String ):void
    {
        trace( "JavaScript says:", messageFromJS );
    }
    }
    }
```

Next, you create the instance of the HTMLLoader object in the constructor of the class and you load the testJS.htm page with the load() method. Then you create an event listener (htmlLoaded) that is triggered as soon as the content of the HTMLLoader object has been completely loaded:

```
    var urlReq:URLRequest = new URLRequest( "testJS.htm" );
    html.load( urlReq );
    html.addEventListener(Event.COMPLETE, htmlLoaded);
```

Once the HTML content has been loaded in an HTMLLoader object, you can access the entire content through the window property of the HTMLLoader object. The window property, typed as Object, contains the global JavaScript object for the content loaded into the HTML control. The window property provides AIR with the same content that the JavaScript window property provides to an HTML page.

So, by accessing this property, you can access JavaScript variables and functions through ActionScript. The htmlLoaded() event handler accesses the messageFromAir variable, declared in the JavaScript code in the testJS.htm page, through the window property, as shown here:

```
    private function htmlLoaded(event:Event):void
    {
        html.window.messageFromAir =
        "Attention, this is an Actionscript
         generated Alert String!!";
        html.window.linkedToAIR = linkedToJS;
    }
```

The messageFromAir variable is in the testJS.htm page you created. This variable is assigned as a parameter to the showMessageFromAir function in the following script block:

```
    <script>
    var messageFromAir = "Not Defined";
    function showMessageFromAir()
    {
```

```
    alert( messageFromAir );
  }
</script>
```

The JavaScript linkedToAIR() function is mapped to an ActionScript method in the ActionScript class, in the htmlLoaded() event handler, with the following syntax:

```
html.window.linkedToAIR = linkedToJS;
```

Then the linkedToJS() method is declared in the ActionScript class and executes a simple trace:

```
private function linkedToJS( messageFromJS:String ):void
{
    trace( "JavaScript says:", messageFromJS );
}
```

In this ActionScript class, you've been able to experiment with the approaches used to make ActionScript communicate with JavaScript code declared in the HTML content loaded by the HTMLLoader class.

To test the class, you can create a Flash AIR project and specify the ActionScript class you've just created as a document class. To access the document class associated with a Flash project, click the Edit class definition icon next to the Class field. The class, which is now only an empty document, will open in Flash. Run the file to test the AIR application.

Having access to the entire content of the page from ActionScript makes it possible to interact with the DOM of the HTML page. This will be the topic of the next section.

Interacting with the HTML DOM from ActionScript

10

The DOM (Document Object Model) is a standard whose specifications have been produced by the W3C. Way back in October 1998, DOM 1 was born, an object model to represent XML, HTML, and related formats. Through JavaScript, you can access and edit an HTML page dynamically using the DOM.

In AIR, the document property for the HTMLLoader class provides access to the whole DOM of the loaded HTML page. The DOM functions and properties that will be mainly used to access and edit DOM elements are the following:

- getElementsByTagName (tag name)
- getElementById (element ID)
- innerText
- innerHTML

getElementsByTagName accepts a string that specifies the tag name to search for, and getElementById accepts a string that specifies the ID of the element.

To see which DOM classes are contained in the WebKit engine, there is a complete list available at the following URL: http://developer.apple.com/documentation/ AppleApplications/Reference/WebKitDOMRef/index.html.

> *For more information about the methods and properties just listed, have a look at* http://webkit.org/docs/a00024.html#2bd21fcb647c704cf308e40f19f0903b.

Create a new HTML page using Dreamweaver CS4 or your favorite HTML editor. Save the page as testDOM.htm. Insert the following HTML code:

```html
<!DOCTYPE html
PUBLIC "-//W3C//DTD HTML 4.01//EN"
"http://www.w3.org/TR/html4/strict.dtd">
<html>
<style>
.button1{
background-color: #ffff00;
font-size: 12px;
}
.button2{
color: #ff0000;
}
</style>
    <script>
var defaultString =
"This text can be updated from
Actionscript via DOM scripting";

function dummy()
{
    return "It's me JavaScript";
}

function resetJSString()
{
document.getElementById("editableContent").innerHTML =
                defaultString;
}
    </script>

<body>

<h2 id="editableContent" style="color:#00ff00;">
This text can be updated from Actionscript via DOM scripting
</h2>
```

```
<button onClick="updateJSString()" class="button1">
        Update string via AS3
        </button>

<button onClick="resetJSString()" class="button2">
        Reset String via JS
        </button>

    </body>

</html>
```

The page only contains two buttons and an h2 header. The two buttons invoke two functions on the click event, and the h2 tag sets the ID to editableContent. You can try accessing the elements of the page using the document property or the window property of the HTMLLoader object.

The HTMLLoader object is in the following ActionScript code. The HTMLLoader object loads the testDOM.htm page. Once the COMPLETE event of the HTMLLoader fires, it is possible to access the DOM elements, variables, and functions of the loaded HTML page in the event handler.

> Before the complete event of the HTMLLoader is dispatched, the HTML content loaded by the HTMLLoader object may not have been parsed or created. That's why it is a best practice to wait for the complete event to be dispatched before accessing the HTML DOM.

Here is the ActionScript code that accesses the DOM element in the completeHandler() event handler using the getElementById() method:

```
var html:HTMLLoader = new HTMLLoader();
html.width = 300;
html.height = 300;

html.addEventListener(Event.COMPLETE, completeHandler);
html.load("testDOM.htm");

function completeHandler(e:Event):void
  {
    // It returns "This text can be updated from
    //  Actionscript via DOM scripting"
     trace(html.window. defaultString);

    // You get "This text can be updated
    // from Actionscript via DOM scripting"
    trace(html.window.document.getElementById(
            "editableContent").innerHTML);

   trace(html.window.dummy()); // Returns "It's me JavaScript"
  }
```

The code to analyze is completely contained in the completeHandler() event handler declared in the previous code. There are three traces, which respectively return the following:

- trace(html.window.defaultString): This returns the string This text can be updated from ActionScript via DOM scripting.
- trace(html.window.document.getElementById("editableContent"). innerHTML): This returns a string that contains the HTML within the editableContent DOM element.
- trace(html.window.dummy()): This returns the string It's me JavaScript.

Please note that, whereas you use the window property of the HTMLLoader object to access variables and functions declared in JavaScript, you use html.window.document to access the DOM elements.

The window property is typed as Object precisely because you can create a reference to complex data types like functions, as well as assign it simple data types.

Creating the AIR project to access the HTML DOM

Now that you're familiar with how to access the DOM elements, variables, and functions of the HTML page loaded by the HTMLLoader object, you can go a bit further and create an AIR project that summarizes the concepts illustrated up to now.

Open Flash and create an ActionScript class, which you save as AccessDOM.as. You can use the same package you've used until now in the other examples: com.comtaste.foed. essentialair.chapter10.

Enter the following ActionScript code in the class:

```
package com.comtaste.foed.essentialair.chapter10
{
import flash.display.MovieClip;
import flash.display.NativeWindowInitOptions;
import flash.display.SimpleButton;
import flash.display.Sprite;
import flash.display.StageAlign;
import flash.display.StageScaleMode;
import flash.events.Event;
import flash.events.MouseEvent;
import flash.geom.Rectangle;
import flash.html.HTMLLoader;
import flash.net.URLRequest;
import fl.controls.TextArea;

public class AccessDOM extends MovieClip
{
public var html:HTMLLoader;
public var textInput:TextArea;
public var loadURL:SimpleButton;
```

```
//Our access to the HTML DOM
private var domWindow:Object;

public function AccessDOM()
{
this.stage.scaleMode = StageScaleMode.NO_SCALE;
this.stage.align = StageAlign.TOP_LEFT;

initLayout();

var urlReq:URLRequest = new URLRequest( "testDOM.htm" );
html.load( urlReq );
}


protected function initLayout():void
{
// draw HTML container
html = new HTMLLoader();
html.width = 460;
html.height = 320;
html.x = 19.35;
html.y = 10;
html.addEventListener(Event.COMPLETE, completeDOMHandler);
this.addChild( html );

textInput.text = "User generated text to use inside HTML tag";

loadURL.addEventListener(MouseEvent.CLICK, updateJSString);
}


private function completeDOMHandler(e:Event):void
{
//Retrieve reference to HTML DOM loaded
domWindow = ( e.target as HTMLLoader ).window;

// overrides default message
domWindow.defaultString = "Attention, this is an
                           Actionscript generated String,
                           that overrides original content
 form JS!!";
// map js function call to as function
domWindow.updateJSString = updateJSString;

// define custom text color for h1 text
domWindow.document.getElementById(
                   "editableContent").style.color =
                   "#990000";
```

```
        // access to CSS style declaration
        var styleSheet0:Object = domWindow.document.styleSheets[0];

        // CSS class '.button1', modify existing properties
        styleSheet0.cssRules[0].style.backgroundColor = "#00ff00";
        styleSheet0.cssRules[0].style.fontSize = "20px";

        // CSS class '.button2', add new prop
        styleSheet0.cssRules[1].style.textDecoration = "underline";
        }

        // set default value to NULL for event object to permit
        // calls from JavaScript
        private function updateJSString( event:MouseEvent=null ):void
        {
        domWindow.document.getElementById(
                        "editableContent").innerHTML =
                        textInput.text;
        }


        }
        }
```

The class creates the instance of the HTMLLoader object and loads the testDOM.htm page with the load() method in the constructor of the class:

```
        var urlReq:URLRequest = new URLRequest( "testDOM.htm" );
        html.load( urlReq );
```

The interesting part of the code for this purpose is contained in the completeDOMHandler event handler, which is invoked on the COMPLETE event of the HTMLLoader:

```
        html.addEventListener(Event.COMPLETE, completeDOMHandler);
```

By accessing the DOM elements in the event listener on the COMPLETE event, you can be sure all the elements have been parsed or created.

The event handler starts by setting the domWindow local property, which contains the reference to the loaded HTML DOM:

```
        domWindow = ( e.target as HTMLLoader ).window;
```

You will use this property to access the elements of the HTML content. Then you overwrite the defaultString variable declared in JavaScript in the HTML page. Finally, you map the call to the JavaScript function with this ActionScript method:

```
        domWindow.defaultString = "Attention, this is an
        Actionscript generated String, that overrides original
        content from JS!!";

        domWindow.updateJSString = updateJSString;
```

The updateJSString method, which is launched at the click of the button created in the HTML page, accesses the h2 tag with the getElementById through its ID. Then it overwrites the text in the innerHTML property with the text the user inserts in the textInput control created in ActionScript:

```
private function updateJSString( event:MouseEvent=null ):void
{
domWindow.document.getElementById(
                    "editableContent").innerHTML =
                    textInput.text;
}
```

When the user clicks the button in the HTML page embedded in the AIR application, the text in the h2 header will be replaced with the text contained in the textInput control.

The event handler concludes with the programmatic creation through CSS ActionScript code. You can access CSS by treating the styleSheets array like a DOM element of the HTML page:

```
// define custom text color for h1 text
domWindow.document.getElementById(
                    "editableContent").style.color =
                    "#990000";

// access to CSS style declaration
var styleSheet0:Object = domWindow.document.styleSheets[0];

// CSS class '.button1', modify existing props
styleSheet0.cssRules[0].style.backgroundColor = "#00ff00";
styleSheet0.cssRules[0].style.fontSize = "20px";

// CSS class '.button2', add new prop
styleSheet0.cssRules[1].style.textDecoration = "underline";
```

To test the class, you can create an AIR project in Flash and specify the ActionScript class you've just created as the document class. To set the document class associated with a Flash project, click the Edit class definition icon next to the Class field. The class, which is now only an empty document, will open in Flash. Run the file to test the AIR application.

Registering JavaScript events from ActionScript

Before concluding the discussion of interaction with the DOM elements, it's important at least to mention the possibility of registering a JavaScript event from ActionScript. There are two different approaches to creating an event listener on a JavaScript event.

The simplest one assigns a function reference to the event handler attribute. This technique is shown in the following example, which adds the function reference in the completeDOMHandler() event handler of the ActionScript class created in this section:

```
private function completeDOMHandler(e:Event):void
{
 ....... cut code
domWindow.document.getElementById(
                "editableContent").onclick =
                onClickHandler;
}
```

The preceding code associates the onClickHandler event handler with the onclick event of the DOM element with the same ID as editableContent (in this testDOM.htm page, it's the <H2> tag).

Once the event listener is created, you can add it to the ActionScript class:

```
private function onClickHandler( event:Object=null ):void
{
domWindow.document.getElementById(
                "editableContent").innerHTML =
                "The H2 tag has been clicked and
 the ActionScript event handler has
 been called" ;
}
```

The second approach to creating an event listener on a JavaScript event uses the addEventListener() method. With this method, it's possible to create event listeners in ActionScript that react to JavaScript events.

Take the following example, which adds the addEventListener() method in the completeDOMHandler() event handler of the ActionScript class:

```
private function completeDOMHandler(e:Event):void
{
 ....... cut code
domWindow.document.getElementById(
"editableContent").addEventListener("click",
                                onClickHandler);
 }
```

There aren't any fundamental differences between the two approaches. It's probably easier for an ActionScript developer to use the addEventListener() method to register the events, whereas a JavaScript developer may be more comfortable with the approach that uses the reference function associated with the event.

In the next section, you'll learn how to provide your users with some of the most classic web browser features when browsing web pages: the HTML history list and the back and forward buttons.

Accessing HTML history

Web navigation practically works on the one-click, one-page concept. However, technologies like Ajax, Flash, and Flex are changing this tendency. The classic web user is accustomed to using the back and forward buttons of the web browser to move between the pages she has visited. For an AIR application that uses HTML content, it is therefore crucial to access the HTML history list to provide the user with the same capabilities that are normally available on a web browser.

Accessing and navigating the history list

The HTMLLoader object offers the historyLength property to get the length of the history list. Furthermore, the HTMLLoader object uses the HTMLHistoryItem objects to access the HTML history list. The HTMLHistoryItem class has the following properties:

- isPost: a Boolean that returns true or false and specifies whether or not the HTML page includes POST data.
- originalUrl: a String that contains the original URL of the HTML page
- title: a String that contains the title of the HTML page.
- url: a String that returns the URL of the HTML page.

To navigate within the history list, you use the following methods of the HTMLLoader class:

- historyBack(): Navigates back in the browser history
- historyForward(): Navigates forward in the browser history
- historyGo(): Navigates the indicated number of steps in the browser history

None of these methods throw errors.

Navigating backward and forward

This section will present an example that allows the user to navigate backward and forward by accessing the history list of an HTMLLoader object. Follow these steps to get started:

1. Open Flash CS4.
2. Create a new ActionScript project.
3. Save it as NavigateHistoryList.as, in the same folder as the other classes you've created so far: com\comtaste\foed\essentialair\chapter10.

Enter the following code in the class:

```
package com.comtaste.foed.essentialair.chapter10
{
import flash.display.MovieClip;
```

10

```
import flash.display.NativeWindowInitOptions;
import flash.display.SimpleButton;
import flash.display.Sprite;
import flash.display.StageAlign;
import flash.display.StageScaleMode;
import flash.events.Event;
import flash.events.MouseEvent;
import flash.geom.Rectangle;
import flash.html.HTMLHistoryItem;
import flash.html.HTMLLoader;
import flash.net.URLRequest;
import fl.controls.TextArea;
import fl.controls.List;
import fl.data.DataProvider;

public class Application extends MovieClip
{

public var html:HTMLLoader;
public var backBtn:SimpleButton;
public var ffBtn:SimpleButton;
public var pastHistory:List;
public var nextHistory:List;

private var currHistoryPos:int = -1;
private var pastDataProvider:Array;
private var nextDataProvider:Array;


public function Application()
{
this.stage.scaleMode = StageScaleMode.NO_SCALE;
this.stage.align = StageAlign.TOP_LEFT;

initLayout();

// prepare HTML container to be shown in a new native window
var initOptions:NativeWindowInitOptions =
      new NativeWindowInitOptions();
var bounds:Rectangle = new Rectangle(50, 30, 500, 400);
// init visible, windows options, show scrollbars, bounding box
html = HTMLLoader.createRootWindow(false, initOptions, true, bounds);
html.stage.nativeWindow.activate();

var urlReq:URLRequest = new URLRequest( "http://www.comtaste.com/en" );
html.addEventListener(Event.COMPLETE, completeHandler);
html.load( urlReq );
}
```

```
protected function initLayout():void
{
pastHistory.addEventListener(Event.CHANGE, historyJump);
nextHistory.addEventListener(Event.CHANGE, historyJump);

backBtn.addEventListener(MouseEvent.CLICK, historyStepBack);
ffBtn.addEventListener(MouseEvent.CLICK, historyStepAdvance);
}


private function completeHandler(e:Event):void
{
html.addEventListener(Event.HTML_RENDER, htmlLocationChanged);
}


private function htmlLocationChanged(e:Event):void
{
// current history position
currHistoryPos = html.historyPosition;

// reset history navigation data providers
pastDataProvider = new Array();
nextDataProvider = new Array();

var temHistoryItem:HTMLHistoryItem;

// regenerate PAST history list
for( var i:int = 0; i < currHistoryPos+1; i++ )
{
temHistoryItem = html.getHistoryAt( i );
pastDataProvider.push( temHistoryItem );
//trace( "past history item[" +i+"]" + temHistoryItem.title );
}
// update data provider
pastHistory.dataProvider = new DataProvider( pastDataProvider );
// define field to use as label
pastHistory.labelField = "title";
// disable icon field to avoid runtime errors
pastHistory.iconField = null;

// regenerate NEXT history list
for( i = currHistoryPos+1; i < html.historyLength; i++ )
{
temHistoryItem = html.getHistoryAt( i );
nextDataProvider.push( temHistoryItem );
//trace( "next history item[" +i+"]" + temHistoryItem.title );
}
// update data provider
```

10

```
nextHistory.dataProvider = new DataProvider( nextDataProvider );
// define field to use as label
nextHistory.labelField = "title";
// disable icon field to avoid runtime errors
nextHistory.iconField = null;

}


private function historyStepBack(e:MouseEvent):void
{
html.historyBack();
}
private function historyStepAdvance(e:MouseEvent):void
{
html.historyForward();
}

private function historyJump(e:Event):void
{
var target:List = e.target as List;
var targetDP:DataProvider = target.dataProvider;

// calculate navigation offset to cover
var index:int = targetDP.length - 1 - target.selectedIndex;
if( e.target == pastHistory )
index = -index;

// jump to desired page
html.historyGo( index );

}
}
}
```

This class controls the two instances of the button symbols created in the FLA file to navigate in the history list (backBtn and ffBtn). The user of the application can navigate in the HTMLLoader and the pages will be displayed in two List components. Each time the user selects one of the items shown in the List components, the historyGo() method will load the web page selected by the user.

Next, create the instance of the HTMLLoader object in the constructor of the class, and then register the COMPLETE event on the completeHandler event handler:

```
private function completeHandler(e:Event):void
{
html.addEventListener(Event.HTML_RENDER, htmlLocationChanged);
}
```

In this event handler, you create another event listener that responds to the HTML_RENDER event of the HTMLLoader object. This event is dispatched when the rendering of content in the HTMLLoader object is completed, and is used to get information when new content is displayed when a user clicks a link or JavaScript in the page renders HTML.

The htmlLocationChanged event handler contains the management of the history list, which keeps track of the user's navigation by updating the data provider.

To populate the pastDataProvider and nextDataProvider properties, you use the for loop construct. It navigates through the history list with the historyPosition property, the current position in the history list, and the getHistoryAt() method. Once you've populated the two properties used as DataProviders, they are passed to the List control that displays the history list to the user, as you can see in the following code:

```
private function htmlLocationChanged(e:Event):void
{
// current history position
currHistoryPos = html.historyPosition;

// reset history navigation data providers
pastDataProvider = new Array();
nextDataProvider = new Array();

var temHistoryItem:HTMLHistoryItem;

// regenerate PAST history list
for( var i:int = 0; i < currHistoryPos+1; i++ )
{
    temHistoryItem = html.getHistoryAt( i );
    pastDataProvider.push( temHistoryItem );
    //trace( "past history item[" +i+"]" + temHistoryItem.title );
}
// update data provider
pastHistory.dataProvider = new DataProvider( pastDataProvider );
// define field to use as label
pastHistory.labelField = "title";
// disable icon field to avoid runtime errors
pastHistory.iconField = null;

// regenerate NEXT history list
for( i = currHistoryPos+1; i < html.historyLength; i++ )
{
    temHistoryItem = html.getHistoryAt( i );
    nextDataProvider.push( temHistoryItem );
    //trace( "next history item[" +i+"]" + temHistoryItem.title );
}
// update data provider
nextHistory.dataProvider = new DataProvider( nextDataProvider );
// define field to use as label
nextHistory.labelField = "title";
```

10

```
// disable icon field to avoid runtime errors
nextHistory.iconField = null;

}
```

In the constructor, you also launch the initLayout() method, which has the sole task of registering the CLICK events of the buttons and the CHANGE event of the List components:

```
protected function initLayout():void
{
pastHistory.addEventListener(Event.CHANGE, historyJump);
nextHistory.addEventListener(Event.CHANGE, historyJump);

backBtn.addEventListener(MouseEvent.CLICK, historyStepBack);
ffBtn.addEventListener(MouseEvent.CLICK, historyStepAdvance);
}
```

The event handlers associated with the CLICK event of the buttons allow the user to navigate backward and forward in the history list. The historyBack() and historyForward() methods of the HTMLLoader object are used:

```
private function historyStepBack(e:MouseEvent):void
{
html.historyBack();
}
private function historyStepAdvance(e:MouseEvent):void
{
html.historyForward();
}
```

Only one event handler is associated with each List component, which uses the historyGo() method to navigate to the page the user selects in the component:

```
private function historyJump(e:Event):void
{
var target:List = e.target as List;
var targetDP:DataProvider = target.dataProvider;

// calculate navigation offset to cover
var index:int = targetDP.length - 1 - target.selectedIndex;
if( e.target == pastHistory )
index = -index;

// jump to desired page
html.historyGo( index );

}
```

Now you can test the class. Create an AIR project in Flash, and specify the ActionScript class you've just created as a document class. Set the document class that is associated with a Flash project by clicking the Edit class definition icon next to the Class field. The class, which is now only an empty document, will open in Flash. Run the file to test the AIR application.

Limitations of the HTML engine used by AIR

There are some limitations that you need to be aware of when you use HTML content in an AIR application. While AIR uses a powerful HTML and JavaScript engine, you can't consider this support as a proper browser with all its active functions. Several JavaScript functions and HTML and CSS declarations aren't supported by AIR. For example, the use of the eval() method is restricted, the JavaScript window object print() method isn't supported, the Scalable Vector Graphics (SVG) format isn't supported, and the CSS opacity property isn't supported.

You should definitely consider the support of the plug-ins that AIR provides. As you have already seen in Chapter 9, AIR allows you to open PDF files using the Adobe Reader plug-in if Acrobat or Adobe Reader 8.1 or a more recent version is installed. The HTMLLoader allows you to check whether a user's system can display PDFs through the pdfCapability property.

AIR also provides the possibility of loading SWF files in HTMLLoader objects through the Flash Player plug-in. Adobe Reader and Flash Player are the only two plug-ins that are supported by the WebKit plug-in in AIR. You won't be able to load, for instance, QuickTime movies that are embedded in a web page. Streaming video that uses Real Player technology is also unavailable in AIR. However, AIR does support the streaming of FLV files with Flash Player.

> For a list of features that the AIR WebKit engine supports, consult the AIR documentation at the following URL: http://livedocs.adobe.com/air/1/devappsflash/AboutHTMLEnvironment_3.html#1042199.

In the next section, you will be introduced to the security model that AIR uses to avoid malicious code being executed on the client's machine.

Understanding the security model in AIR

HTML content is loaded by AIR in two different sandboxes:

- **The application sandbox**: Content loaded from the application directory goes into this sandbox, which has the highest level of privilege.
- **The nonapplication sandbox**: Content that's loaded from a web server and that otherwise isn't loaded from the application directory uses this sandbox.

Depending on the sandbox used, there are different ways to prevent dishonest users from loading malicious JavaScript code. For example, the eval(), innerHTML(), and outerHTML()

10

methods can't be used if they are in the application sandbox. However, JavaScript can access all the AIR APIs in this sandbox (and therefore gain full access to the file system). On the other hand, JavaScript can't access the AIR APIs in the nonapplication sandbox, but it can, for example, access the eval(), innerHTML(), and outerHTML() methods. This guarantees adequate security for users who will install and use the AIR application.

A simple technique called **sandbox bridging** allows you to overcome these limitations by loading a host HTML page into an iframe tag. Because the two HTML pages (the host page and the one loaded into the iFrame) are loaded in two different sandboxes (application and nonapplication), these HTML pages will be able to communicate with one another.

The following example illustrates how to apply this technique. This HTML page, saved as testSandBox01.html in the application directory of the AIR application, contains the following code:

```html
<!DOCTYPE html
PUBLIC "-//W3C//DTD HTML 4.01//EN"
"http://www.w3.org/TR/html4/strict.dtd">
<html>
<script>
var messageFromAir = "Not Defined";
var childInterface;
var bridgeInterface = {};

function showMessageFromAir()
{
    alert( messageFromAir );
}

function engageBridge()
{
// map properties and function to bridge object
bridgeInterface.testProperty = "Property sandbox-bridge enabled";
bridgeInterface.messageFromAir = messageFromAir;
bridgeInterface.showMessageFromAir = showMessageFromAir;

// link mapped interfaces to child property "parentSandboxBridge"
document.getElementById(
"sandbox").contentWindow.parentSandboxBridge =
                        bridgeInterface;
}
</script>

<body style="background-color:#0000cc;">
<center>

<iframe id="sandbox"
style="background-color:#cccccc;color:#330000;margin-top:50px;"
src="http://www.example.com/air/testSandBox01Child.html"
documentRoot="app:/"
```

```
sandboxRoot="http://www.example.com/air/"
ondominitialize="engageBridge()"/>



</center>
</body>
</html>
```

This page will access all the AIR APIs once you load it. The page finishes initializing the DOM of the iFrame when the ondominitialize event is triggered. Then the engageBridge() function is called. In this function, you create the object that will act as a bridge and assign this bridge to the parentSandboxBridge variable within the iFrame content. You also add the reference to some properties and functions of the bridge object, as shown here:

```
function engageBridge()
{
// map properties and function to bridge object
bridgeInterface.testProperty = "Property sandbox-bridge enabled";
bridgeInterface.messageFromAir = messageFromAir;
bridgeInterface.showMessageFromAir = showMessageFromAir;

// link mapped interfaces to child property "parentSandboxBridge"
document.getElementById(
"sandbox").contentWindow.parentSandboxBridge =
                                            bridgeInterface;

}
```

This is the content of the remote HTML page loaded by the iFrame http://www.example. com/air/testSandBox01Child.html:

```
<!DOCTYPE html
PUBLIC "-//W3C//DTD HTML 4.01//EN"
"http://www.w3.org/TR/html4/strict.dtd">
<html>
    <body>

<h2>Show an alert message displaying
an Actionscript generated string,
called via sandbox cross scripting</h2>

<button onClick="window.parentSandboxBridge.showMessageFromAir()">

Which message comes from Adobe AIR ?

</button>

</body>
</html>
```

10

The content of the remote page will be able to access the showMessageFromAir() function contained in its parent, meaning the testSandBox01.html page. When the user clicks the button, the bridge will call the function, through the parentSandboxBridge, and will have full access to the AIR APIs.

It is possible to call properties and functions from the iFrame content to the parent using the childSandboxBridge variable. The childSandboxBridge property allows the child document to expose an interface to content in the parent document by setting it to a function or object in the child document.

Finally, this is the ActionScript class that you can use to test the sandbox-bridging technique with AIR:

```
package com.comtaste.foed.essentialair.chapter10
{
import flash.display.MovieClip;
import flash.display.NativeWindowInitOptions;
import flash.display.SimpleButton;
import flash.display.Sprite;
import flash.display.StageAlign;
import flash.display.StageScaleMode;
import flash.events.Event;
import flash.events.MouseEvent;
import flash.geom.Rectangle;
import flash.html.HTMLLoader;
import flash.net.URLRequest;
import fl.controls.TextArea;

public class SandboxBridging extends MovieClip
{
public var html:HTMLLoader;


public function SandboxBridging()
{
this.stage.scaleMode = StageScaleMode.NO_SCALE;
this.stage.align = StageAlign.TOP_LEFT;

initLayout();

var urlReq:URLRequest = new URLRequest( "testSandBox01.html" );
html.load( urlReq );
}


protected function initLayout():void
{
// draw HTML container
html = new HTMLLoader();
html.width = 400;
```

```
    html.height = 350;
    html.x = 50;
    html.y = 10;
    html.addEventListener(Event.COMPLETE, htmlLoaded);
    this.addChild( html );
    }


    private function htmlLoaded(e:Event):void
    {
        html.window.messageFromAir =
        "Attention, this is an Actionscript
         generated Alert String!!";
        html.window.linkedToAIR = linkedToJS;
    }

    private function linkedToJS( messageFromJS:String ):void
    {
        trace( "JavaScript says:", messageFromJS );
    }


    }
    }
```

The sandbox-bridging technique is simple. However, my recommendation is to use it very carefully to avoid distributing a potentially dangerous and damaging application to your users.

Summary

In this chapter, you've learned how to load, render, and interact with HTML and JavaScript content in AIR applications using the HTMLLoader class. This class allows you to manage the content you need to load and display web pages, which can be directly loaded by a URL or assigned to the object as a string.

Using some of the HTMLLoader properties, you've learned how to cache content and control how AIR loads the HTML content.

The HTMLLoader doesn't render HTML and JavaScript content as static content. AIR allows for communication between JavaScript and ActionScript by invoking functions from the AIR application (ActionScript) to JavaScript functions that are loaded in the HTMLLoader object. Moreover, you've learned that the HTMLLoader class makes it possible to access the whole DOM of the loaded HTML page, as well as the HTML history list.

Finally, you created some examples where JavaScript and ActionScript interacted using the sandbox-bridging technique.

CHAPTER 11

MONITORING NETWORK
CONNECTIVITY

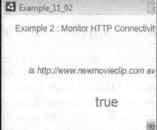

Specify the domain name you want

jetlag.com

Domain Name: JETLAG.COM
Registrar: TUCOWS INC.
Whois Server: whois.tucows.com
Referral URL: http://domainhelp.ope
Name Server: NS1.HOSTCENTRIC
Name Server: NS2.HOSTCENTRIC
Status: ok
Updated Date: 10-sep-2008
Creation Date: 26-sep-1995

In this chapter, you will learn how to monitor network connectivity from within your AIR application. **Network connectivity** is the physical (wired or wireless) connection to a computer network, like the Internet or an office network. Monitoring your network connection comes in very handy when you are using online resources in your AIR application, like an XML file, images, or a web service. AIR applications react differently depending on whether or not a network connection is available.

Suppose that you are building an application that lets you manipulate images by changing their brightness or contrast. When you are connected to the Internet, your application can save your final altered image to an online server. However, when you are disconnected from the Internet (e.g., when you are on a plane), you can save your image locally and upload it to the server when an Internet connection becomes available. This way, your application can easily function online or offline.

Another useful implementation of online/offline connectivity might be a blogging application that allows the user to make changes to their account and content while offline, and syncs the data online when the connection returns. Another might be a shopping application that lets the user order items offline. Then, when an Internet connection becomes available, the ordered items are sent to the server. These applications that are designed to work in both online and offline mode are sometimes called **occasionally connected clients**.

This chapter will tell you how to determine if your application is connected to the Internet. You will also learn to use the Service Monitoring Framework to test connections. Let's start by discussing how you can detect a network connectivity change.

Detecting network connectivity changes

When you design an occasionally connected AIR application, you need a way of monitoring the network connectivity. If a network connection is lost while an application is running, you want to be able to detect that change in order to make the application responses consequently. Lets have a look at how AIR handles this.

How AIR handles network connectivity changes

Writing an application that functions seamlessly both online and offline requires that you be able to detect whether you have a connection. But what is a connection? A **connection** allows the exchange of information between two or more devices. Today, every computer has several kinds of network connections—for example, 3G wireless connections (which allow your computer to talk to a 3G wireless device), virtual networks, virtual private networks (VPNs) (which allow you to connect to your office network securely), and so on. Any of these computer connections can change—for example, the wireless Internet connector might be turned off (as shown in Figure 11-1), the network cable might get plugged in, or the VPN connection might be closed. As a result of these changes, the application's NativeApplication object will dispatch a network change event (Event.NETWORK_CHANGE).

Figure 11-1. Example of network connections that may be available on a PC running Windows Vista

Next, let's build a basic example that alerts you when the network changes (see Figure 11-2).

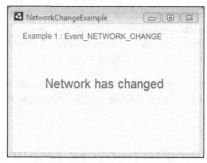

Figure 11-2. Basic AIR application that tells the user that the network has changed

The first thing you need to do is add a dynamic text field on the stage of a new Flash document. In the Document Properties panel, give the text field the instance name statusTextField. You will use this text field to show a message when the network has changed. Also in the Document Properties panel, you link the following document class to the FLA file: com.comtaste.foed.essentialair.chapter11.NetworkChangeExample.

The ActionScript code inside the NetworkChangeExample class looks like this:

```
package com.comtaste.foed.essentialair.chapter11{

import flash.display.*;
import flash.events.*;
import flash.desktop.*;

public class NetworkChangeExample extends MovieClip{
```

```
        public function NetworkChangeExample():void
    {

        NativeApplication.nativeApplication.addEventListener(
        Event.NETWORK_CHANGE,networkChangeHandler);
    }

    private function networkChangeHandler(event:Event):void
    {
        statusTextField.text = "Network has changed";
    }
    }
    }
```

As you see in the preceding code, inside the constructor of your NetworkChangeExample class you define an Event.NETWORK_CHANGE event listener to the application's NativeApplication object. The networkChangeHandler function is executed when the network has changed.

Keep in mind that when the Event.NETWORK_CHANGE event is dispatched, it only alerts you as to whether one of your network connections (of one of your network interfaces) has changed. In other words, there may still be an Ethernet connection to the outside world. So you would not know whether an online resource was available or not. A good way to architect your occasionally connected AIR application is first to listen for a notification of a change in your network connections and then to check if the resource is available or not. If not, then the application has to go in offline mode.

To find out whether the AIR application absolutely has no connection, you need to test if a specific resource is available using the Service Monitoring Framework, which I'll discuss next.

Checking connections to network resources

The Service Monitoring Framework is separate from the AIR framework. It resides in the file servicemonitor.swc.

If you want to use the framework, the servicemonitor.swc file must be included in your build process. You can find the servicemonitor.swc file in the AIK/frameworks/libs/air directory of the Flash CS4 installation directory. You will add the servicemonitor.swc file to the library path of your FLA file. To do so, follow these steps:

1. Go to File ➤ Publish Settings.
2. Choose the Flash tab, and click the Settings button to the right of the ActionScript Version field to open the Advanced ActionScript 3.0 Settings window.
3. Choose the Library Path tab and click the Browse to SWC file button.
4. Browse to the AIK/frameworks/libs/air directory of the Flash CS4 installation directory.
5. Select the servicemonitor.swc file and click Open. Click OK to close the Advanced ActionScript 3.0 window, and click OK again to close the Publish Settings window.

In addition to adding the servicemonitor.swc file in your library path, you also need to add the following import statement to your ActionScript code when working with the Service Monitoring Framework:

```
import air.net.*;
```

The Service Monitoring Framework consists of three classes that can be used for network connectivity detection. The classes are located in the air.net package.

- air.net.ServiceMonitor: Implements the framework for monitoring the status and availability of network services. This is the base class for the service monitors.

- air.net.SocketMonitor: Monitors the availability of a connection to a server on a given port. This class extends the ServiceMonitor class.

- air.net.URLMonitor: Monitors the availability of an HTTP- or HTTPS-based service. This class extends the ServiceMonitor class.

The SocketMonitor and URLMonitor are actually quite similar. They both monitor network connectivity. As you will see later on in this chapter, the SocketMonitor can monitor a lower-level connection and the URLMonitor can monitor HTTP or HTTPS connections. When the connection changes, both the SocketMonitor and the URLMonitor dispatch a StatusEvent.STATUS event. You can listen to that event and react accordingly.

Next, you will take a closer look at how the URLMonitor class works.

Monitoring HTTP/HTTPS connectivity

Imagine that your AIR application uses resources that are loaded from a server on a network (e.g., images loaded from an Internet location). You want to check if the needed resources are available to your desktop application. This is where the URLMonitor class comes in. The availability of any HTTP- or HTTPS-based service can be monitored by using the URLMonitor class.

When you create a new URLMonitor instance, you need to pass in a URLRequest object that holds the HTTP or HTTPS URL that you want to check. Next, you instantiate a new URLMonitor instance, here called monitor, and pass the URLRequest instance to the constructor of the URLMonitor:

```
var url:URLRequest = new URLRequest("http://www.newmovieclip.com");
var monitor:URLMonitor = new URLMonitor (url);
```

The URLMonitor object dispatches events when the connectivity status changes. You can listen for the StatusEvent.STATUS event and define a handler function for it, as shown here:

```
monitor.addEventListener(StatusEvent.STATUS, statusHandler);
```

The StatusEvent.STATUS event is only dispatched when the connection changes. If you want to check it more regularly, you can set the URLMonitor.pollInterval value to, for example, 1000 (milliseconds) to poll every second. This means that the URLMonitor instance will check every second if the resource is available:

```
monitor.pollInterval = 1000;
```

11

By default, the URLMonitor.pollInterval value is 0, which means the URLMonitor instance does not poll at a given interval.

Inside the statusHandler function, you can check the availability of the service by checking the Boolean value of the URLMonitor.available property. That value is true when the connection is available and false otherwise.

After creating the URLMonitor object, you have to call the start() method to begin monitoring the status of the service, as follows:

```
monitor.start()
```

When the URLMonitor is started, the Boolean property URLMonitor.running will return true.

You can call the URLMonitor.stop() method to stop monitoring the service.

Next, let's create a basic example AIR application that monitors whether the URL http://www.newmovieclip.com is available. The application looks like Figure 11-3.

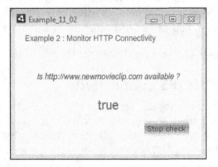

Figure 11-3. Basic AIR application to check if an HTTP resource is available

First, you add a dynamic text field on the stage of a new Flash file (Adobe AIR). You give this dynamic text field the instance name statusTextField. You also place a button on the stage with instance name stopCheckButton. When this button is clicked, you will call the URLMonitor.stop() method to stop monitoring the URL.

You define com.comtaste.foed.essentialair.chapter11.HttpConnectivityExample as the document class of your Flash document. The HttpConnectivityExample document class looks like this:

```
package com.comtaste.foed.essentialair.chapter11{

    import flash.display.*;
    import flash.events.*;
    import flash.net.*;
    import flash.desktop.*;
    import air.net.*;
```

```
public class HttpConnectivityExample extends MovieClip
{

   private var urlToCheck:String =
              "http://www.newmovieclip.com";
   private var monitor:URLMonitor;

   public function HttpConnectivityExample():void
   {
      stopCheckButton.addEventListener(
           MouseEvent.MOUSE_DOWN,
                 stopHttpConnectivityCheck);

      startHttpConnectivityCheck();
   }

   private function startHttpConnectivityCheck():void {
      var url:URLRequest = new URLRequest(this.urlToCheck);
         monitor=new URLMonitor (url);
         monitor.pollInterval = 1000;
         monitor.addEventListener(StatusEvent.STATUS,
                                             statusHandler);
         monitor.start();
   }
   private function stopHttpConnectivityCheck(
                                  event:MouseEvent) :void
   {
         monitor.stop();
   }
   private function statusHandler(
                       event:StatusEvent):void
   {
      statusTextField.text=
              monitor.available.toString();
   }
  }
}
```

When you run this example, try disabling your Internet connection, and you should see the value false inside the statusTextField text field.

Now let's take a look at how to monitor socket connections inside an AIR application.

Monitoring socket connectivity

As mentioned before, the air.net.SocketMonitor class is used to check the availability of low-level socket connections. A **socket connection** exists between a client and a server. To connect to the server and set up a two-way communication link, you need an IP address and a port number. The IP address and port number are called the *endpoint*. When you are connected to the socket, you can read and write binary data. The SocketMonitor class is responsible for monitoring whether you can establish a connection to the socket.

Imagine that you have built an AIR application that has to send e-mail using the Simple Mail Transfer Protocol (SMTP). This protocol initiates a connection to the mail server's port 25. When the connection becomes available, you then have to connect to the socket server.

A SocketMonitor object requires the two following parameters when instantiated—the name of the server (also called the host) and the port number:

```
var monitor:SocketMonitor = new SocketMonitor (host, port);
```

Just like a URLMonitor instance, the SocketMonitor instance dispatches a StatusEvent. STATUS event every time the connection changes. You can listen for the StatusEvent. STATUS event and define a handler function for it as shown here:

```
monitor.addEventListener(StatusEvent.STATUS,statusHandler);
```

Also, if you want to check more often, you can set a SocketMonitor.pollInterval value, like this:

```
monitor.pollInterval = 1000;
```

To start monitoring the socket connection, you call the SocketMonitor.start() method, as shown here:

```
monitor.start();
```

When the SocketMonitor is started, the Boolean property SocketMonitor.running will return true.

To stop monitoring, call the stop() method of the SocketMonitor instance, like this:

```
monitor.stop();
```

In the following basic example, you will create a SocketMonitor instance, and when the connection is available, you will connect to the socket. You will use the WHOIS (for "who is?") server from http://internic.net. WHOIS is a query/response protocol that is used for querying an official database to determine the owner of a domain name or an IP address. You can connect to a WHOIS server on port 43. Worldwide, there are several WHOIS servers available.

Figure 11-4 shows how your final application will look.

Figure 11-4. The final application that illustrates the SocketMonitor class

The first thing you need to do is create the layout of your AIR application. Create a new Flash File (Adobe AIR) and make sure the dimensions are 400 × 400 pixels. Then add these three text fields:

- statusTextField: This is a dynamic text field that you will use to show the status of the connection.

- domainInputText: This is an input text field. The user will fill in this text field with the domain name. This name will be used by the WHOIS service to get the detailed information about that domain.

- resultTextField: This is a multiline dynamic text field. In this text field, you will show the resulting data coming back from the socket server after the SEARCH WHOIS button is clicked.

The button with the SEARCH WHOIS label is just a dark gray rectangle with a text field positioned above it, converted into a button symbol. The button instance name is searchButton.

Now you are ready to write the code to get everything working. First, you define a document class for your Flash file, called com.comtaste.foed.essentialair.chapter11. SocketConnectivityExample. The full SocketConnectivityExample class looks like this:

```
package com.comtaste.foed.essentialair.chapter11{

    import flash.display.*;
    import flash.desktop.*;
    import flash.events.*;
```

11

```
import flash.net.*;
import air.net.*;

public class SocketConnectivityExample extends MovieClip
{

    private var monitor:SocketMonitor;
    private var host:String = "whois.internic.net";
    private var port:int = 43;
    private var socket:Socket;
    public function SocketConnectivityExample():void{

        domainInputText.visible = false;
        searchButton.visible = false;
        resultTextField.visible = false;

        searchButton.addEventListener(MouseEvent.MOUSE_DOWN,doSend);

        monitor = new SocketMonitor (host,port);

        monitor.addEventListener(StatusEvent.STATUS,statusHandler);
        monitor.start();
    }

    private function statusHandler(event:StatusEvent):void
    {
        statusTextField.text = monitor.available.toString();
        if(monitor.available){
            socket = new Socket();

            socket.addEventListener(Event.CONNECT,connectHandler);

            socket.addEventListener(ProgressEvent.SOCKET_DATA,
                socketDataHandler);
            socket.connect(host,port);
        }else{
            domainInputText.visible = false;
            searchButton.visible = false;
            resultTextField.visible = false;
        }
    }

    private function connectHandler(event:Event):void
    {
        trace("You are connected and ready to send/retrieve data");
        domainInputText.visible = true;
        searchButton.visible = true;
        resultTextField.visible = true;
        if(domainInputText.text.length >0)
```

```
        {
            sendData();
        }
    }
    private function doSend(event:MouseEvent):void
    {
        if(socket.connected)
        {
            sendData();
        }else{
            socket.connect(host,port);
        }
    }

    private function sendData():void
    {
        socket.writeUTFBytes(domainInputText.text + "\n");
        socket.flush();
    }

    private function socketDataHandler(event:ProgressEvent):void
    {
        var fullResult:String =
            socket.readUTFBytes(socket.bytesAvailable);
        resultTextField.text = fullResult;
    }
    }
}
```

In the constructor, you first set the domainInputText, resultTextField, and searchButton objects to be invisible, and you start monitoring the socket connection.

You instantiate the SocketMonitor class, named socket, by passing the host and port parameters to it:

```
monitor = new SocketMonitor(host,port);
```

Next, you add a listener for the StatusEvent.STATUS event and start the SocketMonitor instance by calling the start() method:

```
monitor.addEventListener(StatusEvent.STATUS,statusHandler);
monitor.start();
```

When the status of the socket connection has changed, the statusHandler() function is executed. Inside the statusHandler() function, you check the value of the SocketMonitor.available property. If this returns true, you know that the socket connection is available. Because the socket connection is available, you can set up your socket instance like this:

```
socket = new Socket();
```

The flash.net.Socket class makes it possible to create a socket connection and read/write raw binary data. To connect to the server, you need to pass the host and port number to the connect() method of the Socket object, as shown here:

```
socket.connect(host,port);
```

When the socket has received data, a ProgressEvent.SOCKET_DATA event is dispatched. When a network connection has been established, an Event.CONNECT event is dispatched. Next, you listen for both events and define handlers for them:

```
socket.addEventListener(Event.CONNECT,connectHandler);
socket.addEventListener(ProgressEvent.SOCKET_DATA,socketDataHandler);
```

When you are connected, the connectHandler() callback function is executed and makes the user interface controls visible, so the user can type a domain name to look up. When the user clicks the searchButton button to do a search, you send that query as a UTF-8 string to the socket. To send the binary data to the socket, you use the writeUTFBytes() method of the Socket class. When talking with a socket, you must end all data you send with a newline character, represented as \n:

```
socket.writeUTFBytes(domainInputText.text + "\n");
socket.flush();
```

When you write data using the writeUTFBytes() method to the socket, the data is not immediately transmitted to the server; it is queued until the flush() method of the Socket instance is called.

When you receive the resulting data back from the socket, you can read the UTF-8 data by calling the readUTFBytes() method. The readUTFBytes() method asks for a length parameter to pass in. You can use the bytesAvailable property to specify the length parameter. Finally, you show the received result inside the resultTextField:

```
var fullResult:String = socket.readUTFBytes(socket.bytesAvailable);
resultTextField.text = fullResult;
```

Creating a template application

In this section, you will create a blueprint for an occasionally connected AIR application. You can use this template as a starting point when you need to build an AIR application that needs to function online and offline. This template application uses the URLMonitor class to see if one or more resources are available on the network. If the connectivity of one of the resources changes, the AIR application is notified about the change that happened.

The concept is to build a class that can be given an array of one or more resources, and then the class will watch those resources. When one or more resources become unavailable, then the application will be notified.

This is the starting point for your class:

```
package com.comtaste.foed.essentialair.chapter11
{
    public class ApplicationResourceMonitor extends EventDispatcher
{

        private var resourceArray:Array;
        private var interval:int ;

        public function ApplicationResourceMonitor(
            interval:int = 0,resourceArr:Array = null):void
    {

            trace("---Application Resource Monitor started---")
            //
            this.interval = interval;
            //
            if(resourceArr ==null){
                this.resourceArray = new Array();
            }else{
                this.resourceArray = resourceArr;
                checkResources();
            }
        }

        public function addAsResource(path:String):void
        {

            resourceArray.push(path);
            checkResource(path);
        }
    }
}
```

As you can see in the preceding code, you define the two following variables, which are instantiated when a new instance of the AppplicationResourceMonitor class is constructed:

- resourceArray: This is the array that contains the paths (String values) that point to the resources that need to be monitored. You can pass an array of resources when you instantiate a new ApplicationResourceMonitor, or you can add resources manually by using the addAsResource() method.

- interval: This will be the value for the pollInterval property of the URLMonitor instance of each resource that has to be monitored. The default value for this is 0, which means that the availability of the resource will be checked only when a network connection has changed. If you want to poll more frequently, you can specify a specific interval value.

Next, you instantiate a URLMonitor instance for every resource that needs to be monitored. This is done inside the checkResources() method. This method looks like the following, and is added underneath the ApplicationResourceMonitor constructor function:

```
private function checkResources():void
{
    var resourceLength:int = this.resourceArray.length;
    //check if resources are still available
    for(var i:int = 0;i<resourceLength;i++)
    {
    var mon:URLMonitor = new URLMonitor (
                new URLRequest(resourceArray [i]));
    mon.pollInterval = this.interval;
    mon.addEventListener(StatusEvent.STATUS,
                                        resourceStatusHandler);
    mon.start();
    }
}
```

Now you loop through all the resources in the resourceArray with a for loop. Then you start a URLMonitor instance for a given pollInterval if the interval property has been set. When a connection changes, a StatusEvent.STATUS event will be dispatched. When this happens, the resourceStatusHandler() function will be executed.

Recall that a resource that needs to be monitored can also be added at a given moment in your AIR application by using the public addAsResource() method. When a resource is added manually, the checkResource() method is executed. The checkResource() method actually does the same thing as the checkResources() method, except it is only done for one specific resource:

```
private function checkResource(resource:String):void
{
    var mon:URLMonitor = new URLMonitor (new URLRequest(resource));
    mon.pollInterval = this.interval;
    mon.addEventListener(StatusEvent.STATUS,resourceStatusHandler);
    mon.start();
}
```

The resourceStatusHandler() callback function looks like this:

```
private function resourceStatusHandler(event:StatusEvent):void
{
    var myMonitor:URLMonitor = event.target as URLMonitor;
    if(myMonitor.available ==false){
        this.dispatchEvent(new ResourceEvent(ResourceEvent.UNAVAILABLE,
            myMonitor.urlRequest.url,true,true));
    }else{
        this.dispatchEvent(new ResourceEvent(ResourceEvent.AVAILABLE,
            myMonitor.urlRequest.url,true,true));
    }
}
```

The preceding code checks if the connection to a given resource is available. If a connection is available, a ResourceEvent.AVAILABLE event is dispatched; otherwise, a ResourceEvent.UNAVAILABLE event is dispatched. The application can listen for a ResourceEvent to be dispatched by an ApplicationResourceMonitor instance, and this way can be notified which resource became unavailable or available.

The ResourceEvent class is a basic custom event class that looks like this:

```
package com.comtaste.foed.essentialair.chapter11.events
{

    import flash.events.*;
    public class ResourceEvent extends Event
    {

        public static const AVAILABLE: String = "available";
        public static const UNAVAILABLE:String = "unavailable";

        public var URL:String;

        public function ResourceEvent (type:String,resourceURL:String,
                                bubbles:Boolean,cancelable:Boolean):void
        {
            super(type,bubbles,cancelable);
            this.URL = resourceURL;
        }
        public override function clone():Event
        {
                return new ResourceEvent( type, URL, bubbles, cancelable );
        }
    }
}
```

The ResourceEvent custom event class adds an extra custom property called URL that holds the URL (String value) for the resource that is available or unavailable.

Here is the full code for the ApplicationResourceMonitor class:

```
package com.comtaste.foed.essentialair.chapter11{

    import air.net.*;
    import flash.net.*;
    import flash.events.*;
    import flash.desktop.*;
    import
com.comtaste.foed.essentialair.chapter11.events.ResourceEvent;

    public class ApplicationResourceMonitor extends EventDispatcher
    {
```

11

```actionscript
public var resourceArray:Array;
private var interval:int ;

public function ApplicationResourceMonitor(interval:int = 0,
    resourceArr:Array = null):void
{
    trace("---Application Resource Monitor started---")
    this.interval = interval;

    if(resourceArr ==null)
    {
        this.resourceArray = new Array();
    }else{
        this.resourceArray = resourceArr;
        checkResources();
    }
}

private function checkResources():void
{
    var resourceLength:int = this.resourceArray.length;
    //check if resources are still available

    for(var i:int = 0;i<resourceLength;i++)
    {
        var mon:URLMonitor = new URLMonitor (
            new URLRequest(resourceArray [i]));

        mon.pollInterval = this.interval;

        mon.addEventListener(StatusEvent.STATUS,
            resourceStatusHandler);

        mon.start();
    }
}
private function checkResource(resource:String):void{
    var mon:URLMonitor = new URLMonitor (new URLRequest(
                                              resource));
    mon.pollInterval = this.interval;
    mon.addEventListener(StatusEvent.STATUS,
                              resourceStatusHandler);
    mon.start();
}

private function resourceStatusHandler(event:StatusEvent):void
{
    var myMonitor:URLMonitor = event.target as URLMonitor;
```

```
        if(myMonitor.available ==false)
        {
            this.dispatchEvent(
                new ResourceEvent(ResourceEvent.UNAVAILABLE,
                myMonitor.urlRequest.url,true,true));
        }else{
            this.dispatchEvent(
                new ResourceEvent(ResourceEvent.AVAILABLE,
                            myMonitor.urlRequest.url,true,true));
        }
    }

    public function addAsResource(path:String):void
    {
        resourceArray.push(path);
        checkResource(path);
    }
}
}
```

The last topic I'll discuss is how to test the preceding class in an AIR application. You actually just have to instantiate an instance of your ApplicationResourceMonitor class and pass it the resources that need to be monitored.

Here is a sample document class for an online/offline AIR application. The AIR application implements network resource monitoring via your ApplicationResourceMonitor class:

```
package com.comtaste.foed.essentialair.chapter11
{
    import flash.display.*;
    import flash.events.*;
    import
    com.comtaste.foed.essentialair.chapter11.ApplicationResourceMonitor;

    import
com.comtaste.foed.essentialair.chapter11.events.ResourceEvent;

    public class Application extends MovieClip
    {
        public function Application():void
        {
            trace("--START APPLICATION--");
            var resourceArr:Array = ["http://www.newmovieclip.com/images",
                            "http://www.google.com",
                            "http://www.adobe.com/go/air"];
```

```
        //define a resourceMonitor object and
        //pass the resourceArr if exists
        var monitor:ApplicationResourceMonitor =
            new ApplicationResourceMonitor(5000,
                                                        resourceArr)

        monitor.addEventListener(ResourceEvent.UNAVAILABLE,
                                            resourceUnavailableHandler);

        monitor.addEventListener(ResourceEvent.AVAILABLE,
                                            resourceAvailableHandler);

        //add resources manually if needed
        monitor.addAsResource(
        "http://localhost/xml/updateSettings.xml");
    }
    private function resourceUnavailableHandler(
                                    event:ResourceEvent):void
    {
        //implement logic here when a specific
        //resource is NOT available
        trace(event.URL + " unavailable");
        //...
    }

    private function resourceAvailableHandler(
                                event:ResourceEvent):void
    {
        //implement logic here when a specific resource is available
        trace(event.URL + " available");

    }
  }
}
```

This sample application monitors the connection to three URL resources. If one of the connections becomes (un)available, a ResourceEvent will be dispatched.

In the previous example application, you used a URLRequest instance for every resource you want to monitor. Next, you'll see how to work with the URLRequest class in AIR.

Using the URLRequest class in AIR

Imagine you want to load some data from a server (e.g., an XML file) in a typical Flash web application. To do so, you can make an instance of the URLLoader class and pass a URLRequest to the load() method of the URLLoader instance. The following code shows this typical way of working:

```
var urlReq:URLRequest = new
        URLRequest("http://www.newmovieclip.com/rss.xml");
var loader:URLLoader = new URLLoader();
loader.addEventListener(Event.COMPLETE,loadHandler);
loader.load(urlReq);

private function loadHandler(event:Event):void
{
    trace(event.target.data);
}
```

You use the URLRequest instance to capture all kinds of information in a single HTTP request.

When the request/response action is done, the connection between the server and the client is gone. When you need to reconnect after the connection is gone, it is simply a matter of using the URLRequest instance again.

The process described here is identical for an AIR application when loading data from a server. You can also load data from your file system by using the extra app-storage and app URL schemes. The next section discusses these schemes.

Extra AIR URL schemes

Imagine that you want to load content that is installed together with the AIR application. That content is run within the **application security sandbox**, which is the root of every AIR application. When using the URLRequest class to load content in that sandbox, you can use following extra URL schemes:

- app-storage: The application storage directory is unique for every installed AIR application, and is user specific. The location is based on the username, the application ID, and the publisher ID.

- app: This is the root directory of the installed AIR application (the directory that contains the application descriptor file).

> *Each AIR application also contains a number of different sandboxes, depending on what type of content is being loaded, and for what purpose. For more information, read "Introducing the Adobe AIR Security model" by Lucas Adamski, published on the Adobe AIR Developer Center (at www.adobe.com/devnet/air/articles/introduction_to_air_security.html).*

The app-storage scheme

The following example shows how to use URLRequest with the app-storage URL scheme. Imagine that in your application, you have written the userSettings.txt file in the settings directory inside the app-storage directory. If you want to load the *.txt file into your AIR application, you use following code:

```
var req:URLRequest = new URLRequest(
    "app-storage:/settings/userSettings.txt");

var ldr:URLLoader = new URLLoader()
ldr.addEventListener(Event.COMPLETE,completeHandler);
ldr.load(req);

function completeHandler(event:Event):void
{
    trace(event.target.data);
}
```

The app scheme

The following example shows the use of URLRequest with the app URL scheme. This piece of code will load an image from the images subfolder located inside the root directory of the installed AIR application. To test the code, you can add it to the first frame of a new Flash file:

```
var req:URLRequest = new URLRequest("app:/images/image.jpg");
var ldr:Loader = new Loader()
ldr.load(req);
addChild(ldr);
```

Now let's take a look at some extra URLRequest properties that are available when using this class inside your AIR application to load content inside the security sandbox.

URLRequest properties

In addition to the extra URL schemes you can use, the following properties are also available when using the URLRequest class to load content installed together with the AIR application:

- cacheResponse: Boolean value that indicates whether the response data should be cached.

- useCache: Boolean value that specifies whether the local cache should be consulted before the URLRequest fetches data.

- manageCookies: Boolean value that specifies whether or not cookies are managed. If cookies are managed (true), they are added to the request, and response cookies are remembered.

- userAgent: String that specifies the user agent to be used in the HTTP request.

- followRedirects: Boolean value that specifies whether URL redirects are to be followed.

- authenticate: Boolean value that indicates whether authentication requests should be handled.

Let's continue this discussion with some details about the cacheResponse and useCache properties.

cacheResponse and useCache

The default value for cacheResponse and useCache is true. This is understandable because HTTP caching greatly improves the speed of your AIR application. When cacheResponse is true, then the response data will be cached in the operating system's HTTP cache. When useCache is true, then the operating system's HTTP cache will be consulted before the URLRequest fetches data. If one of these two properties is false, it will cause a decrease in the performance of your application because you won't be reducing the number of request/response roundtrips or the number of bytes transferred between the client and the server.

However, you might not want the AIR application to use the operating system's HTTP cache when loading content from inside the application security sandbox. If this is the case, you can set the useCache property of the URLRequest object to false. In the following code snippet, the loaded data is not cached in the operating system's HTTP cache, and the HTTP cache is not consulted when loading the data:

```
var req:URLRequest = new URLRequest("app:/images/image.jpg");
req.cacheResponse = false;
req.useCache = false;
var ldr:Loader = new Loader();
ldr.load(req);
```

manageCookies

Imagine you want to load a web page inside your AIR application. That web page asks you to choose a color for the background of that page. Once you select a color, the color is saved in a cookie on your hard drive. So, the next time you load that page, the background color you had chosen the last time will be still there. This way, cookies are used to maintain state and other data in a website. Once the cookie has been set, it will be sent with each request so that the server will know how to render the page. Cookies can only be read by the website that has placed them. Figure 11-5 shows the typical request/response model when working with cookies. You load the specific web page from the server using a normal request. When the server answers, a response cookie is sent to the client and the client AIR application will remember the response cookie.

11

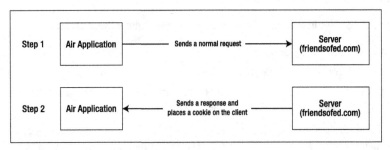

Figure 11-5. The request/response model for your example

Now, when you load another page from the same server, there is a slightly different situation, as you can see in Figure 11-6.

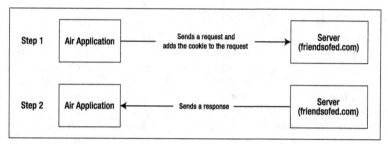

Figure 11-6. Pass the cookie to your remote request.

Now the AIR client already knows the cookie, and sends it together with the request to the server, and the server responds.

The manageCookies property of the URLRequest class gives you the option of not using the standard mechanism just mentioned (for more info see the LiveDocs documentation at http://livedocs.adobe.com/flash/9.0/ActionScriptLangRefV3/flash/net/URLRequest.html#manageCookies). When you set manageCookies to false, cookies are not added to the request and response cookies are not remembered, so actually cookies are disabled. The manageCookies property has a default value of true.

> *AIR uses the cookies from the operating system. On Mac OS X, Safari also uses the operating system cookies. And on Windows, Internet Explorer also does. So, if you want to clear your operating system cookies, the best way is by using one of those browsers, because they have built-in cookie management.*

Follow these steps to clear the cookies in Safari on the Mac:

1. Open Safari.
2. Select Safari ➤ Preferences and open the Security panel.
3. Click the Show Cookies button.
4. Click the Remove All button.

To clear the cookies in Internet Explorer on Windows, follow these steps:

1. Open Internet Explorer.
2. Go to Tools ➤ Internet Options ➤ General.
3. Click the Delete button on the General tab, and then click the Delete Cookies button on the Delete Browsing History panel.

> *If you want more information about the HTTP state management mechanism, have a look at following web page:* www.w3.org/Protocols/rfc2109/rfc2109.

Using the userAgent property

Another property I'll discuss is the userAgent property. The userAgent string describes basic information about the application that requests web content from a server. For example, this might be an AIR application that loads an HTML page. You can check on the server for the user agent that is requesting the content and decide, for example, to display the content according to it.

The default userAgent value varies depending on the runtime operating system (e.g., Mac OS X or Windows), the runtime language, and the runtime version. When you send a request to the server, the user agent is always part of the request. A typical userAgent string looks like this: Mozilla/5.0 (Macintosh; U; PPC Mac OS X; en) AppleWebKit/420+ (KHTML, like Gecko) AdobeAIR/1.0.

You can also set the userAgent string to any value. For this reason, user agent spoofing is not uncommon. Applications can provide false information about their identity that way.

The following example shows a simple AIR application that loads a web page from a server, and the loaded page shows the userAgent you are using. To display the page, you use an HTMLLoader instance. When using an HTMLLoader instance, you must set the userAgent property directly on the HTMLLoader instance instead of on the URLRequest object. In this example, you'll show the HTML page from www.useragentstring.com/. This website shows and explains the userAgent string that the AIR application uses.

First, you'll load the HTML page inside the HTMLLoader component. This way, you can see what the default userAgent string is. The userAgent string will differ depending on the operating system you are using.

When you run the application, the loaded web page will show the default userAgent string from an AIR application.

Here is the code sample:

```
package com.comtaste.foed.essentialair.chapter11
{

    import flash.display.*;
    import flash.events.*;
    import flash.net.*;
    import flash.html.*;

    public class UserAgentStringExample extends MovieClip
    {

        private var req:URLRequest;
        private var myHTMLLoader:HTMLLoader;

        private var url:URLRequest = new
            URLRequest("http://www.useragentstring.com/");
```

11

```
    public function UserAgentStringExample():void
    {
        connect();
    }

    private function connect():void
    {
        myHTMLLoader = new HTMLLoader();
        myHTMLLoader.width = 560;
        myHTMLLoader.height = 400;
        this.addChild(myHTMLLoader);
        //
        myHTMLLoader.load(url);
    }
  }
}
```

If you want to send a different userAgent string, you can simply set the userAgent property of the HTMLLoader instance. Add the following private property to the preceding code:

```
private var userAgentString:String = "MY OWN USERAGENTSTRING";
```

Next, set the userAgent property of the HTMLLoader instance just before you load the url in the connect() method:

```
this.addChild(myHTMLLoader);

myHTMLLoader.userAgent = userAgentString;

myHTMLLoader.load(url);
```

When you run the code again, you should see that the web page now thinks your userAgent string is MY OWN USERAGENTSTRING.

Now let's take a look at how AIR handles URL redirects.

Following redirects

Redirects allow you to make a specific web page send the user to another page. This is sometimes done to make a page with a long URL accessible by a page that has a shorter and easier-to-remember URL.

URL redirects are set on the server. For example, on the comtaste.com server, you can configure http://comtaste.com/foedlogo to redirect to http://www.friendsofed.com/images/logos_and_buttons/logo2.gif.

You can test the preceding redirect by using your browser and surfing to http://comtaste.com/foedlogo. You will see that the URL will change to the much longer URL on the friendsofed server.

When you are loading a URLRequest inside your AIR application, the default value is that redirects are followed. If you do not want that behavior, you can set the followRedirects property of the URLRequest instance to false.

In the following example, you'll load an image file and center it on the stage. The URL where the image resides is a redirect of the http://comtaste.com/foedlogo URL. You can set the followRedirects property of the URLRequest instance to true, and the image will load. When you set it to false, the image will not appear, and instead an IOError that reads as follows will be dispatched:

```
Loaded file is an unknown type.
URL: http://comtaste.com/foedlogo" errorID=2124]
```

Here's the full code for this example:

```
package com.comtaste.foed.essentialair.chapter11
{

    import flash.display.*;
    import flash.events.*;
    import flash.net.*;

    public class FollowRedirectsExample extends MovieClip
    {

        private var req:URLRequest;
        private var ldr:Loader;
        private var path:String= "http://comtaste.com/foedlogo";

        public function FollowRedirectsExample():void
        {
            //connect to XML file
            connect();
        }

        private function connect():void
        {
            req = new URLRequest(this.path);
            //
            req.followRedirects = true;
            //
            ldr = new Loader();
            ldr.contentLoaderInfo.addEventListener(
                Event.COMPLETE,loadCompleteHandler);

            ldr.contentLoaderInfo.addEventListener(
                IOErrorEvent.IO_ERROR,ioErrorHandler);
```

11

```
                    ldr.load(req);
                }

                private function loadCompleteHandler(event:Event):void
                {
                    var bmp:Bitmap = event.target.content as Bitmap;
                    bmp.x = (stage.stageWidth-bmp.width)/2;
                    bmp.y = (stage.stageHeight-bmp.height)/2;

                    addChild(bmp);
                }

                private function ioErrorHandler(event:IOErrorEvent):void
                {
                    trace(event.toString());
                }
        }
    }
```

Now let's take a look at how authentication works.

Using the authenticate property

Here, we'll talk about the authenticate property of the URLRequest class. The default of this property is true. When you load content that requires authentication, your AIR application will show a dialog that requests a username and password. This way, the user can authenticate. When you set the authenticate property to false, the AIR application won't display a login dialog to the user that asks for a username and password.

The following authentication methods are currently supported in AIR:

- **Windows**: HTTP Basic, HTTP Digest, NTLM, Kerberos, and SSL.
- **Mac**: HTTP Basic, HTTP Digest, NTLM, and SSL.

You can find more information about the HTTP Basic and Digest authentication methods at www.ietf.org/rfc/rfc2617.txt.

Kerberos is defined in an open standard so different operating systems can implement it. You can find more information about the Kerberos standard at www.ietf.org/rfc/rfc4120.txt.

The Windows NT LAN Manager (NTLM, not to be confused with LAN Manager) authentication protocol was the default protocol of Windows NT 4.0 and earlier Windows versions. For backward compatibility reasons, Microsoft still supports NTLM in its latest operating systems. The NTLM authentication protocol is not specified in an open standard document; it is a proprietary authentication protocol defined by Microsoft.

Now let's build a little AIR application that loads an XML file from a server. The directory on the server where the XML file resides needs authentication. So you need to log in before accessing the directory using your username and password.

In the code, the first thing you do inside the constructor is set up your TextField instance that you will use to visualize your XML file result. The most important method in the code is the connect method. The connect method instantiates a new URLRequest instance that points to the XML file called data.xml that resides on your server. The XML file is located inside a password-protected directory: foed/essentialair/chapter11/data.xml.

Next, you instantiate a URLLoader object that loads the URLRequest instance. When the data arrives back from the server, the loadCompleteHandler callback method is executed. When the authentication fails, an IOErrorEvent will be thrown and the IOErrorHandler method will be executed.

To authenticate against the server, you set the authenticate property of the URLRequest instance to true, as this code fragment shows:

```
req = new URLRequest(this.serverPath+this.fileName);
req.authenticate = true;
```

The complete code for the authentication example looks like this:

```
package com.comtaste.foed.essentialair.chapter11
{

    import flash.display.*;
    import flash.events.*;
    import flash.net.*;
    import flash.text.TextField;

    public class AuthenticationExample extends MovieClip
    {

        private var req:URLRequest;
        private var ldr:URLLoader;
        private var output:TextField;

        private var serverPath:String =
"http://www.comtaste.com/foed/essentialair/chapter11/";
        private var fileName:String = "data.xml";

        public function AuthenticationExample():void
        {
            output = new TextField();
            output.multiline = true;
            output.width = 400;
            output.height = 400;
            this.addChild(output);

            // connect to XML file
            connect();
        }
```

11

```
    private function connect():void
    {

        req = new URLRequest(this.serverPath+this.fileName);
        req.authenticate = true;
        //
        ldr = new URLLoader(req);
        ldr.addEventListener(Event.COMPLETE,loadCompleteHandler);
        ldr.addEventListener(IOErrorEvent.IO_ERROR,ioErrorHandler);
        ldr.load(req);
    }

    private function loadCompleteHandler(event:Event):void
    {
        var xml:XML = XML(event.target.data);
        // grab the value from the node in the XML file
        output.text = xml.node;
        output.x = (stage.stageWidth-output.textWidth)/2;
        output.y = (stage.stageHeight-output.textHeight)/2;
    }

    private function ioErrorHandler(event:IOErrorEvent):void
    {
        output.text = event.toString();
    }
  }
}
```

When you run the example, the AIR application will show a window like the one in Figure 11-7, which allows the user to log in with a username and a password.

Figure 11-7. A typical window on Windows that asks for user credentials when accessing a server

On the server where the data.xml file resides, you have set permission to access the file only for the user with username airUser with password airPass. So, when you fill in that username and password, the file can be loaded, and the result of the XML file will be shown in the output TextField. When the authentication fails, the error will be shown in the TextField.

If you don't want the user to fill in a username and password, you can set the login details by code. This is done by calling the static setLoginCredentialsForHost() method of the URLRequestDefaults class. You will implement this in the following section, which talks about the URLRequest defaults. So, let's have a look at the URLRequestDefaults class.

Setting default URLRequest values

The URLRequestDefaults class includes static properties that you can set to define default values for the properties of the URLRequest class. You can set values for the following properties:

- cacheResponse
- useCache
- manageCookies
- userAgent
- followRedirects
- authenticate

All of these are static properties, so you don't have to create an instance of the URLRequestDefaults class to set their values. For example, the following code sets the static property authenticate to true:

```
URLRequestDefaults.authenticate = true;
```

Setting the default properties is handy in a large AIR application where you are making a lot of requests and you want to set the properties only once, instead of for every URLRequest instance. Setting the properties for a given URLRequest overrides those static properties set for the URLRequestDefaults class.

There is also one static method available in the URLRequestDefaults class that lets you define the default username and password for a selected host: setLoginCredentialsForHost. You can use this static method as follows:

```
URLRequestDefaults.setLoginCredentialsForHost(
              "www.site.com","username","password");
```

You have to pass the username and password to the setLoginCredentialsForHost() method to make it possible to authenticate against the host domain. By logging in by code, the user will not see the login dialog. In the code of the previous section, add two extra properties in the document class, which hold the values for the username and password:

```
private var userName:String = "airUser";
private var userPass:String = "airPass";
```

In the connect() method, add the default login credentials for the host domain where you are loading the data.xml file from:

```
private function connect():void {

    req = new URLRequest(this.serverPath+this.fileName);
    req.authenticate = true;

    URLRequestDefaults.setLoginCredentialsForHost(
        "www.comtaste.com",this.userName,this.userPass);

    ldr = new URLLoader(req);
    ldr.addEventListener(Event.COMPLETE,loadCompleteHandler);
    ldr.addEventListener(IOErrorEvent.IO_ERROR,ioErrorHandler);
    ldr.load(req);
}
```

When you run the example again, the user will be automatically logged into the server, and the XML data can be read. Next, you will have a look what URLRequest headers are, and how you can use them inside your AIR application.

Setting URLRequest headers

Request headers allow the AIR application to provide information to the server. They give additional details about the nature of the request, and allow the client to have greater control over how the request is processed and how a response is returned by the server. In the specification for the HTTP 1.1 protocol, only the host header is required. The host header field indicates the host and port of the server to which the request is being made.

In some situations, it is handy to add headers to your request. Inside AIR, you can do that by assigning an array of URLRequestHeader objects to the requestHeaders property of the URLRequest instance. Each URLRequestHeader object contains a string name and a string value. These are described following:

- **name**: A string value representing the HTTP request header name (e.g., If-Modified-Since)
- **value**: A string value associated with the name property (e.g., Sat, 28 Jan 2009 19:00:00 GMT)

Let's have a look at an example of when an additional header field is handy because it improves the efficiency of the URLRequest. Imagine a situation where your AIR application loads an XML file from a server. This XML file contains news items to show inside your AIR application. When your AIR application is running on the user's computer, you want it to reload the XML file every 5 minutes to ensure the user always sees the latest news. You can reduce the transaction overhead by adding an extra header field to your URLRequest: If-Modified-Since.

The following snippet shows how an If-Modified-Since URLRequestHeader is instantiated:

```
var header:URLRequestHeader = new URLRequestHeader("If-Modified-Since",
    "Sat Jul 24 00:00:00 2008 UTC");
```

The purpose of the If-Modified-Since header is to allow efficient updates of cached information with a minimum amount of transaction overhead. By using this extra header, no additional download of the XML file will be started if the XML file is not modified. This way, you minimize network traffic.

> *Note that the time used in the request header is the time interpreted by the server, whose clock might not be synchronized with the client.*

If the file has not been modified, a "not modified" code (304) is sent to the client so a cached version of the document can be used; otherwise, the file is returned normally.

> *If you want more information about the different header field definitions, take a look at following web page:* www.w3.org/Protocols/rfc2616/rfc2616-sec14.html.

The following code snippet shows how to add a single HTTP request header to the array for the requestHeaders property of the URLRequest instance. The header indicates that the application should load the requested resource on the server only if the resource has been modified since a given date:

```
var req:URLRequest = new
    URLRequest("http://www.yoursite.com/news.xml");
var header:URLRequestHeader = new URLRequestHeader("If-Modified-Since",
    "Sat Jul 24 00:00:00 2008 UTC");

req.requestHeaders.push(header);

var ldr:URLLoader = new URLLoader();
ldr. addEventListener(Event.COMPLETE, completeHandler);
ldr. addEventListener(IOErrorEvent.IO_ERROR,
    errorHandler);

ldr.load(req);

function completeHandler(event:Event):void{


    trace(event.target.data)
}
function errorHandler(event:IOErrorEvent):void{
    // load not from online, use cached version.
    // ...
}
```

11

This last section discussed how you can set an additional URLRequestHeader to make your server requests more efficient. This can greatly reduce the amount of network traffic your AIR application is using. This way, your AIR application stays connected but eliminates any unnecessary transfers.

Summary

In this chapter, you learned how you can monitor network connectivity, which is very important when building occasionally connected AIR applications. You saw that you can listen for the Event.NETWORK_CHANGE event to monitor a network connectivity change.

This chapter also discussed how you can check if your online resources are still available. This is a very crucial part in building an occasionally connected AIR application. When your resources are not available online, you can, for example, use local resources, and later synchronize your offline data with the online data.

You looked at HTTP/HTTPS connectivity using the URLMonitor class, and socket connectivity using the SocketMonitor class. You bundled that knowledge into a sample occasionally connected AIR application that you can use as a starting point for building larger applications.

Next, I discussed the URLRequest class and its properties for working with issues like authentication, cache control, and cookie management. Using the URLRequestDefaults class, you can set the default values of properties to be used by every URLRequest object inside your AIR application.

You also learned that you can add additional request headers to a request by assigning an array of URLRequestHeader objects to the requestHeaders property of the URLRequest class. Finally, I explained how the If-Modified-Since request header can improve the efficiency of a URLRequest.

CHAPTER 12
SQLITE PROGRAMMING IN FLASH CS4

Adobe AIR can use SQL databases **natively,** which means that ActionScript applications created with Flash CS4 or Flex 3 no longer need to use server-side languages such as Java, PHP, and .NET as intermediaries to manage complex databases. The SQL access offered to ActionScript applications makes it possible to manage data that was initially precluded or difficult to implement solely with Flash.

The AIR runtime includes a SQLite database engine, primarily for its extreme lightness, speed, and flexibility. SQLite offers databases contained in one file, without the necessity of server applications or configuration documents. The SQLite format is multiplatform, making it possible to bring a database created with Windows onto an OS X system and vice versa, without any kind of conversion.

SQLite's multiplatform nature, along with its independence from server-side applications, makes it the ideal candidate for a runtime like AIR. Furthermore, the extreme portability of SQLite has made it the first choice among many software developers for mobile devices. In fact, the SQLite engine has already provided AIR with support for future versions of the runtime. This support should also be compatible with mobile devices such as cellular phones, personal digital assistants (PDAs), and MP3 players.

In this chapter, you will gain better knowledge of relational databases and their use in AIR applications. You'll discover the strong points of using SQLite, and you'll put them into practice with simple examples. You will also see how to create a database from scratch and how to connect to a database that already exists. Through simple examples, you'll see how to execute reading and writing operations for a SQL database in an AIR application.

Introducing SQL: SQLite and AIR integration

For AIR, SQLite offers access to databases contained in a single file that resides on the computer in which the application executes. This means that there aren't any access limits related to remote connections. No network connection is required to use SQL functions in AIR applications. At this time, however, it isn't possible to connect to remote databases without a server-side programming language.

Thanks to the integration with SQLite, AIR applications can be much more than simple desktop integrations of web applications, and they can in fact compete with many desktop applications built with traditional languages and tools.

The implementation of SQLite in AIR is compatible with most of the functionality offered by the SQL-92 specification (www.sqlite.org/omitted.html). The syntax for executing operations on databases is the same as that normally used to interact with SQLite databases.

Every AIR application can connect to as many databases as necessary, and every database is completely contained in a single file. The location, name, and extension of these files are completely left to the discretion of the developer.

Because every database is saved in a single document on disk, it is easy to create a backup of your data. Backups can be used locally or sent to central archives on company networks or the Web. Furthermore, being able to access several data sources at the same time offers many possibilities for creating complex databases.

One example of the use of several databases might be in an application that provides access to various users based on authentication: a database is created for each user, containing only the information and data relevant for that user, and another database will be created for all users for shared information.

Now you know how a SQLite database is structured and what options it provides AIR applications. Before proceeding with some practical examples, though, you need to have an understanding of what a relational database actually is.

Using SQL with relational databases

A relational database stores data in tables that can be arranged to show various relationships between pieces of data. The data in the database is organized in tables, where each row corresponds to an object or some type of information, and each column corresponds to a property or single piece of information regarding the row it belongs to. The contacts section of an e-mail program is a good example of a relational database: each contact corresponds to a row in a table of contacts, and each piece of information associated with it (e-mail address, telephone number, mailing address, IM name, etc.) corresponds to a column of the table.

To operate on relational data, you use SQL (Structured Query Language). This language provides commands to access, read from, and write to a relational database. It gives instructions to the SQL engine regarding the operations to be executed on the data contained in the various tables. In the case of AIR applications, the SQLite engine is used.

Another fundamental characteristic of relational databases is the ability to create relationships among the data. Say you needed to associate an indefinite number of e-mails to any of your contacts. This would be an impossible task using only one table. However, you could create two tables: one for the contacts and one for the e-mails. You could then define a relationship between the two tables. In this one-to-many relationship (i.e., containing many e-mail addresses per contact), it is necessary to define a value that has to be present in both tables as a **relation key**.

Usually, you use a unique name, called an **ID**, for each contact already present in the table as a relation key. If an ID isn't already available, one can be created. This unique name can also be used to access the data of a specific contact. So, in your contacts table, you can create an ID field, containing a value for each contact (e.g., an incremental numerical index). Then, in the emails table, for each defined e-mail, there will be a second id_contact field, used to establish a relation between the e-mail and the correct contact.

Most relational databases also allow you to define **external keys**, which are connections among related data. You can use these keys to update or remove interrelated data. Suppose that you want to delete a contact with an ID value of 7 from your example of address book: you would have to remove all the e-mails with an id_contact equal to 7, as well as remove the relevant row on the contact table. This procedure could be easy, but

12

it requires more code than the external keys approach, especially if you have relationships among several tables. External keys allow you to remove all this data automatically when you delete the contact from the address book.

> Unfortunately, the SQL implementation of AIR doesn't allow you to define external keys; therefore, you will have to remove all the relevant data when it is no longer needed.

It's now time to go deeper and learn how to use the AIR SQLite APIs to work with local databases.

Connecting to a database

SQL allows developers to interact with groups of tables (also known as structures) of relational data. Through SQL, programmers don't set procedures or sequences of operations to be executed, but instead define the data they want to add or extract from the database. How the search is actually carried out depends on the SQL engine being used.

Recall that AIR supports most of the functionality of SQLite directly in SQL code. However, some specific functions of the SQL language, such as managing SQL transactions, are not directly supported by the actual implementation of ActionScript 3. To allow AIR application developers to access these SQL functions, ActionScript functions are provided to allow you to obtain the same results. (You will examine this in further detail later, in the "Using transactions in AIR" section.) ActionScript 3 defines the flash.data namespace, containing the classes that are offered to work on SQL functions. These classes include the following:

- The SQLConnection class, for connecting to local databases
- The SQLStatement class, for executing queries on relational databases
- The SQLResult class, for managing the data returned by database queries

These classes are discussed throughout the chapter.

The SQLConnection class

The SQLConnection class offers functions to create and connect to a database on the local machine. When you connect to a database, you are asked which file it is in; if this file doesn't exist, the SQLConnection class can create it for you while it is creating the connection.

This class also allows you do the following:

- Monitor low-level events regarding activities running on the database
- Delete running operations
- Manage the cache that AIR provides to connect to the database

As mentioned, some standard SQL functions aren't supported in AIR with the query syntax of SQL. Two examples of such functions are accessing table definition patterns and managing SQL transactions. The SQLConnection class implements these missing functions and exposes them through its programming interface.

Synchronous connection to a database

There are two ways to connect to a database: synchronously and asynchronously. Both ways offer advantages and disadvantages; lets examine the differences in more detail.

A **synchronous** connection is a connection that requires the operations to be executed in a sequence, one at a time. Even if some operations could be executed at the same time, each operation is executed only when the previous one has been completed correctly.

To connect to a database in synchronous mode, you use the open() method. When you use this method, all the operations executed on the database you are connecting to will be synchronous. This means that when you access the database in reading or writing mode, your application will wait for the SQL operation to be completed before other operation can be executed.

This type of access may mean that your application could temporary freeze if the operations on the SQL data involve large volumes of information. The freeze can occur because, during the execution of SQL processes, interactions involving the mouse, the keyboard, animations, or graphics can be interrupted, and won't recover their normal functions until the SQL queries have completed.

If your database has a large quantity of information and you want your users to be able to work during the SQL read and write operations, a synchronous connection isn't preferable. On the other hand, if your database is small, this approach is preferred, because it allows the data to be processed in real time with the user's interactions.

If you connect to a database in synchronous mode, you have to enclose all the SQL reading and writing operations in try...catch constructs to intercept any execution exceptions generated by your SQL queries. If you don't use this precaution, every SQL communication error will result in an AIR runtime exception.

When you connect to an AIR database, at least one item of information is required: the file in which the database is contained; therefore, the argument passed into the constructor has to be a valid instance of the ActionScript 3 File class. For example, if you want to connect in synchronous mode to a database that has been saved in a file named MyDatabase. db on the desktop, you could use the following code:

```
// Import needed classes
import flash.data.SQLConnection;
import flash.events.SQLErrorEvent;
import flash.events.SQLEvent;
import flash.filesystem.File;

// instatiate SQLConnection object
var SQLconn : SQLConnection = new SQLConnection();
```

12

```
// create a file object pointing to database file
var dbFile : File =
        File.desktopDirectory.resolvePath( "MyDatabase.db" );

// create a try...catch statement
try {
    // try to connect to database
    SQLconn.open( dbFile );

    // if connection open you are ready to work with database
    trace( "Database created!" );

} catch ( error:SQLError )
{
    // if some error occurs, print details to output console
    trace( "Connection error message: " + error.message );
    trace( "Connection error details: " + error.details );
}
```

Let's put the concepts you have just seen into practice. Open Flash CS4 and load the ch12p01_sync.fla file.

This project was created to start up a synchronous connection to the database. You see two Flash components on the stage: a TextArea, where you write the messages that will keep you updated on the executed operations, and a Button, with which you will start up the request to connect to the database. The stage is shown in Figure 12-1.

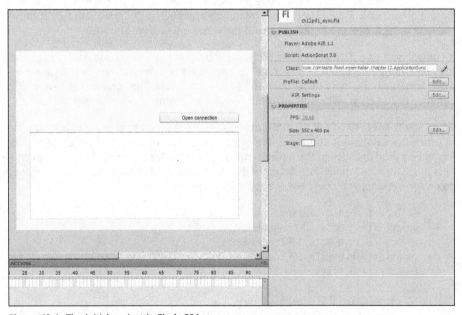

Figure 12-1. The initial project in Flash CS4

On the Properties panel, verify that the Button has been assigned with the button instance name and that the output instance name has been assigned to the TextArea. These labels will allow you to interact with the elements on the stage from ActionScript. Click an empty point on the stage to deselect everything, and access the Document Properties panel. On this panel, under the Publish item, you'll find the Class field, in which the ApplicationSync class is specified (contained in the ApplicationSync.as file). To the right of the Class field, you'll find the Edit class definition icon. Click it to make Flash CS4 open the class associated with this project, as shown in Figure 12-2.

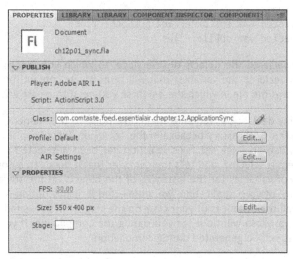

Figure 12-2. The Document Properties panel shows the associated document class.

A new panel in Flash will open, containing the document class of the project, which is ApplicationSync; all the functionality of your AIR application will be defined through this ActionScript class.

Next, declare the classes to be imported. Doing so will allow the Flash compiler to recognize the programming interfaces of the objects that you use. You'll need the following classes to interact with the controls on the stage:

```
package com.comtaste.foed.essentialair.chapter12
{
import flash.data.SQLConnection;
import flash.display.MovieClip;
import flash.errors.SQLError;
import flash.events.MouseEvent;
import flash.filesystem.File;

import fl.controls.Button;
import fl.controls.TextArea;
```

Now the compiler has the necessary information to use the functions you will need in a little while.

12

The following step is to define the variables of the class that you will need to allow the application to function. After the declaration of the class, add the following variables:

```
public class ApplicationSync extends MovieClip
{
    // on Stage objects
    public var button:Button;
    public var output:TextArea;

    // properties
    protected var sqlConnection:SQLConnection;
    protected var dbFile:File;
```

First of all, you declared the objects on the stage, to which you associated an instance name. Then you declared the variables that will respectively contain the instance of the SQL connection and the file in which the database you need to create will be saved.

You must explicitly declare the variables that correspond to the elements on the stage of the application. This is necessary because in the Advanced ActionScript 3.0 Settings panel, the Automatically declare stage instances selection has been deselected (see Figure 12-3). Normally, this item is selected, and tells the compiler that it needs to automatically create the declarations of variables for the instances of the objects on the stage. To be able to have more control of your application, you deselected it. If this option is deselected, you have to declare all the instances of your class on the stage. If it's selected, you don't have to declare them, as Flash will do it for you during the compilation. If you don't deselect this option, errors will be generated during compilation.

The constructor function of the class deals with the following actions, which are included in the subsequent code:

- Starting your application
- Defining the file in which you will create the database
- Registering a click event on the button on the stage

```
public function ApplicationSync()
{
    // register layout events
    button.addEventListener( MouseEvent.CLICK, connect );

    // initialize database file
    initLocalDataBase();
}
```

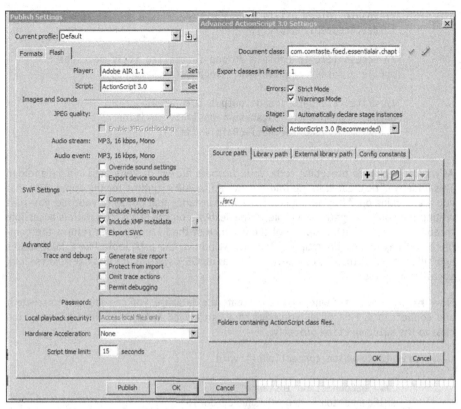

Figure 12-3. The Automatically declare stage instances option

The click event on the button is associated with the connect() method, which deals with calling the connectToDb() method to open the SQL connection:

```
// called pressing connect button
private function connect( evt : MouseEvent ):void
{
    connectToDb();
}
```

The initLocalDatabase() function that is called at the end of the class constructor deals with creating an instance of the File class. The File class allows you to access the file system of the operating system. The initLocalDatabase() method accesses the database file and initializes it if necessary:

```
private function initLocalDataBase():void
{
    // create folder, in application root, to store database files
    var folder:File =
        File.applicationStorageDirectory.resolvePath( "data" );
```

12

```
// ensure folder exists
folder.createDirectory();

// access file to contain db and initialize it if necessary
dbFile = folder.resolvePath( "localDataBase.db" );

// write file path inside output text area
output.appendText( "Database repository position: "
                  + dbFile.nativePath + "\n" );
}
```

As you can see in the preceding code, your database file will be generated in a data folder. This folder will be created in the folder provided by AIR's runtime for the application that you are working on. After having created a valid instance that points to your file, you start writing the complete path to the file in the TextArea on the stage. The path is accessible through the nativePath property of the instance of the File class that returns the complete pathway for the operating system. On Windows, the path looks like C:\Documents and settings\...\localDataBase.db, whereas on OS X systems, it looks like /Users/.../localDataBase.db.

Now that you have a file where you can create the database, you can see how to create it and connect to it. First of all, you have to assign a valid instance of the SQLConnection class to the sqlConnection property:

```
private function connectToDb():void
{
    // SQLConnection instance
    sqlConnection = new SQLConnection();
```

Next, write a message in the TextArea to show that you are about to open the connection:

```
output.appendText( "Opening sync connection...\n" );
```

You start the connection in a try...catch construct to intercept any connection errors to your database. To start the connection you invoke the open() method of your SQLConnection object by passing it as a parameter the dbFile property, which represents the file that contains the database:

```
try{
    // init connection db
    sqlConnection.open( dbFile );
}catch( e:SQLError )
```

If any errors should occur during the connection, the code in the catch() construct will be executed. The information related to the error will be passed on to you through the instance of the SQLError class, defined as an argument of the catch(e:SQLError) instruction. In this case, the only action that you execute is to write the information of the error, defined by the message property of the instance of the SQLError. Then you exit the execution of the method with the return command:

```
    {
        // intercept possible errors
        output.appendText( "Sync connection error: " + e.message
                + " operation type: " + e.operation + "\n" );
        return;
    }
```

If no error occurs and the connection has been opened correctly, you write a message that indicates the completion of the connection process in the TextArea:

```
        output.appendText( "Sync connection opened!\n" );
    }
    }
    }
```

ApplicationSync.as is now complete, and you can proceed with compiling it to verify that it's functioning correctly. Return to the Flash CS4 panel containing your project and select the Test Movie option from the Control menu; the application will be compiled and executed and, if there aren't any problems, you should receive a result like that shown in Figure 12-4.

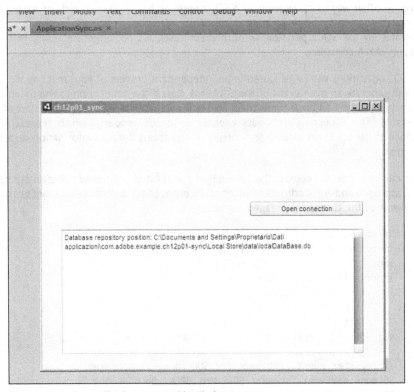

Figure 12-4. The application executed by Flash

Now that you're able to create an AIR application that connects to a database using a synchronous connection, let's take a look at how to operate with an asynchronous connection.

Asynchronous connection to a database

An **asynchronous** connection allows several operations to be executed at the same time. Each operation is executed in an independent process and generates a completion event when it's finished. To execute sequential operations with asynchronous connections, you can start each operation only after a completion event has been received for the previous operation.

To connect to a database in asynchronous mode, you use the openAsync() method. When you use this method, all the operations that will be executed on the database will be asynchronous. The use of asynchronous operations means that during the SQL processes, your application will continue to function normally without freezing.

With this connection mode, you don't have to worry about the volume of processed data, even if it will be considerable. Because the executed SQL operations are asynchronous, to check for their completion or possible execution errors, you will have to register some listener functions. These functions will be called any time a SQL operation fails or completes. Another way to check whether a SQL operation has been executed correctly or has generated errors is to define an instance of a Responder class, which will receive the events generated by the SQL operation. In both these cases, it's no longer necessary to define a try...catch construct.

The SQL operations will be executed in an independent process of your main application. AIR will generate an open event of the SQLEvent class if the connection to the database is opened correctly. If an error is returned, an error event of the SQLErrorEvent class will be generated. The SQLErrorEvent class exposes an error property, which represents an instance of the SQLError class, from which you can access detailed information regarding the error.

Now you'll see how to recreate the connection you created previously, using an asynchronous approach and registering the functions dbConnected() and dbConnectionError() to the events of the successful or failed connection:

```
// Import needed classes
import flash.data.SQLConnection;
import flash.events.SQLErrorEvent;
import flash.events.SQLEvent;
import flash.filesystem.File;

// instatiate SQLConnection object
var SQLconn : SQLConnection = new SQLConnection();

// register event listeners for SQL connection operation
SQLconn.addEventListener( SQLEvent.OPEN, dbConnected );
SQLconn.addEventListener( SQLErrorEvent.ERROR, dbConnectionError );
```

```
// create a file objetct pointing to database file
var dbFile : File =
        File.desktopDirectory.resolvePath( "MyDatabase.db" );

// try to connect to database
SQLconn.openAsync( dbFile );

function dbConnected( event : SQLEvent ):void
{
    // connection opened, now  you are ready to work with database
    trace("Database created!");
}

function dbConnectionError( event : SQLErrorEvent ):void
{
    // some error occurred, print details to output console
    trace( "Connection error message: " + event.error.message );
    trace( "Connection error details: " + event.error.details );
}
```

If you prefer to define an instance of a Responder type object instead of registering the events of the connection manually, you have to remove the event registration and instance the database connection this way:

```
// create a responder instance, mapped to desired functions
var connResponder : Responder =
        new Responder( dbConnected, dbConnectionError );

// instantiate SQL connection passing responder instance
sqlConn.openAsync( dbFile, SQLMode.CREATE, connResponder );
```

The use of Responder objects instead of manual registration of events to control SQL executions offers a more flexible approach that is easy to implement and preferable whenever possible.

Open the ch12p01_async.fla file in Flash CS4 to make an asynchronous connection to the database.

The project that will open is the same one used to test the synchronous connection to a database, so you will find the same Button and TextArea you used before on the stage. The only substantial difference is in the associated document class, which is now the ApplicationAsync class, saved in the ApplicationAsync.as file.

Open the Document Properties panel. In the Class field under the Publish section, you will find ApplicationAsync. Click the Edit class definition icon, which shows a pencil next to the name of the class that is associated with the project, to access the ActionScript code. The panel is shown in Figure 12-5.

12

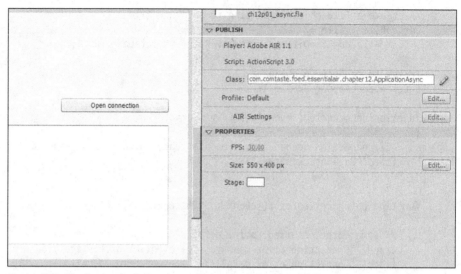

Figure 12-5. The Document Properties panel for the ch12p01_async.fla project

The ApplicationAsync class exposes the same methods and properties of the ApplicationSync class, except for the connectToDb() method. The new implementation of this function, which uses an asynchronous approach to SQL connection, requires the definition of two new functions: sqlConnectionOpenHandler() and sqlConnection➥ ErrorHandler(). These functions are necessary to receive notification of a successful or failed connection of the SQLConnection class. In addition, these functions make it necessary to import two new classes: SQLEvent and SQLErrorEvent. These classes will be used to transport the information regarding the events that will be generated by the SQL operations.

Here's how to create this asynchronous connection to the database:

```
Import flash.events.SQLEvent;
Import flash.events.SQLErrorEvent;

private function connectToDb():void
{
    // SQLConnection instance
    sqlConnection = new SQLConnection();
```

As you can see, the instantiation of the SQLConnection class is the same as it was for the synchronous approach explained previously. Now you have a valid instance of the SQLConnection class.

Before starting up the SQL connection, you have to prepare two callback methods for the events of successful (sqlConnectionOpenHandler()) and failed (sqlConnectionError➥ Handler()) connections; the two events to monitor are respectively the open event of the SQLEvent class and the error event of the SQLErrorEvent class. Then you register the sqlConnectionOpenHandler() method on the connection event and the sqlConnection➥ ErrorHandler() method on the event of failure to open the connection.

```
        // connection event listeners
        sqlConnection.addEventListener( SQLEvent.OPEN,
                    sqlConnectionOpenHandler );
        sqlConnection.addEventListener( SQLErrorEvent.ERROR,
                    sqlConnectionErrorHandler );
```

Once the event listener functions have been registered, you can call the openAsync() function of the SQLConnection class to start up the asynchronous connections.

Like for the open() method, next you pass the previously created dbFile variable as the only argument to the function, which represents the file you have indicated to contain the database you want to connect to:

```
        // try to connect to db
        sqlConnection.openAsync( dbFile );
```

Once the connection has been started up, write a message to confirm that the connection request has been started in the TextArea with the output instance name, and wait for one of the two prepared functions to be invoked at successful or failed connection:

```
        output.appendText( "Opening connection....\n" );
    }
```

Remember, the SQL operations that operate on asynchronous connections, including the opening of the connection itself, don't happen synchronously with the call of the command in question. These operations are processed **in parallel**, thereby allowing your application to continue to function correctly. When the required operation has been completed or fails, specific events are generated for which you should prepare two listener functions.

To manage the successful connection event, you use the sqlConnectionOpenHandler() function. When called, the method will receive an instance of the SQLEvent class from which you can access the specific information of the event. In this case, you only deal with writing a message confirming that the SQL connection was successful in the TextArea:

```
        // SQL connection opened
        private function sqlConnectionOpenHandler( event:SQLEvent ):void
        {
            output.appendText( "Connected to local db...\n" );
        }
```

12

In case of a connection error, the sqlConnectionErrorHandler() method is called. This method, instead of receiving an instance of the SQLEvent class, receives an instance of the SQLErrorEvent class that transports specific information regarding the error. When sqlConnectionErrorHandler() is called, you write an error message in the TextArea by using the information that the received SQLErrorEvent instance has passed on to you. You can access the text representation of the error message through the message property contained in the event object received by the function:

```
    // SQL connection error
    private function sqlConnectionErrorHandler( event:SQLErrorEvent ):void
    {
        output.appendText( "You have problems connecting to local db... "
                + event.error.message + "\n" );
    }
```

Go back to the Flash CS4 panel where your project, ApplicationAsync.as, is located. Select the Test Movie option from the Control menu; your application will be executed, and if no problems occur, you'll see a result similar to Figure 12-6.

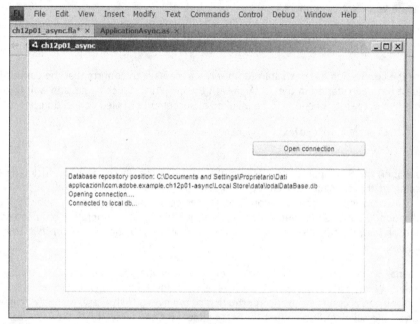

Figure 12-6. The application executed by Flash CS4

By clicking the Open connection button, you will start the request to open the asynchronous connection. In the TextArea, you will receive the messages you prepared in the ActionScript class.

You have seen how to create a local database and how to start synchronous and asynchronous connections to it. The two processes share most of the code. Now it's time to see how to interrupt an open connection regardless of the chosen connection mode.

Creating a test application

Next, let's assemble the functions and the concepts you have just experimented with into an single application. This application will allow you to start synchronous and asynchronous connections. Open the ch12p02.fla file in Flash. The stage will look like Figure 12-7.

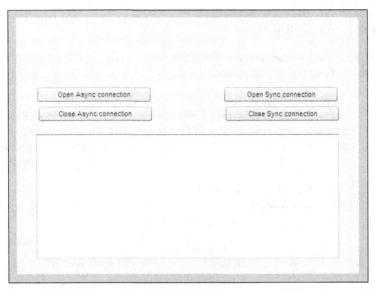

Figure 12-7. The layout of the ch12p02.fla project

For this project, the controls in the ch12p01_sync.fla and ch12p01_async.fla files will start and manage synchronous and asynchronous SQL connections for the database. The buttons have the same names as those used in the previous examples, and the Application class, which is the document class of the ch12p02.fla project, implements the same code as these two applications. You can open the ActionScript class by clicking the Edit class definition icon on the Document Properties panel (the pencil next to the Class field in the Publish section).

In the Application class, you'll add the code to allow and monitor the closing process of the open connection. For the asynchronous connection, you'll prepare event listener functions sqlConnectionCloseHandler() and sqlConnectionErrorHandler() to monitor the closure; whereas for the synchronous connection, you'll use a Responder object to check the outcome of the closure of the connection. The synchronous connection doesn't generate error or completion events like the asynchronous one. The synchronous connection allows you to use a Responder object instead of try...catch constructs to verify the outcome of the executed operations.

If you look at the code of the Application class, you'll find the two new functions closeSyncFunc() and closeAsyncFunc(), which are linked to the click event of the mouse for the two buttons that have been added to the stage. These buttons request the closure of the connection. The connection between the functions and the buttons is defined by the constructor function of the class using the addEventListener() method, as you have already seen for the buttons that deal with the startup of the SQL connection. Now take a look at the constructor function and the closeSyncFunc() and closeAsyncFunc() functions. The declaration of the variables that reference the closeSync and closeAsync buttons have also been added.

12

```
public var closeSync:Button;
public var closeAsync:Button;

// application constructor function
public function Application()
{
    // register layout events
    openSync.addEventListener( MouseEvent.CLICK, connectSyncFunc );
    closeSync.addEventListener( MouseEvent.CLICK, closeSyncFunc );
    openAsync.addEventListener( MouseEvent.CLICK, connectAsyncFunc );
    closeAsync.addEventListener( MouseEvent.CLICK, closeAsyncFunc );

    // initialize database file
    initLocalDataBase();
}

// called pressing close sync button
public function closeSyncFunc( event : MouseEvent ):void
{
    closeSyncDB();
}

// called pressing close async button
public function closeAsyncFunc( event : MouseEvent ):void
{
    closeAsyncDB();
}
```

The closeSyncFunc() and closeAsyncFunc() methods, called when the user interacts respectively with the closeSync and closeAsync buttons, call two new functions. These methods, closeSyncDB() and closeAsyncDB(), are prepared to manage the closure of the SQL connection.

Closing the synchronous connection. Next, you deal with the closure of the synchronous connection. You will use an instance of the Responder class to check the success and failure of the closure of the connection. The closing request is carried out by the closeSyncFunc() method.

First, you write in the TextArea that you are about to start the closing request of the opened synchronous connection:

```
// close async connection to db
private function closeSyncDB():void
{
    output.appendText( "Closing sync connection...\n" );
```

Subsequently, you prepare an instance of the Responder class, to which you associate the function to call in case of a successful operation (syncDbClosure()) or a failed operation (syncDbClosureError()). The Responder class requires that the two functions be passed as arguments during the instantiation of the class:

```
    var syncResponder:Responder =
        new Responder( syncDbClosure, syncDbClosureError );
```

Finally, you call the close() method of the SQLConnection class to start up the closing process of the connection, passing the Responder object as an argument:

```
    sqlConnection.close( syncResponder );
}
```

Now, when the closeSyncDB() method is called, AIR will try to close the synchronous connection you started previously. Depending on the outcome of the operation, one of the two functions will be called through the object of the instanced Responder class.

If the connection is closed correctly, the prepared syncDbClosure() function will receive an instance of the SQLEvent class containing the details relating to the event, and a message will be written in the TextArea notifying you of the correct completion of the requested operation:

```
// closed sync connection
private function syncDbClosure( event:SQLEvent ):void
{
    output.appendText( "closed sync db connection\n" );
}
```

If during the closure of the connection errors occur, the syncDbClosureError() function will be launched. In this function, you have an instance of the SQLError class to access the details of the error. The received error message will appear in the TextArea, containing the message property of the SQLError class:

```
// errors closing sync connection
private function syncDbClosureError( event:SQLError ):void
{
    output.appendText( "Errors closing sync db connection: "
        + event.message + "\n" );
}
```

Now, go back to the project ch12p02.fla, and execute it by selecting the Test Movie item from the Control menu. Once the application has been started, try to start and then close a synchronous connection using the prepared controls shown in Figure 12-8.

12

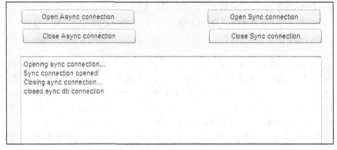

Figure 12-8. The ch12p02.fla application after the opening and closing of a synchronous SQL connection

Closing the asynchronous connection. The closeAsyncDB() method is executed when the user chooses to close an asynchronous connection. The function writes a message regarding the closure of the asynchronous connection in the TextArea and starts the closure by calling the close() method of the SQLConnection class:

```
// close async connection to db
private function closeAsyncDB():void
{
    output.appendText( "Closing async connection...\n" );

    // if error occurs, default error event handler will be called
    sqlConnection.close();
}
```

The event listener methods are as follows:

- sqlConnectionOpenHandler()
- sqlConnectionCloseHandler()
- sqlConnectionErrorHandler()

These methods are necessary to manage the correct closure or failure of the SQL connection. They are defined in the connectAsyncToDb() method before the asynchronous SQL connection is started:

```
// async connection to db
private function connectAsyncToDb():void
{
    // SQLConnection instance
    sqlConnection = new SQLConnection();

    // register callback for needed events
    sqlConnection.addEventListener( SQLEvent.OPEN,
            sqlConnectionOpenHandler );
    sqlConnection.addEventListener( SQLEvent.CLOSE,
            sqlConnectionCloseHandler );
    sqlConnection.addEventListener( SQLErrorEvent.ERROR,
            sqlConnectionErrorHandler );

    // init connection db
    sqlConnection.openAsync( dbFile );
    output.appendText( "Opening async connection...\n" );
}
```

To verify the completion of the closing operation of the connection, you have to register an event listener for the close event, defined as a static constant by the SQLEvent class. Possible closing errors will be intercepted and managed by the same method that is made to manage opening errors in the asynchronous SQL connection, sqlConnectionError➡ Handler(). If the closure happens correctly, the sqlConnectionCloseHandler() will be invoked and will write a closing message in the text area notifying you of the successful asynchronous closure:

```
    // SQL async connection closed
    private function sqlConnectionCloseHandler( event:SQLEvent ):void
    {
        output.appendText( "closed async db connection\n" );
    }
```

Let's go back to the ch12p02.fla project, and execute it by selecting the Test Movie item from the Control menu. Once you have launched the application, start and then close an asynchronous connection using the Open Async connection and Close Async connection buttons (shown in Figure 12-9).

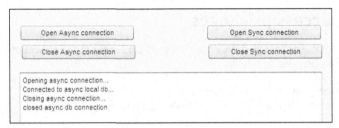

Figure 12-9. The application after the opening and closing of an asychronous SQL connection

You should now be acquainted with applications that use the SQLConnection class offered by AIR. You have seen how to open and close synchronous and asynchronous SQL connections in local SQLite databases. The next section shows you how to modify the behavior of the SQLConnection class to suit your needs.

Using optional connection parameters

When you open a connection to a database, be it synchronous or asynchronous, the only parameter that is required by the connection functions is a valid instance of a File object. This File object is the element that defines the position of the file containing the database in the computer. You can control other aspects of the connection by providing the openMode parameter to the open() and openAsync() functions.

The openMode parameter

The openMode parameter is a string of text that indicates ways in which you can access the database. The possible values are defined in the SQLMode class, and are as follows:

- create
- read
- update

Through this argument, you can tell the SQLConnection how it needs to behave during the access to a SQLite database. The value of the argument will determine whether the executed operations will be able to edit the data or only read the data.

12

> *The variables provided to a method can be called parameters or arguments of the relevant method.*

Using the create parameter shows AIR that the database in question has to be created from scratch if it doesn't exist. It is also possible to choose to access a database in read-only mode. If you use the read parameter, the database will be opened in read-only mode. Use the create or update parameters to give full writing and editing powers for the tables and data.

Assigning access privileges

To access a database through a previously created SQLConnection connection in read-only mode, you can proceed as follows:

```
// open read-only sync connection
sqlconnection.open( file, SQLMode.READ );
```

The SQLMode class defines the static constants corresponding to the access privileges that you can assign to a SQL connection. Those privileges are as follows:

- **Create connection mode**: This is the default value and indicates that you are connecting to a database with reading and writing privileges, and that if the indicated database doesn't exist, it will be created upon connection.
- **Read connection mode**: This indicates that you are connecting to a database with read-only privileges; if the database doesn't exist, an error is returned.
- **Update connection mode**: This indicates that you are connecting to a database with reading and writing privileges; if the database doesn't exist, an error is returned.

Using autoCompact

The autoCompact Boolean value tells the database to use unused space as soon as possible. This option optimizes the dimensions of the database. This option worsens database performance, however, as it must optimize space after every writing operation. Also, this option can occasionally generate a fragmentation of the saved data despite the optimization, slowing down the reading speed. This parameter is valid only when you access a new database created during the connection, or a database that still doesn't contain any tables. To optimize used space and defragment the data at the same time, use the compact() method of the SQLConnection class only when it is necessary, instead of this option.

Here is an example of how you can enable this option for a synchronous connection:

```
// create connection object
var conn:SQLConnection = new SQLConnection();

// point to database file
Var dbFile:File = File.desktopDirectory.resolvePath( "myDatabase.db" );
```

```
// open sync connction with autoCompact active
conn.open( dbFile, SQLMode.CREATE, true );
```

If one of the priorities of your application is to keep the contained dimensions, and you also want the database in use to be continuously forced to have the smallest dimensions possible, you will have to set the autoCompact argument true when you first start up the connection to the database. This behavior will optimize the dimensions of your database, but will have a negative influence on reading and writing performance.

Using pageSize

The pageSize numerical value indicates the size in bytes of the allocated memory for the layout of the tables of the database. The assigned value has to be between 512 and 32768, and it has to be in a power of two; the default value is 1024. This parameter is valid only when you access a new database created during the connection, or a database that doesn't contain any tables yet, and the connection has writing privileges. You can use this parameter to modify the quantity of memory bytes that are available to the database for the layout of the tables. Here is an example of how you can define the pageSize for your database with a size of 512 bytes:

```
// create connection object
var conn:SQLConnection = new SQLConnection();

// point to database file
Var dbFile:File = File.desktopDirectory.resolvePath( "myDatabase.db" );

// open sync connction defining pageSize to 512 bytes
conn.open( dbFile, SQLMode.CREATE, false, 512 );
```

Now you have seen which options are available to check the connection to a database. Next, you will become familiar with the properties and methods of the SQLConnection class itself.

Applying properties and methods of the SQLConnection class

The properties and methods discussed in this section give you more control over the behaviors of a SQL connection. The SQLConnection class offers ways for you to maintain and optimize the databases to which it connects. You can also use SQLConnection to define the behaviors of the database when you access its data.

The properties

Beyond the parameters you can assign to the open() and openAsync() methods, the SQLConnection class provides various properties that allow you to define the behavior of the SQL operations that will be executed.

cacheSize. This property defines the quantity of memory in bytes that can occupy the cache of execution of SQL operations of your connection. By increasing the size of the

12

cache, you can improve the performance of the SQL operations despite the quantity of used system memory. The default value is 2000.

columnNameStyle. The columnNameStyle property defines the format in which the table column names are returned as responses to selection queries on the database. The possible values are defined in the SQLColumnNameStyle class, and are the following:

- long: This indicates that the names of the columns will be returned in long format: [*table-name*]_[*column-name*].

- short: This indicates that the names of the columns will be returned in abbreviated format: [*column-name*]. If the query involves more than one table that contains columns with the same name, only one of these columns will be returned as a result.

- default: The default value, this indicates that the names of the columns will be returned in abbreviated form ([*column-name*]) when the query only involves one table; or, in the case of several tables, when there aren't any conflicts between the column names. Columns with coinciding names will be returned in the extended format: [*table-name*]_[*column-name*].

The methods

In addition to the properties just mentioned, the SQLConnection class also provides various ancillary methods. These methods allow the developer to carry out maintenance and analysis operations on the database.

analyze. This method deals with generating statistics for indexes of database tables. The statistical information obtained supports the SQL query optimization engine, which uses it to determine the best execution strategies. If database tables define the indexes present, but no statistics are generated, the optimization engine uses the indexes anyway. In this situation, the engine can't carry out the best execution choices, even though the performance is reduced.

> *The statistics are not automatically updated after INSERT, UPDATE, and DELETE operations; they need to be explicitly generated for the relevant tables or for the whole database. It's best to avoid obtaining statistical information during the execution of a SQL transaction (even if it's allowed). The changes made by a SQL transaction are effective only when the transaction has been completed. This means that statistics you obtain during a SQL transaction won't take all the transaction operations into account.*

deanalyze. This method allows you to remove the statistical information obtained through the analyze() method, thereby freeing up space in the database file.

attach. The attach() method dynamically adds other databases to your SQL connection. You can add up to ten databases to a single SQL connection; when you add a database to a connection, you need to specify an ID name that will allow you to directly access it. Using different names, you can add the same database to a connection several times.

When you add a database to a SQL connection, you can carry out the same operations and queries that you can for the main database. You can access the data in the tables in reading and writing modes. When you carry out queries on a connection to several databases, the SQL engine looks for the names of the tables that are indicated. It looks first in the main database, and then in the secondary databases, proceeding in the order that they are added onto the connection. This process stops at the first correspondence it finds. To explicitly access a table of a connected database, you use the complete name, made up of the ID name of the database plus the name of the table.

detach. This method removes a dynamically connected database from a SQL connection. It requires the ID name assigned to the database to be specified. It isn't possible to remove a database during the execution of a SQL transaction.

cancel. The cancel() method interrupts any active SQL query. If any SQL transactions are active, they are restored to their initial state. If there aren't any active operations, the cancel() method fails silently. This function can be useful for interrupting queries that are too long.

close. This method closes the connection to a database. By closing a database, all possible running operations are interrupted, and the connections to all additional databases are removed.

compact. This method compacts and defragments the structure of the database file on disk. The insertion and removal of rows in the tables progressively increase the quantity of empty spaces and the fragmentation of information, therefore worsening the performance of the database. It isn't possible to compact a database during a transaction. This operation only applies to the main database of a connection, and it cannot be carried out on databases that are only in temporary memory.

Now that you've explored the methods and properties provided by the SQLConnection class, it's time to get to know the class that is responsible for the execution of SQL operations.

Using the SQLStatement class in database operations

12

Now that you are able to create and manage a connection to one or more SQL databases, you can worry about how to carry out operations on them. In AIR, all the query operations on a database are under the realm of the SQLStatement class. You can use this class to do the following:

- Request data with SELECT operations
- Insert new data INSERT operations
- Update existing data with UPDATE operations
- Remove data with DELETE operations

To carry out queries, an instance of the SQLStatement class has to be connected to a SQL connection through the sqlConnection property; this property allows a SQL instruction to be used at different times on different databases.

To query a database, you need an instance of the SQLStatement class:

```
// crate sql statement instance
var statement:SQLStatement = new SQLStatement();
```

Now you have an object to carry out queries. Next, you must specify which database connection the SQLStatement instance will have to focus on. Assign the instance of the SQL connection to the sqlConnection property as shown here:

```
// link statement to our db connection ('dbConnection'),
// previously created
statement.sqlConnection = dbConnection;
```

Now you have to assign the SQL query that you want to carry out. To do so, you pass the following SQL code to the text property of your object:

```
// create SQL statement string
var sql:String = " SELECT * FROM my_table_name ";

// pass sql string to statement instance
statement.text = sql;
```

Before you can execute the query, you must create a Responder object, of the flash.net. Responder class. This class defines the method to be called at the end of the query or in case of error, as shown here:

```
// create a Responder
var queryResponder : Responder =
    new Responder( sqlStatementResult, sqlStatementError );

// create responder assigned functions
function sqlStatementResult ( result:SQLResult ):void
{
    // statement execution succeeds correctly
    // instruct your application to proceed
}

function sqlStatementError ( error:SQLError ):void
{
    // statement execution fails
    // instruct your application to manage errors that occurred
}
```

Responder objects are valid for synchronous as well as asynchronous SQL connections, and their use is preferable to the use of event listener functions or try...catch constructs. It's preferable because, at every execution of the query, you can, if necessary, redefine the functions that will manage the completion of the query or cases of error.

Alternatively, for asynchronous SQL connections, you can register the sqlStatement➡ Result() and sqlStatementError() methods to your instance of SQLStatement. These methods intercept and manage events of the successful or failed query, as shown here:

```
// register listener methods with addEventListener() function
statement.addEventListener( SQLEvent.RESULT, sqlStatementResult );
statement.addEventListener( SQLErrorEvent.ERROR, sqlStatementError );

// create listener functions
function sqlStatementResult ( event:SQLEvent ):void
{
    // statement execution succeeds correctly
    // instruct your application to proceed
}

function sqlStatementError ( event:SQLErrorEvent ):void
{
    // statement execution fails
    // instruct your application to manage errors that occurred
}
```

Once you have defined the SQL query, assigned the database on which you want to operate, and prepared some functions to manage successful or failed queries, you can execute the SQL instruction.

To start the query, you have to call the execute() method of your instance of SQLStatement; if you are operating on an asynchronous connection and you have prepared listener functions, all you have to do is call the execute() method without any additional parameters:

```
// execute async SQL statement registered with event listeners
statement.execute();
```

If you have prepared the use of a Responder object, you will have to pass it as a parameter to the execute() function. This approach is valid for synchronous as well as asynchronous connections.

```
// execute statement with responder object,
// valid for both sync and async connections
statement.execute( -1,  queryResponder );
```

In the case of synchronous connections, instead of preparing listener functions or Responder objects, you can use a try...catch construct to manage possible errors:

```
// execute sync statement
Try
{
    statement.execute();
} catch ( e:SQLError )
{
    // statement execution fails
```

12

```
        // instruct your application to manage errors that occurred
    }

        // statement execution succeeds correctly
        // instruct your application to proceed
```

The SQLStatement instances so created allow you access the data in the database in read-ing and writing modes, but they don't offer the possibility of easily editing the parameters of the query.

Suppose you have to extract information regarding a certain column of a table at a given time of your application, and then access the content of another column of the same table. In this case, you would have two alternatives: create a new instance of SQLStatement for the new query or redefine the text property of the preexisting instance.

The first option is better in terms of performance, but it entails the allocation of a new object in memory. The second option has no impact on the allocation in memory, but it worsens the execution performance. With the second option, you can keep track of the various queries to use them again later when necessary.

Obviously, neither of these two solutions is optimal if you have to carry out many similar queries at various times in your application. Fortunately, the SQLStatement class provides a third possibility: the use of **parameters** in your SQL instruction. You will explore this function further later on.

Creating tables in a database

The moment has finally arrived to begin creating tables in the database of the ch12p03.
fla application. You will use the CREATE TABLE SQL command in a SQL instruction. Similar to a SELECT or INSERT instruction, this SQL command requires you to specify which col-umns will be present in the table and what kind of data each column will contain.

To create a table, you must do the following:

1. Start a connection to a database with writing privileges.
2. Create a SQLStatement instance to build your SQL query.
3. Define the SQL code to execute.
4. Register the success and failure events of your SQL instruction.
5. Start the query.

In the code for connecting to a database and creating a table, you will create a friends table that simulates an address book that will contain the names, surnames, and e-mail addresses of your friends.

Open the ch12p03.fla file in Flash CS4. The project contains the code you need to con-nect to the database in asynchronous mode and create the friends table. The available methods and elements on the screen are the same as those in the ch12p01_async.fla file, with the addition of a button to create the table and the methods linked to it. You can see the ch12p03.fla stage in Figure 12-10.

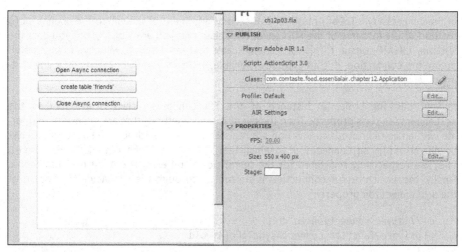

Figure 12-10. The stage in the ch12p03.fla project

Access the document class of the ch12p03.fla project by clicking the Edit class definition icon (the pencil next to the Class field in the Publish section of the Document Properties panel), as shown in Figure 12-10. The event listener functions for the buttons on the stage of the ch12p03.fla project are registered in the constructor method of the class. The three buttons (openSync, closeSync, and createTable) are registered on the connect➥ AsyncFunc(), closeAsyncFunc(), and createTableFunc() methods. The latter function is called when the creation of a database table is requested. Then the initLocalDataBase() method is launched, which instances the SQLConnection object, which will be used by the class. Here is the constructor method of the class:

```
public function Application()
{
    // register layout events
    openAsync.addEventListener( MouseEvent.CLICK, connectAsyncFunc );
    closeAsync.addEventListener( MouseEvent.CLICK, closeAsyncFunc );
    createTable.addEventListener( MouseEvent.CLICK, createTableFunc );

    // initialize database file
    initLocalDataBase();
}
```

The createTableFunc() method is associated with a click on the createTable button. A click on this button will call the method that will create the table in the database:

```
// called pressing create table button
public function createTableFunc( evt : MouseEvent ):void
{
    createMainTable();
}
```

12

579

Starting a connection to a database with writing privileges

In the connectAsyncToDb() method, as a second argument of the call to the openAsync() method of the instance of the SQLConnection class that you are working on, you pass the SQLMode.CREATE constant. This constant indicates that the database will have to be created during the connection, if it isn't already available, and that you will have reading and writing privileges on it.

In the following code, an instance of the SQLConnection class is assigned to the sqlConnection class property. Then the event listener methods that are necessary to operate with an asynchronous connection are registered. These methods are sqlConnection➡ OpenHandler(), sqlConnectionCloseHandler(), and sqlConnectionErrorHandler(). They are respectively registered for the open, close, and error events of the connection. Finally, the asynchronous connection is started up through the openAsync() method of the sqlConnection property:

```
// async connection to db
private function connectAsyncToDb():void
{
    // SQLConnection instance
    sqlConnection = new SQLConnection();

    // register callback for needed events
    sqlConnection.addEventListener( SQLEvent.OPEN,
            sqlConnectionOpenHandler );
    sqlConnection.addEventListener( SQLEvent.CLOSE,
            sqlConnectionCloseHandler );
    sqlConnection.addEventListener( SQLErrorEvent.ERROR,
            sqlConnectionErrorHandler );

    // init connection db
    sqlConnection.openAsync( dbFile, SQLMode.CREATE );
    output.appendText( "Opening async connection...\n" );
}
```

Creating a SQLStatement instance to build your SQL query

When you call the createMainTable() method, the first thing you have to do is create an instance of the SQLStatement class. To do so, you assign a new instance of the SQLStatement class to a local statement variable:

```
// create database table
 private function createMainTable():void
 {
    // create sql statement instance
    var statement:SQLStatement = new SQLStatement();
```

Once the SQLStatement instance has been created, you assign the open SQL connection to the sqlConnection property. By doing so, you specify which database the SQL instruction that you are creating will have to work on:

```
// link statement to our db connection
statement.sqlConnection = sqlConnection;
```

Defining the SQL code to execute

Then you create a string of text containing the SQL instruction to execute on the database to create the friends table. In the SQL code, you insert a control that doesn't recreate the folder if it already exists, so as to avoid unwanted SQL errors, as shown here:

```
var sql:String = "";
sql += "CREATE TABLE IF NOT EXISTS friends ( ";
sql += "friendId INTEGER PRIMARY KEY AUTOINCREMENT, ";
sql += "firstName TEXT, ";
sql += "lastName TEXT, ";
sql += "email TEXT ";
sql += ")";
```

Assign the SQL instruction to the text property of your SQLStatement instance, as shown here:

```
// pass sql string to statement instance
statement.text = sql;
```

Registering the success and failure events

As shown, you register the listener functions for the events that are generated with the successful or failed SQL query:

```
statement.addEventListener( SQLEvent.RESULT,
        sqlStatementResult );
statement.addEventListener( SQLErrorEvent.ERROR,
        sqlStatementError );
```

Starting the query

Now you are ready to execute the SQL instructions. Start by invoking the execute() method, as shown here:

```
// executes SQL query
statement.execute();
}
```

12

Once your SQL instruction has been executed, one of the two registered functions will be called: sqlStatementResult() in case of success, or sqlStatementError() in case of failure.

If an error occurs and the execution fails, the sqlStatementError() method will be invoked. To this method will be passed an object of the SQLErrorEvent type. From this object, you can access the details of the error to understand what hasn't worked properly. You write the content of the error message in the TextArea as shown here:

```
// called when sql statements have errors
private function sqlStatementError( event:SQLErrorEvent ):void
{
    output.appendText( "Errors  in sql execution [ "
            + event.error.operation + " ]... "
            + event.error.message + "\n" );
}
```

If, on the other hand, the SQL call was successful, the registered method will receive a SQLEvent type object, from which you will be able to access more specific information on the result of the operation. In this specific case, the creation of a new table doesn't return any particularly useful information on the processed data, it simply declares that the table has been created correctly and is ready to receive the data to save. Here is the sqlStatementResult() method:

```
// called when sql statement executes correctly
private function sqlStatementResult( event:SQLEvent ):void
{
```

Through the target property of the instance of the SQLEvent class, which has been transmitted to the function, you can access the instance of SQLStatement, which has been executed and has generated the completion event. As shown here, assign the value to a local variable by forcing its type to SQLStatement:

```
// access SQLStatement instance
var statement:SQLStatement = event.target as SQLStatement;
```

Next, remove the event listeners that you previously associated with the executed SQLStatement instance, as shown here:

```
// remove listeners for this statement
statement.removeEventListener ( SQLEvent.RESULT,
        sqlStatementResult );
statement.removeEventListener ( SQLErrorEvent.ERROR,
        sqlStatementError );
```

Write a message confirming correct execution in the TextArea, as follows:

```
output.appendText( "SQL statement executed correctly. \n" );
```

Launch the getResult() method of the SQLStatement class to access the data that the database returns from your query. Being the operation the creation of a table, the method getResult() doesn't return anything. The code is as follows:

```
// access returned data
var sqlResult:SQLResult = statement.getResult();
```

If the data property of the instance of SQLResult returned by the getResult() method of the SQLStatement class is not null, you verify its content; otherwise, you show that the executed SQL query hasn't returned any results in the TextArea. To execute this check, you use two nested if...else constructs:

```
if( sqlResult.data != null )
{
    if( sqlResult.data.length > 0 )
    {
        output.appendText( "SQL statements "
      + "returned some values \n" );
    }else
    {
        output.appendText( "SQL statements "
      + "returned no values \n" );
    }
} else
{
    output.appendText( "SQL statements returned no values \n" );
}
```

The SQLStatement instance contains the possible results of your query, as well as other information such as the number of rows of the database involved in the executed operation (rowsAffected). You write the number of rows affected by the operation in the TextArea, as shown here:

```
// row affected
output.appendText( "SQL statements affected "
        + sqlResult.rowsAffected + " rows \n" );
```

You also write the value of the last automatically generated index as a primary key, in case of data insertion operations in the database (lastInsertRowID). Write the value of the lastInsertRowID property in the TextArea as shown here:

```
// last insert ID
output.appendText( "SQL last insert row id: "
        + sqlResult.lastInsertRowID + "\n" );
}
```

12

Testing the class

Return to the ch12p03.fla Flash project, to which the Application class is associated. Compile the class by selecting the Test Movie item from the Control menu. When the application has started, you can see a preview (as shown in Figure 12-11).

> *You have to be careful working with this application. If the buttons are not clicked in the right order (shown next), the application will generate unpredictable exceptions.*

Follow these steps to test the application:

1. Start the connection.
2. Create the friends table.
3. Close the SQL connection.

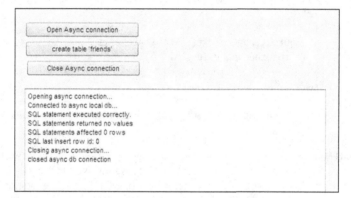

Figure 12-11. The ch12p03.fla application after having opened the connection and created the friends table in the database

Now the application is able to connect to a database in synchronous as well as asynchronous mode. You can even create a table in the database. It's time to see how to add data to this table.

Executing SQL instructions in asynchronous mode

In this section, you'll see how to extend the code you just created to insert data into your table, and also how to access the information passed on to the method called upon completion of the insertion to monitor the status of your database.

Open the ch12p04.fla file and its Application document class. In this project, you'll find the code necessary to create the friends table. The code, originally shown in the ch12p03. fla file, has been modified to use the instance of the Responder class instead of the listener events. Event listener methods are only valid for asynchronous connections that have already been defined previously. You can see a preview of what the stage of the ch12p04.fla project should look like in Figure 12-12.

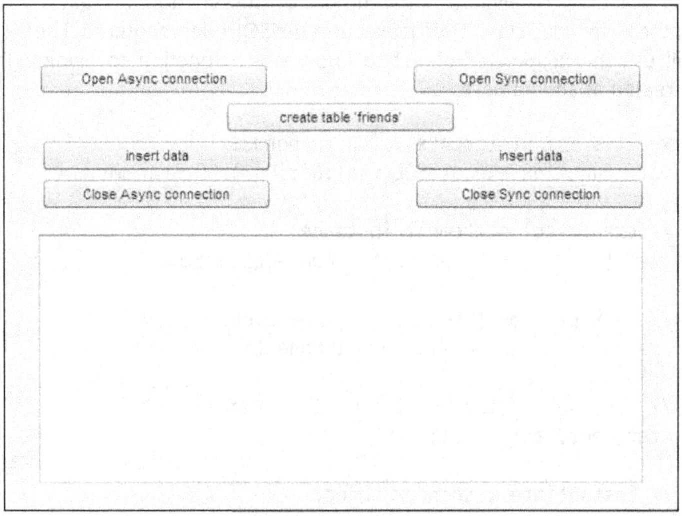

Figure 12-12. The stage of the ch12p04.fla application

This modification allows you to use the createMainTable() method for synchronous as well as asynchronous connections. The Responder objects are allowed for both SQL connection modes.

See how the createMainTable() method has changed:

```
// create database table
 private function createMainTable():void
 {
    // create SQL query
    var sql:String = "";
    sql += "CREATE TABLE IF NOT EXISTS friends ( ";
    sql += "friendId INTEGER PRIMARY KEY AUTOINCREMENT, ";
    sql += "firstName TEXT, ";
    sql += "lastName TEXT, ";
    sql += "email TEXT ";
    sql += ")";
```

After you have created the string of text containing the SQL instruction, you call a new excuteSQL() method to carry out SQL queries. This method will use the instances of the Responder class to manage the success and failure of the requested SQL operations. Launch the method by passing the SQL string to execute as an argument, as shown here:

12

```
        // launch query execution via executeSQL() function
        executeSQL( sql );
    }
```

The executeSQL() method requires the string containing the SQL operations to execute to be passed to it. It begins by creating a new instance of SQLStatement. Then it associates the instance with the opened SQL connection, be it synchronous or asynchronous, and assigns it the SQL code received as an argument of the function. It creates an instance of an object of the Responder class. Then it executes the SQL query required. The SQLStatement instance will use the Responder object to know which function to invoke. The method should be created as shown here:

```
    // executes sql statements using responder
    private function executeSQL( sql:String ):SQLStatement
    {
        // create sql statement instance
        var statement:SQLStatement = new SQLStatement();

        // link statement to our db connection
        statement.sqlConnection = sqlConnection;

        // pass sql string to statement instance
        statement.text = sql;

        // instantiate responder object
        var responder:Responder = new Responder( sqlResponderResult,
            sqlResponderError )
```

> When you use Responder objects with the SQLStatement class, you have to provide the instance created by the Responder class as a second argument for the execute() method. This method has the task of starting the execution of the required SQL operation.

The first argument that has to be provided to the execute() method is an integer value that indicates the maximum number of rows returned from the SQL query. If the SQL operation isn't a selection, this parameter has no influence on the query. Its default value is –1, indicating that all the rows requested by the SELECT operation will be returned.

```
        // execute query
        statement.execute( -1, responder );

        return statement;
    }
```

In the following section, you will see how to use this parameter to gain more control over reading the data in the database.

Inserting data into a database table

To insert a sequence of data in your friends table, you can create as many instances of the SQLStatement class as the number of rows of data to insert, or you can reuse the same instance several times, adding a row at a time.

In AIR, you can start several queries at a time on a database by using various instances of SQLStatement. However, since inserting and editing different data at the same time might cause some problems, the more traditional approach of inserting one record at a time is recommended.

To make a sequential insertion of your data possible, you first have to define an array that will contain the list of data to add to the SQL table. Add the following code at the beginning of your class:

```
public var asyncStatementList:Array = new Array();
```

Now you have to add the list of SQL instructions to the array. To do so, you create a testAsyncStatements() method that will be invoked when you click the insertDataAsync button on the stage of the Flash project:

```
public function testAsyncStatements():void
{
    var sql:String;
```

At every request to insert data, before preparing the list of data to add, empty the friends table of the database. This will keep the number of rows down and limit the number of written messages in the TextArea. Before preparing the insertion instructions, you ask for the table to be cleared, so that each time you access the application, the database won't contain preexisting data. To clear the table, you use the SQL DELETE command, as shown here:

```
// RESET DATA
sql = "";
sql += "DELETE FROM friends; ";
asyncStatementList.push( sql );
```

Create and store into the asyncStatementList array the following SQL INSERT instructions:

```
// insert data
sql = "";
sql += "INSERT INTO friends (firstName, lastName, email) ";
sql += "VALUES ('Bob', 'Smith', 'bob.smith@gmail.com'); ";
asyncStatementList.push( sql );

sql = "";
sql += "INSERT INTO friends (firstName, lastName, email) ";
sql += "VALUES ('Mark', 'White', 'mark.white@gmail.com'); ";
asyncStatementList.push( sql );
```

12

```
sql = "";
sql += "INSERT INTO friends (firstName, lastName, email) ";
sql += "VALUES ('Sarah', 'Lang', 'sarah333@gmail.com');";
asyncStatementList.push( sql );
```

Now that you have created a list of valid SQL strings, you can start executing them one by one. To execute a list of asynchronous SQL operations in sequence, you'll create the nextAsyncStatement() method. To start the sequence of SQL queries, launch nextAsyncStatement() the first time, as shown here:

```
        // start inserting queue
        nextAsyncStatement();
    }
```

The nextAsyncStatement() method will call the executeAsyncSQL() method to execute the SQL strings that have been saved in the asyncStatementList array, as shown here:

```
    public function nextAsyncStatement():void
    {
```

Every time the nextAsyncStatement() method is called, it checks whether the array containing the SQL instructions to execute still contains elements. If there are still available elements, the code execution proceeds; otherwise, the execution of the method is exited using the return command. To check if there are any further SQL instructions to execute, you have to check if the length property of asyncStatementList is equal to 0, as shown here:

```
        // if no statements in queue fails silently
        if( asyncStatementList.length == 0 )
                return;
```

Extract the first available element from the execution list by using the shift() method of the Array class, as shown here:

```
        // get sql to process
        var sql:String = String( asyncStatementList.shift() );
```

Finally, call the executeAsyncSQL() method by passing it the SQL code to execute as an argument:

```
        // executes requested query
        var statementInstance:SQLStatement = executeAsyncSQL( sql );
    }
```

The executeAsyncSQL() method does the following:

- Creates an instance of the SQLStatement class
- Assigns the instance the active connection to the database
- Registers the functions to the necessary events and executes the SQL query

The executeAsyncSQL() method returns the local instance of the created SQLStatement to the caller, therefore making it available for other operations:

```
// executes sql statements in Async mode
private function executeAsyncSQL( sql:String ):SQLStatement
{
    // create sql statement instance
    var statement:SQLStatement = new SQLStatement();

    // link statement to our db connection
    statement.sqlConnection = sqlConnection;

    // pass sql string to statement instance
    statement.text = sql;

    // register event listeners
    statement.addEventListener( SQLEvent.RESULT,
        sqlStatementAsyncResult );
    statement.addEventListener( SQLErrorEvent.ERROR,
        sqlStatementAsyncError );

    // execute query
    statement.execute();

    // return generated statement instance
    return statement;
}
```

Every time a SQL operation is finished correctly, the sqlStatementAsyncResult() method is called. This method will deal with accessing the result returned by the SQL engine and extracting the relevant information. The getResult() method returns the SQL result as an instance of a SQLResult object. Before it finishes, the sqlStatementAsyncResult() method checks whether the list of SQL instructions to execute still contains elements and, if necessary, calls the executeAsyncSQL() method again.

Managing SQL operation completion

Next, we'll examine the sqlStatementAsyncResult() method in detail.

```
// called when sql statement executes correctly
private function sqlStatementAsyncResult( event:SQLEvent ):void
{
```

Once the completion event has been received, you obtain a reference to the instance of the SQLStatement that has just been processed. You can access this instance through the target property of the SQLEvent class:

```
// retrieve sql statement instance via target property of SQLEvent
var statement:SQLStatement = evt.target as SQLStatement;
```

12

Through the reference to the SQLStatement instance, you can manually remove the event listeners that are registered via the addEventListener() command when it is created. By explicitly removing these associations, you facilitate and accelerate the application's **garbage collection** process. You can remove event listener methods as shown here:

```
// remove associated event listeners
// to make the garbage collection process easier
statement.removeEventListener( SQLEvent.RESULT,
        sqlStatementResult );
statement.removeEventListener( SQLErrorEvent.ERROR,
        sqlStatementError );
```

Next, enter the SQL code you have just executed in the TextArea as follows:

```
// output in console executed SQL statement
output.text += "*** Executed query:\n" + statement.text +"\n";
```

Now follow these steps:

1. Access the SQLResult instance that is associated with the SQL operation you have just executed.
2. Check how many rows of the database have been involved in your operation.
3. Write it in the TextArea.

The code for these actions is shown here:

```
// access returned data
var sqlResult:SQLResult = statement.getResult();

// row affected by SQL operation
output.text += "SQL statements affected "
        + sqlResult.rowsAffected + " rows \n" ;

// last insert ID generated, if any
output.text += "SQL last insert row id: "
        + sqlResult.lastInsertRowID + "\n";
```

Once the data-processing operations are completed, check if the list of instructions still contains SQL instructions to execute in asynchronous mode. If necessary, call the nextAsyncStatement() method again, as shown here:

```
// if still there execute queued statements
if( asyncStatementList.length > 0 )
        nextAsyncStatement();
}
```

Managing SQL insertion errors

If the execution of the SQL insertion fails, the sqlStatementAsyncError() method will be called. The method will deal with removing the event listener methods related to the SQLStatement instance that has generated the error. That is done to make it easier to free up memory. Then it displays the details of the error in the output console and, if necessary, proceeds with the execution of the SQL instructions that are waiting:

```
private function sqlStatementAsyncError( event:SQLErrorEvent ):void
{
```

Next, follow these steps:

1. Obtain a reference to the SQLStatement instance that generated an error of execution through the target property of the SQLErrorEvent class.

2. Remove the event listeners associated with the SQLStatement instance.

3. Write the received error in the TextArea.

The code for these actions is shown here:

```
// retrieve sql statement instance via
//target property of SQLErrorEvent
var statement:SQLStatement = evt.target as SQLStatement;

// remove associated event listeners to
//facilitate garbage collection process
statement.removeEventListener( SQLEvent.RESULT,
        sqlStatementResult );
statement.removeEventListener( SQLErrorEvent.ERROR,
        sqlStatementError );

// write error's details in output console
output.text += "SQL statement errors [ "
        + event.error.operation + " ]... "
        +  event.error.message + "\n";
```

If necessary, the following SQL instruction will be executed:

```
// if still there execute queued statements
if( asyncStatementList.length > 0 )
        nextAsyncStatement();
}
```

Return to the Flash CS4 panel containing the ch12p04.fla project, and launch it by selecting Control ➤ Test Movie. Once you've started the application, you'll request the following:

12

1. An asynchronous connection to the database.

2. The creation of the table.

3. The insertion of the data and the closure of the connection, by using the buttons you have prepared on the stage for this purpose. You can see the buttons in Figure 12-13.

When you execute these operations, remember to follow the correct sequence; otherwise, you might cause errors. For example, Flash CS4 will generate an error if you create a table before opening a connection to the database.

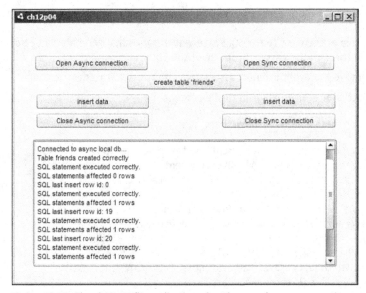

Figure 12-13. The ch12p04.fla application after the asynchronous operations on the database have been executed

In this section, you've seen how to insert data into a database using an asynchronous connection. Next, you'll see how to execute the same operations in synchronous mode.

Executing SQL instructions in synchronous mode

In this section, you'll continue to work on the ch12p04.fla file and its Application class. When you execute queries on the database using a synchronous connection, the instructions are carried out once the command is sent. Then the application waits for the successful or failed conclusion of the operation. Therefore, it isn't necessary to create a recursive function to append data, as you did for the asynchronous approach.

Here's how to create the testSyncStatement() method, which will be executed every time you click the Button with instance name insertSync on the application stage:

```
public function testSyncStatements():void
{
    var res:SQLStatement;
    var sql:String;
```

As with the asynchronous approach, you create the SQL strings to execute, but instead of saving them in an execution list, you start them off one after the other in sequence. Use the executeSyncStatement() method as follows to execute the synchronous SQL instructions:

```
// RESET DATA
sql = "";
sql += "DELETE FROM friends; ";
res = executeSyncSQL( sql );

// insert data
sql = "";
sql += "INSERT INTO friends (firstName, lastName, email) ";
sql += "VALUES ('Bob', 'Smith', 'bob.smith@gmail.com'); ";
res = executeSyncSQL( sql );

sql = "";
sql += "INSERT INTO friends (firstName, lastName, email) ";
sql += "VALUES ('Mark', 'White', 'mark.white@gmail.com'); ";
res = executeSyncSQL( sql );

sql = "";
sql += "INSERT INTO friends (firstName, lastName, email) ";
sql += "VALUES ('Sarah', 'Lang', 'sarah333@gmail.com');";
res = executeSyncSQL( sql );
}
```

As you may know, the executeSyncStatement() method will use a try...catch construct to execute the SQL instructions and intercept possible errors.

The executeSyncStatement() method receives the SQL string to execute as an argument. To execute the required SQL code, you have to do the following:

1. Create a SQLStatement instance.

2. Associate the instance to your SQL connection, which you have already started.

3. Assign the received SQL code to the text property of SQLStatement instance.

The code to accomplish these actions follows:

```
// executes sql statements in Sync mode
private function executeSyncSQL( sql:String ):SQLStatement
{
try
    {
```

12

```
// create sql statement instance
var statement:SQLStatement = new SQLStatement();

// link statement to our db connection
statement.sqlConnection = sqlConnection;

// SQL string
statement.text = sql;
```

You execute the SQL operation by calling the execute() method, as shown here:

```
// execute query
statement.execute();

} catch ( e:SQLError )
{
```

If the SQL operation were to generate errors, the body of the catch() construct would be executed, and you could manage the error situations. In this case, you would return a null value to the calling method to show that the operation wasn't successful. The catch() construct receives an instance of the SQLError class as argument, and through it you can gather detailed information on the error. To return a null value, do the following:

```
// return null when error
return null;
}
```

If the operation executes correctly, you return the SQLStatement instance. Then you can have the testSyncOperation() method access detailed information on the SQL query, if necessary. By doing so, you eliminate the necessity of using functions that are linked to the success and failure events, and even the necessity of having to manage an execution sequence. To return the generated SQLStatement instance, do the following:

```
return statement;
}
```

Testing the application

This approach is definitely faster than the asynchronous connection procedure, but it offers decreased performance if there is a large quantity of data to manage, and it definitely offers less flexibility for the programmer. It's up to you which approach to adopt according to your requirements.

Return to the Flash CS4 panel containing the ch12p04.fla project and execute it (Control ➤ Test Movie). Figure 12-14 shows the application during execution. Once the application has started, you request the following:

1. A synchronous connection to the database
2. The creation of the table

3. The insertion of data

4. The closure of the connection by using the buttons you have prepared to manage the synchronous SQL operations

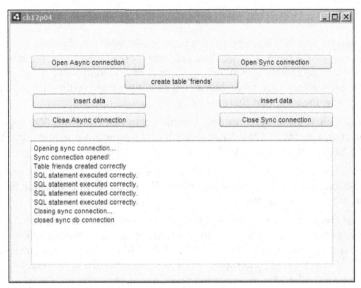

Figure 12-14. The ch12p04.fla application after executing synchronous operations on the database

Now the database table contains data.

Accessing SQL data

The operations for reading SQL data are pretty much identical to those for inserting the data in the database. The differences are mainly in the information to which you have access once the SQL query has been completed and in the SQL command you use, which will be SELECT instead of INSERT. To be able to access and use the data returned by a selection operation, you have to have a better understanding of the SQLResult class. So next, we'll take a minute to look at the properties offered by this class.

Using the SQLResult class

The SQLResult class is used by AIR in response to any executed SQL query. SQL operations get a SQLResult instance from the getResult() method of the SQLStatement class received. This instance contains information on the number of edited rows and any auto-generated indexes.

If the SQL operation is of data selection (SELECT), the SQLResult instance returned from the getResult() method of the SQLStatement class contains the requested data. It also contains the other information returned for the SQL operations. The requested data is exposed through the data property. If data is null, it means that your selection query hasn't produced any results; otherwise, it represents an array containing objects that correspond to the rows of data returned by the SQL operation.

Overall, the SQLResult class has four properties, all of which are read-only:

- complete: This is a Boolean value that indicates when all the available rows from the query have been returned. This property is used when a series of data has been requested by specifying a maximum number of rows returned per call. In this case, complete will be true only when all the rows have been returned; otherwise, it will be false, meaning that there is still data.

- data: This is an array containing the data returned from the SQL engine at the selection operation. If the SQL operation isn't a selection operation or if the selection hasn't produced results, this property will be null.

- lastInsertRowID: This represents the numerical value of the index generated by the database during an INSERT operation. If the operation in question isn't INSERT, this property is equal to 0.

- rowsAffected: This indicates the number of rows that have been edited, deleted, or added to the SQL operation to which the SQLResult instance refers. This property is only valid for INSERT, UPDATE, and DELETE operations; otherwise, it is equal to 0. If it is a DELETE operation, you have to specify the WHERE clause in the SQL expression; otherwise, no value will be indicated, regardless of the number of rows involved in the operation.

Querying the content of the friends table in asynchronous mode

This section extends the example created so far. You will add the code to query the data of the table and to navigate among the returned rows. Begin by opening the ch12p04b.fla file in Flash CS4. Access its Application document class through the Edit class definition icon in the Document Properties panel. You can see a preview of the ch12p04b.fla project in Figure 12-15.

To query the selection of the content of the table, create the following testAsync-Select() method, which will provide the necessary SQL code and start the SQL query:

```
public function testAsyncSelect():void
{
    var sql:String;
```

Use the following SQL SELECT command to return all the rows of data in the friends table and add it to the asynchronous instruction execution sequence:

```
// select data
sql = "";
sql += "SELECT * FROM friends";
asyncStatementList.push( sql );
```

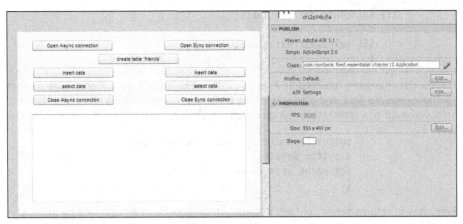

Figure 12-15. The stage of the ch12p04b.fla application

Use the following nextAsyncStatement() method to ask for your SQL selection query to be processed:

```
            nextAsyncStatement();
    }
```

In the sqlStatementResult() method at the end of each asynchronous SQL operation, add the code highlighted in bold. Put it after the SQLResult instance request for the operation that has just concluded:

```
    // called when sql statement executes correctly
    private function sqlStatementResult( evt:SQLEvent ):void
    {
        var statement:SQLStatement = evt.target as SQLStatement;
        statement.addEventListener( SQLEvent.RESULT,
            sqlStatementResult );
        statement.addEventListener( SQLErrorEvent.ERROR,
            sqlStatementError );

        output.appendText( "SQL statement executed correctly. \n" );

        // access returned data
        var sqlResult:SQLResult = statement.getResult();
```

After executing the operations, you check to see if they have returned any data. To do so, you check whether the data property of the returned SQLResult instance from your query is null, or if it contains elements.

If the data property doesn't contain rows of data, you write that the SQL operation hasn't returned data in the TextArea, and continue processing the sequence of asynchronous SQL instructions, as shown here:

12

```
        if( sqlResult.data != null )
        {
            if( sqlResult.data.length > 0 )
            {
```

If some data has been returned as a result of the executed SQL operation, you write that you have received data, and then you list the content of every returned row in the TextArea. To access each row returned by the query, you use a for...each loop as shown here:

```
            output.appendText( "SQL DATA returned:\n" );
            var item:Object;
            for each( item in sqlResult.data )
            {
```

Every row of returned data contains information on the columns requested by the query; therefore, you can access the received data through the properties of the object that represents the row. The names of the properties will correspond to the names of the columns they are associated with. The code to accomplish these actions follows:

```
            output.appendText( "    row: " + item.firstName
    + " " + item.lastName + "\n" );
            }
        }else
            output.appendText( "SQL statements returned no values\n" );

        }else
        {
            output.appendText( "SQL statements returned no values\n" );
        }

        // row affected
        output.appendText( "SQL statements affected "
            + sqlResult.rowsAffected + " rows \n" );
        // last insert ID
        output.appendText( "SQL last insert row id: "
            + sqlResult.lastInsertRowID + "\n" );

        // if still there execute queued statements
        if( asyncStatementList.length > 0 )
            nextAsyncStatement();
    }
```

The added code deals with checking if data has been returned with the instance of the obtained SQLResult class. If the data exists, each row will be examined, and the name and surname of each contact returned from the selection operation on the friends table will be extracted.

Now go back to the Flash CS4 panel containing the ch12p04b.fla project and execute it (Control ➤ Test Movie). Once the application has started, ask for the following:

1. An asynchronous connection to the database

2. The creation of the table and the insertion of data

3. The selection of the inserted data

4. The closure of the connection

You have to execute these operations using the buttons you prepared on the stage to manage the asynchronous SQL operations. You can see the results returned by the SQL selection in the TextArea in Figure 12-16.

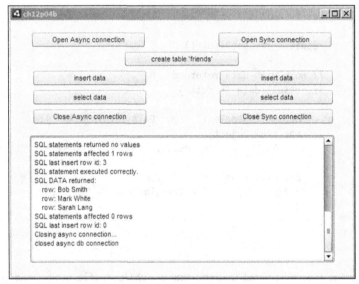

Figure 12-16. The ch12p04b.fla application after executing the selection of data on the database using an asynchronous connection

Querying the content of the friends table in synchronous mode

To query the data using a synchronous approach, you have to create the testSyncSelect() method like you did for the asynchronous approach. The testSyncSelect() method begins by creating the SQL code to execute, as shown here:

```
public function testSyncSelect():void
{
    var result:SQLResult;
    var res:SQLStatement;
    var sql:String;

    // select data
    sql = "";
    sql += "SELECT * FROM friends";
```

```
// executes sync query
res = executeSyncSQL( sql );
```

The creation of and execution request for the SQL query are the same as you've seen for the asynchronous connection. In this case, a SELECT operation will be executed, so you will check if the executed operation has been completed. You will also see if the SELECT operation has returned rows of data through the data property of the SQLResult instance associated with the query. If some data has been returned, you write the information associated with it in the TextArea of your application, as you have already done for the asynchronous connections. The code to accomplish these actions follows:

```
if( res != null )
{
    result = res.getResult();

    // work with data returned
    if( result.data != null )
    {
        output.appendText( "sync DATA returned:\n" );
        var item:Object;
        for each( item in result.data )
        {
        output.appendText( "    row: "
    + item.firstName + " " + item.lastName + "\n" );
        }
    }
}
```

Go back to the Flash CS4 panel that contains the ch12p04b.fla project and compile it (Control ➤ Test Movie). Once the application has started, execute the following operations:

1. A synchronous connection to the database
2. The creation of the table
3. The insertion of data
4. The selection of the inserted data
5. The closure of the connection

These operations have to be executed by using the buttons you have prepared on the stage to manage synchronous SQL operations. Figure 12-17 shows the messages returned once the sequence of requested operations has been completed.

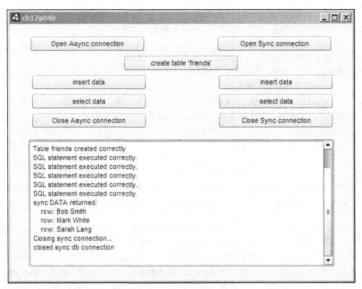

Figure 12-17. The ch12p04b.fla application after executing the selection of data on the database using a synchronous connection

Now you are able to access the data contained in a database. If you are working on a large volume of data, this operation could be very time-consuming, especially if it's synchronous. To avoid this problem, you can ask for the results to be returned on several pages. This concept is explained in the next section.

Splitting returned table data into pages

You know that accessing SQL data in AIR allows you to carry out SELECT operations on data contained in database tables. When you execute SELECT operations, it is also possible to ask the data to be returned in blocks called **pages**, rather than all together.

The SQLStatement class gives you control over how many rows of data should be on each returned page.

Separating data into pages is useful when you are working with large volumes of data, making the execution of SQL selection operations easier and faster. Obviously, receiving 20 rows at a time is much more efficient, for Flash and for you, than receiving 200 or more rows at a time.

To tell the SQLStatement class that you want the requested data divided into pages, you have to provide a parameter to the execute() method. The given value will indicate the maximum number of rows that can be returned on each page. By default, this property has a value of –1, which corresponds to no division into pages. The following block of code shows how to request that the data split into pages:

12

```
// create SQL statement instance
var statement:SQLStatement = new SQLStatement();

// assign previously opened SQL connection
statement.sqlConnection = dbConn;

// assign SELECT instructions
statement.text = "SELECT * FROM friends";
// executes SQL query indicating max 5 rows returned per page
statement.execute( 5 );
```

The preceding code creates a SQL SELECT instruction by specifying that the returned data will have to be split into pages of maximum 5 rows each; this means that if the response to the SQL query contains 30 rows, the data will be returned on 6 pages.

When you ask a database to return data split into pages, the rows returned from the execution of the SQL instruction will correspond to the data of the first returned page. Then, to find out whether there are other pages of data, you have to access the SQLResult instance of the SQL operation it has executed. Finally, you must verify the value of the complete property. If the property returns false, it means that there are other pages of data; otherwise, it means that the page of saved data in the data property of the received SQLResult instance is the last one available.

If other pages are available, to request their content, you have to use the next() method of the SQLResult class. If you call the execute() method instead of the next() method, you'll continue to receive the content of the first page.

The next() method will return the next page of data when it is available. If next() is called on a set of results that doesn't have any other pages to return, a SQLResult instance with a null data property and a true complete property will be returned. You can pass a parameter that corresponds to the maximum number of rows for the following page to the next() method. If a value isn't provided, the SQL query will return all remaining rows of data for the current operation.

In the next section, you will see an example of how you can use this approach to read the data your table returns page by page. You will access the database in asynchronous mode.

Page layout of data in asynchronous connections

Open the ch12p05.fla file in Flash CS4 and access its document class. You can see a preview of the stage of the ch12p05.fla project in Figure 12-18. You want to split the data into pages with a maximum of two rows each. To obtain this result, you have to assign the value 2 to the execute() method as a first argument.

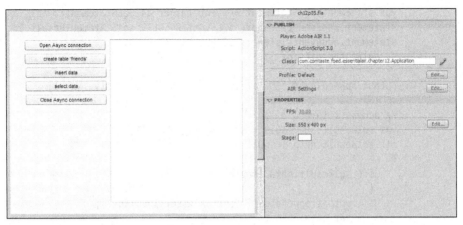

Figure 12-18. The stage of the ch12p05.fla project

Change the executeAsyncSQL() method you created previously as follows:

```
// executes sql statements in Async mode
private function executeAsyncSQL( sql:String ):SQLStatement
{
    // create sql statement instance
    var statement:SQLStatement = new SQLStatement();

    // link statement to our db connection
    statement.sqlConnection = sqlConnection;

    // pass sql string to statement instance
    statement.text = sql;

    // event linsteners
    statement.addEventListener( SQLEvent.RESULT,
        sqlStatementResult );
    statement.addEventListener( SQLErrorEvent.ERROR,
        sqlStatementError );

    // execute query specifying max number of rows for page
    statement.execute( 2 );

    return statement;
}
```

It is also necessary to add the following code to the sqlStatementResult() method. Currently, it doesn't allow you to access the pages of data returned by SQL SELECT queries after the first one.

```
// called when sql statement executes correctly
private function sqlStatementResult( event:SQLEvent ):void
{
```

12

```
var statement:SQLStatement = event.target as SQLStatement;
statement.addEventListener( SQLEvent.RESULT, sqlStatementResult );
statement.addEventListener( SQLErrorEvent.ERROR,
    sqlStatementError );

output.appendText( "SQL statement executed correctly. \n" );

// access returned data
var sqlResult:SQLResult = statement.getResult();
if( sqlResult.data != null )
{
    if( sqlResult.data.length > 0 )
    {
        output.appendText( "SQL DATA returned:\n" );
        var item:Object;
        for each( item in sqlResult.data )
        {
        output.appendText( "    row: "
            + item.firstName + " "
            + item.lastName + "\n" );
        }
    }else
        output.appendText( "SQL statements returned no values\n" );

}else
{
    output.appendText( "SQL statements returned no values\n" );
}

// row affected
output.appendText( "SQL statements affected "
    + sqlResult.rowsAffected + " rows \n" );

// last insert ID
output.appendText( "SQL last insert row id: "
    + sqlResult.lastInsertRowID + "\n" );
```

Now you've enabled the page-splitting function for the SQL selection operations. You have to check if the current query has returned all the available rows before proceeding to the next SQL instruction.

To check if the current set of data in the data property of the SQLResult instance is associated with your SQL operation, you have to check the value of the complete property of the SQLResult instance. If the property in question returns true, it means that all the data available has been returned, whereas if it's false, it means that you still have at least a page of data to receive. Use the following code to check the value of the complete property:

```
if( !sqlResult.complete )
{
```

If complete returns true, you have to ask for the following page of data. You write a page-change message in the TextArea. Then you call the next() method on the SQLStatement instance in execution, passing the number of rows you want to receive in the following page as an argument. The prefetch argument of the next() method asks in the same way as the prefetch argument of the execute() method:

```
output.appendText( "--- request "
+ "next page of SQL result set\n" );

// require next part of resultSets
statement.next( 2 );
```

If there are still pages of data on the same SQL query, interrupt the execution of the method by using the return command, as shown here:

```
    // do not proceed in next queued SQL
    return;
}
```

When all the pages have been returned, the following code will be executed:

```
    // if still there execute queued statements
    if( asyncStatementList.length > 0 )
        nextAsyncStatement();
}
```

Now you can return to the Flash project panel and execute the ch12p05.fla project (Control ➤ Test Movie). Start a connection, insert data, and then read it. Your application should look like Figure 12-19.

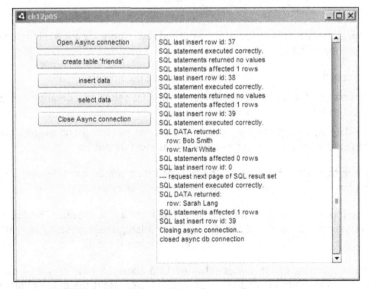

Figure 12-19. The ch12p05.fla applicaton in execution

The next section is about using value objects for returned rows of data. The use of typed value objects allows you to obtain more solid code that is easier to understand.

Accessing data in a table using value objects

A **value object** is a class instance that defines a group of properties. These properties normally refer to a group of correlated data. For example, a class value object could contain the personal data of a person or sales details of a store article.

When you execute a SELECT operation on the tables of an AIR database, it returns the requested data through the data property of the SQLResult class. As you have just seen, AIR allows you to split the rows that have been returned into pages to improve the performance of the execution of your SQL instructions.

Each row is returned as an instance of an object. Each column of the table is converted into a property of the object, using the column name as the property name. This conversion allows you to go through the returned data row by row in for...in loops and access the returned values for each column easily.

While this approach is already quite powerful, the SQLStatement class allows you to go even further, offering you the possibility of explicitly defining the data that is returned by row. To define the data in the returned rows, you have to assign a class to the itemClass property of the SQLStatement instance. By doing so, an instance of the specified class will be created for each returned row, and its properties will be populated with the data of the row in question. The following code shows how to assign a typed class to the itemClass property:

```
// define Class type for returning data
statement.itemClass = FriendVO;
```

To make this automatic conversion of the returned rows, there are a few minimum requirements for the indicated class:

- The constructor of the class must not require parameters.
- Each name of a returned column from the SQL selection operation has to correspond to the name of a property.
- The data type of the properties of the class has to correspond to the data type in the returned columns and these properties must be public.

If you adhere to these requirements, the returned data will be correctly mapped; otherwise, if the mapping isn't possible, generic objects will be returned.

You can use this technique with the returned data from a SQL database. By doing so, you can fully exploit the potential of the ActionScript 3 language, drastically limit the errors due to wrong conversions, and carry out safer checks on the data.

To define the mapping of the values returned to a class you have created, you use the FriendVO class. The following code creates a class to represent the data of your friends table. The class is saved in the src folder of the ch12p06.fla project, and the file is FriendVO.as.

```
// FriendVO class definition
package com.comtaste.foed.essentialair.chapter12
{
public class FriendVO
{
    public var friendId:int;
    public var firstName:String;
    public var lastName:String;
    public var email:String;
```

Next, prepare a personalized toString() method that returns a formatted string containing the saved values in the properties of the class:

```
    public function toString():String
    {
        return " firstName: " + firstName
            + ", lastName: " + lastName
            + ", email: " + email;
    }
    }
}
```

The class created to represent the data of each row correctly exposes a property for each column of the friends table. Because the properties of the class coincide with the database table fields, they can be associated with the rows returned from the selection of the table data.

Now let's see how to use the FriendVO class you have just created in association with the data returned from a SQL selection operation on your friends table. First, you access the Application document class of the Flash project ch12p06.fla. To make the mapping possible, you have to import the value class created as shown here:

```
    Import FriendVO;
```

Then you have to modify the construction of the SQLStatement instances, instructing AIR on how it will have to treat the returned data for the SQL queries. The executeAsyncSQL() method will be updated as follows:

```
    // executes sql statements in Async mode
    private function executeAsyncSQL( sql:String ):SQLStatement
    {
        // create sql statement instance
        var statement:SQLStatement = new SQLStatement();

        // link statement to our db connection
        statement.sqlConnection = sqlConnection;

        // pass sql string to statement instance
        statement.text = sql;
```

12

During the initialization of the SQLStatement instances, you have to pass a reference of the value class to the itemClass property of the SQLStatement class. This is needed to allow the mapping of the rows returned with your value class FriendVO. Thanks to the following assignment, AIR will be able to map the rows of received data correctly:

```
// define associated class for returned rows
statement.itemClass = FriendVO;

// event listeners
statement.addEventListener( SQLEvent.RESULT,
    sqlStatementResult );
statement.addEventListener( SQLErrorEvent.ERROR,
    sqlStatementError );

// execute query
statement.execute( 2 );

return statement;
}
```

Finally, update the sqlStatementResult() method as follows so that the FriendVO value class can be used to access the data returned from the SQL selection queries:

```
// called when sql statement executes correctly
private function sqlStatementResult( event:SQLEvent ):void
{
    var statement:SQLStatement = event.target as SQLStatement;
    statement.addEventListener( SQLEvent.RESULT,
        sqlStatementResult );
    statement.addEventListener( SQLErrorEvent.ERROR,
        sqlStatementError );

    output.appendText( "SQL statement executed correctly. \n" );

    // access returned data
    var sqlResult:SQLResult = statement.getResult();
    if( sqlResult.data != null )
    {
        if( sqlResult.data.length > 0 )
        {
            output.appendText( "SQL DATA returned:\n" );
```

Having defined the FriendVO class as a value of the itemClass property of your queries, every returned row will be automatically mapped to an instance of this class. Ensure that the designated value object class for the mapping process and the data returned for each row of the query have corresponding types and names.

For each row of data returned from the query, enter the returned value from the toString() method you created in the FriendVO value class in the TextArea:

```
                // map any row to FriendVO
                var item:FriendVO;
                for each( item in sqlResult.data )
                {
                output.appendText( "    row: " + item.toString() );
                }
            }else
                output.appendText( "SQL statements returned no values\n" );

        }else
        {
            output.appendText( "SQL statements returned no values\n" );
        }

        // row affected
        output.appendText( "SQL statements affected "
            + sqlResult.rowsAffected + " rows \n" );

        // last insert ID
        output.appendText( "SQL last insert row id: "
            + sqlResult.lastInsertRowID + "\n" );

        if( !sqlResult.complete )
        {
            output.appendText( "--- request next "
            + "page of SQL result set\n" );
            // require next part of resultSets
            statement.next( 2 );

            // do not proceed in next queued SQL
            return;
        }

        // if still there execute queued statements
        if( asyncStatementList.length > 0 )
            nextAsyncStatement();
    }
```

Now, when you receive the requested data, you execute a cast operation on the returned object, declaring it as a FriendVO type.

> A **cast operation** is a conversion operation. This operation tells the Flash CS4 compiler that a given property has to be converted into the specified type. If the conversion isn't possible, Flash Player will generate an exception during the execution of the operation.

Now return to the Flash CS4 panel containing the ch12p06.fla project and execute it (Control ➤ Test Movie). After having executed the possible SQL queries, the TextArea will show the operation details, as you can see in Figure 12-20.

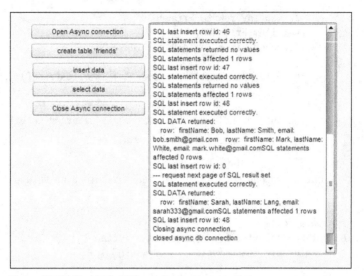

Figure 12-20. The ch12p06.fla application in execution

The next section is about parameters. You have already seen some uses of parameters in SQL instructions. Now you'll see what they have to offer in more detail.

Assigning parameters to SQL queries

Parameters allow you to dynamically update parts of the SQL code at every execution. The parameters are defined in the string of SQL text and can be of two types: **ordinal**, meaning that they can be accessed by order of insertion, or **associated with a label**, meaning that they can be accessed by name. To indicate the insertion of an ordinal parameter, you use the ? character, as shown here:

```
// create SQL statement string with unnamed parameter
statement.text = " SELECT * FROM ? ";
```

In this example, the use of the ? means that the name of the table from which the information has to be extracted is defined by an ordinal parameter. The parameters of a SQL query are saved in the parameters object, which contains both the ordinal parameters without a label and the parameters associated with a label.

The key of the object assigned to the ordinal parameters corresponds to their order of creation in the SQL string, whereas for parameters with a label, the key corresponds to the label itself. Parameters associated with a label are defined using the : and @ parameters, followed by the label itself, as shown here:

```
// create SQL statement string with named parameter using ":"
statement.text = " SELECT * FROM :tableName ";

// create SQL statement string with named parameter using "@"
statement.text = " SELECT * FROM @tableName ";
```

Both examples define a parameter with a name. The first defines the :tableName label and the second defines the @tableName label.

Using parameters is the only way to control the types of the values passed to the queries. As ActionScript 3 is a strongly typed language, it takes typed variables values and assigns them to parameters maintaining the correct type.

Without the use of parameters, the conversion of the values passed through the SQL query string is carried out implicitly by the SQL engine.

Here is an example of how to use parameters with an associated label:

```
// create SQL statement string with named parameter using "@"
statement.text = "SELECT * FROM friends WHERE email = @email ";
// access parameter and set it to a valid value
statement.parameters[ "@email" ] = "mark@comtaste.com";

// execute SQL statement
statement.execute();
```

The same example, if you prefer to use parameters without a label, would look like this:

```
// create SQL statement string with unnamed parameter using "?"
statement.text = "SELECT * FROM friends WHERE email = ? ";

// access parameter and set it to a valid value
statement.parameters[ 0 ] = "mark@comtaste.com";

// execute SQL statement
statement.execute();
```

Parameters are also fundamental for avoiding unwanted interference with your data through **SQL injection attacks**. These kinds of attacks are created by linking SQL code to the text inserted by the user in an editable text field, enabling attackers to run potentially malicious SQL code in your database.

By using parameters, you considerably limit the risk of SQL injections, as the data inserted by the user is processed before being used and not simply linked to the final SQL string.

The assignment of the value of a variable to a parameter happens by copy, not by reference. Therefore, if your reference value changes over time, you will have to update the saved value in the parameter of the SQLStatement instance.

You can use the clearParameters() method to remove all the values associated with the parameters in the SQLStatement class.

Using parameters in the address book example

You have seen how to map the values returned from SQL operations and how to use parameters. Now you'll add these capabilities to your application. First, open the

12

ch12p07.fla file and its Application document class. After the declaration of the class variables, declare the three following properties:

```
protected var insertStatement:String =
"INSERT INTO friends (firstName, lastName, email) "
        + "VALUES ( :firstName, :lastName,  :email );";
protected var selectStatement:String = "SELECT * FROM friends";
protected var deleteAllStatement:String = "DELETE FROM friends; ";
```

These variables contain your SQL instruction strings for the insertion, deletion, and selection of rows from the friends table. The SQL string to insert the rows in the table is saved in a String that exposes three parameters: :firstName, :lastName, and :email. For each row to insert in the table, you save an object that defines three properties with names that correspond to the defined parameters.

To use an execution sequence of SQL instructions that includes parameters to define the values to associate with the SQL query, you need to save two values for each instruction: the string of SQL text and an object containing the parameters that define the values to use for the query. To transport and manage this information, you create an internal class that is only accessible from your Application class.

Then, after closing the class and the package, at the end of the document, you declare the StoredQuery class:

```
class StoredQuery
{
    public var text:String;
    public var parameters:Object;

    public function StoredQuery( text:String,
                     parameters:Object = null )
    {
        this.text = text;
        this.parameters = parameters;
    }
}
```

The internal class is created and exposes two public properties: text (SQL instruction) and parameters (an optional object containing the parameters that can be defined for the SQL instruction).

Next, modify the testAsyncStatements() method and the testAsyncSelect() method. In this update, the array asyncStatementList doesn't contain strings, but instances of the StoredQuery class you have just defined.

```
public function testAsyncStatements():void
{
    var deleteQuery:StoredQuery =
            new StoredQuery( deleteAllStatement );
    asyncStatementList.push( deleteQuery );
```

```
        var insertParams:Object = new Object();
        insertParams[ ':firstName' ] = "Matteo";
        insertParams[ ':lastName' ] = "Ronchi";
        insertParams[ ':email' ] = "matteo@comtaste.com";
        var insertQuery:StoredQuery =
                    new StoredQuery( insertStatement, insertParams );
        asyncStatementList.push( insertQuery );

        insertParams = new Object();
        insertParams[ ':firstName' ] = "Fabio";
        insertParams[ ':lastName' ] = "Bernardi";
        insertParams[ ':email' ] = "fab@comtaste.com";
        insertQuery = new StoredQuery( insertStatement, insertParams );
        asyncStatementList.push( insertQuery );

        insertParams = new Object();
        insertParams[ ':firstName' ] = "Sarah";
        insertParams[ ':lastName' ] = "Lang";
        insertParams[ ':email' ] = "sarah333@gmail.com";
        insertQuery = new StoredQuery( insertStatement, insertParams );
        asyncStatementList.push( insertQuery );

        nextAsyncStatement();
    }

    public function testAsyncSelect():void
    {
        var selectQuery:StoredQuery = new StoredQuery( selectStatement );
        asyncStatementList.push( selectQuery );

        nextAsyncStatement();
    }
```

Proceed by updating the nextAsyncStatement() method. This method extracts the saved objects containing the parameters for the SQL insertion instruction one by one. For any object, the necessary information is passed for the executeAsyncSQL() method.

```
    public function nextAsyncStatement():void
    {
        // if no statements fails silently
        if( asyncStatementList.length == 0 )
            return;
```

Each extracted element from the sequence of SQL instructions is an instance of the internal StoredQuery class. Through this class, you can access the SQL string and possible parameters associated with it, and pass them on to executeAsyncSQL() to start the query. The following code extracts the first object from the array and requests the execution of the associated SQL operation:

12

```
        // get sql parameters object
        var sqlStored:StoredQuery =
                asyncStatementList.shift() as StoredQuery;

        // request query execution
        var statementInstance:SQLStatement;
        statementInstance =
                executeAsyncSQL( sqlStored.text, sqlStored.parameters );
    }
```

Each object extracted from the array is passed on to the executeAsyncSQL() method, which creates the instance of the SQLStatement class with the necessary data, as shown here:

```
// executes sql statements in Async mode
 private function executeAsyncSQL( sql:String,
                                parameters:Object = null ):SQLStatement
{
    // create sql statement instance
    var statement:SQLStatement = new SQLStatement();

    // link statement to our db connection
    statement.sqlConnection = sqlConnection;

    // pass sql string to statement instance
    statement.text = sql;
```

Each time the execution of a SQL instruction is requested, you check if parameters have been passed to be associated with the SQLStatement instance and, if necessary, you associate them with the parameters property of the SQLStatement instance, as shown here:

```
// if parameters are available, pass them to SQL statement
if( parameters != null )
{
        // loop on passed parameters
        var param:String;
        for( param in parameters )
        {
            statement.parameters[ param ] = parameters[ param ];
        }
    }

// define associated class for returned rows
statement.itemClass = FriendVO;

// event listeners
statement.addEventListener( SQLEvent.RESULT, sqlStatementResult );
statement.addEventListener( SQLErrorEvent.ERROR,
    sqlStatementError );
```

```
        // execute query
        statement.execute( 2 );

        return statement;
    }
```

Now your application can implement parameters correctly.

Every time that the testAsyncSelect() method is executed, you will create a new SQL SELECT operation request.

Go back to the Flash project ch12p07.fla and launch it (Control ➤ Test Movie). Connect to the database and execute some operations on it. Figure 12-21 shows what the application should look like during execution.

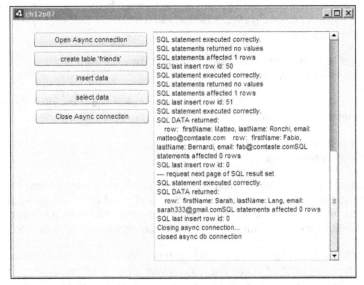

Figure 12-21. The ch12p07.fla application in execution

This chapter has presented many SQL functions provided by AIR. One last important function for executing complex SQL operations remains to be examined: SQL transactions. The next section will provide an introduction to transactions, as well as a practical example of how to use them.

Using transactions in AIR

Working with relational databases often involves manipulating various tables at the same time. Sometimes, the sequence of SQL operations requires a discreet number of operations and every operation depends on the successful completion of the previous one.

What would happen if during the execution of a sequence of operations that depend on each other, one query fails? The probability of compromising the data saved on your database would be high. To face these kinds of situations, the SQL languages offer "protected" execution mechanisms called **transactions**.

A transaction allows you to execute a sequence of SQL operations and, if one of the queries fails, gives you the opportunity to restore the structure of and data contained in the database to the state they were in before starting the transaction.

To start a transaction, you call the begin() method of the SQLConnection class:

```
// INIT TRANSACTION
sqlConnection.begin();
```

From this moment on, all the SQL operations that are executed will be part of the transaction, and if one of these fails, the database will be restored to its initial state. To restore the database to initial conditions in case of failure, you have to call the rollback() method of the SQLConnection class:

```
// go back to last database's valid state
sqlConnection.rollback();
```

If all the operations are successful, you have to complete the transaction by calling the commit() method of the SQLConnection class:

```
// close open transaction
sqlConnection.commit();
```

Some SQL languages allow you to **nest** transaction inside other transactions. This makes it possible to create complex operations that offer conditional behaviors based on the outcome of the internal transactions. This mechanism offers not only the possibility going back to an initial transaction, but also to the last state considered valid by the database.

The SQLite implementation in AIR doesn't currently allow you to create nested transactions; therefore, any attempt at opening a transaction when one is already open will simply be ignored by the SQL engine. The next sections present the use of the commit(), rollback(), and begin() methods provided by AIR for working with SQL transactions.

Using methods of the SQLConnection class

The SQLConnection class was introduced earlier in this chapter. In this section, you'll examine the three following methods of this class in more detail:

- begin()
- rollback()
- commit()

Starting transactions with begin

The begin() method starts the SQL transaction. All the operations executed after this will be grouped together, making it possible to undo them by restoring the database to the state before the transaction, or confirm them by making the executed operations definite and irreversible. One transaction can also include operations carried out on different databases connected via an active SQL connection. This method accepts two optional arguments:

- option: This is a string of text that indicates how the SQL engine will manage the transaction that it is opening. The possible values are defined as constants in the SQLTransactionLockType class, and are as follows:

  - SQLTransactionLockType.DEFERRED: The default value, this means that the databases involved in the transaction will be made inaccessible to other SQL connections only after the first SQL operation has been started.

  - SQLTransactionLockType.EXCLUSIVE: This means that each database linked to the connection will be made inaccessible to other connections as soon as possible, and it won't be unblocked until the conclusion of the transaction.

  - SQLTransactionLockType.IMMEDIATE: This means that every database linked to the connection will be available to other SQL connections in read-only mode and will not be accessible in writing mode until the conclusion of the transaction.

- responder: This is an instance of the Responder class that defines the function to call in case of completion or failure of the opening of the transaction.

Restoring databases with rollback

The rollback() method allows you to restore the database to the last valid state before the SQL transaction. It accepts an instance of the Responder class as its only argument, which defines the functions to call if the database is successfully restored to its initial state.

Confirming changes with commit

The commit() method gives the database the confirmation to make the changes made by the operations included in the transactions permanent. It accepts an instance of the Responder class as its only optional argument, which defines the methods to call if the database is successfully restored to its initial state.

Next, we'll look at a practical application of the use of SQL transactions.

Writing a SQL transaction

Open the ch12p08.fla file and access its Application document class through the Edit definition class icon on the Document Properties panel. This project faithfully reproduces the previous one: it adds the use of the SQL transactions to insert the data in the friends table. This project will restore the database in case the data input generates execution errors.

12

Modify the testAsyncStatements() method by adding the opening of a SQL transaction before executing the insert operations. Remember that you must call the begin() method of the SQLConnection class to start a SQL transaction. All the SQL operations executed on the instance of the involved connection will be grouped, and it will be possible to restore the database to its initial state. The following code shows the method, with the added parts to start the SQL transactions highlighted in bold:

```
public function testAsyncStatements():void
{
    // INIT TRANSACTION
    output.appendText( "-----> BEGIN transaction\n" );
    sqlConnection.begin();

    var deleteQuery:StoredQuery =
        new StoredQuery( deleteAllStatement );
    asyncStatementList.push( deleteQuery );

    var insertParams:Object = new Object();
    insertParams[ ':firstName' ] = "Matteo";
    insertParams[ ':lastName' ] = "Ronchi";
    insertParams[ ':email' ] = "matteo@comtaste.com";
    var insertQuery:StoredQuery =
        new StoredQuery( insertStatement, insertParams );
    asyncStatementList.push( insertQuery );

    insertParams = new Object();
    insertParams[ ':firstName' ] = "Fabio";
    insertParams[ ':lastName' ] = "Bernardi";
    insertParams[ ':email' ] = "fab@comtaste.com";
    insertQuery = new StoredQuery( insertStatement, insertParams );
    asyncStatementList.push( insertQuery );

    insertParams = new Object();
    insertParams[ ':firstName' ] = "Sarah";
    insertParams[ ':lastName' ] = "Lang";
    insertParams[ ':email' ] = "sarah333@gmail.com";
    insertQuery = new StoredQuery( insertStatement, insertParams );
    asyncStatementList.push( insertQuery );

    nextAsyncStatement();
}
```

You have to update the two event listener methods, sqlStatementResult() and sqlStatementError(). These methods are registered for the SQL queries so that you can confirm the changes or restore the database according to the outcome of the executed operations. First, you update the sqlStatementResult() method, which is called after each operation that has been executed correctly. Here is the sqlStatementResult() method:

```
// called when sql statement executes correctly
private function sqlStatementResult( evt:SQLEvent ):void
{
    var statement:SQLStatement = evt.target as SQLStatement;
    statement.addEventListener( SQLEvent.RESULT, sqlStatementResult );
    statement.addEventListener( SQLErrorEvent.ERROR,
        sqlStatementError );

    output.appendText( "SQL statement executed correctly. \n" );

    // access returned data
    var sqlResult:SQLResult = statement.getResult();
    if( sqlResult.data != null )
    {
        if( sqlResult.data.length > 0 )
        {
            output.appendText( "SQL DATA returned:\n" );

            // map any row to FriendVO
            var item:FriendVO;
            for each( item in sqlResult.data )
            {
                output.appendText( "    row: " + item.toString() );
            }
        }else
            output.appendText( "SQL statements returned no values\n" );

    }else
    {
        output.appendText( "SQL statements returned no values\n" );
    }

    // row affected
    output.appendText( "SQL statements affected "
            + sqlResult.rowsAffected + " rows \n" );

    // last insert ID
    output.appendText( "SQL last insert row id: "
            + sqlResult.lastInsertRowID + "\n" );

    if( !sqlResult.complete )
    {
        output.appendText( "--- request next "
        + "page of SQL result set\n" );
        // require next part of resultSets
        statement.next( 2 );

        // dont't proceed in next queued SQL
        return;
    }
```

12

Once you have completed a SQL instruction without any errors, you check if the process-ing sequence still contains instructions to process. When you don't have any more SQL instructions to process, you check if you are inside a SQL transaction, and if you are, you close it and confirm the executed operations with the commit() command of the SQLConnection class. Once you have confirmed the executed operations, it won't be pos-sible to restore the database to the initial state before the transaction. Once the transac-tion is closed, you write a message in the TextArea to confirm the success of the operation, as shown here:

```
// if still there execute queued statements
if( asyncStatementList.length > 0 )
{
    nextAsyncStatement();

} else if( sqlConnection.inTransaction )
{
    // auto-Commit if a transaction still open
    output.appendText( "-----> COMMIT transaction\n" );
    sqlConnection.commit();
}
}
```

All you have left to do is update the sqlStatementError() method, which is called when one of your SQL operations fails, generating an execution error. The following code shows how to edit the sqlStatementError() method:

```
// called when sql statements have errors
private function sqlStatementError( evt:SQLErrorEvent ):void
{
    output.appendText( "Errors in sql execution [ "
        + evt.error.operation + " ]... "
        + evt.error.message + "\n" );
```

If an error occurs during your SQL operations, the sqlStatementError() method will be called. You check if the error happened when the SQL connection had an open transaction and, if possible, restore the database to its state before the transaction.

To restore the initial state of the database, you call the rollback() method of the SQLConnection class. If you are inside a transaction, restore database to its original state using the rollback() method. Otherwise, if the list of SQL instructions still contains ele-ments, you proceed with the execution of the next instruction, as shown here:

```
// rollback TRANSACTION
if( sqlConnection.inTransaction )
{
    output.appendText ( "-----> ROLLBACK "
        + "transaction, 'cause errors..." );
    sqlConnection.rollback();
}else
{
```

```
        // if still there execute queued statements
        if( asyncStatementList.length > 0 )
            nextAsyncStatement();
    }
}
```

Go back to the ch12p08.fla project and execute it (Control ➤ Test Movie). After you connect to the database and insert the data into it, the TextArea should show the following actions:

- The opening of the transaction
- The insertion of data
- The closure of the transaction

Figure 12-22 shows the correctly executed application.

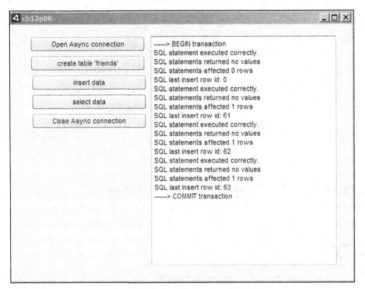

Figure 12-22. The ch12p08.fla application executed without errors

Return to the Application class and to row 121, inside the testAsyncStatement() method. In this part of the example, you'll change the parameter containing the e-mail address of the contact to generate an error. This time, use the @ parameter operator instead of the correct operator, :, as shown in the following SQL string:

```
insertParams[ '@email' ] = "sarah333@gmail.com";
```

Now save the changes and go back to the ch12p08.fla project. Execute the application again and repeat the sequence of operations to invoke the function to insert data in the database. This time, the TextArea will tell you that your database has been restored to its initial state because of an execution error, and you know it's due to the inappropriate use of a parameter in the insertion of the third contact. You can see the error message in Figure 12-23.

> Note that the applications in this chapter are merely examples—not perfect error-free programs—and will crash if the buttons are clicked out of order. Error handling in the code has been omitted to make the point of the examples clearer.

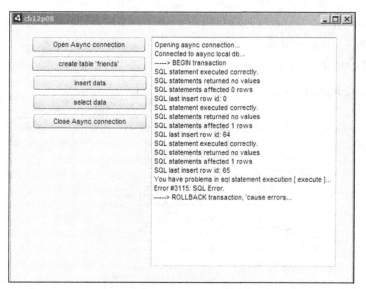

Figure 12-23. The ch12p08.fla application with an error

Summary

In this chapter you have begun to get to know the implementation of the SQL engine for AIR. You've explored how to connect to a local database and operate SQL connections both synchronously and asynchronously.

Throughout the chapter, you've worked on the development of an application made especially for experimenting with the SQL functions in AIR. This application has introduced you to the methods and properties offered by AIR SQL classes, and has shown you how they can help you by reducing the quantity of code necessary to create complex and refined functions.

Now you have the knowledge to create real applications that use local SQLite databases to manage and maintain the processed data. But it's up to you to fully use the new, powerful data management systems that AIR has to offer.

In the next and last chapter, you'll learn how to package and distribute your AIR applications to your end users.

CHAPTER 13

PACKAGING, DISTRIBUTING, AND
INSTALLING AIR APPLICATIONS

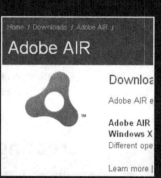

One of the key advantages of developing applications using AIR is the ability for those applications to run on Windows, Mac, and Linux operating systems, irrespective of the platform used by the developer to create the application.

To achieve the vision of write once, run anywhere for desktop applications, Adobe created the AIR file format as a way to package the application logic, supporting resources, and installation settings for an AIR application. The process of **packaging** an AIR application is undertaken when you are ready to distribute the application to end users as an AIR file; this is the format expected by the AIR runtime on each of the supported desktop platforms to install the application on the user's system.

Understanding the role of digital certificates during the application-packaging process is critical in your ability to ensure that users feel confident when installing an AIR application; unlike web-based applications, AIR applications have unrestricted access to a computer's hard disk, and an untrustworthy application could cause irreparable damage to the user's system. The onus is therefore on the application publisher to demonstrate to the user that they can trust the application.

The deployment of web-based applications is relatively simple, as the user simply browses to the relevant page and the latest version of the HTML page or Flash content loads and displays in the browser. _Distributing_ desktop-based applications, however, is more convoluted, with users typically required to download and execute an installer file before the application is available for use. AIR improves upon the traditional desktop install experience, but there are still a number of considerations, such as whether to use the browser-based install badge and/or digitally sign your application with a certificate from a trusted authority. You need to be aware of these decisions to ensure that the application distribution is optimized for the intended audience.

The AIR runtime provides a consistent way for users to install and uninstall AIR applications while conforming to the experience used by the host operating system for managing native desktop applications. Once deployed, it is likely that you will continue to make changes and enhancements to the application, and will need to deliver new versions of the application to the end user; AIR provides a convenient mechanism for updating applications, but planning is essential to ensure that you can alert users when updates are available.

This chapter covers the process of packaging, deploying, installing, and updating AIR applications created using Flash Professional CS4, and will equip you with the necessary information to ensure that you provide the optimal installation experience for end users. Let's start by creating a package for an AIR application.

Creating an AIR package

During the development of an AIR application using Flash, the process for compiling and testing your application is the same as if you were developing content for deployment on the Web.

When you distribute your AIR application to users, you must package the compiled Flash movie (SWF) together with any other assets required by your application (e.g., SWF files, graphics, video, audio, and XML data) in a single AIR installer file, denoted with an .air suffix. You can distribute this AIR installer file just as you would any other file. For example, you can use the following for distribution:

- Website as a download
- E-mail attachments
- Physical media such as a CD-ROM, DVD, or USB drive

With the AIR runtime already installed, the user can double-click the AIR file to install the application. If you are unsure as to whether your users will have the AIR runtime installed, you can use the seamless installer badge to detect the presence of the AIR runtime and install the runtime and/or your application as required.

> *The seamless installer badge is discussed later in this chapter.*

Using Flash to package an AIR application

Flash provides the necessary tools to configure and create the AIR package from an FLA document. To create an AIR package, you must first ensure that the FLA document that you are working with is set to target the AIR runtime, rather than Flash Player. If you initially selected Flash File (Adobe AIR) when you created your FLA, then your Flash document will be configured correctly for AIR; if, however, you are working with a Flash file created by someone else, or you created your FLA file using the Flash File (ActionScript 3.0) option, then you should ensure that the publish settings are adjusted to target the AIR runtime.

Follow these steps to target the AIR runtime:

1. From the File menu, select Publish Settings to display the Publish Settings panel, as shown in Figure 13-1.
2. Select the Flash tab. If the Player option is not set to Adobe AIR 1.x, then you should select this value from the list of player options.
3. Click OK to confirm the amended value and close the dialog.

> *At the time of writing, the latest version of AIR is AIR 1.5. You should ensure that you apply any updates to Flash Professional CS4 to ensure that you are targeting the latest version of the AIR runtime. If multiple AIR runtimes are listed, you should select the version that you wish to target for your application.*

13

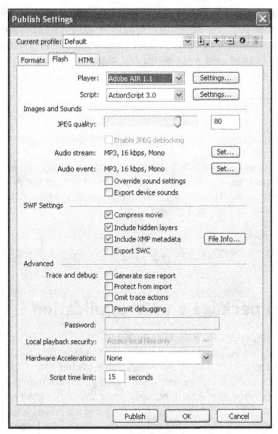

Figure 13-1. The Publish Settings dialog showing Adobe AIR 1.1 selected as the target player

There are a number of configuration properties that you must specify so that the AIR runtime can install the application. As part of the AIR package, these configuration properties are contained within an application descriptor XML file and are used by the AIR runtime during the installation process. Rather than manually editing the values in the application descriptor file, Flash provides a number of dialogs to simplify the process of customizing these options. If you would prefer, however, to write your own application descriptor, you can tell Flash Professional CS4 to use a custom application descriptor file.

Additionally, there are a number of optional settings that you can use to control features such as the visual appearance of the initial application window, the application icons used, the installation location, and whether there are file types associated with your application.

Specifying application settings

From the File menu, select AIR Settings to display the AIR – Application & Installer Settings panel, as shown in Figure 13-2.

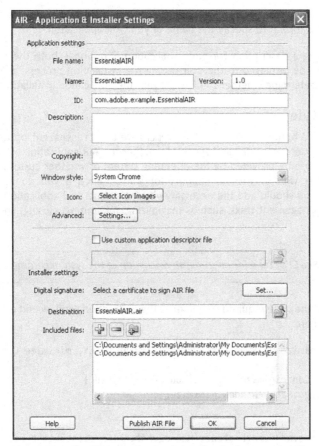

Figure 13-2. The AIR – Application & Installer Settings panel, with default values set

As a minimum you should complete the following options under Application settings:

- File name: The application name that will be displayed to the end user on their computer's file system. The corresponding file will be used to launch the application.

- Name: The application name that will be displayed during the AIR installation process.

- Version: A value that is used to differentiate between each release of your application.

- ID: An application identifier that is used to uniquely identify your AIR application.

The ID option

You should pay particular attention to the ID for your application—this value needs to be unique and, once published, must remain consistent for all future releases of your application should you wish to upgrade existing application installations to a newer version. To ensure that the application ID is unique, it is recommended that you use a reversed DNS domain address format to specify the name of your AIR application.

While specifying a description for your application is optional, both the name and the description will be displayed to the user during the installation process, and as such, will help the user determine whether to proceed with the application installation.

Window style

The Window style option relates to the systemChrome and transparent options within the AIR application descriptor file, and specifies whether the AIR application will use the standard window chrome provided by the operating system or whether custom chrome is to be used—either with or without support for transparency. If you do not use system chrome, then you should add the necessary visual elements and application logic to handle window management tasks, such as maximizing, minimizing, closing, and moving the window.

> See Chapter 4 for an in-depth discussion of the system chrome.

An example of the code required to minimize the application window and exit the application is shown here:

```
btn_minimize.addEventListener(MouseEvent.CLICK, minimize_CLICK);

  function minimize_CLICK(e:MouseEvent):void {
    stage.nativeWindow.minimize();
}

btn_close.addEventListener(MouseEvent.CLICK,closeButton_CLICK);

  function closeButton_CLICK(e:MouseEvent):void
{
    NativeApplication.nativeApplication.exit();

}
```

Selecting icon images

Click the Select Icon Images button to open the dialog shown in Figure 13-3. From here, you can select up to four differently sized PNG graphic files to be used for the application icon. If you do not specify a particular icon size, then AIR will scale one of the supplied images to create the missing icon; if you do not specify any icons, then a default application icon will be used.

Figure 13-3. Custom application icons can be specified within the AIR – Icon Images dialog.

When you have selected the icons for your application, click OK to close the dialog.

Specifying advanced application settings

Click the Settings button to the right of the Advanced item in the AIR – Application & Installer Settings panel. Doing so displays the Advanced Settings dialog, as shown in Figure 13-4. The configuration options in this dialog do not need to be specified to create an AIR package, but provide you with additional control over the behavior of the AIR application.

13

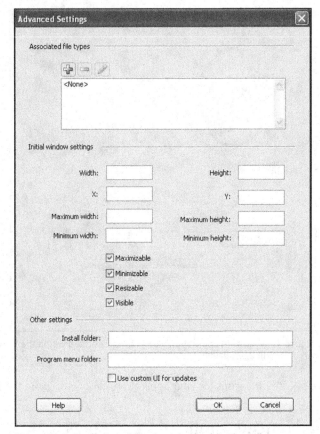

Figure 13-4. Properties within the Advanced Settings dialog
are optional.

Associated file types

You saw how to work with associated file types in Chapter 8, but as these relate to the packaging process, I'll cover them again quickly here. If you would like to associate one or more file types with your AIR application, you should specify a list of file types using the + icon under the Associated file types heading. Doing so will support the launch of your application and loading of the file when the user double-clicks a file of that type. You will also need to add logic to your application to handle an InvokeEvent event when the file is launched by the user—the following code demonstrates loading the selected file using the fileLoader class:

```
import flash.events.InvokeEvent;


var fileLoader:Loader = new Loader();

addChild(fileLoader);
```

```
NativeApplication.nativeApplication.addEventListener(
InvokeEvent.INVOKE, onInvoke);


function onInvoke(event:InvokeEvent):void {

    var args:Array = event.arguments as Array;

    if (args.length) {

        var fileToOpen:String = String(args[0]);

        fileLoader.load(new URLRequest(fileToOpen));

    }

}
```

Initial window settings

The Initial window settings options can be used to configure both the behavior and appearance of the main application window. By default, the AIR runtime will use the height and width of the Flash movie as the size of the initial application window, with no maximum or minimum window size constraints, and will display the window at an arbitrary position on the user's screen. You should enter values for the width, height, maximum width, maximum height, minimum width, and minimum height if you want to restrict how the user can interact with the window. You can also control the initial window position on the user's screen by providing an X and Y pixel location for the top left of the window.

The Resizable option. When allowing the user to resize the window, you need to consider how your content will be displayed—the default will be for the Flash content to scale as the user resizes the window. If this is not the desired effect, you may need to set the stage of the Flash movie as follows so that it does not scale:

```
stage.scaleMode = StageScaleMode.NO_SCALE;
```

Resizing the window may not be appropriate for your application. If this is the case, then you can completely disable the ability to resize the window by unchecking the Resizable option. Additionally, you can disable support for maximizing and minimizing the application window by unchecking the Maximizable and Minimizable options.

The Visible option. You can make the initial window invisible by unchecking the Visible option. This can be useful if you need to load external resources, set up the user interface, or position the window before displaying the application to the user. When you are ready, you can activate the window to make it visible as follows:

```
stage.nativeWindow.activate();
```

13

The install folder and program menu folder options

Other settings that you can control in this dialog include specifying the install folder for the application and, for Windows users, the program menu folder the application will be accessible from. If you do not specify any values for these options, then the AIR runtime will use the name value for the application to determine the installation and program menu folders. Enter values for these options using a forward slash (/) if you wish to specify a subdirectory. For example, to install the application into the Essential AIR/Chapter 13 directory and have it appear in the program menu with the same structure, enter the following values:

```
Install folder: 'Essential AIR/Chapter 13'
Program menu folder 'Essential AIR/Chapter 13'
```

On Mac OS X, the application will be installed in the Applications/Essential AIR/ Chapter 13 folder, whereas on Windows, it will be installed in the C:\Program Files\ Essential AIR\Chapter 13 folder. On Windows, the application will be accessible from Start ➤ All Programs ➤ Essential AIR ➤ Chapter 13.

Specifying installer settings

The final step in the packaging process involves the following tasks:

- Specifying the contents of the package
- Naming the AIR package
- Signing the package with a digital certificate

The AIR package needs to contain all of the supporting assets required by the application, such that when the application is installed and launched for the first time by the user, it can run without any additional resources. It is important to remember that a user may launch your application when offline and therefore you should provide the capability to use the application in a disconnected state, or at a minimum, advise the user that they need to be online to continue using the application.

The resources included in the AIR package will be deployed alongside the main application SWF during the installation process. Depending on the functionality of your application, you might choose to include one or more of the following resources within the AIR package:

- Image files (JPG, PNG, GIF)
- Media files (MP3, FLV, MOV)
- Supporting application data or configuration settings (XML, TXT)
- SQLite database files (DB, DB3)
- Additional Flash libraries or content (SWF)

You can of course choose to load additional resources dynamically at runtime from a web server and use those within your application (subject to sandbox security restrictions), but for each resource type, you should consider whether including resources in the AIR package or loading them at runtime is most appropriate.

Adding resources

To add the resources you want to include in the AIR package, use the + icon next to the Included files item in the AIR – Application & Installer Settings panel, as shown in Figure 13-5. If you wish to add a folder of resources (such as a collection of images), then you should use the folder icon rather than adding each individual file manually.

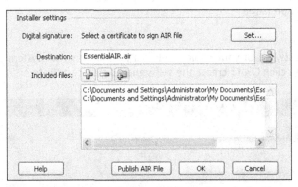

Figure 13-5. You can define the digital signature, destination AIR file, and files to be included using the AIR – Application & Installer Settings panel.

> *If you've specified custom icons for your AIR application, then you need to include those images within your AIR package—they are not included automatically.*

Signing AIR applications

Before you can create the AIR package, you need to sign the application with a digital certificate. AIR applications can either be signed by linking a certificate from an external certificate authority (CA) such as VeriSign or thawte, or by constructing your own certificate. It is important to note that self-signed certificates do not provide any assurance to the end user that the named publisher has genuinely created the application, and as such, self-signed applications represent a security risk.

> *It cannot be stressed enough that you should use a certificate from an external CA when you deploy your application so as to instill confidence that the application is genuine and that it can be trusted—more information on this topic is provided later in this chapter.*

During the development and testing of your application, you might choose to sign the AIR package with a self-signed certificate, and Flash provides an option to create such a certificate. You can create a single self-signed digital certificate for use across each of the AIR applications that you are developing, so once created, you can reference the certificate by clicking the Browse button and navigating to the PFX or P12 certificate file.

13

To create a new certificate, select the Create button on the Digital Signature panel, as shown in Figure 13-6. The Create Self-Signed Digital Certificate dialog will appear, as shown in Figure 13-7. Enter the following information in that dialog:

- Publisher name
- Organization unit
- Organization name
- Country

Then enter a password of your choice. Select a location on your system to save the certificate, and then click OK to create the self-signed digital certificate.

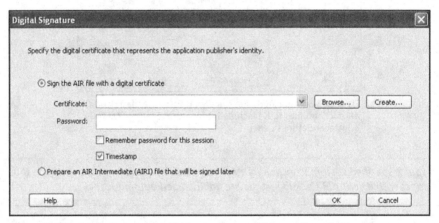

Figure 13-6. A certificate is required before you can publish an AIR application.

Figure 13-7. Creating a self-signed digital certificate requires all fields to be completed.

Once the location of the certificate is defined, you should enter the password you used when creating the certificate and then click OK to continue. If you want to avoid the hassle of reentering the password each time you package the AIR application, you can select Remember password for this session.

After defining the application and installer settings and selecting a digital certificate, you can go ahead and publish the AIR file for your application. Select Publish AIR File, and Flash will do the following:

1. Package the application as an AIR file

2. Sign it using your digital certificate

3. Place the file alongside the FLA document on your hard drive

If you make changes to your Flash application, the supporting resources, or any of the application or installer settings, then you will need to republish the AIR package using this process.

Customizing the AIR application descriptor file

While Flash provides a convenient way to specify most of the configurable options for the AIR application and installer, there are some additional properties that you can only customize by editing the application descriptor file manually; these include configuring the application to allow invocation from a web page and providing support for multiple languages during the installation process.

The application descriptor file for a simple AIR application is shown here:

```
<?xml version ="1.0" encoding="utf-8" ?>

<application xmlns="http://ns.adobe.com/air/application/1.5">

    <id>com.adobe.example.EssentialAIR</id>

    <version>1.0</version>

    <filename>EssentialAIR</filename>

    <description>An example application</description>

    <!-- To localize the description, use the following format for
            the description element.

    <description>

            <text xml:lang="en">English description goes here</text>

            <text xml:lang="fr">French description goes here</text>
```

13

```
                        <text xml:lang="ja">Japanese description goes
                        here</text>

        </description>

        -->

        <name>EssentialAIR</name>

        <!-- To localize the name, use the following format for the name
        element.

        <name>

                        <text xml:lang="en">English name goes here</text>

                        <text xml:lang="fr">French name goes here</text>

                        <text xml:lang="ja">Japanese name goes here</text>

        </name>

        -->

        <copyright></copyright>

        <initialWindow>

                        <content>EssentialAIR.swf</content>

                        <systemChrome>standard</systemChrome>

                        <transparent>false</transparent>

                        <visible>true</visible>

                        <maximizable>true</maximizable>
                        <minimizable>true</minimizable>
                        <resizable>true</resizable>
        </initialWindow>

        <customUpdateUI>false</customUpdateUI>

        <allowBrowserInvocation>false</allowBrowserInvocation>

        <icon>

                <image16x16>AppIconsForAIRPublish/AirApp_16.png
                </image16x16>
```

```
        <image32x32>AppIconsForAIRPublish/AirApp_32.png
        </image32x32>
        <image48x48>AppIconsForAIRPublish/AirApp_48.png
        </image48x48>
        <image128x128>AppIconsForAIRPublish/AirApp_128.png
        </image128x128>
    </icon>

</application>
```

Flash creates the application descriptor file, named by default the same as your FLA document, but appended with -app.xml, and located in the same directory as your FLA document.

Supporting multiple languages

With the release of AIR 1.1, the runtime supports the following languages alongside English:

- Brazilian Portuguese
- Chinese (traditional and simplified)
- French
- German
- Italian
- Japanese
- Korean
- Russian
- Spanish

It is likely that support for further languages will be added in future versions of AIR.

The AIR runtime contains the necessary features to display the installer dialogs and other runtime dialogs in supported languages automatically, based upon the language selected by the user for the operating system. As the developer of the application, you must, however, provide localized strings for use during the installation process so as to display the name and description of your application in the appropriate language.

To do this, remove or comment out the name and description elements within the AIR application descriptor file and instead use a list of text elements containing strings for each of the languages you wish to support. The following example demonstrates how you would specify the application name for English, French, and Japanese:

```
<name>

    <text xml:lang="en">English name goes here</text>

    <text xml:lang="fr">French name goes here</text>
```

13

```
                    <text xml:lang="ja">Japanese name goes here</text>
        </name>
```

The AIR runtime uses the name and description that most closely match the user interface of the user's operating system. If the application defines no languages that directly match the operating system user interface language, then the first value defined in the application descriptor file for name and description are used.

In order to provide full localization support for your application, you must also localize the strings and assets used within your Flash content, as well as implement ActionScript logic to support the display of the appropriate locale-specific resources within your application.

More information on creating localized Flash content for your AIR application can be found in the AIR documentation at http://help.adobe.com/en_US/AIR/1.1/ devappsflash/WSB2927578-20D8-4065-99F3-00ACE6511EEE.html.

Configuring the application to allow browser invocation

You can let users launch your application by clicking a link in their web browser. To do so, you need to explicitly enable this functionality through the application descriptor file, as shown here:

```
        <allowBrowserInvocation>false</allowBrowserInvocation>
```

By changing allowBrowserInvocation to true, the application can be launched from within the web browser. If you choose to use the enhanced install badge described later in this chapter, one of the features available to you when browser invocation is enabled is to allow the user to launch the application from the installer badge if the application is already installed.

Using a custom application descriptor file in Flash

If you choose to amend or not use the default application descriptor file, you can instruct Flash to use a custom application descriptor file that you've written. Within the AIR – Application & Installer Settings panel, select Use custom application descriptor file, and browse to the file you have created. Note that it is not possible to edit the settings for your application using the dialog in Flash if you've provided your own custom application descriptor file.

With the application descriptor file defined, you can now move on to the next step, which is to consider how you're going to digitally sign the AIR package.

Digitally signing an AIR package

When viewing Flash or other content on the Web, the user is guaranteed a certain level of protection by the restrictions placed upon what the content can and can't do when running within the confines of the browser sandbox. For example, a SWF running within Flash Player can only write a limited amount of data to a very specific location on the user's hard drive without direct user interaction.

The limited access to local system resources available to browser content means that users can browse the Web, consume content, and interact with applications without giving much regard to security, except in circumstances when they are explicitly providing personal or sensitive data over the Internet.

Unlike browser-based applications, AIR applications have the same user privileges as native desktop applications, allowing them full access to the local file system. This means that a SWF running within the AIR runtime can read, write, and delete data anywhere on the local system, subject to the restrictions placed upon applications by the operating system.

To mitigate the risk to the user from installing an application, Adobe requires that AIR applications be signed by their publisher, so as to securely associate their identity with the application and to guarantee that after release, someone other than the publisher hasn't amended the application code.

While it is possible to create your own digital certificate for use with AIR applications, such self-signed certificates don't provide the user with the guarantee that you are who you say you are. In order to instill user confidence and guarantee that you are the publisher, it is necessary to obtain a digital certificate signed by a trusted third-party vendor. These trusted third parties, or CAs, validate your identity as a publisher and issue you with a certificate that you can use to sign your AIR application with.

Certificates and the AIR installation process

During the application installation process, the AIR runtime differentiates between applications that are self-signed and those that are signed using a certificate from a trusted third-party vendor.

Because self-signed applications represent a higher risk to the user, the installation dialogs highlight this increased risk by specifying the publisher as UNKNOWN and using red warning icons, as shown in Figure 13-8. The user will still be able to install the application, but by not using a trusted certificate you may find that users are wary of proceeding and choose to cancel the installation process.

13

Figure 13-8. The Application Install dialog displayed when the AIR application is signed using a self-signed certificate

By contrast, applications signed using a certificate from a trusted third party display the name of the application publisher and present a green "trusted" icon next to the publisher name. AIR applications have unrestricted access to the user's system, so there is still some risk to the user—hence the yellow warning icon at the top of the dialog, as shown in Figure 13-9.

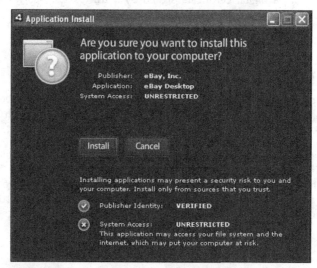

Figure 13-9. The Application Install dialog displayed when the AIR application is signed using a certificate from a CA

Another slight difference during the installation process is that applications signed with a certificate from a trusted third party will display the application icon on the second of the installation dialogs, whereas self-signed applications will not. Figure 13-10 shows the install dialog for the eBay Desktop application, which is signed with a certificate from a trusted third party.

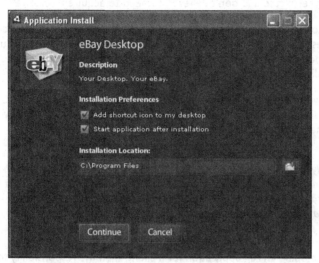

Figure 13-10. The application icon is displayed only when the application is trusted.

It is important to note that signing an application doesn't make the application inherently trustworthy—the user can only trust the application if he trusts the publisher of the application. The AIR runtime provides the user with the opportunity to establish if an application has been signed using a certificate from a trusted third party, but the user must still make the ultimate decision as to whether to trust that publisher and install the application on their system.

Plan early for application signing

Right at the beginning of your project, as you're scoping out the features for your application, you should allocate some time to consider how you're going to sign your AIR application and whether you need to acquire a certificate.

There are a number of possible application-signing options that might be applicable to you, depending upon the type of application you are building and the organization that you are working for. In general, however, one of the following scenarios is likely to apply:

- You will need to acquire a new certificate from a CA to sign the AIR application.
- Your organization already has a class 3–compatible certificate (suitable for user servers and software signing), and you plan to use that to sign the AIR application. More information on certificate types can be found at http://en.wikipedia.org/wiki/Public_key_certificate.

13

- You are developing an application for a client and they will need to sign the application using an existing or a new certificate.

- You are building an application that you are comfortable releasing with a self-signed certificate and don't believe you need to acquire a certificate from a CA.

If you need to acquire a certificate from a CA, you should allow a reasonable period of time to process the necessary paperwork, which may include providing documentation to a regional processing center so that the vendor can verify your organization's identity. The next section discusses how to acquire a digital certificate.

If you know your organization has already published and signed a .NET, Cocoa, or Java application using a class 3, high-assurance code-signing certificate, then you should be able to use that certificate to sign your AIR application.

> You typically cannot use an SSL (Secure Sockets Layer) certificate to sign AIR files; a certificate must be marked for code signing to be suitable. You will want to allocate some time to test the certificate that you would like to use, and allow time to acquire a new certificate should the existing certificate prove to be unsuitable.

If you are developing an AIR application for a client, then the responsibility to procure the appropriate certificate and/or sign the application may fall to the client's IT department. It is unlikely that the client will supply you with the private key for their certificate, and as such, they may insist you provide a build of the application that they sign. In this situation, you will need to supply them with an AIR Intermediary (AIRI) file. This is an unsigned AIR package that cannot be installed, but that can be signed using the ADT (AIR Developer Tool) command-line tool supplied with the AIR SDK (software development kit).

Deploying an application with a self-signed certificate may be an option for you, even with the increased probability that some users will choose not to install the application. While it is possible to migrate from a self-signed certificate to a certificate issued by a CA at a later date, if from the outset you know that you will want to deploy a trusted application, then it is far simpler to release the initial application with a certificate from a CA.

Regardless of whether you need to acquire a new certificate, test an existing certificate, or produce an AIRI file to pass to your client to sign, you should allocate an appropriate amount of time for this as part of your overall project plan and not leave this task until you've finished the development of the application and are ready to deploy it.

Acquiring a digital certificate

While you can choose which CA you acquire your digital certificate from, thawte has worked with Adobe to provide a certificate service specifically for AIR application developers. At the time of writing, this is the easiest way to acquire a certificate to sign an AIR application, and so it's the one you will use in this book.

The use of a thawte certificate is also convenient for end users installing your application; because the AIR runtime relies upon the operating system to establish whether a certificate can be trusted, it is necessary for the operating system to trust a chain of certificates linking the certificate to a known certification authority. Both Windows and Mac OS X operating systems come preinstalled with root certificates from thawte. Thus, your signed AIR application using a thawte certificate can be verified without requiring the user to install any additional root certificates on their machine.

To purchase an AIR Developer Certificate, the thawte website requires that you use the Mozilla Firefox browser, and that you purchase and retrieve the certificate on the same computer and browser. Once you have downloaded the certificate and private key successfully, you can export them from the browser keystore and use them elsewhere.

Follow these steps to purchase a certificate from thawte:

1. Visit the thawte website (www.thawte.com/) and select Products ➤ Code Signing Certificates from the navigation.

2. Navigate to the purchase page by clicking the Click here to buy link or button presented.

3. From the list of available code-signing certificates, select Adobe AIR Developer Certificate, as shown in Figure 13-11. Then click submit.

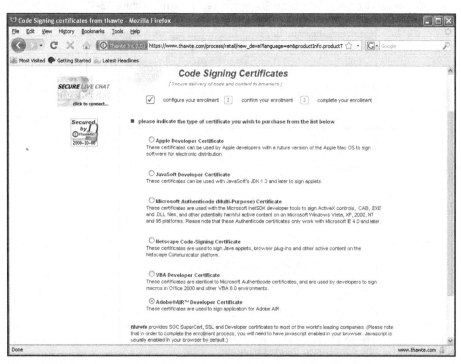

Figure 13-11. Select Adobe AIR Developer Certificate from the listed certificate types.

4. Select whether you want to purchase a certificate for a one- or two-year period, and then enter the requested information about your organization, country, state/province, city/town, and web server domain. It is important that the organization name be spelled correctly and in full, and that it represents the legal identify of the organization within the country in which it operates.

5. Complete the remainder of the three-step enrollment process. thawte will then perform its identity verification process and may request that additional information be provided and/or that documents used to prove the organization's identity be faxed to a local thawte office. The requested documents vary depending upon the type of organization and the country in which it operates, but may include articles of incorporation, VAT certificates, registrations of trade name, partnership papers, or certificates of formation.

6. Once verification is complete, thawte will e-mail you instructions on how to retrieve the certificate. Using Firefox, navigate to the link provided by thawte, log in using the credentials specified during the enrollment process, and fetch the certificate.

7. Your certificate will automatically be saved to the keystore within Firefox. It needs to be exported so that you can use it to sign your AIR application.

8. Within Firefox, open the Preferences dialog from the File menu. Then click the Advanced icon and select the Encryption tab, shown in Figure 13-12.

Figure 13-12. Select View Certificates to view and then export the downloaded thawte certificate.

9. To export your certificate, click the View Certificates button, select the Your Certificates tab, and then select the certificate from the list. Once selected, click the Backup button to export the certificate and private key in a P12 file to a suitable location on your computer.

During the backup process, you will be required to protect your certificate with a password. You will need to use this password during the packaging process within Flash.

Signing your application using Flash

To sign your application using your newly acquired certificate, open the AIR – Application & Installer Settings panel from File ➤ AIR Settings, and then select the Change button next to the Digital signature field. In the Digital Signature dialog, shown in Figure 13-13, browse to the P12 or PFX file, and then enter the password for your digital certificate.

Leave the Timestamp option selected to ensure that the application can be installed even after the certificate has expired. During the signing process, the server of a timestamp authority is queried and the resulting information is embedded in the AIR file; if the timestamp is not obtained, the AIR file ceases to be installable when the certificate expires or is revoked by the CA.

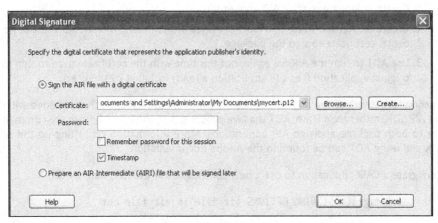

Figure 13-13. Ensure the Timestamp option is selected when packaging the application you intend to deploy.

To publish the AIR file with your new certificate, close the Digital Signature dialog by clicking OK, and then choose Publish AIR File from the AIR – Application & Installer Settings panel.

Migrating from an existing certificate to a new certificate

As part of the packaging process, a publisher ID is created using information from the supplied digital certificate. Because the publisher ID is tied to the certificate used, any changes to the certificate used for signing will alter the publisher ID and cause the AIR runtime to treat intended updates to the application as a completely different application and perform a new installation rather than update the existing installation.

Some of the scenarios that would cause a change to the publisher ID include the following:

- Selecting a different certificate (i.e., for a parent company or otherwise different organization)
- Renewing your certificate with different information
- Changing the certificate provider
- Changing from a self-signed certificate to a commercial certificate

In these situations, you need to sign the updated version of your application with both the new certificate and the original certificate so that the AIR runtime recognizes the original publisher of the application and allows the update to be installed to the existing application.

To change the certificate used, follow these steps:

1. Create an update to your AIR application.
2. Create an AIR file using the tools provided within Flash. You should use the new digital certificate to sign the package.
3. Use ADT to sign the AIR file again, but this time with the certificate used to sign the original application (i.e., the application already installed by the user).

To complete step 3 of the migration process, you must use ADT, which is included within the AIR SDK, rather than Flash. ADT is a Java program that you can run from the command line to both package and sign AIR applications. More information on setting up the AIR SDK and using ADT can be found in the Adobe documentation.

To migrate an AIR application to use a new certificate, use the following syntax:

```
adt -migrate SIGNING_OPTIONS air_file_in air_file_out
```

The signing options identify the private key and certificate with which to sign the AIR file. The air_file_in setting defines the path to the AIR file that has been signed with the new certificate, while the air_file_out setting defines the name of the AIR file to be created.

An example of a complete command that you might use to sign an AIRI file is shown here:

```
adt -migrate -storetype pkcs12 -keystore cert.p12 myApp.air myApp.air
```

When the user installs the updated AIR file, the identity of the application changes because the publisher ID has been altered to reflect the information in the new digital certificate. This does have practical repercussions for your application, including not being able to access any data stored by the previous version of the application in the encrypted local store (ELS). In addition, the location of the application storage directory changes, so that any data used previously by the application is no longer available—data from the previous application storage directory can be copied across to the new storage directory location, but this is not done automatically.

Once an application has been successfully migrated, future updates to the application need only be signed with the new certificate. However, keep the following in mind if you issue updates to the application that are only signed with the new certificate: any users that have failed to update their version of the application using an intermediary update (which is signed with a migration certificate) will get a new install of the application.

Using an AIRI file and the ADT tool to sign applications

Do you work for an organization that has strict control over who has access to the private key for a digital certificate? Or, are you building an application for a third-party client? If either of these are the case, you may need to package your AIR application as an AIRI file. Then you can provide this file, together with the AIR SDK and appropriate documentation, to the person responsible for signing applications.

You can create the AIRI file by selecting Prepare an AIR Intermediate (AIRI) file that will be signed later from the Digital Signature dialog in Flash. To complete the signing process, use ADT as discussed in the previous section. To sign an AIRI file, use the following syntax:

```
adt -sign SIGNING_OPTIONS airi_file air_file
```

The signing options identify the private key and certificate with which to sign the AIR file. The airi_file setting defines the path to the unsigned AIRI file to be signed, while the air_file setting defines the name of the AIR file to be created.

An example of a complete command that you might use to sign an AIRI file is shown here:

```
adt -sign -storetype pkcs12 -keystore cert.p12 unsignedMyApp.airi
myApp.air
```

Once the AIRI file has been signed using a digital certificate, you can continue with the process of deploying your application to your target audience; note that it is not possible for end users to install an AIRI file.

Distributing an AIR application

Once you've packaged your AIR application as an AIR file, you're ready to distribute the application to potential users. There are a number of different ways you can choose to distribute your AIR file, depending on the following factors:

- Whether you want to distribute the application online or on physical media
- How streamlined you want to make the web-based installation experience
- The target audience for the application

If you know that the users of your application will have a high-speed Internet connection, then it is probably most appropriate to deploy the application to your website. This way, as

13

you make changes to the application and publish new versions, you can simply upload the new AIR file to your site and offer the latest version of the application for download.

When distributing the application via a website, you have the following choices, depending upon how streamlined you want to make the web-based installation experience:

- Provide a link to the AIR file for the user to download.
- Use the seamless installer badge that is provided as part of the AIR SDK.
- Use the enhanced seamless installer badge that is provided on the Adobe Developer Connection website, at www.adobe.com/devnet/air/articles/badge_for_air. html (at the time of writing, this badge is in beta).

If, however, you need to distribute the application to users with limited or no Internet connectivity, then providing the AIR file on a CD-ROM, DVD, or USB drive might be necessary. In this case, you will have the following choices:

- Provide the AIR file and the required version of the AIR runtime installer for your target operating systems. The user will need to install the AIR runtime before installing your application.
- Provide a native installation package that combines both the AIR runtime and your AIR application to provide a customized installation experience.

> *Creating a native installation package is beyond the scope of this book.*

When considering deployment of AIR applications with enterprise organizations, many of whom will have corporate IT policies that restrict access to the Internet and the downloading of files, you may be able to distribute the application via physical media. There are some additional choices that you should also consider:

- Provide a link to the AIR file and the AIR installer on an internal server (i.e., all component parts required for installation are hosted within the organization).
- Deploy the AIR runtime and application using standard desktop deployment tools such as Microsoft SMS, Tivoli, or any deployment tools that allow silent installations.

Deployment of AIR applications via a website, on physical media, and within an enterprise environment is covered next.

Deploying an AIR application to your website

The simplest way to deploy your application is to provide a link within an HTML page to the AIR file for your application. Before installing your application, the user must determine whether they have the AIR runtime installed, and if not, download it from the Adobe website prior to launching the AIR file—otherwise, the operating system will not recognize the AIR file type and they will be unable to install the application.

At a minimum, you should provide the user with information advising that they need to install the AIR runtime on your website and provide a link to Adobe's site so that the user can download the correct installer for their operating system. The recommended link to download the AIR installer from is http://get.adobe.com/air/.

The downside to using this approach is that it places the onus on the end user to complete a number of steps in the correct order to guarantee the correct installation of your application. In most cases, using the seamless installer badge will provide a far better installation experience and increase the likelihood of a successful installation. The seamless installer badge is described in the next section.

If you do choose to use this approach, you should ensure that your web server is set up correctly to handle the AIR file type; otherwise, some browsers may download the AIR file with a .zip extension. You may need to add the following MIME content type mapping to your web server configuration:

    application/vnd.adobe.air-application-installer-package+zip .air

Failing to set the correct MIME content type on the server will result in the user downloading a ZIP file that she will not be able to install with the AIR runtime, without first manually renaming the file to have an AIR extension.

Using the seamless installer badge

The seamless installer badge is designed to make it easy to start the installation of your AIR application from the browser—the user simply clicks a link within a Flash-based badge, and the badge can then detect the presence of the AIR runtime. If the runtime isn't already installed on the user's computer, the badge can install both the runtime and your application. If the user does have the AIR runtime, then the badge will start the download process for your AIR application and enable the user to install the application without the need to save and launch the AIR file.

> To use the seamless installer badge, your user will need Flash Player 9 update 3 (version 9.0.115.0) installed in their browser.

There are currently two versions of the seamless installer badge: the original badge included in the AIR SDK, and an enhanced badge, which offers a number of benefits over the original badge, but at the time of writing is still in beta, available from the Adobe Developer Connection website (www.adobe.com/devnet/air/articles/badge_for_air. html).

The features provided by the standard badge include the following:

- Detection of the required AIR runtime version and installation of both the runtime and application if not present on the user's computer
- Simplified installation of AIR applications, without requiring the user to save and launch the AIR file

13

In addition to the standard badge features, the enhanced badge also offers the following:

- Integrated Flash Player express install to upgrade older Flash Player versions to the current version required to enable the seamless installer badge functionality
- Capabilities to detect and launch installed AIR applications from within the browser
- Customizable help text and links to improve the installation experience
- Customizable text within the installer badge

The standard badge can be extended to provide all of the functionality offered by the enhanced badge if you are uncomfortable with using a beta release of the enhanced badge.

The enhanced installer badge is, however, already in wide use with many AIR applications today, and a final release version may ship as part of a future version of the AIR SDK. As such, while I will cover the use of the standard badge, more attention will be given to leveraging the features of the enhanced installer badge.

Using the standard seamless installer badge

A sample implementation of the seamless installer badge, as shown in Figure 13-14, can be found within the AIR SDK—at a minimum, all you need to do to use the badge is customize some parameters within the accompanying HTML page and then upload the HTML page, the badge SWF, and your AIR file to your server.

Figure 13-14.
An example of the standard seamless installer badge

The AIR 1.5 SDK is included within the Flash CS4 installation directory, at Program Files/Adobe/Flash CS4/ AIK1.5/ on Windows, and at /Applications/Adobe Flash CS4/AIK1.5/ on Mac OS X. If you need to download a later version of the AIR SDK, you can always find it on the Adobe website at www.adobe.com/products/air/tools/sdk/.

Once you have downloaded and extracted the AIR SDK to a folder of your choice, look in the samples/badge/ directory to find the following files:

- badge.swf: The seamless installer badge SWF
- default_badge.html: A sample HTML page that embeds the seamless installer badge
- AC_RunActiveContent.js: A JavaScript file containing supporting code for the HTML page

To customize the badge, open the default_badge HTML page in Dreamweaver CS4 or your preferred HTML editor, and look for the following line of code:

```
'flashvars','appname=My%20Application&appurl=myapp.air&airversion=1.0&
imageurl=test.jpg'
```

You will need to edit this line of code to set the name of your AIR application, the URL for your application's AIR file, and the version of your application; there are also additional options that can be used to customize the look and feel of the badge. Here's a full list of the parameters:

- appname **(required)**: The name of your AIR application, displayed by the badge when the AIR runtime is not installed. (This value must be URL-encoded.)

- appurl **(required)**: The absolute URL of the AIR file to be downloaded by the badge (e.g., http://www.mydomain.com/myapp/myapp.air).

- airversion **(required)**: The version of the AIR runtime required by this application. For AIR 1.5, you would set this value to 1.1.

- imageurl **(optional)**: The URL of an image to be used within the badge. The image used should be 215 × 100 pixels in size. While this parameter is optional, you should supply an image that is relevant to your application.

- buttoncolor **(optional)**: The color of the download button, specified as a hex value.

- messagecolor **(optional)**: The color of the text below the button, specified as a hex value.

In addition to customizing the badge itself, you should also edit two further areas within the HTML page. One area ensures the correct information is displayed for users who do not have the required version of Flash Player. The other area is for users who do not have JavaScript support enabled in their browser.

Look for the following line of code and edit the link to your application's AIR file and the name of your application:

```
document.write('<table id="AIRDownloadMessageTable"><tr><td>Download
<a href="myapp.air">My Application</a> now.<br /><br /><span id=
"AIRDownloadMessageRuntime">This application requires the <a href="');
```

Within the noscript block at the bottom of the HTML page, you should again make the necessary edits for your application:

```
<noscript>
<table id="AIRDownloadMessageTable">
<tr>
<td>Download <a href="myapp.air">My Application</a> now.<br /><br />
<span id="AIRDownloadMessageRuntime">This application requires
Adobe&#174; AIR&#8482; to be installed for <a
href="http://airdownload.adobe.com/air/mac/download/latest/
AdobeAIR.dmg">Mac OS</a> or <a
href="http://airdownload.adobe.com/air/win/download/latest/
AdobeAIRInstaller.exe">Windows</a>.</span>
</td>
</tr>
</table>
</noscript>
```

13

With the changes made, you should upload your customized installer badge and test the badge functionality before integrating the code into any existing HTML pages on your website.

If you cannot achieve the level of user interface customization required by editing the badge properties within the HTML page, you can choose to edit and recompile the badge. swf file by modifying the FLA document for the badge in Flash. The source files for the badge can be found within the AIR SDK, in the src/badge/ directory.

Included within the source directory for the badge is the ActionScript class that defines the functionality available within the seamless installer badge. Note, however, that the actual logic that implements the seamless install functionality is contained within an air. swf file that is loaded at runtime from the Adobe website—this enables Adobe to make changes to the code used in all instances of the installer badge in response to any security issues.

The air.swf file provides a number of APIs that can be used within the standard seamless installer badge. These APIs implement the functionality to support a variety of badge features, including the following:

- Checking if the runtime is installed
- Checking from a web page if an AIR application is installed
- Installing an AIR application from the browser
- Launching an installed AIR application from the browser

Note that the default badge only exposes the functionality required to check if the runtime is installed and to install an AIR application from the browser. If you would like to add the functionality to check if your AIR application is installed and, if so, launch that application, then you will need to amend the AIRBadge.as file included in the AIR SDK. More information on this is available within the AIR documentation.

Before implementing any additional functionality in the seamless installer badge, you may like to consider using the enhanced seamless installer badge.

Using the enhanced seamless installer badge

While the enhanced seamless installer badge, shown in Figure 13-15, may be included in a future version of the AIR SDK, at the time of writing it is available from the Adobe Developer Connection website, at www.adobe.com/devnet/air/articles/badge_for_air.html.

Once downloaded, you should extract and look for the following files:

- AIRInstallBadge.swf: The seamless installer badge SWF

- EmbedDemo.html: A sample HTML page that embeds the seamless installer badge

Figure 13-15.
An example of the enhanced seamless installer badge

- Expressinstall.swf: The SWF file required by SWFObject to carry out an express installation of Flash Player (if the user does not have Flash Player 9.0.115.0 or later)
- Swfobject.js: The SWFObject JavaScript Flash Player detection and embed script

As with the standard badge, you will need to edit a number of parameters in the HTML page before you can deploy the badge with your application.

At a minimum, you must provide values for airversion, appname, and appurl—note that this badge uses SWFObject, and thus the following format for defining the parameters is different from the standard badge:

```
so.addVariable("airversion", "1.5");
so.addVariable("appname", "My Application");
so.addVariable("appurl", "http://www.mysite.com/myapp.air");
```

The additional parameters that you can use to customize the enhanced badge are as listed here (all are optional):

- appid: The unique ID that you gave your application in the application descriptor file.
- pubid: Your publisher ID. (This can be found by getting the value of NativeApplication.nativeApplication.publisherID when the deployed application is running.)
- appversion: The version of your application that will be installed by the badge. (This should be the same as the version number set in your application descriptor file.)
- appinstallarg: The value of this parameter will be passed to your AIR application if it is launched after installation via the badge.
- applauncharg: The value of this parameter will be passed to your AIR application if it is launched from the badge.
- imageurl: The URL of an image to be used within the badge. The image used should be 205 × 170 pixels in size. While this parameter is optional, you should supply an image that is relevant to your application.
- helpurl: A URL for the user to get additional help information on installing your application.
- hidehelp: If set to true, hides the help icon within the installer badge user interface.
- skiptransition: If set to true, skips the transition when the image loads.
- titlecolor: The color of all dialog titles, specified as a hex value.
- buttonlabelcolor: The color of button labels, specified as a hex value.
- appnamecolor: The color of the application name, specified as a hex value (only displayed when no image URL is specified).

There are also a number of parameters that can be used to change the text used throughout the badge—check the documentation that comes with the badge for further

13

information. The source files for the badge are also included so that you can alter both the visual appearance and functionality of the badge.

Figure 13-16.
The badge supports the launch of an already installed AIR application from the browser.

While the enhanced installer badge supports the ability to launch an AIR application that is already installed on the user's system, as shown in Figure 13-16, the application to be launched must be configured to enable this functionality. If you want to enable this feature for your application, you should edit the application descriptor file using your preferred text editor and set the allowBrowserInvocation property to true (it is false by default).

When your application is launched, the value specified in the installer badge's applauncharg parameter will be passed to your application in the arguments property of the BrowserInvokeEvent event. An example of the code required to handle the BrowserInvokeEvent event is shown here:

```
import flash.events.BrowserInvokeEvent;

NativeApplication.nativeApplication.addEventListener(
BrowserInvokeEvent.INVOKE, onInvoke);

function onInvoke(event:InvokeEvent):void {

    var args:Array = event.arguments as Array;

    if (args.length) {


        var arg1:String = String(args[0]);

    }

}
```

Distributing the AIR runtime on physical media or within an enterprise environment

If you want to distribute your AIR application on physical media, such as a CD-ROM, DVD, or USB drive; on an intranet site; or through a desktop deployment tool within an enterprise environment, you may want to include the installer for the AIR runtime along with your application—to do this, however, you must enter into an agreement with Adobe to distribute the runtime.

The Adobe AIR Runtime Distribution License Agreement

The AIR distribution license agreement allows you to post the AIR runtime installer on a company intranet site or local network. You are also allowed to distribute the Adobe AIR runtime on a stand-alone basis or on a CD, DVD, or USB drive as part of your software product or other physical media. In order to be eligible to enter into this type of agreement with Adobe, you must submit an application to Adobe in which you provide information about your intended distribution. If accepted, you will be entitled to distribute the AIR runtime in accordance with the terms of the agreement.

There are some limitations with regard to the distribution agreement that you should be aware of:

- You must distribute the AIR installers and files as-is without modification.
- You may not distribute the AIR installer or installer files for the purpose of bypassing installation of the AIR runtime, an AIR application, or the end user license agreement (EULA).
- You may not distribute or use the AIR runtime, runtime libraries or components, or installer files in an undocumented manner.

More information about distributing the AIR runtime can be found on the Adobe website, at www.adobe.com/products/air/runtime_distribution1.html.

Considerations for enterprise deployment

Within an enterprise environment, it is likely that IT administrators will manage the deployment of applications, and as such, individual users may not have administrator rights on their computer; such rights are required to install both the AIR runtime and individual AIR applications.

> *IT administrators can silently install the AIR runtime and your AIR application using tools such as Microsoft SMS, IBM Tivoli, or any deployment tool that allows silent installations that use a bootstrapper.*

IT administrators are able to do the following as part of deployment:

- Suppress the display of the AIR EULA
- Specify the application installation location
- Specify the whether the application's program menu or shortcut should appear on the end user's desktop

In addition, administrators can configure the AIR runtime to prevent installation of additional AIR applications, prevent installation of untrusted AIR applications, and/or disable automatic updates of the AIR runtime. These settings are intended for use only within a closed environment, such as an enterprise where an IT administrator controls the end user's systems.

More information on AIR application deployment within an enterprise environment can be found in the AIR Administrator's Guide, at www.adobe.com/go/learn_air_admin_guide_en.

Regardless of how you choose to distribute your AIR application, it is useful to understand how end users will both install and uninstall the application; this is covered next.

13

Installing and uninstalling an AIR application

When the end user installs an AIR application, either by launching an AIR file on their desktop or by using the seamless installer badge, the AIR runtime is leveraged to provide the following benefits:

- Consistent installation experience for all AIR applications, irrespective of application publisher or application functionality
- Unified installation experience across Windows, Mac, and Linux operating systems
- Localized installation experience for languages supported by the AIR runtime
- Notification of security risks in relation to the installation of the application and whether the publisher can be verified by means of a digital certificate
- Transparent deployment of application resources to create a native OS-specific application (on Windows, an EXE file is created; on Mac OS X, an APP package is created) and access points to launch the application

It is important to understand the installation experience of your users when they install your application. You should also have a sense of how the application publisher can customize the installation experience.

Regardless of the installation method chosen by the user, it is necessary for them to be logged into their computer with administrative privileges to install the AIR runtime, install an AIR application, or update an existing AIR application.

Installing an AIR application using the seamless installer badge

The seamless installer badge is the easiest way for your users to download an installation for your application. Clicking within the badge on a web page will cause the badge to determine whether the user has the appropriate version of the AIR runtime installed; if not, it will offer the user the option to install both the runtime and your application. If the appropriate version of the AIR runtime is already available, then just your application will be downloaded and installed.

The seamless installer badge for the eBay Desktop application is shown in Figure 13-17; this can be seen at http://desktop.ebay.com/.

Figure 13-17.
The seamless installer badge as used on the eBay website

When the user clicks the Install Now button, the badge changes, as shown in Figure 13-18, to advise that the application installation process has started.

Figure 13-18.
The badge shows that the installation process has commenced.

If the correct version of the AIR runtime is not already installed on the user's computer, then the badge will display the message shown in Figure 13-19. The user can choose to proceed or cancel the installation at this point.

Figure 13-19.
If the AIR runtime is not installed, the user will see this dialog.

If the AIR runtime is already installed or the user accepts the prompt to install the AIR runtime, then the application install process continues, as shown in Figure 13-20. If AIR is required as part of the application installation process, then the runtime components will be downloaded automatically. The AIR 1.5 installer will add approximately 15MB on Windows or 21MB on Mac OS X to your application download, and as such, a slight delay may occur while waiting for these components to download.

Figure 13-20. The user is kept informed of the application installation progress.

If the AIR runtime is already installed, the user is presented with three options, as shown in Figure 13-21:

13

- Opening the file
- Saving the file
- Canceling the installation process

Opening the file will continue the install process immediately, while saving the file allows the user to initiate the AIR application installation at a later point in time. If the AIR runtime is not already installed, then the user is not provided with this option; instead, the installation process continues automatically.

Figure 13-21. The user can choose to save or open the AIR file, or cancel the installation process.

After examining the contents of the AIR package, the AIR runtime will present the application install dialog shown in Figure 13-22. This dialog requests that the user confirm that they want to install the application on their computer. If the AIR package has been signed with a certificate from a trusted third party, then the publisher information is displayed and a green check mark is presented next to the publisher name to indicate the publisher identity is verified.

Figure 13-22. The Application Install dialog confirms the application publisher.

If the AIR package is signed with a self-signed certificate, then this dialog will list the publisher as UNVERIFIED, and a red cross will be displayed to warn the user that the publisher identify could not be verified. Regardless of whether the publisher identity is verified or not, the user can continue with the installation process by selecting Install.

Figure 13-23 displays the final dialog in the application process. It shows the application name, a description of the application, and if the publisher identity is verified, the application icon. The information used to present the name, description, and icon is retrieved from the AIR application descriptor file, so it is important that these properties be defined accurately when publishing the AIR package from within Flash.

Figure 13-23. The user can select the installation location for the application.

While the default installation location presented to the user is based upon the path you defined in the application descriptor file, the user can change the installation location by browsing to an alternative folder on their hard drive.

As you can see in Figure 13-24, on Mac OS X–based systems, the dialog differs slightly from Windows and does not present the user with the option to add a shortcut icon to their desktop. The user must create a shortcut or add the application to the dock manually.

13

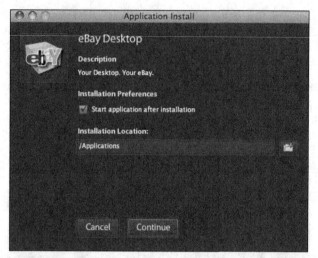

Figure 13-24. The user is not given the option to add a shortcut to their desktop on Mac OS X.

If the user continues with the installation process, the AIR runtime will perform the following actions:

1. Deploy the necessary files to the installation location

2. Create a native application package

3. Launch the installed application

On some versions of Mac OS X and Windows, the user may be presented with an operating system–generated dialog, as shown in Figure 13-25, that asks them to confirm the launch of the application—this occurs on the first launch of the application only.

Figure 13-25. A warning presented to users on Mac OS X before the application is launched for the first time

The installation process for the application is slightly different if the AIR runtime is not already present on the user's computer—in this situation, the installer will install both the AIR runtime components and your AIR application.

On the second installer dialog, an additional item, Install Adobe AIR 1.1, is added under the Installation Preferences heading, confirming that the AIR runtime will be installed (see Figure 13-26). Note that the user cannot deselect installation of the AIR runtime, as it is a required component.

Figure 13-26. If required, the AIR runtime is listed as an install component.

When AIR is installed as part of the application install process, the dialog shown in Figure 13-27 is displayed. It requires the user to accept the warranty disclaimer and software license agreement for AIR. Selecting I Agree in this dialog will complete the installation process.

Figure 13-27. The user must agree to the AIR license agreement during the installation process.

13

Installing an AIR application by launching an AIR file

As an alternative to installing the application via the installer badge, you can choose to distribute your AIR application as a file download from a website, as an e-mail attachment, or as a file on removable media such as a CD-ROM, DVD, or USB drive.

To initiate the installation of your application, the user will launch the AIR file on their system, typically by double-clicking the file. The installation process and dialogs presented to the user are as described in the previous section.

> *The user must have the AIR runtime installed on their system before trying to launch an AIR file; otherwise, the operating system will not know what to do with this type of file.*

The AIR installer can be downloaded from the Adobe website at `http://get.adobe.com/air/`, as shown in Figure 13-28.

If you are creating an application that will be distributed on an intranet or on physical media, you can also distribute the AIR runtime with your application for the convenience of the user, subject to you agreeing to the AIR runtime distribution license agreement on the Adobe website.

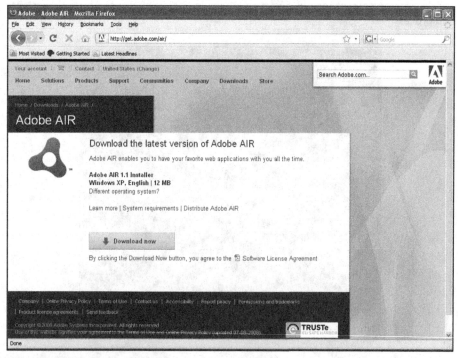

Figure 13-28. The AIR download page on Adobe's website

Installing an update to an existing AIR application

If the user launches an AIR file for the same version of an application that is already installed on their system, the AIR runtime will advise the user that the application is already installed, as shown in Figure 13-29. The user can choose whether to run the application, uninstall the application, or just cancel the dialog. To install an update to an existing application, the user must be logged in with administrative privileges.

Figure 13-29. The user is alerted if the application is already installed.

If the application is already installed, but the AIR runtime identifies that the version of the application in the AIR file is different from the one installed, a different dialog and set of options is presented to the user, as shown in Figure 13-30. It is important to remember that the AIR runtime cannot determine whether a particular version of an application is newer than the one already installed; all the AIR runtime knows is that it is different. As such, it is up to the user to determine whether they should replace the installed version of the application. To help the user make a decision, the numbers of the installed version and the version to be installed are displayed. The user can choose to replace the application, uninstall the application, run the current version of the application, or cancel the dialog.

Figure 13-30. The user is provided with the option to replace the existing application with an alternative version.

13

If you would prefer to have full control over the application update process and not rely upon the user making the decision as to whether one version of your application is newer than another, you can provide an alternative user experience for when the user launches an AIR file that contains an update for your application.

For more information on providing a custom user interface for application updates, see the "Updating an AIR application" section later in this chapter.

Launching an AIR application

Once your application is installed, the user can launch it in the following ways:

On Windows

- Double-click the shortcut icon on the desktop (as long as this option was selected during the installation process).
- Select the shortcut from the Start ➤ All Programs menu.

On the Mac

- Double-click the application within the Application folder (or a subfolder if a custom location was used during installation).

On Mac OS X, the AIR runtime does not automatically add the installed application to the dock; the user can, however, drag the application from the installation location to the dock if a shortcut is required.

Providing a first-run experience upon application launch

You may like to consider providing a first-run experience for your users for their initial launch of your application. This could be used for one or more of the following scenarios:

- You want to present a custom EULA for your application. (Note that it's not possible to display a EULA during the application installation process.)
- You want to provide a welcome page that introduces the user to the application features.
- You want the user to customize the application or configure preferences.
- You want to check that the user has the latest version of the application installed and force them to upgrade if it is out of date.

One way to accomplish this would be to check for the presence of a particular file within the application storage directory. If the file does not exist, then you know the application has not been launched before; you can then display the first-run experience and write the file to the application storage directory so that upon subsequent launches, you know that the application has been launched previously.

You could extend this further to write and check the version number of the application—you could then determine whether the user is running an updated version of your application for the first time and if appropriate, provide information about what's new in this release of the application.

Uninstalling an AIR application

To uninstall an AIR application, the user should follow the standard application uninstall process for their particular operating system.

On Mac OS X, the user should drag the application from the installed directory to the Trash. When the user empties the Trash, the application will be uninstalled from their system.

On Windows, the user should use the Add or Remove Programs dialog from the Control Panel, as shown in Figure 13-31, and select the application they wish to remove.

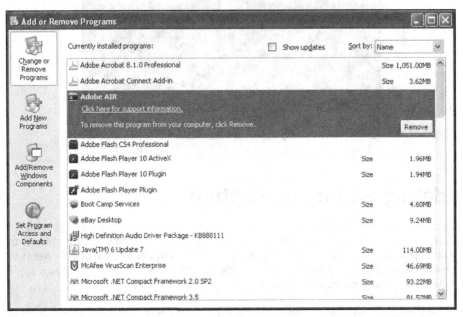

Figure 13-31. Uninstalling an AIR application using Add or Remove Programs on Windows XP

It should be noted that when an AIR application is uninstalled, any data stored within the ELS is not deleted automatically. You may wish to consider checking for the existence of data in the ELS when the user first runs the application and, if present, remove any data stored by a previous version of your application using EncryptedLocalStore.reset().

Uninstalling the AIR runtime

The user can uninstall the AIR runtime using Add or Remove Programs on Windows, or by running the Adobe AIR Uninstaller located in the Applications/Utilities directory on Mac OS X.

If the user tries to uninstall the AIR runtime while there are AIR applications still installed on their system, then they'll be advised that any remaining AIR applications will cease to work if they proceed with uninstalling AIR, as shown in Figure 13-32.

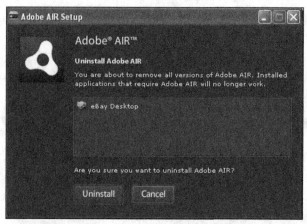

Figure 13-32. The user is alerted if they try to uninstall the AIR runtime when AIR applications are still resident on their computer.

Updating an AIR application

Once you have deployed your AIR application, it is likely that you will continue to enhance your application and add new functionality. Even if you don't plan to make any changes to your application, you might discover a bug or an issue with the application that needs to be addressed. Considering how you will provide updates to users who are using your application is an important aspect of developing desktop applications.

While you can simply publish a new version of your application and upload the AIR file to your website, this does not alert existing users that a new version of the application is available for them to download. Thankfully, the AIR runtime provides a mechanism that enables you to update an AIR application without relying upon the user to go to your website and download the updated AIR file; it does, however, require some preplanning and for you to implement a versioning strategy for your application.

The process for implementing update functionality in your AIR application is as follows:

1. Upon application startup, check with your server to determine if a new version of your application is available.

2. If a new version is available, alert the user and offer to update the application to the latest version. (Note that, depending upon the reason for the update, you might choose to force the user to update their application before they can continue using it.)

3. Download the updated AIR file from your AIR application.

4. Use the flash.desktop.Updater API to update the application to the new version.

I'll cover each of the steps required to update an AIR application in the upcoming sections.

> To update your AIR application, you must repackage all the application logic and required assets within the new AIR file—you cannot package just the resources that have changed. When the updated AIR package is installed, it will replace all installed resources from the previous version of the application.

Implementing a versioning strategy

In order to determine whether a new version of your application is available, you will need to determine both the current version of the installed application and the version number of the latest release of your application.

You can get the version number of the application while it is running by examining the applicationDescriptor property of the NativeApplication class; this property contains all the data in XML format from the application descriptor file that you created and used to package your AIR application. You can retrieve the version number from this property as follows:

```
var descriptor:XML =
NativeApplication.nativeApplication.applicationDescriptor;
var ns:Namespace = descriptor.namespaceDeclarations()[0];
installedVersion = descriptor.ns::version;
```

To compare this version number with the number of the latest release, you must publish that information on a server, which you can then retrieve from within the installed AIR application. There are a number of ways to do this, but using a simple XML file, located within the same directory as the AIR file, is a common approach.

Adobe has published a beta version of an update framework for AIR applications on the Adobe Labs website (http://labs.adobe.com/wiki/index.php/Adobe_AIR_Update_Framework); at the time of writing, this framework is not packaged for use with AIR applications created with Flash, but it will be updated upon final release to work with Flash-authored AIR applications. In the meantime, you can leverage the XML file format defined by Adobe for their update framework, so that it will be simple to migrate to the update framework at a later point. Here's an example:

13

```
<?xml version="1.0" encoding="utf-8"?>
<update xmlns="http://ns.adobe.com/air/framework/update/
description/1.0">
<version>1.7.1</version>
<url>http://www.mysite.com/myapp/myapp_1_7_1.air</url>
<description><![CDATA[

New version includes:
* Feature 1
* Feature 2
* Feature 3

]]></description>
</update>
```

As you can see, the XML defines a version number for the latest release of the application, a URL for the download location of the AIR file, and an optional description, which could detail a list of new features or bug fixes in this release. Each time you upload a new version of your AIR file to your server, you should also update the XML file so that the application version and URL are correct.

While the AIR runtime does not dictate you follow any particular version-numbering strategy, it is essential that you choose a numbering system that allows you to determine whether a particular release is newer than the installed version—should you discover a security issue with an older version of your application, you do not want to allow users to accidently install this over a newer release and expose them to unnecessary risk.

With your XML file in place on the server, you can choose whether to look for a newer version of the application on application startup or at a regularly scheduled interval. Equally, you can choose to offer the user an option to perform a manual check via a menu option within the application. Whichever option you choose, you will need to request the XML file from the server using the URLLoader API, like this:

```
var remoteVersion:String;
var appURL:String;
var loader:URLLoader = new URLLoader();
loader.addEventListener(Event.COMPLETE, loadXML);
loader.load(new URLRequest("http://www.mysite.com/myapp/version.xml"));

private function loadXML(event:Event):void {
    var xmlData = new XML(event.target.data);
    remoteVersion = xmlData.version;
    appURL = xmlData.url;
}
```

Once you have the information from the remote XML file, you can then compare the versions and determine whether you need to download the updated AIR file. Here's how to accomplish this task:

```
if (Number(remoteVersion) > Number(installedVersion)) {
    downloadUpdate();
}
```

Updating the application

Before downloading the updated AIR file, you should alert the user that a new version of the application is available and, optionally, provide an opportunity for her to agree to or defer the application update process. Installing an update will restart the application, and as such, updating the application without advising the user would provide a poor user experience.

Update the application as follows:

1. Download the updated AIR file from the server.

2. Write the AIR file to the application storage directory (you can write the file anywhere, but the applicationStorageDirectory provides a convenient location on the user's system).

3. Call the Updater.update() method, passing a reference to the downloaded AIR file, together with the version number for the updated application, to initiate the AIR update process. The version number must match the value provided in the application descriptor for the AIR package; otherwise, the update will fail.

An example of the code required to complete this task is shown here:

```
var urlStream:URLStream = new URLStream();
var fileData:ByteArray = new ByteArray();

private function downloadUpdate():void {
    urlStream.addEventListener(Event.COMPLETE, installUpdate);
    urlStream.load(new URLRequest(appURL));
}


private function installUpdate():void {
    urlStream.readBytes(fileData, 0, urlStream.bytesAvailable);

    var file:File =
    File.applicationStorageDirectory.resolvePath("appUpdate.air");

    var fileStream:FileStream = new FileStream();
    fileStream.open(file, FileMode.WRITE);
    fileStream.writeBytes(fileData,0,fileData.length);
    fileStream.close();

    var updater:Updater = new Updater();
    updater.update(file,remoteVersion);
    }
}
```

13

Calling the update() method causes the application to exit. The updated version of the application is then installed (the user is shown a progress indicator by the AIR runtime while this is happening), and finally, the new version of the application is launched. If your updated application requires a newer version of the AIR runtime, then this will be downloaded and installed automatically. If the update to your application cannot be installed—for example, because the application ID and publication ID of the existing and new applications don't match—then the AIR runtime presents an error message to the user and the existing version of the application is relaunched.

Presenting a custom user interface for user-initiated updates

In addition to updating the application using the Updater.update() method from within the AIR application, the user can initiate an update by downloading an AIR file and manually launching it on their operating system.

In this situation, the AIR runtime will provide a default update experience that presents the user with the version number of the current application, together with the version number of the updated application. The runtime will ask them to confirm that the updated application should replace the currently installed version. There is no logic within the update process to check that the version to be installed is actually a newer version; this decision is left to the user, based on the version numbers that are displayed.

You may like to provide a custom update experience, rather than rely upon the default dialogs and logic provided by the AIR runtime. To do this, you should check the Use custom UI for updates option within the AIR – Application & Installer Settings panel in Flash (as shown in Figure 13-33), or alternatively, set the customUpdateUI property to true within the AIR application descriptor file.

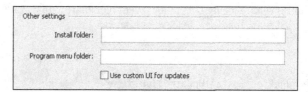

Figure 13-33. Select Use custom UI for updates to replace the standard AIR runtime update experience.

When the user launches an AIR file with the same application ID and publisher ID as your application, the AIR runtime will launch your application and dispatch an invoke event with the arguments parameter set to the path of the AIR file launched by the user. By listening for this event, you can provide a customized interface for the application update process to the user.

One challenge that you will face by providing a custom user interface for updates is how to determine what version of the AIR application the user has launched as an update. Unlike with the web-based update process, there is no XML file that you can reference to get the version number, and you need to know this before you can call the Updater.update() method.

Possible solutions to this issue include naming the AIR file in such a way that you can parse the name of the file and infer the version number from the file name (i.e., myapp_1_7_1. air indicates version 1.7.1). An alternative is writing the appropriate ActionScript code to unzip the AIR file, examine the application descriptor file contained within, and extract the application version number. This second approach is in fact used by the AIR updater framework referenced earlier in the chapter. Before implementing this functionality yourself, you may want to check whether a final release of the updater framework is available for use.

Summary

In this chapter, you learned how to create an AIR package that will enable the user to install your application on their computer. Whether you use Flash to specify the application and installer settings or you provide your own custom application descriptor file, you now understand what you need to specify so that the AIR application can be deployed correctly.

You also learned why it is important to sign an AIR package with a digital certificate issued by a trusted CA, with early planning and the acquisition of an appropriate digital certificate being key to providing the user with an experience that gives them confidence in installing your application.

Finally, by analyzing the installation, update, and uninstall process for AIR applications, you now should understand what your potential users will experience. This knowledge is important so that you can make appropriate decisions as to how you distribute the AIR application and how you manage the process of updating the application once installed by the user.

13

INDEX

U

V